The **Rough Guide** to

Switzerland

written and researched by

Matthew Teller

ROUGH
GUIDES

www.roughguides.com

Contents

Swiss cheese and chocolate colour section following p.184

Mountain excursions colour section following p.376

◀◀ The Zytglogge, Bern ◀ View over Zürich's rooftops

Introduction to
Switzerland

"In Italy for thirty years under the Borgias they had warfare, terror, murder, bloodshed, but they produced Michelangelo, Leonardo da Vinci and the Renaissance. In Switzerland they had brotherly love; they had 500 years of democracy and peace. And what did that produce? The cuckoo clock."

Orson Welles as Harry Lime, in *The Third Man* (1949)

Never has one throwaway movie line done so much to damage the reputation of a whole country. Even now, despite being one of the most visited countries in Europe, Switzerland remains one of the least understood.

The facts are that until national reconciliation in 1848, Switzerland was the most consistently turbulent, war-torn area of Europe (so much for brotherly love), and yet, both before and after it found stability, it brought forth luminaries in the arts and sciences of the calibre of Hans Holbein, Jean-Jacques Rousseau, Albert Einstein, Paul Klee, Hermann Hesse and Alberto Giacometti. So much for the cuckoo clock – a Bavarian invention, anyway.

But two centuries of tourism have left their mark: faced by an ever-increasing onslaught of visitors, these days many Swiss are content to abide by a quaint stereotype of Switzerland that's easily packaged and sold – the familiar Alpine idyll of cheese and chocolate, Heidi and the Matterhorn – while keeping the best bits for themselves. Come for a "Lakes and Mountains" package, or a week of skiing, or a short city-break, and you'll get all the pristine beauty, genteel calm and well-oiled efficiency of the Switzerland that the locals deem suitable for public consumption. The other

Switzerland – the one the Swiss inhabit – needs time and patience to winkle out of its shell, but can be an infinitely more rewarding place to explore.

Within this rugged environment, **community spirit** is perhaps stronger than anywhere else in Europe. Since the country is not an ethnic, linguistic or religious unity, it has survived – so the Swiss are fond of saying – simply through the will of its people to resolve their differences. Today, a unique style of "bottom-up" democracy ensures real power still rests with the people, who vote frequently on referenda affecting all aspects of life from local recycling projects to national economic policy. The constitution devolves power upwards from the people to municipal governments and up again to the regions (known as **cantons**), only as a last resort granting certain powers to the federal government.

▶ Students outside Lausanne's cathedral

Fact file

• Switzerland covers an **area** of 41,285 sq km – roughly the size of Wales or West Virginia. At the most it is 220km from north to south, and 348km from west to east. The highest point is the Dufourspitze at 4634m above sea level, the lowest is Lake Maggiore at 193m. The total **population** is around 7.7 million, of whom 6 million are Swiss citizens.

• The Swiss Confederation is ruled by a seven-member government called the **Federal Council**, with the presidency rotating annually between all seven members. Both this and the **Supreme Court** are elected by the bicameral **Parliament**. Constitutional amendments can be proposed by Parliament or by popular initiative, the latter requiring 100,000 signatures; in either case a referendum ensues, and a double majority – of votes cast both nationally and canton-by-canton – sees the proposal becoming law. Fifty thousand signatures can also put any existing law to a referendum.

• Each of the 26 **cantons** has its own constitution, parliament, government and courts, and there is also a good deal of autonomy vested in the 2942 **communes**, which vary in size from small, crowded city districts to thinly populated tracts of mountain terrain.

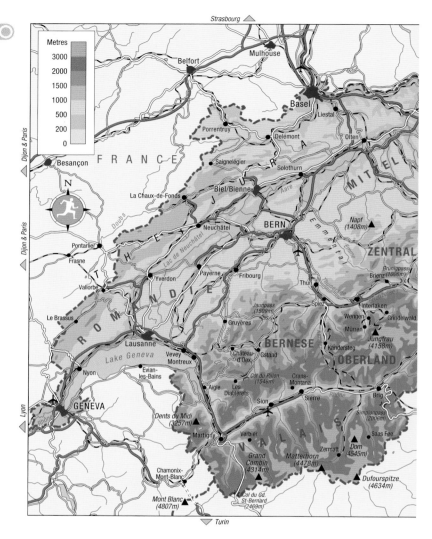

This kind of decentralized structure means that the cantons – which are, in essence, tiny self-governing republics who have volunteered to join together – have mostly held onto their own, unique flavours. Although Swiss people value their shared Swissness above all, they also cherish their own home-town identity and their differences from their neighbours. Tensions exist between the four **language** communities, as they do between Catholic and Protestant, or between urban and rural areas, while **regional characteristics** remain sharply defined and diverse. Local pride is fuelled by a range of traditional **folkloric customs**, most of which stem

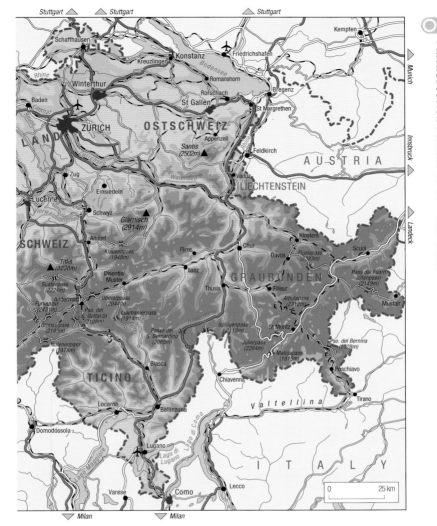

from pagan or medieval Christian festivals. Most prominent of these is **carnival**, held around the country on or around Mardi Gras, the last day before Lent. The most exuberant celebrations, held in Lucerne and Basel, feature bands, masked parades, street dancing and spontaneous partying that belie the stereotype of a placid, unadventurous Switzerland. A host of smaller events fills out the calendar and it's still easily possible to stumble on village festivals that have been staged by local people for centuries past.

This sense of cultural continuity sits oddly with the fact that Switzerland has grown into one of the world's **richest** countries. Its economy is

Schweiz, Suisse, Svizzera, Svizra

For such a tiny country, Switzerland is remarkably polyglot. There are four official languages: about two-thirds of the population have German as their first language; about a fifth French; six percent Italian; while Romansh, a direct descendant of Latin, has clung on in pockets of the mountainous southeast. Around one in ten people use English every day, and many Swiss are comfortably tri- or quadrilingual.

These language divisions are reflected in divisions of culture and identity. In the centre and the east, the old isolation of tight-knit mountain communities lingers on in Swiss German *Kantönligeist* ("little cantonal spirit"), a stubborn parochialism leavened by down-to-earth rumbustiousness.

To the west lies the *Röstigraben*, a comical but slightly discomfiting name given to the invisible language border – a *Graben* is a military trench – between French-speaking Switzerland, where they don't eat the traditional potato dish *rösti*, and German-speaking Switzerland, where they do.

small-scale but thoroughly modern: traditional industries such as watchmaking and textiles now thrive by focusing closely on the luxury end of the market and have ceded prime position to engineering, pharmaceuticals and service industries. **Tourism** has been a high earner since the mid-nineteenth century, when the Alps became both a fashionable destination for wealthy travellers and a prescribed retreat for sufferers from respiratory diseases needing curative sunshine and fresh mountain air. And yet the country still stands alone. In the 1940s, Switzerland was surrounded by hostile Axis powers; these days, it's encircled by the "friendly" EU. Switzerland's dogged **neutrality** rings ever more hollow. Commentators are noting sadly that Switzerland is only now embarking on the kind of multi-ethnic social integration that its neighbours began in the 1950s.

▼ Chalet in Lauterbrunnen

Having taken centuries to bolt their country together from diverse elements, the Swiss seem instinctively to return to their sense of community spirit, expressed most tangibly in the order and cleanliness you'll see on show everywhere. Yet the sterility so decried by Graham Greene (who wrote Harry Lime's jibe about brotherly love), if it characterizes any part of the country, applies only to the glossy, neatly packaged tourist idyll of lakes and mountains. The three great Swiss cities of Geneva, Zürich and Basel are crammed with world-class **museums** and galleries. In Zürich and Lausanne, there's a humming arts scene and underground club culture that feeds **nightlife** as vibrant as anything you'll find in much larger European cities.

The **landscapes** are dominated by the Alps and their foothills, but mountains aren't the only story. In the north and centre are lush, rolling grasslands epitomized by the velvety green hills of the Emmental, traditional dairy-farming country. Vineyards rise tiered above Lake Geneva, the Rhône valley and the Rhine. The southeast is cut through by wild, high-sided valleys, lonely, dark and thickly forested. Most surprisingly of all, bordering Italy in the south you'll find subtropical Mediterranean-style flower gardens, sugarloaf hills and sunny, palm-fringed lakes.

Switzerland may be a small, little-regarded mid-continental country with a serious image problem, but it has plenty more to offer than most visitors suspect.

Where to go – and when

Although Switzerland is best known for its mountain scenery, there are any number of hooks on which to hang a visit, whether you choose to stay in one city or resort, explore a region, or tour the whole country. Getting about is easy, with an unrivalled network of trains, buses and boats. You'll find places to stay and get a hearty meal wherever you end up, even in the wildest of mountain valleys.

The cities

Switzerland has no big metropolises on the scale of Paris or London. Swiss towns and cities were preserved from bombing in World War II, and all of them retain medieval alleys, houses and churches at their centres.

Geneva is positioned at the tip of the idyllic **Lake Geneva** in the south-west, a short distance from the graceful lakeside city of **Lausanne**. In the northeast, **Zürich** too is set on its own lake, within striking distance of the peaceful **Bodensee** (Lake Constance). The diminutive Swiss capital **Bern** has a fine cobbled Old Town, while equally attractive **Lucerne** lies in the centre of the country on its own, famously beautiful, lake. **Basel** is located on the Rhine at the point where France, Germany and Switzerland meet, while at the opposite end of the country, **Lugano** basks on the shores of an azure lake a few kilometres from the Italian border.

CH

UK websites are suffixed .uk, France has .fr, Italy has .it – but Switzerland has .ch. For internet domains, as well as international postal services, vehicle registration and all sorts of other matters, Switzerland dodges the issue of its multilingualism and resorts to its Latin title: Confoederatio Helvetica, meaning the Helvetic (that is, Swiss) Confederation, universally abbreviated to CH.

Any of these – or smaller but no less characterful regional towns such as St Gallen, Schaffhausen, Neuchâtel, Chur, Fribourg, Sion or Bellinzona – could serve as a base for a relaxing short break, especially during the temperate **summer** months (June–Sept). At other times they can get distinctly chilly, although most receive generous dumps of **snow** in the winter, which, combined with glittering sunshine and frozen lakes and rivers, paints the most romantic of urban pictures.

The mountains

There are almost limitless possibilities for exploring the great outdoors. The **Alps** run in a band across the centre and south of the country, with resorts big and small

– plus stunning scenery guaranteed. The two main **seasons** run from June to October, and from mid-December to mid-April; between these times, most mountain resorts close down altogether (see "Basics", p.27 for more).

The best-known Alpine region is the **Bernese Oberland**, focused around the tourist hub of **Interlaken** and boasting such famous names as **Wengen** and **Grindelwald**. To the south, in Valais, sit **Verbier**, **Crans–Montana** and, at the foot of the iconic Matterhorn, **Zermatt**. In Graubünden in the southeast are **Davos**, **Klosters** and **St Moritz**. Justifiably popular, all these places boast some of the best winter skiing and summer hiking in Europe.

It's relatively easy in even the busiest centres (which are still nothing like the mega-resorts of the French and Italian Alps) to head off the beaten path and explore alone, or to aim for smaller, more manageable satellite resorts

▲ Cable car to the Schilthorn

in adjacent side-valleys. However, you may prefer to shun the big names altogether and seek peace and quiet in the hinterlands. Two regions stand out: in the northwest, the scrubby **Jura** mountains are an ideal landscape for long lonely walks and bike rides; while in the south, the wild valleys of **Alto Ticino** lace the southern foothills of the Alps with little-known hiking trails, a world away from the chic lakeside resort of **Locarno** nearby.

Switzerland's climate

The table shows average monthly minimum and maximum temperatures (in °C), and average monthly precipitation (in mm). Precipitation patterns vary widely, with the northern cities (Bern, Zürich) experiencing more overcast skies than, for instance, Lugano, which tends to have long periods of sunshine occasionally punctuated by short downpours.

Average maximum and minimum daily temperatures and monthly precipitation

	Jan	Feb	Mar	Apr	May	Jun	Jul	Aug	Sep	Oct	Nov	Dec
Bern												
Max/Min (°C)	0/-5	4/-3	9/-1	13/3	18/8	20/10	21/11	20/11	17/7	11/4	5/-2	0/-5
Precipitation, mm	56	49	62	77	97	120	118	114	96	71	68	65
Davos												
Max/Min (°C)	-1/-11	-1/-11	3/-8	8/-4	10/1	14/4	18/8	18/7	14/4	10/0	7/-4	1/-8
Precipitation, mm	71	60	57	60	66	121	140	135	90	69	63	70
Geneva												
Max/Min (°C)	3/-2	5/-1	10/0	14/4	19/8	20/10	22/12	22/13	21/11	15/7	9/3	5/0
Precipitation, mm	63	57	55	50	67	92	64	96	102	77	84	59
Lugano												
Max/Min (°C)	6/-2	8/-1	11/2	17/6	20/9	23/11	28/14	29/14	25/11	19/9	13/5	8/0
Precipitation, mm	61	64	96	148	217	199	183	196	160	172	152	95
Sion												
Max/Min (°C)	3/-6	6/-3	9/1	14/3	20/8	21/10	25/11	24/10	21/9	15/4	9/0	5/-3
Precipitation, mm	51	45	40	37	39	46	50	64	65	50	53	62
Zürich												
Max/Min (°C)	0/-5	4/-2	9/0	15/3	20/9	22/11	25/13	23/13	20/11	14/8	9/2	3/-2
Precipitation, mm	75	70	64	81	108	137	144	135	110	80	76	64

23

things not to miss

It's not possible to see everything that Switzerland has to offer in one trip – and we don't suggest you try. What follows is a selective and subjective taste of the country's highlights: beautiful cities and lakes, top mountain resorts, spectacular train journeys and secluded Alpine getaways. They're arranged in five colour-coded categories to help you find the very best things to see, do and experience. All entries have a page reference to take you straight into the guide, where you can find out more.

01 **Bernese Oberland** Page **229** • This legendary Alpine area offers classic Swiss scenery alongside such famous destinations as Interlaken.

I ACTIVITIES I CONSUME I EVENTS I NATURE I SIGHTS I

02 **The Matterhorn** Page **297** • No mountain in the world is so immediately recognizable, dominating the horizon above the world-class skiing, snowboarding and hiking resort of Zermatt.

03 **Zürich** Page **353** • Come to Switzerland's largest city for world-class galleries and museums – but also come for fine dining, atmospheric cafés, lively bars and great nightlife.

www.roughguides.com

04 Schaffhausen Page **394** • This quiet, little-visited market town, replete with medieval frescoed mansions, stands just upstream from the mighty Rhine falls.

06 Wine Page **46** • Switzerland's wine industry is modest, but its products can compete on equal terms with better-known labels from around the world.

05 Lausanne Page **95** • Tiered above Lake Geneva and crowned by a stunning Gothic cathedral (pictured), Lausanne is Switzerland's most visually dramatic city.

07 Davos Page **437** • Boarders and freeriders will find that there are few better destinations in the world than Davos.

08 **Winter sports** Page **51** • Switzerland offers some of the most scenic skiing and snowboarding of anywhere in the Alps.

09 **Lake Geneva** Page **113** • The vineyards of St-Saphorin in Lake Geneva's Lavaux region – protected as part of UNESCO World Heritage – produce some of the country's finest wines.

10 Basel Page **165** • This ancient Rhine-side city straddles the French and German borders, enhanced by fine medieval architecture and one of Switzerland's best art museums, the Fondation Beyeler (pictured).

12 Rhätische Bahn Page **421** • The southeastern corner of Switzerland is the setting for some of Europe's most spectacular train rides aboard the RhB.

11 Montreux Jazz Festival Page **126** • Stellar annual music event in this ritzy lakeside resort, attracting world-class jazz, blues, soul, dance, rock and world music performers.

13 Geneva Page **63** • Take in the cultural attractions of this most urbane of European cities – and then head down to the waterfront to relax and recharge your batteries.

14 Lugano Page **483** • Lugano offers a slice of Italian Lakes-style romance, a stone's throw from Lake Como, with majestic waterfront villas gazing out over blue water.

15 Appenzell Page **410** • Endearingly old-fashioned dairy village, tucked away amidst hilly countryside that is ideal for long walks.

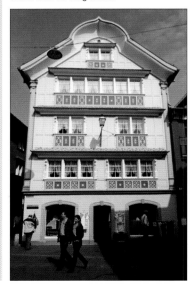

16 **Lake Lucerne** Page **315** • The most dramatically sited of all Switzerland's lakes, ringed by mist-wreathed cliffs.

17 **St Moritz** Page **448** • Switzerland's sunniest mountain resort, boasting outstanding skiing and snowboarding.

18 Walking Page **49** • The high-level route from Schynige Platte past the Bachalpsee and down to Grindelwald is just one of many memorably scenic walks throughout the Swiss Alps.

19 Bern Page **191** • Switzerland's uniquely attractive capital city has a medieval street plan that has survived unchanged for five centuries.

20 **Adventure sports** Page **329** • Whether you're into paragliding, bungee-jumping or canyoning, indulge a taste for adventure in the Jungfrau Region (pictured) or just about any of Switzerland's Alpine areas.

22 St Gallen Page **407** • The library of St Gallen's ancient abbey has one of the most impressive secular Rococo interiors in Europe.

21 Carnival Page **320** • Switzerland has a long tradition of carnival, the best of the bunch being in Lucerne, where thousands pack into the Old Town for parades, music and merrymaking.

23 Alto Ticino Page **469** • The high, remote valleys of this Italian-speaking region offer long hikes and a sense of wilderness unique in the Alps.

Basics

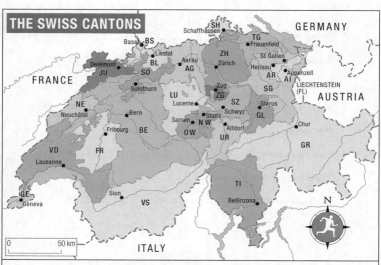

THE SWISS CANTONS

Given is the date of accession to the Confederation, the name (in the local language only), the standard two-letter abbreviation, and the cantonal capital.

1291	Uri (UR) – Altdorf	1501	Schaffhausen (SH) – Schaffhausen
1291	Schwyz (SZ) – Schwyz	1513	Appenzell Ausserrhoden (AR) – Herisau
1291	Obwalden (OW) – Sarnen	1513	Appenzell Innerrhoden (AI) – Appenzell
1291	Nidwalden (NW) – Stans	1803	St Gallen (SG) – St Gallen
1332	Luzern (LU) – Luzern	1803	Graubünden (GR) – Chur
1351	Zürich (ZH) – Zürich	1803	Aargau (AG) – Aarau
1352	Glarus (GL) – Glarus	1803	Thurgau (TG) – Frauenfeld
1352	Zug (ZG) – Zug	1803	Ticino (TI) – Bellinzona
1353	Bern (BE) – Bern	1803	Vaud (VD) – Lausanne
1481	Fribourg (FR) – Fribourg	1815	Valais (VS) – Sion
1481	Solothurn (SO) – Solothurn	1815	Neuchâtel (NE) – Neuchâtel
1501	Basel-Stadt (BS) – Basel	1815	Geneva (GE) – Geneva
1501	Basel-Land (BL) – Liestal	1979	Jura (JU) – Delémont

Basics

Getting there

Switzerland is well served by high-speed trains from across Europe. By air, Zürich is a major intercontinental hub, while Geneva and Basel handle dozens of European flights a day.

Aside from **Zürich** (ZRH), **Geneva** (GVA) and **Basel** (BSL), smaller Swiss airports such as **Bern** (BRN), **Lugano** (LUG) and **Sion** (SIR) are useful entry points to specific regions. **Milan Malpensa** (MXP) – Italy's main intercontinental gateway – is only 25km south of the Swiss border, with good transport links. **Friedrichshafen** (FDH) in Germany, with flights from London, lies just across Lake Constance from the Swiss railhead of Romanshorn.

In this section we cover **independent travel** first. Details of package deals and organized tours follow on p.30.

High and low seasons

The main thing to take into account when planning your trip is the **high and low seasons**, since hotel prices, pressure on rooms and periods of opening of hotels, shops and restaurants – especially in mountain resorts – can fluctuate dramatically.

All across the country, July and August are **high season** (*Hochsaison*, *haute saison*, *alta stagione*), when everything is open but prices are highest. Big cities and lakeside resorts have a **summer season** which extends from at the earliest mid-May until at the latest mid-October. However, the higher in altitude you go, the more the season is truncated: some Alpine pass roads may not be cleared until mid-June, and snow may fall again in mid-September, limiting the opening times of the highest huts to ten or twelve crowded weeks. You may find that some cable cars and mountain railways don't start operation, and trails may not be open for walkers, until well into June, even if hotels and services take bookings for several weeks earlier. If you're travelling specifically for a walking or activity holiday in late May or early September, you should check in advance exactly what will be open, to avoid disappointment.

Countrywide, the **low season** (*Vorsaison*, *Nachsaison* or *Zwischensaison*, *basse saison*, *bassa stagione*) comprises late April to early June, and mid-October to early December: cities and lowland towns still welcome tourists at these times (and, indeed, often have cut-price deals on accommodation), but many mountain resorts – including hotels and shops within them – close down altogether and use the time for renovations.

The **winter high season** matches the ski season, which traditionally opens in the week before Christmas and lasts until the week after Easter (but in practice depends on snow cover); this is when prices in Alpine resorts climb to their peak again. Prices in the mountains are highest around Christmas and New Year, and again in mid-February, whereas the months of January and March are less crowded and less expensive: plenty of resorts offer cut-price skiing packages in mid-December and early April. Resorts with access to slopes above about 2800m tend to extend the season: they may have good snow from mid-November through to early May. Cities and lowland towns are bitterly cold for general wanderings in the winter, and – unless they offer direct access to the mountains – tend to flog accommodation at rock-bottom prices.

"Fly Rail Baggage"

The Swiss have come up with one of the greatest, and simplest, ideas around for easing the stress of air travel. If you're flying into Zürich or Geneva, you can send your bags direct from the **check-in desk** at your home airport through to one of seventy-odd train stations in Switzerland for collection at your convenience, thus eliminating the hassle of airport carousel reclaim and then lugging your bags around. Whoever you're flying with, from any airport in the world, all you need to do is to fill out a special green **customs label** and attach one to each item of baggage. Each label costs the equivalent of US$15/Fr.20; they're obtainable from Swiss Air Lines offices and Rail Europe outlets worldwide, as well as specialist tour operators. Ⓦwww.rail.ch/baggage has full details.

If you choose a station near your arrival airport, your bags may be available for collection as little as two hours after touchdown. For stations further away reckon on proportionately longer (possibly next day): the website has details, including the **opening hours** of the baggage counter at your pick-up station.

The homeward-bound service – by which you can check in at a Swiss train station for your flight home – is covered on p.37.

Flights from the UK

From the UK, there are over fifty flights a day to Switzerland, from a dozen or more UK airports. **Full-service** carriers include British Airways, Swiss, bmi and Aer Lingus. **No-frills** airlines include easyJet, Flybe, Ryanair, Jet2 and bmibaby. Since routes can change – and airlines can fold – with little notice, check under "Destinations" at the website of your home airport and/or an airport in Switzerland (see box below) for up-to-date information on who flies where. **Flight time** from London is around an hour and a half, from the north of England or Scotland two to three hours.

If you book far enough in advance – several weeks at least – you should be able to find a **fare** around £50–70 return, but perhaps only for midweek flights at unsociable hours. For more convenient timings, you may be looking at £100–150 return. No-frills and full-service carriers offer broadly comparable prices. The difference

comes in levels of customer service, both on the ground and in the air.

Airlines in the UK

Aer Lingus Ⓦwww.aerlingus.com.
Baboo Ⓦwww.flybaboo.com.
Blue Islands Ⓦwww.blueislands.com.
bmi Ⓦwww.flybmi.com.
bmibaby Ⓦwww.bmibaby.com.
British Airways Ⓦwww.ba.com.
easyJet Ⓦwww.easyjet.com.
Flybe Ⓦwww.flybe.com.
Jet2 Ⓦwww.jet2.com.
Ryanair Ⓦwww.ryanair.com.
Swiss Ⓦwww.swiss.com.

By train from the UK

Travelling by **train** has regained much of its old romance. As well as the eco benefits, this is a scenic and relaxing way to get to Switzerland – and can often compete with flying on price. If you're travelling from London or southeast England to one of the big Swiss cities (Zürich, Basel, Geneva, Lausanne, Bern, Lucerne), and you compare door-to-door timings, you may even find that flying is only barely quicker, if at all.

Eurostar runs high-speed trains from **London St Pancras** through the Channel Tunnel direct to **Paris Gare du Nord** (2hr 15min). Trains also depart from **Ebbsfleet** (off the M25) and **Ashford** (off the M20), both with ample long-term parking. From Paris, many TGV high-speed trains (for

Swiss airports

Basel Ⓦwww.euroairport.com
Bern Ⓦwww.flughafenbern.ch
Geneva Ⓦwww.gva.ch
Lugano Ⓦwww.lugano-airport.ch
Sion Ⓦwww.sionairport.ch
Zürich Ⓦwww.zurich-airport.com

roughguides.com

Find everything you need to plan your next trip at ⓦ www.roughguides .com. Read in-depth information on destinations worldwide, make use of our unique trip-planner, book transport and accommodation, check out other travellers' recommendations and share your own experiences.

which advance seat reservation is compulsory) serve Switzerland, but not from the Gare du Nord, meaning you have to plan your route in advance and be prepared to lug your bags (or take a taxi). Trains run from **Paris Gare de l'Est**, located beside the Gare du Nord (5–10min walk), to Basel (aka Bâle) (3hr 25min), continuing to Zürich (4hr 25min). Trains run from **Paris Gare de Lyon** on three different routes: to Geneva (3hr 25min); to Lausanne (3hr 50min); and to Neuchâtel (4hr) and Bern (4hr 35min).

You can get complete **timetable information** from London to any station (or bus stop, cable car or ferry halt) in Switzerland at ⓦ www.rail.ch. Eurostar and Rail Europe can book point-to-point tickets to Switzerland from stations all round the UK; rail specialists such as Railbookers can tailor-make an itinerary, book hotels and provide Swiss transport passes as well. ⓦ www .seat61.com has lots of information, photos and links.

Eurostar ☏ 08705 186 186, ⓦ www.eurostar.com.
Railbookers ☏ 020 3327 0800, ⓦ www .railbookers.com.
Rail Europe ☏ 0844 848 4064, ⓦ www.raileurope .co.uk.
Switzerland Travel Centre ☏ 020 7420 4900, ⓦ www.stc.co.uk.

Driving from the UK

Switzerland is just about within reach of the UK on a day's **drive**: the Swiss border is very roughly 850km from the Channel coast and, given an early start and clear *autoroutes*, you could be in Basel, or even Bern or Lausanne, by sundown. Aim for Calais, Reims then Dijon: this route benefits from rapid cross-Channel service and avoids Paris – but the *autoroute* runs out as you

approach the Jura mountains, forcing you onto main roads instead.

Eurotunnel (☏ 0870 535 3535, ⓦ www .eurotunnel.com) runs car-carrying trains from Folkestone to Calais via the **Channel Tunnel**. You can turn up and go, though booking is advisable. Trains run frequently 24 hours a day; journey time is a smooth 35–45 minutes. **Ferries** and **catamarans** from Dover to Calais are currently operated by P&O (☏ 08716 645 645, ⓦ www .poferries.com) and Sea France (☏ 08714 237 119, ⓦ www.seafrance.com). **Fares** by ferry or Eurotunnel vary a lot; travelling at night can cut costs, while travelling at weekends, or in summer, adds a premium. Booking ahead could net you a return ticket for £60–90 per car.

From Ireland

From Ireland, flights from Dublin to Zürich on Swiss are around €200–250 return, matched by Aer Lingus from Dublin and Cork to Zürich and Geneva. On Swiss, transfers which fly you to Zürich and then double back to Geneva or Basel might seem counterproductive, but connection times at Zürich are so well coordinated that they can save time on other airlines' routings, such as BA via Heathrow. Flying Ryanair into Stansted, then on to Basel (or Friedrichshafen in Germany, from where eastern Switzerland is a ferry ride away), saves little.

Aer Lingus ⓦ www.aerlingus.com.
British Airways ⓦ www.ba.com.
Ryanair ⓦ www.ryanair.com.
Swiss ⓦ www.swiss.com.

From North America

From North America Swiss flies from several US and Canadian cities nonstop to Zürich, with a few options nonstop to Geneva. They operate codeshares with United (out of Washington) and Air Canada (out of Montréal/Toronto), giving access to broad domestic networks in both countries. The lowest **fares** are around US$500–700 round-trip from the East Coast, perhaps $650–950 from the West Coast. Flying in peak season can add $500 or more. Deals on routings via other European hubs – for example, Delta/Air France/KLM via Paris or

Five steps to a better kind of travel

At Rough Guides we are passionately committed to travel. We feel strongly that only through travelling do we truly come to understand the world we live in and the people we share it with – plus tourism has brought a great deal of **benefit** to developing economies over the last few decades. But the extraordinary growth in tourism has also damaged some places irreparably, and **climate change** is exacerbated by most forms of transport, especially flying. We feel it's important to **travel thoughtfully and responsibly**, with respect for the cultures you're visiting – not only to derive the most benefit from your trip but also to preserve the best bits of the planet for everyone to enjoy. With Switzerland in mind:

- Consider whether the services you use employ **local people** or source locally grown produce.
- Consider the **environment**. Even in Switzerland biodiversity can be adversely affected by insensitive tourism.
- Travel with a purpose, not just to tick off experiences. Consider **spending longer** in a place, and getting to know it and its people.
- Give thought to your **flights** and try to avoid short hops by air. Good train links exist from the UK to Switzerland, and Swiss public transport is excellent: exploring by train, bus or boat often beats driving.
- Make your trips "**climate neutral**" via a reputable carbon offset scheme. All Rough Guide author flights are offset, and every year we donate money to a variety of charities devoted to combating the effects of climate change.

Amsterdam, or British Airways via London – are comparable in price.

Air Canada ⓦ www.aircanada.com.
British Airways ⓦ www.ba.com.
Delta ⓦ www.delta.com.
KLM ⓦ www.klm.com.
Swiss ⓦ www.swiss.com.
United ⓦ www.united.com.

From Australia and New Zealand

From Australia and New Zealand the most convenient routings are to Bangkok with Thai, who codeshare with Swiss onwards nonstop to Zürich. Flying via London may be cheaper, but adds several hours onto your journey time. Heading east with Qantas, Air NZ or others to Los Angeles, from where Swiss fly nonstop to Zürich, is another option. **Fares** vary tremendously. Expect Aus$1800–2800 from Australia, NZ$2000–3000 from Auckland.

Air NZ ⓦ www.airnz.com.
British Airways ⓦ www.ba.com.
Qantas ⓦ www.qantas.com.
Swiss ⓦ www.swiss.com.
Thai ⓦ www.thaiair.com.
United ⓦ www.united.com.

Packages and organized tours

In addition to fully escorted **package tours**, many agents can put together flexible deals, sometimes amounting to no more than a flight plus accommodation and a rail pass or hire car. Such packages can work out cheaper than the same arrangements made independently. Tour operators offering Switzerland are listed in the Trade pages of the UK, North America and Australia country areas at ⓦ www .MySwitzerland.com.

Ski packages

Many **ski** agents offer at least one or two Swiss destinations. Packages generally include flights, transfers and half-board accommodation (breakfast and an evening meal), but tend to exclude lift passes. Prices vary tremendously depending on the operator, the resort, the style of accommodation and the season (see p.27). Hotels aside, some resorts feature **catered chalets**, which sleep anything from two to fifteen or more. Free or discounted **extras** to look out for include lift passes, equipment, lessons, train passes and reductions for children. Opting to drive to and from Switzerland can cut the package price significantly.

"Lakes and Mountains" and other packages

Lots of travel agents offer packages to Switzerland, often under a "**Lakes and Mountains**" title. The most famous destinations are Interlaken and Lucerne, which offer a wide choice of hotels; prices drop if you choose self-catering accommodation, or stay in less famous resorts. Specialist companies offer small-group summer **walking holidays** around Mont Blanc, the Matterhorn and/or the Bernese Oberland. These can be a great way for experienced hikers and novices alike to get well off the beaten path. Some put you up in campsites, others use mountain huts and refuges, and a few may include vehicle support or porterage. **Cycling holidays** are popular, taking advantage of Switzerland's extensive cycle-path network and high degree of trail support. Some operators make use of the outstanding Swiss public transport system to offer holidays that link together **rail journeys** on classic Alpine routes. Some UK operators offer **city breaks** in summer or winter which can be excellent value (especially in low season), often including a discount travel card. Favoured destinations are Geneva, Lausanne, Bern, Lucerne and Zürich, but some operators offer Lugano, Basel or Alpine resorts.

Tour operators in the UK

Altogold ☎01903 743 193, ⊛www.altogold .co.uk. Family firm offering budget caravan/mobile-home holidays at Interlaken.

Crystal Holidays ☎0870 166 4971, ⊛www .crystalholidays.co.uk. Well-respected winter sports specialists, with destinations including all the top names plus less well-known resorts. Also standard summer city breaks and "Lakes and Mountains" deals.

Esprit ☎01252 618 300, ⊛www.esprit-holidays .co.uk. Specializing in family holidays to Saas-Fee – summer breaks and ski deals.

Exodus ☎020 8772 3936, ⊛www.exodus.co.uk. Experienced adventure tour operator running excellent small-group walking tours in the Swiss Alps at all levels of difficulty, plus novelty expeditions such as snowshoe trekking.

Great Rail Journeys ☎01904 521 936, ⊛www .greatrail.com. Specialists in train tours, with a full range of classic Alpine journeys.

Inghams ☎020 8780 4433, ⊛www.inghams .co.uk. Major operator with summer and winter packages of all kinds, competitive prices and plenty of experience. Especially strong on ski deals.

Interhome ☎020 8780 6633, ⊛www.interhome .co.uk. Swiss-based firm with a massive, easily searchable database of self-catering holiday homes and apartments in towns and villages all over Switzerland.

Keycamp ☎0844 406 0200, ⊛www.keycamp .co.uk. Specialists in summer camping and mobile-home holidays at Alpine sites, with good deals for families.

Kuoni ☎01306 747 002, ⊛www.kuoni.co.uk. A wealth of flexible summer and winter package holidays around Switzerland, taking in all the major resorts and most of the minor ones, with good family offers.

Naturetrek ☎01962 733 051, ⊛www.naturetrek .co.uk. Acknowledged leaders in birdwatching and botanical holidays worldwide, offering sympathetic, expert guidance for small-group summer tours to the Alps.

On the Piste ☎0844 585 8508, ⊛www.otp .co.uk. Swiss specialists, with a wide range of winter and summer deals to Zermatt, Saas-Fee and other destinations, including mountain-bike adventures, women-only groups, golf holidays and more.

Powder Byrne ☎020 8246 5300, ⊛www .powderbyrne.com. Slick, upmarket ski and summer operator, with a Swiss office and plenty of choice at major hotels in top resorts.

Railbookers ☎020 3327 0800, ⊛www .railbookers.com. Expert in tailor-made short breaks and longer holidays to Switzerland by rail, offering first-hand knowledge, flexible service and a wide range of support services.

Ramblers ☎01707 331 133, ⊛www .ramblersholidays.co.uk. Long-standing walking holiday firm, with small-group tours exploring remoter parts of the Swiss Alps and cross-country skiing breaks.

Ski Total ☎01252 618 333, ⊛www.skitotal.com. A decent range of catered chalets at Verbier, Saas-Fee and Zermatt, with flights from around the UK.

Swiss Holiday Company ☎0844 901 1100, ⊛www.swissholidayco.com. Small independent tour operator focusing exclusively on Switzerland, offering a range of destinations and packages.

Swiss Travel Service ☎0844 879 8813, ⊛www.swisstravel.co.uk. Specialist tour operators with a wealth of experience and local knowledge. Almost limitless choices around the country, covering one-centre and two-centre packages, city breaks, train tours, walking weeks, golf holidays, adventure excursions, farmhouse stays, wellness holidays and more. Winter skiing possibilities are equally comprehensive.

Switzerland Travel Centre ☎020 7420 4900, ⓦ www.stc.co.uk. Commercial arm of the national tourist board, with city breaks, fly-drives, tailor-mades and combination possibilities around the country. Options include train itineraries, bike or adventure holidays and gourmet tours, as well as plenty of more orthodox packages and skiing at resorts big and small.

Thomson ☎0871 230 8181, ⓦ www.thomsonlakes.co.uk. "Lakes and Mountains" division of the giant holiday firm, with a range of keenly priced options at leading Swiss resorts.

Travel Definitions ☎020 3327 0878, ⓦ www.traveldefinitions.com. Specialists in tailor-made holidays and city breaks around Switzerland, with excellent local knowledge.

Tour operators in North America

Abercrombie & Kent ☎630/954-2944, ⓦ www.abercrombiekent.com. Five-star guided sightseeing and customized tours.

Adventure Center ☎1-800/228-8747, ⓦ www.adventurecenter.com. Trekking trips in the Swiss, French and Italian Alps; be prepared to camp the whole way.

Adventures Abroad ☎1-800/665-3998, ⓦ www.adventures-abroad.com. Small-group adventure specialists.

Ciao Travel ☎1-800/942-2426, ⓦ www.ciaotravel.com. Jazz festival specialists, with tours to the Montreux Jazz Festival and others.

Classic Travel ☎212/843-2900, ⓦ www.classictravel.com. Luxury specialists, offering a range of upmarket destinations around Switzerland.

Connection Tours ☎416/449-0931, ⓦ www.connectiontours.com. Subsidiary of Carlson Wagonlit, with upscale gastronomy and cultural tours as well as hiking and biking options.

Euro-Bike & Walking Tours ☎1-800/321-6060, ⓦ www.eurobike.com. Cycling and hiking holidays.

Ibex Treks ☎505/579-4671, ⓦ www.ibextreks.com. Guided and self-guided walking tours in the Swiss Alps.

Knapsack Tours ☎925/944-9435, ⓦ www.knapsacktours.com. Small-group budget hikes.

Magic Switzerland ☎1-800/337-9477, ⓦ www.magicswitzerland.com. Destination specialist offering custom itineraries of all kinds to towns and cities around Switzerland.

Maupintour ☎1-800/255-4266, ⓦ www.maupintour.com. Luxury tours by train through Switzerland and Austria.

Mountain Travel Sobek ☎1-888/831-7526, ⓦ www.mtsobek.com. A broad selection of mountain hiking tours, including, unusually, in the Ticino.

Rail Europe US ☎1-800/622-8600, Canada ☎1-800/361-7245; ⓦ www.raileurope.com. Rail, air, hotel and car reservations.

Switzerland Tourism ⓦ www.myswitzerland.com. A vast range of tours and breaks of all kinds, from art and culture to in-line skating to spa and wellbeing retreats, presented by the national tourist board.

Visit Switzerland Tours ☎1-800/255-3537, ⓦ www.visitswitzerlandtours.com. Wide range of options offered by a dedicated specialist team.

Tour operators in Australia & NZ

CIT Australia ☎02/9267 1255, ⓦ www.cittravel.com.au. Tours of the Swiss and Italian lakes.

Explore Holidays Australia ☎1300 731 000, ⓦ www.exploreholidays.com.au. Accommodation and package tours.

Outdoor Travel Australia ☎03/5750 1441, ⓦ www.outdoortravel.com.au. Walking and cycling holidays, both group and self-guided.

Rail Europe ⓦ www.raileurope.com.au, www.raileurope.co.nz. Rail, air, hotel and car reservations.

Swiss Travel Centre ☎02/8270 4866, ⓦ www.swisstravel.com.au. Specialist operator for escorted tours and ski packages; can book car rental, train passes and inexpensive accommodation.

Switzerland Holidays Australia ☎03/9851 8747, ⓦ www.switzerlandholidays.com. A full range, from cycling to rail tours and more.

Switzerland Tourism ⓦ www.myswitzerland.com. A vast range of possibilities from the national tourist board.

Walkabout Gourmet Adventures Australia ☎02/9871 5526, ⓦ www.walkaboutgourmet.com. Classy food, wine and walking tours.

Getting around

The Swiss public transport system remains one of the wonders of the modern world. It's hard to overstate just how good it is: you can get anywhere you want quickly, easily and relatively cheaply; everybody relies on it as a matter of course; and it's clean, safe, pleasant and punctual.

Services always depart on the dot, and **train** timetables are well integrated with those of the **postbuses**, which operate on routes not covered by rail (including remote valleys), as well as **ferry** services on Switzerland's many lakes. **Cyclists** are well served by the Swiss instinct for green thinking; see p.50 for details.

One point can't be stressed enough: Swiss people virtually never pay full fare on their own public transport, and you should follow suit. Unless you're planning to drive or cycle everywhere, you will definitely save money by using a **Swiss travel pass** (see p.35). These are designed for visitors, giving free or discounted travel on trains, buses, boats, cable cars and funiculars nationwide. Most are also valid on urban tram, bus and metro networks in nearly all Swiss cities.

Tickets and ticket machines

If you decide not to get a Swiss Pass (see p.35), which is almost universally valid for free travel, you may find yourself having to tangle with **ticket machines** at some point. Most urban transport networks are divided up into apparently randomly numbered **zones**: in Zürich, for instance, the central area is Zone 10, bordered on various sides by zones 21, 40 and 54. Fares are calculated by how many zones you travel in. You nearly always have to buy your ticket before you board from the machines located at every stop. These are rarely marked in English. First, press a button for your **journey** – either a destination code or an option for travel across, say, one or two zones. This choice often incorporates a **time validity** (eg a short-hop ticket may be valid for unlimited changes within an hour). An alternative is to select a full-day pass. You may then need to choose either **one-way**

(a single arrow) or **round-trip** (a double arrow). Then, press a button for yourself – adult or child. Some machines give you the option to choose **1st class**. You'll also see an option for "**1/1**" or "**1/2**"; press the latter if you hold a pass that permits you to travel half-price. The readout will then show the fare to pay. You may not be able to pay with a banknote, but coins are always acceptable – either Swiss francs or, in some areas, euro coins. Some machines selling long-distance train tickets let you pay by **debit/credit card**.

By rail

The Swiss are the most frequent **train** users in Europe – not surprising, given the quality of the network. Travelling through Switzerland by train is invariably comfortable, efficient and scenic, with many mountain routes an attraction in their own right.

Swiss Federal Railways, or **SBB CFF FFS** (*Schweizerische Bundesbahnen*, *Chemins de fer fédéraux suisses*, *Ferrovie federali svizzere*), retains a monopoly on most of the network, but there are some routes, especially Alpine lines, which are operated by the companies which constructed them often a century or more ago. Two of the largest of these are **BLS**, which runs the pivotal Bern–Lötschberg–Simplon route between the Swiss capital and Milan; and **RhB**, the Rhätische Bahn, which operates trains within Canton Graubünden. There are dozens more, often tiny concerns used by local people to get to and from their nearest town, sometimes (such as the Bernese Oberland's **Jungfraubahn**) massive enterprises ferrying thousands of tourists from valley to summit and back again. However, you don't really need to know which company serves your route, since tickets and passes are universally valid and you never

Scenic routes by train, bus and boat

Although few Swiss journeys are short on scenery, there are a handful of routes marketed as extra-special. On most – after having **reserved** a seat in advance for a few francs – you just sit back, flash your travel pass and drink in the views. Some require you to change from train to boat, or bus to train, but you never have to walk more than the length of a station platform, and timetables are designed so that you're never in a hurry. (Plus, of course, you can always send your heavy bags ahead separately.) Most of these operate with **panoramic** train carriages, either with partial or total glass roofs, but for these – and for extras such as onboard lunches – you must pay a **supplement**. For full information check ⓦ**www .swisstravelsystem.ch** under "Experiences" (or ask at train stations or tourist offices). We've described the journeys in one direction, but you could just as easily travel in the other direction instead.

Note that you can follow the same routes on ordinary trains and pay no extras. You can also get on and off at intermediate points. And, it should be added, these are only the trips in the spotlight: equally scenic routes, such as the Centovalli, the St Bernard Express from Martigny, the Chur to Arosa line, or the tiny Grütschalp to Mürren railway, are just as deserving of your attention. Details of these and others are on the website.

Bernina Express ⓦ www.berninaexpress.ch. From Chur, St Moritz or Davos over the high Bernina Pass and through the Val Poschiavo to Tirano (Italy), where – in summer only – you switch onto a postbus and skirt Lake Como to Lugano. Total 8hr.

Glacier Express ⓦ www.glacierexpress.ch. A spectacular (and very popular) route, which counts as the slowest express in the world (average speed 30kph). From St Moritz (1775m) or Davos down to Chur (585m), then up the Rhine valley to the Oberalp Pass (2033m) and Andermatt, then through a tunnel beneath the Furka Pass and down the Rhône valley to Brig (671m), before climbing to Zermatt (1604m). Total 8hr, 291 bridges and 91 tunnels.

Golden Pass ⓦ www.goldenpass.ch. Flagship panorama route from Lucerne, running over the Brünig Pass to Interlaken and Gstaad, then a spectacular descent through vineyards to the Lake Geneva shore at Montreux. Total 7hr.

Palm Express ⓦ www.postbus.ch/alps. Postbus from St Moritz over the Maloja Pass to Chiavenna (Italy) and Lake Como, then crossing back into Switzerland to end at Lugano. No train track exists on this route. Total 3hr 45min. June–Oct daily; rest of year Fri–Sun only.

Voralpen Express ⓦ www.voralpen-express.ch. Prealpine Express route between Lucerne and Romanshorn on Lake Constance, speeding through the pretty countryside around Mt Rigi, Lake Zürich and St Gallen. Total 2hr 45min.

Wilhelm Tell Express ⓦ www.wilhelmtellexpress.ch. Another beautiful journey, from Lucerne by boat to Flüelen, then a train south, corkscrewing its way up into the Gotthard tunnel beneath the Alps and then through the Ticino to Lugano. Total 6hr. May–Oct only.

---

have to shop around. All trains, apart from local stopping services and mountain lines, have **first-class** and **second-class** sections.

Fares and passes

Swiss **passes** offer the most economical way to get around the country on public transport. There are no ticket gates: onboard inspectors are the sole method of **fare enforcement**, and they'll move through the whole train regularly. Get caught without a valid ticket or pass for your journey and they'll slap a hefty **fine** on you, to which a surcharge is added if you can't pay on the spot. Most regional and local trains are marked with a prominent **swirly eye pictogram**: this means that there's no assigned inspector and that you're trusted to either hold a valid pass or buy a ticket. Roving inspectors may board these trains at any point to check tickets. If you intend to use any kind of multi-day pass or undated ticket, you must stamp it before you board in the little boxes marked with the same swirly eye pictogram on platforms or near escalators.

The Swiss Pass

There are several different **Swiss travel passes**. All are good value, bringing a discount on bike rental from train stations (see p.51) along with other perks: it just takes some untangling to see which is best suited for your trip. Consult ⓦ**www.swisstravelsystem.com** for full details and purchasing.

Top of the pile is the **Swiss Pass**. This gives free unlimited travel on 4, 8, 15, 22 or 30 consecutive days on just about every train in the country, as well as on all boats and postbuses and most city tram-and-bus networks. Where travel isn't free (eg on cable cars and mountain railways), discounts of at least 25 percent apply. The **Swiss Flexi Pass** gives the same privileges as the Swiss Pass on any 3, 4, 5 or 6 days within a month. The Swiss Pass and Swiss Flexi Pass are available online, from Swiss tourist offices abroad and (in francs only) from major stations within Switzerland on production of a foreign passport. Two or more people travelling together (up to a maximum of five) all qualify for 15 percent off the cost of their Swiss Passes or Flexi Passes under the "**Saver**" scheme. The **Swiss Youth Pass** is a standard Swiss Pass discounted for people aged 16–26.

The Swiss Pass, Flexi Pass and Youth Pass can be boosted by the addition of a **free Family Card**, which grants free travel to children under 16 accompanied by their parents (non-family members under 16 pay half the adult price).

All these also double up as a **Swiss Museums Pass**, granting free admission to more than 440 museums nationwide – virtually every museum reviewed in this book (full listing at ⓦwww.museumspass.ch).

Other passes

The **Swiss Transfer Ticket**, only purchasable outside Switzerland, gives one free journey from the airport or border to anywhere in the country, and back again within a month – ideal for skiers.

The **Swiss Card**, purchasable abroad and at airport or border stations within Switzerland, extends the terms of the Transfer Ticket: as well as a free journey at the start and end of your holiday, it lets you buy ordinary tickets for travel by train, bus and boat at fifty percent discount (plus partially reduced fares on most mountain railways) for a month.

The Transfer Ticket and Swiss Card also qualify for a **free Family Card**, described in the section above.

The convenience and universal validity of the Swiss Pass or Flexi Pass are alluring, but it pays to do some sums before you splash out. Depending on the kind of journeys you're liable to take (all of which are fully researchable online), you may find that you'd be better off getting a humble Swiss Card and buying half-price tickets each time, rather than getting an expensive Swiss Pass and travelling for free.

If you're planning to concentrate on one area of the country, but still want the flexibility to move around, it might be more economical to get a **regional pass** for your particular region. These vary across the country in both price and validity, but normally give 5 days' free travel in 15 within a limited region, often including discounts for the other 10 days. Check online at MySwitzerland.com or with local tourist offices for full details.

If you're based in one resort, investigate the terms of the local **guest card** (*Gästekarte*, *carte des visiteurs*, *tessera di soggiorno*), issued for free when you check in at your hotel. These often give free transport on local buses and trains and – sometimes – cable cars and funiculars. Lift passes at ski resorts invariably give free valley-floor transport to and from outlying cable-car stations.

Timetables and information

The most convenient way to consult the national **timetable** (*Kursbuch* or *Fahrplan*, *indicateur* or *horaire*, *orario*), covering all rail, bus, boat and cable-car services, is online (in English) at ⓦ**www.rail.ch**. This lets you research individual journeys on specific dates between any two points in meticulous detail, including complete information on every train, down to platform numbers and the kind of onboard refreshments available, fare quotes, station maps, counter opening hours and loads more. You can also view live arrival and departure boards for every station in Switzerland. Links take you to ⓦ**www .fahrplanfelder.ch** where you can download PDFs of specific pages from the national timetable, to plot alternative connections at your leisure.

Check times carefully if you're travelling in early December, when the timetable is revamped each year. The paper timetable, comprising one book for trains, boats and cable cars, and two books for all the buses, can be ordered online or purchased at larger Swiss stations (Fr.16).

Alternatively, ask ticket-office staff how to get from any station to any other and they'll print out an itinerary for you showing exact connection times. The national train enquiry number is ☏0900 300 300.

Timetables posted on station hoardings are colour-coded: the **yellow timetable** always shows departures (*Abfahrt*, *départ*, *partenza*); the white one always indicates arrivals (*Ankunft*, *arrivée*, *arrivo*). Bus timetables (which are also posted at some stations) look similar: check in the top corner for the relevant pictogram.

Trains are identified on the timetable by an alphabet soup of initials. **ICE** are Inter-City Express services between Switzerland and Germany; **TGV** are high-speed trains between Switzerland and France. Sleeper services are either **CNL** (CityNightLine) or **EN** (EuroNight). Day trains across Europe – that stop at only a few places in Switzerland – are denoted **EC** (EuroCity). If you're holding an ordinary ticket or train pass, all of these are free of any surcharges within Swiss borders; you must pay supplements only if you cross an international frontier, or if the train is marked in the timetable with an R in a square box. In these cases, a seat reservation costs a few francs.

Within Switzerland, **IC** InterCity expresses cross the country stopping only at major cities; those marked **ICN** tilt round corners for extra speed. **IR** InterRegio trains ply between neighbouring regions, stopping at a few more places. **RE** RegioExpress services are one step slower. **R** Regio trains stop at every station.

Also listed on the timetable are **S** "S-Bahn" suburban stopping trains, numbered by route, which feed into the big cities from surrounding towns.

Platforms are marked out in **sectors**, from A to D: beware of short local trains departing from Platform 3 Sector A while you're standing 150m away at Platform 3 Sector D tapping your watch.

For mainline services, the PA announcement (and a detailed plan in **blue** posted beside the timetable boards) tells you which sectors the first- and second-class carriages will arrive at, saving you running up and down the train. Sometimes two short trains will depart in opposite directions from different sectors of the same platform.

Stations and services

It takes something of a leap of faith to realize, but in Switzerland a **train station** (*Bahnhof*, *gare*, *stazione*) isn't the dregs-of-the-earth place it might be in another country. Many Swiss stations harbour genuinely good restaurants (going out for a nice meal at the station is a new experience for most visitors) and many also shelter the only shops and supermarkets in their town that are open late.

Just about all stations, bar village halts, have **luggage lockers**, priced roughly Fr.3/5/8 for small/large/huge. Once they're locked, you can open them only once. Leave stuff for longer than a week or so and it may be impounded: ask beforehand what the time limit is. Access to lockers may be prohibited between midnight and 5am.

Many stations also have a staffed **left-luggage office** (around Fr.5 per item per day), open daily for long hours, and often combined with a **lost-property office**, a **bike-rental counter** (see p.51), and the **airport check-in** service (see box opposite). Other common facilities include **bureaux de change** and spotless toilets (free or Fr.1–2). Some unstaffed halts, marked X in the timetable, are a **Request Stop** (*Halt auf Verlangen*, *Arrêt sur demande*, *Fermata a*

Airport check-in at the train station

This is the outward-bound flipside of the "Fly Rail Baggage" incoming service (see box, p.28). If you're flying out of Zürich or Geneva with Swiss, British Airways (restrictions apply), Flybe, bmibaby, Jet2 or many other airlines (easyJet is excluded, as are all flights to the USA) you can **check your bags in** ahead of time for Fr.20 per item at any of about fifty Swiss train stations and, at the same time, pick a seat on your flight and receive a **boarding card**, thereby cutting out all hassle at the airport and letting you proceed directly to the departure gate. Your bags are transported independently and loaded onto your flight; the next time you see them is on the baggage-reclaim carousel in your home airport. Station staff will need to see a print-out of your flight e-ticket, as well as a train ticket or pass to prove that you'll be travelling to the airport by train. Full details are at Ⓦ www.rail.ch/baggage.

You can do a station check-in at the **earliest** 24 hours before your flight departure. Check online or with station staff for the **latest** possible check-in time (which might be the night before you fly).

richiesta): to get the train to stop for you, press the button on the platform (or in the train) well beforehand. Gesturing to the driver will not work.

Instead of lugging your bags around, you can register them (max 25kg each) at the station baggage counter for sending ahead. The standard service (Fr.10 per item), which operates between any two stations, takes at least 36hrs – you'll probably prefer the **Fast Baggage** option (Fr.20 per item), which lets you check your bag by 9am at any of about fifty major stations for collection the same day after 6pm. Full details at Ⓦ www.rail.ch/baggage.

By bus

Backing up the train network is a comprehensive system of **buses**, which get to every village, covering ground – such as in the high mountains or deep countryside – not served by rail. They exist not to compete with the trains but to complement them. The bus and train **timetables** are coordinated, ensuring watertight connections from one to the other (Swiss buses stick to their schedules with utter reliability). Bus stations are nearly always located beside train stations, and all Swiss travel passes are valid for travel on buses as well as trains.Most long-distance bus lines are operated by yellow **postbuses** (Ⓦ www.postbus.ch). Various regions have their own local bus companies, either instead of or as well as postbuses, but all are equally reliable. Note

that some longer bus routes – such as over the Alpine passes – require either advance **seat reservation** and/or a small supplement around Fr.10 to be paid: check online or with bus-station staff ahead of time.

By boat

All of Switzerland's bigger lakes, and many of its smaller ones, are served by regular **ferries**. Most run only during the summer season – which at its broadest covers April to October – and are primarily pleasure-oriented, duplicating routes which can be covered more quickly by rail. However, a leisurely cruise through the Alpine foothills to Interlaken, for example, or across Lake Geneva, beats the equivalent train journey hands down. All Swiss travel passes grant free travel by boat everywhere except on Lake Maggiore, which is mostly in Italy. Otherwise the **Swiss Boat Pass** (Fr.70) lets you travel half-price on most larger lakes for a year; the **Swiss Family Boat Pass** (Fr.90) also lets the kids travel free.

By car

Driving gives you extra freedom to explore. Switzerland's road network is comprehensive, and although the mountainous terrain can make for some circuitous routes there is the compensation of scenic – if sometimes hair-raising – mountain drives. However, Swiss transport policy means that cars are being given the squeeze, with tough parking regulations and strict law enforcement.

Driving your own vehicle

Minimum driving age is 18 and **third-party insurance** is compulsory. You must carry a red warning triangle and the vehicle registration documents. If you plan to drive on Swiss motorways, you have to stick a **vignette** inside your windscreen (details at Ⓦwww.ezv .admin.ch). This costs Fr.40 for any vehicle up to 3.5 tonnes and remains valid until January 31 of the following year; buy it from the customs officials when you first cross the border (or at post offices, petrol stations and Ⓦwww.swisstravelsystem.com). Trailers or caravans must have their own, additional, vignette. Getting caught without one lays you open to a hefty fine. Note that you can choose to avoid motorways altogether and stick to ordinary main roads, which are free and – outside cities at least – reasonably fast.

Renting a car

Car rental (*Autovermietungen* or *Mietwagen*, *location des voitures*, *noleggio di automobili*) can be expensive: cut costs by renting in advance from the big international agencies. To rent a car, you need a clean UK, EU or international **driving licence** that you've held for more than a year. All rental cars have the motorway vignette prepaid and, in winter, are fitted with snow tyres and supplied with snow-chains (and even a ski rack) for free. Although it's usually no problem to drive **across borders** you should check the rules with your rental company in advance: Switzerland is not in the EU, although it's surrounded by EU countries. Border controls can be time-consuming. Be certain before you drive out of Switzerland that you're not going to inadvertently break customs regulations or passport/visa requirements on your way back in. For convenience (if not price) it's hard to beat Swiss Railways' **Click and Drive** scheme (Ⓦwww.rail.ch/clickdrive), which lets you rent a car by the hour, the day or longer. Reserve online or by phone and pay one all-in price that includes fuel, mileage and insurance. The first time you rent you have to show your driving licence, but then you get a Mobility keycard which lets you drive away unchecked from any of 350 stations nationwide. The card stays valid for future rentals.

On the road

Switzerland and Liechtenstein drive on the **right**, **seatbelts** are compulsory for all, and penalties for **drink driving** are tough (one glass of beer has you on or over the limit). Always drive with **dipped headlights**, day and night. Beware of driving with sunglasses on, since there are hundreds of **road tunnels**, many of them single-bore with one lane in each direction and no central divider: you can be plunged from sunshine into scary blackness with little warning. If you're in a traffic jam in a tunnel, waiting for temporary traffic lights at roadworks or at level-crossing barriers, copy the locals and **switch your engine off**.

Swiss motorways/freeways are **signed in green**, while main roads are signed in blue; it's common to see a green sign and a blue sign to the same place pointing in opposite directions. A motorway (*Autobahn*, *autoroute*, *autostrada*) has a national number (N) and a pan-European number (E), eg N2/E35. **Speed limits** are 120kph (75mph) on motorways, 80kph (50mph) on main roads, 50kph (30mph) in urban areas, and 30kph (18mph) or less on residential streets. There are dozens of cameras, radars and laser traps to catch speeders, with spot fines levied.

At junctions, yellow diamonds painted on the road show who has **priority**; if in doubt, always let trams and buses go first, and give way to traffic coming from your right. On gradients, vehicles heading **uphill** have priority over those coming down; some narrow mountain tracks have controlled times for ascent and descent. If you hear an outrageously loud horn or klaxon sounding on country lanes or twisting mountain roads, it means that a **postbus** is approaching: it always has priority, up or down, so get out of the way. In cities, it's forbidden to overtake **trams** when they're at their stops. In the winter, signs indicate where **snow-chains** are necessary (practise fitting and removing them beforehand).

You can find **fuel** everywhere. **Unleaded** (*Bleifrei*, *sans plomb*, *senza piombo*; green

Breakdown assistance ☏140

pumps) is the standard. Diesel (black pumps) is widely available. Unstaffed 24-hour automatic filling stations – where you feed cash or a credit card into a machine – are cheapest.

You might have unexpected problems with **navigation**, since motorway signs often show the names of distant Alpine passes as indicators of direction, rather than naming the next major town. To drive on the *autoroute* from Geneva to Montreux, for instance, follow signs to "Simplon" and "Grand-St-Bernard", since these are the passes that lie at the end of the road, hundreds of kilometres beyond Montreux (there are no signs to Montreux until you're almost upon it). The main motorway heading south from Zürich and Lucerne is simply signed "Gotthard".

Signs to specific towns are always in the language of that town: Geneva is always "Genève", never "Genf" or "Ginevra". As for crossing the language border, there'll just come a point speeding between Fribourg and Bern when you'll notice that the exits, previously marked "Sortie", suddenly become "Ausfahrt".

Parking

Parking can be limited and prohibitively expensive. In full car parks you might find queues of cars, their engines off, drivers waiting patiently for the next person to finish their shopping and liberate a space.

Covered **parking garages** are signposted in all cities. Prices can be extraordinary: Fr.30 per day or more in central Geneva and Zürich, about Fr.15 per day around the country, and rarely less than Fr.1 per hr anywhere. Out-of-town car parks, often located near motorway exits and tagged **P+R**, are sometimes free or discounted; they're always served by a bus or tram heading into the town centre, for which you must pay.

On-street parking and open **car parks** are colour-coded. Spaces delineated with white lines – the **White Zone** – are most common, controlled either by individual meters or, more usually, a central pay-point (marked *Zentrale Parkuhr*, *Parcomètre collectif*, *Parchimetro collettivo*). These take coins only; costs can vary from Fr.0.50 per hr in small towns to Fr.4 per hr in cities. In most cases, White Zone spaces are time-limited. If your space is numbered, key that number into the machine, then pay. Sometimes that's enough; other times, you must press another button to get a ticket to display in your car. If your space isn't numbered, then just pay and display your ticket. Outside the hours posted on the pay-point, and where there isn't a machine at all (in a small village, say), White Zone spaces are free, unless there's a sign reserving them – as in *nur für Kunden*, "only for customers" of a particular shop nearby.

You can park in **Blue Zone** spaces if you have a special parking disc, supplied in the glove-box of all rental cars (also available for free from tourist offices, car rental agencies, police stations and banks). Spin the wheel round to show your time of arrival and leave it on your dashboard: this gives you 90 minutes' free parking if you arrive between 8 and 11.30am or between 1.30 and 6pm. If you arrive between 11.30am and 1.30pm, you're safe until 2.30pm. If you arrive after 6pm, you're OK until 9am next day. Rarer **Red Zone** spaces are free for up to 15 hours, as long as you display the disc. Spaces marked in **yellow** indicate private parking for, say, staff of a nearby company or guests of a local hotel; the only way to know is to ask.

Parking rules are enforced strictly and fines of Fr.50–100 for minor transgressions (such as having a tyre outside the marked bay) are common.

City transport

The most common form of transport within cities is **buses**, either petrol-driven or electric-powered **trolley buses**. Many cities also have **trams**, and a few have **funiculars**. Larger cities have suburban rail networks (**S-Bahn** in German, **RER** in French), which extend to neighbouring towns. Lausanne has the only true **metro**.

Within each city, all transport is integrated under one **ticketing system**, with no limitations on changing from buses to trams to funiculars or even boats within the time validity of your ticket. The Swiss Pass and Swiss Flexi Pass cover free travel within 38 towns and cities (see the map that comes with the card). Tourist-oriented regional passes give free travel within their allotted area; and city tourist offices sell various **day passes** of their own giving free or discounted travel, which can be excellent value. You must always hold a valid ticket before boarding. Ticket inspections are common within cities.

Metered **taxis** are always available, but given the density of public transport they're rarely necessary – and besides, you need to be on a Swiss salary to afford them. A base price of Fr.6, plus Fr.4 per kilometre, is normal.

Accommodation

As a general rule, you can turn up in any Swiss town at any time of the year and find a hotel room. However, booking ahead – especially in the summer and winter high seasons – is strongly advised. Fr.90–120 will buy you some kind of double room in any town in the country.

Swiss accommodation is relatively expensive but rarely disappointing: expect high standards, conscientious management and good service just about everywhere.

Tourist offices always keep lists of hotels, hostels, campsites and apartments in their area. They may also have a display board on the street with details of the local hotels, often with a courtesy phone. In many cases you'll find these boards at train stations as well. All towns and cities, and many villages, display distinctive **yellow-and-brown signposts** directing drivers to named hotels; you're allowed to drive to the door to load and unload, even in a pedestrian-only zone.

Tourist offices will always make a booking for you, either for free or for a small fee, and may run special discount offers on accommodation in their town. Wherever you check in, ask for a **guest card** (*Gästekarte*, *carte des visiteurs*, *tessera di soggiorno*), as this free perk for overnight visitors, where available, can give substantial discounts for local attractions and transport.

Some towns quote accommodation prices **per person**, while others quote prices **per room**. Our code system (see box below) standardizes them across the board, but you should ascertain what the terms are if you ask for prices direct from a hotel or tourist office. Most establishments post prices in both **CHF** (Swiss francs) and **EUR** (an approximate equivalent in euros): make sure you don't mix the two up. Bear in mind the fluctuating **high and low seasons** between lowland and highland resorts, described on p.27.

Accommodation price codes

All the hostels and hotels in this book have been graded according to the following price codes, which indicate the price for the **cheapest double room** available during high season. Single rooms cost roughly sixty to eighty percent of the double-room rate. Bear in mind that an establishment graded as a ❸ may also have better rooms at ❹ prices, and/or may have different rates for the summer and winter peak seasons, reflected by a range (eg ❸–❺). See opposite for guidance on bed prices in hostels and mountain inns.

❶ Fr.100 and under   ❹ Fr.201–250   ❼ Fr.351–400
❷ Fr.101–150   ❺ Fr.251–300   ❽ Fr.401–500
❸ Fr.151–200   ❻ Fr.301–350   ❾ Fr.501 and over

Hotels

Swiss **hotels** concentrate on value for money: you'll find that even the cheapest places have rooms that are perfectly comfortable, clean and respectable. **Breakfast** is included in the room price at virtually all hotels apart from the very cheapest and the most expensive. Note that in many mountain resorts, hotel prices quoted for the summer season are **bed and breakfast**, whereas those quoted for the winter season are **half-board** (ie also including an evening meal); we've marked this differentiation clearly in our reviews where relevant, but you should check what you're paying for at the time of reservation. A hotel advertising itself as "**garni**" has no restaurant, and serves only breakfast to its overnight guests.

Hostels and "backpackers"

If you're travelling on a budget, a **hostel** or "**backpacker**" is likely to be your accommodation of choice. They can often be extremely good value, and offer clean and comfortable dorms as well as a choice of rooms (doubles and sometimes singles). City and country locations can get very full between June and September, when you should book in advance. There are no age barriers.

Switzerland has two main hostel associations. The 70-odd properties of **Swiss Youth Hostels** (ⓦ www.youthhostel.ch) are the only ones to use the specific term "youth hostel" (*Jugendherberge*, *auberge de jeunesse*, *albergo/ostello della gioventù*). They're affiliated to Hostelling International (ⓦ www .hihostels.com) and are referred to throughout this book as "**HI hostels**". They're of a universally high standard. Most are closed for cleaning between roughly 10am and 6pm, and lock their doors sometime between 10pm and midnight (although checked-in guests can use night entry systems). Most close down in the low seasons: spring and autumn in the mountains, winter in the cities. Prices vary, covering the range Fr.23–42 (average about Fr.30) for a dorm bed including breakfast and bedding. Evening meals, where available, cost a bargain Fr.13–16 or so. Non-HI members pay an extra Fr.6, or can buy

annual membership on the spot for Fr.33 (under-18s Fr.22). Membership is automatic after any six nights of paying the supplement.

Swiss Backpackers (ⓦ www.swissback packers.ch) is a rival grouping of independent hostels. These lively places – referred to throughout this book as "**SB hostels**" – are less institutional than HI hostels, often in prime locations in the centres of cities and resorts, and priced competitively (average about Fr.29). Most are busy, sociable, resourceful places in the mould of backpacker joints everywhere, with kitchen and/or cheap restaurant attached and no curfew. No membership is required. They're all listed – along with practical information for getting around Switzerland on the cheap – in the magazine *Swiss Backpacker News* (ⓦ www.backpacker.ch), published two or three times a year and available for free in hostels and tourist offices.

All ski resorts have places offering **dormitory** accommodation (*Touristenlager*, *Massenlager* or *Matratzenlager*, *dortoir*, *dormitorio*) – often just one room with as many mattresses as possible squeezed into it side by side. The 150 or so **Alpine huts** (see p.50) have similar dorm accommodation, with bed prices rising according to how remote the place is.

Naturfreunde hostels (ⓦ www.nfh.ch) fall midway between countryside hostels and mountain inns, mostly historic buildings well off the beaten track, lovingly restored and maintained, and run by individuals with a passion for nature.

Mountain inns

Whole books have been written about the joys of staying in a Swiss **mountain inn** (*Berghaus*, *Berggasthaus*, *Berggasthof* or *Berghotel*, *auberge de montagne*). The term is a tricky one to pin down, since it can refer to varying styles of simple rustic accommodation. All, though, possess unique character, by dint both of their often spectacular isolated location (generally accessible only by foot, and then often involving long, hard hikes) and of their history – many are farmhouses converted more than a century ago to meet the needs of holidaying British gentlemen and ladies on their summer tours of the Swiss Alps. In general you can expect a wooden building in the local architectural style, with rustic decor (window boxes, antiques on the sideboard, grandfather clocks) and an informal atmosphere of cosy communality. Hikers are the main clientele, and Swiss families may return season after season to walk their favourite paths and catch up on news from their favourite *Berghaus*.

Most *Berghäuser* have chunky old beds smothered under plump duvets. Very few offer private bathrooms, some may not have showers, and a handful have no hot water, or must generate their own electricity. Most also offer **dorm** places (*Massenlager* or *Matratzenlager*). Food is universally good. Prices are very reasonable – say on average Fr.130 for a double, or Fr.45 for a dorm place, both including dinner and breakfast – but you invariably have to pay in cash. It's customary to settle your bill the night before you depart.

Farm-stays, B&Bs and private rooms

Schlaf im Stroh, *Aventure sur la paille* or **Sleeping in the Straw** (@www.abenteuer -stroh.ch) is a great way to get a feel for country life while guaranteeing accommodation at a fixed price wherever you are. Hundreds of farming families all over the country collaborate in the scheme, which runs from May to October only, each offering 10–15 places to sleep on straw in a barn (but as fresh and wholesome a barn as you could wish for), sometimes also offering beds within the farmhouse, and occasionally a place to pitch a tent. An overnight stay costs Fr.20–30 including breakfast (less for children). You must bring your own sleeping bag if you want to sleep on straw. Your host family can also offer a range of services for modest fees, including assembling a picnic, serving a home-cooked dinner, providing horses, renting bikes and offering guided tours.

Slightly less raw are the 250 **Swiss Holiday Farms** (@www.bauernhof-ferien .ch), which offer apartments and rooms for daily or weekly rent, year-round.

Bed and breakfasts, where you lodge in a room in someone's home, are becoming more popular. Tourist offices have details of B&Bs in their area, or consult @www.bnb.ch. Average costs are roughly Fr.30–40 per person. You may also come across signs in rural areas offering **rooms** in private houses (*Zimmer frei*, *chambres à louer*, *affitasi camere*).

Chalets and apartments

Self-catering accommodation in holiday **chalets**, bungalows and apartments is very popular: in Zermatt, Verbier, Gstaad and so on, you should book six months or more ahead. Interhome (@www.interhome.ch) is one of the largest **international agencies**, handling more than 5000 properties all over Switzerland. Prices start from about Fr.25 per person per night. High-season bookings are for a minimum of seven nights (Saturday to Saturday), but in the low season you may be able to find properties for three or four nights only.

Camping

The typical Swiss **campsite** is well equipped and well maintained. The higher the altitude the more limited the opening times: many close outside the summer season (May or June until Sept or Oct). There are sites everywhere, classified from one to five stars. Average **charges** are Fr.8–12 per person, plus Fr.6–10 for a tent and Fr.4–6 for a car. Booking ahead is recommended. The Swiss Touring Club **TCS** (@www.reisen-tcs.ch) runs a network of sites and is a useful source of information, publishing maps and a detailed *Camping Guidebook* (*Campingführer*, *Guide Camping*, *Guida dei Campeggi*). The **Camping Card International (Carnet)** gives discounts and covers you for third-party insurance. It's available in the UK from Camping & Caravanning Club (@www .campingandcaravanningclub.co.uk) and in North America from Family Campers and RVers (@www.fcrv.org). **Camping rough** is illegal, but in the mountain wilds – as long as you are discreet and take care to clean up properly after yourself – it's hard to envisage how anyone could complain.

Food and drink

Switzerland has a wide range of local cuisines, absorbing influences from French, German and Italian cooking while sticking close to its Alpine roots. Beyond the national staples, you'll find regional dishes relying on local ingredients and idiosyncratic styles of preparation that are unknown in the next valley, let alone the next country.

The Swiss take the joy of communal eating to heart. You'll often find rustic decor, wood beams, plenty of Swiss kitsch (cow-bells, alphorns and the like) and a hearty atmosphere – and that may just be in a lunchtime diner in Zürich's financial district. Urban chic aside, your most memorable meals may come from the simplest of kitchens and most ordinary-looking restaurants. See p.56 for advice on **tipping**.

Swiss cooking is firmly rooted in **dairy products**: cheese, milk, cream, butter and/or yoghurt find their way into most dishes. It's not hard to find good-quality, interesting and varied **vegetarian** options – many places offer vegetarian set menus alongside the standard meaty ones – but veggies should be aware that most restaurants default onto **meat-based** dishes: tomato soup may be garnished with bacon bits, and fresh salads may come layered with ham. Alternative-minded restaurants run by local cooperatives, found in many town centres, offer budget vegetarian and vegan meals as standard.

Breakfast

Hotel **breakfasts** tend to be **buffets** of juices, croissants, crusty bread, hard and soft cheeses, cold meats, fruit, yoghurt, boiled eggs and tea or coffee. You're also likely to find cereals including **Birchermuesli**, a lumpy concoction of pre-soaked muesli mixed with fruit and yoghurt (named after Dr Maximilian Bircher-Benner of Zürich who invented the stuff around 1900).

Bread differs from canton to canton. As a rule you'll find light, white breads in the French- and Italian-speaking regions, and heartier loaves in the German-speaking cantons: Basel's double loaf is thick and doughy, Zürich's drier and oval-shaped. Rye bread abounds in Graubünden (Poschiavo's is flavoured with aniseed) and in the Valais, where nuts are often added. The Emmental has *Züpfe*, a plaited white loaf made with milk.

Main meals

The line between a **café** and a **restaurant** is blurred: either can normally do you a meal, although generally only at set times (mostly noon–2pm & 6–10pm), with only snacks available in between. A *Restaurant*, *restaurant* or *ristorante* is more or less the same as an **inn** (*Beiz*, *Gasthof*, *Gaststätte* or *Gasthaus*; *auberge*; *grotto* or *osteria*), although somewhere with the latter name probably serves more traditional local cuisine. Both generally take one or two days a week off (*Ruhetag*, *jour de repos*, *giorno di chiusura*). Bans on **smoking** in public places, including restaurants – enacted canton by canton, rather than nationally – are taking effect in many areas.

Eating out is expensive. To avoid haemorrhaging cash, make lunch your main meal, and always plump for the "*menu*", or dish of the day (*Tagesmenu*, *Tagesteller* or *Tageshit*, *plat/assiette du jour*, *piatto del giorno*) – comprising two or even three courses of substantial, quality nosh, whether in a café or a proper restaurant, often for around Fr.18–22. The English term can be confusing: note that the **menu** is always the daily dish or dishes, while the list from which you make your choice is called the *Karte* or *Speisekarte*, *carte*, *carta*. Lunch *menus* are by far the least expensive way to sample the best of Swiss cuisine, and even fine-dining restaurants will offer multi-course lunches for Fr.30–45 (excluding wine). The same meal in the evening, or choosing à la carte anytime, can easily cost double.

Eating on the cheap

Budget travellers should head for the often surprisingly good **self-service restaurants** in town-centre department stores nationwide. **Manora** (ⓦ www.manora .ch) is often best, but Migros and Co-op are good standbys. These places offer a variety of generic dishes – soups, casseroles, pasta and the like – with buffets of fresh salads and chicken-and-rice staples, plus fresh-squeezed juices and fruit smoothies. Veggies and vegans can gorge. With pricing generally going by the size of the plate, you can easily get a full meal for Fr.15; some places, though, charge by weight (say Fr.2.50 per 100g), which works out more expensive.

For **picnic supplies** Migros is also the largest chain of **supermarkets**, with outlets everywhere. Denner is another. Aperto is a chain of convenience delis with usefully long opening hours found at main train stations. Most towns also have specialist food shops, such as a baker (*Bäckerei*, *boulangerie*, *panetteria*), grocer (*Lebensmittelgeschäft*, *épicerie*, *negozio alimentari*), cheese shop (*Käserei*, *fromagerie*, *bottega del formaggio*) and health-food shop (*Reformhaus*, *magasin diététique*, *erboristeria*).

Fondue

These days, you'll find **cheese fondue** everywhere, but it's really a speciality of French-speaking Switzerland. The word "fondue" refers to the broad, shallow earthenware or cast-iron pot used to heat the cheese, but that's where agreement runs out. Myriad varieties are served nationwide.

The classic style, found in the fondue heartland of Fribourg and the Vaud countryside, is a **moitié-moitié** ("half-and-half"), using either **Gruyère** and **Vacherin Fribourgeois**, or Gruyère and **Emmental**. Others may use several grades of Gruyère, or mix in some local Alpine cheese, Valaisian raclette cheese or Appenzeller. Whichever, it's a winter dish designed to be sampled with friends: a restaurant offering it in the summer is a restaurant to be avoided. Also, since they're never eaten alone, fondues are generally priced as a two-person (or more) deal, or as "fondue à discrétion" or "fondue à gogo" (both of which mean "all you can eat").

There's a ritual surrounding fondue consumption, which most Swiss take rather seriously. The cheeses are melted together behind the scenes, generally with a shot of some kind of alcohol (cider in the orchard-rich east, Kirsch in the cherry-growing central regions, white wine in Neuchâtel and Vaud), after which the aromatic pot is brought steaming to your table and set over a small paraffin burner. You use a special long fork to spear a small cube of bread from a separate dish (some places also serve little chunks of boiled potato and/or vegetables), swoop it through the cheese, twirl off the trailing ends, and pop it in. Don't be shy to give it a good vigorous swirl through the pot, since this helps stop the cheese mixture from separating. Lose your bread in the fondue, though, and traditionally the drinks are on you. The trick, as the pot gets emptier, is to regularly adjust the heat: have it high enough to keep the cheese from solidifying, but not so high that the mixture boils or scorches the pot.

With 150–250g of molten cheese consumed per person, a fondue can be quite a heavy load on your system. The Swiss-German remedy is to gulp plenty of hot herbal tea, thus making sure the cheese doesn't solidify in your innards, but the fearless Romands go the other way and chug chilled white wine throughout. Their *coup de milieu* of a shot of Kirsch (or some other spirit) halfway through the meal supposedly helps things settle.

On menus nationwide you'll also see **fondue chinoise**, where you dip slivers of meat into spicy bouillon; **fondue bourguignonne**, which involves dousing lumps of red meat in hot oil; **fish** fondues; Valaisian **fondue Bacchus** using mulled wine; and even novelty **chocolate** fondues.

Swiss regional specialities

All across German Switzerland you'll find plentiful variations of **Rösti** or **Röschti**, shredded potato formed into a large patty and fried golden-brown on both sides. This can either be an accompaniment to a main course, or, with the embellishment of ham, melted cheese, a fried egg and/or bacon bits, be a comfortably affordable main course.

Älpler Magrone is macaroni cheese with extra onion, bacon, potatoes and cream, often served with puréed apples with cinnamon. **Käseschnitten** is Welsh rarebit (toasted cheese), while *Spätzli* and *Knöpfli* are tiny buttons of boiled dough served drizzled with butter.

In and around Bern, you'll find **Bernerteller** or *Bernerplatte*, a hefty pile of cold and hot meats including pork sausage, bacon, various hams, smoked pork, knuckles and beef tongue, served with beans and *Sauerkraut*.

Zürich has **Züri Gschnetzlets**, diced veal in a creamy mushroom sauce, served with *Rösti*, while St Gallen is known for its pale, milky veal sausages. In Basel, winter menus offer **Basler Mehlsuppe**, a heavy brown brew of onions, pork lard and cream, thickened with flour and topped with grated Sbrinz cheese.

Graubünden is best known for **Bündnerfleisch**, prime beef air-dried and served paper-thin as part of an aromatic plate of mixed meats known as a *Bündnerteller*, or as prime ingredient in **Bündner Gerstensuppe** (barley cream soup with vegetables). You'll also see **game** on autumn menus, such as stews (*Pfeffer*, *fratem*) of chamois (*Gemse*, *chamutsch*) or deer (*Hirsch*, *tschierv*).

Zug and Lucerne are famous for their black **cherries**; Basel has a dark-red variety. **Meringue** was invented in or near Meiringen, and most Emmental and Bernese Oberland villages offer their own cream-laden meringue creations.

The prime speciality of French Switzerland is **fondue**. Another cheesy dish, **raclette**, is known countrywide but best savoured in the Valais: a large half-round of cheese is held in front of a fire, and as it melts it's scraped (**raclé**) onto a plate, and served with boiled potatoes, pearl onions and pickles.

The **saucisson vaudois**, or pork and beef Vaud sausage, is famous for its delicately smoked flavour, served boiled or steamed alongside *papet vaudois*, a puree of potatoes and leeks. Lakeside resorts prepare fresh fish in a hundred different ways, most deliciously as **truite meunière**, fresh trout floured and sautéed in butter.

Autumn heralds **wild mushrooms** (*Pilzen*, *champignons*, *funghi*), from simple *croûtes aux champignons* (creamy mushrooms on toast) up to flavourful game and mushroom casseroles.

Ticino (Italian Switzerland) has its own cuisine, more akin to the flavours and methods of neighbouring Piedmont and Lombardy. **Polenta** (cornmeal), **risotto**, leafy salads dressed lightly with olive oil and fresh pastas and **gnocchi** (bite-sized potato dumplings) with tomato or pesto sauces, are all staples. The Ticinesi also love their sausages, especially rich **luganega**. Spicy *mortadella* is unlike the Italian version, and is either cooked or air-dried for eating raw.

Drink

Swiss **cafés**, open from breakfast onwards, often sell alcohol and might also be called **bars**, although the latter tend to open their doors for late afternoon and evening business only. After work, bars and terraces fill up with people enjoying an **apéro**, a universally recognized term derived from the French *apéritif*, meaning a drink before dinner. A cosy *Bierstube* or *Stübli* – replete with wood beams and Swiss kitsch – is the evening meeting place of choice in many parts of German-speaking Switzerland, while daytime places for tea and cakes are dubbed **tearooms**, or left as nameless nooks attached to a *Konditorei*, *pâtisserie* or *confiserie*, *pasticceria*.

Coffee, tea and water

Coffee has some local variations. In German-speaking areas *Kaffee creme*, coffee with sugar and cream, is popular, as is *Milchkaffee*, with fresh milk. A *Kaffee fertig* is coffee with Schnapps. In Romandie, *café renversée* is the local name for a French-style *café au lait*. **Tea** (*Tee*, *thé*, *tè*) is invariably drunk without milk. A **herbal tea** is *Krautentee*, *tisane* or *infusion*, *tisana*. **Soft drinks** include a fizzy soda called Rivella that tastes all right until you discover that it's made from milk serum.

Water is safe to drink everywhere, whether from taps or public street-fountains. These fountains, even though they (or the horse-trough beneath them) may look grimy, invariably flow with spring water purer than anything you can buy in bottles. The only exceptions are fountains clearly marked "kein Trinkwasser", "eau non potable" or "acqua non potabile", with a pictogram of a crossed-out drinking glass. It's only ever worth paying for bottled **mineral water** (Mineralwasser, eau minérale, acqua minerale) if you want sparkling (mit Kohlensäure, gazeuse, gassata). Still mineral water comes out of every tap.

Beer and spirits

Beer (Bier, bière, birra) on draught (vom Fass, à la pression, alla pressione) comes as a flavourful lager-type brew, always served with a large head of foam. The standard measure (e'Schtange, une pression, una birra) is three decilitres (3dl, a third of a litre), which costs about Fr.3–4, or you can ask for a Grosses Bier, demi, birra grande, which will either turn up a half-litre of the same, or possibly a 0.58-litre bottle. A smaller 2dl chaser is universally known as a Herrgöttli. A panaché is a mixed beer-lemonade shandy. Alcoholic **cider** is suure Most, cidre, sidro. (Note that in Swiss German if you just ask for Most you may end up with non-alcoholic apple juice, aka Süssmost.)

The most famous **distilled spirit** or liquor (Schnapps, eau de vie, aquavite) is Kirsch (cherry spirit) from Zug and around Lake Lucerne. Plums and quetsches go to make Zwetschgenwasser or eau de vie de quetsche – similar to Damassine, a plum spirit from the Jura. Apple spirit comes as Träsch, Gravensteiner and many more, while Valaisian pears go to make aromatic Williamine. You'll also see grappa, a heady firewater made from grape-skins, stalks and pips.

Wine

Wine is one of Switzerland's best-kept secrets, since viticulture is flourishing, quality is high and annual production tops 200 million bottles, but – in the usual Swiss way

– many wines don't leave their local market. Just one percent of Swiss wine is exported.

Ask for the wine list (Weinkarte, carte des vins, carta dei vini) or – more affordably – for Offene Wein, vin ouvert, vino aperto, a few house reds and whites chalked up on a board and sold by the decilitre. Standard measures are 1dl and 2dl, which come to you in glasses, and 3dl and 5dl, which come in a small carafe. Paying around Fr.3–6 per decilitre is normal.

Switzerland's best-known wines come from the steeply terraced vineyards of the **Valais**. Of the whites, bright and floral Fendant is king, named for the ripeness of its golden Chasselas grapes, which se fendre, or split, rather than squish. Other Valais whites include fruity and alcoholic Johannisberg, sweeter Ermitage, and Malvoisie from the Pinot Gris grape (the late harvests, marked flétri, or shrivelled, are particularly sought-after). Valais' reds, led by Dôle, a blend of Pinot Noir and Gamay grapes, are equally respected. The connoisseur's Valais red is a Humagne Rouge. Dôle blanche is a rosé.

Canton **Vaud** hosts the **Côte** and **Lavaux** vineyards above Lake Geneva. Chasselas is ubiquitous, and Vaudois vignerons, particularly at Dézaley, St-Saphorin and Epesses, produce some of the best of all Swiss wines. Yvorne and Aigle in the **Chablais**, southeast of Montreux, are also renowned, and Canton **Geneva** produces affordable Gamays which have taken on imported French Beaujolais with some success.

Around **Neuchâtel**, Murten and Biel/Bienne there are dozens of local producers, with Chasselas still dominating. In the German-speaking north and east, the Riesling-Sylvaner grape is best known on Lake Zürich's "**Gold Coast**". The Rhine banks at **Schaffhausen** mostly feature Pinot Noir (aka Blauburgunder), while the warm southern Föhn wind nurtures Pinot Noir in the **Bündner Herrschaft**, where Graubünden, St Gallen and Liechtenstein meet. **Ticino** is dominated by Merlot: Bellinzona has less success than Lugano and Mendrisio, but a bad Merlot del Ticino is rare anywhere.

The media

The Swiss have a healthy disregard for the mass media: the German Swiss watch the least TV in Europe. To make up for it they read more, and more locally oriented, newspapers than anyone else on the continent.

Newspapers and magazines

Most of Switzerland's 200-plus **newspapers** report local and regional affairs in detail, but relegate the rest of Switzerland, let alone the world, to a few inside columns. Two exceptions are Zürich's conservative, highbrow **Neue Zürcher Zeitung** (Ⓦwww.nzz.ch) and its more progressive francophone equivalent, Geneva's **Le Temps** (Ⓦwww.letemps.ch). English-language magazines include *Swiss News* (Ⓦwww.swissnews.ch), a business and lifestyle monthly, and culture-oriented *Passages*, published on free subscription by Switzerland's Arts Council, *Pro Helvetia* (Ⓦwww.prohelvetia.ch).

Television and radio

The public broadcaster SRG-SSR (Ⓦwww.srg.ch) runs seven national **TV stations**: three from Schweizer Fernsehen (SF), plus two each from Télévision Suisse Romande (TSR) and Radiotelevisione Svizzera Italiana (RSI). Expect game-shows, chat, sport and dubbed US drama. SRG also runs Romansh-language Televisiun Rumantscha (TVR) in Graubünden. There's also a hundred-odd local and regional stations run by private operators.

SRG runs national **radio stations** in all four languages, as well as the English-language World Radio Switzerland **WRS** (88.4FM in Geneva and on DAB around the country; Ⓦwww.worldradio.ch), broadcasting news and music in amongst local programming. More than fifty private local and regional stations fill out the airwaves. SRG's foreign arm, **Swissinfo** (Ⓦwww.swissinfo.ch), delivers English news online, with audio and video options.

Foreign media

You'll find many British and international **newspapers** on sale the same day at kiosks in main train stations, some city centres and larger resorts. Prices are high. Hotels with satellite **TV** offer thirty or forty channels; expect CNN and often BBC World News, plus occasionally BBC Prime, showing British soaps and comedy, and one or two other English channels. As for **radio**, you might pick up the BBC World Service on 648kHz medium wave; otherwise listen online (Ⓦwww.bbc.co.uk) or if you're lucky via your hotel TV. World Radio Switzerland (88.4FM in Geneva, and on DAB around the country) broadcasts BBC news on the hour.

Festivals and annual events

Switzerland has masses of festivals (Feiertage, jours féries, festività), from town jamborees up to international extravaganzas.

Listing them all would be impossible, and anyway would ruin the experience – well within the bounds of possibility – of stumbling by chance into a village's annual knees-up of folk-dancing, street-barbecuing and general merriment. There's an encyclopedic events calendar at www.myswitzerland.com.

In **music**, the biggest show is July's **Montreux Jazz Festival**, featuring as much rock, dance and world music as jazz and blues, alongside open-air summer rock festivals at Bern, Nyon and St Gallen. Zürich's August **Street Parade** attracts a million techno revellers from all over Europe. Top dog for classical music is the **Lucerne Festival**, comprising separate events in March, August and November. The **Locarno International Film Festival** is one of the top five in the world.

Of **folklore festivals**, carnival in mid-February is celebrated best in Lucerne and Basel. Spring festivals in Zürich and Lausanne, and autumn harvest festivals all round the country, keep alive traditions of costume and cuisine stretching back to the Middle Ages. Keep an eye out for weekends of **Schwingen**, traditional Swiss wrestling that's hugely popular in rural areas and is generally accompanied by traditional markets, beer-quaffing and hearty sausage-feasting; they're held in central and eastern Switzerland over the summer months. There are also springtime **yodelling** events, culminating in July's Swiss Alpine Yodelling Championships.

Events calendar

Feb/March Carnival: The biggest events, which run contiguously, are in Lucerne (six days, from the Thursday before Mardi Gras up to Mardi Gras night; www.luzerner-fasnacht.ch), Bern (two days, beginning on the Thursday evening after Mardi Gras; www.baernerfasnacht.ch), and Basel (three days, from the Monday morning after Mardi Gras; www.fasnacht.ch). Many towns and villages stage Carnival celebrations big and small.

March www.lucernefestival.ch. Lucerne Festival – classical music.

April www.sechselaeuten.ch. Zürich – Sechseläuten: spring festival, with parades and fireworks.

June–July www.estivaljazz.ch. Lugano – Estival Jazz.

July 4 www.genevatourism.ch. Geneva – US Independence Day celebrations: the biggest outside the US.

July www.avenches.ch. Avenches Opera Festival: open-air performances in the Roman amphitheatre.

July www.montreuxjazz.com. Montreux Jazz Festival: eclectic showcase of global beats.

July www.paleo.ch. Nyon – Paléo Festival: huge rock and dance happening.

July–Sept www.menuhinfestivalgstaad.ch. Menuhin Festival Gstaad: top classical performances.

July/Aug www.verbierfestival.com. Verbier Festival: world-renowned classical event.

Aug 1 Swiss National Day: fireworks, folkloric shows, parades and more, in every part of the country.

Aug www.pardo.ch. Locarno International Film Festival.

Aug www.streetparade.ch. Zürich – Street Parade: techno/dance gathering.

Aug–Sept www.lucernefestival.ch. Lucerne Festival: one of Europe's leading classical music events.

Nov www.lucernefestival.ch. Lucerne Piano Festival.

Nov www.markt-bern.ch. Bern – Zibelemärit: onion market, doubling as town fair.

Dec 6 Celebrations around Switzerland for the arrival of St Nicholas (Santa Claus).

Sports and outdoor activities

Switzerland is heaven for outdoorsiness of all kinds: kids start skiing as toddlers, and it's common to see Swiss grandparents hiking and cycling on Alpine trails. Safety standards are very high.

Walking

You don't have to be a mountaineer to enjoy an active holiday in the Alps: Switzerland has some of Europe's finest **walking** terrain (Ⓦ www.wanderland.ch), with enough variety to suit every taste. In the northwest the wooded Jura hills provide long views across the lowlands to Alpine giants. The Bernese Alps harbour a glacial heartland but also feature gentle valleys, pastoral ridges and charming hamlets with well-marked trails weaving through. On the south side of the Rhône Valley the Pennine Alps are burdened with snow and glaciers, yet walkers' paths lead along their moraines. In the mountains of Ticino, which are almost completely ice-free in summer, you'll find trails galore linking modest, lake-jewelled peaks. In tourist areas walkers can use chairlifts, gondolas and cable cars in summer and autumn to reach high trails. For more information see Ⓦ www.swisshiking.ch.

Paths and signposts

Paths are well maintained, and clearly marked with regular yellow signposts displaying the names of major landmark destinations, often with an estimate of the time it takes to walk to them. Most signposts also have a white plate giving the name and altitude of the spot you're standing on. There are three major types of path.

A **Wanderweg**, *chemin de randonnée pédestre* or *sentiero escursionistico* remains either in the valley or travels the hillsides at a modest altitude, is sometimes surfaced and will be graded at a relatively gentle angle. **Yellow** diamonds or pointers show the continuation of the route. (You may also spot some cultural trails – old pilgrims' roads and the like – signposted in **brown**.)

A **Bergweg**, *chemin de montagne* or *sentiero di montagna* is a mountain path which runs higher or steeper and can be quite demanding, sometimes rough or narrow. They're marked with the same yellow signposts, but with a **red-and-white** pointer instead of yellow. Waymarks feature similar white-red-white bars. You may occasionally come across cairns directing the way across boulder slopes, or where poor visibility could create difficulties.

Higher, technical Alpine trails, marked in **blue**, are only for those accompanied by a mountain guide and carrying specialist equipment.

Switzerland Mobility

Switzerland Mobility (Ⓦ www.switzerlandmobility.ch) is a scheme bringing together routes for "non-motorized transport" – that is, walking, cycling, mountain-biking, skating and canoeing. In essence this means that information, maps and guides in English are available from a single online portal, as well as local tourist offices. Waymarking has been standardized with all routes numbered under a single national system, options for wayside services such as accommodation and baggage transport are easier to source, and routes have been fully integrated with public transport, enabling straightforward access to trailheads. It's an extraordinary system, typically (and admirably) Swiss in scale and vision. Everything is researchable online.

Planning your walk

No one should venture into the mountains without consulting a good **map**. Local shops and tourist offices usually stock a selection, including walkers' maps with routes and times. **Guided walks** are sometimes arranged by tourist offices in mountain areas, which may be free of charge for guests staying in local hotels. A series of excellent English-language **guidebooks** for walkers covering many parts of Switzerland is published by Cicerone Press in the UK, most written by Kev Reynolds (see "Books", p.512).

Always check the **weather** forecast before setting out. The local tourist office or mountain guides' bureau will display a two- or three-day forecast. Needless to say, do not venture to high altitudes if bad weather is expected. It's sensible to take a fleece and waterproof wherever you go. On more ambitious outings it is essential to be properly equipped with wind- and water-proof clothing and good footwear. Frequent official **avalanche bulletins** are published online (Ⓦ www.slf.ch) and publicized widely in mountain areas.

One-day walks

Never embark on a walk that under normal conditions cannot be completed **well before dark**. Reasonably fit walkers carrying a light rucksack should be able to manage 4.5kph on the flat, plus an additional hour for every 350m of ascent. Carry food for the day, including emergency rations, and at least one litre of water per person. On some *Bergweg* routes, fixed ropes are provided as safeguards. Elsewhere there may be sections of metal ladder fitted to enable walkers to overcome a short stretch of rock. Always check these first before committing your weight to them. Do not stray onto glaciers and snowfields, where crevasses lurk. Above all, don't be too proud to turn back should the weather deteriorate or the route become difficult.

Multi-day walks

When tackling **hut-to-hut walks** carry a map and compass – and know how to use them. You should also take a first-aid kit.

Don't rely on a mobile phone, since mountain coverage may be patchy; always carry a whistle and torch/flashlight. Leave a note of your planned itinerary and expected time of return with a responsible person who's staying behind in a fixed location, and when staying in mountain huts enter your route details in the book provided. If for some reason you can't reach your expected destination, try to send a message ahead to prevent the mountain rescue team being called out. In an emergency, give the **International Distress Signal**: six short blasts on a whistle (or flashes with a torch), followed by a minute's pause. Repeat until you receive an answer; the response is three signals followed by a minute's silence. Switzerland has no free mountain rescue service, and the cost of an accident can be extremely high. Standard travel **insurance** policies do not cover such emergencies, so if you are planning serious walks, choose a policy which specifically covers mountain activity and includes emergency rescue.

Mountain huts

Mountain huts (*Hütte*, *refuge*, *rifugio* or *cabane* or *capanna*) provide simple accom-modation for climbers and walkers and are invariably situated in remote, scenic locations. Most are owned by local groups of the **Swiss Alpine Club** (Ⓦ www.sac-cas.ch). Many are staffed by a guardian during the summer months – usually from mid-June to mid-September – who will prepare simple meals and drinks. Mixed-sex dormitories with large, side-by-side sleeping platforms are the norm. Blankets and pillows, but not sheets, are supplied: bring a sleeping bag liner with you. Prices vary, but are around Fr.25–30 for a bed, plus the same again if you include dinner and breakfast. Most huts have a phone and as a matter of courtesy you should phone ahead to book a place. Find more info at Ⓦ www.bergtourismus.ch. Membership of an Alpine club in your home country may entitle you to reduced overnight charges in SAC huts.

Cycling and mountain biking

Cycling (Ⓦ www.veloland.ch) is not the easiest way of exploring the Alps, but the scenery more than compensates for the extra effort required. It's a very popular Swiss pursuit, with dedicated routes countrywide integrated into the Switzerland Mobility network (see box, p.49) under the banner of *Veloland Schweiz*, *La Suisse à vélo*, *La Svizzera in bici*. **Mountain biking** (ⓦwww .mountainbikeland.ch) is also popular: many Swiss resorts produce their own guides to local trails and there's tons of information online. If you're arriving with **your own bike**, you have to buy a **vignette** from post offices for Fr.6, which covers road tax and third-party insurance for a year.

To **transport a bike** by train anywhere in Switzerland buy a day-pass for Fr.15. You have to load and unload it yourself using the specially marked carriage and you must have a ticket or pass for the same destination. On ICN tilting trains you must also buy a bike reservation (Fr.5). Full information, including trains where bikes are prohibited, is at ⓦwww.rail.ch/bicycle.

Bike rental

You can **rent** a new seven-gear country bike or a quality 21-gear mountain bike from Rent-A-Bike (ⓦwww.rentabike.ch), located at most Swiss train stations (look for *Mietvelos*, *location de vélos*, *bici da noleggiare*). If there's no dedicated bike office, you normally rent from left-luggage counters. **Prices** (which include a helmet) are Fr.25/33 for a half/full day – or Fr.20/28 if you hold any kind of Swiss travel pass. A one-way rental (for a full day) attracts a Fr.7 surcharge; you must let staff know when and where you intend to leave the bike. Prices drop (and one-way rental is free) if you rent for longer than a day. Kids' bikes and seats for children which you can attach to an adult's bike are also available, as are tandems.

Station bike rental is massively popular, especially throughout the summer months, and you should always **reserve** well in advance (at least a day or two). Even so, on summer weekends, city-centre stations like Bern and Zürich that hold dozens of bikes for rent can be completely cleaned out. If so check online, where you might find bikes available at a quieter station in the suburbs. Zürich, Bern, Geneva and a few other cities also offer **free bike rental**, invariably from

depots beside or opposite the train station. All you do is pay a Fr.20 deposit and leave some ID.

Skating and canoeing

The Switzerland Mobility network (see box, p.49) also include full details of **in-line skating** (ⓦwww.skatingland.ch), another massively popular pursuit. Three national routes cross the country, supplemented by lots of shorter local and regional trails. Boats and equipment for windsurfing are available for rent on almost all lakes, where **canoeing** (ⓦwww.kanuland.ch) is also popular.

Skiing and winter sports

It goes without saying that Switzerland is one of the best **winter sports** destinations in the world, with generally small-scale resorts that make a virtue of their village atmosphere and character. Expect peaceful, mostly entirely natural Alpine runs – many starting well above the tree line and set against spectacular mountain vistas. In addition, Swiss resorts are higher than most, and thus have guaranteed snow cover; lower resorts are beginning to feel the pinch from global warming. The **winter season** runs from mid-December to mid-April – though at altitudes above about 3000m the season extends from November to May.

Skiing, snowboarding and beyond

Skiing is split into two varieties. Alpine or **downhill skiing** (*Skifahren*, *ski alpin*, *sci*) is the more popular, and involves swooshing down the mountain on **blue** (easy), **red** (intermediate) or **black** (difficult) runs, according to your ability, or – if you're entirely confident of your skills and take all necessary precautions – venturing off-piste. Nordic or **cross-country skiing** (*Ski Langlauf* or *Ski Wandern*, *ski de fond* or *ski nordique*, *sci di fondo*) is seen as much harder work for much less thrill, but it benefits from no lift queues and allows you to get way out into the countryside. Prepared cross-country trails, known as *Loipen* or *loipes*, are laid on signposted routes fanning out from most resorts.

Snowboarding is massively popular, with resorts hosting half-pipes, lessons for all abilities and boarding tournaments all winter long. **Mono-skiing**, like head-on snow-boarding, uses a single extra-wide ski into which both feet are strapped side by side. **Ski-joring** involves being pulled along by galloping horses. **Snow-biking** or **snow-bobbing** are essentially cycling on snow. Many resorts have great facilities for **tobogganing** or sledding.

Ski destinations

The **classic destinations** include Davos, Klosters, Saas-Fee, Zermatt, St Moritz, Verbier, Crans-Montana, Wengen, Mürren, Grindelwald, Gstaad, Engelberg and Laax.

However, you might find slightly less famous resorts more rewarding, especially for novices or first-timers: they're cheaper and less crowded, but also lack that daunting competitive edge. A sample of these might include Arosa, Kandersteg, Andermatt, Braunwald, Villars-Gryon-Les Diablerets, Leysin, Lenzerheide, Savognin, Adelboden-Lenk, the Aletsch region, or Airolo. Year-round **summer skiing** is possible in a few resorts with access to glacier pistes above 3000m, including Verbier, Zermatt, Les Diablerets, Engelberg, Crans-Montana and Saas-Fee.

Ski passes and equipment

Passes for the ski lifts and cable cars in and around each resort vary hugely in price: a rough average is Fr.40–50 per day, decreasing for longer periods; the big names charge upwards of Fr.60, smaller or harder-to-reach places as little as Fr.20. You can always get half-day passes, and most resorts offer an array of multi-day passes, non-consecutive day passes, weekday discounts, early- and late-season offers,

and more. You can often get a bargain if you buy your pass before the season starts (by, say, November). Use of buses and other valley transport in and around resorts is invariably free.

You can always **rent** any amount of equipment after you arrive: one day's downhill gear is approximately Fr.45–50, cross-country gear around Fr.20–25. Inter-Sport (ⓦ www.intersport.ch) and SwissRent (ⓦ www.swissrent.com) have outlets in virtually every resort. All Swiss resorts have **ski schools** (ⓦ www.snowsports.ch), where you can, in most cases, just turn up and pay for a day's or a week's tuition in a group or one-to-one. Five mornings' tuition costs roughly Fr.150–200. Joining a **ski club** at home gives you access to impartial recommendations and details of specialist tour operators. The Ski Club of Great Britain (ⓦ www.skiclub.co.uk) has particularly good information.

Swiss sports

The classic Swiss sport is **Hornussen** (ⓦ www.ehv.ch): one person launches the *hornuss*, a puck, into the air by hitting it along a curved track with a long cane; the other players, standing well back, try to knock it aside with large wooden bats before it falls to the ground. **Schwingen** (ⓦ www.esv.ch) is an idiosyncratic kind of sumo-wrestling, in which both participants wear leather or canvas over-shorts; you've got to keep at least one hand on your opponent's shorts at all times, while trying to heave him onto his back within a laid-out circle of sawdust. Champs become rural folk heroes. **Steintossen** involves flinging a massive rock as far as possible. Foreign onlookers rarely make any sense of it all.

Travel essentials

Costs

Contrary to the stereotype, it's no more expensive to travel in Switzerland than in parts of Germany, Italy or England – and Swiss standards of service and facilities across all budgets far outstrip those elsewhere. Value for money is the national motto, and in most situations you get what you pay for.

A comfortable double room in a two- or three-star city hotel is on average Fr.140–180 (£80–100/US$130–170). Two people using this kind of accommodation, eating lunch and dinner in modest restaurants, taking in a scattering of sights and a luxury or two, are likely to shell out roughly Fr.300–350 (£170–200/$280–330) a day between them. Remember to add in a public transport pass: see p.35 for details of the numerous options available.

Staying at rural inns or guesthouses, avoiding cities altogether, and spending your days hiking or just relaxing in reasonable comfort is unlikely to set you back more than Fr.150 per day each (£85/$140), but going up a mountain – which may be the whole point of you visiting Switzerland in the first place – can wipe out a day's budget. A journey to the Jungfraujoch, for instance, costs roughly Fr.130 (£75/$122): hiking part or all of the way up or down can bring big savings.

If you're prepared to cut all corners by walking or cycling your own bike around the country, staying in hostels or campsites, and never eating out, you could scrape by on Fr.50 (£28/$48) a day.

Crime and policing

Switzerland has only a small force of plainclothes federal **police** (*Polizei*, *police*, *polizia*). Most policing is managed by the cantons, which have uniformed forces

Police emergency ☏117

operating in conjunction with municipal police. You must carry your **passport** at all times. All drugs are illegal: if you're caught in possession, expect either prison or deportation plus a criminal record. If you're a victim of **theft**, go to the nearest police station to get a report filled out (you'll need it for your insurance).

Electricity

220v, 50Hz (the same as in the rest of continental Europe). Plug sockets are mostly the round or flat two-pin type. British appliances will need a plug adaptor, while North American appliances will also need a 220-to-110v transformer.

Entry requirements

All EU nationals and citizens of the US, Canada, Australia and New Zealand need only a valid passport. Switzerland is part of the Schengen area; Liechtenstein is not. **Swiss embassies** maintain websites at Ⓦ www.eda.admin.ch. **Duty-free allowances** (Ⓦ www.ezv.admin.ch) are 2 litres of alcohol under 15 percent, 1 litre of alcohol over 15 percent, and 200 cigarettes or 50 cigars or 250g of tobacco.

Gay and lesbian travellers

Switzerland is very tolerant towards gay (*schwul*, *gai*, *gay*) and lesbian (*lesbisch*, *lesbien*, *lesbico*) lifestyles. The age of consent is 16. All towns have lobby organizations which serve as a focus for the local scene; national mouthpieces are Ⓦ www .pinkcross.ch and www.los.ch. Also check Ⓦ www.myswitzerland.com/gay.

Health

If you're arriving from Europe, North America or Australasia, you don't need any jabs. EU citizens are entitled to discounted emergency medical care in Switzerland and Liechtenstein on production of an **EHIC**

Ambulance emergency ☎144

(European Health Insurance Card), available in Britain at ⓦwww.dh.gov.uk ("Health advice for travellers"). You normally have to pay the full cost of treatment upfront and claim it back when you get home (minus a small excess); make certain you hang onto full doctors' reports, signed prescription details and all receipts.

Every **pharmacy** (*Apotheke, pharmacie, farmacia*), if closed, will have a sign in the window telling you where the nearest open one is. Virtually every Swiss **hospital** (*Spital, hôpital, ospedale*) has some kind of 24-hour emergency service. Wherever possible, seek advice from your embassy in Bern as well as your insurer at home before getting hospital treatment. You can get **sunburnt** very quickly in the mountains. High-factor sunscreen, a hat and total sunblock for lips, nose and ears are essential. UV sunglasses protect your eyes. **Hypothermia** is most often brought on by cold, wind and rain, with hunger and fatigue also factors. Symptoms include exhaustion, lethargy or dizziness, shivering, numbness in the extremities and slurring of speech. Get the sufferer under cover, replace any of their clothing that is wet (with your own dry garments if necessary), give them hot liquids and high-calorie sugary foods (chocolate), and reassure them by talking. Do not give them alcohol. Above 3000m **altitude sickness** can kick in. If the symptoms of headaches, dizziness and breathlessness don't pass after a day or two, the only treatment is to head down.

Insurance

It's essential to have good **travel insurance** to cover against theft, loss of property and illness or injury. Before paying for a new policy, however, it's worth checking whether you're already covered: home insurance may cover your possessions when overseas, many private medical schemes include cover when abroad and premium bank accounts and/or credit cards often have travel insurance included. After exhausting these possibilities, contact a specialist travel insurance firm.

Mail

Post offices (☎0848 888 888, ⓦwww.post.ch) – identified by a yellow logo and *Die Post, La Poste* or *La Posta* – generally open Monday to Friday 7.30am to noon and 1.30pm to 6pm, and Saturday 8am to 11am, although watch out for regional variations and restricted hours in smaller branches. Some main offices stay open over the lunch break. Sending a postcard or a 20g letter costs Fr.1.30 to Europe, Fr.1.80 worldwide.

Maps

Our **maps** of town centres and regions should be fine for most purposes; otherwise tourist offices always have maps, either free or for a few francs. The Federal Office of Topography (ⓦ**www.swisstopo.ch**) publishes a full-country two-sheet set at 1:200,000, detailed 1:100,000 regional maps and 1:50,000 and 1:25,000 hikers' maps, as well as specialist maps of cycling and skating routes, ski runs, cultural attractions and more. **Hallwag** and

Rough Guides travel insurance

Rough Guides has teamed up with WorldNomads.com to offer great **travel insurance** deals. Policies are available to residents of over 150 countries, with cover for a wide range of **adventure sports**, 24hr emergency assistance, high levels of medical and evacuation cover and a stream of **travel safety information**. Roughguides.com users can take advantage of their policies online 24/7, from anywhere in the world – even if you're already travelling. And since plans often change when you're on the road, you can extend your policy and even claim online. Roughguides.com users who buy travel insurance with WorldNomads.com can also leave a positive footprint and donate to a community development project. For more information go to ⓦ**www.roughguides.com/shop**.

Kümmerly & Frey are two major Swiss cartographic publishers with worldwide distribution and a host of products.

Money

Prices in Switzerland and Liechtenstein are in **Swiss francs** (*Schweizer Franken*, *francs suisses*, *franchi svizzeri*). The most common abbreviation is "Fr." – but you may also see "fr", "sFr", "Sfr", "SF", "FS", or the official bank abbreviation "**CHF**". Each franc is divided into 100; these are called *Rappen* (Rp.) in German-speaking areas, *centimes* (c) in francophone areas, and *centesimi* (also c) in Italian-speaking areas. There are coins of 5c, 10c, 20c, 50c, Fr.1, Fr.2 and Fr.5, and notes of Fr.10, Fr.20, Fr.50, Fr.100, Fr.200 and Fr.1000.

The currency in all the neighbouring countries is the **euro** (€), divided into 100 cents. Across Switzerland, you'll find vending machines, ticket dispensers and phone booths which may accept euro coins as well as Swiss coins. Tourist brochures often quote hotel prices in CHF and EUR: check which column you're reading.

Almost all Swiss banks have English-language **ATMs** (cash machines) which accept foreign **debit and credit cards** in a panoply of brands including Visa, Master-Card, EC, Maestro, Cirrus and Plus. You can pay for most goods and services using plastic – but lots of places still accept cash only, and some ticket machines accept only coins, not banknotes.

The best place to **change cash** or **travellers' cheques** is usually the desk beside the ticket counters at larger train stations (see ⓦ www.rail.ch/change). Rates are identical with the banks, no commission is charged (except at some airport locations), and they're usually open seven days a week for long hours.

Opening hours and public holidays

Outside larger towns you'll find that most shops and services (even public transport) take a break between noon and 2pm, to allow staff to go home for lunch. Otherwise **shop** opening hours are roughly Monday to Friday 9am to 6pm, Saturday 9am to 4pm. Quiet Sundays are sacrosanct. Most towns have late opening until 9pm for one day a week, often Thursday. Exceptions to all this are shops and cafés located beside or within train stations, which generally open daily for long hours. **Banks** in cities generally open Monday to Friday 8.30am to 4.30pm, sometimes with a break for lunch; town and village branches have shorter hours, some others also open on Saturday. Many **museums** and public attractions close on Mondays.

Public holidays

National **public holidays** – when almost everything is closed – are listed below.

Jan 1 New Year's Day, *Neujahr, Nouvel An, Capodanno*

March/April Good Friday, *Karfreitag, Vendredi saint, Venerdì Santo*

March/April Easter Monday, *Ostermontag, lundi de Pâques, Lunedì di Pasqua*

May Ascension Day, *Auffahrt/Christi Himmelfahrt, Ascension, Ascensione*

May/June Whit Monday, *Pfingstmontag, lundi de Pentecôte, Lunedì di Pentecoste*

Aug 1 Swiss National Day, *Nationalfeiertag, Fête nationale, Festa nazionale*

Dec 25 Christmas Day, *Weihnachten, Noël, Natale*

Dec 26 Boxing Day, *Stefanstag, St-Etienne, Santo Stefano*

Most cantons supplement these with local religious holidays: common ones include Jan 2 (St Bertold's Day, *Berchtoldstag*), Jan 6 (Epiphany, *Dreikönigstag, Epiphanie, Epifania*), May 1 (Labour Day, *Tag der Arbeit, Fête du Travail, Festa del Lavoro*), late May's Corpus Christi, Aug 15 (Assumption, *Mariä Himmelfahrt, Assomption, Assunzione*) and Nov 1 (All Saints' Day, *Allerheiligen, Toussaint, Ognissanti*).

Liechtenstein has all the same Swiss public holidays except Aug 1: its national holiday is on Aug 15 instead. It also celebrates May 1 (*Tag der Arbeit*).

Phones

For calls **within Switzerland** you must **dial all ten digits**, even if you're in the same area. Numbers beginning ⓣ0800 are free; ⓣ0900 are expensive; ⓣ0848 are charged as local calls. To use your **mobile phone** (cell phone), check with your provider in advance about roaming and charges.

Public phones

There are lots of **public phones** – always at post offices and train stations, and often at remote mountain refuges and rural hamlets, mostly provided by the former public utility **Swisscom**. A few accept coins (both Swiss francs and euros, which you can put in together), but the majority take cards only. Discount cards exist, but the easiest option is to insert a Swisscom phonecard (known as a "**taxcard**"), available from news kiosks, post offices, many hotels, train station ticket counters and some vending machines in Fr.5, Fr.10 and Fr.20 denominations. You can also swipe a credit/charge card (Visa, MasterCard, Diners, Amex and others). Pressing button L on the phone switches the display to English. Local calls are straightforward (dial all digits), but calling between Liechtenstein and Switzerland counts as international (see "Calling from abroad" below).

Phoning home

To call **internationally** it's easiest to use a Swisscom taxcard to dial direct from public phones; even quite a long call costs only a few francs. You can save money by asking for an international discount taxcard at kiosks: these quote a toll-free number to call, then you type in the PIN printed beneath a scratch-off layer on the card to access that carrier's lines. You can also use **credit cards** in public phones (Visa, MasterCard, Amex, etc), with no surcharges – you're charged only for the call cost.

Useful numbers

Emergencies
Police ☎117
Fire ☎118
Ambulance ☎144
Helicopter rescue
– Rega ☎1414; Air Glaciers ☎1415

Information
Enquiries/Operator ☎1181

Calling Switzerland and Liechtenstein from abroad

First dial your **international access code** (00 from the UK, Ireland and New Zealand; 011 from the US and Canada; 0011 from Australia), followed by **41** for Switzerland, followed by the local number **excluding the initial zero**.

To call **Liechtenstein**, dial your international access code (from Switzerland it's 00), followed by **423**, followed by the seven-digit local number.

Time

Switzerland is on Central European Time (CET), one hour ahead of London, six hours ahead of New York, and eight hours behind Sydney.

Tipping

All bar, restaurant and hotel bills are calculated with fifteen percent service included: staff are on proper salaries and tipping is officially abolished. Nonetheless, unless service was truly diabolical, everyone rounds up to the nearest franc. In restaurants, it's common to add two or three francs.

Tourist information

ⓦ **www.MySwitzerland.com** is the encyclopedic homepage of Switzerland Tourism, with a vast quantity of information including full details about visiting all corners of the country, virtual tours around every resort, weather forecasts, live pictures, maps, links, downloads, booking details, special offers and tons more.

All Swiss cities, virtually all towns, and a sizeable number of villages have a **tourist office** (*Verkehrsverein*, *Verkehrsbüro* or *Tourismus*, *Office du Tourisme*, *Ente Turistico*). These are almost always located beside, opposite, or within five minutes' walk of the train station, and are well signposted. Most staff nationwide speak at least some English and can provide you with free local maps, lists of hotels, restaurants, campsites and rental apartments, and information on local sights, events and transport. Most

Calling home from Switzerland

Note that the initial zero is omitted from the area code when dialling the UK, Ireland, Australia and New Zealand from abroad.

Australia 00 61   **UK** 00 44   **Ireland** 00 353
New Zealand 00 64   **US and Canada** 00 1   **South Africa** 00 27

offices sell hiking maps and guides to the surrounding area. Some sell transport tickets and parking permits. Staff may phone around local hotels to book a room for you for free; some extend the service nationwide (for which a fee – Fr.10 or so – is usually charged). Bear in mind that much of the information offered over the counter is also available online: we've noted tourist office websites throughout this book.

During the low season (in the mountains this means mid-Oct to mid-Dec plus April & May; elsewhere Sept–June), many tourist offices outside major cities and resorts have limited **seasonal hours**, perhaps only Monday to Friday 9am to noon and 2pm to 5pm, plus Saturday morning. If you miss these times it's still worth going to the office: many keep racks of leaflets outside for passers-by to take, and almost all post lists of local hotels in the window. Alternatively, ask at the train station: staff often keep brochures behind the counter.

Switzerland Tourism

ⓦ **www.MySwitzerland.com**
UK Freephone ☎ 00 800 100 200 30.
US ☎ 1-877 SWITZERLAND (794-8037).
Canada ☎ 1-800 794-7795.
Ireland Freephone ☎ 00 800 100 200 30.
Other countries Try the global toll-free number ☎ +800 100 200 30 (add your international prefix:

0011 from Australia, 00 from New Zealand, etc), or call direct to Zürich ☎ +41 43 210 5500.

Useful websites

ⓦ **www.meteoswiss.ch** Detailed weather forecasts.
ⓦ **www.swissinfo.ch** Primary source of Swiss news; also lots of excellent features on travel, culture and Swiss heritage.
ⓦ **www.swissworld.org** National information portal.

Travellers with disabilities

Switzerland is one of the most enlightened European countries for travellers with disabilities. There's a wealth of information to help with planning, and you'll find most facilities have been designed with everybody in mind. There's lots of material at MySwitzerland .com: look for the section "Guests with Special Needs".

Active Motion ⓦ www.activemotion.ch. Snow sports school for people with disabilities.
Mobility International Switzerland ⓦ www .mis-ch.ch. Useful information and links.
Rollihotel ⓦ www.rollihotel.ch. Wheelchair-friendly hotels.
SBB Call Center Handicap ☎ 0800 007 102 or +41 51 225 7150, ⓔ mobil@sbb.ch, ⓦ www.rail .ch/mobil. Info about all forms of public transport, plus arrangements for travel anywhere in Switzerland.

Guide

Guide

Geneva

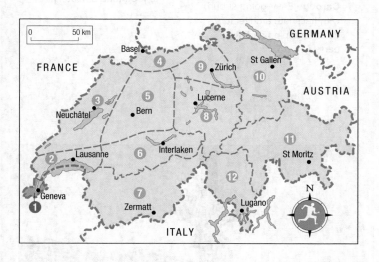

CHAPTER 1 # Highlights

* **Jet d'Eau** Giant fountain, symbol of the city. See p.70

* **Cathédrale St-Pierre** The seat of Calvin's Reformation, at the heart of Geneva's Old Town. See p.74

* **Fondation Baur** Museum of exquisite Chinese and Japanese art and ceramics. See p.76

* **Carouge** Easy-going suburb with Italianate architecture, good shopping and lively bars. See p.77

* **Les Pâquis** Gritty, multiethnic district with diverse restaurants and engaging street life. See p.79

* **Musée de la Croix-Rouge** Superb museum-with-a-conscience, devoted to the history of the Red Cross. See p.80

* **The UN tour** Stand in the footsteps of history. See p.82

▲ The Jet d'Eau

Geneva

GENEVA is an anomaly, the nearest thing the world has to an international city, and yet with nothing of the pizzazz such a description might suggest. From its profile in world events, you'd imagine a megalopolis on the scale of London or New York, but Geneva is little more than town-sized. From its demographic diversity – 38 percent of the population is non-Swiss – you'd imagine its streets to be thronged with the nationalities of the world, but across most of the city centre you'd be hard-pushed to spot a non-white face or eavesdrop on a conversation that wasn't in French or US-accented English. It's in the most beautiful of locations, centred around the point where the River Rhône flows out of **Lake Geneva** (Lac Léman in French), flanked on one side by the Jura ridges and on the other by the first peaks of the Savoy Alps, but for all that, Geneva is a curiously unsatisfying place to spend more than a few days.

The spiritual father of the city is the Reformer **Jean Calvin**, the inspiration behind Puritanism and Scottish Presbyterianism, who turned Geneva into what was dubbed a "Protestant Rome" in the sixteenth century. His parsimonious spirit remains the motive force behind this wealthiest and least exuberant of city-states. The "Republic and Canton of Geneva" is only nominally within Switzerland's borders, squeezed into a bulge of land that shares just 4km of internal border with the neighbouring Swiss canton but 108km with France all around. Some thirty thousand French *frontaliers* commute daily to their workplaces in Geneva from dormitory towns just over the border, benefiting from a high Swiss salary and relatively low French living expenses. Equally large numbers of Genevois save money by doing cross-border shopping in France. And Calvinism is so ingrained that the conservative Genevois – surrounded as they are by some of the world's most expensive shops and most exquisite restaurants – can't quite bring themselves to indulge, and leave most of the high living to the global glitterati who've taken up residence on the lakeside hills.

Instead, Geneva has become the businessperson's city *par excellence*, efficient, unrufflable and packed with hotels. The cobbled **Old Town**, high on its central hill, is atmospheric but strangely austere, with abiding impressions of high, grey walls and the stern tap-tap of passing footsteps. At the heart of the city is the huge **Cathédrale St-Pierre**, surrounded by top-class **museums**, including the giant Musée d'Art et d'Histoire and an impressive gallery of East Asian art, the Fondation Baur. Livelier residential neighbourhoods on both banks of the Rhône, such as **Les Pâquis** and **Plainpalais**, offer better wandering, while a short way south of the centre is **Carouge**, an attractive eighteenth-century suburb built in Sardinian style to be a place of decadence and freedom beyond Geneva's control; its reputation lives on in its population of artists and designers.

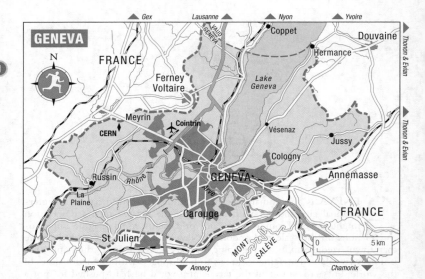

Last but not least, Geneva is home to dozens of international organizations. Two of them – the **United Nations**' European headquarters and the International Committee of the **Red Cross**, the latter with an award-winning museum – allow visitors a glimpse of the unseen lifeblood of the city, the diplomatic and administrative flair that has made Geneva world capital of bureaucracy.

Some history

Pile dwellings on the lakeshore date back to 3000 BC, but Geneva's high ground wasn't inhabited until 500 BC, when the Celtic Allobroges tribe settled. By 58 BC, **Rome** had taken over: the first recorded use of the name *Genua* was by Julius Caesar. The town was a bishopric by 400 AD but, located on the turbulent mid-line of Europe, was continually conquered and reconquered, by Burgundians, Franks, Merovingians, Carolingians and more, until the fifteenth century, when it gained a reputation as a trading capital. The dukes of **Savoy** held power until 1530, when citizens took matters into their own hands and formed a pact with Bern and Fribourg. The Savoyards granted Geneva independence shortly after.

In 1535, the Genevois accepted the **Reformation**; the following year, the preacher **Jean Calvin** visited. Born in Picardy in 1509, Calvin was expelled from the University of Paris for his heterodox views, and arrived by chance in Geneva, where priest Guillaume Farel asked him to help consolidate the Reformation. After two years battling city politicians both were expelled, only to return in 1541. Calvin then began instituting sweeping social and political reforms. Geneva became a beacon of **refuge**: French Huguenots and Italian Protestants flooded into the city. The Geneva Bible of 1560 was the first English translation to be organized with numbered verses, and the city's printing presses turned out hundreds of radical texts, unprintable elsewhere.

In 1602, forces of the Duke of Savoy tried to retake Geneva, but were repulsed in an event that is still commemorated today, in a celebration of the city's independent, patriotic spirit, as **L'Escalade**. Wave after wave of refugees settled in Geneva. Commerce, banking and watchmaking all flourished, and in 1792 the aristocracy was overthrown and a **Republic** declared with political equality for all. Geneva was annexed by France in 1798 and, following the defeat of Napoleon, threw in its lot with the Swiss Confederation in 1815. A Genevan businessman, Henri Dunant, shaped the **Geneva Convention** of 1864, setting down for the first time rules for soldiers' conduct in war. This led to the creation of the **Red Cross**, designed to help soldiers or civilians caught up in war or natural disasters (see p.80).

After World War I, Geneva was chosen as the seat of the League of Nations and, in 1945, as the European headquarters of the **United Nations**. Since then, the city has looked outwards for inspiration, away from the rest of Switzerland and towards the international community, many of whose conflicts have been negotiated away in the halls and chambers of Geneva's Palais des Nations.

Arrival and information

Geneva's **airport** (Ⓦ www.gva.ch) is 5km northwest at Cointrin. A machine in the baggage reclaim hall dispenses free transport tickets valid for 90 minutes on all public transport (including the train into town). The **tourist information** desk (daily 6am–midnight) is in plain view, offering free maps and hotel reservation. To the left is a revolving door giving access into the adjacent train station ("Gare CFF"), from where all **trains** stop at Geneva's main station (6min) before continuing direct to towns across Switzerland, including Lausanne, Montreux, Fribourg, Bern, Zürich, Sion, Neuchâtel and more. **Taxis** charge around Fr.35–40.

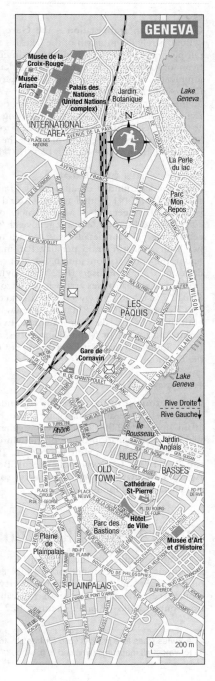

By train

Geneva's main **train** station – the **Gare de Cornavin** – couldn't be more central, barely 300m north of the lake. It's also a terminus of the French SNCF rail network: if you're arriving on an intercity train (TGV or not) from Paris, Lyon or Grenoble you'll pass through customs and passport control before joining the throng within the station proper. In the station is a TPG office (*Transports publics genevois*; Mon–Fri 7am–7pm, Sat 9am–6pm; ⓦ www.tpg.ch), giving out tram and bus maps and selling tickets. French SNCF local trains from Evian, Chamonix and Annecy, connecting at Annemasse and La Roche, arrive at the tiny **Gare des Eaux-Vives**, well to the east of the centre; opposite is a terrace of houses, to the right of which the Rue de Savoie heads 50m up to the main road, from where trams #12/#16/#17 head right into the centre.

By car, bus and boat

Geneva is surrounded on all sides by France: the only Swiss **autoroute** into the city is the N1 from Lausanne. You'd do well to arrange **parking** with your hotel or get rid of your vehicle on the city limits. Parking garages citywide are listed at ⓦ www.geneve.ch/parkings. On-street parking in the centre (see p.39 for details) is very hard to find; garages charge roughly Fr.2 per hour or a stiff Fr.35 per day. Parking de Cornavin (ⓣ 022 827 44 90), under the train station square, is cheapest on the lowest levels, and is also discounted for train users (Fr.22 per day).

All international **buses** arrive at the Gare Routière, on central Place Dorcière (ⓣ 022 732 02 30, ⓦ www.coach-station.com).

CGN **boats** (ⓣ 0848 811 848, ⓦ www.cgn.ch) village-hop their way along both shores of the lake from Lausanne, Evian and Nyon. Boats drop off at the Jardin Anglais and/or Mont-Blanc jetties, at either end of the Pont du Mont-Blanc. Some also call in at Eaux-Vives, east of the Jet d'Eau, and Les Pâquis, near the Casino.

Information

Geneva's **tourist office** covers the city and canton. The main branch is near the station at 18 Rue du Mont-Blanc (Mon 10am–6pm, Tues–Sat 9am–6pm, Sun 10am–4pm; ⓣ 022 909 70 00, ⓦ www.genevatourism.ch), and there's also a desk within the information office of the Municipality of Geneva, situated on the Pont de la Machine (Mon noon–6pm, Tues–Fri 9am–6pm, Sat 10am–5pm; ⓣ 022 311 99 70, ⓦ www.ville-ge.ch). Both stock the free weekly **Genève Agenda** (ⓦ www.le-guide.ch), a useful source of information on sightseeing and current exhibitions.

City transport and tours

Walking is feasible for the heart of Geneva – even getting to further-flung attractions such as Carouge or the UN takes only twenty or thirty minutes on foot – but you'll probably resort to **city transport** once or twice. Renting a bike (see p.57) can make sense. You can hail **taxis** in the street, take them from public ranks or order them (ⓣ 022 331 41 33, ⓦ www.taxi-phone.ch)

A **Swiss Pass** (see p.35) is valid for free city transport in Geneva and free admission to almost all museums reviewed in this book.

– but with a Fr.6.30 flagfall, Fr.3.20 per kilometre (more on Sundays and at night), plus Fr.1.50 per piece of luggage, they're only a ski-mask short of daylight robbery.

Trams, buses and boats

You can travel free on Geneva's **trams**, **buses** and **boats** with a Swiss Pass (see p.35) or a transport card, which is given free when you check-in to any of the city's hotels or hostels and remains valid for the duration of your stay.

Otherwise you must buy tickets – which are valid on all trams, buses and boats within the relevant zones – before you board from the Unireso machines (Ⓦwww.unireso.com) at every stop. They accept **coins only** (Swiss francs and euros). For city-centre trips stick to the "**Tout-Genève**" fare tariff, which includes a short-hop fare (three stops only; Fr.2); a ticket for unlimited travel within one hour (Fr.3); the **carte dès 9 heures**, valid for unlimited journeys from 9am to midnight (Fr.7); and the **carte 24 heures** (Fr.10; on Sat & Sun valid for two people travelling together). Information offices (Ⓦwww.tpg.ch) in the train station and at the large Rond-Point de Rive interchange northeast of the Old Town (both Mon–Sat 7am–7pm, Sun 10am–6pm) can help.

Little ferries (**mouettes**) run by SMGN (Ⓦwww.swissboat.com) carry passengers across the mouth of the lake on four routes, labelled M1–M4 (all Mon–Sat 7.30am–7.30pm, Sun 10am–5pm; June–Aug Sun until 7pm). All citywide tickets and passes are valid.

City tours and walks

For **self-guided walks**, the best option is to pick up an audioguide from the tourist office for an informative 25-point walk in the Old Town at your own pace (Fr.10 plus Fr.50 deposit; max. 4hr). Alternatively, the tourist office publishes eight "Geneva On Foot" brochures detailing themed city walks. Official **guided walks** through the Old Town depart from the tourist office (Sat 10am; June–Sept also Mon–Fri 10am plus Tues & Thurs 6.30pm; 2hr; Fr.15).

The CGN (Ⓦwww.cgn.ch) has plenty of cruises, starting from the Mont-Blanc jetty, including **Les Belles Rives Genevoises** – an hour-long circular tour of both lakeshores (4–6 daily; Fr.17) – and dozens of eat-aboard brunch,

---

Easy day-trips from Geneva by train

Château de Chillon p.128. Fairy-tale lakeside castle. Change at Vevey onto bus #1. 1hr 30min.

Château d'Oex p.265. Stunning scenery on the Golden Pass line (p.131) to this quiet Alpine resort. Change at Montreux. 2hr.

Fribourg p.218. Wander the medieval lanes of this relaxed, bilingual university town. Direct. 1hr 20min.

Lausanne p.95. Lively, colourful city with outstanding galleries and a trendy waterfront promenade. Direct. 35min.

Les Diablerets p.275. Tiny mountain village on a scenic train line, offering year-round glacier skiing at 3000m. Change at Aigle. 2hr 10min.

Mont Salève p.88. Cable-car ride near Geneva for views and walks. Passport needed. City bus #8 to Veyrier-Douane. 50min.

St-Cergue p.117. Refresh yourself with mountain air and tranquil views from 1047m. Change at Nyon. 50min.

St-Saphorin p.119. Beautiful old wine village set amidst the Lavaux vineyards. Change at Lausanne. 1hr.

lunch and evening cruises for around Fr.25–40 (meals Fr.40–80 extra). Smaller companies ranged along both lakefronts tend to offer more regular departures; just wander along until you see a trip you fancy.

Accommodation

Geneva has a good selection of budget and mid-range **accommodation**, adding to the palace hotels catering to diplomats and the international glitterati. Booking ahead is essential, since all affordable rooms can easily get snapped up by delegates to the continuous round of conferences and international events that are the lifeblood of the city. Check Ⓦ www.genevatourism.ch for weekend or off-peak deals. All these places are keyed on the maps on p.71 (Rive Gauche), p.73 (Old Town), p.77 (Carouge) or p.78 (Rive Droite).

Camping and hostels

Camping d'Hermance is a pleasant **campsite** 14km northeast by the French border, at 44 Rue du Nord (Ⓣ 022 751 14 83; April–Sept), reachable on bus E and with free access to the lake. Also check with the tourist office for details of student dorms providing budget accommodation out of term-time.

Auberge de Jeunesse (HI hostel) 30 Rue Rothschild, Les Pâquis Ⓣ 022 732 62 60, Ⓦ www .youthhostel.ch & www.yh-geneva.ch. Big, bustling and well-maintained hostel. Tram #13/15 to Butini. ❶–❷

City Hostel (SB hostel) 2 Rue Ferrier, Les Pâquis Ⓣ 022 901 15 00, Ⓦ www.cityhostel.ch. Functional backpacker place with good facilities. Tram #13/15 to Môle. ❶

Hotels

Plenty of **inexpensive** hotels pack the centre of town – although bear in mind that parts of the Pâquis district in particular can get sleazy. There's a wealth of choice in **mid-range** rooms, with some bargains available from hotels which haven't yet updated to the slick, generic style that tends to prevail. The Geneva-only chain Manotel has six classy hotels (3 three-star, 3 four-star) located within five minutes of each other in the Pâquis, often with exceptionally good-value deals. Stratospherically **expensive** hotels abound.

Inexpensive hotels

Rive Droite: Station area and Les Pâquis

At Home 16 Rue de Fribourg Ⓣ 022 906 19 00, Ⓦ www.hotel-at-home.ch. Clean, modern, sound-proofed rooms, convenient for the location. ❸
Balzac 14 Rue de l'Ancien-Port Ⓣ 022 731 01 60, Ⓦ www.hotel-balzac.ch. Quiet and very spacious rooms – albeit rather bizarrely old-fashioned – just off the Place de la Navigation. Parking Fr.12 per day. ❸–❹
De la Cloche 6 Rue de la Cloche Ⓣ 022 732 94 81, Ⓦ www.geneva-hotel.ch/cloche. Eight spotless, characterful, high-ceilinged rooms in what was formerly a private apartment in a quiet area of the Pâquis 50m from the lake. The pleasant atmosphere is enhanced by period fittings such as original fireplaces and wood floors. Regularly full. ❷
Ibis 10 Rue Voltaire Ⓣ 022 338 20 20, Ⓦ www .ibishotel.com. Generic, functional chain hotel in the city centre, characterless but low-priced. ❸
International & Terminus 20 Rue des Alpes Ⓣ 022 906 97 77, Ⓦ www.international-terminus .ch. Clean and comfortable, a stone's throw from the station. Ask for an upper floor to avoid the worst of the street noise. ❸–❹
Des Quatre-Nations 43 Rue de Zurich Ⓣ 022 732 02 24. Divey little Pâquis den above a lowlife Portuguese bar, with blithely unhelpful staff (if you

can find them; reception closed 1–6pm) and dead-cheap shower-free rooms. ❶

Old Town area

🏃 **Bel'Espérance** 1 Rue de la Vallée ☎022 818 37 37, ⓦ www.hotel-bel-esperance.ch. Excellent modern hotel on a steep Old Town alley. Rooms are bright and simple (those at the back are very quiet), with free use of kitchen and great views. ❸

Central 2 Rue de la Rôtisserie ☎022 818 81 00, ⓦ www.hotelcentral.ch. Quiet, comfortable, renovated top-floor rooms just below the Old Town, all with balconies. Prices depend on the room size, but are all excellent value. ❷–❸

Mid-range hotels

Rive Droite: Station area and Les Pâquis

Edelweiss Manotel 2 Place de la Navigation ☎022 544 51 51, ⓦ www.manotel.com. Comfortable three-star, entirely done-up with Swiss kitsch – carved light pine, images of St Bernard dogs and Alpine flowers and, to top it all, folkloric dinner-shows nightly in the basement restaurant. Beneath the veneer, this remains an excellent city-centre small hotel, with courteous, switched-on staff and good facilities (all rooms have a/c). Ask for a top-floor room, facing back over a quiet rooftop panorama. ❹–❺

🏃 **Kipling Manotel** 27 Rue de la Navigation ☎022 544 40 40, ⓦ www.manotel.com. A touch of airy, exotic class in the heart of the Pâquis, with this sophisticated three-star hotel, air-conditioned throughout. Rooms are styled with some care: fabrics are rich, woods are dark and highly polished, and artefacts attempt to evoke the colonial era of the Raj. Parking available. ❹–❻

Montbrillant 2 Rue du Montbrillant ☎022 733 77 84, ⓦ www.montbrillant.ch. Award-winning family-run hotel overlooking the station, with some style, plus quiet and atmospheric modern rooms – those under the sloping roof are particularly good. Sound-proofing throughout. ❺–❻

Royal Manotel 41 Rue de Lausanne ☎022 906 14 14, ⓦ www.manotel.com. Flagship four-star Manotel property spread over four buildings. Rooms (all a/c) are elegantly designed; superb top-floor suites feature effortless, modern luxury styling – canopied bed, parquet floor, Jacuzzi. Facilities include a sauna, hammam and small gym, plus secure underground parking. ❺–❼

Strasbourg 10 Rue Pradier ☎022 906 58 00, ⓦ www.hotelstrasbourg.ch. Best Western chain hotel on a quiet backstreet very near the station, renovated in classic style, with good service and cosy, if generic, rooms. ❹

Windsor 31 Rue de Berne ☎022 715 16 00, ⓦ www.hotel-windsor.ch. Comfortable and central hotel, with newly renovated modern rooms. Higher floors avoid the Pâquis street noise. ❹

Rive Gauche

Tiffany 20 Rue de l'Arquebuse ☎022 708 16 16, ⓦ www.hotel-tiffany.ch. Highly successful, attractive and charming *belle-époque* hotel near Plainpalais, with efficient, helpful staff and classic Art Deco styling throughout – from stained glass to swirly bathroom tiles to a stunning painted ceiling. ❼–❽

Out of town

Auberge d'Hermance 12 Rue du Midi, Hermance ☎022 751 13 68, ⓦ www.hotel-hermance.ch. Charming inn set amidst the medieval lakeshore village of Hermance 15km northeast of Geneva, with eight cosy and attractive rooms and suites. The restaurant is celebrated for its excellent French cuisine. ❺

Expensive hotels

🏃 **Les Armures** 1 Rue du Puits St-Pierre ☎022 310 91 72, ⓦ www.hotel-les-armures.ch. Quiet seventeenth-century building in the heart of the cobbled Old Town, with a mix of modern and traditional rooms, the latter featuring characterful wood beams and frescoed decor. The height of tasteful, understated luxury. ❾

Beau Rivage 13 Quai du Mont-Blanc ☎022 716 66 66, ⓦ www.beau-rivage.ch. Dreamy classical-style palace, centred on a huge atrium with tinkling fountain and characterized by luxury redolent of its 1865 foundation. The same family tends to the hotel's guests now as then, and a farther cry from international business-class anonymity you couldn't find. Its tragic claim to fame is that Empress Elisabeth ("Sissi") of Austria died in one of the drawing rooms in 1898, stabbed by an Italian anarchist. ❾

Des Bergues 33 Quai des Bergues ☎022 908 70 00, ⓦ www.fourseasons.com. The oldest of

Geneva's palace-style hotels, this much-loved 1834 landmark, renovated to glittering international standards, is now part of the Four Seasons chain, yet retains its atmosphere of discreet and unassailable opulence. ❾

Bristol 10 Rue du Mont-Blanc ☎022 716 57 00, ⓦwww.bristol.ch. A venerable city-centre institution, dating from 1896, with subtle modern decor and calm, efficient service. ❽–❾

Intercontinental 7 Chemin du Petit-Saconnex ☎022 919 39 39, ⓦwww.interconti.com. A vast Sixties high-rise out near the UN, with some rooms boasting spectacular lake views, which is the favoured choice of politicos and visiting international delegations. Cosy decor softens the generic interior, but sombre, world-affairs formality is the tone. The visitors' book reads like a roll call of history, running through the last half-dozen US presidents, the late King Hussein of Jordan, Fidel Castro and Nelson Mandela, to name a few. ❼–❾

President Wilson 47 Quai Wilson ☎022 906 66 66, ⓦwww.hotelpwilson.com. Outstanding five-star palace on the Rive Droite, with a sparkly silver-walled lobby, contemporary styled public areas and cool, airy and spacious modern rooms with uncluttered lake views. ❾

The City

Genevans orient the city centre around the Rhône, which flows west into France from the **Rade**, the narrow lake harbour flanked by grand facades. The **Rive Gauche**, on the south bank, takes in a grid of waterfront streets which comprise the main shopping district (Les Rues-Basses) and the adjacent high ground of the Old Town. Just south is the university, spilling over into Plainpalais; beyond is lively **Carouge**, characterized by artisans' workshops.

Six bridges, including the main Pont du Mont-Blanc, link the Rive Gauche to the **Rive Droite** waterfront, where most of Geneva's grand hotels sit. Behind them lies the main train station, alongside the cosmopolitan and occasionally rough Les Pâquis district. The **international area**, centred on Place des Nations 1.5km north, is home to the European headquarters of the UN, set amidst a clutch of world bodies – not least the International Committee of the Red Cross, which has, as a sideline, one of Switzerland's best museums.

The Rive Gauche

Geneva's **Rive Gauche** (Left Bank, or southern bank) is lined with dozens of bank buildings, behind which the arrow-straight **Rue du Rhône** – principal

---

Liquid asset

The **Jet d'Eau** fountain (May to mid-Sept daily 9.30am–11.15pm; March, April & mid-Sept to Oct Mon–Fri 10am–sunset, Sat & Sun 10am–10.30pm) is Geneva's icon, emblazoned on every piece of tourist literature – and illuminated after dark.

In 1886, new hydraulic turbines on the Rhône were found to build up excessive water pressure every evening after the city's craftsmen had closed the valves in their workshops and gone home. While a reservoir system was being developed to get around the problem, an engineer created a temporary outlet which spurted a 30m fountain to release the pressure. But by the time the reservoir was in operation and the fountain had thus become unnecessary, a few wily Genevois had caught on to its power as a tourist attraction. By then purely decorative, it was moved from the river to an exposed lakeside location, and furnished with more and more powerful pumps. Today, the height of the jet is an incredible 140m, with 500 litres of water forced out of the nozzle every second at about 200kph. Each drop takes sixteen seconds to complete the round-trip from nozzle to lake and, on windy days, the plume can rapidly drench the surroundings (they turn it off if the wind picks up). It's worth risking a dousing by walking out onto the jetty to appreciate the force and noise of the thing close up.

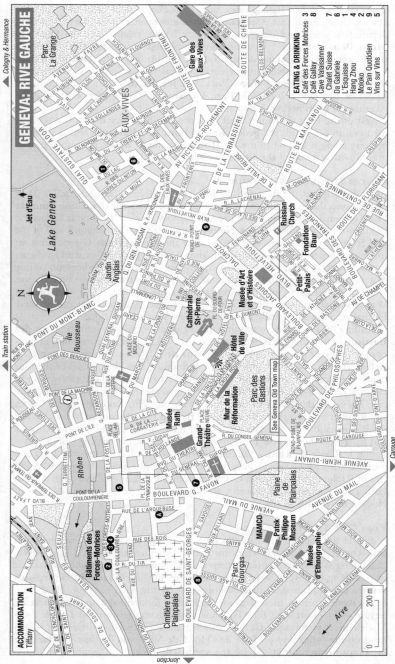

GENEVA: RIVE GAUCHE

EATING & DRINKING
Café des Forces Motrices	3
Café Gallay	8
Cave Valaisanne/ Chalet Suisse	7
Da Gabrièle	6
L'Esquisse	1
Hang Zhou	4
Moloko	2
Le Pain Quotidien	9
Vins sur Vins	5

ACCOMMODATION
Tiffany .... A

0   200 m

thoroughfare of Les Rues-Basses, once a dockside slum and now Geneva's fanciest shopping district – stretches 1km or more east, crammed with jewellers, department stores and designer boutiques. Traffic streams over the **Pont du Mont-Blanc** beneath a view of Europe's highest mountain (4807m), which stands some 80km distant. At the foot of the bridge is the **Jardin Anglais**, focused around a double statue celebrating Geneva's joining the Confederation in 1815 and the famous Flower Clock. The **Jet d'Eau** spouts 400m along the lakeshore (see box, p.70), while **Parc La Grange**, 1km further east along the lakeshore, is crammed with displays of roses.

West of the Pont du Mont-Blanc, past the bustling Place du Molard with its medieval tower, stands the pedestrianized **Pont des Bergues**, with a footpath midway along it linking to the **Île Rousseau**, now a minuscule public garden graced with a statue of the Genevan philosopher.

Place Neuve and around

At its western end, the Rue du Rhône feeds into hectic Place Bel-Air. The Pont de l'Île spans the river here across an island, which boasts the diminutive **Tour de l'Île**, last remaining tower of a thirteenth-century château. Rue de la Corraterie heads south to grandiose **Place Neuve**, dominated by the retaining wall of the Old Town. The street joins the square beside the **Musée Rath**, Geneva's first art museum, opened in 1826, and still holding a changing series of world-class art shows (Tues & Thurs–Sun 10am–5pm, Wed noon–9pm; admission varies; Ⓦ www.ville-ge.ch/mah). Adjacent is the **Grand-Théâtre**, Geneva's opera house, which only just clung onto its facade after the fire of 1951, when a rehearsal of Wagner's *Walkyrie*, in which Brunhilde is encircled by flames, got out of hand. Further round is the equally imposing Conservatoire de Musique.

Heading off Place Neuve through the big gates brings you into the **Parc des Bastions**, a tranquil patch of green below the Old Town ramparts amid university buildings. At its eastern edge is the **Mur de la Réformation**, a 100m-long wall erected in 1917 and dominated by forbidding, 5m-high statues of the four major Genevan reformers: Guillaume Farel, first to preach the Reformation in Geneva; Jean Calvin, leader of the Reform movement and spiritual father of the city; Théodore de Bèze, successor to Calvin; and John Knox, friend of Calvin and founder of Scottish Presbyterianism. Behind runs the motto of the city and the Reformation, *Post Tenebras Lux* ("After the Darkness, Light"). Various figures and bas-reliefs show scenes from Protestant history: just to the right of the main statues is Roger Williams, a Calvinist Puritan who sailed on the *Mayflower* and founded the city of Providence, Rhode Island. The English Parliament's 1689 Bill of Rights – which barred Catholics from the throne – is also depicted, but Luther and Zwingli, with whom Calvin came to disagree, are relegated to plain blocks carved with their surnames.

The Old Town

A gate at the back of the Parc des Bastions brings you up to a small junction and Rue St-Léger, which winds further up into the atmospheric **Old Town**, characterized by quiet, cobbled streets and tall, shuttered, grey-stone houses that give nothing away. Rue St-Léger arrives at the split-level **Place du Bourg-de-Four**, a marketplace since medieval times occupying what was probably the site of the Roman forum, these days adorned with a fountain and lined with relaxed terrace cafés. From here, Rue Fontaine descends to the north to Temple de la Madeleine, a picturesque Gothic church with Romanesque tower, but if you head up the other way on Rue de l'Hôtel-de-Ville, you'll come to **Place de la Taconnerie**, dominated by the cathedral. Tucked on your right is the

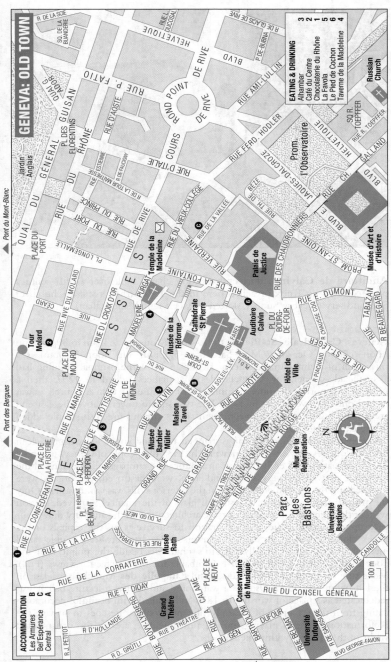

GENEVA: OLD TOWN

ACCOMMODATION
Les Armures B
Bel Espérance C
Central A

EATING & DRINKING
Alhambar 3
Café du Centre 2
Chocolaterie du Rhône 1
La Favola 5
Le Pied de Cochon 6
Taverne de la Madeleine 4

▲ Alleys in the Old Town

Auditoire de Calvin, a thirteenth-century chapel built over a fifth-century predecessor. John Knox preached here in the 1550s (there's still a Church of Scotland service every Sunday, slotted between Dutch and Italian).

Cathédrale St-Pierre

Geneva's **Cathédrale St-Pierre** (June–Sept Mon–Sat 9.30am–6.30pm, Sun noon–6.30pm; Oct–May Mon–Sat 10am–5.30pm, Sun noon–5.30pm) is a mishmash of architectural elements. Begun in 1160, the original building had a small side-chapel, the Chapelle des Macchabées, added in 1397; then a Neoclassical portico – more reminiscent of a museum than a church – was tacked onto the west front in 1752. The two square towers above the east end are totally dissimilar, and between them rises a curious greenish steeple added in the late nineteenth century.

As you enter, though, confusion is stripped away and you're left with the clean lines of dour, severely austere stonework. In 1535 the people of Geneva accepted the Reformation and embarked on an iconoclastic rampage: all the altars in the cathedral, as well as every statue and icon, were destroyed, the organs were smashed and the painted decoration on the interior walls was whitewashed. Only the **pulpit** and, by chance, the stained glass of the chancel, survived. As you wander through the soaring interior, the architecture and the austerity, draw your gaze upwards; almost the only decoration to survive is on the capitals of the nave's clustered pillars, grotesque monsters and a bare-breasted double-tailed mermaid. What is purportedly **Calvin's chair** sits beside the pulpit, near the door to the North Tower, which is climbable for the spectacular views (Fr.4). Make sure to spend time in the delightful **Chapelle des Macchabées**, last on the left before you leave. Used as a warehouse and later as a lecture hall, it was rededicated as a place of worship in 1878 and is filled with beautiful decoration dating from then. Copies of the only fifteenth-century frescoes to survive the Reformation – angels playing musical instruments – are on the ornamented vaults of the chancel within the chapel.

The cathedral is built on the remains of occupation going back to around 350 AD. From then on, the hill on which the cathedral stands saw almost continuous building and rebuilding. Since 1976, archeologists have been working to expose walls, rooms and mosaic floors beneath the cathedral, and the **archeological site** is open to the public (Tues–Sun 10am–5pm; Fr.8; Ⓦwww.site-archeologique.ch), rarefied stuff but well presented, subterranean catwalks weaving around and over the crumbling remains. The free audioguide helps explain what's on view.

On the north side of the cathedral, at 4 Rue du Cloître, the eighteenth-century Maison Mallet houses the airy **Musée International de la Réforme** (Tues–Sun 10am–5pm; Fr.10; Ⓦwww.musee-reforme.ch), dedicated to exploring the ideas behind the Reformation in engaging displays, from polemics and theological debates to music, the trades practised by Huguenot refugees and the rights of women in Protestantism.

Maison Tavel

From the cathedral portico, an alley leads you on to the Rue du Puits-St-Pierre. A few metres left, at no. 6, is the distinctive grey-blue sandstone facade – etched with *trompe l'oeil* mortar-lines – of Geneva's oldest house, now the **Maison Tavel** museum (Tues–Sun 10am–5pm; free; Ⓦwww.ville-ge.ch/mah). Built by the Tavel family in the twelfth century, the house was renovated after a fire in 1334 and bought by the city in 1963 to showcase the history of Geneva. The cellars are the oldest part of the house, and they and the three upper floors are filled with diverting items – massive carved doors, painted inn signs and a complete twelve-room apartment showing everyday life in the seventeenth century. The highlight is in the attic, a giant **relief map of Geneva** dating from 1850, showing the city complete with its star-shaped fortifications, before the Pont du Mont-Blanc or the railway had been built.

Around the Old Town

It's a few steps west from the Maison Tavel to a cobbled crossroads. To the right, parallel to Grand-Rue, is **Rue des Granges**, named "Street of Barns" after the huge mansions built by Geneva's nobility in the eighteenth century. Looming over the junction is the **Hôtel-de-Ville**, ranged around an internal arcaded courtyard. Ahead is the Alabama Room, where the Geneva Convention on the humanitarian rules of war was signed by sixteen countries in 1864, and where, in 1872, conflict between two states was solved in a neutral state for the first time, when Britain and the US settled a disagreement. The League of Nations also gathered here for the first time in 1920. You can work your way up the internal ramp to the top – feeling like an Escher drawing come to life – but all the doors are firmly locked. Behind the building is the lovely **Promenade de la Treille**, with a view over the city framed by chestnut trees and the longest wooden bench in the world, at 126m. The last tree on the left, bent forward, is the official tree of Geneva: the chief city councillor has recorded the day its first bud blossoms as the beginning of spring every year since 1818.

Back along the Rue du Puits-St-Pierre, you'll come to a set of stairs leading down towards the Rues-Basses. Off to the left is Rue Calvin, with, at no. 10, the **Musée Barbier-Müller** (daily 11am–5pm; Fr.8; Ⓦwww.barbier-mueller .ch), housing a beautifully displayed collection of non-European sculpture and artwork. Notes are copious, guiding you from a room filled with antique African gold to carved masks from Oceania, and more.

Musée d'Art et d'Histoire

A few metres east of the Old Town is the **Musée d'Art et d'Histoire**, 2 Rue Charles-Galland (Tues–Sun 10am–5pm; free; Ⓦ www.ville-ge.ch/mah), a gigantic museum that covers in encyclopedic fashion the whole sweep of Western culture from antiquity to the present. To do it justice would take days, but you could spend a worthwhile few hours absorbing the different areas.

For the **fine art** collection, head up the grand staircase. At the top is a heart-stoppingly romantic sculpture in marble by Canova of Venus and Adonis, standing alone and lit by a skylight. Nearby are two Rodins, *The Thinker* and *The Tragic Muse*. The collection begins in Hall 401 to the right. Room 402 holds Konrad Witz's altarpiece (1444), showing Christ and the fisherman transposed onto Lake Geneva. Rembrandt and other Dutch and Flemish artists are in room 406, with Vallotton, Pissarro, Cézanne, Renoir and Modigliani in rooms 412–14 and some striking Hodlers nearby, including a mystical *Lac de Thoune* (1909) in room 425.

Back downstairs, the **applied arts** collection is on the mezzanine gallery and the ground floor, a wealth of silverware, pewter, armour and costume. The Cartigny room, with 1805 wood panelling by the Genevois craftsman Jean Jaquet, shows elegant Louis XV and XVI furniture. The ground floor also often features temporary exhibits (admission charged). The lower floor is given over to the massive **archeological** collection. Turn right for the Egyptian rooms, including sections from the Book of the Dead and a beautiful granite statue of the goddess Sekhmet, with the body of a woman and the head of a lioness, from the fourteenth century BC. The halls devoted to Ancient Greece and Rome are no less impressive, filled with statuary and glassware.

South and west of the Old Town

Within sight of the Musée d'Art, on the high ground opposite, rise the gilded onion domes of the **Russian Church** (Cathédrale de l'Exaltation de la Sainte Croix; open sporadically), built in 1863 on the remains of a sixteenth-century Benedictine priory with money donated by Grand Duchess Anna Feodorovna Constancia, aunt of Queen Victoria and a longtime Geneva resident. The surrounding neighbourhood of town houses lining long boulevards, known as Les Tranchées, remains grand and quiet today. Five minutes from the church, at 8 Rue Munier-Romilly, is the **Fondation Baur** (Tues–Sun 2–6pm; Fr.5; Ⓦ www.fondation-baur.ch), a splendid museum of East Asian art. Start at the top floor, with a display of nineteenth-century Japanese ceramics. One floor down is the Chinese collection, with luminescent yellow Yongzhang ceramics in room 8. The ground floor has older Chinese work, including Ming porcelain in room 3 and other rooms with Qing jade.

Plainpalais

The broad Boulevard des Philosophes traces a path around the Parc des Bastions and the university district to the Rond-Point de Plainpalais, on the eastern tip of a diamond of open space known as the **Plaine de Plainpalais**. If Geneva still has a village green or a marketplace, this is it. Most days see some kind of market, whether fruit and veg or the Wednesday and Saturday flea markets.

Just to the west is **MAMCO**, the Musée d'Art Moderne et Contemporain, 10 Rue des Vieux-Grenadiers (Tues–Fri noon–6pm, Sat & Sun 11am–6pm; Fr.8; Ⓦ www.mamco.ch), its high-quality collection of installations, video art, photographs, sculptures and painting produced since the 1960s displayed in the fluorescent-lit concrete rooms of a former factory. Next door, the **Centre d'Art Contemporain** (Tues–Sun 11am–6pm; Fr.5; Ⓦ www.centre.ch) also stages temporary shows of young Swiss artists, while down the road at no. 7 is the **Patek Philippe Museum** (Tues–Fri 2–6pm, Sat 10am–6pm; Fr.10; Ⓦ www.patekmuseum.com), a fine horological collection. Nearby is the vast **Musée d'Ethnographie**, 65 Bd Carl-Vogt (Tues–Sun 10am–5pm; free), especially strong on weapons and art from Edo-period Japan.

From the Place du Cirque at Plainpalais' northern tip, Boulevard de St-Georges heads due west through one of Geneva's most engaging young neighbourhoods. A short way along, a brick wall conceals the **Cimitière de Plainpalais**, permanent home to, among others, Sir Humphry Davy, who invented the miners' lamp. Gravestone #707, close to the wall, is marked only with a faint "J.C.": this is presumed to be where Calvin lies. Behind, Rue de la Coulouvrenière feeds into the atmospheric **Place des Volontaires**, with a scattering of cafés and the **L'Usine squat**, Geneva's biggest alternative arts venue, with galleries, a theatre space, music venue, café and more. The riverfront here, also with cafés and clubs, is dominated by the arched windows of the **Bâtiments des Forces Motrices**, which once housed gigantic hydraulic turbines supplying the city with water and which has now been converted into a space for opera and drama. Further along Boulevard de St-Georges is run-down **Jonction**, at the point where the Arve meets the Rhône; residents have a tradition, in the torrid days of summer, of flinging themselves off the Pont de Sous-Terre for a refreshing float downstream.

Carouge

Carouge (Ⓦ www.carouge.ch), 2km south of the centre, is a quite different experience from Geneva proper. In 1754, the township – then, as now, beyond the city limits – was granted to Victor Amideus, King of Sardinia (ruling from Turin). He envisioned Carouge as a trading competitor to Geneva and turned it into a refuge for Catholics, Protestants unable to stomach Geneva's puritanical ways and, uniquely in Europe for the time, even Jews. Turinese architects developed a chessboard design of crisscrossing streets planted with trees, and low houses with wooden, Mediterranean-style galleries looking into internal gardens. Between 1774 and 1792, this hamlet of a hundred people grew to a bustling town of four thousand and, although Carouge never overtook Geneva, it's still something of a refuge from the city, its quiet, attractive streets packed with artists' workshops, old-style cafés and some of the city's best small-scale nightlife.

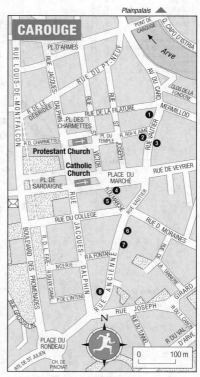

EATING & DRINKING

Bar du Nord	8	Cave à Bière	6
La Bourse	4	Le Chat Noir	3
Café des Amis	7	Le Marchand de Sable	1
Café de la Plage	2	Martel Tea Room	5

Trams #12/13/14 from the city centre can drop you at the **Place du Marché** in the heart of Carouge, still used as a marketplace. Adjacent **Rue St-Joseph** is shoulder-to-shoulder artisans, from carpenters to milliners to horologists. Check out the delicate artworks in the florist Les Cinq Sens round the corner on **Place du Temple**. A major feature of Carouge is the delightful internal galleried gardens which lurk behind almost every gate: most are open, so feel free to explore.

The Rive Droite

Explorations on Geneva's **Rive Droite** (Right Bank), on the north side of the Rhône, focus on the Pâquis for café life and Les Grottes for architecture. Broad **Rue du Mont-Blanc**, Geneva's landmark street, slopes down the hill from the

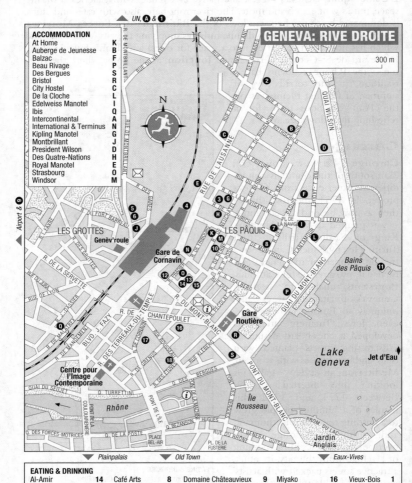

GENEVA: RIVE DROITE

0   300 m

ACCOMMODATION	
At Home	K
Auberge de Jeunesse	B
Balzac	F
Beau Rivage	P
Des Bergues	S
Bristol	R
City Hostel	C
De la Cloche	L
Edelweiss Manotel	I
Ibis	Q
Intercontinental	A
International & Terminus	N
Kipling Manotel	G
Montbrillant	J
President Wilson	D
Des Quatre-Nations	H
Royal Manotel	E
Strasbourg	O
Windsor	M

EATING & DRINKING								
Al-Amir	14	Café Arts	8	Domaine Châteauvieux	9	Miyako	16	Vieux-Bois	1
Bains des Pâquis	11	Café de Paris	12	El Mektoub	13	Mr Pickwick	2	Zara	4
La Bretelle	18	Le Diwane	7	Jeck's Place	10	Au Petit Chalet	15		
Buvette Cropettes	6	Le Dodo	5	Manora	17	Teranga	3		

train station, lined with airline offices and souvenir shops; what happens either side is of more interest. The **St Gervais** quarter, just west, was formerly the preserve of watchmakers, jewellers and goldsmiths. These days it is swamped by traffic and commerce, although its old Gothic church survives on Rue du Temple, on the same street as the **Centre pour l'Image Contemporaine**, at no. 5 (Tues–Sun noon–6pm; free; ⓦ www.centreimage.ch), with temporary shows often devoted to video art.

Les Pâquis and around

Spreading east of Rue du Mont-Blanc is the cosmopolitan, rough-edged district of **Les Pâquis**, centred on the long Rue de Berne – not a pretty place but crammed with restaurants and cafés devoted to every conceivable cuisine from Senegalese to Filipino. Equally visible are the numerous sex shops and street prostitutes of Geneva's flourishing red-light trade. The further north you go, the quieter it gets; conversely, you could head out to the lakeside Quai du Mont-Blanc for a tree-shaded stroll north, past the **Bains des Pâquis** artificial beach, the marina and ranks of luxury hotels on Quai Wilson, to the beautiful Parc Mon-Repos, first of several adjoining lakefront parks on the edge of the international area.

Immediately behind the train station is a small residential area known as **Les Grottes**, a web of twisting lanes and mostly unrenovated nineteenth-century houses. On Rue Louis-Favre, just off the main Rue de la Servette, looms a public-housing estate which looks as though it's been thrown together from plasticine. This is **Les Schtroumpfs** ("The Smurfs"), a whimsical exercise in Gaudí-esque architectural fantasy by Robert Frei, Christian Hunziker and Georges Berthoud (1982). All the buildings have lumps and blobs, giant mushrooms holding up balconies with cobweb railings, fairy-tale spiral staircases and twisted-liquorice columns, everything in a riot of primary colours. By all accounts the residents love it.

The international area

A little over 1km north of the train station, at the heart of the so-called **international area**, is the open square of the **Place des Nations**, surrounded by offices of the dozens of international organizations headquartered in Geneva – everything from the World Council of Churches to Eurovision. Gates on the square open to the **Palais des Nations**, now occupied by UNOG, the United Nations Office at Geneva; the huge monolith just off the square to the west (like a bent playing card on its edge) is WIPO, the World Intellectual Property Organization; the high-rise to the south is ITU, the International Telecommunications Union; just to the east is UNHCR, United Nations High Commission for Refugees…and so the alphabet soup continues. Most of these are just ordinary office buildings filled with working people; only the ICRC (International Committee of the Red Cross) and the UN are open to visitors.

The giant **Broken Chair** which looms over the square was installed in 1997 for the international conference at Ottawa banning the use of land mines, a graphic symbol of the victims of such weapons. The Place des Nations is an easy walk from the station, or you can take trams #13 or #15. An array of buses – #8, #F, #V and #Z – continues past the square to Appia, the best stop for the museums.

There's a **map** showing the international area on p.65.

International Red Cross Museum

Housed within the headquarters of the International Committee of the Red Cross (ICRC), the **Musée International de la Croix-Rouge et du Croissant-Rouge**, 17 Avenue de la Paix (Mon & Wed–Sun 10am–5pm; Fr.10; Ⓦ www.micr.org), uses video displays and interactive technology (in English) to

The Geneva Conventions and the ICRC

The creation of modern humanitarian law, as expressed in the 1949 Geneva Conventions, is closely tied to the history of the **International Committee of the Red Cross** (Ⓦ www.icrc.org).

On a single day – June 24, 1859 – during the war of Italian Unification, over 40,000 people were killed or wounded at a battle near the northern Italian town of **Solferino**. Genevan businessman **Henri Dunant**, who happened to be travelling in the area, was shocked at the sight of thousands of wounded soldiers left to fend for themselves with little or no medical provision. Thousands perished where they fell, despite Dunant's efforts to rally local people to give aid. On his return to Geneva, Dunant wrote *A Memory of Solferino*, which ended with appeals for the formation of an internationally protected nursing corps to care for the wounded during times of war. The book was read in translation all over Europe. The Geneva Public Welfare Society, a local charity, set up a committee in 1863 to look at Dunant's proposals; this body, which used a reversed red-on-white Swiss flag to identify its workers in the field, later became known as the **International Committee of the Red Cross**.

In 1864, a conference of sixteen states – chaired by Dunant – signed the "Geneva Convention for the Amelioration of the Condition of the Wounded in Armies in the Field", the first instrument of international humanitarian law. As the ICRC expanded its work, more treaties were agreed by states around the world – banning poison gas and bacteriological warfare, defining combatants and non-combatants, and more. These culminated in the four **1949 Geneva Conventions**, which still provide the legal foundation for humanitarian law and are among the most widely ratified of all treaties. The first and second conventions cover protection of members of armed forces in the field and at sea, the third is concerned with the rights of prisoners of war, and the fourth concentrates on protection of civilians in wartime. **Protocols** adopted in 1977 extend the conventions to cover victims of civil wars.

The Geneva Conventions laid down rules of war which are taken for granted today – for instance, that **prisoners of war** are entitled to withhold all information from their captors except their name, rank, serial number and birth date. Some definitions have changed: under the 1949 conventions, **journalists** – who often covered conflicts while armed and uniformed – were regarded as combatants, but, with the developing independence of the media, the 1977 Protocols explicitly recognized them to be non-combatant civilians as long as they identify themselves as such, which is why war correspondents now emblazon their flak-jackets with the word "PRESS".

Governments are responsible for enforcing the Geneva Conventions, but the ICRC remains the only organization recognized to carry out relief activities for the victims of armed conflicts. It publicizes the rules of war to all sides involved in hostilities and, through national Red Cross and Red Crescent societies around the world, serves as a global network to help trace prisoners of war and civilians displaced by conflict, and provide aid to civilians during and after wars, as well as monitoring conflict conditions. Four-fifths of its budget of about **Fr.1 billion** (US$700m) is spent on relief work. Its **red cross** emblem is now one of the world's best-known symbols, almost universally recognizable as indicating an impartial source of medical care; the **red crescent**, which has enjoyed equal status since 1876, is widely used in the Muslim world. In 2005 a new, deliberately non-religious emblem – the **red crystal** – was approved in order to allow countries where neither the cross nor the crescent is seen as neutral to join the ICRC federation.

▲ Red Cross Museum

chronicle the history of modern conflict, and the role the Red Cross has played in providing aid to combatants and civilians caught up in war and natural disasters. The displays are strikingly affecting, always using clear single images to tell a story instead of swamping you with facts and figures, and always avoiding judgement or ideological point-scoring.

You enter through a trench in the hillside opposite the UN, emerging into an enclosed glass courtyard, surrounded by reflected images of yourself beside a group of stone figures, bound and blindfolded, representing the continual worldwide violation of human rights. Inside, above the ticket desk, is a quotation in French from Dostoevsky: "Everyone is responsible to everyone else for everything." An audioguide (Fr.5) takes you through the museum, which examines the history of kindness from the Good Samaritan and Saladin to the experiences of nineteenth-century Genevan businessman **Henri Dunant** which prompted him to found the Red Cross (see box opposite). One area features aisle after aisle of **record cards** from World War I – seven million of them – detailing prisoners' particulars in order that they could be traced and reunited with their families. In another is a **reconstructed cell**, 3m by 2m, which an ICRC delegate reported housed seventeen prisoners: 34 footprints on the cell floor only go some way towards helping imagine the conditions. Also memorable is the eye-opening **Wall of Time**, an ingenious representation of those wars and natural disasters which have killed more than 100,000 people, year by year since the Red Cross's foundation.

Palais des Nations: the UN building

The **Palais des Nations** was built from 1929 to 1936 to serve as the world headquarters of the League of Nations, an organization set up to prevent a recurrence of war on the scale of World War I but stymied soon after its birth by the outbreak of World War II. When the organization was re-founded in 1945 as the **United Nations** (*l'Organisation des Nations Unies* in French, abbreviated to ONU), with its headquarters at New York, this complex became European HQ and was retitled UNOG ("the UN office at Geneva"). Since then it has burgeoned, and now encompasses offices administering a vast array of economic and social development work, as well as bodies dealing with the negotiation and signing of treaties and conventions of all kinds. It's also the hub of UN operations to deliver humanitarian aid and uphold human rights around the world.

The UN tour

Some areas are open to the public for **guided tours** (July & Aug daily 10am–5pm; April–June, Sept & Oct daily 10am–noon & 2–4pm; Nov–March Mon–Fri 10am–noon & 2–4pm; Fr.10; takes 1hr; ⓦwww.unog.ch). The tours – in any of the UN's fifteen official languages – are only moderately interesting, but are packed with star quality for those who want to hobnob with history. This is the world's single largest conference centre for multilateral diplomacy and top-level international politicking: when the news has reports of "negotiations taking place in Geneva", they mean here. If this impresses, then you'll enjoy the visit; if it signals only the dreary prospect of traipsing along corridors and standing in empty conference halls, you should probably take your francs elsewhere.

The main entrance of the Palais des Nations, facing onto Place des Nations, is for UN staff only; the **public entrance** is up Avenue de la Paix opposite the Red Cross Museum. To enter, you'll have to hand in your **passport** and go through airport-style security procedures (you're effectively leaving Switzerland and entering international territory). Walk down the hill to the left, towards **Porte 39** in the new wing, from where tours depart. You may have to wait a little for the next tour in English and you must carry your bags with you.

The tour starts with a potted history of the UN as you're led to the great Assembly Hall, visitable today in more or less the same condition as when it was inaugurated in 1937. The Council Chamber, which hosted the negotiations to end the 1991 Gulf War, is decorated with gold-and-sepia murals painted in 1934 by the Catalan artist José Maria Sert, depicting the progress of humankind; all very heroic. Indeed, the whole style of the main wing – granted to a consortium after Le Corbusier's visionary modernist design had been rejected because he hadn't used Indian ink for his drawings as instructed – is, rather ironically, a prime example of 1930s Fascist architecture, complete with cold marble floors, gigantic bronze doors and the hard lines of Neoclassicist Art Deco. The building's rear extension, added in the late 1960s, resembles the worst of London or Paris's inner-city office blocks.

Musée Ariana

Just down the hill from the Palais des Nations, in a distinctive 1880s Neo-Baroque mansion, is the **Musée Ariana** (Mon & Wed–Sun 10am–5pm; free; ⓦwww .ville-ge.ch/mah), devoted to seven centuries of glass and ceramics from Europe and the East. Unless you're a fan, though, the building – semicircular galleries overlooking an internal atrium – is likely to be at least as inspiring as its contents, which include faïence and porcelain from the sixteenth to eighteenth centuries, the earth tones of Spanish ware contrasting with creamy French colours and light Italian pastels. There are English notes aplenty.

Eating and drinking

With more than a thousand restaurants in the city, you could **eat** and **drink** your way around the world in Geneva. The most visible establishments might give you the impression that you could afford nothing more adventurous than a filled baguette, but Genevois café culture is alive and well, and inexpensive diners do exist. If you're prepared to splash out, you could dine as grandly as in Paris, London or New York.

Cafés

Almost every corner has its **café**, and the following list is highly selective, serving as much to give pointers as to what to expect in each neighbourhood as to recommend these particular establishments over others. The Old Town's Place du Bourg-de-Four, for instance, is lined with busy terrace cafés offering coffees, *apéros* and snacks to fuel hours of reading and people-watching: pick any one you fancy. Wherever you are in the city, you'll have no trouble finding somewhere congenial to rest your feet and sample a little something. All of these places are keyed on the maps on p.71 (Rive Gauche), p.73 (Old Town), p.77 (Carouge) or p.78 (Rive Droite).

Rive Droite: Station area and Les Pâquis

Bains des Pâquis 30 Quai du Mont-Blanc. Excellent and very popular café-bar attached to the lakefront swimming areas, renowned for some of the best people-watching in the city – atmospheric, colourful and cool. May to mid-Sept in good weather only. Closes 8pm (or earlier if custom is slow).

Buvette des Cropettes Place Gruet, off Rue de Montbrillant. Tiny atmospheric six-table wood-floor café-bar tucked behind the station, opposite the sunny Cropettes park. Closed Sun eve & Mon lunch.

Café de Paris 26 Rue du Mont-Blanc, ⓦwww .cafe-de-paris.ch. Very central café that does one meal only, but does it very well – entrecôte steak in a special herb-and-butter sauce with golden chips and salad, for Fr.40. Otherwise, it's a perfect place for downtime, seconds from the station.

Old Town area

Alhambar 10 Rue Rôtisserie ⓦ www.alhambar .com. Relaxed glittery bar behind a Rues-Basses cinema, with a yuppyish tone, plenty of tapas and evening DJs. Sunday's laid-back piano-brunch (winter only) is worth checking out. Closed Sat lunch & Mon eve.

Chocolaterie du Rhône 3 Rue de la Confédération. Outlet for fine handmade chocolates, with a small tearoom in the back serving heavenly cakes and confections to accompany tea and coffee. Closed Sun.

Rive Gauche

Café des Forces Motrices Place des Volontaires. Directly opposite *L'Usine* (see p.86), this is one of the best options in a buzzing area, not grand or trendy, but just calm, friendly, attractive and welcoming.

Café Gallay 42 Boulevard St-Georges. Friendly neighbourhood café-bar opposite Plainpalais cemetery, attracting an arty young crowd of students and theatre people. Good, inexpensive food (from Fr.17) and shared tables add to the appeal. Closed Sun and Mon eve.

Moloko In L'Usine squat, Place des Volontaires. Graffitied upstairs bar-café that once sported a rough-edged clientele puffing clouds of sweet smoke to a background of heavy noise. These days it's been cleaned up a bit, but is still a good place to step into the city's alternative scene. Solid meals for around Fr.15.

Le Pain Quotidien 21 Boulevard Helvétique. No-nonsense café ("Daily Bread") with a well-deserved reputation for superb breakfasts (Fr.14–16) and weekend brunches (Fr.30) – or good at any time for an inexpensive snack. Seating is on benches at long wooden tables. Closes 6pm.

Carouge

Martel Tea Room 4 Rue du Marché. Perfect spot to punctuate an afternoon walk around Carouge, founded in 1818 and still offering exquisite chocolates and pastries as well as good, inexpensive salads, sandwiches and light meals. Closed Mon.

Restaurants

Geneva's excellent Swiss **restaurants** are boosted by numerous French places, chiefly drawing on influences from *haute-cuisine* Lyon. The **Old Town** in particular (around the Place du Bourg-de-Four) has a host of atmospheric Swiss eateries. **Carouge** is a foodie's paradise, with plenty of sometimes pricey choices. **Eaux-Vives** is much more down-to-earth, with some quality inexpensive

Italian joints. **Les Pâquis** has dozens of low-priced, authentic Arabic, East Asian, South American and African cafés and restaurants. All these places are keyed on the maps on p.71 (Rive Gauche), p.73 (Old Town), p.77 (Carouge) or p.78 (Rive Droite).

Inexpensive and mid-range restaurants

Rive Droite: Station area and Les Pâquis

Al-Amir 3 Rue Chaponnière. Excellent Lebanese café dishing up a quality range of *mezze* (Fr.7–15 each), plus chicken or lamb *shawerma*, tajines and so on (Fr.15). Top choice of the many Pâquis kebab dens. Hole-in-the-wall branch nearby at 22 Rue de Berne.

Le Diwane 6 Rue de Zurich ☏022 732 73 91. Excellent, authentically prepared Arabic cuisine, with classy *mezze* (Fr.12–14) plus grills and kebabs (Fr.28–39) – either way, don't miss the delicious *maamoul* (orange-scented cookies) afterwards. July–Sept daily; rest of year closed Sat lunch & Sun.

Le Dodo 20 Rue de Montbrillant ☏022 734 39 57, ⓦ www.ledodo.ch. Much-loved Mauritian restaurant, with a dodo on the bar and an intriguing menu of meat and seafood dishes blended to perfection with Indian-style spicing. Under Fr.20 for lunch; double that in the evenings. Closed Sat lunch & Sun.

El Mektoub 5 Rue Chaponnière ☏022 738 70 31, ⓦ www.elmektoub.com. Discreet central hideaway for quality North African cooking in a pleasant ambience. Excellent couscous (including veggie options) and a wealth of tajines are Fr.27–35. Closed Sun lunch.

🏃 **Jeck's Place** 14 Rue de Neuchâtel ☏022 731 33 03, ⓦ www.jecksplace.ch. Excellent Thai restaurant, with nice wood-and-rattan decor and superb authentic food that is surprisingly affordable (around Fr.30, or half that at lunch). House speciality is a range of Singaporean dishes, mixing influences from Malaysia, China and India. Closed Sat lunch & Sun lunch.

Manora 4 Rue de Cornavin. Excellent, down-to-earth self-service nosh at this huge outlet of the Swiss chain (see p.44). With such a fast customer turnover, its food is very fresh as well as rock-bottom cheap: you can easily stuff yourself for around Fr.15.

Au Petit Chalet 6 Rue Chaponnière. Unpretentious city-centre Swiss place for fondues, *rösti* and pizza (Fr.20–25) in a refreshingly untouristic dark-wood setting. Closed Mon.

Teranga 38bis Rue de Zurich ☏022 731 15 22, ⓦ www.terangaresto.ch. Tiny backstreet Senegalese place, down a side alley, attractively decorated, with good service and great food, including plantains, *yassa* (braised chicken in onion sauce) and fresh ginger juice. Mains around Fr.25. Closed Sat lunch & Sun.

Zara 25 Rue de Lausanne. Simple little Eritrean/Ethiopian café-restaurant near the station, with mains (meat and vegetarian) for Fr.20–25.

Old Town area

Les Armures 1 Rue du Puits-St-Pierre ☏022 310 34 42, ⓦ www.hotel-les-armures.ch. Traditional stone-floored Old Town institution on three storeys, refreshingly kitsch-free and once graced by Bill Clinton and family (with a plaque by the door to prove it). The menu offers a full range of perfectly prepared fondues and other Swiss dishes from Fr.30, plus cheaper pizzas and pastas.

🏃 **Café du Centre** 5 Place du Molard ☏022 311 85 86, ⓦ www.cafeducentre.ch. A very handy Rues-Basses pit stop with terrace seating in summer. The smell of the sea hits you as you push the door and that's really what this plain, very popular café-restaurant is all about, offering everything from a plate of periwinkles up to a dozen fresh oysters, backed by a huge wine list. Not cheap for dining, at Fr.30–50, but worth having a coffee just to sample the old-style atmosphere. Also good terrace tables.

La Favola 15 Rue Jean Calvin ☏022 311 74 37, ⓦ www.lafavola.com. Charming little family-run restaurant on a cobbled Old Town alley, with a small menu of choice Ticinese specialities to dally over in an atmospheric setting. A romantic evening tête-à-tête will top Fr.50 each; lunches cost much less. Closed Sat & Sun.

Le Pied de Cochon 4 Place du Bourg-de-Four ☏022 310 47 97, ⓦ www.pied-de-cochon.ch. One of Geneva's best-loved bistros, serving meaty Genevois and Lyonnais rib-stickers (Fr.35), including the namesake grilled pigs' trotters, to a clientele not short of a *centime* or two.

Taverne de la Madeleine 20 Rue Toutes-Âmes. Quite possibly the oldest restaurant in the city, now an alcohol-free café-bistro, serving lunches only: solid home-made fare (Fr.15–20) – pasta, pizza, salads and steaks – in a tiny old dining room below the Old Town. Closed Sun.

Rive Gauche

Cave Valaisanne/Chalet Suisse Place du Cirque Ⓦ www.chaletswiss.ch. Touristy place for those seeking that authentic fondue experience. The chalet side is all dim lights, dark wood-beamed interior and endless Swiss kitsch; the *cave* side less contrived and so slightly less grating. The food is fine at both, albeit a touch pricey, with fondues for Fr.25–35.

Da Gabriele 7 Rue Cherbuliez Ⓣ 022 736 30 40, Ⓦ www.dagabriele.ch. Eaux-Vives has many Italian restaurants, but this is one of the best, boasting freshly made pasta, a wood-fired pizza oven, relaxed open decor and friendly service. Meals are not expensive, mostly under Fr.20.

L'Esquisse 7 Rue du Lac Ⓣ 022 786 50 44. Set in the unlikely surroundings of an Eaux-Vives backstreet, this "bistro gourmand" (which also serves as a gallery for local artists) offers fine French cuisine at relatively affordable prices, from a short menu of carefully crafted meat and seafood dishes (Fr.37–45). Closed Sat lunch & Sun.

Hang Zhou 19 Rue de la Coulouvrenière Ⓣ 022 781 41 47. Excellent inexpensive Chinese, with a good range of vegetarian and meat dishes, plus *dim sum* menus (Fr.16–25). Closed Sun.

Vins sur Vins (Café Huissoud) 51 Rue du Stand Ⓣ 022 310 25 83, Ⓦ www.cafe-huissoud .ch. This chic modern restaurant pays homage to five decades of French pop music, with photos and record sleeves adorning the walls, Charles Aznavour crackling over the speakers and a range of meat and fish dishes (mains Fr.27–55) on the table.

Carouge

La Bourse 7 Place du Marché Ⓣ 022 342 04 66. Celebrated nineteenth-century café-brasserie in the heart of Carouge, offering a mix of meat and fish dishes – and, in winter, a good range of seafood taking in mussels, oysters and a protein-packed *marmite du pêcheur* (Fisherman's Pot). A quality lunch *menu* can be had for around Fr.20. The cellar doubles as a pizzeria. Closed Sun & Mon.

Expensive restaurants

Le Chat Botté In *Hôtel Beau-Rivage*, 13 Quai du Mont-Blanc Ⓣ 022 716 66 66. Classic French fine dining in this most traditional of hotels, with a choice between the somewhat stuffy formal dining room and, in summer, the lighter, easier-going terrace overlooking the lake. Mains Fr.50–90; lunchtime *menu* around Fr.70. Closed Sat lunch & Sun.

Domaine de Châteauvieux 16 Rue Châteauvieux, Peney-Dessus, Satigny Ⓣ 022 753 15 11, Ⓦ www .chateauvieux.ch. An atmospheric château a short drive west of the city, in the heart of Geneva's wine region, complete with a cobbled approach, ancient beams, old stones and a giant open fireplace dominating the dining room (or, in summer, views from the terrace over the vineyards). The fine, traditional cuisine with some innovative modern touches, emphasizing simplicity and seasonal, local ingredients, is highly acclaimed – not least by Michelin, who give the place two stars. Mains around Fr.100. Closed Sun & Mon.

Miyako 11 Rue de Chantepoulet Ⓣ 022 738 01 20, Ⓦ www.miyako.ch. Superb Japanese restaurant, calm, modern and attractive, with three separate areas. The sushi and sashimi bar is first as you walk in, downstairs is a quiet dining room, with low tables and traditional seating, but the best location is the lively main *teppan-yaki* area in the rear, ranged at counters around several open hotplates, where chefs expertly slice, dice, toss and sauté your meal in front of you. Quality is outstanding, with everything melt-in-the-mouth fresh. There are four *teppan-yaki* menus (Fr.70– 110), plus less pricey sushi and sashimi menus (Fr.55), as well as other Japanese classics such as shabu shabu and sukiyaki. Leave space for the exquisite *glace au thé vert* (green-tea ice cream). Closed Sun.

Vieux-Bois 12 Avenue de la Paix Ⓣ 022 919 24 26, Ⓦ www.vieux-bois.ch. High-quality showcase of the world-famous catering school L'École Hôtelière de Genève: all the chefs and waiting staff are students, which means you'll get sharp, attentive service and an *haute cuisine* lunch – French, with light, inventive touches and veggie options – for a fraction of prices elsewhere. Scoff a four-course meal for as little as Fr.50, or choose from the daily specials for half that, and then retire to the garden for coffee. Hours are erratic: at least Mon–Fri noon–2.30pm, but check the website for details.

Bars, clubs and live music

Geneva's **nightlife** is unlikely to set your pulse racing. Many venues cater to visiting businesspeople – yawnworthy cabaret, strip-shows and hostess bars –

▲ Café Arts

but aside from checking out the handful of alternative arts venues, it's not easy to find what young Genevois get up to, often because they've vanished up the road to the cutting-edge **clubs** in and around Lausanne instead. Best advice is to aim for the bars and clubs around Rue Vautier in Carouge.

Rive Droite: Station area and Les Pâquis

La Bretelle 15 Rue des Etuves. Tiny kitsch tavern just off the Rive Droite, a glitz-drenched haven from the mean streets outside, that pulls in plenty of camp, alternative young-at-hearts, especially for the live accordion and/or drag cabaret (Thurs–Sat nights).

Café Arts 17 Rue des Pâquis. Bright café-bar with a young, excitable clientele. A pleasant slice of sleaze-free Pâquis. Daily 5pm–midnight.

Mr Pickwick 80 Rue de Lausanne ⓦwww .mrpickwick.ch. Generic, rather down-at-heel English pub – a bit expensive, but nonetheless with the right kind of atmosphere and live football on the telly.

Sud des Alpes 10 Rue des Alpes ⓦwww .amr-geneve.ch. Jazz buffs' mecca, with live music roughly four nights a week from 9.30pm.

Rive Gauche/Old Town

L'Usine Place des Volontaires ⓦwww.usine.ch. Alternative arts squat venue, featuring live bands at the Salle PTR ("Post Tenebras Rock"), experimental dance and drama at the Théâtre de l'Usine and non-commercial movies at the Cinéma Spoutnik.

XS 21 Grand-Rue. Easy dancing to reggae, disco and popular tunes. Tues–Sat 10pm–5am.

Carouge

Bar du Nord 66 Rue Ancienne. Dark, plasticky and filled with young designerish Carougeois carousing beneath murals by a local cartoonist. Closed Sun.

Café de la Plage 10 Rue Vautier. Trendy alternative hangout, with long carved wooden benches and a pleasant, talkative ambience, regularly spilling drinkers out onto the street. It's a long way from any kind of *plage*, though.

Café des Amis 23 Rue Ancienne. Oldest of the traditional cafés on Ancienne, full of atmosphere from an age now past. Join the locals for a trip down memory lane.

Cave à Bière 19 Rue Ancienne. Bar with almost 400 beers from around the world that attracts connoisseurs and serious drinkers in equal measure. Closed Sun.

Chat Noir 13 Rue Vautier ⓦwww.chatnoir.ch. Bar and cellar venue dedicated to live performances, with three or four concerts a week, featuring anything from *chanson* to drum'n'bass, acid jazz and acoustic blues. DJs follow. Tues–Sat 6pm till late.

La Marchand de Sable 4 Rue Vautier. Noisy little nook with a rough edge and student clientele, packed most nights.

Out of town

Weetamix 114 Route de Vernier, about 4km west Ⓦ www.weetamix.com. House and techno weekend all-nighters, with international DJs.

Entertainment

The **Fêtes de Genève** (Ⓦ www.fetesdegeneve.ch) is the city's premier annual arts festival, held in early August on the waterfront, with music of all kinds, theatre, funfairs and street entertainers. What's-on **listings** are published weekly in **Genève-Agenda**, a free city guide available from the tourist office and hotels.

Classical music and opera

There's plenty of **classical music** in Geneva. The Orchestre de la Suisse Romande (Ⓦ www.osr.ch) shuttles between Geneva and Lausanne, and often performs – in amongst big-name visiting orchestras and soloists – at the Victoria Hall, 14 Rue Général-Dufour. The Grand Théâtre (Ⓦ www.geneveopera.ch), on Place Neuve, stages classical concerts, chamber music and **opera**, and the Conservatoire de Musique, also on Place Neuve, hosts a competition for young soloists in late September as well as recitals all year round. Innovative opera productions, as well as concerts and some dance events, take place at the lofty Bâtiments des Forces-Motrices (Ⓦ www.bfm.ch), 2 Place des Volontaires. There are also free classical concerts in many of Geneva's churches year-round, and open-air concerts at the Hôtel-de-Ville in July and August.

Listings

Bike rental The station has the usual bike-rental facilities (see p.51) or you could take advantage of the *Genèv'Roule* scheme, behind the station at 17 Place de Montbrillant (May–Oct daily 8am–9pm; Nov–March Mon–Sat 8am–8pm; Ⓦ www .geneveroule.ch). Bikes are free for the first four hours (with ID and Fr.20 deposit) or Fr.12 per day, and they offer mountain bikes and child seats.

Boat rental You can rent boats from a handful of quayside operators, including Les Corsaires, 33 Quai Gustave-Ador (Ⓦ www.lescorsaires.ch), and Marti Marine, 31 Quai du Mont-Blanc: roughly, a pedalo is Fr.20 per hr, a small motorboat around Fr.50 per hr.

Books Aside from the large Payot, 5 Rue Chantepoulet, the best place for English-language books is Off The Shelf, 15 Boulevard Georges Favon, in Plainpalais. L'Inédite, 15 Rue St-Joseph, in Carouge, has a quirky selection of English books by, for and about women.

Consulates Australia, 2 Chemin des Fins Ⓣ 022 799 91 00; Canada, 5 Ave de l'Ariana Ⓣ 022 919 92 00; New Zealand, 2 Chemin des Fins Ⓣ 022 929 03 50; UK, 58 Ave Louis-Casaï Ⓣ 022 918 24 00;

US, 7 Rue Versonnex Ⓣ 022 840 51 60. Embassies are listed on p.211.

Flight enquiries Geneva-Cointrin Ⓣ 0900 571 500, Ⓦ www.gva.ch.

Gay and lesbian Geneva Aim for Dialogai, 11 Rue de la Navigation (Ⓣ 022 906 40 40, Ⓦ www.dialogai.org), which, as well as being a library and resource centre, has a regular programme of events. Every week, they put on a mass candlelit dinner in a back room, guys crowding at long tables for the home-made food (Wed 7–10pm; Fr.17).

Markets Flea market on the Plaine de Plainpalais (Wed & Sat 8am–5pm); general market on Place de la Madeleine (Mon–Sat 8am–6pm); and crafts (Thurs 8am–6pm) and books (April–Oct Fri 8am–5pm), both on Place de la Fusterie. Plainpalais also has big fruit & veg markets (Tues, Fri & Sun).

Medical facilities The Cantonal Hospital, 24 Rue Micheli-du-Crest (Ⓣ 022 372 33 11), has a 24hr emergency room.

Post office 18 Rue du Mont-Blanc (Mon 10am–6pm, Tues–Sat 9am–6pm, Sun 10am–4pm).

Around Geneva

If you're on an unhurried visit, there's plenty of opportunity to get out into the beautiful countryside of **Canton Geneva**, Switzerland's smallest. The tourist office can provide a map showing local walks and cycle routes, but it's also easy to strike out alone and discover bucolic villages, châteaux and views of the mountains or lake for yourself. Many vineyards offer **free wine-tastings** on Saturday mornings; the tourist office brochure *Viticulteurs genevois* lists them all, with opening hours and what's on offer. Spots to aim for include **Mont Salève**, the nearest high mountain to Geneva – a perfect place for sunshine when the lake is foggy – as well as the atmospheric and easy-to-reach Rive Gauche village of **Cologny**.

Mont Salève

First ridge of the Alps rising southeast of Geneva is **Mont Salève** (1380m), the city-dwellers' principal retreat into nature, with countryside for walking or skiing, plus views over the city and Jura hills opposite. There are footpaths galore on top (which become cross-country skiing trails in winter), both through woodland and, higher up, across green meadows. In contrast to the sheer face presented to Geneva, the other, southern side of the mountain is a gentle slope, looking out onto Mont Blanc and the Savoy Alps.

  Bear in mind that Salève is across the French border, so you should carry your passport. Bus #8 terminates on the border at Veyrier, from where it's a short walk through customs to the **cable car**, which rises to a crest of the ridge (May–Sept daily; April & Oct closed Mon; check at other times). TPG offices at Gare de Cornavin and Rive, and the Place Dorcière coach station, sell a day pass that includes the cable-car round-trip for Fr.19. There's a panoramic restaurant on top (Ⓦ www.restaurant-horizondusaleve.com). You can do the trip to the summit and back in a couple of hours.

Cologny and Hermance

The Rive Gauche lakeside slopes are dotted with peaceful, attractive villages that can offer beautiful walks. **COLOGNY**, 6km northeast of the city (bus A), has long been known as an exclusive and somewhat refined suburb, and the difference from Geneva is striking, with country lanes weaving between fields and woods, and many large detached houses set back behind walls. **Byron** wrote the third canto of *Childe Harold* in 1816 while staying at the Villa Deodati, 9 Chemin de Ruth, in Cologny, and waxed lyrical about the rarity of seeing Mont Blanc reflected in the lake from up here. **Milton**, too, came visiting in 1639. If you follow Chemin de Ruth north, you'll come to the district of Montalègre, and the Maison Chapuis, where **Shelley** and Clairmont stayed in 1816 with **Mary Godwin**, who began writing *Frankenstein* here. Cologny still has its fair share of resident big names: the tourist office has obligingly dubbed

---

Rafting and paragliding

Rafting Genève (☎079 301 41 40, Ⓦ www.rafting.ch) runs canoeing, rafting and kayaking trips daily on the Arve's 7km of rapids, as well as whitewater trips on the Dranse and elsewhere, from about Fr.50–75 per person. They also rent canoes and kayaks and make tandem paragliding jumps off Mont Salève (Fr.150). Their info-shack is on Quai des Vernets south of Plainpalais (May–Oct only).

it the "Beverly Hills of Geneva". There's also an esoteric museum attraction, the **Bibliotheca Bodmeriana**, 19 Route de Guignard beside the bus stop (Tues–Sun 2–6pm; Fr.15; ⓦ www.fondationbodmer.org). One of the greatest private libraries ever assembled, it includes illuminated medieval manuscripts, one of the few copies of the Gutenberg Bible and the oldest surviving text of the Gospel of St John.

Some 10km further along the lakeshore on a minor road, the village of **HERMANCE**, on the French border and reachable on bus E (or summertime boats), is even quieter, with remnants of its thirteenth-century walls and many medieval houses.

Travel details

Full timetables for all trains, buses, trams, boats and cable cars in Switzerland – as well as international connections – are searchable at ⓦ www.rail.ch.

Trains

Geneva to: Basel (every 30min; 2hr 40min); Bern (every 30min; 1hr 45min); Biel/Bienne (hourly; 1hr 30min); Fribourg (twice hourly; 1hr 20min); Geneva airport (every 10min; 6min); Lausanne (every 15min; 35min); Martigny (3 hourly; 1hr 20min); Montreux (4 hourly; 1hr 5min); Neuchâtel (hourly; 1hr 10min); Nyon (every 15min; 15min); Sion (3–4 hourly; 1hr 45min); Vevey (4–5 hourly; 50min); Zürich (every 30min; 2hr 45min).

Boats

Following is a summary of May–Sept summer services; fewer boats run in other months, generally Sat & Sun only, if at all. Full details are at ⓦ www.cgn.ch.

Geneva to: Evian, France (2 daily; 2hr 45min); Hermance (1 or 2 daily; 45min); Lausanne (2 daily; 3hr 30min); Nyon (3 daily; 1hr–1hr 30min).

Lausanne and Lake Geneva

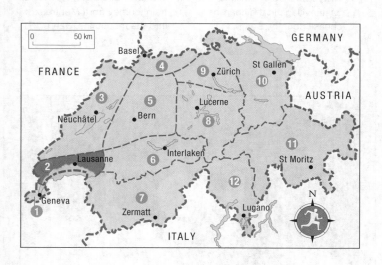

CHAPTER 2 **Highlights**

✳ **Collection de l'Art Brut**
Moving and highly memorable
gallery of "outsider" art.
See p.103

✳ **Cathédrale Notre-Dame**
Lausanne's elegant Gothic
centrepiece. See p.104

✳ **Ouchy waterfront** Lakeside
catwalk for bladers and
old-fashioned promenaders
taking the air. See p.106

✳ **Gruyères** Medieval hilltop
castle-village in the heart of
cheese country. See p.111

✳ **Vevey** The most refined and
alluring of lakeside towns.
See p.120

✳ **Montreux** Lake Geneva's
most upmarket destination
– beautiful, expensive and
exclusive. See p.125

✳ **Château de Chillon** One of
the best-preserved medieval
castles in Europe, perched
over deep water. See p.128

✳ **Golden Pass** Superbly scenic
train journey from Montreux
into the mountains. See p.131

▲ Views of Lake Geneva

Lausanne and Lake Geneva

Y ou can find the whole of Switzerland on the shores of **Lake Geneva**: snowy mountains, bucolic wine-villages, city nightlife, the sound of cow-bells in rolling pastureland, castles, cathedrals and the beautiful blue lake itself (Lac Léman in French). The southern shore of the lake is in France, taking in the Savoy Alps as well as Mont Blanc a little further south. The northern shore forms the economic and cultural focus of French Switzerland, centred around **Lausanne**, an energetic, endearing city that's too often skimmed over.

Aside from Geneva in the southwest and fragments of Valais in the southeast and Fribourg in the northeast, this is all **Canton Vaud** (pronounced *voh*; Ⓦ www.lake-geneva-region.ch), economically and politically the strongest of the French-speaking cantons, with a turbulent past. A 1798 revolution backed by France returned control to the Vaudois after two centuries of rule by Bernese bailiffs, a struggle commemorated by Napoleon, who formally created a new canton out of the territory. Vaud duly joined the Swiss Confederation in 1803 under a green-and-white flag which still flies in towns and villages to this day

Exploring Lake Geneva

Mainline CFF **trains** trace an arc around the northern lakeshore, from Geneva to Lausanne and Montreux. Smaller lines branch off at various points – into the Jura foothills in the west and the Prealps in the east. However, don't miss the chance to take to the water: CGN **boats** (Ⓦ www.cgn.ch) link all points on the Swiss and French shores, most hopping between villages, some also crossing the lake to Yvoire, Thonon and Evian in France (don't forget your passport). **Swiss Pass** holders travel free.

Regional Pass

The excellent **regional pass** is publicized through the GoldenPass train line (Ⓦ www.goldenpass.ch): it's available online, at train stations and tourist offices. Coverage is wide, taking in buses, trains and boats across the whole lake from Geneva airport to Montreux (including the French shore), as well as routes into the Vaud Alps and to Gruyères and Gstaad. For Fr.94, you get five consecutive days of validity: any two days of free travel, plus three days at half-price. The seven-day pass – including three days' free travel – costs Fr.114. Pay more to travel first class.

LAUSANNE & LAKE GENEVA

Gstaad

Dent de Broc (1830m)

Les Merlas (1908m)

Vanil Noir (2389m)

Vanil Carré (2198m)

Château-d'Oex

Broc

Fribourg

Bulle

Gruyères

Sarine

Les Milliets (1886m)

Montbovon

Planachaux (1925m)

Mont d'Or (2175m)

Les Diablerets

Villars

Le Gibloux (1206m)

Le Moléson (2002m)

1069m

1072m

Romont

Fribourg

Moléson

1413m

Niremont (1514m)

Vanil Blanc (1827m)

Dent de Lys (2014m)

1993m

Dent de Jaman (1875m)

Rochers de Naye (2047m)

Pointe d'Aveneyre (2027m)

Tour de Mayen (2326m)

Leysin

Aigle

Bex

Martigny

Payerne

Moudon

Oron

Palézieux

Châtel-St-Denis

Pralet (1630m)

Les Pléiades (1397m)

1360m

Molard (1752m)

Les Avants

Caux

1527m

Villeneuve

Rhône

VAUD

VALAIS

Yverdon

Échallens

GROS DE VAUD

Cossonay

Orbe

VAUD

FRIBOURG

Mt. Pèlerin (1080m)

Chexbres

Cully

LAVAUX

St-Saphorin

Lutry

Ouchy

LAUSANNE

Vevey

La Tour-de-Peilz

Montreux

Château de Chillon

St-Gingolph

Pic de Blanchard (1472m)

La Dent d'Oche (2222m)

Mt. Gardy (2198m)

Les Cornettes de Bises (2206m)

Mt. Chauffé (2095m)

Mont de Grange (2433m)

Vallorbe

St-Saphorin

Apples

Vufflens

Tolochenaz

Morges

Aubonne

Rolle

LA CÔTE

Lake Geneva

Evian-les-Bains

2432m

Mt. Ouzon (1881m)

1808m

1808m

Pic de la Corne (2084m)

Mt. Bénant (1285m)

1420m

FRANCE

1441m

1409m

1389m

1384m

MONT RISOUX

VALLÉE DE JOUX

Mont Tendre (1679m)

1264m

Le Brassus

1389m

1494m

Mts. de Bière (1530m)

Bière

Thonon-les-Bains

Mt. Billat (1895m)

FRANCE

1532m

Les Bégnines (1545m)

1357m

1419m

Yvoire

N

Mont Pelé (1532m)

St-Cergue

La Barillette (1528m)

La Dôle (1677m)

Luins

Vinzel

Prangins

Nyon

Céligny

Coppet

Hermance

Divonne

ROUTE SUISSE

VAUD

GENÈVE

FRANCE

GENEVA

Rhône

10 km

0

bearing the words "Liberté et Patrie". The ambience of the region is thoroughly Gallic: historical animosity towards Catholic France has given way to a yearning on the part of most urban francophone Swiss to abandon their heel-dragging compatriots in the more stolid east and embrace the EU. The short train ride from the Swiss-German cities of the Mittelland crosses more than just a linguistic boundary: it seems to span a whole continent of attitude.

Lausanne

[From] the terrace of the cathedral, I saw the lake above the roofs, the mountains above the lake, the clouds above the mountains, and the stars above the clouds. It was like a staircase where my thoughts climbed up step by step and broadened at each new height.

Victor Hugo

LAUSANNE tends to inspire hyperbole. In a country of spectacular natural beauty it is the most beautiful of cities – Switzerland's San Francisco – a place of incredibly steep hills, tiered above the lake on a succession of compact, south-facing terraces. Vistas of blue water, glittering sunlight and the purple and grey of the white-capped Savoy Alps peep through between gaps in buildings or at the ends of steeply dropping alleys. Much of the city is still wooded and the lakefront promenades spill over with beds of vibrantly colourful flowers. Attractive, interesting, worldly, and well aware of how to have a good time, it's simply Switzerland's sexiest city.

The comparisons with San Francisco don't stop at the gorgeous setting. If Switzerland has a counterculture, it lives in the clubs and cafés of Lausanne, a fact which lies broadly within the city's long tradition of fostering intellectual and cultural innovation. From medieval times, Lausanne has stood at the Swiss cultural avant-garde. Back then, the **cathedral** crowned the city the most influential of the region; it still sits resplendent on an Old Town hill, Switzerland's most impressive Gothic monument. After the Reformation, students flocked to Lausanne's pioneering university, and in the eighteenth and nineteenth centuries restless Romantics found inspiration in the city's setting on Lake Geneva. It remains grand, full of shuttered foursquare mansions and ritzy shopping streets, and with its own glamorous lakeside resort of **Ouchy**. For decades the municipality has subsidized art and culture of all shades, resulting in a range of festivals, live music, clubs, theatre, opera and dance to rival a metropolis ten times bigger.

A defining feature of Lausanne is its international population of **students**, attracted to the prestigious university, Switzerland's biggest, and the French-language arm of the Federal Institute of Technology. Hundreds of language schools and private academies enhance the city's reputation for learning, along with the world-famous École Hotelière, training ground for top chefs and hotel staff. This youthful, outgoing spirit, and the city's hilly aspect, have also given Lausanne a new role as European **blading** and **skateboarding** capital: when the sun shines, every public space hisses with the spinning of tiny wheels, and the Ouchy waterfront echoes with the clack of skateboards.

The International Olympic Committee has been headquartered in Lausanne since 1915, and has attracted to the city an array of world governing bodies in sports ranging from chess to volleyball. This has lent the city its marketing tag of **"Olympic Capital"** – a meaningless title which you'll see used everywhere to plug the city's rather vapid Olympic Museum.

Some history

Vidy, beside Lausanne, was a focus of settlement from **Neolithic** times onwards, and was where the **Romans** founded Lousonna in 15 BC. During troubled times in the fourth century, the lakefront site was abandoned for a better-defended spot on the heights above, today the site of the Old Town. In 590, Bishop Marius transferred his bishopric from Avenches to Lausanne, confirming the city's rising influence. Succeeding bishops gathered power until by the thirteenth century they were overseeing one of the largest cities in the region, with some nine thousand inhabitants.

During the fourteenth and fifteenth centuries, Lausanne was buffeted by a series of fires and plague epidemics, as well as increasing social disorder stemming from the division between the opulent lifestyle of the bishops in their lofty palace and the poverty of the people in the **Ville Basse**, or lower town. In 1525, the Lausannois made a pact of mutual military assistance with Bern and Fribourg; eleven years later when the **Bernese** army, fired with the zeal of the **Reformation**, swept down towards Lake Geneva, the Lausannois were finally able to eject the bishops. Their independence was short-lived, though, since no sooner had the bishops departed (founding a new see in Catholic Fribourg) than the Bernese installed bailiffs of their own and reduced Lausanne to the status of a subject city.

Lausanne's university was founded in 1540 as the first French-language centre of Protestant theology, but the city remained a Bernese-run backwater until, in 1803, **Napoleon** hived Canton Vaud away from Bern and granted Lausanne the status of Vaudois capital. Shortly after, the municipality filled in the rivers Flon and Louve, which wound between the city's summits, and threw grand arching bridges over the ditches to link disparate neighbourhoods for the first time. Artists, romantics and adventurers soon flocked to Lausanne and the adjacent *commune libre et indépendante* of Ouchy, turning the place into a rather genteel stop on the Grand Tour of Europe. By the turn of the century, Lausanne was hosting a thriving community of expats and boasted English churches, boarding schools, a cricket pitch, a football field and an English library serving afternoon tea. Lausanne had a quiet twentieth century, flourishing commercially, socially and culturally while content to remain in the shadow of its over-illustrious, sober and considerably less desirable neighbour, Geneva.

Orientation

Lausanne's topography looks straightforward on the map, but can be confusing on the ground: places which appear to be beside each other may in reality be far apart in elevation. At the top of the city is the **Old Town**, in the middle are the train station and commercial districts, and at the bottom are the lakefront cafés of **Ouchy**. But the gradients are no joke: Mont Jorat, only 10km northeast of the city, rises to 927m; just north of the Old Town is a viewpoint at 643m; the central districts are ranged around 475m; while residential neighbourhoods slide on down for another kilometre to the lakeshore at 372m.

Lausanne's festivals

It can seem like there's always some celebration or other happening in Lausanne. All summer long, the **Ouchy waterfront** hosts informal music events – from techno to chamber music to African dance – just about every weekend, and always free. **Lausanne Estivale** (Ⓦwww.lausanne.ch/lausanneestivale) is a summer-long programme of free music, dance and culture at various locations around the city.

Lausanne's biggest party is the **Festival de la Cité** (Ⓦwww.festivaldelacite.ch) held in early July – more spontaneous and cutting-edge than the Montreux Jazz Festival happening at the same time just down the road, not least because everything is free and out in the streets. Performances start at dusk and run until the small hours on more than half a dozen open-air stages. Otherwise aim for the **Cully-Lavaux Jazz Festival**, 8km east of Lausanne, in late March (Ⓦwww.cullyjazz.ch); the **Carnaval de Lausanne** in March/April (Ⓦwww.carnavalausanne.ch); the **Fête de la Musique**, impromptu music in the streets in mid-June (Ⓦwww.lausanne.ch/fetedelamusique); or the **Paleo Rock Festival**, a July event near Nyon (see p.115) which draws top-name artists and a crowd of a quarter of a million. Chilly January hosts the acclaimed **Prix de Lausanne** (Ⓦwww.prixdelausanne.org) competition and workshop for young dancers.

Focus of the city centre is **Place St-François**, hub of bus routes and heart of the shopping district. Gilt-edged **Rue de Bourg** entices shoppers uphill from St-François, while beside it Rue St-François drops down north into the valley and up the other side to the cobbled **Place de la Palud**, an ancient, fountained square in the heart of the Old Town. The elegant Gothic turrets of the **cathedral** rise loftily above, while the foursquare **château** stands even further up, at the highest and most northerly tip of the Old Town. Beyond rise forests and open parkland.

Northwest of St-François, the Grand-Pont soars over the warehouse district of **Le Flon**, hotbed of Lausanne's burgeoning club culture, to **Place Bel-Air** and on to Place Chauderon at the head of the Pont Chauderon, which also rises above Le Flon. The steep slope south of St-François ends at the main **train station**, south of which residential districts trickle down to **Place de la Navigation** on the **Ouchy** waterfront. Lakeside promenades lead in both directions from Ouchy, east to the villages of **Pully** and **Lutry**, west to the parkland of **Vidy** and the lakeside campus of the **university**.

Arrival and information

Lausanne's imposing **train station** is served by trains from all corners of Switzerland as well as TGVs from Paris. **Boats** dock at the CGN jetty in Ouchy, more or less opposite which is a metro station, with regular shuttles on line M2 climbing to the train station ("Gare CFF") and across the city centre.

By **car**, the *autoroutes* describe an awkward jink through the outskirts, and it's easy to go wrong. Following *autoroute* signs for "Lausanne-Centre" can get you snarled in suburban traffic; instead, aim for "Lausanne-Sud" – this brings you directly to the Maladière roundabout, a scant kilometre west of the city centre and Ouchy. If you're approaching from Vevey or Montreux, follow blue signs for Lausanne along the lakeshore road.

Parking is expensive or awkward, or both. The largest car park is under Place de la Riponne (Ⓦwww.parking-riponne.ch), but it's cheaper to use one of the easy-to-find **P+R** (Park and Ride) car parks in Ouchy or Croisettes, at either end of the metro.

From **Geneva airport**, trains run direct to Lausanne (every 10min; 45min). Alternatively, book in advance for an Airport Shuttle Express minivan (☎021 311 66 66, ⓦwww.airportshuttleexpress.ch), which will bring you and your luggage to anywhere in Lausanne (from Fr.49 per person).

Lausanne has two **tourist offices**, one in the train station (daily 9am–7pm; ☎021 613 73 73, ⓦwww.lausanne-tourisme.ch), and the other beside Ouchy metro station (daily 9am–7pm; Oct–May closes 6pm). Both have stacks of information on the whole lake region. For more focused information on cultural happenings and the life of the city, drop into the municipality's **information office**, in the Hôtel de Ville (Mon–Fri 7.45am–noon & 1.15–5pm; ☎021 315 25 55, ⓦwww.lausanne.ch). Geneva's *Le Temps* newspaper is the best source of **listings** and reviews of cultural events (although all in French). The tourist office puts out its own bimonthly offering.

City transport and tours

Although the Old Town is compact, maps can only give half the story: you'll soon find that negotiating Lausanne's mountainous gradients and cat's cradle of valleys and bridges can be wearying. You can **travel free** on Lausanne's excellent public transport (ⓦwww.t-l.ch) with a Swiss Pass (see p.35) or a transport card, which is given free when you check-in to any of the city's hotels or hostels and remains valid for the duration of your stay. Otherwise you must buy tickets: a short journey costs Fr.1.90; a one-hour pass is Fr.2.60; and a *Carte journalière* day pass is Fr.7.60.

The easiest way to move around is on the smart, modern **metro**. Most useful for visitors is the steep M2 line (known as *la Ficelle*, "the string"), which runs from the Ouchy waterfront north to the train station (Gare CFF) and city centre, terminating at Croisettes in the suburbs. Line M1 runs from Flon west to the university and Renens. For a **taxi**, call ☎0844 814 814. For details of **boat** services on the lake, see p.93.

Walking tours

Two-hour multilingual **walking tours** of the Old Town start from the Place de la Palud (May–Sept Mon–Sat 10am & 3pm; Fr.10). Alternatively the tourist office provides self-guided walking tours – either pay Fr.10 (plus deposit) for an audioguide, or download the same MP3 files yourself for free at ⓦwww.lausanne-tourisme.ch.

Accommodation

Lausanne has **accommodation** to suit all budgets and aspirations. There's only a couple of **hotels** within the Old Town, plus a few more in the heart of the city centre; those on the Ouchy lakefront have a more gracious ambience, although the lakefront road sees plenty of traffic. Any number of **luxury** establishments

A **Swiss Pass** (see p.35) is valid for free city transport in Lausanne, free boat transport on Lake Geneva and free admission to almost all museums reviewed in this book.

capitalize on Lausanne's topography to offer romantic lake views, but the best-value deals come at the business hotels, where you'll find weekend discounts and special offers. Lausanne's **hostels** are good.

Camping and hostels

Jeunotel (HI hostel) 36 Chemin du Bois-de-Vaux ☏ 021 626 02 22, ⓦ www.youthhostel.ch. Huge place right beside the *Vidy* campsite, with good four-bed dorms plus a range of private rooms. ❶–❷

🏃 **Lausanne Guest House (SB hostel)** 4 Chemin des Epinettes ☏ 021 601 80 00, ⓦ www.lausanne-guesthouse.ch. Quality hostel occupying a fine old nineteenth-century town house a couple of minutes' walk behind the train

station. All rooms have lake views, with doubles (some with separate private bathrooms) and four-bed dorms. ❶–❷

Vidy ☏ 021 622 50 00, ⓦ www.camping lausannevidy.ch. A five-star campsite sandwiched between the Roman ruins and the International Olympic Committee's château. From St-François take bus #2 (direction Bourdonette) to Bois de Vaux, or from the station take bus #1 to Maladière and walk for 5min.

Hotels

Inexpensive

Formule 1 67 Rue de l'Industrie, Bussigny ☏ 021 701 02 02, ⓦ www.hotelformule1.com. Chain motel offering generic rooms priced unbeatably low: less than Fr.75 for single, twin or triple occupancy. Located 6km northwest of the centre, close to the Crissier/Bussigny *autoroute* exit, with free parking. Bussigny train station is a 500m walk away but to reach Lausanne it's easier to take bus #35 (not Sun) from nearby Croix-de-Plan to Renens, then either the metro, a train or bus #7 into town. ❶

Pension Bienvenue 2 Rue du Simplon ☏ 021 616 29 86, ⓦ www.pension-bienvenue.ch. Decent and respectable women-only guesthouse a few metres behind the station, with 25 rooms. Reception closed 11.30am–5pm. ❷

Le Raisin 19 Place de la Palud ☏ 021 312 27 56. A handful of rooms above an old café in the heart of the Old Town, with character and atmosphere but few facilities. ❷

Mid-range

AlaGare 14 Rue du Simplon ☏ 021 617 92 52, ⓦ www.alagare.com. Decent, serviceable, mid-sized hotel in a quiet pedestrian zone just below the station. ❸–❹

Aulac 4 Place de la Navigation, Ouchy ☏ 021 613 15 00, ⓦ www.aulac.ch. Large *belle-époque* building looming over the Ouchy waterfront beside the metro station. Rooms are simple and comfortable – the more expensive ones at the front have balconies and lake views (but are also exposed to street noise). Those at the back are cheaper and quiet. ❹

🏃 **Elite** 1 Avenue St-Luce ☏ 021 320 23 61, ⓦ www.elite-lausanne.ch. Extremely pleasant, very quiet and well-run hotel, surrounded

by greenery and centrally located between the train station and St-François. Top-floor balconied rooms perch you above the roofs for views over the lake. Best value in this bracket. ❸–❹

🏃 **Du Port** 5 Place du Port, Ouchy ☏ 021 612 04 44, ⓦ www.hotel-du-port.ch. Quality little three-star lakefront hotel, in the same family for decades and now fully upgraded, with excellent facilities and some lake-view rooms. Road noise can be a problem, though: ask for a room on an upper floor. Closed late Dec & Jan. ❹

Regina 18 Rue Grand St-Jean ☏ 021 320 24 41, ⓦ www.hotel-regina.ch. Friendly little place owned by an English-speaking couple, steps from the central Place de la Palud, offering quality renovated rooms in modern style, with marvellous views from the top floor. ❸–❹

Expensive

Alpha Palmiers 34 Rue du Petit-Chêne ☏ 021 555 59 99, ⓦ www.fhotels.ch. A swanky business hotel, very well located on a busy central pedestrian street just up from the station, boasting interior palm gardens and ultra-modern rooms – the antithesis of the grand palace hotels. ❺–❽

Angleterre & Residence 11 Place du Port, Ouchy ☏ 021 613 34 34, ⓦ www.angleterre-residence.ch. Classy hotel occupying four eighteenth-century mansions on the Ouchy waterfront, including the one where Lord Byron is reputed to have written *The Prisoner of Chillon*. Historic features remain, and the tone is one of refined, tasteful comforts, with a range of rooms in both traditional and contemporary styles, and top personal service. Guests can use all facilities of the *Beau-Rivage Palace* alongside. ❼–❽

www.roughguides.com

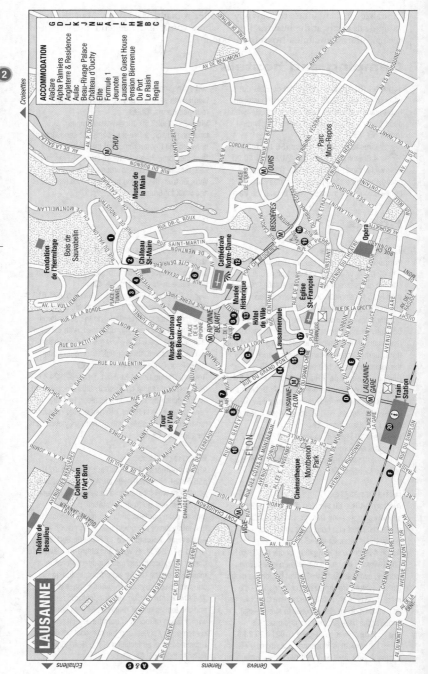

LAUSANNE

ACCOMMODATION

AlaGare	G
Alpha Palmiers	D
Angleterre & Residence	L
Aulac	K
Beau-Rivage Palace	J
Château d'Ouchy	N
Elite	A
Formule 1	I
Jeunotel	F
Lausanne Guest House	H
Pension Bienvenue	M
Du Port	B
Le Raisin	C
Regina	

Croisettes

Théâtre de Beaulieu

Collection de l'Art Brut

Fondation de l'Hermitage

Bois de Sauvabelin

Musée de la Main

CHUV

Parc Mon-Repos

TOURS

Château St-Maire

Cathédrale Notre-Dame

Musée Historique

Hôtel de Ville

Musée Cantonal des Beaux-Arts

Lausanneroule

Opéra

Tour de l'Ale

FLON

Cinémathèque

Montbenon Park

Église St-François

LAUSANNE-FLON

LAUSANNE-GARE

Train Station

Echallens

Renens

Geneva

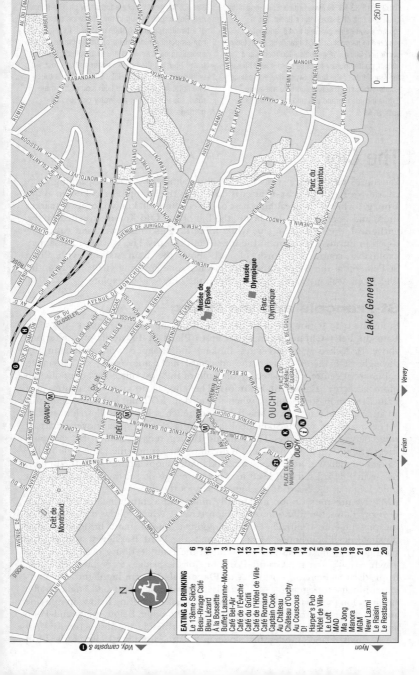

▲ Fribourg ▲ Vevey ▲ Pully

250 m

0

Parc du
Denantou

Musée de
l'Elysée

Musée
Olympique

Parc
Olympique

Lake Geneva

OUCHY

▼ Vevey

▼ Evian

▼ Nyon

Crêt de
Montriond

N

EATING & DRINKING

Le 13ème Siècle	6
Beau-Rivage Café	J
Bleu Lézard	16
À la Bossette	1
Buffet Lausanne-Moudon	3
Café Bel-Air	7
Café de l'Evêché	12
Café du Grütli	13
Café de l'Hôtel de Ville	11
Café Romand	17
Captain Cook	19
Au Château	4
Château d'Ouchy	N
Au Couscous	19
D!	14
Harper's Pub	2
Hôtel de Ville	5
Le Loft	8
MAD	10
Ma Jong	15
Manora	18
MGM	21
New Laxmi	9
Le Raisin	B
Le Restaurant	20

▲ Vidy, campsite & ℹ

Beau-Rivage Palace 17 Place du Port, Ouchy ⊕ 021 613 33 33, ⊛ www.brp.ch. Lausanne's top hotel and one of Switzerland's finest, set in ten-acre waterside gardens and sparklingly restored to its original 1861 grandeur. Sumptuous decor and fittings, huge, balconied rooms and stylish, contemporary touches raise it well above the standards of the many Swiss five-star palace hotels, while sharp service adds to the allure. Extras include a grand spa and award-winning cuisine. ⑨

Château d'Ouchy 2 Place du Port, Ouchy ⊕ 021 331 32 32, ⊛ www.chateaudouchy.ch. Grandiose neo-Gothic pile put up in the 1890s on the ruins of a twelfth-century bishop's palace. Its suave, contemporary minimalism offers an unusual but appealing contrast with the atmospheric Gothic tower housing the hotel's seven suites, most with dreamily romantic lake views. This is the one hotel situated on the lake side of the main road, separated from the water only by lush gardens. ⑥–⑧

The City

Lausanne's **city centre** spans several hilltops, linked by bridges spanning deep, riverless gorges. **Place St-François** dominates the hilltop district known as the **Bourg**, formerly the wealthiest part of the city and still known for its upmarket shops and boutiques. To the north, the hill of the **Old Town**, crowned by the **cathedral**, dominates the city, while more heights to the west and east were roped in during expansion in the nineteenth century. The whole of Lausanne's explorable centre lies north of and above the train station, with Place St-François at the edge of a pedestrian-only zone covering virtually the entire Old Town. Walking is the best, and often the only, way to explore.

St-François and the Bourg

From the train station, a gap between buildings directly ahead marks the steep **Rue du Petit-Chêne** which winds up to **Place St-François** on the terrace above. Bedecked with bus-wires, buskers and shoppers, with traffic surging through, St-François – given the adenoidal nickname *Sainf* – is Lausanne's commercial centre, dominated by the bulk of the post office and, opposite, the more attractive **Église St-François**. The church stood at the centre of a Franciscan monastic complex when founded in 1272, but although it remains an atmospheric retreat from the bustle, not much is left of its illustrious past.

   The quarter in which St-François stands, the **Bourg**, spreads over a narrow ridge between two gorges. The **Rue de Bourg**, today a fashionable shopping street rising steeply from behind the church, had much the same style in the past, lined then with restaurants, inns and luxury shops. In the 1780s, the English historian Edward Gibbon lived in a house on the site of the St-François post office, right at the heart of the high society of the day.

   Massive urban expansion in the early nineteenth century included the razing of many slums, the filling in of the Flon River – which followed the course of the present Rue Centrale – and the construction of grand bridges unifying disparate neighbourhoods. Most dramatic is the **Pont Bessières**, spanning the Flon gorge from the eastern (top) end of the Rue de Bourg over to the Old Town. A walk over the **Grand-Pont**, first of the bridges to be built (in 1844), from Place St-François northwest to **Place Bel-Air**, can highlight Lausanne's extraordinary topography – stairs and alleys running off at odd angles, traffic surging along the valley road way beneath, the lake glittering below on one side and the cathedral crowning the hill above on the other. Below the Grand-Pont, and also accessed by stairs leading down from beside the distinctive Bel-Air tower (Switzerland's modest first skyscraper, dating from the 1930s), is the **Flon** district. Once full of merchants and traders, today its warehouses have been converted into clubs, alternative cafés, galleries and theatre spaces.

Collection de l'Art Brut

A fifteen-minute walk northwest of Bel-Air (or bus #2 from St-François or Bel-Air to Beaulieu) brings you to one of Switzerland's most original art galleries, the **Collection de l'Art Brut**, 11 Avenue des Bergières (Tues–Sun 11am–6pm, July & Aug also Mon same hours; Fr.10, free on 1st Sat of month; Ⓦ www.artbrut.ch). This unique collection, founded by Jean Dubuffet, is devoted to what's been called "outsider art", the creative output of people with no artistic training at all – often loners, psychotics or the criminally insane. What results is art entirely free from any conception of formal artistic rules or conventions, challenging both how we tend to view such "outsiders" and our expectations of what art should be about.

Short biographies alongside each piece tell some heart-rendingly sad or disturbing stories. One highlight is the work of Henry Darger, a hospital porter in Chicago, who died alone, an old man unknown by his neighbours; it was only after his death that his 19,000-page novel, illustrated with dozens of detailed watercolours, came to light. There's art on show from a factory worker whose talent was only discovered because he pinned his drawings up in his workshop, from an illiterate Glaswegian trader whose whimsical art is reminiscent of Escher, from a postman who believed his hand was being directed by an external force, and so on. Both the permanent collection and the regular temporary exhibitions are worth going some distance out of your way to see.

The Old Town

Located in the tranquil core of Lausanne's **Old Town**, the cobbled **Place de la Palud** is a perfect spot for people-watching. With shopping streets cascading through the square from all sides, plenty of pavement cafés and the **Fontaine de la Justice** usually ringed with people perching on its wide rim, it's a tempting spot for a reviving *café renversée*, especially if the Wednesday and Saturday morning markets are in full swing. On the hour, mechanical figures emerge on the wall behind the fountain for a little chiming display. Dominating the south side of the square is the arcaded **Hôtel de Ville** (Town Hall), built in 1675 on the site of a covered marketplace dating back to the fourteenth century.

Place de la Riponne and around

From the Place de la Palud, Rue Madeleine leads up to **Place de la Riponne**, an expanse of concrete usually dotted with students sitting on the steps of the **Palais de Rumine** on the far side – a grandiose late nineteenth-century neo-Renaissance structure adorned with lions, angels and pink marble, designed by a Parisian architect who hadn't actually bothered to visit Lausanne beforehand. The palace is now home to a clutch of museums, most interesting of which is the **Musée Cantonal des Beaux-Arts** (Tues & Wed 11am–6pm, Thurs 11am–8pm, Fri–Sun 11am–5pm; free; Ⓦ www.beaux-arts.vd.ch). Most of its collection is in storage, pending decisions about relocation. Instead it displays some Swiss early-modern works and devotes its resources to high-quality changing shows of contemporary art.

From Riponne, Rue Haldimand heads down to the church of **St Laurent**, in the heart of the old quarter also known as St-Laurent. The Rue de l'Ale and Rue de la Tour bring you further west – past the crooked **Pinte Besson**, the city's oldest tavern, to the stout, circular **Tour de l'Ale** atop the hill, built in

1340 during a reorganization of the city's defences. The traffic hub of Place Chauderon is a few metres south and downhill, at the head of the **Pont Chauderon**, third of the major bridges spanning the Flon valley. On the south side of the bridge is the Montbenon park; here, tucked into the trees, are the Swiss film archives, housed in the *fin-de-siècle* casino building now transformed into the Cinématheque Suisse.

Cathédrale Notre-Dame

Stairs lead up from both Place de la Palud and Place de la Riponne to the higher points of the Old Town. The atmospheric **Escaliers du Marché**, covered wooden stairs heading up from Palud, deliver you to Rue Viret, circling around the pinnacle of the hill, from where more stairs bring you up to the **Cathédrale Notre-Dame** (April–Sept Mon–Fri 7am–7pm, Sat & Sun 8am–7pm; Oct–March until 5.30pm; free; Ⓦ www.grandesorgues.ch), Switzerland's finest Gothic building, on a par with the greatest of French Gothic architecture. Elegant and proportioned towers, turrets and spires claw their way up into the sky; the south facade is studded with a spectacular giant Gothic rose window of stained glass, and flying buttresses encircle the exterior of the choir and ambulatory. The foundations of the current building were probably laid in the mid-twelfth century, with construction continuing from 1190 through to the cathedral's consecration in 1275. Despite extensive renovations and alterations just before the Reformation, and the loss of the altars, screens, and most of the statuary, paintings and glass during and after it, the cathedral has lost none of its grace and poise.

You enter through the west portal, bedecked with figures and dubbed the **Montfalcon portal** after a sixteenth-century bishop. The interior **Great Porch**, an unusual lofty open arcade with its recessed doorway and two tiers of columns, echoes similar setups in English cathedrals such as Lincoln and Canterbury, and it's been suggested that Notre-Dame's main architect, Jean de Cotereel, may have been Norman or part English himself. Just beyond, a squarish vestibule gives into the vast, broad **Great Bay** which, prior to 1504, was actually an open thoroughfare which connected the Rue Cité-Devant (to your left) with the Rue St-Étienne (to your right).

The interior of the cathedral is stunning, every line and detail drawing your eye dizzily up to the lofty vaulted heights. On the south wall of the nave is the impressive **Painted Portal**, dating from 1215–30; its exterior is still encrusted with original statues, but has suffered badly from weathering in recent years, and may still be covered for protection. The crossing and transept, a few steps up from the nave and filled with light, are endowed on the south side with a glowing thirteenth-century **rose window**. Opposite is the doorway to the former cloister, above which columns in front of the rectangular windows have

---

The nightwatch

Lausanne suffered from many devastating medieval fires, and is the last city in Europe to keep alive the tradition of the **nightwatch** (*le guet*). Every night between 10pm and 2am, after the bells have struck the hour, a sonorous-voiced civil servant calls out from all sides of the cathedral's 75-metre tower "*C'est le guet; il a sonné l'heure*" ("This is the nightwatch; the hour has struck"), assuring the lovers and assorted drunks sprawled under the trees below that all is well. Having fulfilled his civic duty, he then retreats to a comfortable little room within the tower for the next 59 minutes.

▲ Cathédrale Notre-Dame, Lausanne

been snapped off to allow more light to enter the building. A few steps up again is the **choir**, housing some beautiful thirteenth-century carved choir stalls; on the left is the tomb of Otto of Grandson, a rather diminutive figure for such a celebrated medieval knight (see p.148). With a view over the whole of the city and most of Lake Geneva too, climbing the southwest **tower** (Mon–Sat 8.30–11.30am & 1.30–5.30pm, Sun 2–5.30pm; Fr.2) is one of the highlights of visiting Lausanne.

Beside the cathedral is the Ancien Évêché, the old Bishop's Palace, which has been converted into the **Musée Historique** (Tues–Thurs 11am–6pm, Fri–Sun 11am–5pm, July & Aug also Mon 11am–6pm; Fr.8, free on 1st Sat of month; Ⓦ www.lausanne.ch/mhl). Crammed with displays illustrating the history of Lausanne, its highlight is the giant scale model of the city in the basement, with an excellent accompanying commentary (in English) detailing the history of the various neighbourhoods since medieval times.

North of the cathedral

Two parallel streets, Rue Cité-Devant and Rue Cité-Derrière, lead up from the cathedral to the top of the Old Town. Old-timers bemoan the fact that the **Ancienne Académie** at 7 Rue Cité-Devant, built in the 1580s as Lausanne's first university, formerly lay at the heart of a bustling student quarter, but that the students have all departed since the new out-of-town campus opened. It's true that the alleyways are now quiet, but they're also atmospheric, the blank facades giving away little of their long history. A number of cellar theatres, as well as mouthwatering smells wafting from small bistros, hint that the quarter is far from dead. At the top of the Old Town sits the unshakeable **Château St-Maire**, begun in the fourteenth century and completed in brick by northern Italian masons a century later. The structure symbolizes political power; in former times it was the residence of the Bernese bailiffs, and today it is the seat of the Vaud cantonal government.

Rue de la Barre continues north, rising over the workaday district known as **Tunnel**, busy with traffic and home to many students, accessed by stairs down to the left (west) of the street. Place du Tunnel is ringed by bars, cafés and music venues, while the eponymous tunnel itself – a major traffic route – cuts beneath Rue de la Barre and the whole Old Town hill through to the eastern districts of the city.

The open **Bois de Sauvabelin**, the beginnings of the Jorat forests, flanks Rue de la Barre northwards. Set into the park some way up (and this is no mean hill; take bus #16) is an expansive, beautifully preserved nineteenth-century villa housing the **Fondation de l'Hermitage** art gallery, 2 Route du Signal (Tues–Sun 10am–6pm, Thurs until 9pm; Fr.18; Ⓦwww.fondation-hermitage.ch). The foundation owns a permanent collection taking in Degas, Sisley and Magritte, but displays only portions of it to complement the two or three world-class shows it mounts each year.

Ouchy and the lakefront

As if Lausanne weren't relaxed enough already, it has **Ouchy** as a lakeside terrace on which to stroll, chill out and enjoy the mountain views and fresh breezes. Officially – and proudly – a separate commune from Lausanne, Ouchy for years survived as a fishing port, but these days it's one of the more chic of the Swiss lakeside resorts, with classy hotels and waterfront cafés abounding.

Musée Olympique

A couple of hundred metres past the opulent **Beau–Rivage Palace** hotel, set in its own grounds, you'll come to the Parc Olympique, home of Lausanne's much-touted **Musée Olympique** (daily 9am–6pm; Nov–March closed Mon; Fr.15; Ⓦwww.olympic.org). It's a grand affair, with formal gardens and fountains preluding the sweeping pomp of the interior design, but rather unsatisfying, a showcase more for the IOC administrators (International Olympic Committee, headquartered in Lausanne) than for the achievements of the athletes. Displays on the Olympics of ancient Greece and the restoration of the games in modern times are good, but the main focus of the museum – banks of video screens replaying past games to the accompaniment of stirring music – ends up as little more than glorified TV. Rows of medals, sheets of Olympic postage stamps, and cases of objects from athletes past (signed swimming trunks, basketballs and Carl Lewis's old running shoes) do little to help tell any special

---

Across the lake to Evian

One of the best excursions from Lausanne is the short but scenic voyage across the lake to the French spa town of **EVIAN**, almost directly opposite Ouchy. The best bit of the trip is on the water: little Evian has been gentrified almost to stupefaction, and there's not much to do other than stroll the boulevards, poke around the backstreets and gawp at the modern spa complex that exploits the famous mineral springs. One of the grand nineteenth-century edifices, the **Hall d'Exposition** on Rue Nationale, has an exhibition on the town's watery past (May–Sept daily; free), and can take bookings for a visit to Evian's giant bottling plant, 5km out of town (June–Sept; €2, includes transport). The **tourist office** is on Place d'Allinges (Ⓦwww.eviantourism.com). Take your pick of the cafés and restaurants that line every street: all of them are shameless about flogging the local product.

In high summer, **boats** run from Lausanne-Ouchy to Evian almost hourly until 11pm; service is reduced in other seasons, but this is one of the few Lake Geneva routes that runs daily, all year round. You can **change money** on arrival, or withdraw euros from an ATM. Don't forget your **passport**.

Turn to p.114 for coverage of the lakeshore west of Lausanne, known as **La Côte** – and p.118 for the wine-villages of the **Lavaux**, east of Lausanne towards Vevey. Yverdon and the lakes of the Jura are covered in Chapter 3.

stories, and the museum's video archive offers only disappointing snippets of action; even for sports fans, it's a washout.

Musée de l'Elysée

On an upper level in the same park, set back from the Olympic Museum, you'll find the much more worthwhile **Musée de l'Elysée** (Tues–Sun 11am–6pm; Fr.8, free on 1st Sat of month; Ⓦwww.elysee.ch), dedicated to photography from the earliest daguerrotypes to contemporary photojournalism. Its rotating exhibitions are generally outstanding.

Vidy

A kilometre or so west of Ouchy is the district of **VIDY**, marked by a boxy building on stilts in a lakeside park: this is the Théâtre de Vidy, home of Switzerland's leading contemporary drama company. The parkland just beyond the theatre was the location of the first settlements in the Lausanne area, in Neolithic times, and then later under the Romans. Approaching through the park, you'll discover remnants of the Roman town of Lousonna, an assembly of low walls and tumbled stones with an explanatory board nearby. A short distance beyond, at 24 Chemin du Bois-de-Vaux, is the modern and well-laid-out **Musée Romain** (Tues–Sun 11am–6pm, July & Aug also Mon 11am–6pm; Fr.8, free on 1st Sat of month; Ⓦwww.lausanne.ch/mrv). Finds include glassware, mosaic work and interesting displays of Roman artefacts.

Eating and drinking

If all you want is a reviving drink and somewhere to take the weight off your feet, the city centre and the Old Town can offer dozens of **cafés** and **café-bars**: almost every corner has its local haunt, mostly offering food as well.

Aside from the city's reasonable choice of ethnic eateries, there are plenty of **restaurants** offering Vaudois specialities. A **tomme** is a round soft cheese baked to melting point within its white Brie-like rind, and often served on a bed of leafy salad. A local speciality of the La Côte region just west of Lausanne is a **malakoff**, a hot, fried round of cheese served on a bread or pastry base; the nearby villages of Vinzel and Luins (see p.118) compete for whose *malakoff* is the best, but you can also find Lausannois versions. The **saucisson vaudois**, a smoked pork and beef sausage – the highest-quality labelled reverentially with the green cantonal flag – is served hot accompanied by **papet vaudois**, a puree of leek and potato.

Cafés and café-bars

À La Bossette 4 Place du Nord, east of Tunnel. Comfortable and uniquely friendly local café on a patch of green beneath the château, serving a range of specialities along with excellent food. Closed Sat all day & Sun lunch.
Buffet Lausanne-Moudon Place du Tunnel. Popular and attractive local joint with pleasant outdoor seating plus a better-than-average range of food (including several veggie options) at below-average prices: *plats du jour* are around Fr.16–22.
Café de l'Évêché 4 Rue Curtat. Atmospheric little haunt of talkative students and local old-timers just below the cathedral – perfect for morning coffee, authentic fondue (Fr.23–27) or beer and dominoes.

Café de l'Hôtel de Ville 10 Place de la Palud. Wonderful little intimate wood-floor café, specializing in salads of every description (Fr.18–27) using the freshest of local produce, along with some Vaudois specialities. Or just come for a drink. Closed Sun, Mon, Tues eve & Sat eve.

Café Romand Place St-François. Much-loved city-centre retreat with clunky wooden furniture, a sociable atmosphere and a good range

of heavy Swiss fare, featuring lots of meat and cheese. Closed Sun.

MGM 14 Rue du Lac. Café-bar in Ouchy, the best of the bunch, with a young, laid-back atmosphere and good tunes.

Le Raisin 19 Place de la Palud. Prime people-watching terrace café in the Old Town. Also does a range of meaty mains (Fr.27–35) plus cheaper pizzas.

Restaurants

Inexpensive and mid-range

Bleu Lézard 10 Rue Enning. Fashionable and lively spot on a busy corner, with a comfy, colourful interior. The mood is of a busy café at lunchtimes, mutating into restaurant territory in the evenings: expect reasonably priced meat and fish mains (Fr.22–28). There's also a lively downstairs club.

Café du Grütli 4 Rue de la Mercerie. Venerable old tile-and-dark-wood brasserie in the heart of the Old Town, with affordable *menus* (Fr.17 or so) and *à la carte* options ranging from horse steak to a dozen snails. Head past the pavement tables and make for the hum of conversation within. Closed Sun.

Au Couscous 2 Rue Enning ☏ 021 321 38 40. Long-standing Arabic restaurant in a lively part of town, lacking some atmosphere but making up for it with excellent couscous and tajines (Fr.29–33) and *mezze* (Fr.8 each), with veggie dishes too. *Menus* from Fr.18. Closed Sun lunch.

Ma Jong 3 Escaliers du Grand-Pont. Just down from *Manora*, with excellent pan-Asian fast food (around Fr.17) ranging from chicken satay through to *yaki-niku* (Japanese fried beef) and curries. Closed Sun lunch.

Manora 17 Place St-François. Self-service place with a wide range of excellent cheap food. Daily 7am–10.30pm or so.

New Laxmi 5 Escaliers du Marché ⊛ www.laxmi .ch. Excellent North Indian restaurant, with well-prepared meat, fish and veg standards (Fr.18–30). Budget all-you-can-eat buffet lunches are Fr.20, or Fr.17 for veggies. Students get a ten percent discount. Closed Mon lunch & Sun.

Le Restaurant (Buffet de la Gare) In the train station. Atmospheric station café-restaurant, with high ceilings, wood-panelled walls and more than a hint of the age of steam. If your eye's on the minute hand, ask for the *assiette express*.

Expensive

Beau-Rivage Café 17 Place du Port, Ouchy ☏ 021 613 33 33, ⊛ www.brp.ch. The *Beau-Rivage Palace* hotel boasts several top-class restaurants, including one with three Michelin-starred chef Anne-Sophie Pic at the helm – but for a less stratospherically pricey experience, book for the "café" (actually a stylish brasserie restaurant). It's an excellent place to splash out on fish and shellfish, such as Creole-influenced jambalaya.

Château d'Ouchy 2 Place du Port, Ouchy ☏ 021 331 32 32, ⊛ www.chateaudouchy.ch. Chic, contemporary-style restaurant attached to the *Château d'Ouchy* hotel, now occupying the nineteenth-century lakefront château. The Mediterranean-influenced cuisine concentrates on fresh market produce, with international touches: expect, for example, local perch but also Maine lobster.

Hôtel de Ville 1 Rue d'Yverdon, Crissier ☏ 021 634 05 05, ⊛ www.philippe-rochat.ch. Once the domain of the legendary Frédy Girardet, said to be the greatest chef in the world in his day, now the shop window of culinary star Philippe Rochat. Many consider this Switzerland's best restaurant – Michelin give it three stars. The style is classic, the presentation and service are impeccable. Reserve two months ahead for dinner, two weeks ahead for lunch. Located 7km west of the city. Closed Sun & Mon, and early Aug.

Nightlife and entertainment

Lausanne's **nightlife** and cultural offerings are second to none in Switzerland, with a vast range of music and performance to check out, aside from the festivals listed in the box on p.97.

Bars, clubs and live music

Bars and nightlife abound. First place to look is Le Flon, a low-lying warehouse district bounded by Bel-Air, Grand-Pont and the metro station, where following your ears after dark will lead you to the best hangouts of the moment. Otherwise, there's a good concentration of bars around Rue Enning, Le Tunnel, and around Place du Tunnel, and, on a more sedate note, the streets immediately behind the château. The bars listed here all close at 1–2am, the clubs at 4–5am.

2

LAUSANNE AND LAKE GENEVA | Listings

Le 13ème Siècle Rue Cité-Devant. Atmospheric cellar DJ-bar in an Old Town street above the cathedral.

Bleu Lézard 10 Rue Enning ⓦ www.bleu-lezard .ch. Trendy cellar venue beneath a lively bar/restaurant (see opposite), staging DJ nights, live music, jam sessions, dance nights and more.

Captain Cook 2 Rue Enning. Crammed and smoky pub in the heart of the action, screening English football.

Au Château 1 Place du Tunnel. Funky music bar serving flavourful home-brewed beers – pale, dark and red – to an excitable crowd.

D! Place Centrale ⓦ www.dclub.ch. Highly respected Flon basement club, close and sweaty, playing house and jungle, and pulling in some international DJs. Entry Fri & Sat Fr.15. Closed Mon–Wed.

Harper's Pub 8 Rue de la Barre, directly above the tunnel. Hilltop Irish pub in a peaceful spot behind the château. Closed Sat & Sun lunch.

Le Loft 1 Escaliers Bel-Air ⓦ www.loftclub.ch. No-frills little club on the stairs up from Flon, with a range of music on different nights – anything from reggae to techno. Closed Mon, Tues & Thurs.

MAD (Moulin à Danse) 23 Rue de Genève ⓦ www.mad.ch. Infamous and hugely popular Flon club with adjoining theatre, gallery and alternative-style café. The club is open from 11pm, and hosts a range of local and international DJs playing anything from trance to retro crowd-pleasers. Also organizes party cruises on Lake Geneva. Entry Fr.15–25. Open Thurs–Sat.

Classical music, opera, dance and film

The Théâtre de Beaulieu, 10 Avenue des Bergières (ⓦ www.beaulieu.org), is the main venue for **classical music** – the Orchestre de la Suisse Romande (ⓦ www.osr.ch) performs here when not in Geneva – and is also famous as the place where the **Béjart Ballet** (ⓦ www.bejart.ch) presents new material every June and November. The **Opéra de Lausanne** performs at Beaulieu too, as well as at its home at 12 Avenue du Théâtre (ⓦ www.opera-lausanne.ch), while the **Orchestre de Chambre de Lausanne** (ⓦ www.ocl.ch) stages concerts at the stunning Salle Métropole (ⓦ www.sallemetropole.ch), also the venue for many Béjart productions. The arts centre at 36 Avenue Sévelin is the home of **contemporary dance**, with continuous productions year-round. Don't miss the cycle of free Friday evening concerts in the **cathedral** (June–Oct, plus Easter, Whitsun and Christmas; ⓦ www.grandesorgues.ch) – mostly, but not exclusively, organ recitals. The **Cinématheque Suisse**, in Montbenon park (ⓦ www.cinematheque.ch), has a programme of non-commercial movies from around the world, occasionally with English subtitles.

Listings

Bike and blade rental Bikes can be rented at the station or for free at Lausanneroule, in the archway under Rue du Grand-Pont (daily 8am–9pm; Fr.20 deposit) – but even the locals have to get off and wheel them up and down the city's hills. Where bikes score is if you fancy a day out of the city, perhaps cycling through the vineyards either side

of Lausanne. To blend in with the locals, rent blades from the kiosk at 6 Place de la Navigation in Ouchy (June–Sept daily 11am–10pm, April, May & Oct Sat & Sun 11am–7pm); they also rent scooters and bikes, including 21-speed tandems.

Boat rental Rowing boats and pedalos are available to rent from opposite the *Hôtel* d'Angleterre on the Ouchy waterfront for around Fr.20 per hr, motorboats for about Fr.45 per hr.

Gay and lesbian Lausanne VoGay (ⓦwww .vogay.ch) is the local gay association. *Le Saxo*, 3 Rue de la Grotte (ⓦwww.lesaxo.com), is a central bar-restaurant. Many clubs run gay nights; check with VoGay or the tourist office.

Markets The Place de la Palud hosts a lively food market (Wed & Sat 6am–2.30pm) as does the Petit-Chêne (Fri 6am–1pm). There's a crafts market at Palud (March–Dec 1st Fri of month 6am–7pm), and a flea market on Place Chauderon (Thurs 6am–7pm). During December, Place de la Riponne hosts a Christmas market, with stalls for mulled wine and roast chestnuts.

Medical facilities The Centre Hospitalier Universitaire Vaudois (CHUV) is at 46 Rue du Bugnon ⓣ021 314 11 11. The train station has a pharmacy (daily 6am–9pm).

Post office The most convenient large office is at Place St-François (Mon–Fri 7.30am–6.30pm, Sat 8am–noon).

Sport Prime arena for Lausanne's passion, blading and skateboarding, is the giant indoor La Fièvre skatepark, also called HS36 (36 Ave Sévelin; ⓦwww.fievre.ch), open daily – you'll also find dance companies, artists' ateliers and music rehearsal rooms in the same complex. For summer swimming, the beach is free at Vidy.

North of Lausanne

Past the hills **northeast of Lausanne** you encounter classic rural Swiss scenery – rolling green hills backed by distant peaks and tinkling with the neck-bells of happily munching cows. Vaud's cantonal boundary is only about 20km northeast of Lausanne, and most of the sights in this region fall inside **Canton Fribourg**; however, unless you have your own transport, Fribourg's famous cheese-making centre of **Gruyères** is most easily accessible by train from Lausanne. **Romont**'s Gothic church and thirteenth-century town centre make a beautiful detour on the journey to or from Fribourg itself (see p.218), while the untouristed **Gros de Vaud** region north of Lausanne is perfect for countryside cycling.

The northern stretches of Canton Vaud – Yverdon, Payerne and Avenches, as well as the Vallée de Joux – are covered in Chapter 3.

La Gruyère region

The walls and turrets of **Gruyères**' fairy-tale castle, 50km northeast of Lausanne, bristle atop a single crag rising above the rolling lowlands of Canton Fribourg. The whole region – of which Gruyères village is the best-known attraction – is known as **LA GRUYÈRE** (ⓦwww.la-gruyere.ch), taking in the long Lac de la Gruyère and the Sarine valley south of Fribourg, the market town and regional transport hub of **Bulle**, and a handful of resorts clinging to the slopes of the Prealpine peaks which prelude the Pays d'Enhaut (see p.264) further south. Dominating the landscape is the **Moléson**, a jutting chunk of mountain rising to 2002m with plenty of hiking possibilities and some gentle skiing in winter. This is dairy country, the most famous product being Gruyère cheese, run a close second by the local butterfat-rich double cream, served with forest fruits in Gruyères' heavenly, artery-clogging version of afternoon tea.

The chocolate factory at Broc

Some 30km northeast of Lausanne, **BULLE** isn't lacking in charm, but there's little reason to visit other than to switch transport. On the road to Gruyères, you'll pass through **La Tour de Trême**, its eponymous thirteenth-century tower plumb in the middle of the village.

On the edge of the village of **BROC**, which lies 4km east of La Tour astride the route leading up through the tiny resort of Charmey to the Jaun Pass, you'll detect luscious scents emanating from the Cailler **chocolate factory** (April–Oct

The Swiss Chocolate Train

One of the region's top excursions is a full-day package on the first-class **Swiss Chocolate Train**. Classic luxury Pullman carriages, built in 1915, and modern panoramic carriages run from **Montreux** (July & Aug daily; May, June, Sept & Oct Mon, Wed & Thurs) on the spectacular climb above Lake Geneva to **Gruyères**, where there's a stop to visit a cheese factory as well as two hours free in the village to visit the château and have lunch. In the afternoon, you move on to **Broc** for a visit to the Nestlé-Cailler **chocolate factory**, and then, around 4pm, settle back for the scenic return journey from Broc to Montreux. If you hold a Swiss Pass, you pay Fr.49/39 in 1st/2nd class (otherwise the full fare is Fr.89); this includes your seat reservation, coffee and a croissant on the morning train, bus transfers and all admission fees. You must buy your own lunch in Gruyères (or carry a picnic). Reserve at any station in Switzerland or at Ⓦ www.goldenpass.ch.

daily 9.30am–4pm; free; Ⓦ www.cailler.ch). Founded in 1898, this is the sole production facility for Nestlé's Cailler brand, named after one of the nineteenth-century pioneers of chocolate-making. On arrival, you're led through to watch a super-schmaltzy costume-drama movie about life, love and chocolate in a small Swiss town, after which a guide leads you on an explanatory tour of part of the factory. The climax comes in the Tasting Room, where you're let loose on tables piled with bite-sized chunks of every Cailler product, in unlimited quantities. Just beyond lies a shop where you can buy discounted Nestlé chocolate.

The factory, signposted on all approach roads, is a short walk from Broc-Fabrique **train station**, which is served by local trains from Bulle and La Tour and also by the **Swiss Chocolate Train**, a packaged excursion from Montreux (see box above).

Gruyères

A perfectly preserved old castle-village, isolated on its crag but within easy reach of Lake Geneva, **GRUYÈRES** is one of Switzerland's most photogenic sights and attracts hordes of day-trippers throughout the summer season, come to stroll on the village's only street and explore the impressive château. By 10am in season, the village can get uncomfortably crowded and can stay so until late afternoon. Cars are banned, but you'll find several large parking areas on the hillside just below.

At the foot of Gruyères village in **Pringy** (the location of Gruyères train station) is the **Maison du Gruyère**, a working dairy (daily 9am–7pm, Oct–May closes 6pm; Fr.7; Ⓦ www.lamaisondugruyere.ch) where you can watch the cheesemaking process close up (production runs 9–11am & 12.30–2.30pm). There's also a restaurant and shop, both concentrating on local produce. Also in the village is the new Tibet Museum, at 4 Rue de Château (April–Oct daily 11am–6pm; Nov–March Tues–Fri 1–5pm, Sat & Sun 11am–6pm; Fr.12; Ⓦ www.tibetmuseum.ch), with a selection of sculpture, paintings and ritual objects displayed in an attractive renovated chapel.

Up on the hill, the **Château de Gruyères** (daily: April–Oct 9am–6pm; Nov–March 10am–4.30pm; Fr.6.50, joint ticket with Giger Museum Fr.17; Ⓦ www.chateau-gruyeres.ch) was occupied from 1080 to 1554 by the nineteen counts of Gruyères, but was decimated by a fire in 1493 which destroyed virtually everything but the dungeons. Michel, the last count, ran up huge debts reconstructing the living quarters in Savoyard style and then fled, leaving his creditors – the governments of Fribourg and Bern – to divide up his lands between them. A rich Geneva dynasty, the Bovy and Balland families, bought the castle in 1848 and supported a number of artists in residence, including the French landscape painter Corot, before the cantonal government of Fribourg assumed control in 1938. To approach, you must walk the length of Gruyères' dipping, picturesque main street with its central fountain and quaint old houses on either side bedecked with hanging signs. A huge **gate** affords entry to the castle grounds. Highlights include Flemish **tapestries** decorating the count's bedchamber, Corot's room with landscapes painted by the man himself, and other rooms with grand fireplaces, heraldic stained glass, often featuring the dynastic symbol of a crane (*grue* in French), and booty from the Battle of Murten (see p.153) where Louis II of Gruyère fought. Beside the castle, Gruyères' **church** is in an exceptionally beautiful location, backed by valley vistas.

You'll find a couple of odd counterpoints to the grandeur of the castle at its gate (both covered by the same entrance fee and opening hours). The first is the **Centre International de l'Art Fantastique**, a small gallery devoted to modern fantasy art – which is fine if you like that kind of thing. This, though, is nothing compared with the truly nasty **H.R. Giger Museum** adjacent (April–Oct daily 10am–6pm; Nov–March Tues–Fri 11am–5pm, Sat & Sun 10am–6pm; Fr.12, joint ticket with château Fr.17; Ⓦ www.hrgiger.com). Giger is a Swiss graphic artist, most famous for designing the special effects for the movie *Alien* – for which he won an Oscar – as well as *Poltergeist II*, *Alien 3* and others. He has turned one of Gruyères' old houses into a showcase for his unique brand of grotesque art – sexualized surrealist visions of machine-like humanoids, nightmarish cityscapes and fantasy porn. "Giger," enthused Timothy Leary, 1960s acid guru, "you give us courage to say hello to our insectoid selves." Afterwards, scuttle over to the *Alien*-style bar alongside.

Practicalities

Trains from Lausanne to Fribourg pass through **Palézieux**, where you must change for the local GFM trains that trundle through the countryside to **Bulle**, and then on to **Gruyères-gare** at the foot of the village; it's a short but stiff walk from the station up the hill to Gruyères, or you could time your arrival to coincide with one of the half-dozen buses a day shuttling between Gruyères-gare and Gruyères-ville. The Palézieux–Gruyères trains terminate at **Montbovon**, on the MOB line between Montreux and Gstaad. If you're approaching from Fribourg, take an express bus to Bulle and switch onto a train there. Occasional buses go direct to Gruyères-ville from Bulle station.

Everything in Gruyères is on the village's single street. The **tourist office** is at the car park end (May–Oct daily 9am–noon & 1.30–5.45pm; rest of year Mon–Fri 10am–noon & 1.30–5pm; ℡026 921 10 30, Ⓦ www.gruyeres.ch). There are only a few **hotels**, most of which take one or two days a week off in the winter. Whichever side of the street you're on, getting a room at the back gives you a view over the valley. The pinewood *Fleur de Lys* (℡026 921 82 82, Ⓦ www.hotelfleurdelys.ch; ❸) is a sound choice; the grand *Hôtel de Ville* (℡026 921 24 24, Ⓦ www.hoteldeville.ch; ❸–❹) takes a step up in comfort and cuisine; and nicest of the lot is the *Hostellerie des Chevaliers* (℡026 921 19 33, Ⓦ www.gruyeres-hotels.ch/chevaliers; ❸–❹), just outside the village.

Finding a place to **eat** isn't difficult: everywhere offers terraces on both the village side and the valley side at which to sample cheesy delights or bowls of berries slathered in silky *crème-double*. The *Auberge de la Halle* is one of the least pretentious places to get a proper meal, with *menus* around Fr.19. All the hotels offer quality traditional Gruyères and French cuisine, with the *Hostellerie St-Georges* (℡026 921 83 00) top choice within the village.

Moléson

Ten minutes on the bus past Gruyères-gare is **MOLÉSON** village (Ⓦ www
.moleson.ch), a small resort giving access to the heights of **Le Moléson**
mountain (2002m), via a funicular and gondola; panoramic views from the
summit take in Lake Geneva, the Prealps and even Mont Blanc. There are plenty
of ridge-top walks and, in winter, easy-to-medium ski runs.

Romont and the Gros de Vaud

Train tracks and minor roads between Lausanne and Fribourg pass by **ROMONT**,
a medieval town perched atop an isolated round hill, with lofty 360-degree views.
From the train station, it's a steep ten-minute walk up to the thirteenth-century
ramparts. Romont consists of little more than two broad streets with a distinctive
round tower at each end. The focus is the **castle**, parts of which have been
converted into the **Vitromusée** (Stained Glass Museum; April–Oct Tues–Sun
10am–1pm & 2–6pm; Nov–March Thurs–Sun 10am–1pm & 2–5pm; Fr.10;
Ⓦ www.vitromusee.ch), holding mostly modern examples. Nearby is the beautiful
Gothic collegiate **church**, replete with original woodcarving from a rebuilding
in 1434. The **tourist office** is at 112 Rue du Château (Mon–Fri 10am–noon &
2–4pm, April–Oct also Sat 10am–noon; Ⓣ 026 652 31 52, Ⓦ www.romont.ch).

To the west, the peaceful country between Lausanne and Yverdon is known as
the **Gros de Vaud** (Ⓦ www.gros-de-vaud.ch), rural heart of the canton and
Switzerland's breadbasket. **ECHALLENS** (Ⓦ www.echallens.ch), 15km north of
Lausanne, is the main centre, formerly an important market town but now a
popular retreat for young families. Despite its sometimes twee touches, it's still a
picturesque place, with a thirteenth-century château and many eighteenth-century
buildings. The LEB narrow-gauge **railway** (Ⓦ www.leb.ch) – Switzerland's oldest,
opened in 1873 – runs here from Lausanne; in summer especially, this is a lovely,
scenic ride.

Lake Geneva

The croissant-shaped **LAKE GENEVA** (Lac Léman in French), bluest of the
Swiss lakes, is ringed with villages, castles and gorgeous walks that demand
attention. This is wine country, with vineyards carpeting the lakeshore and

---

Lake Geneva factoids

Lake Geneva is the largest freshwater lake in Western Europe, holding some 89
trillion litres. It's a big bulge in the course of the River Rhône, which rises at the
Furkapass and flows westwards between the mountains of Canton Valais to enter the
lake near Villeneuve. Its water takes an estimated seventeen years to cover the 73km
to Geneva before flowing on through France to reach the Mediterranean near
Marseille. Although the lake is only 14km wide at its broadest point, it plunges to
310m maximum depth and is subject to heavy winds which rip across the surface,
causing stormy conditions not unlike an inland sea.

the first slopes of the hills which rise behind. Genteel small towns such as **Nyon** and **Vevey**, either side of Lausanne, have made a living recharging the batteries of frazzled urbanites for generations. Over the decades, the lake has also attracted some of the world's wealthiest people, and the shores around the jet-set playground of **Montreux** in particular are lined with opulent villas – although a lakeside stroll can still let you taste the unspoilt beauty which drew Byron and the Romantic poets. Relaxing on one of the boats which crisscross the lake beneath the looming presence of the Savoy Alps and the Dents-du-Midi mountains on the French side helps bring home the full grandeur of the setting.

La Côte

The gently curving northwestern shore of the lake from Geneva to Lausanne (some 65km) is known as **La Côte** (ⓦ www.lacote.ch), characterized by a succession of hamlets and small villages, almost without exception pretty, well kept and pristinely picturesque. Those along the minor shoreline road, the *Route Suisse*, are less numerous and more visited than those placed back behind the main *autoroute* on the first slopes of the Jura foothills, amongst vineyards producing some of the highest-prized **wine** in Vaud.

Things are much less developed here for **wine-tasting tours** than in the Lavaux region east of Lausanne (see p.118). However, if you rent a bike from larger train stations for a day's gentle exploration along the narrow **Route des Vignerons**, which winds from vineyard to vineyard along the slope, you'll find plenty of *caveaux* (wine cellars) offering *dégustations* (tastings) of local products. You have to pay for the tasting – which generally comprises a few choices of wine, in 1dl glasses – but this can work out a bargain if you choose to buy a bottle. Countless *auberges* and *pintes* (country taverns) along the way offer local home-cooked specialities.

You'll also pass dozens of **châteaux**, evidence both of the region's key strategic significance in medieval times, and its attraction to Europe's nobility in more recent centuries. Some are now museums, but most remain in private hands. Major stopoffs include the historic **Château de Coppet**, close to Geneva, the attractive little harbour-town of **Nyon** with its own château and Roman museum, and the nearby **Château de Prangins**, housing an excellent museum devoted to Swiss history.

Coppet

COPPET, 2km inside Vaud, sits astride the lakeshore *Route Suisse* and has an attractive arcaded main street, yet is unremarkable but for the **Château de Coppet** (ⓦ www.swisscastles.ch). Entry is only on the multilingual **guided tours** (Easter–Oct daily 2–6pm; July & Aug also 10am–noon; Fr.8), which run every half-hour or so, according to demand.

The house was built by **Jacques Necker**, Minister of Finance to the French king Louis XVI from 1776 until the Revolution in 1789. Necker seems to have been rather disgusted by the excesses of the regime he was publicly responsible for, and built up a dossier documenting the extent of financial corruption which, it's said, helped to initiate the Revolution. During the

There's a **map** of the La Côte region on p.94.

1780s, his daughter **Germaine** gained a reputation in the Paris *salons* for her intellect and vivacity. Necker retired to Coppet in 1790, from when Germaine's (now **Madame de Staël**'s) literary and philosophical *salon* began to attract the leading intellects of the day, gaining the nickname "the Parliament of European Opinion". Schlegel, Chateaubriand and Byron were among regular visitors to the musical *soirées*, playlets, debates and discussions which often continued late into the night. Madame de Staël died in 1817 and the château is still in her family.

The approach to the château is beneath a vaulted arch into a peaceful interior courtyard, open on one side to the gardens behind a wrought-iron gate surmounted with the elaborate initials "N.C.", demonstrating the partnership between Jacques Necker and his wife Suzanne Curchod. Nine rooms are open to the public, including the library, formerly the main reception room, filled with Empire and Directoire furniture; Madame de Staël's bedroom, with her Louis XVI bed draped in Lyon silk; Juliette Récamier's bedroom next door, hung with exquisite eighteenth-century Chinese wallpaper; and, upstairs, a drawing room and a gallery of family portraits.

Coppet also boasts the splendid **hotel** *Du Lac*, 51 Grand'Rue (☎022 960 80 00, ⓦwww.hoteldulac.ch; ⑤–⑥). This wood-beamed inn was classified as a *grand logis* in 1628: after ducking in off the busy road, you trail through grand dining rooms and antique-laden drawing rooms until you reach the shady, perfectly calm lakeside terrace at the back. It's a fine, atmospheric retreat.

Céligny

Occupying an enclave of Canton Geneva, surrounded by Vaud, gentle **CÉLIGNY** is about as endearing a rural gem as you could hope to find, enjoying waterside lawns, vineyards all around and, through the village, an atmospheric church and château (not open to the public). The air of undisturbed tranquillity proved particularly balming for the actor Richard Burton, who spent the last few years of his life here. If you walk up into the village from the train station, across the square and then head left, cutting around a parking area, you'll find the Vieux Cimitière, a mossy grove by a stream that is Burton's final resting place.

Nyon

NYON – a major town under the Romans which has mellowed into an attractive little port, 9km north of Coppet – is a perfect stopover on a leisurely tour of the area. The town is spread out among fields and lawns which reach down to the water, and is backed by acres of vineyards. There's a château and an excellent Roman museum, and the nearby **Château de Prangins** houses the regional branch of the National Museum.

After Julius Caesar conquered Gallia Comata (Long-Haired Gaul) in 52 BC, he retired his cavalry veterans to the **Colonia Julia Equestris**, built over the

---

Paleo Rock Festival

Nyon's biggest party is also one of Europe's biggest – the giant **Paleo Rock Festival** (ⓦwww.paleo.ch), which takes place over a week in late July in a field outside town, with a consistently excellent line-up of musicians attracting hundreds of thousands of fans. Acts in past years have been as diverse as Ruben Gonzalez, Massive Attack and Mika. Day tickets go for around Fr.40; a full six-day pass for around Fr.300. Transport between Nyon and the festival site is free. The tourist office has festival-plus-hotel packages.

old Helvetian settlement of Noviodunum. The third century AD saw attacks from Alemans and Franks, and by the mid-fifth century the colony was virtually deserted. Only its name survived, "Colonia" truncated to the single nasal syllable "Nyon". The region was passed from lord to lord until the Bernese conquered Vaud in 1536. In 1781 a French entrepreneur opened a **porcelain** workshop, staffed by local artisans who produced work of exceptionally high quality, rapidly establishing Nyon as a centre for the craft: museums around Europe now display Nyon porcelain alongside the best of Limoges china as some of the highest-prized ceramic art of the period. These days, Nyon's claim to fame is as the location of football cup draws: the European governing body **UEFA** is headquartered in the town.

Arrival and information

Plenty of **trains** serve Nyon, although note that not all trains heading east go to Lausanne: some branch off at Morges on their way to Yverdon. Regular **boats** arrive from Geneva and Lausanne. The **tourist office** is one minute's walk from the station, at 8 Avenue Viollier (Mon–Fri: mid-May to mid-Sept 8.30am–noon & 2–5.30pm, closed Wed pm; rest of year 8.30am–12.30pm & 1.30–5.30pm; ☎022 365 66 00, Ⓦwww.nyon-tourisme.ch), with a summer office by the landing-stage (mid-May to mid-Sept daily 10am–4pm, July & Aug until 6pm).

The Town

Heading southeast from the train station towards the lake for a couple of minutes will bring you into the compact Old Town, centred on **Place du Château**, a charming, shaded square with terrace cafés. It is backed by the château itself, a twelfth-century turreted fortress looking out over the lake, which houses the **Musée Historique** (Tues–Sun 10am–5pm, Nov–March 2–5pm; Fr.8 joint ticket with Musée Romain and Musée du Léman, 1st Sun of month free; Ⓦwww.chateaudenyon.ch), with displays of silver, fine art and a comprehensive collection of Nyon porcelain. Opposite, at 4 Place du Château, is the headquarters of Focale (Ⓦwww.focale.ch), a leading association of Swiss photographers; their cramped **bookshop** is excellent, as is the gallery downstairs. Heading west off the square, Rue Maupertuis passes a statue of Julius Caesar on the way to the **Musée Romain** (Tues–Sun 10am–5pm, Nov–March 2–5pm; Fr.8 joint ticket with Musée Historique and Musée du Léman; Ⓦwww.mrn.ch). The museum is housed in a Roman basilica, originally part of Nyon's forum; a trompe l'oeil fresco of the basilica's interior on the wall outside, as well as a model in the museum, give an idea of the size of Nyon's public buildings in its Roman heyday. The museum's extensive collection is well laid out with zones devoted to daily life, crafts, architecture and religion.

Follow Rue Maupertuis round to the junction with Rue du Vieux-Marché, just beyond which you'll find the small **Église Notre-Dame**, dating from 1110, its dark interior enlivened only by some colourful modern stained glass and an unusual asymmetrical design. The arched Porte Ste-Marie round the corner gives onto the **Esplanade des Marronniers** (Chestnut Trees), exposed to fresh lake breezes and dominated by two and a half Roman columns, sited impressively against the blue. Walking along the city walls east and down to the lakefront delivers you to the little **Musée du Léman**, 8 Quai Louis-Bonnard (Tues–Sun 10am–5pm, Nov–March 2–5pm; Fr.8 joint ticket with Musée Historique and Musée Romain; Ⓦwww.museeduleman.ch). The ground floor has informative displays on the lake's fauna, with large aquariums, while upstairs are paintings, models of ships and disquisitions (in French) on how to protect the lake. Beyond the museum, Rue de Rive heads east, lined with fine old

Above Nyon – St-Cergue

Rising above Nyon are the final stretches of the Jura range within Switzerland, known as the **Pied du Jura**, sliced across by the international border separating the French Pays de Gex from the Swiss mountain resort of **ST-CERGUE**. This unassuming town is set in some wild countryside, with hiking trails that see few ramblers; the tourist office on Place Sy-Vieuxville (Tues–Fri 8.30am–noon & 1.30–4.30pm, Sat & Sun 9.30am–3.30pm; ☎022 360 13 14, ⓦwww.st-cergue.ch) has details. In winter, St-Cergue provides easy downhill **skiing** for families, and plenty of excellent cross-country routes. The *desalpe*, or annual descent of cattle from the high pastures to winter quarters in the valley, accompanied by much floral decoration and folkloric celebrations, is a highlight of St-Cergue's calendar, taking place on a Saturday in late September. Riding on the little red narrow-gauge NStCM **trains**, which depart from the forecourt of Nyon station on a winding route up into the hills, is worth an afternoon in itself, whether you get off at St-Cergue or continue over the **Col de la Givrine** (1228m) to the hamlet of **La Cure** on the border.

shuttered town houses. At the end, Rue de la Colombière continues uphill. Turn right at the junction with Rue de la Porcelaine and head a short distance downhill to find Nyon's **Roman amphitheatre**, currently under renovation. It's virtually the same size as the one at Avenches (see p.152) but much more ruined and unfortunately now hemmed in by modern housing.

Accommodation and eating

Nyon's top **hotel** is the *Beau-Rivage*, 49 Rue de Rive (☎022 365 41 41, ⓦwww.leshotelsderive.ch; ❻–❼), a grandiose pile that's been in business since 1481 and boasts large, traditionally furnished rooms, about half of them facing the lake. The charming *Hostellerie du XVIe Siècle*, 2 Place du Marché (☎022 994 88 00, ⓦwww.16eme.com; ❷–❸), occupies an arcaded building in the cobbled Old Town. Rue de Rive has any number of places to **eat** fresh fish, but the fillet of perch (Fr.39) served at *Du Cheval Blanc* at no. 62 must rank with the best. More affordable pizzas and pasta (Fr.17–35) can be found at *Le Léman*, 28 Rue de Rive, or at half-a-dozen other cafés nearby.

Château de Prangins

A kilometre or two east of Nyon is the village of **PRANGINS**, in the midst of which, set in formal English gardens, is the **Château de Prangins** (Tues–Sun 10am–5pm; Fr.7; ⓦwww.musee-suisse.com), built in the 1730s in the French style, and now an arm of the **Swiss National Museum** devoted to the history of Switzerland in the eighteenth and nineteenth centuries. It's a huge place holding an imaginative collection that's well worth a couple of hours. All the rooms are numbered sequentially, but the layout can be confusing. Exhibits on the **ground floor**, outlining the ideals of aristocrats and the bourgeoisie around 1800, and in the cellars, detailing Switzerland's pre-industrial rural economy, are less engaging than those on the **two upper floors**, which are devoted to Swiss cultural history from 1750 into the twentieth century. Each room has English notes, with items from everyday life displayed next to historically significant objects. Reconstructed interiors, such as that of a late nineteenth-century schoolroom, display uncanny attention to detail. Outside, an extensive kitchen garden has been planted with fruit and vegetables according to eighteenth-century accounts of horticulture. **Buses** #5 and #31 run every twenty to thirty minutes (hourly at weekends) from Nyon's train station to Prangins, stopping in the village a couple of minutes' walk from the château.

Luins and Vinzel

Some 10km northeast of Nyon on the **Route des Vignerons** are the neigh-bouring wine villages of **LUINS** and **VINZEL**, both famous for their *malakoffs*. These little gastronomic curiosities – a rich, fried cheese-and-egg mixture served hot on a round bread base – are a local speciality, renamed to celebrate the triumphant return of a band of Vaudois mercenaries under the Russian general Malakoff from the 1855 siege of Sebastopol. The two villages, which are ten minutes' walk apart, have competed since then for whose *malakoff* is better. Take the taste test at the *Auberge Communale* in Luins (☎021 824 11 59), then wander down the road past the vineyards to *Au Coeur de la Côte* in Vinzel (☎021 824 11 41) – both are open daily, serving *malakoffs* for around Fr.7 each; while you're at it, take the chance to compare and contrast the excellent village wines. A good hike reaches above Luins to a tiny church-with-a-view dating from 1393, and on up past the vineyards into woods of beech, oak and chestnut.

The Lavaux wine villages

The compact stretch of Lake Geneva shore east from Lausanne to Vevey – known as the **Lavaux** (⊛www.lavaux.com), a UNESCO World Heritage Site – is one of the most alluring of all Swiss regions, its floral waterside promenades flanked on one side by wide expanses of vines and on the other by vistas across to the Savoy Alps rising behind the Dents-du-Midi on the far shore. Trains heading to Montreux and beyond hug the shoreline, seeming to whisk you along centimetres above the glittering lake. Some of the country's best **wines** come from the vineyards clustered cheek by jowl along the steep Lavaux slopes: this is perfect country for gentle walks and bike rides punctuated by samplings of the local nectar. Cafés and *pintes* abound, set in the cobbled streets of picturesque villages.

Tourist offices have information to guide you through the Lavaux's **wine villages**, a line of hamlets strung along the slopes between Lausanne and Vevey, devoted to the art of viticulture. Between May and October, most reliably on weekends (Thurs–Sun), you'll find *caveaux* (cellars) and *carnotzets* (cellars with rough benches and tables for extended wine- and food-sampling sessions) open in every village, some of them belonging to that commune's *vignerons* associa-tion, others attached to private châteaux or independent *vignobles*. The website and tourist offices have full details.

Exploring the Lavaux

The best road to follow through the Lavaux is termed the **Corniche**, winding sceni-cally through the vineyards between the main lakefront traffic road and the *autoroute* and Lausanne–Bern train tracks on a terrace higher up. The **Grande Traversée** route, marked with a "GT" signpost, starts in Ouchy, follows the lakefront to Lutry, then snakes up to the Corniche, ending 32km away at Chillon. You can follow any number of shorter trails on and around the Corniche, marked with **Parcours Viticole** (Vineyard Trail) signposts. Local **trains** along the lakefront line are plentiful, meaning you can hop on and off at will; alternatively, the narrow-gauge **"Train des Vignes"** shuttles hourly from Puidoux-Chexbres station (on the line between Lausanne and Fribourg) on a short but steep track down through the vineyards to Vevey (takes 12min). Another option is to rent a **bike** in Lausanne, Vevey or Montreux, while local tourist offices can also provide a **hiking map** of the area. **Boats** stop at Lutry, Cully and Rivaz.

There's a **map** of the Lavaux region on p.94.

Cully

The shuttered village of **CULLY** (pronounced "kwee"), 8km east of Lausanne, is full of *caveaux* and *carnotzets* offering the forest-fruity wines of nearby Epesses, Calamin, Riex, Villette and Lutry. The last Friday in November is Cully's **Nuit du vin cuit**, a masked musical parade accompanied by quaffing of mulled must (new unfermented wine). The **Cully Jazz Festival** (March/April, Ⓦwww .cullyjazz.ch) is an intimate affair.

Cully's tourist office is at the train station (Mon–Fri 9am–noon & 1–5pm, Ⓣ021 962 84 54). The thirteenth-century town hall has been converted into a characterful hotel, *Auberge du Raisin*, 1 Place de l'Hôtel de Ville (Ⓣ021 799 21 31, Ⓦwww.aubergeduraisin.ch; ❸–❹), filled with period furniture. Its restaurant is outstanding, acclaimed by Michelin, Gault Millau and others, but not cheap (expect Fr.75 and upwards). Otherwise head to the lakeside *Au Major-Davel* (Ⓣ021 799 94 94, Ⓦwww.hotelaumajordavel.ch) in the village, which serves up superb local produce; *menus* from about Fr.45.

St-Saphorin and east to Vevey

About 3km east of Cully are the vineyards of **Dézaley**, producing some of the highest-rated *grand cru* wines in Switzerland. From the landing-stage at nearby **Rivaz**, it's 1km east to **ST-SAPHORIN** – about as romantic and photogenic a waterside hamlet as you could ever hope for, piled up on steep slopes above the lake, with an old church, skinny cobbled alleys that crook their way up between crumbling old cottages, and superb flinty, smoke-perfumed wines best sampled at the village's central ⚜ *Auberge de l'Onde* (Ⓣ021 925 49 00, Ⓦwww .aubergedelonde.ch; closed Mon & Tues). This atmospheric old inn, once a halt for stagecoaches plying between Geneva and Italy, is splendid: its languorous combination of wood-beamed quaintness, day-fresh perch sautéed delectably in

▲ Wine from the barrel in St-Saphorin

herb-butter and a heady carafe or three of the village wine could easily charm you into abandoning all plans for the rest of the day.

Strolling 2km up the hill from St-Saphorin brings you to picturesque **CHEXBRES**; aim for the beautiful lounge-restaurant in the *Baron Tavernier* hotel (℡021 926 60 00, Ⓦwww.barontavernier.com), set in a vineyard with panoramic views. It's 4km further east to **Chardonne**, on the slopes of Mont Pèlerin, from where an amble under the funicular tracks brings you down to Corsier, on the edge of Vevey.

Vevey

At the little town of Vevey, there is a particularly comfortable hotel…The entertainment of tourists is the business of the place, which, as many travellers will remember, is seated upon the edge of a remarkably blue lake – a lake that it behoves every tourist to visit.

Henry James, from *Daisy Miller* (1878)

Whereas brassy Montreux, a few kilometres down the road, has freely embraced all that glisters, its old-fashioned neighbour **VEVEY** is more discriminating. Vevey quietly cleans its streets, tends its flowerbeds, makes sure it has enough, but not too many, hotels and then waits for visitors to find the town for themselves. With an ambience of tasteful, restrained gentility, it is enchanting, a world apart (or a remnant of a world now past). You may find yourself lulled into staying.

Henry James set his *Daisy Miller* – the story of a headstrong young woman on the Grand Tour who broke the rules of propriety by visiting the Château de Chillon unchaperoned, and so got her comeuppance – in Vevey, specifically at the *Hôtel des Trois Couronnes*, which seems much the same now as it must have been in James's day. In a similar vein, **Anita Brookner** set her Booker Prize-winning novel *Hotel du Lac* in a taciturn but anonymous lakeside town

Nestlé

Henri Nestlé was born in Frankfurt in 1814, and moved to Vevey in his 20s, a merchant and small-scale inventor. He began experimenting with recipes for baby-food to help mothers unable to breastfeed. In 1867, he fed his "*farine lactée*" to a premature baby boy whose mother was dangerously ill; the boy survived, and Nestlé's reputation skyrocketed. The following year he opened an office in London to cope with the quantity of orders, and within five years was exporting to South America and Australia. In 1874 he sold his company for a million francs. In 1929, Nestlé bought out Peter, Cailler and Kohler – pioneers in making milk chocolate – and started to diversify, launching the world's first instant coffee, Nescafé, in 1938. More takeovers followed, and by the 1960s Nestlé was Switzerland's biggest company. Today, still based in Vevey and having swallowed up cosmetic firm L'Oréal in 1974 and British confectioner Rowntree's in 1991, Nestlé employs almost a quarter of a million people, and buys up more than ten percent of the world's entire crop of coffee and cacao beans. Yet its most controversial product is its original one: baby formula. For years parents' organizations and health watchdogs have been lobbying for boycotts of Nestlé products, to force the company to take a role in helping educate mothers in the developing world to breastfeed whenever possible and to buy formula only as a last resort. The company maintains it is merely offering mothers a choice. The dispute shows few signs of resolution.

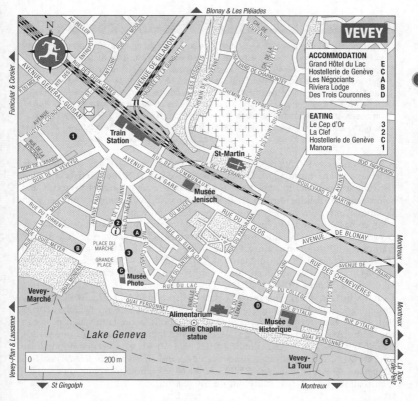

ACCOMMODATION
Grand Hôtel du Lac	E
Hostellerie de Genève	C
Les Négociants	A
Riviera Lodge	B
Des Trois Couronnes	D

EATING
Le Cep d'Or	3
La Clef	2
Hostellerie de Genève	C
Manora	1

opposite the Dent d'Oche (the huge 2222m mountain on the French shore facing Vevey).

Generations of tourists return to Vevey to stroll the flowered promenades, muse on the Dent d'Oche, venture across the water on the *belle-époque* ships, and take high tea in grand hotels. Yet there's more to do than this suggests: Vevey's shops, museums and local life are far more engaging than in Montreux, and if big cities such as Lausanne or Geneva don't appeal, you could easily use small-town Vevey as a comfortable base from which to explore the whole lake region.

Arrival, information and accommodation

Vevey's **train station** is 300m north of the lakeshore on a busy east–west main road: cross over and head towards the lake on the Rue de Lausanne, and within a minute or two you'll come to the huge central square of Grande-Place, also known as Place du Marché, which fronts directly onto the lake. The Old Town alleys are clustered to the east. The town has three **ferry stops**: Vevey-Plan is to the west, behind the Nestlé building; Vevey-Marché is metres from Place du Marché in the town centre; and Vevey-La Tour is to the east, close to La Tour-de-Peilz.

Vevey's **tourist office** is in the pillared Grenette building on Grande-Place (mid-May to mid-Sept Mon–Fri 9am–6pm, Sat 8.30am–noon; rest of year Mon–Fri

Vevey–Montreux transport

If you're shuttling between Vevey and Montreux, you might prefer to abandon the train in favour of the handy electric **city bus #1** (Ⓦ www.vmcv.ch). This runs on a straight lakeside route from Vevey's funicular station (west of the centre), past Vevey train station, through La Tour-de-Peilz and Clarens into Montreux town centre, on through Territet (stopping outside the Château de Chillon), and terminating in Villeneuve. Buses run every ten minutes; journey time is twenty minutes. **Swiss Pass** holders travel **free** on buses, trains and boats between Vevey and Montreux (and further afield) and also gain free admission to almost all museums reviewed in this book; see p.35.

8.30am–noon & 1–5.30pm, Sat 9am–noon; Ⓣ 0848 868 484, Ⓦ www.montreux riviera.com). The most colourful annual event is August's **Street Artists' Festival** (Ⓦ www.artistesderue.ch), when the town is taken over by jugglers, acrobats and mime artists. A "**folkloric market**" is held every Saturday morning in summer, with live music and street theatre, plus lots of local food and wine.

Vevey has a limited, but high-quality, range of accommodation options. Stay overnight and you qualify for a free **Riviera Card**, covering free public transport and other discounts. Right in the centre of town is the SB **hostel** ⚘ *Riviera Lodge*, 5 Place du Marché (Ⓣ 021 923 80 40, Ⓦ www.rivieralodge .ch; ❶), with spotless modern dorms and rooms. You can **camp** 3km west at lakeside *La Pichette* (Ⓣ 021 921 09 97).

Of the **hotels**, ⚘ *Les Négociants*, 27 Rue du Conseil (Ⓣ 021 922 70 11, Ⓦ www .hotelnegociants.ch; ❷), and *Hostellerie de Genève*, 11 Place du Marché (Ⓣ 021 921 45 77, Ⓦ www.hotelgeneve.ch; ❹–❺), are both good, family-run places in the centre. At the top end of the scale, both with literary associations (see p.120), *Grand Hôtel du Lac*, 1 Rue d'Italie (Ⓣ 021 921 10 41, Ⓦ www.grandhoteldulac .ch; ❽–❾), offers small-scale, understated grandeur, while ⚘ *Hôtel des Trois Couronnes*, 49 Rue d'Italie (Ⓣ 021 923 32 00, Ⓦ www.hoteltroiscouronnes.ch; ❽), retains all its period style, stuffy but utterly charming.

The Town

The best way to get the flavour of Vevey is simply to wander: its narrow Old Town alleys, enclosing the huge **Grande-Place** (or **Place du Marché**) in a cat's cradle of arcades and shuttered facades, are alive with people, shops and activity. Arrive on a Tuesday or Saturday and you'll find the marketplace packed with stalls: food, crafts, wine or all three. The pillared building dominating the square is the Grenette, or town granary, dating from 1808 and now housing the tourist office. On the south side of the square stands the fine **Musée Photo** (Camera Museum; Tues–Sun 11am–5.30pm; Fr.8; Ⓦ www.cameramuseum.ch), an absorbing survey of the history of photography, with dozens of antique cameras and other kit; pick up an English-language audioguide.

Vevey's excellent fine art museum is the **Musée Jenisch**, 2 Avenue de la Gare (closed for renovation at time of writing, due to reopen spring 2011; formerly Tues–Sun 11am–5.30pm; Fr.8–15, depending on the exhibition; Ⓦ www .museejenisch.ch). The museum was built in 1897 with a donation from a Hamburg émigré family named Jenisch (no connection with the Jenisch gypsy people; see p.428). It stages changing exhibitions of Swiss art, along with lithographs and other graphic work by Rembrandt, Dürer, Le Corbusier and others as well as works by Austrian expressionist Oskar Kokoschka.

About 500m west of the centre, the giant green building on the waterfront is Nestlé's world HQ (see box, p.120). A little uphill on the Chemin de Meruz is

Walks around Vevey

Vevey's tourist office runs a two-hour **guided walk** around the town (April–Sept Wed–Fri 10am; Fr.10), starting from their office; check in advance about the availability of an English-speaking guide. One of the area's most pleasant long walks is the three-hour **"Chemin Fleuri"** (Flowered Path), covering the sumptuous 9km lakefront promenade between Vevey and Villeneuve (aside from a short stretch east of La Tour-de-Peilz, where private lakefront properties force you back into the town). Another possibility is the engaging **"Poets' Ramble"**, which starts in Vevey and heads east through Clarens to Montreux, Glion, Territet, the Château de Chillon and Villeneuve. This takes in major sights as well as a series of "Speaking Benches", each dedicated to a writer with some connection to that particular location – press a button to hear a short extract of their work while you sit down and enjoy the view. The complete walk takes around five hours (longer if you stop at all the museums en route), but it's easy enough to just select one or two sections from the maps in the guidebook (Fr.5 from tourist offices).

the village of **CORSIER**; on the right of the road you'll find a small cemetery, location of the graves of Oona and Charlie Chaplin, who moved here in the 1950s as an escape from McCarthyite America and never left. Their house, the Manoir de Ban, is in the process of becoming the **Charlie Chaplin Heritage Site** (Ⓦ www.chaplinmuseum.com), a new interactive museum based on Chaplin's life and movies.

Back on the main lakefront Route de Lavaux, some 200m west of the Nestlé building you'll find the **Villa Le Lac** (guided tours March–Oct Wed 1.30–5pm; Fr.5), an elegant white bungalow designed by modernist architect Le Corbusier for his parents in 1924, which also holds much original Corbusier furniture.

To the east, Vevey merges with its neighbour, the colourful port village of La Tour-de-Peilz. On the way along Quai Perdonnet, you'll pass a photogenic statue of a bowler-hatted Chaplin staring intently at an incongruous sculpture of a large fork, which announces the presence of the nearby **Alimentarium** (Tues–Sun 10am–6pm; Fr.12; Ⓦ www.alimentarium.ch), a rather dull Nestlé-sponsored exhibition on food and nutrition. Another 200m brings you to the **Musée Historique**, 2 Rue du Château (Tues–Sat 10.30am–noon & 2–5.30pm, Sun 11am–5pm; Nov–Feb Tues–Sun 2–5.30pm; free; Ⓦ www.museehistoriquevevey.ch), with a large section devoted to Vevey's Fête des Vignerons (Wine-Growers' Festival), a mammoth celebration in music, costume and dance, staged about every 25 years – most recently in 1999. The Quai d'Entre Deux Villes leads you on into **LA TOUR-DE-PEILZ**, 1km east of Vevey and dominated by its white château (the towers of which were once roofed with animal pelts – hence the odd name). Inside is the **Musée Suisse du Jeu** (Tues–Sun 11am–5.30pm; Fr.8; Ⓦ www.museedujeu.com), an absorbing museum of games from ancient Egyptian dice to the latest handheld devices; you're encouraged to tinker.

Eating and drinking

Vevey has plenty of pavement **cafés** and **restaurants**. There are cafés all around Place du Marché offering simple *plats du jour* for under Fr.20. On the east side of the square the sociable terrace restaurant at the *Hostellerie de Genève* serves up good-value pizza and pasta (Fr.16–28) plus more expensive meat and fish mains, while *Le Cep d'Or* has a particularly good terrace for people-watching. Just off the north side of the square, *La Clef*, 1 Rue du Théâtre, is an atmospheric little corner bistro, once a haunt of Jean-Jacques Rousseau, serving up steaming Vaudois specialities (Fr.23–34, plus a good selection of *plats du jour* from Fr.17). The boss of the nearby hotel *Les Négociants* rolls up his sleeves of an evening and cooks solid, unpretentious fare in the hotel brasserie. There's also a self-service *Manora* on the second floor of the St Antoine mall opposite the station.

Above Vevey

Aside from the little Train des Vignes (see box, p.118), there are two routes for excursions by train into the hills above Vevey.

From Vevey-Funi station opposite the Nestlé building (at the terminus of bus #1), a **funicular** (every 20min; April–Oct only) rises through the wine village of Chardonne to a terrace on the slope of **MONT-PÈLERIN** at 800m, where you'll find plenty of places to appreciate the views with a little something to whet the whistle – for example at *Le Mirador Kempinski* (☏021 925 11 11, ⓦwww .mirador.ch; ➒), a huge luxury spa hotel. A stiff hike (at least 1hr) up to the summit brings you to a TV tower, with its high-speed **Plein-Ciel** glass lift whisking you up to the even better views at 1100m (lift Fr.5; funicular & lift Fr.16).

More dramatic is the curving train line from Vevey station up to the vantage point of **LES PLÉIADES**, perched in the hills at 1364m. The section beyond **Blonay** village – a junction for the line down to Montreux as well as the old steam railway to **Chamby** (see p.131) – is rack-and-pinion to cope with the gradient. Beside the penultimate station, **Lally**, is the cosy old-world *Hôtel Les Sapins* (☏021 943 13 95, ⓦwww.les-sapins.ch; ➌), with great food and a little spa. From here, it's a quarter-hour climb (or the last six minutes of the train ride) to the summit, face to face with the mighty Dent de Jaman peak, only 1875m but prominent and pyramidal enough to earn the nickname of the Vaudois Matterhorn. Views yawn out in all directions, as do hiking trails – a leg-stretching one leads east across the hilltops to Les Avants (see p.131).

Taking to the water

The part of Lake Geneva around Vevey and Montreux – the **Haut-Lac Supérieur** – dominated by the Dent d'Oche on one side, the heights above Montreux on the other, and glimpses of the snowy Pennine Alps further south, is spectacular: it's best appreciated **by boat**. Daily in summer (mid-May to mid-Sept), CGN (ⓦwww.cgn.ch) operates a ferry continuously from 10am to 6pm on a circuit between Vevey, Montreux, Château de Chillon, Le Bouveret, St-Gingolph and back to Vevey: you can get on anywhere and be taken round for two hours back to your starting point. If you don't have a Swiss Pass (see p.35), the fare is Fr.31.

A few kilometres round the lakeshore from Chillon, across the Rhône, **LE BOUVERET** is a family-friendly holiday village. Its **Swiss Vapeur Parc** (mid-May to mid-Sept daily 10am–6pm; mid-March to mid-May & mid-Sept to Oct Mon–Fri 1.30–6pm, Sat & Sun 10am–6pm; Fr.14, under-16s Fr.12; ⓦwww.swissvapeur.ch) is a miniature railway complex featuring replica locomotives pulling passengers around 1.5km of track. A stroll away is **Aquaparc** (daily 10.30am–7.30pm; ⓦwww.aquaparc .ch) a heated, indoor waterpark complete with multiple flumes, slides, rides and eateries; a full-day adult ticket costs Fr.46; children and families get discounts.

About 5km west is **ST-GINGOLPH** (ⓦwww.st-gingolph.ch), half in Switzerland and half in France. Apart from the busy border crossing, it's a soporific village that lives a quite different life from its lake neighbours: trains run not to Montreux but to the Valais villages south along the Rhône. Down by the water on the Swiss side are cafés and restaurants; on the French side is a supervised beach, with pedalos for rent. **Evian** (see p.106) is about 20km west.

Montreux and around

If you want your soul to find peace, go to Montreux.

Freddie Mercury

MONTREUX can be a snooty place, full of money and not particularly exciting. It's spectacularly located, bathed in afternoon sunshine and protected from chill northerlies by a wall of mountains, but once you've had your fill of window-shopping and strolling beneath the palm trees, it can be a bit dull. The main reasons to visit are to absorb the panorama of the Dents-du-Midi peaks across the lake, to visit the unmissable **Château de Chillon** and to catch the stellar annual **Montreux Jazz Festival**.

From the early nineteenth century, Montreux was one of the centres for pan-European – and particularly British – tourism to Switzerland, following on from the importance of the medieval **Château de Chillon** 3km away as a controlling presence on the transalpine road. An edict dated 1689 authorized the building of inns to accommodate travellers, and since then travel and tourism have been mainstays of the local economy. The name Montreux formerly referred to just one village in a loose affiliation of 24 vineyard-communes spread around the neighbouring hills, including picturesque **Clarens** to the west and **Territet** to the east. Both these are now super-plush suburbs, their visitors' books taking in the great and the good, crowned heads of Europe and Russia, and literary and artistic personages galore.

Arrival, information and accommodation

Montreux occupies a bulge of land jutting out into the lake, with the landmark Casino on the tip of the bulge. The **train station** is set on a terrace above and slightly west of the town

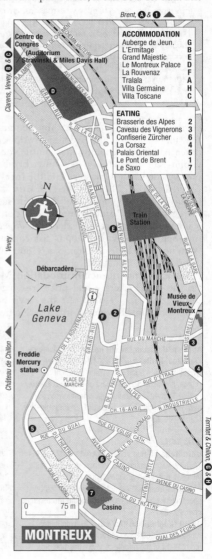

ACCOMMODATION
Auberge de Jeun.	G
L'Ermitage	B
Grand Majestic	E
Le Montreux Palace	D
La Rouvenaz	F
Tralala	A
Villa Germaine	H
Villa Toscane	C

EATING
Brasserie des Alpes	2
Caveau des Vignerons	3
Confiserie Zürcher	6
La Corsaz	4
Palais Oriental	5
Le Pont de Brent	1
Le Saxo	7

MONTREUX

Montreux's festivals

The star-studded **Montreux Jazz Festival** (Ⓦ www.montreuxjazz.com) – featuring world-famous artists from R.E.M. to B.B. King – takes place over two weeks in early July, mainly at the two stages (Auditorium Stravinski and Miles Davis Hall) within the Congress Centre, plus at the Casino. It covers the gamut of music from around the world, these days only very loosely committed to formal jazz. Check online for tickets (Fr.40–130); otherwise, just enjoy the street parties and free entertainment which spring up on the lakefront. Montreux is turned upside down during festival time, with only mornings remaining relatively normal: from mid-afternoon onwards, the main roads are blocked off, with free buses shuttling to and from huge car parks set up on the outskirts. Bars and restaurants do a roaring trade and there's a constant thrumming of music from buskers and live stages on the lakefront into the early hours. All accommodation is booked solid, and special post-event trains and buses run every night from about 1am onwards, returning festival-goers to towns as far afield as Sion and Bern. Montreux's other big events include April's **Choral Festival** (Ⓦ www.choralfestival.ch) and the classical "**Septembre Musical**" (Ⓦ www.septmus.ch).

centre; stairs and escalators within the station raise you up to the Old Town on the slopes above, while Avenue des Alpes, the street outside the station's ticket office, has stairs and a lift which shuttle you down to the main central boulevard, Grand-Rue. A patch of park sandwiched between Grand-Rue and the lakefront promenade has at its western end the **ferry** *débarcadère*, and at its eastern end the covered market, Place du Marché. **Bus #1** (see p.122) from Vevey runs along Grand-Rue, stopping below the train station, at the *débarcadère*, the covered market and the Casino, before heading on to Chillon.

The **tourist office** is next to the *débarcadère* on the lakefront (mid-May to mid-Sept Mon–Fri 9am–6pm, Sat & Sun 10am–5pm; rest of year Mon–Fri 9am–noon & 1.30–5.30pm, Sat & Sun 10am–2pm; ☏0848 868 484, Ⓦ www .montreuxriviera.com).

When it comes to **accommodation** Montreux favours its high-rollers more than its backpackers – and prices rise across the board in summer. Early July (during the Jazz Festival) sees the town booked solid. Stay overnight and you qualify for a free **Riviera Card**, covering free public transport and other discounts.

Hostel

Auberge de Jeunesse (HI hostel) 8 Passage de l'Auberge, Territet ☏021 963 49 34, Ⓦ www .youthhostel.ch. Good hostel with dorms and rooms. It's located 1.5km east of Montreux centre, beside Territet train station (slow trains only) and near the L'Eaudine stop on bus #1. Closed mid-Nov to mid-Feb. ❶

Hotels

L'Ermitage 75 Rue du Lac, Clarens ☏021 964 44 11, Ⓦ www.ermitage-montreux.com. A waterside villa set in its own grounds, with only seven rooms, all fresh and attractive, accompanied by spectacular gastronomic delights from the resident chef. ❻–❼

Grand Hôtel Suisse-Majestic 45 Avenue des Alpes ☏021 966 33 33, Ⓦ www.suisse-majestic .com. Right in the middle of town, this fine old

belle-époque establishment has much of the traditional style and atmosphere of *Le Montreux Palace* (albeit with far fewer creature comforts) at around half the price, including a fine waterside terrace restaurant and wonderful views from lake-facing rooms. ❻–❼

Le Montreux Palace 100 Grand-Rue ☏021 962 12 12, Ⓦ www.fairmont.com. Legendary luxury palace hotel, dominating the Montreux lakefront. This giant *belle-époque* folly was opened in 1906 and later expanded both along the main street and across the road to the *Petit Palais* restaurant and teahouse, set in its own gardens on the lake. Rooms are spacious, superbly well equipped and retain much of their original character; plump for one of the lakeside balconies with sweeping panoramic views over the water. The public areas are effortlessly grand, and the associations with Vladimir Nabokov (he occupied the older wing's penthouse apartment – now suite no. 65 – for his last sixteen years) still resonate. **9**

La Rouvenaz 1 Rue du Marché ℡021 963 27 36, ⓦwww.montreux.ch/rouvenaz-hotel. Six comfy enough rooms in this central but quiet family-run place with an Italian restaurant. **3**

Tralala 2 Rue du Temple ℡021 963 49 73, ⓦwww.tralalahotel.ch. Modern designer hotel in a quiet, attractive corner of the Old Town, a stiff 10min walk uphill from the centre. Rooms come in various sizes, decorated in functional but attractive minimalist style and adorned with images of jazz

and pop luminaries in concert at the Montreux Jazz Festival. **2**–**3**

Villa Germaine 3 Avenue Collonge, Territet ℡021 963 15 28, ⓦwww.montreux.ch/villa-germaine. Attractive *fin-de-siècle* villa, considerably more characterful than in-town options, and well out of the hubbub to boot. **2**

Villa Toscane 2 Rue du Lac ℡021 966 88 88, ⓦwww.villatoscane.ch. A fabulous white Art Nouveau creation on the Montreux waterfront, with balconies, meticulous service and a good deal of style. **6**

The Town

Aside from rubbing shoulders with the hoi polloi of international tourism on thronging Grand-Rue and Avenue de Casino – everyone looking at everyone else wondering where all the rich people are – there's actually precious little to do in Montreux. Backing onto the Place du Marché, with impressive views across the water to the Dents-du-Midi, stands the town's most popular photo-op: a flamboyant bronze statue of long-time local resident **Freddie Mercury**. His group Queen first recorded an album in Montreux in 1978 and returned many times afterwards, with Freddie eventually buying an apartment on the Territet waterfront (still private property) where he spent his last few months in 1991.

Associations with rock music continue at the **Casino**, on Rue du Théâtre: this dour modern building replaced the grand original, which opened in 1883 and was burned to the ground on December 4, 1971, during a concert by Frank Zappa and the Mothers of Invention. During the show, someone in the audience let off a rocket-flare which set the ceiling on fire; everyone got out without injury, but the building continued to burn all night. Ian Gillan, lead singer of the band Deep Purple, who were holed up in a hotel nearby, watched the flames leaping into the sky and was thus inspired to write his seminal rock classic "Smoke On The Water".

The zigzagging streets and hillside terraces of the steep Old Town above the train station are of marginally more interest. A group of eighteenth-century buildings houses the modest **Musée de Vieux-Montreux**, 40 Rue de la Gare (April–Oct daily 10am–noon & 2–5pm; Fr.6; ⓦwww.museemontreux.ch), illustrating the town's history.

Eating and drinking

There are plenty of inexpensive places to **eat** around the station on Avenue des Alpes. Elsewhere options abound at all price brackets, but with Montreux a whistle-stop tourist town you may need to choose with care to avoid high prices and/or disappointing quality.

Walks around Montreux

There's a two-hour **walking tour** of the town, which leaves from the tourist office (April–Sept Wed–Sat 10am; Fr.10); check in advance about the availability of an English-speaking guide, and beware too that the walk involves a steep haul up the slopes into the Old Town and down again. Montreux is also part of the self-guided "Poets' Ramble" walk, which starts in Vevey; see p.123 for details.

Brasserie des Alpes 23 Rue des Alpes. Cheery little brasserie serving up inexpensive salads, pasta and vast pizzas (Fr.17–25), plus a few pricier meat and fish mains.

Caveau des Vignerons 30 Rue Industrielle. Homely little place with a menu featuring fondues, plus Swiss meat and cheese dishes (Fr.21–39) and cheaper pasta concoctions. Closed Mon–Fri lunch & Sun eve.

Confiserie Zürcher 45 Avenue du Casino. Montreux's most venerable old tearoom (since 1894), with plate-glass windows for crowd-watching, exquisite cakey creations and a range of daytime à la carte offerings (Fr.15–39). Closed Mon.

La Corsaz 24 Rue de la Corsaz. No-frills local diner dishing up traditional meaty fare – liver, horse and so on – plus more standard Swiss offerings (Fr.19–35). Closed Sun & Mon.

A Palais Oriental 14 Quai du Casino ☏021 963 12 71, ⓦwww.palaisoriental.ch. This rather odd-looking place (done up like a Moroccan palace inserted into a Swiss chalet) is the most appealing place to eat in town, offering a selection of Middle Eastern, Persian and Indian dishes (Fr.32–45) and set menus, plus Arabic *mezze* (Fr.10–20).

Le Pont de Brent Brent, 3km west of town ☏021 964 52 30, ⓦwww.lepontdebrent.com. Unassuming luxury restaurant, which has garnered three Michelin stars for the excellence of its haute cuisine. Set dinner *menus* start around Fr.185, though weekday lunch *menus* are a slightly more affordable Fr.85. Closed Sun & Mon, late July & Christmas.

Le Saxo Montreux Casino ☏021 962 83 83, ⓦwww.casinodemontreux.ch. Suave modern brasserie-restaurant, chic but surprisingly inexpensive, with a good range of Italian and Swiss food (Fr.15–39) and an attractive lakeside terrace.

Château de Chillon

There are seven pillars of Gothic mould,
In Chillon's dungeons deep and old,
There are seven columns massy and grey,
Dim with a dull imprison'd ray,
A sunbeam which hath lost its way...

Lord Byron, *The Prisoner of Chillon*

The climax of a journey around Lake Geneva is the thirteenth-century **Château de Chillon** (daily: April–Sept 9am–6pm; March & Oct 9.30am–5pm; Nov–Feb 10am–4pm; Fr.12; ⓦwww.chillon.ch). This impressive specimen, among the best-preserved medieval castles in Europe, is in Veytaux, about 3km south of Montreux; whether you opt for the 45-minute shoreline walk, bus #1 from Vevey or Montreux, a bike, or best of all a boat, your first glimpse of the castle is unforgettable – an elegant, turreted pile jutting out into the water, framed by trees and craggy mountains.

Some history

Although the scenery all around the castle is impressive enough, the **location** of the building is the key to its history. The mountains in front of the castle fall directly into the lake, with only the narrowest of through-routes between the sheer rock wall and the water. Directly opposite the defile, a razor-edge, sheer-sided islet rises from the water, of which only the very top is visible. The road is narrow, the heights are virtually unscaleable and there's no other way to pass: whoever controlled the castle could control the traffic.

In **Bronze Age** times, there was no path around the lake: travellers had to climb the steep, 200m slopes at Chillon to a village on the heights above, then drop back down to rejoin the path. The **Romans** cut a narrow ledge along the lakeshore, and also opened up the Grand-St-Bernard Pass over the Alps further

A **Swiss Pass** (see p.35) is valid for free transport within and around Vevey and Montreux (including to/from Chillon), free boat transport on Lake Geneva and free admission to almost all museums reviewed in this book.

south, turning the road past the then–unfortified islet into the only mountain route connecting northern and southern Europe. By the **Middle Ages**, the quantity of traffic meant the road had to be widened and also that a form of toll could be set up. The village above was abandoned in favour of a new town (*ville neuve*, today's Villeneuve) built on open, accessible land a little way south on the valley floor. The first surviving mention of a "guardian of the stronghold of Chillun" dates from 1150.

The Counts of **Savoy**, particularly Pierre (1203–68), made Chillon a princely residence, also developing Villeneuve into a major trading centre which poured tolls and customs duties into Chillon's coffers. Pierre's architects and engineers transformed Chillon, rebuilding the half facing the shore as a fortress with three strong towers and a keep, and filling the half facing the water with grand halls and royal apartments.

As the Savoyards began to threaten the Habsburgs, Chillon became their military and naval headquarters. The castle was both the centre of court life and a much-feared prison. By the fourteenth century, the Gotthard Pass further east was in use, and the transfer of traffic away from Chillon and the Grand-St-Bernard led to the castle's terminal decline as a military fortress, although it remained handy as a secure jail. In 1530, the Savoyards imprisoned a scholar, **François Bonivard**, at Chillon for inciting the Genevois people to form an alliance with the Swiss against Savoy. They left him shackled to a pillar in the dungeons for six years, until his release in 1536, when the **Bernese** army took control.

Fortunately for posterity, Chillon became a quiet backwater. In 1816, after Vaud had won independence from Bern, **Byron** (aged 28) and **Shelley** (24) visited the castle on their tour of the lake. A guide took them into the dungeons where Bonivard had been shackled and wove enough of a tale around him, and around the castle's history, to catch the poets' imaginations. In his Ouchy hotel, Byron scribbled out his *Prisoner of Chillon*, a long narrative poem supposedly spoken by Bonivard (but entirely fictitious throughout), which celebrates the cause of individual liberty, and which brought Chillon to the attention of the wealthy tourists who were starting to explore the Alps. Archeologists and historians launched renovations of the crumbling infrastructure in the late nineteenth century, which restored a great deal of the castle's original grandeur. Work to maintain the castle continues today.

Visiting the Château de Chillon

As throughout history, the **road** passes outside the castle walls – these days, it's the Montreux–Villeneuve highway, served by bus #1. The eighteenth-century **gatehouse** is supported on stilts, replacing the original drawbridge. At the ticket window you'll get a follow-the-numbers pamphlet, which plunges you straight down into the vaulted and atmospheric **dungeons** (rooms 4–7) where the dukes of Savoy imprisoned François Bonivard: he was manacled to the fifth pillar along, which still bears a ring and a length of chain. Bonivard wrote that the dungeon was excavated to below the water-line, and Byron also wrote about the damp, but the room is in fact above the water and quite airy. The Irish novelist Maria Edgeworth, visiting in 1820, perhaps missed the point when she brightly chipped in: "If I were to take lodgings in a dungeon I should prefer this to any I have ever seen because it is high and dry with beautiful groined arches and no bad smells." She also noted that Byron's name was cut into the third pillar of the dungeon, as it still is. A grille in the external wall gives onto the lake, facilitating a rapid exit by rowing boat should things have ever got nasty up above.

▲ The Château de Chillon

The real wonder of the castle lies in the rooms upstairs, gloriously grand knights' halls, secret twisting passages between lavish bedchambers, Gothic windows with dreamy views, a frescoed chapel, and more. The **Grand Kitchen** (room 8) still has its original wooden ceiling and two massive oak pillars, installed around 1260. The **Bernese Bedchamber** (room 10) has original bird and ribbon decorations dating from the 1580s, while the expansive **Hall of Arms** (room 12), complete with fireplace and windows over the lake, is covered with escutcheons of the Bernese bailiffs. The **Lord's Chamber** adjacent (room 13) retains its original thirteenth- and fourteenth-century wall paintings, rustic scenes of animals in an orchard with St George slaying the dragon on the chimney-piece. The **chapel** (room 18) features an impression of the full glory of the fourteenth-century decoration, with slides projected onto the partly decorated walls. Next door, the breathtaking **Great Hall of the Count** (room 19) has slender black marble pillars, shimmering chequered wall decoration, a coffered ceiling dating from the fifteenth century, and four windows over the lake topped by a beautiful four-leafed clover design.

Above Montreux

Montreux's train station is served by three different gauges of track. As well as the mainline CFF trains running west along the lake and south into the Valais, there are two different narrow-gauge lines operated by **MOB** (Montreux-Oberland-Bernois; ⓦ www.mob.ch) climbing up into the hills above Montreux, which offer spectacular viewpoints, excellent hill walking, and panoramic rides through the countryside towards the high Alps of the Bernese Oberland.

The smaller line has creaking trains winding their way northeast up to the giant Rochers-de-Naye summit (Swiss Pass holders – who travel free to Caux – pay Fr.25 return for the Caux–Naye section). Emerging from a series of corkscrew tunnels you come to **GLION**, an eyrie of a village perched amidst fields of narcissi directly above Montreux, with jaw-dropping views over the lake and the Rhône. There are a couple of luxury old-world hotels up here, including the stately *Victoria* (℡021 962 82 82, Ⓦwww.victoria-glion.ch; ❺–❼). A steep **funicular** also serves Glion from Territet on the lakeside below. The summit is the rugged vantage point of **ROCHERS-DE-NAYE** (2045m), with incredible views over the lake and plenty of hiking trails over the grassy hilltops – you can even stay the night up here in a Mongolian yurt (details at Ⓦwww.mob.ch).

The Golden Pass line: Montreux–Gstaad–Interlaken

The more important MOB narrow-gauge line above Montreux climbs northwest through the steep hills into Canton Bern. This is the route of the **Golden Pass** (Ⓦwww.goldenpass.ch; free with Swiss Pass), one of the showcase journeys of Swiss railways (see p.34) – a small supplement must be paid on the special panoramic trains, but not on the ordinary ones. A little above Montreux is **CHAMBY**, one end of the Chemin de Fer-Musée (Museum Railway; May–Oct Sat & Sun 10am–6pm; Ⓦwww.blonay-chamby.ch), which has steam trains running on a three-kilometre stretch of track to and from **Blonay** (Fr.16 return), on the Vevey–Les Pléiades line (see p.124), as well as a depot full of old rolling stock.

The trains from Montreux continue up on a spectacular route, coiling through the village of **LES AVANTS** – starting point of a number of beautiful walks – to **Montbovon**, junction point for trains north into the countryside around **Gruyères** (see p.111).

The Golden Pass line continues east to **Château d'Oex** and **Gstaad** (see p.262), but runs out at **Zweisimmen**, where you must change for connections to Interlaken and Lucerne.

Travel details

Full timetables for all trains, buses, trams, boats and cable cars in Switzerland – as well as international connections – are searchable at Ⓦwww.rail.ch.

Trains

Lausanne to: Basel (twice hourly; 2hr 10min); Bern (twice hourly; 1hr 10min); Biel/Bienne (twice hourly; 1hr); Brig (twice hourly; 1hr 40min); Echallens (every 30min; 35min); Fribourg (twice hourly; 45min); Geneva (every 10min; 35min); Interlaken Ost (twice hourly; 2hr 10min); Martigny (twice hourly; 50min); Montreux (every 15min; 20min); Neuchâtel (twice hourly; 40min); Nyon (4 hourly; 30min); Palézieux (for Gruyères; 4 hourly; 20min); Sion (twice hourly; 1hr); Vallorbe (hourly; 45min); Vevey (every 15min; 15min); Yverdon (3 hourly; 20min); Zürich (twice hourly; 2hr 10min). **Montreux** to: Caux (hourly; 25min); Geneva (4 hourly; 1hr 5min); Gstaad (hourly; 1hr 20min); Lausanne (every 15min; 20min); Martigny (twice hourly; 30min); Vevey (4 hourly; 6–9min).

Nyon to: Geneva (4 hourly; 15min); Lausanne (4 hourly; 25min); Neuchâtel (hourly; 55min); St-Cergue (every 30min; 35min); Yverdon (hourly; 35min).
Vevey to: Geneva (twice hourly; 1hr); Lausanne (every 15min; 15–20min); Martigny (every 30min; 35min); Montreux (4 hourly; 6–9min).

Buses

Bulle to: Fribourg (twice hourly; 35min); Gruyères-ville (4 daily; 20min).
Montreux to: Chillon (every 10min; 10min); Vevey (every 10min; 20min).
Vevey to: Chillon (every 10min; 30min); Montreux (every 10min; 20min).

Boats

Following is a summary of May–Sept summer services; fewer boats run in other months, generally Sat & Sun only, if at all. Full details at Ⓦwww.cgn.ch.

Chillon (Château) to: Lausanne (4 daily; 1hr 45min); Montreux (4 daily; 20min); Vevey (4 daily; 35min).

Lausanne (Ouchy) to: Coppet (2–3 daily; 2hr 45min); Evian, France (10–15 daily; 40min); Geneva (3 daily; 3hr 30min); Montreux (3 daily; 1hr 20min); Nyon (2 daily; 2hr 10min); Vevey (4 daily; 1hr).

Montreux to: Chillon (4 daily; 20min); Lausanne (3 daily; 1hr 20min); Vevey (5 daily; 20min).

Nyon to: Geneva (3 daily; 1hr–1hr 30min); Lausanne (2 daily; 2hr 10min).

Vevey to: Chillon (4 daily; 35min); Lausanne (4 daily; 1hr); Montreux (5 daily; 20min).

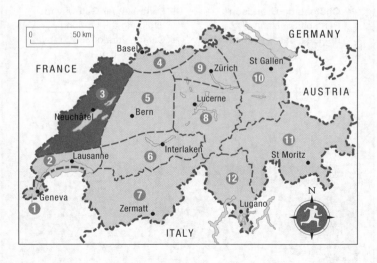

The Arc Jurassien

3

CHAPTER 3 # Highlights

* **The three lakes** Ferries crisscross their way between the scenic lakes of Neuchâtel, Murten and Biel/Bienne. See p.138

* **Neuchâtel** Attractive, graceful city with a fine old quarter. See p.138

* **Yverdon** Sci-fi fans will love the outlandish "House of Elsewhere" museum. See p.145

* **Château de Grandson** Perhaps Switzerland's grandest castle. See p.148

* **Vallée de Joux** High, remote Jura valley, perfect for lonely hikes and cross-country skiing. See p.151

* **Payerne** A superb Romanesque abbey dominates this quiet country town. See p.152

* **Avenches** Former Roman capital, whose amphitheatre is still used for opera and shows. See p.152

* **Saignelégier** Gateway to exploring the far-flung Canton Jura on foot or by bike. See p.161

▲ Ferry on the lake at Neuchâtel

The Arc Jurassien

The northwest frontier dividing Switzerland from France is the **Jura** mountain range – line after line of northeast-southwest ridges that trap between them a succession of sausage-shaped lakes. The Jura are nothing like the Alps: much lower to start with (rarely more than 1500m), with none of the majesty but all of the ruggedness. Scrubby hilltops and deep, parallel valleys are dotted by windswept, privately minded villages nursing a weatherbeaten Gallic culture cut off for centuries from both France and Switzerland.

The slice of territory linking Geneva and Basel, dubbed the **Arc Jurassien**, takes in the three connected lakes of Neuchâtel, Murten/Morat and Biel/Bienne, the highlands of the Jura Vaudois (and smaller Jura Bernois) and the remote countryside of cantons Neuchâtel and Jura. This is all well off the beaten track of most visitors, and doesn't easily fit into the usual Swiss pigeonholes. If you choose to venture out here, you'll find a minimum of tourist hype and few actual sights other than the main towns of **Neuchâtel** and **Biel/Bienne**, but what exists in abundance is virtually untouched nature – and this is why the Swiss know and love the place. The recent brainwave to market the region as "**Watch Valley**" (Ⓦ www.watchvalley.ch) – despite the fact that it isn't a valley, and only some areas have a tradition of watchmaking – rather misses the point of its rural charm.

On p.185, we've outlined a long, multi-day walk through the area, which starts near Zürich, winds through the whole Jura region and ends up at Lake Geneva.

Language issues: Crossing the Röstigraben

The majority of the area covered by this chapter is francophone, and yet it straddles the linguistic divide, the *Röstigraben*, between French- and German-speaking Switzerland (see p.8).

Neuchâtel is entirely French-speaking, but German speakers call it Neuenburg and expect you to understand. The Lac de Neuchâtel is one and the same as the Neuenburgersee. Nearby is the majority-German-speaking resort of Murten (known to French speakers as Morat), on the shore of the Murtensee (Lac de Morat). Kerzers, a town with a key rail junction, is announced in French as Chiètres. The lake to the north is called both the Bielersee and Lac de Bienne, with the officially bilingual town at its foot signposted as Biel/Bienne.

Further north is German-speaking Solothurn (Soleure in French), abutting the Jura Bernois – Canton Bern's only francophone region. Beyond lies franco-phile Canton Jura, nudging at the borders of Alsace and Basel.

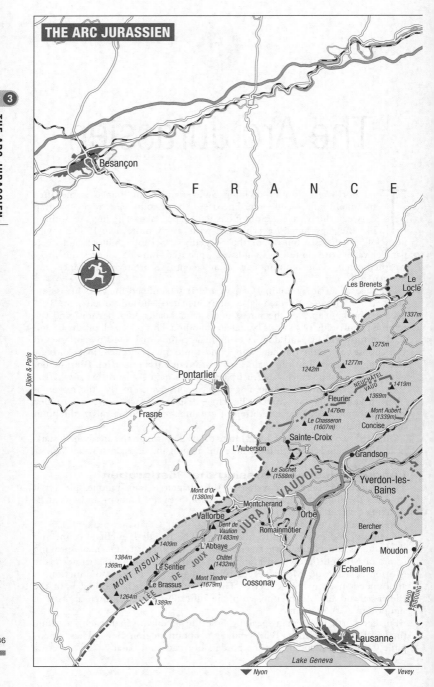

THE ARC JURASSIEN

Besançon

F R A N C E

N

Les Brenets

Le
Loclé

▲ 1337m

▲ 1275m

1242m ▲   ▲ 1277m

NEUCHÂTEL
VAUD

Pontarlier

Fleurier   ▲ 1419m

▲ 1369m

1476m ▲

Mont Aubert
(1339m) ▲

Le Chasseron
(1607m) ▲

Concise

Frasne

Dijon & Paris ◄

Sainte-Croix

L'Auberson ●

Grandson ●

Le Suchet
(1588m) ▲

Yverdon-les-
Bains

VAUDOIS

Mont d'Or
(1380m) ▲

Montcherand ●

JURA

Vallorbe ●   ● Orbe

Dent de
Vaulion (1483m) ▲

Romainmôtier ●

Bercher ●

1409m ▲

L'Abbaye ●

Moudon ●

1384m ▲
1369m ▲

Le Sentier ●

Châtel
(1432m) ▲

Echallens ●

MONT RISOUX

DE

JOUX

VALLÉE

Le Brassus ●

Mont Tendre
(1679m) ▲

Cossonay ●

VAUD
FRIBOURG

▲ 1264m

▲ 1389m

Lausanne

Lake Geneva

▼ Nyon

▼ Vevey

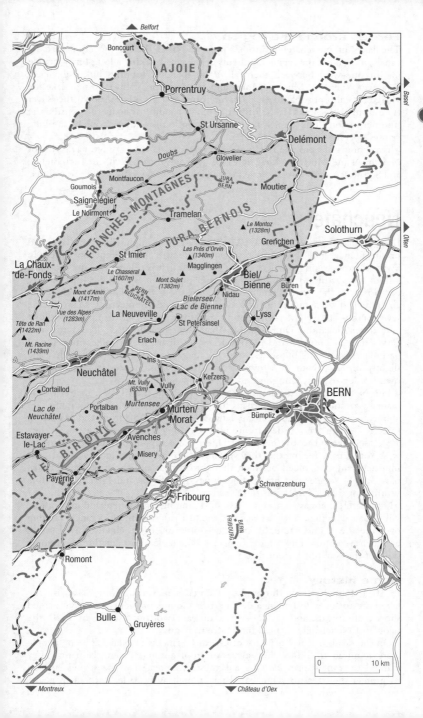

Belfort

Boncourt

AJOIE

Porrentruy

Basel

St Ursanne

Delémont

Doubs

Glovelier

Montfaucon

JURA
BERN

Moutier

Goumois

Saignelégier

Le Noirmont

FRANCHES-MONTAGNES

Tramelan

JURA BERNOIS

Le Montoz
(1328m)

Solothurn

Olten

St Imier

Les Prés d'Orvin
(1340m)

Grenchen

La Chaux-
de-Fonds

Le Chasseral
(1607m)

Magglingen

Biel/
Bienne

Büren

Mont d'Amin
(1417m)

Mont Sujet
(1382m)

BERN
NEUCHÂTEL

Bielersee/
Lac de Bienne

Nidau

Vue des Alpes
(1283m)

La Neuveville

Lyss

Tête de Ran
(1422m)

St Petersinsel

Mt. Racine
(1439m)

Erlach

Ins

Neuchâtel

Kerzers

BERN

Cortaillod

Mt. Vully
(653m)

Vully

Lac de
Neuchâtel

Portalban

Murtensee

Bümpliz

Estavayer-
le-Lac

THE B:R:O:Y:E

Avenches

Murten/
Morat

Payerne

Misery

Schwarzenburg

Fribourg

BERN
FRIBOURG

Romont

Bulle

Gruyères

0   10 km

Montreux

Château d'Oex

Ferries around the region

The lakes of Neuchâtel, Murten/Morat and Biel/Bienne are connected by canals, and one of the scenic highlights of the area is taking a long **ferry cruise** (3–4hr one-way) between them all. Point-to-point routings link Neuchâtel, Estavayer, Yverdon, Murten/Morat and Biel/Bienne with a host of lakeside villages. It's also possible to take a **river journey** (2hr 40min) down the River Aare from Biel/Bienne to Solothurn. Only a handful of boats run outside the summer season (June–Sept), and then only on local routings: none of the long cruises operates in winter.

Two companies provide this service: Navigation LNM (ⓦ www.navig.ch) for Neuchâtel and Murten/Morat, and BSG (ⓦ www.bielersee.ch) for Biel/Bienne and Solothurn, with some overlap between the two. Swiss Pass holders travel free.

Neuchâtel

Beam yourself down into **NEUCHÂTEL**, and you might think you've ended up in France. The Neuchâtelois people are the most French-oriented in Switzerland, speaking a dialect of Swiss French that is celebrated – by those for whom such a thing is significant – as the "purest" in Romandie (that's to say, the closest to the "true" French spoken over the border). The town's dignified air is fuelled by a profusion of French-influenced architecture. Many of the seventeenth- and eighteenth-century buildings are made from local yellow sandstone: Alexandre Dumas wrote that Neuchâtel looked "like a toytown carved out of butter". And the modern and disarmingly Gallic street life of pavement cafés and brasseries, studenty buzz and designer fashion has the slightly unreal flavour of a town actively seeking influences from beyond its own borders – a rare thing indeed in Switzerland.

The Neuchâtelois, for whom the issue of joining the EU is a matter of the plainest common sense, are perhaps the epitome of the Swiss mystery: they are about as far removed in attitude, language and outlook from the people of Lucerne – with whom their future is inextricably linked – to the east, as they are closely related to the people of Dijon – the supposed foreigners – to the west. You get the feeling that they've thrown up their hands in disbelief at such injustice, and, ensconced between their broad lake and the mountain border, have sought solace in a life of fine wines, rich foods and French TV while waiting for their compatriots to see sense.

Neuchâtel's main attractions are its café-lounging atmosphere and its location, with boats weaving across the lake and the first ridges of the Jura range standing over the town. The Musée d'Art offers some diversion, chiefly for its set of eighteenth-century mechanical figurines which demonstrate the exceptional skills of the watchmakers of that era.

Some history

In 1011, Rudolf III of Burgundy presented a new castle (*neu-châtel*) on the lakeshore to his wife Irmengarde. The first Counts of Neuchâtel were named shortly afterwards, and in 1214 their domain won city status. In 1530, the people of Neuchâtel accepted the **Reformation**.

On the death in 1707 of Mary of Orléans, Princess of Neuchâtel, the people were required to choose her successor from among fifteen claimants. They wanted their new prince to be a Protestant, and also to be strong enough to protect their territory but based far enough away to leave them in peace.

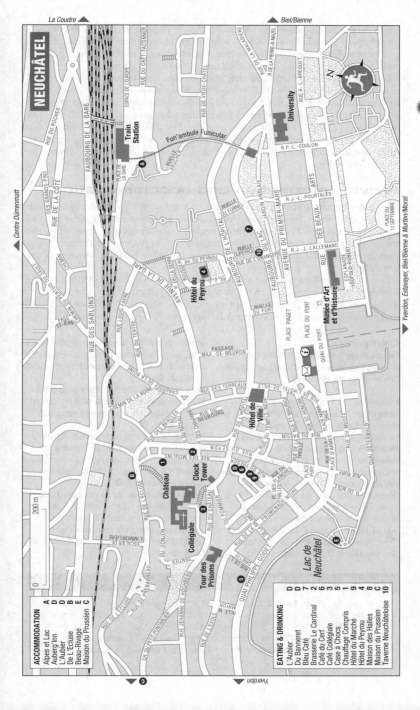

NEUCHÂTEL

La Coudre ▲

▲ Biel/Bienne

Train Station

Fun'ambule Funicular

University

Hôtel du Peyrou **4**

7

10

Musée d'Art et d'Histoire

Hôtel de Ville

Château

Clock Tower

Collégiale

Tour des Prisons

1
2
3
5

6
8
9

Lac de Neuchâtel

0   200 m

ACCOMMODATION
Alpes et Lac	A
Auberg'Inn	D
L'Aubier	D
De L'Écluse	B
Beau-Rivage	E
Maison du Prussien	C

EATING & DRINKING
L'Aubier	D
Du Banneret	D
Bleu Café	7
Brasserie Le Cardinal	2
Café du Cerf	6
Café Collégiale	3
Case à Chocs	5
Chauffage Compris	1
Hôtel du Marché	9
Hôtel du Peyrou	4
Maison des Halles	8
Maison du Prussien	C
Taverne Neuchâteloise	10

▲ Centre Dürrenmatt

▼ Yverdon

▼ Yverdon, Estavayer, Biel/Bienne & Murten/Morat

Louis XIV actively promoted the many French pretenders, but the Neuchâtelois people ignored the Sun King's wishes and chose instead Frederick I, king of **Prussia**. Thereafter the city entered a golden age, with commerce, banking and industry (including watchmaking and lace) steadily growing.

In 1805 **Napoleon** forced the defeated Prussian king to surrender Neuchâtel in order to keep Hanover. Following Napoleon's own defeat, Frederick III of Prussia reasserted his rights by proposing that Neuchâtel be linked with the other Swiss cantons (the better to exert influence over the lot of them). On September 12, 1814, Neuchâtel became the 21st canton, but confusingly also remained a Prussian principality. It took a bloodless revolution for the region to shake off Prussian control and declare itself, in 1848, a **republic** within the Swiss Confederation.

Arrival, information and accommodation

Neuchâtel's **train station** is perched above the town; it's a walk of about ten minutes, or a short hop by bus, down to the lakefront town centre focused around Place Pury. The Fun'ambule underground **funicular** runs from the station down to the university, 400m east of Pury on Avenue du Premier-Mars. Pury is 100m west of Place du Port, arrival point for **boats** from around the three lakes.

The **tourist office** is in the main post office on Place du Port (July & Aug Mon–Fri 9am–6.30pm, Sat 9am–4pm, Sun 10am–2pm, rest of year Mon–Fri 9am–noon & 1.30–5.30pm, Sat 9am–noon; ☏ 032 889 68 90, ⓦ www.neuchatel tourisme.ch). City-centre **accommodation** is good, if unadventurous.

Camping

Paradis-Plage Colombier ☏ 032 841 24 46, ⓦ www.paradisplage.ch. Good waterfront campsite 7km west (bus #5). March–Oct.

Hotels

Alpes et Lac 2 Place de la Gare ☏ 032 723 19 19, ⓦ www.alpesetlac.ch. Fine old mansion opposite the station with spacious restored rooms, airy views and a good restaurant. ③–④

Auberg'Inn 1 Rue Fleury ☏ 032 721 44 20, ⓦ www.auberginn.ch. Small backpacker-style hotel insinuated into an old town house. Rooms are compact, facilities basic (you get a mini-kitchen, but no breakfast) but everything's cosy enough – and the location is perfect. ②

🏃 **L'Aubier** 1 Rue du Château ☏ 032 710 18 58, ⓦ www.aubier.ch. Lovely little hotel tucked away in an Old Town alley, run along eco-friendly lines and annexed to an organic farm in the Neuchâtel countryside. Decor is fresh, staff are cheerily welcoming and the food is – of course – delicious. ②–③

Beau-Rivage 1 Esplanade du Mont-Blanc ☏ 032 723 15 15, ⓦ www.beau-rivage-hotel.ch. Five-star lakefront palace, with super-swanky rooms and views to match. ⑦

De L'Ecluse 24 Rue de l'Ecluse ☏ 032 729 93 10, ⓦ www.hoteldelecluse.ch. Simple, beautiful rooms, characterized by ochre tones, tasteful wrought-iron furniture and stone floors, in this fine small hotel above the town centre. ③

Maison du Prussien Gor du Vauseyon ☏ 032 730 54 54, ⓦ www.hotel-prussien.ch. A restored sixteenth-century mill beside a stream 2km west of town, with seven comfortable, well-appointed wood-beamed rooms and three pricier suites. ③–④

Above Neuchâtel – Chaumont

From the suburb of **La Coudre**, 4km east of the centre (bus #7), a panoramic funicular (ⓦ www.tnneuchatel.ch) rises through thick forests to the village of **CHAUMONT** (1087m). Set on a balcony atop the first of the Jura ridges, the viewpoint of Le Signal (1171m), a short walk from the funicular station, offers a vista over lakes, fields and forests clear across Switzerland to the distant snowy fringe of the Bernese Alps.

The Town

Random wanderings through the steep alleys of Neuchâtel's **Old Town** are as good a way as any to appreciate the golden beauty of the architecture, as well as the 140-odd street fountains, some of which date from the sixteenth century. From the rather anonymous **Place Pury** – hub of buses and shoppers alike – alleys to the west lead into **Place des Halles**, perpetually filled with talkers and drinkers lounging at terrace cafés. The square itself is overlooked by fine Louis XIV architecture, notably the shuttered facades and the turreted oriels of the sixteenth-century **Maison des Halles**. You'll find informal lunchtime *boules* sessions on nearby Rue du Coq d'Inde, a tranquil courtyard away from the bustle, while a two-minute walk east on Rue de l'Hôpital brings you to the 1790 **Hôtel de Ville** (Town Hall), designed by Louis XVI's chief architect Pierre-Adrien Paris.

The highlights of the Old Town loom above, accessed by the steeply winding Rue du Château. The **Collégiale church** (daily 9am–8pm; Oct–March closes 6.30pm), begun in 1185 and consecrated in 1276, is a graceful example of early Gothic. The east end of the church boasts three Norman apses; the main entrance, to the west, is crowned by a giant rose window. Inside, the transept, lit by a lantern tower, holds the beautiful Cenotaph of the Counts of Neuchâtel on the north wall of the choir. Begun in 1372, and the only artwork of its kind to survive north of the Alps, the monument comprises fifteen near-life-size painted statues of knights and ladies from Neuchâtel's past, framed by fifteenth-century arches and gables.

Beside the church is the imposing **château**, begun in the twelfth century and still in use as the offices of the cantonal government: entry is only on guided tours, which start on the hour from the signposted Door no. 1 (April–Sept daily 2–4pm, Tues–Fri also 10am–noon; free). Nearby, the turreted Tour des Prisons (April–Sept daily 8am–6pm; Fr.2), part of a medieval bastion, has panoramic views along with some historical background.

▲ The Old Town, Neuchâtel

Musée d'Art et d'Histoire

The **Musée d'Art et d'Histoire**, Esplanade Léopold-Robert (Tues–Sun 11am–6pm; Fr.8, free on Wed; ⓦ www.mahn.ch), is well worth a visit. The galleries of fine and applied art keep a focus on interdisciplinary themed exhibits – painting sharing a space with crafts or coins or historical documents, inducing you to make connections between diverse works. But the most extraordinary exhibits are the **Automates Jaquet-Droz**, three mechanical figurines built to the most exacting technical standards by a Neuchâtelois watchmaker in the 1770s (see box below) and still in perfect working order. They are displayed static behind glass, with a fascinating accompanying slide-show in English, but you should really time your visit to tie in with one of the regular public demonstrations (1st Sun of month at 2pm, 3pm & 4pm; extra shows in summer; free). Alternatively, you can book ahead for a private showing with an English guide (Fr.130).

The **Draughtsman** is a child sitting at a mahogany desk; his right hand, holding a pencil, performs extraordinarily complex motions over a sheet of paper to produce intricate little pictures of a dog, the god Eros in a chariot pulled by a butterfly, or a noble profile of Louis XV. The **Writer**, a chubby-cheeked little boy, also sits at a mahogany desk, with a goose quill in his right hand and a tiny pot of ink nearby for dipping. He writes in a florid and chunky style, and can be "programmed" to produce any text of up to forty characters: watching him write, for instance, "email" lifts the hairs on the back of your neck. While he writes, his eyes follow the words across the page. The most charming of the three is the **Musician**, a gracious young girl with slender fingers who plays a small organ – a real instrument, not a disguised musical-box. As her fingers strike the keys, her eyes, head and body move subtly in time, her chest rising and falling in an imitation of rhythmic breathing. Her melodies were composed by Henri-Louis Jaquet-Droz; having them played by this exceptional machine forms a unique auditory time capsule, delivered intact from the 1770s. It is all quite flabbergasting.

The celebrated Monsieur Jaquet-Droz

Pierre Jaquet-Droz (1721–90) was born in La Chaux-de-Fonds into a wealthy local family. Working in Neuchâtel he combined his interest in mathematics with the skills of applied mechanics used in the watch industry, quickly gaining a reputation for technical brilliance. In 1758 he travelled to the Spanish court to show off the skill of Neuchâtelois clockmakers; his "Shepherd's Clock" is still on display in Madrid.

By then wealthy enough to retire, Jaquet-Droz withdrew to concentrate on building complex mechanical figurines designed to do particular tasks – the earliest of robots. He trained his son, Henri-Louis, and a colleague, Jean-Frédéric Leschot, to work with him; together, they produced the **Writer**, the **Draughtsman** and the **Musician**, and presented all three to the public in La Chaux-de-Fonds in 1774. People flocked to see such extraordinary works of whimsy and technical skill. The craftsmen showed their figurines in drawing rooms and palaces across Europe, to universally high acclaim.

Perhaps aware of impending revolution in France and Switzerland, Jaquet-Droz sold the figurines in 1778. They reappeared after the conflicts, in Paris in 1812, becoming the centrepiece of Martin and Bourquin's "Museum of Illusions", which toured Europe throughout the nineteenth century. In 1906 Neuchâtel bought the figurines back, and they have been on display in the town's museum ever since, in virtually the same condition as when they were first made, over 230 years ago.

Centre Dürrenmatt

On the hillside above Neuchâtel (bus #9) stands the **Centre Dürrenmatt**, 74 Chemin du Pertuis-du-Sault (Wed–Sun 11am–5pm; Fr.8; ⓦwww.cdn.ch), a museum devoted to the Swiss writer and artist Friedrich Dürrenmatt (1921–90), who lived most of his life in Neuchâtel. Dürrenmatt's papers and his Expressionist-style paintings aside, the chief reason to visit is the architecture: the Ticinese architect Mario Botta has designed a sleek, curving gallery partly buried in the hillside below Dürrenmatt's former home. It is eye-popping: enjoy it, along with spectacular lake views, from the terrace café.

Eating and drinking

Neuchâtel takes **eating and drinking** seriously, with dozens of pavement cafés and relaxed bistros all over town. Local specialities include tripe in wine, *tomme panée* (baked cheese) and fresh lake fish. A *fondue neuchâteloise* takes full advantage of the nearby vineyards, with local whites splashed liberally into the bubbling pot of cheese to make an especially convivial dinner.

Restaurants and cafés

L'Aubier 1 Rue du Château (see "Hotels"). Friendly, informal café on a quiet Old Town square, serving only organic, locally produced food (plus organic coffees and teas). A haven. Closed Sun.

Du Banneret 1 Rue Fleury ☎032 725 28 61. Peaceful little restaurant in a crook of the Old Town's steep alleys. The food is consistently good – regional specialities, lightly prepared, with fresh fish a staple. *Menus* Fr.25 and up. Closed Sun & Mon.

Bleu Cafe 27 Faubourg du Lac ⓦwww.bleucafe .ch. Lively student hangout near the university that looks cheap – and is: pay as little as Fr.12–15 for a decent *menu* at lunch or dinner. Arthouse cinema alongside.

🏃 **Brasserie Le Cardinal** 9 Rue du Seyon ☎032 725 12 86, ⓦwww.lecardinal -brasserie.ch. A wonderful old-fashioned interior, complete with colourful tilework and brass lamps, boosted by classic brasserie fare: mussels, veal, rack of lamb and so on. Expect around Fr.40. Closed Sun.

Café de la Collégiale 10a Rue de la Collégiale ⓦwww.cafedelacollegiale.com. Tiny café just below the church, with a cobbled terrace and delicious light bites. Mon–Fri 8am–2.30pm only.

Chauffage Compris 37 Rue des Moulins ⓦwww .chauffage-compris.ch. Sociable Old Town café-bar with an alternative bent (and good, inexpensive food), attached to a small arts centre.

Hôtel du Marché Place des Halles ⓦwww .hoteldumarche.com. Central Old Town landmark, serving hearty Swiss and French cuisine for Fr.20 or so. Service can be brusque, but it's decent enough. Closed Sun & Mon lunch.

Hôtel du Peyrou 1 Avenue du Peyrou ☎032 725 11 83, ⓦwww.dupeyrou.ch. Immense villa in its own grounds, built in 1770 by Pierre-Alexandre Du Peyrou, friend and publisher of Jean-Jacques Rousseau. Its lavish interior now hosts the town's best fine-dining restaurant, with seasonal specialities presented on *menus* ranging from Fr.50 at lunch to three times that at dinner.

Maison des Halles Place des Halles ☎032 724 31 41, ⓦwww.maisondeshalles.ch. Town-centre institution occupying the fairy-tale turreted building directly beside *Hôtel du Marché* – wood-fired pizza and simple dishes at ground level (from Fr.20), and a posher restaurant up above.

Maison du Prussien Gor du Vauseyon (see "Hotels"). One of Neuchâtel's gourmet highlights, with characterful French-oriented *menus* from around Fr.60. Closed Sun.

Taverne Neuchâteloise 5 Rue de l'Orangerie ☎032 725 27 01. Plain café that serves some of Neuchâtel's best fondues: choose from ten varieties (Fr.20–40). Mon–Sat 7–10pm, also Wed & Thurs noon–2pm.

Bars and clubs

Café du Cerf 4 Rue de l'Ancien Hôtel-de-Ville ⓦwww.cafeducerf.ch. Lively central bar, serving beers from around the world.

Case à Chocs 16 Quai Philippe-Godet ⓦwww .case-a-chocs.ch. Club and venue, with DJ nights of anything from ska to drum'n'bass. Thurs–Sat.

Around Canton Neuchâtel

Above Neuchâtel, roads and train tracks rise steeply into the Jura – known within the canton as the **Montagnes Neuchâteloises**. This is wild country, characterized by remote, windswept settlements and deep, rugged valleys. It is also the heartland of the celebrated Swiss watchmaking industry, centred on the once-famous towns of **La Chaux-de-Fonds** and **Le Locle**, both UNESCO World Heritage Sites. The River Doubs marks the border with France, set down in a gorge; the impressive **Saut du Doubs** waterfall and nearby **Lac des Brenets** together make a pleasant day.

La Chaux-de-Fonds

LA CHAUX-DE-FONDS is an oddity. More people live there than in Neuchâtel, although you'd never guess it from the bleakness and lack of street life. This rather unprepossessing place was once a household name across Europe, the humming centre of the Swiss **watchmaking** industry, which in its heyday of the late eighteenth and nineteenth centuries was largely respon-sible for establishing Switzerland's reputation – which survives today – for producing refined luxury goods of the highest quality. Yet in 1794 the town burned to the ground and was rebuilt on a grid system. Its enormously long boulevards, all parallel and perpendicular, suck any character out of the city. Visit for the museums, or to pay homage to its most famous son, modernist architect **Le Corbusier**.

If you're approaching from Neuchâtel (on the winding minor road or through the motorway tunnels), stop off at the **Vue des Alpes** (1283m), a magnificent viewpoint just short of La Chaux-de-Fonds, giving a broad panorama out towards the snowy Bernese Alps. From the **train station**, turn right to follow Rue des Musées past a mall and over a mini-roundabout to reach the Neoclassical **Musée des Beaux-Arts**, 33 Rue des Musées (Tues–Sun 10am–5pm; Fr.8; ⓦcdf-mba .ne.ch). The permanent collection takes in a Modigliani, a couple of Van Goghs, Delacroix and Renoir. A portrait of local artist Léopold Robert, by his son Aurèle, shows a troubled face; Robert cut his own throat in 1835 at the age of 41 after the failure of an unhappy relationship with Charlotte Bonaparte. The museum houses plenty of Robert's romantic images of Venetian sailors, exotic peasant women and rogueish mountain bandits.

Immediately adjacent is La Chaux-de-Fonds' main draw, the award-winning **Musée International d'Horlogerie**, 29 Rue des Musées (Tues–Sun 10am–5pm; Fr.15; ⓦ www.mih.ch). It holds hundreds of items tracing the art of keeping time, with many beautiful pieces from La Chaux's heyday in the eighteenth and nineteenth centuries as well as ultra-modern atomic and electronic clocks. In the park outside is a giant tubular-steel **carillon** with digital readout – all the rage when it was built in 1980 – that chimes every quarter-hour.

The world-renowned modernist architect Charles-Edouard Jeanneret, known as **Le Corbusier** (his face adorns the Swiss ten-franc note), was born in 1887 at 38 Rue de la Serre. Dotted around town are several examples of his work, including the **Maison Blanche**, 12 Chemin de Pouillerel (Fri–Sun 10am–5pm; Fr.10; ⓦ www.maisonblanche.ch), built for his parents following a journey aged 25 to Istanbul, and the Mediterranean-style **Villa Schwob** or Villa Turque, 167 Rue du Doubs (1st & 3rd Sat of month 11am–4pm; free; ⓦ www.ebel.ch), which now houses the public relations arm of the Ebel watchmaking firm. The tourist office can point you in the direction of several more Le Corbusier landmarks around town.

Practicalities

With your back to the Musée des Beaux-Arts, follow Rue du Casino for three blocks to the main Avenue Léopold-Robert, a broad arrow-straight boulevard. Here, in the Espacité glass tower, resides the **tourist office** (July & Aug Mon–Fri 9am–12.15pm & 1.45–6.30pm, Sat 10am–4pm; rest of year Mon–Fri 9am–noon & 1.30–5.30pm, Sat 9am–noon; ☎032 889 68 95, ⓦ www.neuchateltourisme.ch). *De France* is a serviceable **hotel** opposite the station (☎032 913 11 16; ❷); *Fleur-de-Lys*, 13 Avenue Robert (☎032 913 37 31, ⓦ www.fleur-de-lys.ch; ❸), is a cosier choice.

The bland *Citérama* **café**, on the 14th floor of the Espacité tower, is worth a look only for its bird's-eye city views – best after dark. For classic French fine dining, head to the *Hotel de Ville* **restaurant**, Place de l'Hotel de Ville (☎032 968 46 66, ⓦ www.hotel-de-ville-2300.ch; closed Sun): expect Fr.25 at lunch, upwards of Fr.50 in the evening. *Casapagni*, nearby on Place du Marché (☎032 968 18 08, ⓦ www.casapagni.com; closed Sun & Mon), offers light, well-prepared Tuscan fare, or for a less formal ambience try *ABC*, 11 Rue du Coq (☎032 967 90 40, ⓦ www.abc-culture.ch; closed Mon), a café-restaurant within a cinema and arts centre.

There's some **live music** downstairs, as well as good inexpensive food, at the vaulted *Petit Paris*, 4 Rue du Progrès (closed Sun; ⓦ www.petit-paris.ch), while the *Bikini Test* club, 3 Rue Joux-Perret (ⓦ www.bikinitest.ch), hosts everything from folky jazz to death metal.

Le Locle and around

The small town of **LE LOCLE**, 8km west of La Chaux by train or bus #60/61, is where Swiss watchmaking was born. Daniel Jeanrichard, a native of Neuchâtel (where he made his first watch in 1681, aged 16), settled in Le Locle in 1705 and taught the trade to his family and a small group of apprentices, who then took the skill around the Jura. The **Musée d'Horlogerie** in the Château de Monts above the town (Tues–Sun: May–Oct 10am–5pm, Nov–April 2–5pm; Fr.8; ⓦ www.mhl-monts.ch) features eighteenth-century rooms crammed with ticking timepieces of all kinds.

Postbuses towards La Brévine stop at the Col-des-Roches **underground mills** (May–Oct daily 10am–5pm; Nov–April Tues–Sun 2–5pm; Fr.12.50; ⓦ www.lesmoulins.ch), 2km west of Le Locle. These dank chambers were chiselled out in the seventeenth century to take advantage of the water flowing down to the Doubs: there are various mills and other bits of heavy machinery down there. English notes accompany the obligatory hour-long guided tour.

A side road branches 3km north from the Col-des-Roches down to the riverside village of **LES BRENETS**, where the Doubs broadens into the Lac des Brenets (known to the French on the other bank as the Lac de Chaillexon), which freezes over in winter to form the largest natural ice rink in Europe. Narrow-gauge trains from Le Locle pull into Les Brenets station; walk left down through the village for twenty minutes to the riverbank to reach the landing stage, which is also served by direct buses from Le Locle. From here, you can take a fine boat trip (20min; ⓦ www.nlb.ch) east through a craggy gorge to the 27m-high **Saut du Doubs** waterfall.

Yverdon-les-Bains and around

A market town on the southern tip of Lac de Neuchâtel, **YVERDON-LES-BAINS** is best known for its thermal springs – celebrated at least since Roman times – and is handy as a jumping-off point both for the terrific old castle at

Johann Heinrich Pestalozzi

Johann Heinrich (Henri) Pestalozzi, born in Zürich in 1746, devoted his life's work – twenty years of it in Yverdon – to giving underprivileged children access to a decent education. In 1804, after four years in Bern as a schoolteacher, Pestalozzi was invited by the Yverdon municipality to establish an educational institute. He took in up to 150 boys aged 7 to 15 who would otherwise have been begging on the streets, fed and clothed them, and organized a flexible school curriculum suited to each child's abilities, covering mathematics, languages, music, gymnastics, biology and more. His efforts gained worldwide attention. Two years later, he set up a similar school for girls, followed in 1813 by Switzerland's – and one of the world's – first schools for children with hearing and/or speech disabilities.

Pestalozzi died in 1827, but there still remains a great deal of interest in his methodology. His vision of education for all was seized upon by Victorian reformers in Britain and elsewhere as a cornerstone of the development of welfare policy. When Pestalozzi wrote, "Development of a child's mind should be made continuously relevant to that child's personality and everyday life", such an idea was laughable. Today it seems obvious, largely due to his example.

nearby **Grandson**, and for trips into the Vaudois hinterland around **Vallorbe** (see p.150) and into the **Vallée de Joux** (see p.151).

Yverdon was founded in 1260 when Pierre of Savoy built a castle on what was then the lakefront to defend against attack from the east (the lake has since silted up so that the fortress is now the best part of a kilometre inland). However, prehistoric standing stones and Roman remains show that the Savoyards were not the first to see the strategic importance of Yverdon's location: the shortest routes from central France to Italy, and from southern France to Germany – not to mention the vital water route linking the Rhône and the Rhine – all passed through Yverdon, whose name derives from the Gallo-Roman Eburodunum ("Fortress of the Yew Tree").

The Town

Yverdon's central **Place Pestalozzi** is dominated by the broad-fronted Louis XV-style Hôtel de Ville and, next to it, the foursquare turreted **château**, built after 1260 by Pierre II of Savoy, occupied by the Bernese in 1536, and seized during the Vaudois revolution in 1798. From 1805 to 1825 the château housed an educational institute set up by the visionary reformer Johann Heinrich Pestalozzi (see box above); Yverdon's school children continued to be taught within the castle walls right up until 1974. Today it's the home of the **Musée d'Yverdon** (Tues–Sun 11am–5pm; Oct–May 2–5pm; Fr.8; ⓦwww.musee-yverdon-region.ch), which includes Gallo-Roman dugout canoes, a rather homesick Egyptian mummy in the Jew's Tower and a costume collection.

More engaging is the **Maison d'Ailleurs** ("House of Elsewhere"; Wed–Fri 2–6pm, Sat & Sun 11am–6pm; Fr.9; ⓦwww.ailleurs.ch). This self-billed "museum of science fiction, utopia and amazing journeys", housed in the old prison opposite the château, holds a massive collection featuring antiquarian books (notably a 1631 Amsterdam edition of Thomas More's *Utopia* in Latin) and sci-fi paperbacks galore, as well as the "Espace Jules Verne", exhibiting an extraordinary array of models and ephemera connected to the acclaimed author. Changing exhibits might cover fantasy art, sci-fi magazines, unpublished drawings from Hollywood movie designers, or original toys (1950s ray guns, original Superman dolls, Star Trek and Star Wars figures, and more). You're welcome to browse through their English library.

Yverdon is suffixed "-les-Bains" for its **spa** waters, 14,000-year-old mineral springs bubbling up from 500m below ground and rich with all kinds of curative properties. The water emerges at between 28 and 34°C, and is corralled into indoor and outdoor pools at the Centre Thermal, off Avenue des Bains 1km southeast of the Old Town (Mon–Sat 8am–10pm, Sun 8am–8pm; Fr.19; Ⓦwww.cty.ch).

Practicalities

Yverdon's **train station** is 100m northeast of the Old Town, and about 600m southwest of the lakeshore. **Boats** dock at the *débarcadère* on Quai de Nogent near the racecourse; walk fifteen minutes south along the River Thièle and under the train tracks (or take bus #2) to reach the Old Town. The **tourist office** is by the station, 2 Avenue de la Gare (Mon–Fri 9am–noon & 1.30–6pm; April–Oct also Sat 9am–noon; ℡024 423 61 01, Ⓦwww.yverdonlesbains-tourisme.ch).

Yverdon's spa **hotels** aren't up to much; aim instead for *Du Théâtre*, 5 Avenue Haldimand (℡024 424 60 00, Ⓦwww.hotelyverdon.ch; ❸), a characterful, modern hotel near the tourist office, with king-size beds and a fresh, uncluttered feel. Behind the station is *Gîte du Passant*, 14 Rue du Parc (℡024 425 12 33, Ⓦwww.gite-du-passant.ch; March–Nov; ❶), a friendly **hostel** with dorms from Fr.29. *Des Iris* **campsite** is on the lakefront (℡024 425 10 89; April–Sept).

For **restaurants** try *Crêperie l'Ange Bleu*, 11 Rue du Collège (closed Mon), for salads, crêpes and light *menus* (around Fr.12). *Don Camillo*, 10 Rue du Pré (Ⓦwww.don-camillo.ch; closed Sun), has good pizza/pasta dishes, while Yverdon's poshest dining is at the restaurant or adjacent brasserie within *Hôtel La Prairie*, 9 Avenue des Bains (℡024 423 31 31, Ⓦwww.laprairiehotel.ch; closed Sun) – expect contemporary decor and classic fare, priced highly.

The Clendy stones

About 1.5km northeast of Yverdon, between the suburb of **Clendy** and the lakeshore, are **standing stones**, or menhirs, some five thousand years old.

▲ The Clendy stones

Take bus #1 to Clendy, walk left (north) under the railway bridge, and then head straight along a footpath beside a wood for about 50m. Cut right on paths through the trees, and you'll emerge into a neatly mown clearing set with the stones.

The Clendy stones were reset in their original positions in 1986, just one of many significant clusters of **Neolithic** stone circles and dolmens on the north shore of Lake Neuchâtel. These pitted and blotchy stones – big, but no Stonehenge – form a rough rhomboid shape; they may have been connected with worship and/or ley lines, since Yverdon sits at a conjunction of ancient roads. The atmosphere of the place is tangible, but the stones now stand beside a main road, shielded by trees from all but the sound of modern traffic.

Grandson

A lakeshore village 4km north of Yverdon, **GRANDSON** resonates in the mind of every Swiss schoolchild as the location of one of the three greatest victories ever won by a Swiss army, against Charles of Burgundy in 1476. Its castle, the focus of the battle, now houses one of the best **castle museums** in the country.

Although a tower was built as early as 1050, the main buildings date from 1281, when Otto I of Grandson returned from the Eighth Crusade wealthy enough to build a new castle, a Franciscan cloister in the village (of which the beautiful Romanesque St-Jean-Baptiste survives, five minutes' walk southwest from the castle up Rue Haute) and a Carthusian monastery further along the lake near Concise. Otto's tomb is prominent within Lausanne cathedral.

In 1475, during clashes with Charles the Bold, duke of Burgundy, the Swiss confederate army besieged Grandson for the first time; after less than a month, the Burgundian garrison surrendered and was allowed to escape. In February 1476, Charles retook Grandson. Treacherously, the Swiss garrison of 412 men were hanged from the apple trees in the castle orchard. Two days later, the Swiss army met Charles in battle north of Grandson. "The sun was opposite them," reported an eyewitness, "and their weapons sparkled like mirrors. The raised bugles of Uri and the Luzerner battalion were bellowing, and the din was such that the Duke's men took fright." After the Burgundians had run away, the Swiss discovered that Charles had abandoned his vast riches on the battlefield: 400 decorated tents and precious tapestries, countless items of gold and silver, 400 cannon, 10,000 horses, 600 flags, 300 tons of powder…booty which remains on display in Grandson and other Swiss museums.

Soon afterwards, the Swiss defeated Charles again at Murten and conclusively at Nancy, thus eliminating the principal threat to the French throne and, at least in a small way, permitting France instead of Burgundy to grow as a united imperial force in the centuries following.

Grandson castle

Grandson's **train station**, 700m west of the castle along Rue Basse, has only one or two slow trains on the Lausanne–Neuchâtel line (via Yverdon). It's better to get the regular **postbus** from Yverdon to Gorgier-St-Aubin, which can drop you in Grandson's Place du Château (takes 10min), or the **boat**.

At the castle ticket desk (daily 8.30am–6pm, Nov–March closes 5pm; Fr.12; ⓦ www.chateau-grandson.ch) – which doubles as the tourist office (same hours; ⓣ 024 445 29 26) – it's worth pausing to soak up the atmosphere of the lake and the massive fortress above. Highlights inside include the Torture Chamber (room 3), with executioner's axe; vast quantities of booty from 1476, as well as a life-size mock-up of Charles the Bold's war tent (room 12); the claustrophobic Prison (room 16); and a ramparts walk. Also inside is an incongruous Vintage Car Museum (rooms 17–19), whose dream machines include Greta Garbo's 1927 Rolls-Royce Phantom.

The Jura Vaudois

West of Yverdon is a stretch of hilly countryside known as the **Jura Vaudois** (Ⓦ www.juravaudois.ch), characterized by rushing streams (and the remnants of iron-working industries which exploited their power), hidden valleys and cobbled villages. The area lies wholly within Canton Vaud hard up against the French frontier – one of Europe's oldest borders, unchanged since 1186.

The main town of the region is **Vallorbe**, at the southern end of a pass that has been used since antiquity as a route from France to the Grand-St-Bernard road over the Alps to Italy. Early twentieth-century railway engineers followed the same route when they tunnelled beneath the Jura to form a chain of railways linking Paris to Venice (and onwards to Istanbul) – the classic Orient Express line. The same route through Vallorbe is used by TGV high-speed trains to this day.

The Jura Vaudois was also a stopoff for medieval pilgrims following the Chemin de St-Jacques from Germany to Santiago de Compostela in Spain: Romanesque and Gothic churches at **Orbe** and **Montcherand** and a priory at **Romainmôtier** fulfilled both spiritual and material needs on the journey. Guarded by high peaks, the secluded **Vallée de Joux** offers some great walking and cross-country skiing.

Sainte-Croix and L'Auberson

A small Jura village, 19km northwest of Yverdon on a tortuous road, **SAINTE-CROIX**'s claim to fame is its 200-year history of making musical boxes, on show at the **Musée CIMA**, 2 Rue de l'Industrie (guided tours Mon 3pm, Tues–Sun 10.30am, 2pm, 3.30pm & 5pm; hours curtailed in winter; Fr.17; Ⓦ www.musees.ch). The tours, which are in French with English notes, last an hour and a quarter, and take in the history, design and development of the art, with demonstrations. Some 6km west of Sainte-Croix is the village of **L'AUBERSON**, with – on much the same lines – the **Musée Baud**, 23 Grand-Rue (July–Sept daily 2–5pm; rest of year Sat 2–5pm, Sun 10am–noon & 2–6pm; Fr.10; Ⓦ www.museebaud.ch), displaying a Parisian fair-organ from 1900 and other musical figurines. Northeast of Sainte-Croix, a sharp-edged ridge culminates in **Mont Chasseron** (1607m), one of the highest of the Jura peaks, commanding a majestic panorama across the whole sweep of the distant Alps.

Narrow-gauge trains climb from Yverdon to Sainte-Croix, terminating at the lower end of Rue de l'Industrie. The **tourist office** is at 10 Rue Neuve (Mon–Fri 8.30am–noon & 1.15–4.30pm; ☎024 455 41 42, Ⓦ www.ste-croix.ch). Buses shuttle to L'Auberson. **Hotel** *De France*, 25 Rue Centrale (☎024 454 38 21, Ⓦ www.hotel-defrance.ch; ➋–➌), is a fine three-star with comfortable renovated interiors, or plump for the spacious south-facing balconied rooms at pine-shaded *Grand Hôtel des Rasses* in nearby Les Rasses (☎024 454 19 61, Ⓦ www.grandhotelrasses.ch; ➌–➍).

Vallorbe

VALLORBE, right on the Franco-Swiss frontier, is today just a stop on the TGV line between Paris and Lausanne, but in times past this small, rather austere town, loomed over from the southwest by the Dent de Vaulion peak, was the centre of a thriving iron industry. This is commemorated in the riverside Grandes-Forges building, dating from 1495 and now housing the **Musée du Fer et du Chemin de Fer** (Iron and Railway Museum; April–Oct daily 9.30am–noon & 1.30–6pm, closed Mon am; rest of year Tues–Fri 1.30–6pm; Fr.12; ⓦwww.museedufer.ch). The main draw is the working smithy, powered by waterwheels on the River Orbe outside. Upstairs is the railway section, housing memorabilia from the Venice-Simplon Orient Express.

Several fast buses per day run to Vallorbe from Yverdon, beating the train. Vallorbe's train station is perched on a terrace high above the town; it's a ten-minute walk down to the museum, which also houses the **tourist office** (ⓣ021 843 25 83, ⓦwww.vallorbe-tourisme.ch). **Accommodation** is basic: go for the *Auberge Pour Tous* hostel, 11 Rue du Simplon (ⓣ021 843 13 49, ⓦwww.aubergepourtous.ch; ❶). The main street, Grand-Rue, has inexpensive **eating** options; cosy *Café de la Poste* is on parallel Rue de l'Ancienne Poste.

Around Vallorbe

Wild countryside surrounds Vallorbe. Local trains and buses go everywhere but they're less convenient than your own transport.

Just over 2km southwest of Vallorbe are **Les Grottes de Vallorbe** (April–Oct daily 9.30am–4.30pm, June–Aug until 5.30pm; Fr.15), caves replete with stalactites and stalagmites and an exhibition of minerals dubbed Le Trésor des Fées (Fairy Treasure). About forty minutes' walk from Le Day train station near Vallorbe is the **Fort de Pré-Giroud** (July & Aug daily 11am–4.45pm; May, June, Sept & Oct Sat & Sun 11.30am–4.15pm; Fr.12), a military complex dug into a hillside in 1937 to defend against incursion by enemy forces from France. An innocuous chalet on the surface hides vertical shafts giving access to a subterranean bunker complete with kitchen, dorms and a hospital.

ROMAINMÔTIER, a small village about 14km east of Vallorbe near Croy, is dominated by its fine Romanesque priory church. Switzerland's oldest monastery was founded on the same site in about 450, and the current building was constructed by Cluniac monks in 990–1028. The church (daily 7am–6pm) is approached beneath a picturesque fourteenth-century clock-tower. As you enter, you pass into the harmonious nave, with a vividly painted thirteenth-century vault. On the left of the choir and chancel, with fourteenth-century frescoes, is a beautiful medieval statue of Mary in the Chapel of the Holy Virgin. The remains of the cloister run along the outside of the south wall.

In **MONTCHERAND**, a tranquil village 8km northeast of Romainmôtier, a small but notable tenth-century church (daily 8.30am–8.30pm, Oct–April closes 6.30pm) houses a striking set of twelfth-century frescoes, depicting saints in brilliantly restored colours.

ORBE, halfway between Vallorbe and Yverdon by bus or train, is a picturesque old town up on a rock, with steep cobbled streets and another atmospheric church, dating from the fifteenth century. Orbe was known to the Romans as *Urba*, and 2km north of the town at Boscéaz are some of the best Roman mosaics to be seen in Switzerland (Easter–Oct Mon–Fri 9am–noon & 1.30–5pm, Sat & Sun 1.30–5.30pm; Fr.6; ⓦtourisme.orbe.ch), including hexagonal depictions of gods and goddesses with central medallions showing the deities of the seven days of the week.

The Vallée de Joux

About 5km southwest of Vallorbe, the sharp Dent de Vaulion rises to 1483m, standing guard over the **Vallée de Joux**, a long thin valley sandwiched at 1000m between the Grand Risoud pine forest, which conceals it from France, and the parallel Mont Tendre range, which cuts it off from Lake Geneva. This is perfect summer walking country, with many routes along the valley floor beside the **Lac de Joux**, while the thickly wooded valley sides turn into cross-country skiing heaven in winter. The valley has its own, bracing microclimate, reminiscent of Alpine areas 400m higher in altitude: temperatures of -20°C on the valley floor are not unknown in winter, and precipitation tops 1800mm a year. It's no surprise that the first people to consider settling in the windblown valley were ascetic monks: even by 1700 there were still just 173 inhabitants, plus 22 bears.

Between the small Lac Brenet and Lac de Joux is **LE PONT** village. In front of the train station is what's left of a colossal hangar, used between 1880 and 1936 to store ice, which was hacked from the lakes and then transported by fast train to Paris, Lyon and Geneva. Roads run west from Le Pont along both shores of the Lac de Joux, meeting at **LE SENTIER**, a one-time watchmaking centre to rival those in the Neuchâtel mountains: Audemars Piguet, Blancpain and Breguet still make watches hereabouts. The Espace Horloger, 2 Grand-Rue (Tues–Sun 2–5.30pm; Nov–Feb Thurs–Sun same times; Fr.11; ⓦ www.espacehorloger.ch), has a fine collection of historic timepieces. **LE BRASSUS**, 4km southwest, is pretty and quiet, set amid wild nature. From here all the way southwest to the Col de la Givrine above Nyon extends the protected Parc Jurassien Vaudois (ⓦ www.parc-jurassien.ch).

Practicalities

Trains from Vallorbe (connecting with services from Lausanne at Le Day) run along the north shore of the Lac de Joux, terminating at Le Brassus. One **boat** a day in summer does a circular cruise of the lake, to and from Le Pont. A **road** from Le Brassus (open summer only) surfs over the mountains at Marchairuz before dropping down to Lake Geneva.

The well-equipped **tourist office** for the valley is in the sports centre at the southern end of Le Sentier (daily 9am–noon & 1–6pm; ☎021 845 17 77, ⓦ www.myvalleedejoux.ch). They rent ice skates, mountain bikes and kayaks and have simple, cheap dorms. For **hotels**, *La Lande* (☎021 845 44 41, ⓦ www .hotellalande.com; ❷–❸) in Le Brassus is pleasant and newly renovated. **Camp** year-round at *Le Rocheray* in Le Sentier (☎021 845 51 74).

The Broye

The mellow countryside between Yverdon and Bern is named after the **River Broye** which flows gently through the area. Not much happens here, but it's good cycling country: reasonably flat, with small villages and the shores of both Lake Neuchâtel and the Murtensee (Lake Morat) to explore. **Estavayer-le-Lac** is a lakeside resort town with peace and quiet as its main attributes; nearby **Payerne** is home to a splendid Romanesque abbey, while **Avenches** was once the capital of Roman Switzerland. **Murten/Morat**, on the line where French-speaking Western Europe meets German-speaking Central Europe, has a well-preserved medieval core.

Estavayer-le-Lac

The centre of **ESTAVAYER-LE-LAC** – a picturesque little yachties' town on Lake Neuchâtel 19km northeast of Yverdon – has remained largely unchanged since 1599. Today Estavayer occupies a little enclave of Canton Fribourg within Canton Vaud, and is known for its roses.

A ten-minute walk from the station leads northwest along Route de la Gare to Place du Midi on the edge of the Old Town. Heading east from here takes you to the Gothic **St-Laurent** church; turn left (north) to reach Place de Moudon, the medieval marketplace which formerly looked over the lakeshore. Over to the east is the turreted **Château de Chenaux**, added to over 450 years. South of the church, Grand-Rue heads out of town via the Porte des Religieuses. Partway down, Rue du Musée branches off to the **Musée des Grenouilles** (March–Oct Tues–Sun 10am–noon & 2–5pm; July & Aug also Mon; rest of year Sat & Sun 2–5pm; Fr.5; Ⓦ www.museedesgrenouilles.ch), featuring 108 small frogs, stuffed by François Perrier, a retired captain of the Vatican's Swiss Guard, in the 1860s and posed in glass cases to mimic the social life of the period. It's perhaps the world's most pointless museum; the frogs don't look impressed in the least.

Estavayer's **train station** – on the slow Yverdon–Fribourg line – is 600m southwest of Place du Midi. The **tourist office** is at 16 Rue Hôtel de Ville (May–Sept Mon–Fri 9am–noon & 1.30–6pm, Sat & Sun 10am–3pm; rest of year Mon–Fri 9am–noon & 1.30–5pm; Ⓣ 026 663 12 37, Ⓦ www.estavayer-payerne .ch). **Boats** arrive from Yverdon and Neuchâtel. The most appealing **hotel** is ⚑ *My Lady's Manor*, 7 Route St-Pierre (Ⓣ 026 663 23 16, Ⓦ www.myladysmanor .org; ❷), a romantic old house only open to guests in summer. Otherwise, try the pleasant *Hôtel de Ville* in the centre (Ⓣ 026 663 92 92, Ⓦ www.hotel-de-ville .info; ❸–❹), which has a fine restaurant and terrace.

Payerne

Some 8km inland from Estavayer is the market town of **PAYERNE**, centred on its **Abbatiale** (Tues–Sun 10am–noon & 2–6pm, Oct–March closes 5pm; Fr.3 or more, depending on exhibition; Ⓦ www.payerne.ch), one of Switzerland's finest examples of Romanesque architecture. There's a wealth of detail in the five-naved church, which dates from the eleventh and twelfth centuries; its square, turreted **tower**, with a slender **twisted spire**, dominates the town. Within the lofty barrel-vaulted interior, natural light reflects off the variegated sandstone pillars of the nave to set the whole space glowing. Carved **capitals** in the transept and detailed **frescoes** from around 1200 on the vaultings of the porch and in the narthex are gorgeous. However, the church has not been used as a house of worship since 1562, and you may find modern art exhibitions filling the space with distractions.

Avenches

About 10km northeast of Payerne, **AVENCHES** was the capital of Roman Switzerland, at one time supporting a population of 20,000. After defeat at the hands of Julius Caesar, the Helvetians founded their new capital of Aventicum in the early first century BC (Aventia was the local Celtic goddess of water). Emperor Vespasian granted it the status of colony in 72 AD, and during the second and third centuries the city wall boasted 73 watchtowers; many of the public buildings of that period – a baths, temples, the amphitheatre, and more – have been excavated. Aleman tribes raided in around 277, and by 450 Aventicum's glory days were over.

Avenches' festivals

Every July, little Avenches hosts an **opera festival** (⊛ www.avenches.ch/opera), with open-air productions in the 8000-seat amphitheatre that draw thousands of promenading spectators. Performances start around 9pm and last until after midnight – many people stay overnight, booking the town's few hotels out months ahead of time. Tickets cost well over Fr.100, with some limited-view seats available on the day. Every August, the same amphitheatre stages the **Rock oz'Arènes** festival (⊛ www.rockozarenes.com), with headliners like P.J. Harvey, the Wailers and Asian Dub Foundation, plus jugglers, acoustic sets and more.

Climbing the hill from the train station, the first thing you come to is the large **amphitheatre** crowning the eastern edge of the Old Town, well restored and now the scene of an annual summer opera festival (see box above). The tower at the rear of the arena houses the excellent **Musée Romain** (Tues–Sun: April–Sept 10am–noon & 1–5pm; Oct–March 2–5pm; Fr.4). The ground floor is filled with statuary and mosaics, while upstairs are impressive exhibits on Roman life. Dotted around town are seven other (free) Roman sites, all well signposted; the tourist office can advise.

Avenches' **train station** is on the Murten–Payerne line. There are also plenty of **buses** from Fribourg. Avenches' **tourist office** is at 3 Place de l'Église (Mon–Fri 8am–noon & 1.30–5.30pm; ☎ 026 676 99 22, ⊛ www.avenches.ch). There is an HI **hostel** five minutes' walk south at 5 Rue du Lavoir (☎ 026 675 26 66, ⊛ www.youthhostel.ch; April–Oct; ❶), while the grandest **hotel** is the *Couronne*, 20 Rue Centrale (☎ 026 675 54 14, ⊛ www.lacouronne.ch; ❸–❹), which also has the poshest brasserie around (*menus* Fr.27). There are pavement cafés along Rue Centrale.

Murten/Morat

Belying its historical resonance for the Swiss, **MURTEN**, 6km northeast of Avenches, has the air of a holiday town, its neat suburban streets and low-key waterfront promenade reminiscent of the English south coast. It lies bang on the *Röstigraben* (linguistic divide), though German-speakers outnumber French, who call the place **MORAT**. It's also one of the best preserved of Switzerland's medieval towns, still encircled by its fifteenth-century walls, now offering the simple pleasures of strolling on cobbled lanes, sipping drinks at lakeview terrace cafés and taking the odd ferry.

The town's name is derived from the Celtic *moriduno*, meaning "lakeside fortress". Fire in 1416 led to rebuilding in stone, a useful move since, in 1476, Murten allied itself with Bern and Fribourg against the Burgundians and found itself facing down a siege from Charles the Bold. The town hung on for thirteen days until a Bernese force arrived to slaughter the Burgundians: 10,000 died, and local legend tells of bones still being washed up eighteen years later. A runner took news of the victory 17km to Fribourg, but expired after recounting his tale; his exploit is commemorated by thousands who take part in a fun run between the two towns on the first Sunday in October.

Murten's **Old Town** is a simple three-street affair, full of picturesque medieval architecture. From the castle (closed to the public) – which has a peaceful courtyard with lake views – Rathausgasse leads east, lined with hotels whose rear terraces afford prime views across the lake to the Vully vineyards. Parallel to the south are Hauptgasse, crammed with bars and eateries, and tranquil Schulgasse/Deutsche Kirchgasse. One of the best ways to see Murten is from the ramparts, accessible at a number of points along Deutsche Kirchgasse. The main eastern gate is the Berntor, or Porte de Berne, with a distinctive clock face. Five minutes west of the harbour, an old mill houses **Museum Murten** (April–Oct Tues–Sat 2–5pm, Sun 10am–5pm; Fr.6; ⓦwww.museummurten.ch), with a diverting collection gathered when dredging of nearby marshes revealed evidence of Neolithic settlement.

Practicalities

The **station** – with trains from Fribourg and Payerne, as well as connections from Neuchâtel and Bern – is a five-minute walk west of the Old Town. **Boats** (ⓦwww.navig.ch & www.bielersee.ch) cruise in summer to and from Neuchâtel and Biel/Bienne. The **tourist office** is at Französische Kirchgasse 6 (April–Oct Mon–Fri 9am–noon & 2–6pm; May–Sept also Sat 10am–2pm; July & Aug also Sun 10am–2pm; Nov–March Mon–Fri closes 5pm; ⓣ026 670 51 12, ⓦwww.murtentourismus.ch).

Top **hotel** is the *Vieux Manoir au Lac*, 1km west of town at 18 Rue de Lausanne (ⓣ026 678 61 61, ⓦwww.vieuxmanoir.ch; ❽), a romantic manor house set in its own gardens, with private beach and harbour. In town, *Murtenhof & Krone*, Rathausgasse 1 (ⓣ026 672 90 30, ⓦwww.murtenhof.ch; ❸–❹), is prime choice, its medieval buildings renovated throughout, many boasting original beams. Otherwise the *Adler*, Hauptgasse 45 (ⓣ026 672 66 69, ⓦwww.adler-hotel.ch; ❹), has pleasant, artistically decorated rooms within a splendid medieval building on the main drag.

Eating and **drinking** are well taken care of at the Hauptgasse cafés and hotel restaurants, although many cater for day-trippers and so can be overpriced; the *Murtenhof* menu is long and inexpensive, with veggie options, while *Anatolia*, Hauptgasse 45 (ⓦwww.anatolia.ch), can do pizza or kebabs for around Fr.20. For formal dining aim for *Le Vieux Manoir au Lac* (see above): their top-rated French cuisine (*menus* around Fr.100) is served in a delightful waterside dining room.

Biel/Bienne and around

The double-barrelled town 32km northeast of Murten, and almost exactly halfway between Geneva and Zürich, can get a little confusing. German-speakers call it **BIEL** (*beel*), French-speakers know it as **BIENNE** (*bee-yen*), but it's Switzerland's only officially **bilingual** town and so all road signs, documents and public information must be produced in both languages. Train timetables, maps and books always call the place "Biel/Bienne", and the locals cheerfully straddle the *Röstigraben* without a second thought – perhaps chatting with a friend in German whilst ordering lunch in French. The **lake** stretching southwest from the town is both the Bielersee and the Lac de Bienne. In addition, some forty percent of the population originate from outside Switzerland, with prominent numbers of Italian and Spanish residents as well as Turks, Slavs, Arabs and more. Eavesdropping can be an entertaining pastime.

Biel/Bienne is a dynamic, modern town, very different in both style and mood from its near-neighbours Neuchâtel and Bern: it was only when the railway arrived in the late nineteenth century that it began to expand beyond its old walls. Watchmaking had been a mainstay of the regional economy for a century or more, but had been suffering from the inefficiency of tiny cottage industries: there were some 350 enterprises throughout the Jura at one point,

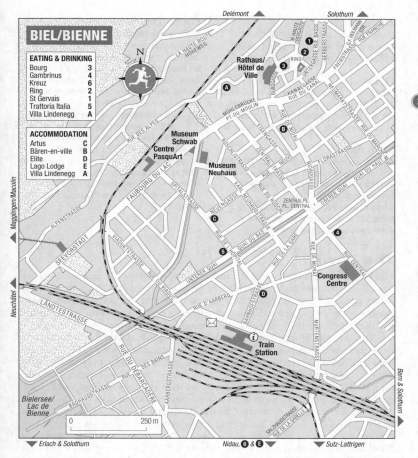

each employing a few artisans working by hand. Mechanization meant that production could be expanded and made more competitive, and Biel/Bienne took on the role of factory centre, initially for watchmaking and subsequently for precision machinery and other industries. To this day, firms such as Omega, Rolex and Swatch maintain factories and headquarters here.

Arrival, information and accommodation

The **train station** is between the town and the lakeshore: it's a 500-metre walk northeast along Bahnhofstrasse/Rue de la Gare to the main Zentralplatz/Place Centrale – from where the Old Town is the same distance again northwards. **Boats** dock at the *Schifflände/débarcadère*, some 500m southwest of the station. The **tourist office** occupies a kiosk in the station forecourt (Mon–Fri 8am–12.30pm & 1.30–6pm, Thurs until 8pm, Sat 9am–3pm; ☎032 329 84 84, ⓦwww.biel-seeland.ch). Most **accommodation** is geared towards businesspeople: character tends to take a back seat, but rates are often slashed at weekends.

Campsite

Lindenhof Sutz-Lattrigen ☏ 032 397 10 77, Ⓦ www.camping-lindenhof.ch. Decent site 4km southwest by narrow-gauge train. April–Oct.

Hostel

Lago Lodge (SB hostel) Uferweg 5, Nidau ☏ 032 331 37 32, Ⓦ www.lagolodge.ch. Pleasant, attractive spot just south of the centre, with its own microbrewery onsite. Bus #4 to Schloss Nidau. ❶

Hotels

Artus Neuengasse/Rue Neuve 6 ☏ 032 323 02 36, Ⓦ www.hotel-artus-biel.ch. Quiet, family-run hotel and bistro on a pretty corner, with plain but comfortable rooms. ❸

Bären-en-ville Nidaugasse/Rue de Nidau 22 ☏ 032 322 45 73, Ⓦ www.risto.ch. A creaky, simple two-star in the town centre. ❸

Elite Bahnhofstrasse/Rue de la Gare 14 ☏ 032 328 77 77, Ⓦ www.hotelelite.ch. Very central four-star business hotel, built in 1930 and renovated in Art Deco style. It looks chic, classy and quite elegant, but rooms are rather small. Ask for one on the corner side: bars on the main road generate noise late into the night (every room is kitted out with a free set of earplugs). ❹–❺

🏃 **Villa Lindenegg** Lindenegg 5 ☏ 032 322 94 66, Ⓦ www.lindenegg.ch. A fine mansion built in 1831 in its own little park in the Old Town, bought by the city in 1985, renovated by three local women and reopened in 1996 as a bistro and hotel. All eight rooms are different, each of them fresh, light and wood-floored, the best (room 4) with a balcony over the garden. ❸–❹

The Town

Heading from the station along the main shopping streets of Bahnhofstrasse/Rue de la Gare and then Nidaugasse/Rue de Nidau, the bustle and high-street brand names suddenly fade painlessly away as you cross into the cobbled **Old Town**. Burggasse climbs past the old Zeughaus (arsenal), rejuvenated as the city's theatre, and the impressive 1676 step-gabled Rathaus (Town Hall), now police headquarters, into the open **Burgplatz/Place de Bourg**. Quaint old shuttered houses line the square, which centres on the Fountain of Justice, dating from 1714. Continue uphill, and head right to the **Ring**, core of the Old Town and named for the circle of head shakers who would sit here to deliberate on the fate of criminals brought for trial. Head east along arcaded Obergasse/Rue Haute, and then double back onto Untergasse/Rue Basse to stroll past the town's oldest houses.

Best of the town's museums is **Centre PasquArt**, Seevorstadt/Faubourg du Lac 71 (Wed–Fri 2–6pm, Sat & Sun 11am–6pm; Fr.10; Ⓦ www.pasquart.ch), devoted to contemporary art and photography. A stroll away are **Museum Neuhaus**, Schüsspromenade/Promenade de la Suze 26 (Tues–Sun 11am–5pm, Wed until 7pm; Fr.7; Ⓦ www.mn-biel.ch), a good local history museum, and **Museum Schwab**, Seevorstadt/Faubourg du Lac 50 (Tues–Sat 2–6pm, Sun 11am–6pm; Fr.6; Ⓦ www.muschwab.ch), focused on archeology.

A fine way to fill an afternoon is on the **boat trip** (2hr 30min; Ⓦ www .bielersee.ch) down the River Aare from Biel/Bienne to Solothurn, passing the stork colony at Altreu on the way.

Above Biel/Bienne

A **funicular** from Seevorstadt/Faubourg du Lac, west of the station, heads up through the forested slopes to the village of **MAGGLINGEN/MACOLIN** 400m above, for ridge-top hiking trails; you'll be in fit company, since Magglingen is home to the Federal Institute of Sport. With strong legs, you can get 16km west to **Le Chasseral** (1607m; Ⓦ www.parcchasseral.ch), the highest summit in the Swiss Jura, where you'll find a simple hotel and mountain restaurant, *Chasseral* (☏ 032 751 24 51, Ⓦ www .chasseral-hotel.ch). Buses run down the other side of the ridge to **St-Imier**, on the train line between Biel/Bienne and La Chaux-de-Fonds.

Eating and drinking

Biel/Bienne has some good **restaurants** and **café/bars** both within the Old Town and around the city centre.

Bourg Burggasse/Rue de Bourg 12. Uncomplicated local café-restaurant on a characterful Old Town cobbled street, with a friendly welcome and simple *menus* from Fr.16. Closed Mon.

Gambrinus Zentralstrasse/Rue Centrale 57 Ⓦ www.gambrinus-loungeria.ch. Classy bar and hangout, open from mid-afternoon, dubbing itself a "loungeria" – think white sofas, DJ chillout beats and sparkly decor. Closed Mon.

🏃 **Kreuz** Hauptstrasse/Rue Principale 23 in Nidau ☎ 032 331 93 03, Ⓦ www .kreuz-nidau.ch. Relaxed co-operative-run café and restaurant in this pleasant little town contiguous with Biel/Bienne to the south (a short walk, or bus #4). Old wood floors inside, and a garden terrace out back – the food is excellent, organic and veggie (*menus* from Fr.17). Closed Wed.

Ring Ring 16. Cheery, much-loved local restaurant on this cobbled Old Town square, mainly serving uncomplicated pastas and pizzas (Fr.25–35). Closed Sun.

St Gervais Untergasse/Rue Basse 21 Ⓦ www .stgervais.ch. Lively, friendly, alternative-style joint in the Old Town with quality inexpensive food; not the only choice on this street. Closed Tues eve.

Trattoria Italia Spitalstrasse/Rue de l'Hôpital 26 ☎ 032 322 92 50. A pleasant terrace restaurant on a quiet corner. Pizzas are around Fr.20, and there's a choice of risottos and a range of *menus* for around Fr.30. Closed Sun.

Villa Lindenegg Lindenegg 5 (see "Hotels"). A fine bistro with gourmet evening *menus* (around Fr.23) with or without meat, using market-fresh produce inventively and attractively. Renowned for Sunday brunches (10am–2pm). Closed Mon.

Around Biel/Bienne

Walking or cycling through the **vineyards** and wine villages on the northern shore of the Bielersee/Lac de Bienne can be a peaceful way to spend an afternoon. The tourist office has information.

From Erlach/Cerlier, opposite Biel/Bienne at the southwestern end of the lake (served by plenty of boats), a footpath leads out for an hour-and-a-half's stroll along a causeway to the car-free **St Petersinsel/Île de St-Pierre**. No longer an island (the level of the lake dropped in the late nineteenth century during hydro-engineering work), this little dot of forest was first populated by Cluniac monks, who built a monastery here in 1127. Its most famous resident was the Genevois philosopher Jean-Jacques Rousseau, who spent two months here in 1765, later calling it the happiest time of his life. The renovated monastery buildings, idyllically set amidst vineyards, now house a gourmet **restaurant** (*menus* around Fr.25) and award-winning historic **hotel** (☎ 032 338 11 14, Ⓦ www.st-petersinsel.ch; March–Oct; ④–⑤), full of character.

Northeast of Biel/Bienne is the **Taubenloch Gorge**, accessible on bus #1 or on foot from Magglingen above. There's a well-engineered path running through the defile above the fast-flowing River Schüss/Suze for about 2km. Entry is free. Check with the Biel/Bienne tourist office for details of local adventure operators running canyoning trips in the gorge.

Canton Jura

Ignored by most travellers, but well loved by the Swiss themselves, **Canton Jura**, in the far northwest corner of Switzerland, is a rural gem, perfect if all you want from your holiday is to walk or cycle your way through rolling countryside and dark forests, with only the smallest of villages and simplest of hotels (or campsites) to provide material comforts. This little bulge of land has

Chemins de fer du Jura (Ⓦ www.les-cj.ch) runs many of the region's trains and buses. Swiss Pass holders travel free. Otherwise, there are several good-value local passes, including the **Régio CJ** one-day pass (Fr.19) and the **Railévasion** pass (Fr.48), valid for any three days' travel in 14.

over the centuries been shunted from pillar to post: from the dukes of Burgundy to the bishops of Basel, seized by the Swiss, ruled by the French, handed to the Bernese, and finally in the 1970s – after decades of political turmoil that briefly threatened to ignite violent conflict (see box opposite) – granted independence to form its own government. The towns, including the cantonal capital **Delémont**, have retained a graceful, historic, Gallic air.

More than forty churches and chapels around the canton are decorated with stained glass by modern and contemporary artists, including Fernand Léger; the tourist office has put together an itinerary, with notes, at Ⓦ www.juravitraux.ch.

Delémont

An ancient town first mentioned in 737, **DELÉMONT** is an atmospheric place to stop over for an afternoon or a day. Its main historical claim to fame was as the summer residence of the prince-bishops of nearby Basel from the Middle Ages through to the Revolution. Last century, the stirrings for Jurassien independence (see box opposite) led to Delémont being named in 1976 as cantonal capital, but it retains a small-town charm – only around 12,000 people live here – and has good access into the rolling Jura countryside for walks and rides.

Turn left out of the station past the post office and then right on Rue Texerans: it takes five minutes to cross the river into the Old Town. The main street is Rue du 23-Juin, longer and more impressive than you might expect for a little town, and home to the eighteenth-century **Hôtel de Ville**, set skewed to the road and shaded by a huge tree. This ornate building was the scene, in 1947, of a historic demonstration which sparked the subsequent liberation movement. A few steps west is the **Église St-Marcel**, built in the 1770s in a mixture of Rococo and formal Neoclassical, with some lovely dark oak-wood stalls. Beside the church is the **château**, built in 1721.

At the western end of the road is the Porte de Porrentruy, one of the old city gates. Alongside is the Fontaine du Sauvage and modest **Musée Jurassien d'Art et d'Histoire** (Tues–Sun 2–5pm; Fr.6; Ⓦ www.mjah.ch). Star exhibit of this interesting museum is the beautiful golden mitre of St Germain, first abbot of Moutier in the seventh century. It's a shame Germain's twisted old leather sandals – far more evocative – get shorter shrift.

Practicalities

Delémont's **tourist office** is by the station, 9 Place de la Gare (Mon–Fri 9am–noon & 2–5.30pm, Sat 9am–noon; ☎032 420 47 71, Ⓦ www.juratourisme.ch). A kilometre east of the centre is an excellent HI **hostel**, 185 Route de Bâle (☎032 422 20 54, Ⓦ www.youthhostel.ch; April–Oct; ❶), with good facilities and quality food. *Hôtel du Boeuf*, 17 Rue de la Préfecture (☎032 422 16 91; ❷), is a clean, well-run **hotel** within the Old Town. Pavement cafés aside, places to **eat** include *La Cigogne* nearby at no. 7 (closed Sun lunch & Tues), a stylish modern brasserie serving wood-fired pizzas (around Fr.18), and rustic *La Bonne*

Discontent and secession

From the 1940s to the 1970s, Switzerland underwent serious political crisis, as a group of disaffected, historically marginalized people from the Jura pushed the flexibility of Swiss democracy to its limits. The origins of the conflict can be dated back to the 1815 Congress of Vienna which handed the area to Canton Bern. Bern welcomed the **Protestants** who lived in Biel/Bienne and the southern districts of the Jura around Moutier, but were powerful enough to ignore the destitute French-speaking **Catholic** peasants of the northern districts around Delémont and Porrentruy. Bernese moved into the region, bringing a new language and culture with them. Economic boom in the nineteenth century brought prosperity to Biel/Bienne yet largely passed Porrentruy by – but any rumblings of discontent in the north were quelled by the extreme hardship suffered by the whole region in the depression of the 1930s.

On September 20, 1947, a Jurassien member of Bern's parliament was refused election to the cantonal government because he spoke French. The outrage that followed led to the formation of a hardline anti-Bern grouping, which garnered popular support throughout the northern districts, and which got enough backing to force a controversial **cantonal referendum** on splitting the Jura away from Bern. The voters of Canton Bern rejected the proposal. However, it surprised the separatists that Jura too had voted against it: Porrentruy, Delémont and Saignelégier had supported separation two-to-one, but Moutier and its neighbours had rejected it by three-to-one. The francophone, separatist Catholics of the north, a minority within Protestant, German-speaking Bern as a whole, and also a minority within the Jura itself, decided to resort to direct action. **Paramilitaries** – with their slogan "Jura libre" – seized a police station in Delémont and the Swiss Embassy in Paris, sabotaged Bern's trams, and, in a show of support for Walloon separatists, simultaneously stormed the Belgian Embassy in Bern and the Swiss Brussels.

In 1973, Bern's cantonal government accepted terms for a **referendum on separation**, and on June 23, 1974, over ninety percent of eligible voters turned out, with a majority backing separation. This shocked the Protestant southern districts of the Jura and precipitated the formation of a pro-Bern, **anti-separatist bloc**, which threatened violence against the Catholics of the north and demanded another referendum to allow the south to detach itself from the Jurassien independence movement and thereby remain part of Bern. On March 16, 1975, this proposal was carried, but with a majority in Moutier of just 286 votes. Amidst the accusations of manipulation that followed, a pro-Jura demonstration turned into a full-scale riot, with 800 militants involved in an all-night running battle with police. Discontent simmered throughout the year.

Nonetheless, after a series of commune-by-commune referenda, popular opinion was shown to favour both the formation of a new canton in the north, and the adherence of the south to Bern. The split became inevitable. Moutier remained in Bern, and a new **Canton Jura** came into existence on January 1, 1979. Individual communes continued to shift over the next two decades: in 1989, the residents of Laufenthal voted to leave Bern and join Canton Basel-Land, and in 1995, Vellerat (population 70) voted to leave Bern and join Canton Jura.

As Jonathan Steinberg notes in his excellent book *Why Switzerland?* (see p.513), it was this minute concentration on opinion within the tiniest linguistic, cultural or ethnic units, as well as a political structure able to take such micro-referenda into account, that meant the Swiss could address Jurassien discontent, allow it to be expressed (with a minimum of violence and no casualties) and then have the flexibility to incorporate it into a new national order. Most countries facing similar discontent have neither the political structures nor the flexibility to effect similar solutions.

Auberge, 32 Rue du 23-Juin (🅦www.labonneauberge.ch), using market-fresh ingredients in heavy, French-influenced dishes (Fr.30–50) – think Chateaubriand steak, veal kidneys and the like.

Porrentruy

From Delémont, a good half-day driving tour heads from Develier, on the western outskirts, through hilly countryside up to the **Les Rangiers** pass (856m) – a Rhône/Rhine watershed – and down to the forest-bound hamlet of **Pleujouse**, where the tenth-century *Château de Pleujouse* is now a fine **restaurant** (☎032 462 10 80, 🅦www.juragourmand.ch/le-chateau; closed Mon & Tues), with *menus* of classic local dishes for around Fr.50. Head on through **Alle**, a village where the River Allaine flows down the main street, to reach the graceful town of **PORRENTRUY**.

In the heart of the **Ajoie** region – the bulge of Canton Jura that sticks out into France – Porrentruy's cobbled streets, filled with eighteenth-century buildings, have a vivacity lacking in towns twice the size. Walking 500m west from the train station brings you onto the main Grand-Rue, dotted with medieval fountains and lined with ornate facades, including the **tourist office** housed in the old hospital at no. 5 (Mon–Fri 9am–noon & 2–5.30pm, Sat 9am–noon; ☎032 420 47 72). Following the street down to the river leaves you a few metres west of the fourteenth-century **Porte de France** and at the foot of the impressive **château** towering above.

Hôtel Lion d'Or, 12 Rue Malvoisins (☎032 476 13 77; ❷), is a little **hotel** in the Old Town with geraniums in the windowbox and decent rooms. The same street has many pavement cafés, including jolly *Aux Deux Clefs* at no. 7, while *Le Faucon*, 15 Rue des Annonciades (🅦www.le-faucon.com; closed Sun), is a brasserie and lively bar. In November, the huge St-Martin **fair** is an excuse for scoffing vast quantities of the local pork *saucisse d'Ajoie* at stand-up stalls.

St-Ursanne

South of Porrentruy, the River Doubs loops into Swiss territory for the only time, enclosing a neck of land known as the **Clos de Doubs**: the scenic road running alongside the valley is dubbed, romantically, the Corniche du Jura. **ST-URSANNE** is a picturesque old walled village on the river, 10km from Porrentruy, blessed with both a twelfth-century church and several hotels. The one-kilometre walk down from the station is lovely, and you approach the village through its eastern, sixteenth-century Porte de St-Pierre. The same road passes through to the Porte de St-Paul at the village's western end, while midway along, an alley branches south through the Porte de St-Jean to an ancient, narrow bridge over the river. The beautiful **collégiale** church in the heart of the village, with its sculptured and painted south doorway, has a Romanesque choir filled with Baroque ornament. Above the nave, which has fifteenth-century frescoes, the vaulting is crowned with carved keystones giving the date 1301, and you'll find fewer more peaceful corners to spend a sunny hour or two than the Gothic cloister alongside.

The **tourist office** is on Place Roger Schaffter (June–Sept Mon–Fri 9am–noon & 2–6pm, Sat & Sun 10am–noon & 1.30–5.30pm; shorter hours in winter; ☎032 420 47 73). Of the several hotels, the *Demi-Lune* (☎032 461 35 31, 🅦www.demi-lune.ch; closed Nov–Feb; ❷–❸) and *Couronne* (☎032 461 35 67, 🅦www.hotelcouronne.ch; ❷–❸) are fine choices for both lodging and dining. St-Ursanne's **Fête Médiévale** in July (🅦www.medievales.ch) features minstrels, dancers and jugglers.

Saignelégier and Franches-Montagnes

The stretch of the Jura mountains within Canton Jura is called **Franches-Montagnes**. Following wars between local lords in the twelfth and thirteenth centuries, Bishop Imier de Ramstein granted tax exemptions (*franchises* in French) to the whole area as a way to encourage repopulation, thus giving the area its name. It's a beautiful landscape of rolling green hills and wide meadows flanked by fir trees, and is fiercely loved by the locals: one writer commented, "A Franc-Montagnard who sells off the land for profit is considered a traitor."

SAIGNELÉGIER is the main – indeed only – town in the region, just a shop or two larger than a village. The **tourist office** is in the sports centre (Mon–Fri 9am–noon & 2–5.45pm, Sat & Sun 9.30am–1.30pm; ☎032 420 47 70, Ⓦ www.juratourisme.ch), with an array of information, as well as local crafts and bottles of the delectable local firewater – a plum-based *eau-de-vie* called *Damassine* – for sale. In mid-August, the Marché-Concours National de Chevaux rolls into town (Ⓦ www.marcheconcours.ch), a horse market and show with parades and races.

There are limitless possibilities for hikes and cycle routes through the countryside: aim southeast to the Étang de la Gruère lake, or southwest along the ridge to the ancient village of **LE NOIRMONT**, or north, down into the Doubs valley for the riverside forest trails around the border hamlet of **GOUMOIS** – also known for its canoeing and kayaking.

You can **camp** at *Sous La Neuvevie* (☎032 951 10 82, Ⓦ www.campingsaignelegier.ch; May–Oct), 2km south of Saignelégier, or at the municipal site in Goumois (☎079 314 19 38; April–Oct). **Hotels** abound, in every hamlet and scenic spot. The friendly ⛺ *Café-Hôtel du Soleil*, two minutes south of the station in Saignelégier (☎032 951 16 88, Ⓦ www.cafe-du-soleil.ch; ❷), doubles as an arts centre, with concerts and exhibitions as well as good veggie food in their restaurant. *Hôtel du Doubs*, by the riverside border crossing in Goumois (☎032 951 13 23, Ⓦ www.juragourmand.ch/hoteldudoubs; closed Jan & Feb; ❷), offers comfortable rooms as well as fine local cuisine.

▲ Horseriding at Saignelégier

Your own transport gives easy access to a couple of excellent **restaurants**. 🍴 *Le Theusseret* (☎032 951 14 51; closed Wed & Dec–Feb), just uphill from Goumois, is an atmospheric restaurant in an old mill beside a weir, specializing in fresh local produce and melt-in-the-mouth fish (*menus* from Fr.23). *Restaurant Georges Wenger* in Le Noirmont (☎032 957 66 33, ⓦwww.georges-wenger.ch; closed Mon & Tues & Jan) has won national acclaim; the fresh, locally inspired cuisine has two Michelin stars, while the hotel embraces a handful of classic, individually styled guest rooms (➏–➐).

Travel details

Full timetables for all trains, buses, trams, boats and cable cars in Switzerland – as well as international connections – are searchable at ⓦwww.rail.ch.

Trains

Biel/Bienne to: Basel (twice hourly; 1hr 5min); Bern (3 hourly; 25min); La Chaux-de-Fonds (twice hourly; 40min); Delémont (hourly; 30min); Lausanne (hourly; 1hr); Neuchâtel (3 hourly; 15min); Solothurn (4 hourly; 15min); Yverdon (twice hourly; 35min).

Delémont to: Basel (twice hourly; 30min); Biel/Bienne (hourly; 30min); Neuchâtel (hourly; 50min); Porrentruy (twice hourly; 25min); St-Ursanne (hourly; 20min).

Murten/Morat to: Bern (hourly; 35min); Fribourg (hourly; 25min); Payerne (hourly; 20min).

Neuchâtel to: Bern (twice hourly; 35min); Biel/Bienne (3 hourly; 15min); La Chaux-de-Fonds (twice hourly; 30min); Delémont (hourly; 50min); Geneva (hourly; 1hr 10min); Lausanne (hourly; 40min); Porrentruy (twice hourly; 1hr 25min); Solothurn (twice hourly; 40min); Yverdon (twice hourly; 20min); Zürich (hourly; 1hr 30min).

Yverdon to: Biel/Bienne (twice hourly; 35min); Estavayer (hourly; 15min); Fribourg (hourly; 55min); Geneva (hourly; 50min); Neuchâtel (twice hourly; 20min); Sainte-Croix (hourly; 35min).

Buses

Avenches to: Estavayer (4 daily; 45min); Fribourg (8 daily; 25min).

La Chaux-de-Fonds to: Le Locle (every 30min; 25min).

Orbe to: Croy-Romainmôtier (3 daily; 10min).

Yverdon to: Orbe (hourly; 25min); Vallorbe (11 daily; 30min).

Boats

Following is a summary of June–Sept summer services; fewer boats run in other months, generally Sat & Sun only, if at all. Full details at ⓦwww.navig.ch & www.bielersee.ch.

Biel/Bienne to: Erlach & St Petersinsel (at least 3 daily; 45min–1hr); Neuchâtel (2 daily except Mon; 2hr 20min); Murten/Morat (1 daily; 2hr 50min); Solothurn/Soleure (at least 4 daily except Mon; 2hr 30min).

Estavayer-le-Lac to: Neuchâtel (at least 3 daily except Mon; 1hr 30min); Yverdon (at least 3 daily except Mon; 1hr 25min).

Murten/Morat to: Biel/Bienne (1 daily; 3hr 45min); Neuchâtel (at least 4 daily; 1hr 40min).

Neuchâtel to: Biel/Bienne (at least 1 daily; 2hr 20min); Estavayer (at least 3 daily except Mon; 1hr 35min); Murten/Morat (at least 4 daily; 1hr 45min).

Yverdon to: Estavayer (at least 3 daily except Mon; 1hr 25min).

4

Basel and around

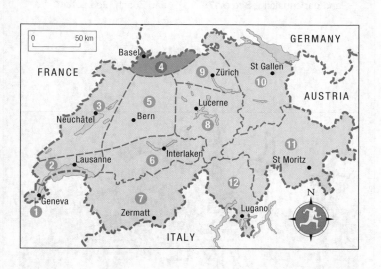

CHAPTER 4 # Highlights

✴ **Fasnacht** Basel's carnival, an exultant three days of music, parades and merry-making. See p.174

✴ **The Münster** Highlight of a cathedral visit is a peaceful stroll around the adjoining cloisters. See p.175

✴ **Basler Papiermühle** Delightful little riverside museum devoted to printing and papermaking. See p.178

✴ **Museum Tinguely** A stunning home for the mechanical sculptures of Switzerland's best-loved artist. See p.178

✴ **Fondation Beyeler** Basel's best gallery, where the architecture sets off the modernist art within to serene effect. See p.178

✴ **Baden** Attractive provincial town partway between Basel and Zürich. See p.184

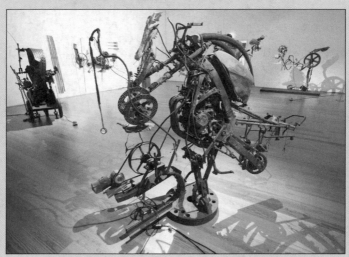

▲ Sculptures at the Museum Tinguely

Basel and around

ou might expect **BASEL** (**Bâle** in French, and often anglicized to **Basle**), situated on the Rhine exactly where Switzerland, Germany and France touch noses, to be the focal point of the continent, humming with pan-European idealism. It's not quite that – but Basel's voters are the most fervently pro-European of all Switzerland's German-speakers and their enthusiasm for close neighbourly relations has palpably energized the city in recent years, drawing what was formerly an introverted place out of its shell. The success of Basel's international airport and new high-speed rail links to Strasbourg, Paris, Frankfurt and Milan have helped to blow the cobwebs away. Basel is a city rejuvenated.

Its historic centre, dominated by the soaring **Münster**, is definitely worth seeing, but with a long history of banking excellence, a major port on the Rhine – Switzerland's only outlet to the sea – and the research headquarters of several pharmaceutical multinationals, Basel still cherishes its reputation as Switzerland's wealthiest city. Yet, oddly, what's made the biggest difference has been the city's resolutely high taxes: recent years have seen an exodus of the rich to the lower-tax haven of the Fricktal in nearby Canton Aargau. In their place have come artists, young professionals and, most notably, international expats: the Swiss pharmaceuticals giant Novartis recently created forty thousand new jobs in Basel, helping to draw new lifeblood into the city.

In short, business is booming. New restaurants with fresh ideas are springing up all over town and the city's long-standing patronage of the arts has resulted in dozens of first-rate **museums and galleries**. Three annual events above all define the city for different markets. Every June the art fair **Art Basel** is one of contemporary art's highest-profile gatherings, with world-famous artists, dealers and wannabes packing the city amid glitzy shows and events. **BaselWorld** every March is the most prestigious jamboree in the more traditionally Swiss world of watchmaking and jewellery. Expect every hotel room in the city to be taken at these times.

But the most accessible is the extraordinary annual carnival, **Fasnacht**, held in the week after Ash Wednesday – see p.174 for full details. For the spectacle and the partying, Fasnacht alone merits a special trip to Basel.

Some history

A **Celtic** town stood on the hill now occupied by Basel's cathedral in the first century BC, but the city is traditionally dated to 44 BC, when the nearby Roman city of Augusta Raurica (see p.184) was also founded. By 374 AD, **Basilia** was seat of a bishopric. In 1225, Bishop Heinrich II of Thun built the first **bridge** across the Rhine – ancestor of today's Mittlere Brücke – which

Dr Hofmann's problem child

It was a Friday afternoon, April 16, 1943, in the laboratories of one of Basel's major pharmaceutical companies, Sandoz. The 37-year-old **Dr Albert Hofmann**, who had worked for Sandoz for fourteen years, was doing research into the various properties of rye fungus in a search for a cure for migraine. During the afternoon he began to feel peculiar, and went home to lie down. "With eyes closed," he wrote, "I perceived an uninterrupted stream of fantastic pictures, extraordinary shapes with intense, kaleidoscopic play of colours." Unwittingly, Dr Hofmann had taken the first ever acid trip: he had synthesized lysergic acid diethylamide, or **LSD**, from the fungus and had absorbed the drug through his fingertips.

After the weekend, he decided to experiment on himself with more scientific precision. This time, though, his apprehension at exploring an untested area of pharmacology led to unforeseen paranoias. "A demon had invaded me," he later wrote. Thinking that milk would act as an antidote to the drug, he knocked on his neighbour's door to ask for some, only to discover that "she was no longer Mrs R., but rather a malevolent, insidious witch." He took to his bed. Next morning, though, he wrote, "breakfast gave me extraordinary pleasure… [and] the garden glistened and sparkled."

Dr Hofmann continued his quiet work into the psychoactive properties of both LSD and other **hallucinogens**, while the drug itself – his so-called "problem child" – escaped the confines of the laboratory. A small band of writers were attracted to LSD: Aldous Huxley's *Doors of Perception* (1954) is probably the most famous creative work to stem from experiments with mescalin, an LSD derivative. Underground tests on volunteers by the British and American military were so dramatic that subsequent top-secret reports suggested that if LSD could be deployed in a missile fired at the Soviet Union, it could at a stroke put the entire Red Army out of action.

Massive controversy persists as to the medical uses of LSD and other hallucinogens such as cannabis. In 1993 Dr Hofmann told the British *Independent* newspaper: "LSD is not addictive, it is not toxic. The danger is this very deep change in consciousness: it can be beautiful, it can be terrifying. The next step is that it should be put into the hands of the psychiatrists. Fifty years' experience is nothing. For a substance which exhibits such new and extraordinary properties you must have much longer."

Those hopes might yet be realized. To celebrate Dr Hofmann's 100th birthday in 2006, Basel staged an international symposium on LSD, as a prelude to the restart of clinical studies in the US under the auspices of the Multidisciplinary Association for Psychedelic Study (🌐 www.maps.org). Dr Hofmann died in 2008, but his "problem child" lives on.

coincided with the opening of a road over the Gotthard Pass into Italy, thus ensuring Basel's continuing growth as a natural focus for trade.

For almost twenty years (1431–49), the ecumenical **Council of Basel** pushed the city into the European limelight, as the Church set about reforming itself; Pope Felix V was crowned in Basel in 1440 as merchants, philosophers, emperors, princes and bishops flocked in, spurring the growth of papermaking, printing, and the development of ideas and trade. In 1460 Pope Pius II founded Basel's **university**, Switzerland's oldest and a major centre for humanism – home to the philosopher **Erasmus of Rotterdam** in the 1520s and 1530s.

During the following century, Protestant refugees from France, Flanders and Italy expanded Basel's industries. In 1831, disaffected residents in the rural communities around Basel launched a **rebellion** against the city oligarchs and after a brief civil war managed to secede, forming their own half-canton of Basel-Land (countryside), separate to this day from Basel-Stadt (city).

Throughout the nineteenth century, industrial growth spurred construction of huge **port** facilities on the Rhine, which still handle a large proportion of Swiss import/export trade. But Basel is best known these days as a centre of both banking and chemical industry: the companies which started out dyeing silk ribbons woven by Huguenot refugees centuries ago are now the world's largest **pharmaceutical** companies, with their headquarters and laboratory facilities still in Basel.

Arrival and information

Basel has two **train stations** straddling three countries. **Basel SBB** is the main one; most of it is in Switzerland, although platforms 30–36 at the far end, used by trains to and from France, form an area known as **Bâle SNCF** which is in French territory, divided from the main concourse by passport control. Lots of trams pass through Centralbahnplatz outside the main doors; trams #8 and #11 run to Barfüsserplatz and the city centre. Some fast trains from Germany serve Basel SBB, but others stop short at Basel Badischer Bahnhof (**Basel Bad.** for short), run by Deutsche Bahn (DB) and located within an enclave of German territory in Kleinbasel; passport control separates the platforms from the ticket hall. Tram #6 from outside runs to Barfüsserplatz.

The **airport** (Ⓦ www.euroairport.com) is 5km north in France, shared between Basel (Switzerland), Mulhouse (France) and Freiburg (Germany). A special customs-free fenced road links the Swiss terminal with Switzerland proper, along which express bus #50 shuttles frequently all day to and from Basel SBB station (takes 15min); if you don't have a Swiss Pass, buy a ticket for Fr.8. A taxi into the centre costs about Fr.45.

By **car**, the Basel-City *autobahn* exit delivers you directly to parking at SBB station, but car parks in Basel-Nord at the Messe and beneath Basel Bad. station are less outrageously priced – or try short-term car park S5 at the airport (Fr.16.50 for 24hr).

The main **tourist office** is in the city centre, in the Stadtcasino on Barfüsserplatz (Mon–Fri 8.30am–6.30pm, Sat 9am–5pm, Sun 10am–4pm; ☎061 268 68 68, Ⓦ www.basel.com), with a branch office inside the main SBB train station (Mon–Fri 8.30am–6.30pm, Sat 9am–5pm, Sun 9am–4pm). The **BaselCard** (Fr.20/27/35 for 24/48/72 hours) covers free entry to all the city's museums, plus Augusta Raurica and the Vitra museum, free guided walking tours, free ferry rides, discounts at restaurants, bars and clubs, and more. You'll find listings and cultural information in the *Basler Zeitung* newspaper.

City transport and tours

If you don't already have a Swiss Pass, pick up a free **Mobility Ticket** when you check into your hotel: it gives free tram and bus travel throughout Basel for the duration of your stay (not valid to/from the airport).

Basel's public transport – run by BVB (Ⓦ www.bvb.ch), part of the TNW Tarifverbund Nordwestschweiz (Ⓦ www.tnw.ch) – focuses on **trams**, virtually

A **Swiss Pass** (see p.35) is valid for free city transport in Basel and free admission to almost all museums reviewed in this book.

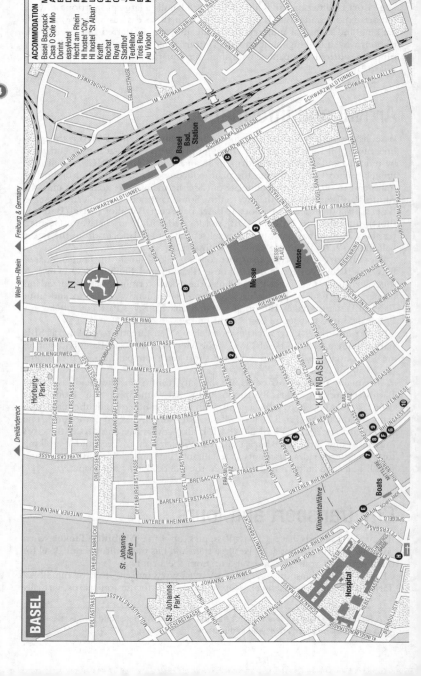

BASEL

ACCOMMODATION	
Basel Backpack	M
Casa O Sole Mio	A
Dorint	B
easyHotel	D
Hecht am Rhein	F
HI hostel 'City'	N
HI hostel 'St Alban'	L
Krafft	G
Rochat	C
Royal	J
Stadthof	H
Teufelhof	I
Trois Rois	E
Au Violon	K

EATING & DRINKING

Acqua	27
Atlantis	25
Bar Rouge	3
Bird's Eye	19
Café Damas	20
Café Spitz	8
Fischerstube	10
Fumare non fumare	15
Les Garçons	1
Gifthüttli	13
Grenzwert	9
Hirscheneck	11
KaBar	5
Küchlin	23
Kunsthalle	22
Kuppel	27
Manora	6
Mr Wong	21
Noohn	24
Paddy Reilly's	26
Parterre	4
Pfalz	17
RhyWyera	7
Stucki	28
Teufelhof	1
Au Violon	K
Wilhelm Tell	14
Zum Goldenen Fass	2
Zum Goldenen Sternen	18
Zum Isaak	16
Zum Roten Engel	12

Rhine

Solitude Park

Museum Tinguely

St. Alban-Fähre

Basler Papiermühle

St Alban-Tor

Museum für Gegenwartskunst

Münsterfähre

Kunstmuseum

Antiken Museum

Münster

Museum der Kulturen & Naturhistorisches Museum

Historisches Museum

Martins-kirche

Rathaus

Kunsthalle

Theatre

Peterskirche

University

Leonhardskirche

Puppenhaus-museum

Jüdisches Museum

Spalentor

Airport Bus

Bâle SNCF

Basel SBB Station

Rosenfeld Park

▲ Airport & France

▲ M & N

4

BASEL AND AROUND

500 m

0

all of which pass through Barfüsserplatz. Swiss Pass holders travel **free**; otherwise, a short-hop ticket costs Fr.1.90, a cross-town journey Fr.3, a suburban ride Fr.3.80 or a day pass Fr.8. Ticket machines take Swiss coins and euros, but rarely notes. Basel's **taxis** are ferociously expensive.

Ferries

There are three city-centre bridges, but a more fun way to cross the Rhine – and a method used by many locals – is on one of the traditional **cable-ferries** (ⓦ www.faehri.ch). The most useful, from north to south, are the *Vogel Gryff*, or Klingentalfähre; the *Leu*, or Münsterfähre; and the *Wild Maa*, or St Alban-Fähre. All three run continuously during the day, with restricted hours in winter. A ride costs Fr.1.60.

The **ferry** company Basler Personenschifffahrt (ⓣ 061 639 95 00, ⓦ www .bpg.ch) runs several eat-aboard **cruises** as well as scheduled boats to nearby points on the Rhine (May–Oct only), including a round trip to the German border at Dreiländereck and longer journeys east to Kaiseraugst and Rhein-felden. Boats depart from Schifflände in the city centre, where there's a ticket booth (April–Oct Tues–Fri 9am–6.30pm, Sat 9.30am–4pm, Sun 9am–2.30pm; rest of year Mon–Fri 11am–6pm).

Tours

Guided **walking tours** of the Old Town start from the tourist office (May–Oct Mon–Sat 2.30pm; Fr.15; takes 2hr). Otherwise, you can follow any of five **self-guided** historical wanders, all starting from Marktplatz (corner of Sattelgasse) and marked by small blue information signs: the Erasmus Walk (red on blue; 30min); Burckhardt Walk (light blue on blue; 45min); Platter Walk (yellow on blue; 45min); Paracelsus Walk (grey on blue; 1hr); or Holbein Walk (green on blue; 1hr 30min). Enhance your wanderings with the **iGuide**, a handheld device with pictures and sound (Fr.15 for 4hr; Fr.22 per day). Alternatively, roll through the city for an hour on a restored **vintage tram**, with an English commentary describing highlights; the ride

▲ Cable ferry on the Rhine

starts in front of the SBB train station (Sun 10.30 & 11.30am; Fr.20; reserve at the tourist office). For something a little different opt for one of the tourist office's **tours by Segway** (4 people minimum; book one day ahead; driving licence needed) – around the Old Town (Fr.90 per person; 1hr 30min) or further afield (Fr.120 per person; 2hr 30min).

Accommodation

Basel thrives on the conference and convention trade: the Messe in Kleinbasel is Switzerland's largest exhibition centre, and attendees to major events often fill all **accommodation** in the city (and most in neighbouring cities too). Reserving ahead is strongly advised. Basel's hoteliers tend to focus more on providing comforting extras, such as minibars and big-screen cable TV, than on character. You'll also find prices hiked during the week and/or while a big trade fair is on. The **B&B Agency Basel** (T061 702 21 51, W www.bbbasel.ch) controls 150 inexpensive private rooms and furnished apartments in and around the city. All hotels, hostels and guesthouses offer overnight guests a **free Mobility Ticket**, covering city transport (see p.167). All our recommendations are keyed on the map on p.168.

Hostels

Basel Backpack (SB hostel) Dornacherstrasse 192 T061 333 00 37, W www.baselbackpack.ch. Friendly, independent hostel about 10min walk behind the main SBB train station, with a mix of rooms and dorms. ❶
Jugendherberge Basel City (HI hostel) Pfeffingerstrasse 8 T061 365 99 60, W www .youthhostel.ch. Fresh, modern hostel with rooms

and dorms, located 2min walk behind the SBB train station. March–Oct. ❶
Jugendherberge Basel St Alban (HI hostel) St Alban-Kirchrain 10 T061 272 05 72, W www .youthhostel.ch. Pleasant riverside hostel – quiet, spotless and well run. Now in sparkling condition after a top-to-toe refit completed in 2010. ❶

Hotels

Inexpensive

Casa O Sole Mio Gatternweg 41, Riehen T061 641 54 16, W www.basel-bed-breakfast.ch. Fine

B&B on the outskirts (tram #6 to Pfaffenloh), decorated in Laura Ashley style, with three separate two-room apartments, a studio apartment,

---

Basel's festivals

Basel's huge **carnival**, Fasnacht (see p.174), held over three days from the Monday following Mardi Gras, attracts attention from all over Switzerland, as does January's **Vogel Gryff** festival, centred specifically on Kleinbasel (see p.177).

The most prestigious of the city's many events is **Art Basel** (W www.artbasel.com), the largest contemporary art fair in the world, held at the Messe in mid-June. Although more trade- than public-oriented, it's fascinating to attend (tickets are around Fr.30 per day), with major galleries exhibiting a range of work and many arty happenings staged citywide.

The night before the Swiss National Day – **July 31** – sees a festival of folk music on the Rhine, with stalls, traditional foods and a huge fireworks display, and the last Saturday in October marks the start of Basel's two-week **Autumn Fair**, Europe's longest-running traditional fair, held without a break since 1471 and now comprising funfairs and street jollity.

and five B&B rooms, all demonstrating the kind of personal touch no hotel can manage. Keen prices, large breakfasts and free use of bikes make this an excellent choice. ❸

easyHotel Riehenring 109 ☎0900 327 927, Ⓦwww.easyhotel.com. Reliably good-value budget chain hotel. You get a tiny room with a double bed, a shower, toilet and washbasin, and one towel per person; everything else, including food, drinks, TV and housekeeping, costs extra. Most rooms have windows; those that don't have a/c. ❶

Hecht am Rhein Rheingasse 8 ☎061 690 15 15, Ⓦwww.hotelbasel.ch. Unfussy little one-star, priced a touch high for the superb riverside location. ❷

Rochat Petersgraben 23 ☎061 261 81 40, Ⓦwww.hotelrochat.ch. Central two-star option beside the Peterskirche, with pleasant, if generic, rooms and a modestly cosy atmosphere. ❸–❹

Stadthof Gerbergasse 84 ☎061 261 87 11, Ⓦwww.stadthof.ch. Plain and simple little hotel, bang on the main shopping drag (and so prone to noise). No en-suite rooms. ❷–❸

🎿 **Au Violon** Im Lohnhof 4 ☎061 269 87 11, Ⓦwww.au-violon.com. Once a convent, then a women's prison, this is now beautifully renovated to offer comfortable, stylish rooms above a quiet Old Town courtyard. Service is faultless. ❸

Mid-range and expensive

Dorint Schönaustrasse 10 ☎061 695 70 00, Ⓦwww.dorint.com. Excellent business hotel in Kleinbasel's Messe district: the surrounding streets are dull, but the comfortable rooms compensate with multi-channel TV and hi-tech bathrooms. Onsite parking is an added bonus. Discounts for early booking and/or weekend stays. ❹–❻

Krafft Rheingasse 12 ☎061 690 91 30, Ⓦwww.krafftbasel.ch. Atmospheric old pile on the Kleinbasel waterfront which has had a complete makeover: rooms are now swish and elegant, with contemporary, minimalist styling. Riverside rooms are pricier. ❺–❻

Royal Schwarzwaldallee 179 ☎061 686 55 55, Ⓦwww.royal-hotel.ch. Unusually good-value four-star, opposite the Basel Bad. (German) train station. The unremarkable exterior preludes swish, contemporary interiors, with bright colours, clean lines and good use of space. ❹–❺

🎿 **Teufelhof** Leonhardsgraben 47 ☎061 261 10 10, Ⓦwww.teufelhof.com. Outstanding boutique hotel in the heart of the city centre. The prestigious "Kunsthotel" section has eight rooms, redecorated every two or three years by a different artist; if you're prepared to do without minibars or TVs, you get the opportunity to live inside a work of art. The "Galeriehotel" bit, with 25 rooms, is less lavishly done up, and so less expensive, but still reworked annually by a local artist. A breath of fresh air compared with Basel's standard business hotels. ❻–❽

Trois Rois Blumenrain 8 ☎061 260 50 50, Ⓦwww.lestroisrois.com. The oldest hotel in Europe, which began life as a small inn in 1026; that year it hosted Emperor Conrad II, his son Heinrich (later Heinrich III) and Rudolf III of Burgundy – the three kings of the title – who met to thrash out the details of Switzerland's absorption into the German Empire. These days, having received most of the crowned heads of Europe over the past millennium, it's still the haunt of presidents and royalty – who of course occupy the beautiful Rhineside suites. ❾

The City

The River **Rhine** describes an elegant curve through the centre of Basel, flowing from east to north and dividing the city in two. On the south/west bank is **GROSSBASEL** (Greater Basel), focused on the historic Old Town. Shopping streets connect **Barfüsserplatz** and **Marktplatz**, the two main Old Town squares, while medieval charm is retained in the steep lanes leading off to either side, where you'll find leafy courtyards surrounded by sixteenth-century town houses, medieval churches and the majestic steepled **Münster** dominating the skyline from its Rhineside terrace. The Old Town and surrounding districts comprise the main business, shopping and nightlife areas of the city.

On the north/east bank of the Rhine is down-to-earth **KLEINBASEL** (Lesser Basel), more residential and less historical than its neighbour, with some laid-back nightlife around Claraplatz diluting the weighty presence of the giant Messe conference centre nearby.

The **international border** with France is on the west bank of the Rhine, about 2km north of the city centre. The border with Germany is on the east bank, about 3km north of the centre.

Barfüsserplatz and around

The focus of the Old Town is **Barfüsserplatz**, crisscrossed by trams and surrounded by terrace cafés. Rubbing shoulders with the fast-food joints and raucous pubs, on the corner with Steinenvorstadt, is the **Yellow House**, designed by Roger Diener, a yellowish concrete building adored by architects but ignored by the general public. Across the way is the **Puppenhausmuseum** (Doll's House Museum; daily 10am–6pm; Fr.7; ⓦwww.puppenhausmuseum .ch), with displays of doll's houses and plenty of venerable old teddy bears.

Historisches Museum

Overlooking Barfüsserplatz are the soaring, pointed-arch windows of the **Barfüsserkirche**. This elegant white church, built by and named after the bare-footed Franciscans, dates from the fourteenth century, was deconsecrated in the eighteenth, and is now home to the **Historisches Museum** (Tues–Sun 10am–5pm; Fr.7; ⓦwww.hmb.ch), devoted to documenting Basel's cultural pre-eminence during the Middle Ages. Restoration work was ongoing at the time of writing; the layout when you visit may be different from what's described here.

Once you've absorbed the detail of the monumental **choir stall** (1598) facing into the church, the highlight of the ground floor is the collection of sumptuous fifteenth-century **tapestries** (press the button to raise the protective blind shielding each one). These vivid, wall-sized pieces were woven to decorate private houses and churches, specifically in Basel and Strasbourg, and are excep-tionally rare, both for their artistic quality and their excellent condition. Only three of the sixteen pieces show religious imagery – and one of the best is no. 235 (from 1490), the allegorical *Garden of Love*, showing two lovers playing cards inside a summer pavilion. The man has just slapped down a card with the words, "That last play of yours was a good one", while the woman nods in anticipatory triumph: "And it's won me the game!"

Downstairs you'll find an excellent detailed survey of Basel's history, including a board locating ancient buildings, maps and globes galore, the original 1640 **Lällekeenig** (see p.174), and bedchambers and elaborate wood-panelled rooms from the seventeenth century. Head to the back to see the **treasury** of Basel cathedral, including two silver-and-copper busts dating from 1270–1325, of St Pantalus (no. 251) and, with an almond-eyed gaze, a Buddhic St Ursula (no. 253). Another highlight is a series of paintings showing the **Dance of Death**, originally part of a sixty-metre-long mural covering the inside of the cemetery wall of Basel's Dominican convent until its demolition in 1805. The mural depicts, in a graphic reminder of human mortality, people of all different ages and professions on a macabre procession, which leads, eventually, to the cemetery's charnel house.

Marktplatz and around

Shop-lined Gerbergasse and Freiestrasse, as well as a dense network of narrow, sloping medieval alleys such as Schneidergasse (Tailor Street), Sattelgasse (Saddle Street) and Imbergässlein (Ginger Alley), run north from Barfüsserplatz to **Marktplatz**, the Old Town's other main square, crowded every morning with fruit-and-veg stalls. Lighting up the broad rectangular space with a splash of

Basel Fasnacht

Basel is famous for its ancient masked carnival, or **Fasnacht** (🕸 www.fasnacht.ch), a three-day affair starting on the Monday after Ash Wednesday.

Some history

The earliest documented record of the carnival is from 1376, although celebrations undoubtedly date back to well before that (earlier city records were destroyed in a fire in 1356). In the fourteenth century, carnival took the form of **knightly tournaments** held on Münsterplatz. Through the **Middle Ages**, theologians railed against both excessive drinking at carnival time and the use of devilish masks and disguises: it's no coincidence that the iconoclasm which marked the beginning of Basel's Reformation broke out on Mardi Gras (Shrove Tuesday), 1529. Over time, celebrations drifted one week later (Basel still celebrated carnival despite its embrace of Protestantism after the Reformation), and were transformed into a series of **processions** organized by the city's guilds. Drum-and-pipe bands accompanied the display of weaponry, dancing and fancy-dress revelry. The carnival of today sees some 12,000 people take part under the auspices of several hundred **Cliques**, groups or musical bands, which must apply in advance to the Fasnachts-Comité for permission to march.

The night before

On the Sunday after Mardi Gras, thousands of *Fasnächtler* kick off their celebrations in **Liestal**, 17km south of Basel, where the **Chienbesen** parade centres on giant mobile bonfires, flames as high as the houses and people crammed shoulder to shoulder brandishing flaming torches. The tradition dates back to at least the sixteenth century, but it's been dogged by controversy – from the Church, which once regarded it as diabolic, and more recently from the fire service. Despite the raging inferno dragged through Liestal's narrow streets each year, no harm has yet been done. Neighbouring **Sissach** has similar fiery revels, with the torching of a 10m-high effigy, the Chluris, while in **Biel-Benken** people fling burning wooden discs into the night sky in an equally mesmeric fire-orgy termed the Reedlischigge.

eye-catching colour is the elaborate scarlet facade of the **Rathaus** (Town Hall), its central arcaded section sixteenth-century, the tower and side annexe both late nineteenth-century. Feel free to wander into the frescoed interior courtyard.

At the northern end of Marktplatz is the small **Fischmarkt**, with its central fountain, just beyond which is **Schifflände** at the southern end of the **Mittlere Brücke**, a modern construction at the site of what was for centuries the only bridge over the Rhine between the Bodensee (Lake Constance) and the North Sea. On a facade looking along the bridge, you'll spot an odd little bust of a bearded man: this is the **Lällekeenig**, or Tongue King. The original adorned the gate of the bridge from the mid-seventeenth century, greeting arrivals to the city until the gate's demolition in 1839, and had a clockwork motor so that he rolled his eyes and stuck out his tongue in time with the ticking. He was probably made to demonstrate what Grossbaslers thought of their down-at-heel Kleinbasel neighbours, but these days the city is united, the clockwork original is in the Historisches Museum, and the Lällekeenig staring along the bridge is a static copy.

From Marktplatz and Fischmarkt, quiet old lanes climb steeply west towards the former city walls; up here is the Gothic **Peterskirche** (Tues–Sun 10am–5pm) on Petersgraben, the plain exterior of which harbours late-medieval frescoes. The narrow Spalenvorstadt leads west to the **Spalentor**, most elaborate of the surviving city gates, with massive wooden doors and a huge

Morgestraich, Schnitzelbängg and Guggemuusige

Well after midnight, everyone decamps back to Basel in preparation for the **Morgestraich**, a parade of huge illuminated lanterns through the city centre which begins in invariably freezing darkness at 4am on the Monday morning. From lunch time, masked *Cliques* parade through the city in a **Cortège**, with much music, dancing and jollity, followed in the evening by masked bands and small groups of drummers and fife-players roving through the Old Town. The ornately decorated Morgestraich lanterns are displayed in Münsterplatz from Monday evening through to Wednesday morning.

Baslers take their costumes seriously (half-masks and face paint are taboo), and many people spend weeks making huge, cartoonish papier-mâché heads and sewing lavish jester-like costumes. However, it's a feature of Basel's carnival that unless you're part of a performing *Clique*, you have to remain an **observer** – unlike, for instance, in Lucerne, where carnival is an all-in street party. You're encouraged to contribute to the *Cliques'* expenses by buying a **Blaggedde**, a metal badge produced each year in various denominations; get them on the street, from kiosks and hotels, or the tourist office. You'll come across places selling *Fasnachtsküchli*, a thin round cake covered in icing sugar, and *Fastenwähe*, a kind of caraway-seed pretzel.

During the Monday and Wednesday evenings, it's a tradition for locals to recite **Schnitzelbängg**, satirical verses directed at local bigwigs, in the city's taverns and restaurants. Tuesday night sees **Guggemuusige** concerts of comical oompah, played on old and dented brass instruments by bands gathered in Barfüsser-, Clara- and Marktplatz. Musical groups and masked *Cliques* continue to prowl through the Old Town until nightfall on Wednesday – whereupon everybody turns in.

If you're serious about attending, get hold of Peter Habicht's excellent book *Lifting The Mask* (see p.512), the most evocative description in English of the topsy-turvy few days, replete with personal anecdotes.

portcullis. The small **Jüdisches Museum der Schweiz**, Kornhausgasse 8 (Jewish Museum; Mon & Wed 2–5pm, Sun 11am–5pm; free; Ⓦwww .juedisches-museum.ch), has interesting historical items and an excellent short video (in English) on the history of the Jews in Basel.

Both Leonhardsgraben and the lovely Heuberg trickle on through an old residential quarter to the beautiful **Leonhardskirche**, a Gothic construction built after the 1356 earthquake with portholed windows and an elaborate cat's cradle of vaulting within. The gallery is accessible, but only up the tightest, narrowest spiral staircase imaginable.

The Münster

Sixteenth-century lanes lead up behind Barfüsserplatz to Basel's cathedral, the impressive **Münster** (Easter–Oct Mon–Fri 10am–5pm, Sat 10am–4pm, Sun 1–5pm; rest of year Mon–Sat 11am–4pm, Sun 2–4pm), built in the thirteenth century of red sandstone with a patterned roof and rebuilt following an earthquake in 1356. The tower of St George, on the left of the main frontage, has some white stonework dating from the original church (consecrated in 1019), as well as a thirteenth-century statue of the saint impaling a dragon. Stone carving from 1280 above the main portal shows the cathedral's founder, Emperor Heinrich II, holding a model of the church, with his wife Kunigunde to the left. To the right is a Foolish Virgin with her Satanic seducer.

Inside, the north aisle holds the tomb of the Renaissance humanist Erasmus. Close by is the **St Vincent panel**, a Romanesque relief from around 1100 telling the story of the martyr who was killed in 312 AD: on the top left, Vincent speaks up for his bishop and is flogged for it; to the right he is tortured and led into a furnace; below, angels carry his soul to heaven while ravens protect his body before it is dumped at sea, retrieved and buried in a proper tomb. The lacy **pulpit** was carved – incredibly – from a single block of stone in 1486. On the north side of the choir, which has some intricate capitals, is the **tomb of Queen Anna**, wife of Rudolf of Habsburg, who chose to be buried in Basel alongside her three-year-old son Karl in an attempt to make up for her husband's cruelty whilst ruling the town during the 1270s. In the crypt you'll find ninth-century remains of an earlier cathedral along with some late-Romanesque frescoes.

One of the highlights of Basel is a wander through the memorably atmospheric **cloisters** adjoining the cathedral to the south, filled with timeworn tombs. You emerge onto the **Pfalz**, an open, tree-lined terraced bastion behind the cathedral choir which overlooks the Rhine. Carved elephants and grotesque creatures support the external arches of the choir, and round the corner, on the north side of the church, is the **St Gallus Doorway**, a rich piece of Romanesque carving, with Christ at top centre.

Tranquil alleys run northwest from Münsterplatz, amongst them Augustinergasse, with, at no. 2, the **Museum der Kulturen** (Tues–Sun 10am–5pm; Fr.7; Ⓦwww.mkb.ch) housing a massive anthropological collection, and, separately in the same building, the equally daunting **Naturhistorisches Museum** (same hours and ticket; Ⓦwww.nmb.bs.ch).

The narrow lane Rheinsprung leads on to the **St Martinskirche** with, beside it, the little **Elftausendjungfern-Gasse**, or Alley of the Eleven Thousand Virgins. Its curious name commemorates the martyrdom in Cologne of St Ursula and her legendary company of female supporters. Follow the tiny lane down to reach the Mittlere Brücke.

▲ Cloisters at the Münster

East of Barfüsserplatz

From Barfüsserplatz, Steinenberg climbs east. A short way up, past the sputtering Tinguely fountain in the grounds of the theatre, is the **Kunsthalle** (Tues–Fri 11am–6pm, Thurs until 8.30pm, Sat & Sun 11am–5pm; Fr.10; ⓦwww .kunsthallebasel.ch), its big white rooms staging a continual flow of cutting-edge contemporary art shows. The same building houses the **Architekturmuseum** (same hours & ticket; ⓦwww.architekturmuseum.ch), showcasing the work of Swiss and international contemporary architects. One of Basel's most impressive recent buildings is the Zentralstellwerk, a giant signal-box sitting beside the train tracks alongside the Münchensteinerbrücke (take tram #10 or #11 from the junction outside the museum a couple of stops past SBB station). Designed by award-winning Swiss architects Herzog and de Meuron, it is a mesmerizing structure encased in shimmering twisted copper sheets.

At the top of Steinenberg, St Alban-Graben heads northeast to the river. The **Antikenmuseum** at no. 5 (Tues–Sun 10am–5pm; Fr.7; ⓦwww.antiken museumbasel.ch) houses superb Greek and Etruscan pottery. The basement holds temporary exhibitions, often of Egyptian or Middle Eastern antiquities.

The Kunstmuseum

Basel's world-famous **Kunstmuseum** is at St Alban-Graben 16 (Tues–Sun 10am–5pm; Fr.15, also gives entry to Museum für Gegenwartskunst; free on 1st Sun of month; ⓦwww.kunstmuseumbasel.ch). It's a rather stern Neoclassical building – all marble floors, high ceilings and grand staircases – but don't let yourself be put off. There's a dazzling array of **twentieth-century art**, including Dalí's nightmarish *Perspectives*, roomfuls of paintings by Arp, Klee, Léger, Munch, Braque and the Impressionists, a fantastically attenuated cat by Giacometti, and fluid sculptures in wood by Kirchner and Scherer. In 1967, the Basel electorate voted to use Fr.6 million of public funds to buy two Picassos for the museum, *Arlequin assis* and *Les deux frères* – and then stumped up another Fr.2.4 million to guarantee the purchase. The artist was so impressed by this popular enthusiasm that he personally donated four more works.

The gallery's modern art, and its large collection of nineteenth-century German, French and Swiss painting, is, however, overshadowed by its vast and absorbing **medieval** collection. Dozens of rooms are devoted to works by the

---

Vogel Gryff

Dating back at least to the thirteenth century, Kleinbasel's strange **Vogel Gryff** festival (ⓦwww.vogel-gryff.ch) incorporates pagan rituals in the guise of fêting the head of one of the three guild associations of Kleinbasel. It takes place on January 13, 20 or 27, depending on which association holds the baton that year. At 11am, a raft carries the **Wild Maa** (a man in a hairy costume symbolizing fertility) down the Rhine to the Mittlere Brücke; he holds an uprooted pine sapling and dances – with his back turned to Grossbasel – to an ancient drum march. The **Leu** (lion) and **Vogel Gryff** (griffon) meet him on the bank to the accompaniment of booming cannon, and at noon the three of them stand at the midpoint of the Mittlere Brücke and dance a traditional, highly ritualized dance to the sound of a drum. Everyone then heads into Kleinbasel for the **Gryffemähli**, a luncheon for the three guilds (where the symbolic dance is repeated), and a procession through the streets accompanied by four jingling jesters who collect money for the poor. The evening is filled with drinking and merrymaking, while the three figures continue to dance their odd and mysterious dance in the older Kleinbasel restaurants.

prolific Holbein family in particular, including the extraordinary two-metre-long *Body of the Dead Christ in the Tomb* (1521), a painting which obsessed Dostoevsky when he visited the museum in 1867. He climbed on a chair to get a better view of it, and then started to yell "Holbein was a great painter and a poet!" His wife, who thought he was about to have a fit, had to usher him from the room. The work subsequently popped up in Dostoevsky's novel *The Idiot*, when a character's recollections of it lead him to question the existence of God.

Down to the river

St Alban-Vorstadt continues east to the **St Alban-Tor**, a thirteenth-century city gate. Nearby, down by the river, is the **Museum für Gegenwartskunst**, St Alban-Rheinweg 60 (Contemporary Art; Tues–Sun 11am–5pm; joint admission with Kunstmuseum), its installations by Frank Stella, Joseph Beuys and others sharing space with recent German painting. An annexe, the **Schaulager** (Ⓦ www.schaulager.org) – a vast concrete box, designed by Herzog and de Meuron, located south of the centre at Ruchfeldstrasse 19 (tram #11) – holds part of the collection in storage, accessible during occasional public shows.

A stroll away, in a restored medieval waterfront mill at St Alban-Tal 37, is the **Basler Papiermühle** (Basel Papermill), housing the wonderful Schweizerisches Papiermuseum (Swiss Museum of Paper, Writing and Printing; Tues–Sun 2–5pm; Fr.12; Ⓦ www.papiermuseum.ch). The waterwheel alongside, remnant of the growth of the industry in the fifteenth century, still functions, and, in amongst exhibits of paper and typography, the museum stages demonstrations of typecasting, typesetting, bookbinding and – most engagingly – papermaking, where you can work through the whole process yourself, from pulp to final product.

A landing-stage across from the mill marks the St Alban ferry *Wild Maa*, which can scoot you across the Rhine to the north bank for the leisurely stroll east along Solitude Promenade to the Tinguely Museum.

Museum Tinguely

On the north bank of the Rhine, in Solitude Park under the Schwarzwald-brücke – and also reached by ferry from Schifflände in the city centre – is the outstanding **Museum Tinguely** (Tues–Sun 11am–7pm; Fr.15; Ⓦ www.tinguely.ch), occupying a building designed by Swiss architect Mario Botta that is a work of art in its own right. Jean Tinguely, who was born in Fribourg in 1925 and died in Bern in 1991, is perhaps Switzerland's best-loved artist, a maverick postmodernist who broadened the confines of static sculpture to incorporate mechanical motion. Living for years on a farm in the Swiss countryside with his long-time partner and fellow artist Niki de St-Phalle, Tinguely used scrap metal, plastic and bits of everyday junk to create room-sized Monty-Pythonesque machines that – with the touch of a foot-button – judder into life, squeaking, clanking and scraping in entertaining parody of the slickness of our modern performance-driven world. Most are imbued with an irreverent sense of humour (*Klamauk*, or Din, is a moving tractor complete with banging bells and cymbals, smoke, smells and fireworks), but some, such as *Mengele Dance of Death*, are darkly apocalyptic. Elsewhere in the city, a Tinguely fountain spits and burbles outside the Kunsthalle.

Fondation Beyeler

If you had to pick just one of Basel's many top-rated museums to visit, go for the gallery run by **Fondation Beyeler**, at Baselstrasse 101 in the northeastern suburb of Riehen (daily 10am–6pm, Wed until 8pm; Fr.25, reduced fee Fr.17

4

One of Basel's curiosities is its location at the meeting point of France, Germany and Switzerland. If you take tram #8 to its terminus amongst the warehouses and shipping cranes at Kleinhüningen, cross to the north bank of the River Wiese, head left 200m to the Rhine, then right (north) along a spit of land beside more warehouses and train sidings for 300m, you'll come to **Dreiländereck** (Three Countries' Corner), marked by a futuristic rounded steel-and-glass building. This is about as far as you can go in Switzerland; ahead is Germany, while the other bank of the Rhine is France. Boats depart from here back to Basel Schifflände.

applies all day Mon and after 5pm on Wed; tram #6; @www.beyeler.com). A masterfully elegant building, designed by Renzo Piano, houses a small but exceptionally high-quality art collection featuring works by some of the twentieth century's best artists – Picasso, Giacometti, Warhol, Rothko, Rodin, Klee, Kandinsky, Bacon, Miró and more. Matisse's paper cutouts (*Nu bleu* and others) and Mondrian's geometric abstractions – familiar from innumerable posters and T-shirts – still have the power to startle as full-size originals.

For some gentle relief, sink into a huge white sofa opposite a giant Monet to indulge in dreamy contemplation both of the waterlilies in front of you and, through the floor-to-ceiling window, the watery gardens outside.

Vitra Design Museum

Across the border in Germany, 10km north of Basel, is the small town of **WEIL-AM-RHEIN**, unremarkable but for being the location of Vitra, a famous design company which collaborates with top international designers to produce office and home furniture, and whose premises – on an out-of-town greenfield site – are the work of some of the world's leading contemporary architects. Design buffs will love the **Vitra Design Museum** (Charles Eames Strasse 2; daily 10am–6pm, Wed until 8pm; €8; @www.design-museum.de). Bus #55 from Claraplatz and Basel Bad. station takes twenty minutes to the museum (passport needed); a ticket costs Fr.3.80 – Swiss passes and the free Mobility Ticket you get from your hotel are not valid.

The building is engaging enough to start with, a teetering, almost Cubist concoction by US architect Frank O. Gehry, while inside are temporary exhibitions on various themes of design, anything from furniture – with original chairs by Frank Lloyd Wright, Charles and Ray Eames, Philippe Starck and others – to lighting or industrial design. It's also possible to join a two-hour guided **architectural tour** of the array of avant-garde buildings comprising the Vitra site (daily 11am, 1pm & 3pm; €9.50, joint ticket with museum €13.50), which includes two factory units by Nicholas Grimshaw, an elegant, award-winning fire station by Zaha Hadid (now used as an extension to the museum), Tadao Ando's serene conference centre and Alvaro Siza's assembly hall.

Eating and drinking

Drawing influences from the cuisines of France and Germany into its native Swiss culinary tradition, Basel deftly manages to sit on the fence as far as **eating and drinking** go. Beer and sausages is the snack of choice, but it's equally possible to find venues in which to savour classic French cuisine and, if the city could be said to have a local speciality, it's salmon (originally plucked from the Rhine but these days more likely to be imported) marinaded in the fruity local white wine and topped with fried onions. All our recommendations are keyed on the map on p.168.

Cafés

There are plenty of **cafés** and *Bierstuben* around Marktplatz and Barfüsserplatz, with nearby Steinenvorstadt also core snacking territory. Perfect accompaniment to a Basel teatime is the local speciality *Leckerli*, a melt-in-the-mouth ginger biscuit made with honey, spices, almonds and candied orange- and lemon-peel: buy over the counter at the *Läckerli-huus* patisserie at Gerbergasse 57 or in *Café Spitz* (see "Restaurants").

Grossbasel

Fumare non fumare Gerbergasse 38 ⓦ www
.mitte.ch. Atmospheric, high-ceilinged espresso
bar on a people-watching junction in the midst
of the city-centre bustle, also with its own beer.
Open late.
Pfalz Münsterberg 11. Tiny, bright nook, with fresh
juices, sandwiches, quiches and a salad buffet.
Closed Sat & Sun.
🏃 **Zum Isaak** Münsterplatz 16 ⓦ www
.zum-isaak.ch. A tranquil, much-loved
tea-drinkers' café by the cathedral that knows its
Darjeeling from its Lapsang Souchong, and also
offers lovingly prepared snacks and full meals. Also
has a courtyard terrace and cellar theatre.
Zum Roten Engel Andreasplatz 15. Cosy den on a
secluded Old Town courtyard, with trestle tables
outside and amiable, alternatively minded regulars

scoffing veggie snacks, fresh juices and full meals
(around Fr.18).

Kleinbasel

Hirscheneck Lindenberg 23 ⓦ www.hirscheneck
.ch. Graffitied budget café-bar-restaurant, co-op
owned and popular with a rough-edged crowd,
offering grungy music and simple food in generous
portions (around Fr.16).
🏃 **KaBar** Klybeckstrasse 1b ⓦ www.kaserne
-basel.ch. An alternative-style café-restaurant
beside a quiet lawn in Kleinbasel, with a minimalist
contemporary styled interior and shady outdoor
tables and benches. Great for a relaxed latte, also
offering light lunch *menus* from Fr.18 and a very
popular weekend brunch buffet. Transforms into a bar
in the evenings, with much the same atmosphere
(gay night Tues from 7pm). Closed Sun.

Restaurants

The host of international visitors to Basel with access to high-end expense accounts pushes up **restaurant** costs, but it's also not hard to uncover cosy local eateries for home-cooked fare in all corners of the city centre. Aside from those reviewed below, you'll find straightforward places on all the main squares, although we've bypassed the clutch of rather stiff restaurants within the big business hotels around the Messe. When there's a major event on, most restaurants abandon their regular day(s) off and stay open all week.

Inexpensive

🏃 **Café Damas** Steinenberg 23. Budget Syrian
restaurant on one side of Barfüsserplatz,
offering takeaway falafel and kebabs as well as
budget-priced fare such as *magloubah* (chicken
with rice) and a range of *mezze* in a comfortable,
friendly setting replete with Arabian-style decor.
Manora Greifengasse 22. Good self-service
restaurant within this chain department store (see
p.44). Mon–Fri 8.30am–8pm, Sat 8am–6pm.

Mr Wong Steinenvorstadt 1a ⓦ www.mister-wong
.ch. Popular fast-food joint just off Barfüsserplatz
that piles your dish high with fresh-cooked Asian
food for Fr.15 or so. There's another branch by the
SBB train station.
Wilhelm Tell Spalenvorstadt 38 ☎ 061 261 15 38.
Cosy, quiet den for solid Swiss fare – *Rösti*,
sausages and more, from Fr.22. Closed Sun.

▲ Zum Goldenen Sternen restaurant

Mid-range

Grossbasel

Atlantis Klosterberg 13 ⓦ www.atlan-tis.ch.
Universally known as "Tis", and one of Basel's
most popular café-bar-restaurant-lounge venues.
Come for the buzz as much as for the proficient but
familiar range of international cuisine; after dark,
the place fills up with a lively, easy-going crowd of
sociable drinkers. Also hosts live bands and DJ
nights. Closed Sat lunch, all day Sun, Mon eve.
Gifthüttli Schneidergasse 11 ⓣ 061 261 16 56,
ⓦ www.gifti.ch. Great place for traditional local
cooking (even the menu is in Basel dialect),
whether in the standard *Stube* downstairs or
the more formal restaurant upstairs. They
specialize in *cordon bleus* – slabs of cheese-
slathered meat – with thirteen choices (around
Fr.33), as well as plenty of other Swiss belt-
bulgers. Closed Sun & Mon.
Küchlin Steinenvorstadt 55 ⓣ 061 205 00 50,
ⓦ www.kuechlin.ch. Classic Basel brasserie
attached to an Art Deco-fronted cinema on one of
the city's busiest shopping streets – prime people-
watching territory. Stop for a coffee or a beer, or
plump for hearty dishes such as steak, rack of
lamb, *escargots* or *Flammkuchen* – an Alsatian *tarte
flambée* of thin pastry topped with cheese and
onions. A blowout will cost Fr.55 or more, but lighter
fare will stay south of that. Closed Sun lunch.
Kunsthalle Steinenberg 7 ⓣ 061 272 42 33,
ⓦ www.restaurant-kunsthalle.ch. Contemporary art
gallery with a leafy terrace café favoured by Basel's

sizeable crowd of arty literati. The restaurant
section is a reliable city-centre choice, open daily,
with bistro fare for around Fr.40.

Noohn Henric Petri-Strasse 12 ⓣ 061 281
14 14, ⓦ www.noohn.ch. Classy lounge and
minimalist restaurant occupying a vast semi-
industrial space on the ground floor of a city-centre
office building – think dark wood, exposed
concrete, lots of black. Come to chill on the sofas,
head up to the roof terrace for cocktails or pick at
the artfully presented Asian fusion-style cuisine.
Very popular. Closed Sun.

Au Violon Im Lohnhof 4 ⓣ 061 269 87 11,
ⓦ www.au-violon.com. Very pleasant
brasserie in a renovated old building near the
Leonhardskirche, offering seasonal specialities
prepared with care. *Menus* from about Fr.35.
Closed Sun & Mon.
Zum Goldenen Sternen St Alban-Rheinweg 70
ⓣ 061 272 16 66, ⓦ www.sternen-basel.ch.
Gracious old riverside wood-beamed inn, perfectly
restored, serving upmarket, old-fashioned French
cuisine in the banqueting room and the waterfront
garden terrace, with a number of highly regarded
fish dishes. Expect to pay Fr.50 and up.

Kleinbasel

Parterre Klybeckstrasse 1b ⓦ www.parterre.net.
Round the corner from *KaBar* (see "Cafés") and in
similar style – fancy-free wooden tables and hearty
home-cooking popular with artists, musicians and

other alternative types. Lunch *menus* under Fr.20; evening *à la carte* roughly double that. Closed Sun.

RhyWyera Unterer Rheinweg 10 ☏ 061 683 32 02, ⓦ www.rhywyera.ch. A play on words (pronounced "riviera", but recalling the Basel dialect word Rhy, meaning the Rhine), this bright, cheery little Mediterranean-style hideaway is located right next to the river, with a beautiful waterfront terrace. Modern art covers the walls and terracotta tiles cover the floor. The place is small: book ahead for

their straightforward dishes of pasta, fish and salads, all carefully prepared and served with a smile. *Menus* around Fr.25. Closed Sun & Mon.

Zum Goldenen Fass Hammerstrasse 108 ☏ 061 693 34 00, ⓦ www.goldenes-fass.ch. Quality formal restaurant with an informal air, in a Kleinbasel residential neighbourhood. Excellent, top-quality organic food, lightly prepared (plus veggie options), for around Fr.45. Open evenings only. Closed Sun & Mon, and July & Aug.

Expensive

Acqua Binningerstrasse 14 ☏ 061 564 66 66, ⓦ www.acquabasilea.ch. Super-trendy contemporary Italian restaurant occupying an ex-industrial space near the station (once a water-purification plant, then a car workshop). There is no sign: head along Binningerstrasse towards the zoo and, opposite the city jail, you'll see a small red Campari sign beside some gates on the right: this is the place. Head inside to rub shoulders with Basel's beautiful people under chandeliers and exposed pipework – and expect to share a table. *Menus* are around Fr.70–80. Closed Sat lunch, Sun & Mon.

Café Spitz In *Hotel Merian*, Rheingasse 2 ☏ 061 685 11 11, ⓦ www.hotel-merian.ch. Historic hotel building in the Kleinbasel district, with a fine riverside terrace and the best fish in Basel, if not Switzerland. Expect upwards of Fr.70.

🏃 **Les Garçons** In Basel Bad. station, Schwarzwaldallee 200 ☏ 061 681 84 88, ⓦ www.lesgarecons.ch. A remarkably good contemporary fusion restaurant in an unlikely location – within an Art Deco railway station (hence the pun: *gare* meaning station, mixed with *garçons* meaning boys), with tables on the forecourt terrace.

Expect a dozen flavours on a single plate: swordfish in purple curry, for instance, or pan-fried organic beef with ginger and noodles, or roasted sardine fillets with lemon, strawberry and rocket. The combination of memorably good food, excellent service and the unusual surroundings makes for a dinner to remember. Expect Fr.70 and up.

Stucki Bruderholzallee 42 ☏ 061 361 82 22, ⓦ www.stuckibasel.ch. One of Switzerland's best-known restaurants, awarded a Michelin star for its classic style and inventive touches. Expect lunch *menus* around Fr.70–80, or Fr.150+ in the evening – if you can book far enough ahead to secure a table, that is. Closed Sun & Mon.

Teufelhof Leonhardsgraben 47 ☏ 061 261 10 10, ⓦ www.teufelhof.com. Gourmet restaurant ("Bel Étage") attached to a super-trendy design hotel. The food is of impeccable quality, although the cuisine is like the art: avant-garde. No classics here, with a constantly changing menu marrying diverse flavours and styles with panache. A broad array of wines by the glass and bottle completes the picture. Expect to pay well over Fr.100 a head. Closed Sat lunch, Sun & Mon.

Bars, clubs and live music

Basel's **nightlife** can be difficult for outsiders to access: even the locals quite often prefer to skip across the border to nearby towns in Germany or France to let their hair down. That said, some of the city's trendier restaurants (see p.180) double up as DJ lounges, and there's a handful of subculture bars to sample.

Grossbasel

Bird's Eye Kohlenberg 20 ⓦ www.birdseye.ch. Great venue for live jazz and/or jazz DJ-ing – very popular, very lively. Around Fr.15. Closed Sun & Mon; June–Aug also closed Tues.

Kuppel Binningerstrasse 14 ⓦ www.kuppel.ch. Loud music venue and club alongside *Acqua* (see "Restaurants"), hosting a broad range of acts.

Paddy Reilly's Steinentorstrasse 45 ⓦ www .paddys.ch. Standard Irish pub, Guinness and all.

Also serving up fish and chips and cottage pie for under Fr.20.

Teufelhof Leonhardsgraben 47 ⓦ www.teufelhof .ch. Trendy wine bar attached to the art-hotel of the same name.

Kleinbasel

Bar Rouge Messeplatz 12 ⓦ www.barrouge.ch. After-work bar on the top (31st) floor of Switzerland's tallest inhabited building, the Messeturm. It has its own street entrance and lifts, round the side of the Ramada Plaza hotel. At the top, you emerge into an eye-catching interior – mainly red (obviously), but also with nicely designed lighting and funky decor. The clientele, like the music, is pretty mainstream but it's an unusual space. Come before sunset for Basel's best views.

🏃 **Fischerstube** Rheingasse 45 ⓦ www .uelibier.ch. Excellent backstreet beerhall, full of atmosphere, that brews its own beers as a snub to the big-name breweries and so attracts dedicated, single-minded drinkers. Salted pretzels hanging from wooden stands on every table, a

dark, smoky interior, rich, powerful beer plus a uniquely hearty clientele make for a memorably convivial evening.

Grenzwert Rheingasse 3 ⓦ www.grenzwert.ch. Cool, jazzy, spotlit little bar, attracting black-clad Kleinbaslers by the score. Closed Sun.

Hirscheneck Lindenberg 23 ⓦ www.hirscheneck .ch. Grungy hardcore, metal and ska acts play at this café-bar venue, generally on weekends.

KaBar Klybeckstrasse 1b ⓦ www.kaserne-basel .ch. Focus of Kleinbasel nightlife, a café-bar with adjacent venue for live bands, DJs, readings and other events. Gay night Tues. Closed Sun.

Entertainment

For **classical music**, the Basel Symphony (ⓦ www.sinfonieorchesterbasel .ch) and Chamber (ⓦ www.kammerorchesterbasel.com) orchestras both perform at the central Stadtcasino, along with a host of guest performers. The Musik–Akademie, Leonhardsstrasse 6 (ⓦ www.musik–akademie.ch), has an international reputation, often presenting concerts and recitals from students and visiting soloists.

Basel's main draw is its burgeoning **theatre** scene – universally in German. The celebrated Baseldytschi Bihni, Im Lohnhof 4 (ⓦ www.baseldytschibihni .ch), can provide an entertaining but truly incomprehensible evening of drama in the local dialect.

Listings

Bike rental At the station (see p.51).

Books Bergli Bookshop, Rümelinsplatz 19 ⓦ www .bergli.ch, near Marktplatz, is the hub of Basel's sizeable English-speaking community, with a broad range of books in English, community information and regular events. Bider & Tanner, Aeschenvorstadt 2, is the city's top bookshop, a multi-department outlet with a diverse English-language section.

Flight enquiries ☏ 061 325 31 11, ⓦ www .euroairport.com.

Gay and lesbian life The local support group HABS (ⓦ www.habs.ch) has information and links. *KaBar*, Klybeckstrasse 1b, is the place to start: on

Tuesdays (7pm–1am) it transforms into *ZischBar* (ⓦ www.zischbar.ch), a popular lesbian and gay get-together.

Markets Basel's main fruit and veg market is in Marktplatz (Mon–Sat mornings; also Mon, Wed & Fri afternoons); otherwise, check out the flea markets in Barfüsserplatz (2nd & 4th Wed in month) and Petersplatz near the university (Sat).

Medical facilities 24hr emergency room at Kantonsspital Basel Universitätsklinik, Hebelstrasse 30 ☏ 061 265 25 25.

Post office The most central office is on Rüden-gasse, with another near the station.

Around Basel

There's little to stop for in the countryside around Basel, known as the Baselbiet, although you may find yourself having to change trains at **Olten**, in Canton Solothurn, which has a quiet, attractive old quarter. An impressive set of Roman ruins stands on the Rhine at **Augusta Raurica**, while further east, just fifteen minutes from the outskirts of Zürich, is the pleasant spa town of **Baden**.

Augusta Raurica

In its heyday, **AUGUSTA RAURICA** – a Roman Rhineside provincial capital 20km east of Basel near the modern village of **Kaiseraugst** – was home to twenty thousand people. These days it comprises the largest set of Roman ruins in Switzerland, and is an easy day-trip from Basel.

Augusta was founded in 44 BC, in the territory of the Gallic Raurici tribe. Its initial prosperity was ended by an invasion of the Alemanni tribes around 260 AD. Many of its stones were pilfered during the Middle Ages, but it nonetheless still hosts the best-preserved classical theatre north of the Alps, temples, a forum, taverns, many public buildings and more.

Focus of the site is the well-signposted **Römermuseum** (Roman Museum; Glebenacherstrasse 17; Mon 1–5pm, Tues–Sun 10am–5pm; Nov–Feb from 11am; Fr.7; ⓦ www.augusta-raurica.ch). Fight your way through the school parties to take in the finds, which include a reconstruction of a Roman house. Staff can give you a map of the whole site (which is open and **free**): the ruins spread out around the museum and down to the river. The 10,000-seat **theatre** is opposite the museum, with a small sculpture garden to one side. Schönbuhl Hill in front of the theatre is topped by a **temple**. Some 200m south is a large **amphitheatre**, near the **forum** and an exhibition of mosaics in the basement of the **curia** (Town Hall). Down on the riverbank beside the boat jetty, 500m north, is an enclosed **fortress**, housing an extensive baths complex. Plentiful display panels ensure you're never short of information.

Two or three slow **boats** a day (May–Oct only) from Basel to Rheinfelden stop at the jetty at Kaiseraugst, about fifteen minutes' walk below the Roman Museum. Otherwise take **bus** #70 (every 30min) from Basel's Aeschenplatz to Augst village, ten minutes' walk from the museum.

Baden

A pleasant, relaxing spa town on the River Limmat, 24km downstream from Zürich in Canton Aargau, **BADEN** makes for a good stopover on a journey across the north of the country. There's not an awful lot to do, other than enjoy the ancient Old Town, take in a fine collection of Impressionist art, and perhaps take a soothing dip in the warm spring waters… but that's the point. People have been coming to Baden for centuries to sit around doing very little, and there are few more congenial towns in the country in which to follow suit.

On a more prosaic note, Baden also functions well as a picturesque, small-town base for exploring northern Switzerland: frequent fast trains serve Zürich (15min) and Basel (50min), the last ones returning well after midnight.

The town is divided into two, with the station in the middle. South of the station is the centre, focused around the **Old Town** with the ruined castle above. North of the station, in a bend of the Limmat, is the low-lying **spa area** (signed as *ThermalBaden*). The main Badstrasse, which becomes Bäderstrasse, connects the two neighbourhoods, running along a terrace above the Limmat valley.

The Town

At Schlossbergplatz at the southern end of Badstrasse is the turreted fifteenth-century **Stadtturm**, gateway into the Old Town. On a hill above to the west, and visible from all over town, is the **Stein castle**, partially destroyed in 1712 by the Protestant forces of Bern, Basel and Zürich during a battle against the

Swiss cheese and chocolate

Cheese is an institution in Switzerland, with individual varieties savoured like ales in Britain or wines in France. Some are still made in the traditional way – by hand on summer mountain pastures – and so represent the essence of Swissness. Chocolate, meanwhile, is also a way of life: the Swiss eat a world-beating 11.6kg per person each year, compared with 9.2kg in the UK and 5.4kg in the US. Swiss chocolate is held to be the best in the world, rich with cocoa butter, super-smooth and, above all, creamy. Like cheese, chocolate stands as one of the iconic Swiss exports.

Cheese at the Saturday market in Bellinzona ▲

Vendor at a cheese market ▼

Origins

Cheese has been around in Switzerland at least since the Romans. For centuries, cheesemaking was a skill of mountain farmers, isolated for the summer months with their herds, but these days, some twelve hundred village dairies are in operation, processing fresh milk from local cows. Pasteurization is frowned upon by most cheesemakers, who claim it undermines the body and aroma of the cheese; all Swiss cheese is made from **raw milk** unless otherwise stated (and is thus not a good option for pregnant women).

For years, Switzerland had no system controlling use of the names of its cheeses. In 2001 an **AOC** mark (Appellation d'Origine Contrôlée) was established – too late, in many cases. Swiss Emmental now comprises only 2.5 percent of world Emmental production, and must rely on the wording "Emmentaler Switzerland" to identify it in the marketplace.

Alpine cheeses

Most cheese is now produced in the valleys, but the tradition of making **Alpine cheese** continues over the short summers on high pastures.

Only cheese which has been made on the alp with raw milk processed from cows fed on fresh grass, wildflowers and clover can qualify for the Bergkäse (alpine cheese) name. The cheese is produced by hand, allowed to ripen, then handed out to local farmers at summer's end, according to how many head of cattle they own. Many are sold to specialist cheese shops and market stalls around the country, where they are much in demand for their richness and individual nuances of flavour. Check out ⓦwww .switzerland-cheese.com for the full story.

Top 10 Swiss cheeses

▶▶ **Appenzeller** Ⓦwww.appenzeller.ch. Family name for some of the world's smelliest cheeses. The most pungent, Räss, gains its odour from a herb-and-brine marinade.

▶▶ **Emmental** Ⓦwww.emmentaler.ch. The holey mousetrap classic with a subtle, nutty flavour. A massive 55,000 tonnes are produced annually in Emmental and across the German-speaking lowlands.

▶▶ **Gruyère** Ⓦwww.gruyere.com. Smooth, rich and creamy-tasting hard cheese, with a distinctive salty-dry sharpness that makes it the favourite of the Swiss themselves. A prime ingredient in fondue.

▶▶ **Raclette** Ⓦwww.raclette-suisse.ch. Spicy, easily meltable cheese produced throughout Switzerland for the popular Alpine winter dish raclette.

▶▶ **Sbrinz** Ⓦwww.sbrinz.ch. Originating in Brienz, but now produced around Lucerne, this is Switzerland's Parmesan, matured over three years – crumbly, grainy and powerful.

▶▶ **Schabziger** (Sapsago) Ⓦwww.schabziger.ch. Distinctive green conical cheese made in Glarus for centuries according to the same recipe, using a herb known as melilot, originally imported from the Middle East by returning Crusaders.

▶▶ **Tête de Moine** Ⓦwww.tetedemoine.ch. First made at Bellelay monastery in the Jura in the twelfth century, and still made only in the Jura, at just nine dairies.

▶▶ **Tilsiter** Ⓦwww.tilsiter.ch. Creamy, full-flavoured semi-hard cheese produced in the eastern cantons bordering the Bodensee.

▶▶ **Vacherin Fribourgeois** Ⓦwww.vacherin.ch. A recipe reputed to have been brought back from Catalonia by a Swiss monk in the thirteenth century, and produced only in Canton Fribourg since then. The fondue cheese *par excellence*.

▶▶ **Vacherin Mont d'Or** Ⓦwww.vacherin-montdor.ch. A mild, creamy soft cheese made only in winter at fifteen dairies in the Jura Vaudois.

▲ Swiss cheese counter

▼ Traditional cheese fondue

Swiss chocolate

Many of the pioneers of chocolate-making were Swiss. In 1819, **François-Louis Cailler** started production at Vevey, soon followed by **Philippe Suchard** in Neuchâtel. Until the 1870s, all chocolate was dark and bitter; in 1875, Vevey-based Daniel Peter (aided by his neighbour Henri Nestlé) invented **milk chocolate**, and then, in 1879, **Rodolphe Lindt** of Bern invented "conching", a process which created the smooth, melting chocolate familiar today. **Jean Tobler**, also of Bern, was another pioneer.

Their names live on. The Swiss food giant **Nestlé** today incorporates the **Cailler** marque, Kraft/Philip Morris controls brands such as **Toblerone**, **Suchard** and **Milka**, while **Lindt** remains an independent concern.

As well as robust daily consumption – the chocolate aisle in Swiss supermarkets is quite a sight – Switzerland has a long tradition of confectioners producing hand-filled luxury chocolates for special occasions. Aside from chocolate bunnies at Easter, you'll see **chocolate chestnuts** in autumn and **chocolate flowers** in spring. *Chocolatiers* in the Jura make **chocolate watches**, while **chocolate bears** are a Bernese favourite.

Sumptuous Swiss chocolates ▲

The world-famous Toblerone ▼

Swiss confectionery counter ▼

Chocolate factories

Several Swiss chocolate factories are open for public visits, including:
▶▶ **Alprose** (p.492)
▶▶ **Maestrani** (p.407)
▶▶ **Nestlé** (p.110)
And don't miss the "Swiss Chocolate Train" (p.111).

Walking the Jura Höhenweg

The **Jura Höhenweg** (or High Route; ⓦ www.jura-hoehenwege.ch) makes for a multi-day hiking tour through a region unlike any other in Switzerland, stretching 299km along the length of the Swiss Jura from Dielsdorf, 12km east of Baden, to Borex near Geneva. End to end it takes about fourteen days: you can often find yourself walking for long distances without seeing signs of habitation. In this limestone country there's a rich flora in summer and long views to the snowy Alps. The notes below are meant as a guideline only: you shouldn't set off without a good **map** and *The Jura* by Kev Reynolds and R. Brian Evans (see p.512), which outlines the route in good detail. See p.49 for the basics.

Dielsdorf slumbers amid farms and market gardens, but within an hour of setting out the path goes through **Regensberg** which, with its thirteenth-century castle turret and cobbled square, is the finest village of the whole route. You'll also pass through **Baden** and **Brugg** on the first day, but thereafter the true nature of the Jura becomes evident, with the well-marked trail undulating to the horizon through steep green hills. Beyond **Staffelegg** the route almost reaches 1000m on the wooded summit of the Geissflue. Edging above **Olten**, on day four the route joins a track across the 1098m Belchenflue engineered by Swiss soldiers during World War I, adorned with carved and painted regimental insignia. Later the same day reinforced timber steps take the path up towards the Roggenflue to emerge on a prominent limestone cliff with more expansive views before descending to **Balsthal**. Day five ends on the **Weissenstein** (1284m), while, on reaching **Frinvillier** you pass from German to French Switzerland on the way up the 1607m **Chasseral**. On day nine the trail edges a huge limestone cauldron, the **Creux du Van**, before leading down to **Sainte-Croix** (see p.149). A steady climb then gains an open plateau close to the French border, before a sharp pull culminates on the summit of Le Suchet at 1588m. Day 12 brings you to the source of the River Orbe in a woodland soggy with newborn streams. After the view from Mont Tendre (1679m), the last two days are spent mostly on the ridge among flowers, from where 1200m of descent brings you to **Borex** above Lake Geneva.

Catholic cantons. Rathausgasse runs east from the Stadtturm just inside the walls, and partway along you'll find the **Stadthaus** (Town Hall): take a look inside at the whimsical modern ceiling murals of clouds and sky, and then head two floors up to the **Tagsatzungssaal** (Meeting Hall), for three centuries the meeting place of the Confederate Diet (Switzerland's parliament of the day), with a restored interior dating from 1497, complete with wood panelling and original stained glass showing the Swiss cantonal flags. You'll have to ask in one of the offices on the same floor for the key, since the door to the hall is kept locked.

An alley from Rathausgasse leads through to Kirchplatz, with its atmospheric **church**, built in 1420 (and retaining its Gothic arches) but later renovated in a surprisingly frill-free Baroque style. Stairways and steep alleys head down to a covered **wooden bridge** of 1813, leading to the bailiff's castle on the other bank. If the rock nearby looks oddly flat, it's because after the rainy night of June 25, 1899, the whole top of the crag sheared off and crashed into the river – a momentous event that is still talked about today.

It's a short walk north along the banks of the Limmat, on a footpath fragrant with wild garlic, to the **spa area**. Baden's nineteen **springs** were well known to the Romans, who called the place *Aquae Helveticae* and built a lavish baths complex to exploit the hot water, a million litres of which emerges every day at a toasty 47°C. The spa hotels which formerly ringed little Kurplatz were all undergoing complete renovation at the time of writing, as were the spa buildings themselves. It's unclear what the end result will be; by the time you visit, everything may be open for business again.

Museum Langmatt

At Römerstrasse 30, 150m west of the spa area, is the **Museum Langmatt** (March–Nov Tues–Fri 2–5pm, Sat & Sun 11am–5pm; Fr.12; Ⓦ www.langmatt .ch), housing a small but excellent collection of French Impressionist art. The charming house, dating from 1900–05, belonged to one Sidney Brown, a founder of the engineering multinational ABB, which is still headquartered in Baden. Off the reception area, the **Venetian salon** (room 3) hosts Louis XV and XVI furniture; next door you'll find work by Cézanne, Renoir and Pissarro. A wonderful Degas nude is curiously hung in a corridor (room 7) opposite the toilets. The atmospheric **library** (room 8) has landscapes by Corot and Degas, while the purpose-built gallery (room 9) is hung with, among other works, the beautiful *Portrait of Suzanne Valadon plaiting her hair* by Renoir. Upstairs rooms are mostly devoted to the history of the family.

Practicalities

The **tourist office** is opposite the station (platform 1 exit), Oberer Bahnhof-platz 1 (Mon noon–6.30pm, Tues–Fri 9am–6.30pm, Sat 9am–4pm; ⓣ 056 200 87 87, Ⓦ www.baden.ch). On the east side of the Limmat, about 200m south of the wooden bridge, is the HI **hostel** *Jugendherberge*, Kanalstrasse 7 (ⓣ 056 221 67 36, Ⓦ www.youthhostel.ch; March–Dec; ❶). Of the **hotels** *Blue City*, Hasel-strasse 17 (ⓣ 056 200 18 18, Ⓦ www.bluecityhotel.ch; ❹–❺), is a fine upmarket city hotel, with contemporary styled decor, warm service and a convenient location two minutes behind the station. Weekend discounts apply. While the spa district is under renovation, the swankiest spa hotel is the *Limmathof*, Limmatpromenade 28 (ⓣ 056 200 17 17, Ⓦ www.limmathof.ch; ❺–❻), with spacious rooms, chic designer interiors and a host of wellness packages.

For **eating**, *Himmel*, Bahnhofplatz 9, is a much-loved café/patisserie in the pedestrian zone with tea and cakes to die for. Roughly opposite is *Schwyzerhüsli*, Badstrasse 38 (ⓣ 056 222 62 63; closed Sun), a popular place to sit and watch the world go by over a salad, or more substantial Swiss fare, with *menus* from about Fr.22. In an unlikely location off the main shopping street behind Credit Suisse bank is *Hirschli*, Badstrasse 9 (ⓣ 056 210 09 55, Ⓦ www.hirschli.ch; closed Sun lunch), an atmospheric Italian/Asian-fusion restaurant; sit out on the vine-shaded terrace or in the sleek, dark-wood interior, for prawns in coconut-curry sauce, truffle ravioli or diced beef in Cognac cream. Expect Fr.50 or more.

Lengnau and Endingen

Amid the Aargau countryside stand **LENGNAU**, 8km north of Baden, and **ENDINGEN**, 3km further. Up until about a century ago these two villages were almost exclusively Jewish. Since the thirteenth century Jews had lived in Basel and Zürich: Jewish financing, for instance, made it possible for Basel's bishops to build the first bridge over the Rhine. On January 16, 1349, the Basel government decided to pack the town's Jews into a wooden house on an island in the Rhine and burn it to the ground; those who escaped were expelled six months later when plague arrived, accused of poisoning the city's water supply. Jews were allowed back after the 1356 earthquake to finance rebuilding work, but were again expelled in 1397. They took refuge in Lengnau and Endingen, where Jewish life in Switzerland was concentrated for more than four centuries.

Today, the two villages – despite being largely depopulated of their Jews – still bear many traces of the past. Lengnau's little square is overlooked not by a church, but by a large **synagogue**, and the village has many characteristic old double-doored houses, not seen elsewhere. Endingen's **domed synagogue** has been renovated. Nearby stands an overgrown **Israëlitischer Friedhof** (Jewish Cemetery), with graves dating back to 1750. Staff at the Basel tourist office, or the Jüdisches Museum (see p.175), can – with notice – put you in touch with a specialist guide.

Travel details

Full timetables for all trains, buses, trams, boats and cable cars in Switzerland – as well as international connections – are searchable at Ⓦ www.rail.ch.

Trains

Baden to: Basel (twice hourly; 50min); Bern (twice hourly; 1hr 10min); Zürich (every 15min; 15min).
Basel SBB to: Baden (twice hourly; 50min); Bern (every 30min; 1hr); Biel/Bienne (hourly; 1hr 5min); Interlaken Ost (twice hourly; 2hr 10min); Kaiseraugst (twice hourly; 10min); Lausanne (twice hourly; 2hr 10min); Lucerne (hourly; 1hr 10min); Neuchâtel (twice hourly; 1hr 25min); Zürich (every 15min; 55min).

Boats

Basel (Schifflände) to: Kaiseraugst (May–Oct 1–3 daily; 2hr 10min).

Bern and around

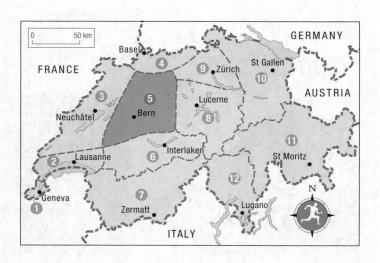

CHAPTER 5

Highlights

* **Old Town, Bern** Wander the atmospheric cobbled streets, dipping in and out of the arcades on a street plan unchanged since medieval times. See p.198

* **Münster, Bern** Switzerland's tallest steeple adorns this mighty cathedral. See p.202

* **Zentrum Paul Klee, Bern** The world's largest Klee collection, housed in a splendid modern gallery. See p.205

* **The Emmental** Home region of the best-known Swiss cheese, featuring classic scenery of velvety green hills. See p.212

* **Kemmeriboden** Tiny trailhead village in the upper Emmental that produces meringues to die for. See p.215

* **Solothurn** The finest Baroque city in the country, a day-trip from Bern, Basel or Zürich. See p.216

* **Fribourg** Switzerland's best-kept secret, a genial, bilingual university town with a fine tradition of fondues. See p.218

▲ Bern's Old Town

5

Bern and around

T he giant Canton Bern takes in a swathe of diverse countryside from Alpine peaks to rolling farmland. The north of the canton is focused around **Bern** itself, Switzerland's low-key and attractive federal capital. At the fulcrum of Swiss history, Bern has often dominated the fortunes of the country's populated west-central heartland, or **Mittelland**. This arc of territory stretching from Lake Geneva to Zürich has always held Switzerland's most fertile country, densest population and greatest wealth. The Reformation may have begun in Zürich, and flourished in Geneva, but it was the Bernese army that seized hearts and minds in the countryside between the two. For centuries after the Burgundian wars, the patrician nobility of Bern controlled a city-state covering the entire Mittelland. A French-backed revolution in 1798 saw Bern stripped of its Lake Geneva breadbasket (carved out to form Canton Vaud) and northern farmland (Canton Aargau). Nonetheless, Bern was a natural choice for Swiss federal capital under the 1848 constitution.

Every Swiss values his or her home canton above all the others, but the Bernese draw on a particularly deep wellspring of nationalistic pride. They're famous for their slow, deliberate manner, reflected in the lethargic, sing-song Bernese dialect of Swiss German that you'll doubtless overhear. The population is still relatively static and self-possessed. Many people feel little affinity with neighbouring Luzerners and Fribourgeois, with whom the Bernese share a nationality but neither a cultural, linguistic nor religious identity.

Around Bern, the picturesque farming region of the **Emmental** holds plenty of rustic charm, while two nearby cities are worth making time for: **Solothurn** to the north and **Fribourg** to the southwest. The Alpine region of the Bernese Oberland, in the south of the canton, has its own chapter, beginning on p.227.

Bern

Of all Swiss cities, **BERN** (**Berne** in French) is perhaps the most immediately charming. Crammed onto a steep-sided peninsula in a crook of the fast-flowing River Aare, its quiet, cobbled lanes, lined with sandstone arcaded buildings straddling the pavement, have changed little in over five hundred years but for

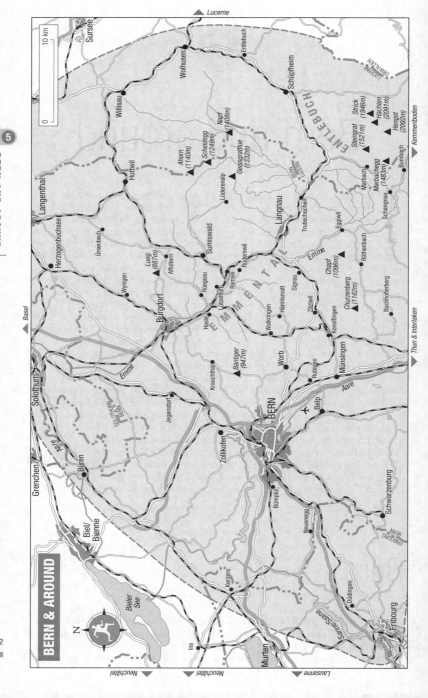

BERN & AROUND

N

Lucerne

Sursee

Wolhusen

Entlebuch

Schüpfheim

ENTLEBUCH

Strick
(1946m)

Hächlen
(2091m)

Willisau

Steingrat
(1521m)

Hengst
(2092m)

Kemmeriboden

Napf
(1408m)

Scheidegg
(1249m)

Ahorn
(1140m)

Geissgrattlue
(1332m)

Marbach

Marbachegg
(1483m)

Langenthal

Huttwil

BERN / LUZERN

Schangnau

Bumbach

LUZERN / OBWALDEN

Lüderenalp

Langnau

Trubschachen

Eggiwil

Herzogenbuchsee

Sumiswald

Röthenbach

Chapf
(1096m)

Emme

Ürsenbach

Lueg
(887m)

Affoltern

Rüegsau

Ramsei

Rüderswil

E M M E N T A L

Signau

Zäziwil

Churzenberg
(1162m)

Buchholterberg

Wynigen

Burgdorf

Hasle

Lützelflüh

Hämlismatt

Konolfingen

Walkringen

Basel

Bantiger
(947m)

Worb

Münsingen

Rubigen

Krauchthal

Aare

Thun & Interlaken

Emme

Jegenstorf

BERN

Belp

Solothurn

Zollikofen

Bümpliz

Aare

Grenchen

Büren

Neuenegg

Schwarzenburg

Biel/
Bienne

FRIBOURG / BERN

Bieler
See

Kerzers

Murten

Ins

Didingen

Sarine/Saane

Fribourg

Neuchâtel

Neuchâtel

Lausanne

Neuchâtel

0   10 km

modern signage and the odd car or tram rattling past. The hills all around, and the steep banks of the river, are still wooded. Views over the Old Town's clustered roofs, with the Alps on the horizon, are breathtaking. Coming from Zürich or Geneva, it's hard to remember that tiny Bern – once voted Europe's most floral city – is the nation's capital.

Despite its political pre-eminence, Bern has a population under 130,000 and retains a small town's easy approach to life. Traffic is kept out of the Old Town and you could spend days just wandering the streets and alleyways, café-hopping and – if it's warm – joining the locals for a plunge into the river. The medieval street plan, with its arcades, towers and street fountains, persuaded UNESCO to name Bern a World Heritage Site. In a competition for the world's most beautiful and relaxing capital city, it's hard to think what could knock Bern into second place.

Some history

A castle probably stood at **Nydegg**, on the eastern tip of Bern's peninsula, from the eleventh century, before Berchtold V, Duke of Zähringen, chose the strategic spot to found a new city in 1191. He named it – so the legend goes – after his first hunting kill in the area, a **bear** (*Bär* in German). Bern's coat of arms, sporting a bear, first appeared in 1224. To this day bears remain indelibly associated with the city.

The Aare encircles Bern's Old Town on three sides; Berchtold's fourth defence was a wall, which initially ran through the Zytglogge tower. The city expanded rapidly. By 1256 it had a new wall at the present Käfigturm, and a century later it reached as far as the Christoffelturm (at the present-day train station). In 1339, at the Battle of Laupen, Bern defeated **Burgundy**, and asserted its new-found independence by joining the Swiss Confederation in 1353.

Shortly before 5pm on May 14, 1405, **fire** broke out in Brunngasse and tore through the timber-built city, killing one hundred. Subsequent rebuilding in local sandstone gave the city much of its present character, including the street arcades, surviving town plan and monumental public buildings such as the Rathaus and Münster. In 1528, Bern embraced the **Reformation**, its nobility gathering greater and greater power, putting down a series of citizens' revolts before finally falling prey to **French invaders** in 1798. The 1814 Congress of Vienna forced Bern to surrender land (creating cantons Aargau and Vaud), but donated parts of the Jura in recompense; the Bernese complained that they'd lost their granary and cellar, and been given an attic. Nonetheless, the city was a popular choice for **federal capital** in 1848.

Einstein published his Special Theory of Relativity in Bern in 1905, and **Hermann Hesse** spent the World War I years in Bern, when the city was already known as a hub of politically progressive ideas, hosting the anarchists Kropotkin and Bakunin. Throughout the century Bern continued to expand, new bridges linking to suburbs such as **Kirchenfeld**, a planned district to the south characterized by grand 1920s–30s mansions. To the west, **Bümpliz** has mushroomed to accommodate most of the city's rapid new growth, its low-income housing and high proportion of Arab, South Asian and Slavic immigrants contrasting dramatically with the settled affluence and ethnic homogeneity of the city centre.

Recent years have brought a number of prestigious **architectural** commissions to Bern, including Renzo Piano's **Zentrum Paul Klee** gallery (see p.205) and Daniel Libeskind's **Westside** mall (Ⓦwww.westside.ch). The old Wankdorf football stadium, in the northeast suburbs, has been transformed into the state-of-the-art **Stade de Suisse** (Ⓦwww.stadedesuisse.ch). Bern is arriving, characteristically unhurried.

Arrival and information

Bern's **train station** is centrally situated at the western edge of the Old Town, within a few minutes' walk of practically all the hotels and sights. The **Old Town** stretches to the east, occupying the central high ground of a thin, finger-like peninsula: three long, parallel cobbled streets (which all change their names along their length) define the Old Town area: Aarbergergasse-Zeughausgasse-Rathausgasse-Postgasse is the northernmost; Spitalgasse-Marktgasse-Kramgasse-Gerechtigkeitsgasse is in the centre; Schauplatzgasse-Amthausgasse-Münstergasse-Junkerngasse is to the south. The Zytglogge clock-tower is in the centre of the Old Town; the Bärengraben (Bear Pits) are to the east; and the main museums are clustered around Helvetiaplatz to the south.

Bern's tiny **airport** (Ⓦwww.flughafenbern.ch) is 9km southeast in Belp, served by the irregular city bus #334. Otherwise book ahead for a minibus (misleadingly named "Airport Taxi") into the city, or take a taxi (around Fr.40).

Most of the centre is off-limits to traffic. Unless you can find a blue-zone space (see p.39), **parking** (Ⓦwww.parkingbern.ch) is expensive; the large car park at the station (Ⓦwww.bahnhofparking.ch) charges Fr.4 per hour (Fr.30 per day). Others are at Waisenhausplatz, Casinoplatz and behind the Rathaus.

Bern's friendly **tourist office** is on the upper level of the train station (June–Sept daily 9am–8.30pm; Oct–May Mon–Sat 9am–6.30pm, Sun 10am–5pm; ☏031 328 12 12, Ⓦwww.berninfo.com). There's a smaller tourist information desk at the Bärengraben (June–Sept Mon–Sat 9am–6pm; March–May & Oct Mon–Sat 10am–4pm; Nov–Feb Fri–Sun 11am–4pm).

Bern's festivals

The **Zibelemärit** (Onion Market) – held on the fourth Monday in November, preceded by a mass swim in the Aare the day before – is Bern's major annual festival, an excuse, despite the food stalls and the rustic-sounding name, for people to run around Spitalgasse throwing confetti and brandishing blow-up bananas. It is claimed that the spectacle originated after the fire of 1405, when people from nearby Fribourg helped Bern clean up the mess and, in gratitude, the Bernese granted the Fribourgeois the right to sell their onions in the city (down the centuries, the onions developing into blow-up bananas). In fact, Bern's Zibelemärit began – much more mundanely – in the mid-nineteenth century, when rural women, selling onions and other vegetables, began to turn up in Bern on the first day of the city's Martinmas Fairs, which had been celebrated since the Middle Ages to mark the transition to winter. The quality of the produce, and the engaging demeanour of the vendors, meant that news of the women's market spread rapidly, until the newspapers in 1860 proclaimed the Onion Market to be the "traditional" start of Martinmas. The tale quickly wove its way into popular thinking, somehow getting muddled with the 1405 fire and the Fribourgeois along the way.

Zibelemärit aside, Bern's biggest party is its **carnival** (Ⓦwww.fasnacht.be), spread over a weekend between the carnivals in Lucerne (before) and Basel (after). There's a **jazz festival** in May (Ⓦwww.jazzfestivalbern.ch) and the **Gurten festival** (Ⓦwww.gurtenfestival.ch) of rock, dance and folk in July.

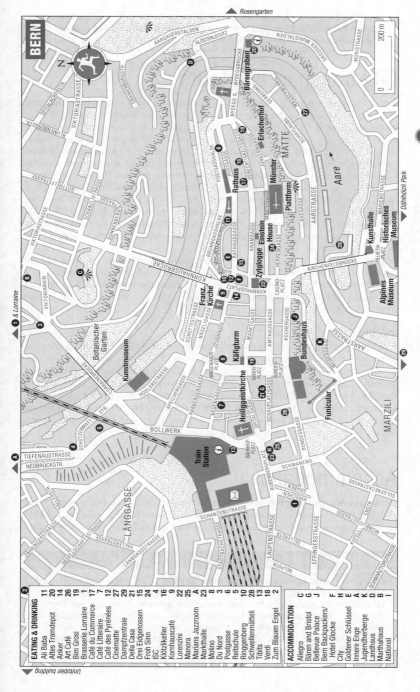

▲ Untitober building

▲ & Lorraine

Dählhölzli Park ▶

EATING & DRINKING	
Ali Baba	11
Altes Tramdepot	20
Anker	14
Art Café	26
Bim Grosi	19
Brasserie Lorraine	1
Café du Commerce	17
Café Litteraire	7
Café des Pyrénées	12
Cinématte	27
Dampfzentrale	29
Della Casa	21
Drei Eidgenossen	15
Froh Sinn	24
ISC	4
Klötzlikeller	16
Kornhauscafé	9
Lorenzini	22
Manora	25
Marians Jazzroom	23
Markthalle	8
Molino	3
Du Nord	6
Postgasse	10
Ringgenberg	5
Retschule	13
Schwellenmätteli	28
Tibits	18
Verdi	2
Zum Blauen Engel	2

ACCOMMODATION	
Allegro	C
Bären and Bristol	G
Bellevue Palace	J
Bern Backpackers/	
Hotel Glocke	F
City	H
Goldener Schlüssel	E
Innere Enge	A
Jugendherberge	K
Landhaus	D
Marthahaus	B
National	I

200 m

0

> A **Swiss Pass** (see p.35) is valid for free city transport in Bern and free admission to almost all museums reviewed in this book.

City transport and tours

Bern's city centre is small enough that you can easily **walk** everywhere: the stroll from the train station to the Bärengraben is only around twenty minutes and takes in the length of the Old Town on the way. Walking is the only way you're going to be able to get a sense of the atmosphere of the arcades – and it's the principal delight of Bern – but a close second-best comes in the form of **horse-drawn carriages**, which ply for trade in the central squares during the summer months.

Bern's network of **buses and trams** (Ⓦ www.bernmobil.ch) is comprehensive. Pretty much all lines run through Bahnhofplatz. Swiss Pass holders travel free; otherwise a **fare** for up to six stops is Fr.2 (valid 30min), for seven or more stops Fr.3.80 (valid 1hr), while a Tageskarte (Fr.12) is valid all day, all buyable from the machines at every stop. The **BernCard**, buyable from the tourist office and all hotels, gives unlimited travel and free admission to all museums; it costs Fr.20/31/38 for 24/48/72hr.

Bern's **taxis** are vying to be the most expensive in Europe: with a Fr.6.80 flagfall, plus Fr.3.80 per kilometre (more at nights and Sundays), they're about twice as pricey as London's. There are public ranks at the train station, Casinoplatz and Waisenhausplatz; two companies are Bären (℡031 371 11 11) and Nova (℡031 331 33 13).

Tours

The tourist office runs a **guided walk** through the Old Town, starting from the office in the train station (April–Oct daily 11am; Fr.18; lasts 1hr 30min), or you could tackle a self-guided walk with an iPod as your audioguide (Fr.18, plus deposit). One of the more interesting ways to see the city is from a **river dinghy** – ask at the tourist office for details of where to meet for such a tour. Otherwise, there are plenty of **bus tours** of the city and various **boat trips** on the river (Fr.25–35), as well as day-trips to Lake Thun and into the mountains. Most of the tours run in the summer season only.

Accommodation

Bern's **accommodation** is good value: it's easy to choose an inexpensive hotel and still find yourself in a tasteful, tranquil room overlooking historic cobbled streets, with only voices and church bells as background. Standards, even within

---

Sightseeing by bus

Bern's most useful bus line is the electric **bus 12** (every 6min). Aside from trams along Marktgasse, this is also the only public transport running through the Old Town. From the train station (direction Zentrum Paul Klee), the bus heads to the Zytglogge, then on down picturesque Kramgasse and Gerechtigkeitsgasse, and across the Nydeggbrücke to the Bärengraben, terminating in the eastern suburbs at the Zentrum Paul Klee gallery. In the other direction (signed Länggasse), bus 12 climbs the hill from the train station west to the university.

historic buildings, are high – the only drawback is the need always to book ahead. None of these places is more than ten minutes' walk from the train station, or a few stops on a tram or bus.

Campsite

Eichholz Strandweg 49 ☎031 961 26 02, ⓦwww.campingeichholz.ch. Decent site on the riverbank in Wabern, a few minutes south of the city by tram #9 (to Gurten). Mid-April to Sept.

Hostels

Bern Backpackers/Hotel Glocke (SB hostel) Rathausgasse 75 ☎031 311 37 71, ⓦwww .bernbackpackers.com. Old Town fixture benefiting from a perfect central location and excellent dorms and facilities, with some pleasant, bargain-priced singles and doubles too. ❷

Jugendherberge (HI hostel) Weihergasse 4 ☎031 311 63 16, ⓦwww.youthhostel.ch. Well-run place, with good facilities and a nice riverside location in Marzili – it's regularly chock-full. They also do good solid lunches and inexpensive evening meals. Walk down from the Bundesterrace, or take the funicular and then the lowest of three left-hand streets when you emerge. ❶

Landhaus (SB hostel) Altenbergstrasse 4 ☎031 331 41 66, ⓦwww.landhausbern.ch. Attractive building in an old part of town by the river, with beds in quiet, super-clean partitioned dorms; you can use the kitchen for free, and there's a café downstairs. Bus #12 to Bärengraben. Also has rooms, see below. ❷

Inexpensive hotels

City Bubenbergplatz 7 ☎031 311 53 77, ⓦwww .fhotels.ch. Geared towards a business clientele, with slick designer interiors. Directly opposite the train station and not at all bad; a sound choice for facilities and location. Street-side rooms are marginally noisier. ❸–❹

Goldener Schlüssel Rathausgasse 72 ☎031 311 02 16, ⓦwww.goldener-schluessel.ch. Comfortable place on a quiet Old Town street, with efficient, pleasant service. Simple, spacious rooms are clean and smart, recently renovated to a good standard. ❸

🏃 **Landhaus** Altenbergstrasse 4 ☎031 331 41 66, ⓦwww.landhausbern.ch. The most attractive budget rooms in town, in an historic, renovated building (with spiralling wooden stairs but no lift) overlooking a curve in the river. Spacious, modern design prevails throughout, with en-suite or shared facilities, and some rooms have floor-to-ceiling windows and balconies. Bus #12 to Bärengraben. ❷–❸

Marthahaus Wyttenbachstrasse 22a ☎031 332 41 35, ⓦwww.marthahaus.ch. Excellent value.

A characterful hotel-pension on a quiet cul-de-sac a few minutes out of the Old Town, friendly, well run and cosy. Most rooms are en suite, and are spotless, fresh and airy. Bus #20 to Gewerbeschule. ❷

National Hirschengraben 24 ☎031 381 19 88, ⓦwww.nationalbern.ch. Something of an institution, with a restaurant, theatre and – up above – a hotel occupying a lovely old building on an atmospheric tree- and tram-lined street. The ancient wooden lift rattles you up to characterful, renovated rooms with big windows and wood floors; some are en suite. ❷–❸

Mid-range and expensive hotels

Allegro In the Kursaal building, Kornhausstrasse 3 ☎031 339 55 00, ⓦwww.allegro-hotel.ch. Innovative business hotel set in the Kursaal building (which also boasts a large casino). Super-slick postmodern design swishes you into stylish rooms – go for the ones with Warhol decor. Top-floor balconies with Alpine vistas cost more. Weekend discounts can make this the best-value, and least traditional, top-end accommodation in the city. Tram #9. ❻–❽

Bären and **Bristol** Within 50m of each other at Schauplatzgasse 4 & 10 ☎031 311 33 67, ⓦwww.baerenbern.ch & www.bristolbern.ch. Two identical hotels seconds from the Bundeshaus, with different owners but shared Best Western management. Rooms are modern, well designed and comfortable, though rather soulless. ❺–❻

Bellevue Palace Kochergasse 3 ☎031 320 45 45, ⓦwww.bellevue-palace.ch. Top hotel in the city, right beside the Bundeshaus. This is the haunt of presidents, diplomats and billionaires, with as much palatial grandeur as you'd expect plus the added bonus of views of the river and, in the distance, the snowcapped Alps. Rooms are spacious, sumptuous, traditionally styled and horribly expensive. ❾

🏃 **Innere Enge** Engestrasse 54 ☎031 309 61 11, ⓦwww.zghotels.ch. Lovely choice, well out of the city on the edge of open parkland but only 5min by bus from the centre. This fine old building, which hosted Empress Josephine in 1810, features superb Art Nouveau styling throughout; the 26 rooms are characterful and quiet, many with expansive views of the Alps. Breakfast – which is optional – is served in the octagonal Park Pavilion. Free parking. Bus #21. ❻

The City

Wandering through Bern's UNESCO-protected **Old Town** can be a magical experience: few cities in Europe are so visibly wedded to their distant past, with architecture and a street plan essentially unchanged since medieval times. The most hectic shopping goes on in the **western half** of the Old Town, on Marktgasse and Spitalgasse in particular; the older, **eastern half** is slower-paced. However, not for nothing does the tourist office tout the famous arcades, lining both sides of every street in the Old Town, as being "the longest covered shopping promenade in the world". In a strange turnaround of expectations, it's when you walk under the crowded arcades that you get a full-on blast of modern consumerism, with music, shop windows and advertising vying for your attention. Step a few metres to the side to walk in the open air and – with a little imagination – it's easy to picture yourself in the Bern of the sixteenth century.

The Zytglogge

An imposing presence at the centre of the Old Town, the **Zytglogge** (*tseet-klok-uh*), Zeitglockenturm or Clock Tower, is as much the symbol of Bern as the bear. The focal point of public transport and walking routes within the Old Town – and both the benchmark of official Bern time and the point from which all distances in the canton are measured – its squat shape, oversized spired roof and giant, gilded clock face will imprint themselves on your memory of the city.

The tower was originally constructed partly in wood as the westernmost city gate in 1218–20, but by 1256 the city walls had moved west to the Käfigturm; the tower was then converted into a prison for prostitutes who made a living servicing the clergy. After the devastating fire of 1405, the tower was rebuilt in stone with a new, squat design, a turreted staircase to one side (still used today) and a clock mechanism. The clock soon broke and stayed broken for 122 years until one Caspar Brunner designed an elegant new mechanism which has

▲ The Zytglogge

functioned since he installed it in 1530, and which is still complete with nearly all its original parts. Below the main east face of the clock is an intricate astronomical and astrological device, which, in one small diameter, displays a 24-hour clock, the twelve hours of daylight, the position of the sun in the zodiac, the day of the week, the date and the month, the phases of the moon and the elevation of the sun above the horizon, everything kept accurate by linkage to the main clock mechanism. The external appearance of the Zytglogge dates from Baroque embellishments of 1770–71.

The main draw of the thing is generally touted to be a rather underwhelming little **display** of mechanical figures – a crowing cock, a parade of bears, Chronos with his hourglass and a dancing jester – which is set into motion four minutes before every hour on the clock's east face. What's more interesting is to see close-up (and have explained) the actual inner workings of the mechanism as the pendulum swings and linked cogs turn gracefully: check with the tourist office for details of their fascinating **guided tour** of the tower.

On Kornhausplatz, below the west face of the Zytglogge, stands the **Kindlifresserbrunnen**, or Ogre Fountain (1544), topped by a statue of a man devouring a struggling baby. The Bernese authorities would have you believe this is a light-hearted carnival scene, but the nightmarish statue was once painted yellow (the colour used to stigmatize Jews) and may possibly be an unusually graphic representation of the suspicion held throughout medieval Europe that Jewish religious ritual involved the murder of children. Whichever, Bern's happy shoppers of today seem unfazed by images of cannibalistic infanticide in their midst.

The eastern Old Town

From the Zytglogge, the atmospheric lanes of the Old Town branch out in all directions. The meandering walking tour outlined here covers notable sights, but it's just as appealing to follow your nose and explore unremarkable alleys and passageways that cut through and around the main routes.

The impressively wide main cobbled thoroughfare of the Old Town stretches away on both sides of the Zytglogge: the **western Old Town** is covered on p.203, while elegant **Kramgasse** runs east, featuring many Baroque facades which were added to the medieval arcaded buildings early in the eighteenth century. At no. 49 is the **Einstein–Haus** (April–Sept daily 10am–5pm; Feb, March & Oct–Dec Mon–Fri 10am–5pm, Sat 10am–4pm; closed Jan; Fr.6; ⓦ www.einstein-bern.ch), the apartment and workplace of the famous scientist. He developed his Theory of Relativity in 1905 while working in the Bern Patent Office, having graduated from the Zürich Institute of Technology a few years before.

On Kramgasse are more of Bern's many ornamented **fountains**. First is an armoured bear holding the standard of the city's founder, Berchtold von Zähringen (dating from 1535). Halfway along the street is another, with a copy of a 1545 statue of Samson, and just before the Kreuzgasse junction is a statueless fountain dating from 1779. At this eastern end of Kramgasse, and above head height, you'll also spot several eighteenth-century oversized figures mounted on pedestals, which indicated the location of Bern's various craft guilds: the Moor represented the clothworkers, the ape stonemasons and bricklayers, and the axe-wielding carpenter graphically demonstrates his own trade.

While the main street continues ahead, changing its name to **Gerechtigkeitsgasse**, the small Kreuzgasse heads left (north), past a quaint little shop which has been a pharmacy since 1571, to **Rathausplatz**, dominated by the double-staircased **Rathaus**. Although the building dates from 1406–17, it's been much altered over the centuries. Opposite is a 1542 fountain sporting a Bernese standard-bearer

The Old (Christ) Catholic Church

In 1870, the **First Vatican Council** confirmed the rule of the Pope over the whole of the Catholic Church and asserted the doctrine of papal infallibility. At the same time, political unification in Italy, and Bismarck's *Kulturkampf*, or Culture Struggle, in Germany – a thinly veiled assault on church authority – drew Switzerland into conflicts between church and state. Swiss liberals in particular saw the Vatican's dogmatism as challenging the basic principles of the church and the right to individual freedoms. In a meeting in Olten in 1872, they were troubled enough to form a separate church hierarchy. When the Bishop of Basel began to excommunicate priests who refused to accept the notion of papal infallibility, cantonal authorities in the north of Switzerland deposed him, and the dissenting priests formed a new church.

Known in Germany, Austria and the Netherlands as "Old Catholic" but generally in Switzerland as "**Christ Catholic**", the church flourishes today in northern areas influenced by political liberalism, principally cantons Bern, Basel, Aargau and Solothurn, with scattered communities as far apart as Geneva and St Gallen. About 140,000 Swiss consider themselves Christ Catholics, as opposed to Roman Catholics (of which there are 3.2m); they follow a church which holds that there is a priesthood of all believers, that priests are allowed to marry, that women can be ordained as deacons, and that services should always be performed in the language of the congregation. This has brought it closer in spirit to Anglicanism than to Roman Catholicism, with which relations have often been bitter and strained.

in full armour. Next to the Rathaus is the **St Peter & St Paul-Kirche**, built in 1858 as the first Catholic parish church to go up in the city since the Reformation. It's a cool, musty place in a mock-Gothic style, which since 1875 has belonged to the heterodox Christ Catholic Church (see box above). This is one of the most peaceful and atmospheric corners in the Old Town. **Rathausgasse** to the west retains its facades, though many of the old upper floors have been converted into luxury apartments, while to the east, tiny **Postgasse**, with a handful of cafés and antiquarian booksellers, trickles its way down the slope towards the oldest part of the city around Nydegg.

An alternative route heads the other way on Kreuzgasse, right (south) onto tranquil **Junkerngasse**. The apse of the Münster (see p.202) is opposite, but if you head east (left), down the street, you'll pass a succession of fine town houses on the route to Nydegg. First, set back from the street on the right at no. 59, is the Beatrice von Wattenwyl-Haus, its frontage and arcades dating from the 1440s, the south wing and upper floors from a major expansion in 1705. At no. 51 is the sixteenth-century Zeerlederhaus, with neo-Gothic heraldic exterior murals done in 1897. The main draw, at no. 47, is the **Erlacherhof**, the grandest patrician mansion in the city, designed in 1746 around its own courtyard; it's been the seat of the municipal government since 1832 and for a decade after 1848 housed the federal government. A short stroll past the Louis-XVI Lerberhaus at no. 43 and Morlothaus at no. 32 leads on down to Nydegg.

Nydegg

The three most characterful streets in the Old Town – Postgasse, Gerechtigkeitsgasse and Junkerngasse – meet at the **Nydeggbrücke** (*nee-dek*), the easternmost point of Bern's peninsula and the location of Nydegg Castle, built probably before the 1191 founding of Bern and the spur to the city's construction. It was destroyed in the mid-thirteenth century and its location is now marked by the **Nydeggkirche**, although parts of its massive stone foundations survive here and there. The church is a mishmash of elements added to an original 1341 building, and it's worth stopping to savour the tranquil atmosphere of the courtyard outside, with a well which originally stood within the precincts of the twelfth-century castle, and a picturesque view of the medieval houses clustering on the slopes all around. The covered Burgtreppe steps lead down from the courtyard to **Gerberngasse**; at the bottom, if you cross the street and walk 20m or so left, you'll find more steps leading down to the riverside, through a thirteenth-century arch which originally belonged to the **Ländtetor**, landing stage for the first ferry across the river. The wall fresco beneath the arch depicts the neighbourhood in the early nineteenth century.

Matte and Marzili

Emerging back onto Gerberngasse, to the right (northeast) is **Läuferplatz**, its fountain-statue of the city herald standing at the head of the low **Untertorbrücke**, one of the oldest bridges in Switzerland (1468). To the left (southwest), Gerberngasse follows the bend of the river down into one of the most appealing districts of the Old Town, **Matte** (Ⓦ www.matte.ch). For many centuries this was a self-contained district of craftspeople and dockworkers which long retained its own dialect, related to the Jenisch language of the Swiss gypsies (see p.428) and dubbed *Mattenenglisch* by the other Bernese, to whom it was an incomprehensible language (as obscure as *Englisch*) spoken in a meadow (*Matte*). Gentrification of the neighbourhood in the 1970s brought sweeping social changes. The river is still channelled into an open canal along the main street, and there are plenty of crooked half-timbered houses all around, but a look at wall plaques will turn up more software companies and design partnerships than you could shake a stick at. During the disastrous floods of 1999 and 2005, Matte spent several weeks underwater: you may still see evidence of high-water marks.

From Matte, the least energetic way to get back to the Old Town is to continue southwest along the riverside Schifflaube until Badgasse, where there is a **lift** (Mon–Sat 6am–8.30pm, Sun 7am–8.30pm; Fr.1) to whisk you up to the Münsterplattform overhead. Many flights of steps wend their way up the hillside all around too. Otherwise, you could continue a riverside stroll under the Kirchenfeldbrücke into **Marzili**, a peaceful residential district with a handful of old industrial buildings on the riverbank now converted into music venues and arts centres. The Aare is particularly fast at Bern; summer sees hordes crowding the riverbank lawns, and many people leave their possessions at the pool complexes at Marzili or Lorraine and walk or take public transport south to a convenient jumping-in point. The strong current floats them back north again. Cheapskates wrap their clothes up in a plastic bag and tie it to their wrist as they float along.

Across the Nydeggbrücke

There are few attractions on the eastern bank of the Aare. At the bridgehead across the river are the **Bärengraben** (Bear Pits; freely accessible) – now also known as the **Bärenpark** (Bear Park; Ⓦ www.baerenpark-bern.ch) – which have housed a collection of shaggy brown bears, the symbol of Bern, since the early sixteenth century. The area has been newly renovated so the bears can roam widely and even swim in the river.

The tourist complex adjacent, housed in a century-old converted tram depot, has a restaurant-bar and tourist information desk, as well as the much-touted **Bern Show** (every 20min: June–Sept daily 9am–6pm; March–May & Oct daily 10am–4pm; Nov–Feb Fri–Sun 11am–4pm; Fr.3), where – having waited for the English version to come round – you sit on benches to watch a potted history of Bern, evoked by a large model of the city and clever use of lights and pictures. It's a valiant attempt to bring history to life, but is just too cheesy for its own good.

Heading left up the steep hill next to the Bärengraben will bring you to the **Rosengarten** (Rose Garden), which has a lovely collection of flora (220 varieties of rose, 200 of iris, and more) and spectacular morning views over the Old Town.

The Münster

Bern's late Gothic **Münster** (Easter–Oct Mon–Sat 10am–5pm, Sun 11.30am–5pm; Nov–Easter Tues–Fri 10am–noon & 2–4pm, Sat until 5pm, Sun 11.30am–4pm; ⓦwww.bernermuenster.ch) is unmistakable, its feathery spire – the highest in Switzerland – towering over the Old Town and its sonorous bells dominating the quiet city. It's a reverential place, both for its lofty, gloomy interior and the terrific views from its tower.

The first chapel on the site – recorded in 1224 – probably dated from the founding of the city. On March 11, 1421, when just five thousand people lived in Bern, Matthäus Ensinger, a master builder from Strasbourg who already had three cathedrals under his belt, started construction on the new minster using the greenish local sandstone. Work continued according to his original plans until the mid-sixteenth century and, after a gap of three centuries or so, was finally completed in 1893 with the addition of the spire. Bern was a rapid convert to the Reformation and most of the church's treasures were destroyed in or soon after 1528, although some notable pieces such as the portal sculpture, choir stalls and stained-glass windows survived.

Outside the cathedral, cobbled **Münsterplatz** features the imposing Baroque facades of, among other buildings, the chapterhouse, and a 1790 fountain showing Moses, fired with the zeal of the Reformation, pointing to the Second Commandment (the one forbidding idolatry). It's worth stopping at the **central portal** of the cathedral before heading inside – this spectacular depiction of the **Last Judgement** is one of the only remaining unified examples of such late Gothic sculpture in Europe. The 170 smaller figures are the fifteenth-century originals (the 47 larger freestanding pieces were replaced by copies in 1964, the originals now sitting in the Bernisches Historisches Museum). The left half of the portal depicts the saved, the right half the damned: you can imagine that the graphic, didactic counterpoint between the beatific smiles of one side and the naked, screaming torment of the other would have appealed even to the iconoclastic Reformers, who chose to spare it from destruction. In the centre is Justice, flanked by angels, the Wise and Foolish Virgins and, above, the Archangel Michael wielding a sword and scales.

Entry is through the right-hand gate, and the hushed **interior** is immediately impressive. The immense roof span is laced around with vaulting (1572–3), the aisles are flanked by rows of porches and small chapels, and the nave, with square pillars placed diagonally and a pulpit dating from 1470, channels attention towards the stained glass of the choir. Keystone busts of saints, Mary, Christ and others were left untouched by the Reformers, possibly because they were too high to reach. The 1520s **choir stalls** are marvellous, carved with faces of the prophets and much intricate detail of ordinary life. The gorgeous **stained-glass windows** of the choir date from 1441–50, although a hailstorm in 1520 damaged the right-hand windows (two replacements were installed in 1868).

You can also climb the **tower**, the tallest in Switzerland. The way up is just inside the church door (closes 30min early; Fr.4), but be warned: this is a hundred-metre climb up a narrow spiral of 254 stone stairs. (You might want to ask in the church when the bells will be rung and make your ascent to coincide, since the experience of standing beside a gigantic, tolling ten-and-a-half-ton bell – the largest in the country, cast in 1611 – is one you and your ribcage will remember.) The 360-degree vistas over the whole city, most of the surrounding countryside, and out towards the Alps, are dreamy.

On the south side of the church is the **Münsterplattform**, a buttressed terrace above the Aare which took about a hundred years from 1334 to build. Abandoned icons were dumped here during the Reformation, but later it was planted with lime and chestnut trees and given elegant Baroque corner pavilions in order to serve as an open promenade, which is how it has remained. The views of the Aare and of silhouetted trams creeping along the soaring Kirchenfeldbrücke are spectacular. The net below the parapet was added a few years ago as a disincentive to desperate Bernese who chose this rather dramatic and beautiful spot to end it all.

The western Old Town

Some 100m west of the Münster is Casinoplatz – the Casino itself is a concert venue – from where trams head south to the Helvetiaplatz museums (see p.206).

Nasty, brutish and short?

There was much social unrest in Switzerland in 1980, most noticeably among radical leftists. Zürich's Autonomous Youth Centre (AJZ) – intended as a police-no-go building where young people could run their own entertainment free from mainstream commercial and social pressures – was violently suppressed, and a similar AJZ movement in Bern which took over the **Reitschule** (an abandoned city-owned former riding school, also known as the **Reithalle**; W www.reitschule.ch) was also evicted by the police. The situation simmered until late 1987 when, following the eviction of the riverside Zaffaraya community, thousands demonstrated in the city centre, a large group re-squatted the Reitschule and, perhaps most significantly, retailers reported a ten-percent loss in profits over the Christmas shopping season. In the face of such a groundswell of discontent, the police and city council adopted a damage-limitation policy, and left the Reitschule squatters to their own devices.

Despite problems with violent anarchist gangs in the early 1990s, the Reitschule – now an arts centre and activist collective – has come to be highly valued by alternatively minded Bernese, and has even gained a certain official legitimacy while remaining in a curious legal grey area. Its cinema, for instance, is licensed with the council but the bar next to it is illegal; the concert venue pays its taxes, while the adjacent café is packed with dope-smokers. Unlike the similar *Rote Fabrik* movement in Zürich (see p.355), the Reitschule cooperative has consistently rejected proposals to accept funding from the city council, sticking tight to its counter-cultural principles ("No violence, no sexism, no commercial exploitation") by raising its own money through ticket sales, bar profits and a popular annual fundraising party. Through effective word-of-mouth networking, it's been able to stage gigs by British, European and American bands and DJs, raising its profile still further, yet to this day the police don't venture into the complex, turning a deliberate blind eye to such a self-contained concentration of – mostly very innocuous – lawbreaking. It's a run-down, heavily lived-in place and an obvious honeypot for drug dealers (who are barred from entry, but nonetheless gather outside), yet these days is quite safe. More to the point, it's become an icon of opposition to the city council, which has been trying for years to turn it into a multistorey car park and supermarket. A huge graffito as you approach reads *Reitschule bleibt autonom* ("Reitschule still rules itself"). In a remarkably effective and purposeful demonstration of communal self-government, virtually unknown in other European countries and running entirely counter to the Swiss stereotype, it's true.

A few steps north on Kornhausplatz is the Zytglogge; just beyond, past the Kindlifresserbrunnen (see p.199), stands the **Kornhaus** (Granary; ⓦwww .kornhaus.org), now occupied by offices, a chic bar and restaurant and the attractive **Kornhausforum** exhibition space, used for shows of design and media (ⓦwww.kornhausforum.ch). Behind is the **Französische Kirche** (French Church; ⓦwww.paroisse.gkgbe.ch), the city's oldest, which originally formed part of a thirteenth-century Dominican monastery. The compact but beautiful interior (Mon–Fri 9–11am & 2–5pm, Sat 11am–3pm) has been much renovated, but retains its stalls (1302) and a rare frescoed rood screen (1495).

From the main **Kornhausplatz**, trams weave their way west along Markt-gasse, heart of the city-centre shopping district, neatly avoiding the fountain statues of a musketeer in full armour and Anna Seiler, founder of Bern's first hospital. Just beyond the Seilerbrunnen is the **Käfigturm**, an early city gate (1256–1344) which was used as a prison from 1642 until 1897. The broad, sunny marketplace of **Bärenplatz** opens beyond, and a little further west along hectic Spitalgasse, with its bagpiper fountain, stands the late 1720s **Heiliggeist-kirche** (Holy Spirit Church; Tues & Wed 11am–6.30pm, Thurs 11am–8.30pm, Fri 11am–4.30pm; ⓦwww.heiliggeistkirche.ch), acclaimed as Switzerland's finest example of Protestant church-building, boasting a fine Baroque pillared-and-galleried interior.

The train station – metres away – marks the limit of the medieval city: several sections of excavated city wall are exposed on the lower shopping concourse.

The Bundeshaus

Immediately south of Bärenplatz is **Bundesplatz** (ⓦwww.bundesplatz.ch), with a display of 26 fountains – one for each canton of Switzerland – spouting in front of the **Bundeshaus**, or Federal Assembly building, built in Renaissance style in 1902 and inscribed *Curia Confoederationis Helveticae* (Assembly Building of the Swiss Confederation). When the parliamentarians are not in session, you can join a free 45-minute guided tour (on the hour Mon–Fri 9–11am & 2–4pm; arrive 25min early at the security entrance on the east side), which takes you through the various chambers, decorated with coats of arms, statues and paintings commemorating events in Swiss history. When the assembly is sitting (the flag overhead will be flying), you can watch proceedings from the public gallery. The building sits on a cliff-edge above the Aare, and the **Bundesterrasse** behind rests on a massive retaining wall. On one side, a quirky little **funicular** runs down to the riverside district of Marzili (daily 6.30am–9pm; Fr.1).

The Kunstmuseum

Bern's **Kunstmuseum** is five minutes' walk northeast of the train station, in an impressive building at Hodlerstrasse 8–12 (Tues 10am–9pm, Wed–Sun 10am–5pm; Fr.7; temporary shows Fr.8–18; ⓦwww.kunstmuseumbern.ch). Aside from often excellent changing exhibits, the permanent collection comprises large numbers of works by Kandinsky, Modigliani, Giacometti, Rothko, Miró, Pollock and more, including some by Paul Klee (although most now reside at the Zentrum Paul Klee). Cézanne's *Self-portrait with Black Felt Hat* (1879) stands out, as does a depressing, dark Picasso drinker from 1902 and the accomplished, late *Blue Blouse* by Matisse (1936). The finest work in a small group of Old Masters is a luminous gold *Maestá* by Duccio (1290) – rather out of place amidst the rest. Elsewhere, you'll find a range of works by contempo-rary artists, a wide selection from **Swiss artists** such as Anker and Hodler, as well as the curious naïve art of Adolf Wölfli (1864–1930), a paedophile farmworker who spent most of his life confined to a Bernese asylum creating thousands of pages of writing, musical scores and drawings (his work is also displayed at the Collection de l'Art Brut in Lausanne; see p.103).

Zentrum Paul Klee

Alongside the A6 *autobahn* in the eastern suburbs, linked to the city centre by bus #12, rises the **Zentrum Paul Klee** (Tues–Sun 10am–5pm; Fr.22; Ⓦwww .zpk.org), built to showcase the artist's creative output. This magnificent building, opened in 2005, was designed by the architect Renzo Piano with a steel roof that undulates in three fluid, graceful waves, or "hills". The northern "hill" is dedicated to Klee the teacher and musician; below this part of the roof is a children's museum, Creaviva, and a subterranean concert hall staging works inspired by Klee's art. The southern "hill" focuses on Klee the researcher and mathematician, housing a research centre and archive relating to the artist.

However, the main draw is the superb **gallery** occupying the central section of the building. This holds over four thousand works by Klee, the largest such

▲ The Zentrum Paul Klee

collection in the world, comprising almost half of his total output. The permanent exhibition on the ground floor displays two hundred works at a time, changed twice a year, while the basement level stages rotating shows focusing on Klee's contemporaries or highlighting cultural/historical themes. This means that you can't be certain which works will be on display when you visit – but the experience of viewing any of Klee's art in such a space is well worth the visit. Check the website for details of the occasional gallery tours in English (free) and the regular programme of music events. On site are a shop, café and restaurant.

The Helvetiaplatz museums

Most of Bern's museums are clustered together around **Helvetiaplatz**, on the south side of the Kirchenfeldbrücke. Trams #3 (direction Saali) and #5 (direction Ostring) shuttle from the train station and the Zytglogge to Helvetiaplatz.

Bernisches Historisches Museum

The **Bernisches Historisches Museum** (Tues–Sun 10am–5pm; Fr.13; Ⓦwww.bhm.ch), housed in a castle-like folly off Helvetiaplatz, is packed with interest. Start in the basement, which houses displays on the history of Bern, including a model of the city from around 1800 and a series of macabre paintings showing "**The Dance of Death**"; these are 1649 copies of originals (now lost) that were painted in 1516–17 on the wall of Bern's Dominican monastery. The sequence of 24 vivid images, showing a hideously grinning and fooling skeleton leading kings, prostitutes, nuns and lawyers alike to their inevitable fate, sends a chill down your spine – as, no doubt, it was intended to. Also here are the original sandstone figures from the **Last Judgement** portal of the Münster, fascinating for the chance to view their details up close. The ground floor, as well as major temporary shows, has galleries dedicated to Celtic and Roman pieces, as well as art from Asia and Oceania, including a spectacular **Islamic collection**, with daggers galore, a mounted Turkestan warrior in full armour, jewellery, ceramics and a reconstructed Persian sitting room. Upstairs is a gallery devoted to an impressive series of wall-sized medieval **Flemish tapestries** – including the "**Thousand Flowers Tapestry**", the only one surviving of a set of eight made in Brussels in 1466, which was looted by Bern during the Burgundian wars of 1474–77 – while upstairs again are sections devoted to the work of Albert Einstein in Bern (confusingly dubbed the **Einstein Museum**, as if it were a separate institution). The topmost floor houses absorbing displays of ephemera and household items showcasing the history of Bern in the twentieth century.

Schweizerisches Alpines Museum

Beside the Historical Museum, the **Schweizerisches Alpines Museum** (Mon 2–5.30pm, Tues–Sun 10am–5.30pm; Fr.12; Ⓦ www.alpinesmuseum.ch) is surprisingly good, taking an intelligent, sensitive look at all aspects of life in the mountains, from tourism, the history of mountaineering and the social identity of mountain dwellers to surveys of Alpine flora and fauna and the impact of industry on the mountain environment. There's plenty to play with and read up on (in English). Crowded all over the museum are dozens of examples of relief mapmaking gone berserk, with mountains, whole valley systems and complete Swiss ranges rendered in perfect scale detail, almost rock by rock, by enthusiasts whose energy and patience can only be imagined.

Other museums

On or very close to Helvetiaplatz are plenty of other museums, as well as the Swiss national library and federal archives. Worth aiming for are the porticoed **Kunsthalle**, Helvetiaplatz 1 (Tues–Fri 11am–6pm, Sat & Sun 10am–6pm; Fr.8; Ⓦ www.kunsthalle-bern.ch), with changing exhibits of contemporary art, usually of high quality, and the **Museum für Kommunikation**, Helvetiastrasse 16 (Tues–Sun 10am–5pm; Fr.12; Ⓦ www.mfk.ch), which surveys media and communication from postage stamps to the web and beyond.

Outer districts

If you're on an extended visit to Bern, or if you just fancy something a bit different from medieval history at every turn, more modern districts can provide a little urban realism. Easiest to reach – just a short walk north of the train station across the river – is **Lorraine** (Ⓦ www.lorraine.ch). Once a dyed-in-the-wool working-class district, in the last decades Lorraine has attracted a

---

Above Bern – Gurten

A favourite Bernese getaway – if one were needed from such a gentle, slow-paced capital – is to the hill of **Gurten** (Ⓦ www.gurtenpark.ch), which towers over the city from the south. Take tram #9 to Gurtenbahn, in the neat suburb of Wabern, and walk 100m along Dorfstrasse to the **funicular** (every 10–20min; Fr.10 return; passes valid; Ⓦ www.gurtenbahn.ch). The whole journey from the train station to the summit only takes about half an hour. On top you'll find a kids' play area, a lavish folly of a castle (housing the gourmet restaurant *Bel Étage* and the more down-to-earth eatery *Tapis Rouge*) and wide expanses of countryside laced with hiking trails that give views over Bern, out towards the Jura, and across the peaks of the Bernese Oberland. In winter the hill and snowy slopes are crowded with sledding families; in summer, you might have difficulty escaping the hikers and picnickers. Every year, for a weekend in mid-July, Gurten plays host to a very popular **rock festival** (Ⓦ www.gurtenfestival.ch); ask for details at the tourist office.

growing population of students and young people. They have created a funky, relaxed community atmosphere, which nonetheless doesn't exclude the many old-timers still in the neighbourhood. Lorrainestrasse and the streets around still retain much charm. On the way, you pass the **Botanischer Garten**, Altenbergrain 21 (daily 8am–5pm; free; ⓦwww.boga.unibe.ch), a fixture since 1858 with Alpine flora as well as hothouses to explore.

If you follow Schanzenstrasse up behind the train station, a short climb will bring you to Länggassstrasse, heart of the bustling university district of **Länggasse**. The **Unitobler** building, at no. 49a, 300m along on the left (bus #12 stops outside), was formerly the factory where, for most of the twentieth century, the famous Toblerone chocolate was produced. In the 1980s, production moved to a more modern site outside Bern, and the building was renovated for use by the university (hence the Unitobler name), subsequently receiving numerous architectural awards for sensitivity of renovation. You're basically free to explore: the student café spills onto a sunny plaza behind the building, and the library occupies an extraordinary site between two wings of the building that has been converted into an impressive three-storey atrium space. Just behind Unitobler, on Freiestrasse, is the elegant **Pauluskirche**, dating from 1905 and one of the best examples of Art Nouveau in the country.

Eating and drinking

Bern's compact Old Town groans with **eating and drinking** possibilities, and you'll have no trouble finding something to suit your palate and your budget. The broad Bärenplatz, always busy with people, performers and market stalls, has no fewer than eleven cafés side by side – one of them, *Gfeller*, is a Bernese institution. This square is top choice for coffee and an ice cream in the sunshine, but there's a host of places all through the cobbled lanes offering *al fresco* consumption during the summer and firelit warmth in winter.

Cafés

Altes Tramdepot Beside the Bärengraben ⓦwww .altestramdepot.ch. Weave your way past the tourist crowds and into this fine old high-ceilinged place, formerly a tram depot and now a microbrewery, offering three house beers and a speciality monthly brew. The food is solid Bernese, Viennese and Bavarian fare, heavy on game, sausages and rich desserts. It's a sociable place, with good panoramic views from the garden terrace. Daily until 12.30am.
Art Café Gurtengasse 3 ⓦwww.artcafe.ch. Bright, trendy café just off the main shopping streets that morphs into a rather cool lounge bar after the shops shut. Open until after midnight. Closed Sun.
Brasserie Lorraine Quartiergasse 17 ⓦwww.brasserie-lorraine.ch. Just about the last café in Bern still owned by a cooperative, with excellent, inexpensive food, wood floors and a summer terrace. Games galore fill the cupboards (free to use) and the Sunday brunch is

the best in Bern. A cosy, calm meeting place for alternative types and politicos. Take bus #20 to Lorraine; Quartiergasse is a little ahead on the left. Closed Mon.
Café Littéraire In Stauffacher bookshop, Neuengasse 25. Cosy espresso bar in Bern's largest bookshop, with snacks and newspapers. Closed Sun.
Café des Pyrénées Kornhausplatz 17 ⓦwww .pyri.ch. Jovial and unpretentious meeting place for artists, alcoholics and others with loud voices. Equal quantities of twenty- and forty-somethings crowd the place out nightly. Closed Sun.
Kornhauscafé In the Kornhaus. The vaulted and renovated interior of the city's former granary is now home to a postmodern-style café, with coiffed customers and pricey desserts and sandwiches. A cool contrast to the raucous *Pyrénées* opposite. Downstairs is a rather posh restaurant (closed Sun lunch) and a swanky, upmarket lounge bar (open from 5.30pm daily).

Du Nord Lorrainestrasse 2 ☏ 031 332 23 38. A quality Lorraine café-bar and eatery, offering a nice mixture of heavy meat-and-potatoes dishes and lighter veggie options. A meal might only come to Fr.25 in the evening, or as little as Fr.15 at lunchtime. All the food is organic and comes from small local producers ensuring freshness, and monthly dance events and occasional concerts add to the allure. Bus #20 to Gewerbeschule. Closed Wed.

Reitschule (aka Reithalle), graffitied buildings next to the railway bridge 5min north of the station ⊛ www.reitschule.ch. See also box, p.203. Cooperative-run bastion of Bernese counterculture. The hash-smoky café-bar (named *Sous Le Pont*) is uniquely amiable; however, if sharing a scratched-up table with a green-haired character in a holey sweater rolling a joint isn't your idea of fun, you should head elsewhere. Tues–Thurs 11.30am–midnight, Fri 11.30am–2am, Sat 7pm–2am, Sun 10am–4pm; food generally noon–2pm & 6–10.30pm, during which dope-smoking is discouraged.

Zum Blauen Engel Seidenweg 9b ⊛ www .zumblauenengel.ch. Cosy student café near the university, with *objets trouvés*, worn gilt mirrors, hosts of candles and a crowd of young, arty regulars creating a pleasantly seductive atmosphere in which to while away the evening. Eat before you come, though, since the food is disappointing. Bus #12 to Mittelstrasse – Seidenweg is first right. Closed Sun & Mon.

Restaurants

Ali Baba Rathausgasse 18 ☏ 031 311 91 09, ⊛ www.alibaba-partyservice.ch. Wonderful little Turkish restaurant in the heart of the Old Town lanes, run by Ali Biçer, a Kurdish writer who sought asylum in Switzerland and now compiles books of recipes. This is a jovial place to indulge in a range of authentic dishes, from perfect *Iskender* kebab and pilav to veggie spinach pastries, in a sleekly stylish interior (mains Fr.16–25). Open Mon–Fri evenings only; Sat all day. Closed Sun.

Anker Kornhausplatz 16 ⊛ www.roeschti.ch. Cosy pub, with a restaurant section in the back where you can scoff Swiss stomach-liners such as fondue, *Rösti* and a meat-laden Berner-Teller (around Fr.22).

Bim Grosi Bärenplatz 3 ☏ 031 305 08 88, ⊛ www.bimgrosi.ch. The cheeriest and least fusty of the many eating places on this central square, offering local dishes such as Emmentaler Bratwurst or a farmer's salad with sheep's cheese. Slightly overpriced (reckon on Fr.35–45 for a meal), but the location is unbeatable.

Café du Commerce Gerechtigkeitsgasse 74 ☏ 031 311 11 61. One of Bern's best-loved local restaurants, a fixture here since 1947, with a plain, cosy interior and sociable buzz. Specializes in Spanish cuisine, with fine paella and *zarzuela* – a thrown-together dish of fish and seafood. The gazpacho is excellent, as are the scampi and octopus. Closed Mon lunch & Sun.

Cinématte Wasserwerkgasse 7 ☏ 031 312 21 22, ⊛ www.cinematte.ch. Pleasant riverside nook attached to Bern's premier arthouse cinema. *Menus* (meat or veggie) and the à-la-carte choice are varied and not expensive. It's a small place, though, so booking is advised. Closed at lunch, and all day Tues & Wed.

Della Casa Schauplatzgasse 16 ☏ 031 311 21 42, ⊛ www.della-casa.ch. An unprepossessing exterior preludes a fine old Bernese institution serving high-quality Swiss fare. The Bernerplatte – a plateful of half a dozen varieties of meats with potatoes and sauerkraut – is a house speciality, but doesn't come cheap: you'd be lucky to walk out with change from Fr.60. Closed Sat eve & Sun.

Froh Sinn Münstergasse 54 ☏ 031 311 37 68, ⊛ www.froh-sinn.ch. A popular *beiz* (local-style tavern) in the Old Town, sociable and informal, serving light international cuisine – pastas, steaks, grills – in a bistro atmosphere. Reckon on around Fr.40. Closed Sun.

Klötzlikeller Gerechtigkeitsgasse 62 ☏ 031 311 74 56, ⊛ www.kloetzlikeller.ch. Another Bernese institution, a fine old traditional restaurant occupying an atmospheric seventeenth-century cellar space off one of the main Old Town streets. The high, barrel-vaulted interior – lined with dark-wood panelling – is a great place to tuck into hearty Swiss cooking: think sausages, steaks, proper cheese fondues, schnitzel and the like. Mains are roughly Fr.20–30. Closed Sun (summer also closed Mon).

Lorenzini Theaterplatz 5 ☏ 031 311 78 50, ⊛ www.lorenzini.ch. High-flying young professionals flock here both for the café-bar and the top-drawer Tuscan cuisine, although you'll be looking at well over Fr.50 for a meal. Closed Sun.

Markthalle Bubenbergplatz 9 ⊛ www.markthalle -bern.ch. A convenient indoor mall devoted to food from around the world – espressos, tapas, cheese, wine, bread, chocolates and more. There's a host of different ways to satisfy munchies, at counters and small eateries serving inexpensive sushi, pizzas, Thai food, Indian curries, Indonesian rice platters, Turkish kebabs and more. Closed Sun.

Molino Waisenhausplatz 13 Ⓦ www.molino.ch. White-aproned waiters bustle around doling out pizzas and other staple fare at this reliably good Italian bistro in a good central location, with a nice roof terrace. Open daily from breakfast until around midnight. Expect about Fr.35.

Postgasse Postgasse 48 ☎ 031 311 60 44, Ⓦ www.cafepostgasse.ch. Tiny old den on the quietest of alleys, with wood tables and an intimate, cosy atmosphere. The menu is good and not expensive (around Fr.25), but the joy of the place is its tasteful, convivial ambience. Closed Sun & Mon, and Tues lunch.

Ringgenberg Kornhausplatz 19 ☎ 031 311 25 40, Ⓦ www.taberna.ch. Warm and comfortable place that styles itself as a *Brasserie Bernoise*, serving rather posh Mediterranean-style cuisine (around Fr.40). Closed Sun eve.

Schwellenmätteli Dalmaziquai 11 ☎ 031 350 50 01, Ⓦ www.schwellenmaetteli.ch. Attractive, popular riverside restaurant serving light Mediterranean dishes (mains around Fr.20–30) to a rather cool,

fashion-conscious clientele – many of whom come as much for the fine terrace as the food. Closed Sat lunch & Mon.

Tibits Bahnhofplatz 10 Ⓦ www.tibits.ch. Bernese branch of the successful Swiss mini-chain of cool, contemporary-styled cafés-cum-veggie restaurants, located within the main train station. The food is excellent and moderately priced – high-quality light bites, salad buffets, sandwiches and full meals, plus fresh juices and coffees. Open daily from breakfast time until around midnight.

🏃 **Verdi** Gerechtigkeitsgasse 5 ☎ 031 312 63 68, Ⓦ www.bindella.ch. One of Bern's finest restaurants, a superb Italian tucked away at the bottom end of the cobbled Gerechtigkeitsgasse. The interior breathes class – candles, white tablecloths, an atmospheric galleried back room – while the food is to die for: stand-out dishes include veal *saltimbocca* in a marsala sauce, or fettucine with prawns, spinach and vine tomatoes (mains Fr.24–45).

Bars, clubs and live music

Dampfzentrale Marzilistrasse 47 Ⓦ www .dampfzentrale.ch. An old steam factory down on the riverbank, now hosting hugely popular nights featuring jazz, drum'n'bass, dance, theatre and film, as well as a daytime café-bar.

Drei Eidgenossen Rathausgasse 69. A small, noisy bar in the Old Town, very popular with a loquacious, alternative young crowd.

ISC Neubrückstrasse 10 Ⓦ www.isc-club.ch. Popular venue and club.

Marians Jazzroom At *Hotel Innere Enge* Ⓦ www .mariansjazzroom.ch. Celebrated basement jazz venue in a genteel out-of-town hotel.

Mühle Hunziken 13km south of town near Rubigen Ⓦ www.muehlehunziken.ch. An old wooden mill out in the countryside that has, over the years, hosted a jaw-dropping array of top-flight international jazz, blues and soul performers in an intimate, raucous setting more reminiscent of a delta juke-joint than the Swiss capital. If you see a gig advertised here, it's worth the taxi ride. Make friends quickly in order to nab a lift back to town after the show.

Reitschule (aka Reithalle Ⓦ www.reitschule.ch; see also box p.203). Heart of the city's underground. Facilities include a cinema, concert venue, disco, women-only area and the *Sous Le Pont* café-bar.

Entertainment

Bern's **nightlife** is surprisingly vibrant, with music, dance, theatre and film all getting a substantial look-in. **Classical music** is well served by the Bern Symphony Orchestra (Ⓦ www.bsorchester.ch), which performs regularly at the Casino (Herrengasse 25) and the Stadttheater (Kornhausplatz 20), the latter also staging occasional **opera**. Posters all over town advertise events, or otherwise you can find complete city nightlife **listings** in *Agenda*, the Thursday supplement of the *Berner Zeitung* newspaper, available free from many cinemas. For cutting-edge news about clubs and music events (in German), pick up the free *Bewegungsmelder* from the tourist office and elsewhere (Ⓦ www.bewegungsmelder.ch).

Listings

Bike rental The station has the usual paid bike-rental facilities (daily 7am–9pm), but in summer (May–Oct), the municipality runs *Bern rollt* (ⓦwww.bernrollt.ch), a free bike-rental scheme to help unemployed people get back to work. There are pick-up points on Bahnhofplatz and Waisenhausplatz (both daily 7.30am–9.30pm), with new city bikes, electric bikes, kickboards and scooters; for a Fr.20 deposit plus your passport, you can ride away for free.

Books Bern's biggest bookstore, with a quality range in English, is Stauffacher, Neuengasse 25 (Mon–Sat 8am–6.30pm, Thurs until 9pm).

Embassies Australia: embassy in Berlin ⓣ004930/880 0880; consulate in Geneva. Canada: Kirchenfeldstrasse 88 ⓣ031 357 32 00. Ireland: Kirchenfeldstrasse 68 ⓣ031 352 14 42. New Zealand: embassy in Berlin ⓣ004930/20 6210; consulate in Geneva. UK: Thunstrasse 50 ⓣ031 359 77 70, ⓦukinswitzerland.fco.gov.uk. US: Sulgeneckstrasse 19 ⓣ031 357 70 11, ⓦbern.usembassy.gov.

Flights Flight enquiries from Bern-Belp ⓣ031 960 21 11, ⓦwww.flughafenbern.ch.

Gay and lesbian life Start by checking ⓦwww.gaybern.ch for details of events and happenings. The Reitschule (see p.203) has regular gay and lesbian club nights.

Markets Bern has a wealth of markets (ⓦwww.markt-bern.ch). There are general markets on Tuesdays and Saturdays on Waisenhausplatz, Bundesplatz and Bärenplatz, with extra late-opening markets on Thursdays in summer. The Münster hosts a handicrafts market on the first Saturday of every month, and there's a riverside flea market on Mühleplatz in Matte on the third Saturday of the month (May–Oct only). In December Münsterplatz and Waisenhausplatz host Christmas markets (ⓦwww.weihnachtsmarktbern.ch).

Medical facilities The Inselspital university hospital on Freiburgstrasse (ⓣ031 632 21 11) has a 24hr emergency room. Bahnhof Apotheke Hörning is a pharmacy on the upper level of the train station, open daily 6.30am to 10pm.

Police Waisenhausplatz 32 (ⓣ031 321 21 21).

Post office Main office (Mon–Fri 7.30am–9pm, Sat 8am–4pm, Sun 4–9pm) is on Schanzenstrasse behind the train station.

Around Bern

To the east of Bern, a bucolic region of farmhouses and dairies, undulating hills and peaceful villages spreads through and around the **Emmental**, the valley (*tal*) of the River Emme. Despite the presence of a show dairy and the region's prominent place in the hearts of the rurally minded, cheese-loving Swiss, the Emmental has managed to escape heavy tourist development. It's a wonderful place for long country walks or bike rides. To the north, generic suburban prosperity quietly covers the land as far as the dignified old city of **Solothurn**,

---

Exploring the Mittelland

You can get information on the whole Mittelland region from the **Schweizer Mittelland tourist office** (ⓣ031 328 12 28, ⓦwww.smit.ch), which forms part of the Bern tourist centre, located in Bern's train station. They have plenty of contacts with companies running multi-day adventure packages in the area, and can put together any kind of itinerary covering hikes or long-distance cycling or inline skating on the hundreds of trails through the Mittelland, often throwing in extras such as canoeing on the Aare or panning for gold in the Emmental hills. Pro Emmental (ⓦwww.emmental.ch) also has details of deals in the area.

capital of its own canton, and now included, along with the Bernese Mittelland, under the rather awkward tourist-office rubric of the "Schweizer Mittelland".

To the west and south, the Mittelland merges into the lakeside country of Canton Fribourg and the Broye (see p.151), with the attractive city of **Fribourg** a short way southwest of Bern on the French–German language border.

The Emmental

Just outside the eastern city limits of Bern rises the Bantiger mountain (947m); behind it stretches the **EMMENTAL**, a quintessentially Swiss landscape of peaceful, vibrantly green hills dotted with happily munching brown cows, sleepy rustic hamlets and isolated timber-built dairies. This is where Emmental **cheese** (the one with the holes) originates. A local nineteenth-century clergyman celebrated the sturdiness and moral rectitude of Emmentaler dairy farmers in a series of novels under the pseudonym Jeremias Gotthelf; since then the place has gathered to itself an atmosphere of earnest rural stability and honesty. The salt-of-the-earth locals have the reputation of being the most reliable, the most sensible, the most Swiss of all the Swiss – a reputation which, in a distasteful modern turnaround, has been exploited by politicians: the

Customs and festivals in the Mittelland

The Mittelland is one of the more traditional areas of the country, and has hundreds of **folk customs and festivals** surviving in various forms, many of them dating back to the pre-Christian pagan religions of the Celts. "Chilbi" is the generic name given to the summer highland festivals of the Emmental, raucous events taking in folk singers and dancers, yodellers, flag-throwers, alphorn blowers and more. The **Lüderenchilbi** is one of the most famous, held on the Lüderenalp meadow every second Sunday in August and centred on a Schwingfest, a traditional Swiss wrestling contest held in a sawdust ring. The winner gets to take home a heifer decked out in garlands. The **Schafsheid**, or sheep-sorting, held in Riffenmatt, 20km south of Bern, on the first Thursday in September, is a colourful event, when the sheep, after spending the summer on the alp, are sorted out by owner, amidst market stalls and celebrations. The **Sichlete** is a communal autumn meal, where in years gone by everyone who'd worked to bring in the harvest would sit down to gorge on stew, sausages, hams and fresh garden produce, helped down by huge meringues and local apple Schnapps; these days, with increasing farm mechanization (and so fewer seasonal farmhands taken on), the Sichlete has become an excuse for two or three villages to get together for a feast and a knees-up. In Burgdorf, the last Monday in June sees the **Solennität**, a 250-year-old festival for children, featuring contests, games and traditional costumes.

Many pagan New Year's Eve rituals survive in the villages of the Mittelland. Laupen's **Achetringele** stems from a Celtic exorcizing of evil spirits and demons on the winter solstice; now shifted to December 31, it involves all the boys in the village chasing away the old year either as one of the masked *Bäsemänner* (broomsweepers) or as a noisy, cowbell-swinging *Tringeler* (bell-ringer). One of the most bizarre customs survives in Schwarzenburg, 8km north of Riffenmatt, where the **Altjahrsesel** (Old-Year Donkey) – these days a man dressed in a donkey suit – is whipped and beaten before being led away by a grim figure representing death. Other characters take part in the ritual, including a bride and groom, representing joy in the year to come, the devil, a priest, and, most chillingly of all, a two-faced woman, the *Hinnefürfraueli*, whose beautiful front face looks forward to the new year, while her hideous rear face despatches the old year to memory.

extreme right-wing SVP (Swiss People's Party) has expanded out of its traditional base in Lucerne to make significant gains in the Emmental countryside on a tide of anti-immigration, anti-foreigner rhetoric.

Emmentaler **architecture** is distinctive, the local timber-built inns and dairies crowned by huge roofs with overarching eaves, ringed by wooden balconies, and encrusted with rows of tiny windows, each with its window box and neatly tied-back set of net curtains.

Emmentaler **cooking**, featuring cheese or cream with everything, is renowned around the country (this is where you can find some of Switzerland's finest meringue creations) and protected by the **Ämmitaler Ruschtig** mark (ⓦ www.aemmitaler-ruschtig.ch), which guarantees quality local ingredients and methods. Many inns and restaurants offer – among other dishes – the Ämmitaler Ruschtig *menu*, a gut-busting four-course blowout. Starting with *Beeri Schämpis* (sparkling berry wine) and a cheese salad served with the local *Züpfe* plaited bread, it takes in soup with whipped cream and *Chlepfer Ännis Schwynsschnitzu* (pork escalope in cream sauce, with creamy mashed potatoes and vegetables), then moves on to *Meielis Merängge Gschlaber* (fresh meringue with whipped cream, ice cream and caramelized cream), before rounding it (and you) off with Schnapps-laced coffee. Local tourist offices and the website have the full list of *Ämmitaler Ruschtig* establishments.

Burgdorf and the northern Emmental

On a pleasant road 19km northeast of Bern through Krauchthal village, the picturesque old town of **BURGDORF** is built on a prominence above the Emme. From the train station, follow Bahnhofstrasse south and then head east on Oberstadtweg to meander up into the Old Town, an atmospheric quarter characterized by steep cobbled streets. At the top is the mighty **Schloss Burgdorf**, the Zähringens' largest castle, begun in the seventh century and expanded in the twelfth. Several rooms grouped around an attractive courtyard comprise the **Schlossmuseum** (April–Oct Mon–Sat 2–5pm, Sun 11am–5pm; Nov–March Sun 11am–5pm; Fr.5; ⓦ www.kulturschloss .ch), outlining local history; the ticket also lets you into the adjacent **Goldmuseum** (same hours), tribute to the history of gold-panning in these hills. Below, the late Gothic **Stadtkirche** features an elaborate choir screen that looks rather too grand for the church housing it. Every Thursday, the Old Town hosts Burgdorf's weekly **market**.

Roads climb northeast from Burgdorf to a viewpoint at **Lueg** (887m), offering classic panoramas over the rolling countryside. Nearby is **AFFOLTERN**, a pleasant village that's home to the Emmental's flagship **Schaukäserei** (Show Dairy; daily 8.30am–6.30pm; free; ⓦ www.showdairy.ch), a rather hectic place often full of busloads of excitable Swiss-German old ladies. As well as being able to watch the various cheesemaking processes – the dairy gets through some seven billion litres of milk a year – you can take in plenty of English-language videos on the cheese industry. A noisy and rather pricey café-restaurant adjacent serves the *Ämmitaler Ruschtig Menu*. Plus, of course, you can buy any amount of cheese, ranging from a bag of "Schnouserli" (bite-sized cubes of different strengths of Emmental) up to a full 9kg round of Emmental shipped direct to your door.

Hasle-Rüegsau and Lützelflüh

Roads drop back down from Affoltern into the Emme valley at **HASLE-RÜEGSAU**, two small villages which, over the years, have grown to hate each other like only next-door neighbours can. Pressured by economic hardship a century or so ago, the farmers of Rüegsau were forced to move down from their original hillside village (tiny Rüegsbach) through an intermediate settlement (Rüegsau itself) to a village down on the Emme (Rüegsauschachen), alongside the settled folk of Hasle; spurred on by displacement, they've since developed a strong community and prosperous commercial base. Static, conservative Hasle has been left behind, and is now struggling with old-fashioned, unrenovated buildings and a stagnating economy. To this day, the two merely tolerate each other: Rüegsauschachen has carefully kept gardens, modern houses and an air of suburban pride, and tends to regard its neighbour as backward, while in Hasle resentment and bitterness run high. This stretch of the Emme has become known locally as the River Jordan, symbolizing the depth of feeling on both banks.

The two were formerly linked across the river by the largest arched wooden bridge in Europe, **Holzbrücke**, an impressive 69m-long construction built in 1839. Unfortunately it was damaged by cars in 1955 and – another nail in the coffin of neighbourly relations – was shifted 800m downstream to its current position, a five-minute walk west in a hard-to-spot woodsy location behind the train tracks. Hasle and Rüegsau now have an undistinguished modern bridge that seems to divide them as much as join them.

Along the valley floor 8km is a turning for **LÜTZELFLÜH**, a charming village at the heart of the Emmental that was home to the novelist Gotthelf from 1831 to 1854. On the outskirts of the village you'll pass the **Kulturmühle**, an old mill from 1821 that has been turned into a cultural centre (ⓦ www.kulturmuehle.ch), staging everything from the Emmentaler Cock-Crowing Contest to monthly classical music concerts which attract the Bern cognoscenti out into the sticks. The small garden nearby, laid out in French Baroque style, isn't out of place: you can find similar examples outside farmhouses throughout the Emmental – a legacy of French influence over Bern following the 1798 revolution – though today the formal squares and circle patterns are just as likely to be planted with carrots and lettuces. From Lützelflüh, back roads climb to Affoltern, while the main valley road runs on south beside the Emme.

Langnau and the southern Emmental

Some 17km southeast of Bern, the tranquil town of **Konolfingen** marks the start of a scenic road along the Kiese valley through Zäziwil to **LANGNAU**, the main town of the Emmental, but a singularly sleepy place nonetheless, with little traffic and fewer than 10,000 people. A small **tourist office** in a travel agent off the main square at Dorfmühle 22 (Mon–Fri 8am–noon & 1–6pm, Sat 9am–4pm; ☏034 409 95 95, ⓦ www.langnau-tourismus.ch) has information on the region, including details of local walking routes, as does Pro Emmental, Schlossstrasse 3 (Tues & Fri 8.30am–noon & 2–5pm; ☏034 402 42 52, ⓦ www.emmental.ch).

East of Langnau, the main road passes through the picturesque village of **Trubschachen**, with big old wooden Emmentaler houses lining the street and a demonstration **pottery** turning out examples of the pretty local ornamental ware. To the north rises the **Napf** (1408m), the most famous of the Emmental's hills and a mecca for hikers and Sunday hill walkers. East of Trubschachen, the road crosses briefly into Canton Lucerne and an area known as the **ENTLEBUCH** (ⓦ www.tourismus-entlebuch.ch), with its small countryside resort of **Marbach** boasting a couple of ski lifts serving the Marbachegg (1483m). The Entlebuch is now a UNESCO-affiliated Biosphere Reserve (ⓦ www.biosphaere.ch) – a move intended to protect this rural area and kick-start sustainable development.

Less than 5km southwest, and back in Canton Bern again, is **Schangnau** village, at the upper end of the Emme valley. A minor road southeast from here winds dramatically between the cliffs, which rise to 2000m on both sides, through tiny **Bumbach** (with lifts up to the wedge-shaped Hohgant, towering overhead at 2197m) and on to **KEMMERIBODEN** (976m). This end-of-the-road hamlet, sliced through by the rushing, tumbling Emme – a mountain torrent at this stage – is the place to get the single best **meringue** in Switzerland (see p.259), and is also the trailhead for many wilderness hikes, principally the tough path through the mountains to the 2350-metre, Brienzer Rothorn (7hr), from where a rack railway can take you down to Brienz (see p.257).

From Schangnau, the main road crosses the Emme and heads north through **Eggiwil** to Langnau, crossing nine picturesque wooden covered bridges that are typical of the area. From Eggiwil, you can also reach Langnau by a parallel road further west over the crest of **Chuderhüsi** (1103m), which offers spectacular views over the Emmental hills and valleys backed by the snowy Alps.

Emmental practicalities

The best way to get around in the Emmental is **by bike** or **on foot**, both of which allow you to set your own itinerary and pace; stations at Bern, Langnau and Burgdorf have bikes for rent. A scenic **train** line between Bern and Lucerne passes through Konolfingen and Langnau, while a branch line runs north from Langnau through Hasle to Burgdorf, shadowing the Emme through verdant countryside. **Postbuses** from Marbach run through Schangnau to Kemmeriboden.

Tourist offices in Bern and Langnau heavily tout **hiking**, with maps and route suggestions galore. Walking through hillside pastureland from Burgdorf to Affoltern, for instance, takes about three hours; from Burgdorf along the riverbank to Hasle, or from Walkringen (above Konolfingen) to Lützelflüh, a little less. For a ramble down the Emme from Langnau to Burgdorf, or a stiffer hike from Langnau up to the Napf, reckon on a leisurely six hours or more. Pro Emmental also has details of companies that can inexpensively transport your bags around the region, enabling you to spend the day walking unencumbered.

Accommodation and restaurants

There are **campsites** around the area: modest *Mettlen* at Gohl, 2km north of Langnau (☎034 402 36 58, ⓦwww.campingemmental.ch), or the modern, eco-friendly *Sternen* at Marbach (☎078 878 41 05, ⓦwww.camping-sternen.ch). The spartan HI **hostel** *Jugendherberge*, Mooseggstrasse 32 in Langnau (☎034 402 45 26, ⓦwww.youthhostel.ch; closed Oct; ❶), has dorms, as do the mountain inns on the summits of the Napf (☎034 495 54 08, ⓦwww.hotelnapf.ch; ❷) and the Marbachegg (☎034 493 32 66, ⓦwww.marbach-egg.ch; ❶).

Otherwise, every hamlet has its choice of small-scale country inns which double as **hotel** and **restaurant**, virtually all of which, big and small, use farm-fresh produce and ingredients brought straight into the kitchen from the morning's market – bad Emmentaler cooking is a contradiction in terms. Affoltern, for instance, has the *Sonne* (☎034 435 80 00, ⓦwww.sonne-affoltern .ch; ❷), with a few pleasantly renovated rooms above a good local restaurant; while dominating the centre of Langnau is the excellent *Hirschen* (☎034 402 15 17, ⓦwww.hirschen-langnau.ch; ❸), a huge inn in typical Emmentaler style. In far-flung Kemmeriboden is the wonderful *Kemmeriboden-Bad* (☎034 493 77 77, ⓦwww.kemmeriboden.ch; ❹), with comfortable rooms, superb local cooking and delectable home-made meringues.

Solothurn

SOLOTHURN (Soleure in French), some 35km north of Bern at the confluence of the Emme and the Aare, is touted as the most beautiful Baroque city in Switzerland. Its compact but characterful Old Town is crammed with an odd architectural mix of Swiss-German sturdiness and Italianate excess dating from the town's heyday in the seventeenth and eighteenth centuries. It's an easy day-trip from points all over the Mittelland, with a couple of fine Baroque churches, a worthwhile art gallery and a high viewpoint nearby for breezy walks.

In Celtic times, Salodurum was a fortified town; after Roman domination and Alemannic invasion, it was only in the tenth century that Solothurn rediscovered some stability. With the demise of the Zähringen dynasty in 1218, the city expanded its territory to form a buffer zone between Bern and Basel, and joined the Swiss Confederation in 1481. In the decades following, despite the turmoil of the Reformation all around, Solothurn remained Catholic and so, in 1530, was chosen by the Catholic ambassadors of the king of France as their place of residence. For more than 250 years, these **French ambassadors** oversaw Solothurn's redevelopment in the contemporary **Baroque** style. Some destruction followed the 1798 revolution, but much of Solothurn's graceful Old Town has survived. These days it's a lively, cosmopolitan place, with thriving industry (watchmaking and precision manufacturing figure large) and a varied mixture of ethnicities on its streets.

Arrival, information and accommodation

Solothurn is on the main SBB **train** line between Biel/Bienne and the big rail junction at Olten. It's also served by regular mini-trains from Bern operated by RBS (Ⓦwww.rbs.ch); these don't appear on the big departures board in Bern station – aim instead for platforms U1–4. Solothurn's **train station** is a few minutes' walk south of the river: Rötistrasse is the highway heading north from in front of the station, but quieter Hauptbahnhofstrasse, one street to the left, will deliver you to the pedestrian-only Kreuzackerbrücke, which leads into the Old Town. **River boats** on the *Aarefahrt* route to and from Biel/Bienne (May–Oct; see p.154; Ⓦwww.bielersee.ch) dock at the Romandie jetty beside the railway bridge, two bridges west (upstream) of the Kreuzackerbrücke.

The **tourist office** is in the Old Town at the foot of the cathedral steps, Hauptgasse 69 (Mon–Fri 8.30am–12.30pm & 1.30–6pm, Sat 9am–noon; ⓉU032 626 46 46, Ⓦwww.solothurn-city.ch & www.mysolothurn.com), and runs excellent ninety-minute **walking tours** of the town beginning from the Baseltor (May–Oct Sat 2.30pm; Fr.10).

Hostel

Jugendherberge (HI hostel) Landhausquai 23 ⓉU032 623 17 06, Ⓦwww.youthhostel.ch. One of the country's best hostels, modern steel-and-glass decor insinuated into a seventeenth-century building on the Old Town riverbank just west of the Kreuzackerbrücke. There's a wide choice of dorms and rooms with and without river views, as well as all the usual services, including bike rental. March–Nov. ❶

Hotels

Baseltor Hauptgasse 79 ⓉU032 622 34 22, Ⓦwww.baseltor.ch. Popular and friendly

brasserie with just six en-suite rooms, all appealingly simple and fresh, and so generally snapped up well in advance. Worth booking for. ❸

Kreuz Kreuzgasse 4 ⓉU032 622 20 20, Ⓦwww.kreuzkultur.ch. Rough-and-ready cooperative, offering simple rooms – spartan with creaky wood floors (newer rooms are upstairs) – plus discounts for stays beyond one night and free kitchen use. ❶

Krone Hauptgasse 64 ⓉU032 626 44 44, Ⓦwww.hotelkrone-solothurn.ch. Top choice in town, its Baroque decor preluding solidly comfortable traditional rooms in either Biedermeier or

Louis XV style, with stout, tasteful furnishings and airy rooms at the back looking over the cathedral steps. ④–⑤

Zunfthaus zu Wirthen Hauptgasse 41 ☎032 626 28 48, ⓦwww.wirthen.ch. An all-wood guild-house with plasticky but spacious rooms, some en suite. ②–③

The Town

Centrepiece of the town is the massive **St-Ursen-Kathedrale** (daily 8am–noon & 2–7pm; Oct–Easter closes 6pm), an Italianate vision in local grey-white stone that seems to float above the main Hauptgasse. It's crowned by a greenish tower which rises to 62m. Overhead, the Latin inscription in gold running around the building refers to Solothurn's patron saints, Ursus and Victor, who refused to worship Roman gods and were martyred. The bright, soaring wedding-cake interior has a riot of intricate stucco covering the white stone walls that is typical of the lavish late Baroque era in which the church was built (1762–73).

Sandwiched between shopfronts barely 100m along Hauptgasse is the atmospheric **Jesuit church**: push the unremarkable door to gain entry to the extremely remarkable interior, dating from the 1680s and encrusted with a dizzying amount of lacy stuccowork. Halfway along Hauptgasse, overlooking the central Marktplatz, is the **Zytglogge**, Solothurn's oldest building, the lower part dating from the twelfth century, the upper part from 1467, and the astronomical device in the centre from 1545. The hour hand on the giant clock face is longer than the minute hand.

A few steps north of the cathedral is the doughty **Altes Zeughaus** (Old Arsenal), housing a moderately interesting museum of militaria (May–Oct Tues–Sat 10am–noon & 2–5pm, Sun 10am–5pm; Nov–April Tues–Fri 2–5pm, Sat & Sun 10am–noon & 2–5pm; Fr.6). This massive collection documents Solothurn's history of battles and booty, most impressively with a hall full of swords and suits of armour. Some 50m east is the **Baseltor**, a city gate dating from 1508. Hug the walls north to the corner bastion of the Old Town and you'll come to the circular **Riedholz** tower, now the location of a summer cycle of prestigious classical concerts.

Across the lawns to the north lies the **Kunstmuseum** (Tues–Fri 11am–5pm, Sat & Sun 10am–5pm; free; ⓦwww.kunstmuseum-so.ch). Highlights of this surprisingly good collection are Holbein's *Solothurner Madonna* (1522), on a panel backed by the *Madonna in the Strawberries* (1425), painted by the anonymous Master of the Garden of Paradise. Some spectacular Alpine canvases are led by Ferdinand Hodler's much-reproduced portrait of a Herculean William Tell emerging from a break in the clouds. One of Hodler's famous

---

Above Solothurn – the Weissenstein

One of the best viewpoints in the Swiss Jura is the **Weissenstein**, a ridge rising to 1284m with a breathtaking panorama towards the Bernese Alps. Local **trains** from Solothurn to Moutier stop at Oberdorf, from where you can either hike up or take the **chairlift** to the summit (ⓦwww.seilbahnweissenstein.ch). At the time of writing the chairlift was closed for renovation work, and there was some uncertainty about when (or whether) it might reopen. At the top is the slick *Weissenstein Hotel* (☎032 628 61 61, ⓦwww.weissenstein.ch; ③), complete with gourmet restaurant and a lovely Alpine garden. Plenty of walks branch out from the hotel, mostly along the crest of the ridge; you could also do a chunk of the long-distance Jura Höhenweg walk from here (see box, p.185).

sequences of larger-than-life moving bodies decorates the stairs, while Klimt's luscious *Goldfish* is another highlight.

Last but not least, way on the other side of town, on the southern bank near the river-boat landing stage, is the highly odd **Krummer Turm**, or Twisted Tower, a fortification of the town dating from the 1460s. Looked at from any point other than its axis of symmetry, it appears to be hopelessly lopsided; in fact, though, its base is an irregular pentagon (due to the tower's original location at the sharp corner of a bastion of entrenchments). The spire, although it seems about to topple off any minute, has been safe and secure these past five centuries. From the tower, you can cross to the northern bank and hike the riverside road for two hours west to the stork colony at **Altreu**.

Eating and drinking

At the many Old Town terrace **cafés**, look out for the local delicacy *Solothurner Kuchen*, a tart of nut fondant and whipped cream piled on a biscuit base, served best at *Suteria*, Hauptgasse 65 (ⓦwww.suteria.ch). *Kaffeehalle*, Gurzelngasse 26, is a fine place for coffee and cake by the Bieltor, while *SolHeure*, on the Aare at Ritterquai 10 (ⓦwww.solheure.ch; closed Sun lunch & Mon lunch), is a wonderfully relaxed bar and lounge, serving mojitos and light bites on a lazy riverfront terrace.

Of several good **restaurants** in the Old Town, try *Zum Fritz*, Judengasse 2 (closed Sun & Mon), a classy, informal stop for reasonably priced home-made pasta, steaks and fondues, or the posher *Stephan*, Friedhofplatz 10 (ⓣ032 622 11 09, ⓦwww.alterstephan.ch; closed Sun & Mon), where hearty fare such as rack of lamb or lemon sole takes centre-stage on a five-course menu (Fr.50 at lunch; Fr.100 in the evening). *Kreuz* and *Baseltor* hotels have cooperative café-restaurants (both closed Sun lunch) serving up delectable organic food, but otherwise aim for ⚤ *Pittaria*, Theatergasse 12 (ⓦwww.pittaria.ch; closed Sun & Mon), a jovial little nook run by Sami Daher, a Palestinian who has lived in Solothurn since the mid-1980s: his kebabs and falafel are spot on, and he has done the place up very nicely with family photos and Arabian-style decor.

Fribourg

Some 34km southwest of Bern, **FRIBOURG** (Freiburg in German) is one of Switzerland's best-kept secrets, its winningly attractive medieval Old Town set on a forested peninsula in a meander of the River Sarine. Steep, cobbled streets, bedecked with wrought-iron lamp standards and ornate inn signs, are pictur-esque and characterful. Six bridges, from medieval wooden fords to lofty modern valley spans, provide woodcut-pretty views of the town's old houses piled up together on the slopes.

Behind its visual charm, you'll find Fribourg to be an amiable place, thoroughly modern at heart despite the medieval appearance of some quarters. The university – one of Switzerland's most prestigious – attracts ten thousand students from all over the country and beyond, generating a lively cosmopoli-tanism that is tangible on the streets.

The River Sarine (Saane in German), which carves a path through the town, is the local defining line of the *Röstigraben*: Fribourg is split roughly 70:30 between French Swiss, who call their town *free-boor* and are a majority on the western bank, and German Swiss, to whom the place is *fry-borg* and who form a majority on the eastern bank. Almost everyone is instinctively bilingual.

Some old-timers still use the ancient Bolze dialect, a mixture of French and German which you might be able to catch in the taverns of the Basse-Ville (Lower Town).

Within easy reach of both Bern and Lausanne, Fribourg is an understated town. For the "must-see" visitor, it merits barely an hour or two – which is all the better for those on a long, slow journey of familiarity around Switzerland, who could spend a week in the place and not see it all.

Some history

Bertold IV of Zähringen founded Fribourg in 1157 as part of his consolidation of regional power, which also saw the establishment of Bern, Thun and other towns. The Zähringens were succeeded by the Counts of Kyburg, who were themselves bought out in 1277 by the Austrian Habsburgs. Savoy took over in 1452, although in the Burgundian wars shortly afterwards Fribourg backed the victorious Swiss against Savoy, and so became a free city. In 1481, it joined the Swiss Confederation.

Fribourg remained Catholic throughout the Reformation, becoming a place of refuge for the exiled bishops of Geneva and Lausanne. The ruling families retained power even through the 1798 upheavals, and in 1846 Fribourg joined the reactionary Sonderbund, fighting against Protestant liberalism all around. It lost, and suffered expulsion of its Jesuits as revenge. Intolerance was short-lived, though: Jews were allowed to return to Fribourg in 1866 after almost 400 years of banishment, and a local entrepreneur, Georges Python, founded the Catholic university in 1889. The boom of the last few decades has brought new wealth and energy to the town.

Arrival, information and transport

Fribourg's **train station** is on a hill to the west of the town centre. As you emerge, shop-lined Avenue de la Gare heads left down to Place Python (pronounced *pee-tohh*), where the Old Town begins. Rue de Lausanne runs east down to the **Bourg** district, centred on Place de Notre-Dame (aka Place Tilleul) and the cathedral, below which steep lanes descend to **Neuveville** and **Auge**, the oldest parts of the Old Town. It's a walk of about 1.5km – downhill all the way – from the station to Auge.

Turn right out of the station for the **tourist office** (Mon–Fri 9am–6pm, Sat 9am–3pm; Oct–April Sat closes 12.30pm; ☎026 350 11 11, ⓦwww.fribourg tourism.ch & www.fribourgregion.ch). Cheery staff can provide information on the city and the whole canton, which extends south to Gruyères (covered in Chapter 2) and includes Murten/Morat and Estavayer-le-Lac (in Chapter 3).

Fribourg's festivals

In February, Fribourg's **carnival** focuses on the ritual torching of the Grand Rababou effigy, bearer of evil and the winter. **Bénichon** (Kilbi in German) is a harvest feast held in early September, with food stalls devoted to seasonal specialities such as mild mustard spread on oven-hot bread, *poires à botzi* (sweet pear compote), and *beignets* (sugared pastry leaves). Early October hosts a **fun run** over the 17km between Murten/Morat and Fribourg, to commemorate the messenger who brought news of victory at the Battle of Murten in 1476 (see p.153). **St Nicholas Day**, in early December, sees a parade headed by a jolly old man with a long white beard, who rides in on a donkey distributing *biscômes* (spicy cake squares) to the children of the town.

▲ Fribourg's Old Town

Markets occupy Place Python (Wed morning) and Place de l'Hôtel de Ville (Sat morning). Place du Petit-St-Jean hosts a flea market (April–Sept: first Sat of month).

Fribourg is definitely a **walking** city, but the Old Town alleys are steep enough that you may want to take advantage of **bus** #4, which runs every fifteen minutes on a handy route between Auge and the station ("Gare CFF"), via Place du Petit-St-Jean, Planche-Supérieure and Neuveville. Swiss Pass holders travel free; otherwise check fares at ⓦ www.tpf.ch.

Accommodation

Business **hotels** excepted, Fribourg has some characterful accommodation, well located in or next to the Old Town and covering a range of budgets.

Hostel

Auberge de Jeunesse (HI hostel) 2 Rue de l'Hôpital ☎ 026 323 19 16, ⓦ www.youthhostel.ch. Good-quality hostel – if a tad institutional – occupying part of the old city hospital a few minutes' walk north of the station. March–Oct. ❶

Hotels

Elite 7 Rue du Criblet ☎ 026 350 22 60, ⓦ www .elitefribourg.ch. Plain but adequate, within a few minutes' walk of the station. Weekend discounts. Cheaper attic rooms. ❷–❸

Faucon 76 Rue de Lausanne ☎ 026 321 37 90, ⓦ www.hotel-du-faucon.ch. Fresh little hotel in the pedestrianized Old Town, renovated in light, pastel shades, with good facilities. ❷–❸

Hotel de la Rose 1 Rue de Morat ☎ 026 351 01 01, ⓦ www.hoteldelarose.ch. Cosy and very central, with efficient, friendly staff. Good value, featuring modern, renovated rooms and a good onsite restaurant. ❹

🏃 **Sauvage** 12 Planche-Supérieure ☎ 026 347 30 60, ⓦ www.hotel-sauvage.ch. Comfortable rooms, spacious and individually decorated with charm and character, in a sixteenth-century town house on a lovely old square. Part of the Romantik hotel group. Free parking. Bus #4 stops outside. ❺

The Town

Skip the commercial shopping streets nearest the station – mocked by one of Jean Tinguely's sculptural **fountains**, a spouting, spitting affair on **Grands-Places**

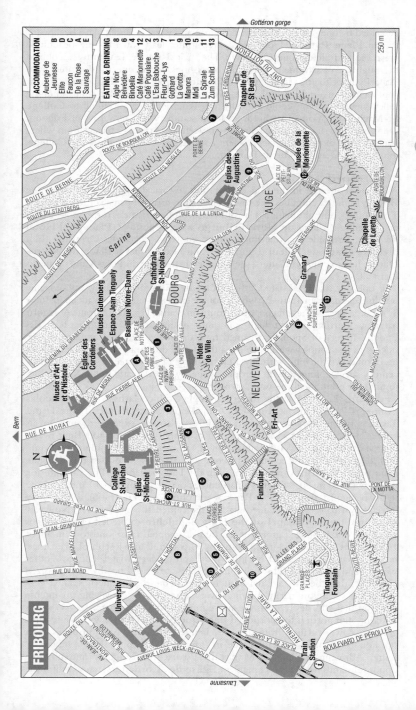

FRIBOURG

ACCOMMODATION	
Auberge de Jeunesse	B
Elite	D
Faucon	C
De la Rose	A
Sauvage	E

EATING & DRINKING	
Aigle Noir	8
Belvédère	6
Bindella	4
Café Marionnette	12
Café Populaire	2
L'Eau Babouche	3
Fleur-de-Lys	7
Gothard	1
La Grotta	9
Manora	10
Midi	5
La Spirale	11
Zum Schild	13

described by one critic as "a firework in iron and water" – and make a beeline for central **Place Python**. From here, three routes lead you into the beautifully preserved and picturesque Old Town. The main **Rue de Lausanne**, a cobbled thoroughfare of pavement cafés and bookshops, heads directly downhill from Place Python. To the right, quieter **Rue des Alpes** (duck through an arch) is another option – take a look, first, over the nearby railings for some stunning valley views – or you could cut left from Rue de Lausanne uphill to **Collège St-Michel**, for most of its history a Jesuit seminary and now part of Fribourg University. The shaded grounds are very peaceful, and there's a terrace from where you can look out over the city. Ancient covered steps, the **Escaliers du Collège**, join the lower end of Rue de Lausanne.

The Bourg

All routes converge in the Old Town's most historically important district, the **Bourg**, home to churches, the town hall and an array of patrician town houses. The Bourg's central square is a small space with four names. At the foot of Rue de Lausanne is **Place de Nova-Friburgo** with, opposite it, **Place de l'Hôtel de Ville**; alongside is a tree-lined square known as Place des Ormeaux (Elm Trees) or **Place de Tilleul** (Lime Tree); and next to that is **Place de Notre-Dame**. Just to confuse matters, the indeterminate Rue du Pont-Muré connects them all.

To one side stands the late Gothic **Hôtel de Ville** (Town Hall), a photogenic building dating from 1501–22, whose double exterior staircase was added in 1663. St George spears the dragon on a fountain statue (1525) in front. A regular Saturday morning market here spills into nearby streets, including Rue des Épouses (Street of Spouses), spanned by a decorative old sign attesting to the fidelity of the couples who once lived there. The dourly impressive **Grand'Rue** heads off down the hill, a virtually intact example of a seventeenth- to eighteenth-century street, complete with Baroque, Regency, Rococo and Louis-XVI facades jostling for position all the way down.

Fribourg's highlight is the towering, High Gothic **Cathédrale St-Nicolas** (Mon–Fri 9am–6pm, Sat 9am–4pm, Sun 2–5pm), just off Place Notre-Dame. Take a moment to view the soaring, buttressed **tower**, exposed to view for its entire 73-metre height clear to the ring of feathery spires on top. Built over a church dating from the city's foundation in 1157, the present building was begun in 1283, and took two centuries to complete. Traffic swishes past the elaborate main portal, featuring a tympanum with the Last Judgement. The vast interior, musty with old incense, features a particularly ornate **pulpit** (1516) and, opposite it, an octagonal **font** (1499). The tracery **choir screen** (1466) is dazzlingly intricate. Virtually all the stained glass in the cathedral is modern Art Nouveau. Don't miss the tiny **Chapel of the Holy Sepulchre**, to the left of the door as you head out: it holds a group of ten figures, sculpted from sandstone in about 1430. Christ is being laid in the tomb by Nicodemus and Joseph of Arimathea; behind, Mary is supported by John the Baptist, Mary Magdalene, two other women and two angels. Three sleeping soldiers are placed nearby. The life-sized ensemble, drenched in a blueish submarine light from modern stained-glass windows, is extraordinarily moving, every stony figure conveying an intense emotion that effortlessly spans the six centuries it has stood here.

About 50m north is the porticoed **Basilique Notre-Dame**, with white-and-gold stuccowork dating from the late eighteenth century. Samson prises apart the lion's jaws on a fountain statue in front (1547), copied from a design by Dürer. Adjacent on Rue de Morat, the Espace Jean Tinguely museum (see opposite) stands beside the Franciscan **Église des Cordeliers**, renovated in the eighteenth and nineteenth centuries but with original medieval decor, including a vast altar painting (1480) showing the crucifixion and, on the opened wings, the adoration. High Gothic oak choir stalls (1300), the oldest in Switzerland, and a larger-than-life 1438 statue of Christ at the whipping post also stand out. Behind is the **Musée Gutenberg** (Wed–Sat 11am–6pm, Thurs until 8pm, Sun 10am–5pm; Fr.10; Ⓦ www.gutenbergmuseum.ch), with engaging displays of printing and bookbinding.

Espace Jean Tinguely and Musée d'Art

In front of the Musée Gutenberg stands the excellent **Espace Jean Tinguely– Niki de St-Phalle**, 2 Rue de Morat (Wed–Sun 11am–6pm, Thurs until 8pm; Fr.6; Ⓦ www.fr.ch/mahf), devoted to the twentieth-century Swiss kinetic artist, who was born in Fribourg, and his artist wife. Housed in an old transport depot, this museum complements the more famous one in Basel (see p.178), documenting Tinguely's whimsical but trenchantly purposeful sculptural machines. Old rusty wheels, bits of iron and *objets trouvés* are all recycled in constructions which use a lot of energy and demonstrate great skill and ingenuity – but which go absolutely nowhere. One of the grandest on display is the *Retable de l'Abondance occidentale et du Mercantilisme totalitaire*; press the foot button to set things in eccentric but somehow poetic motion.

Walk 150m north to reach the **Musée d'Art et d'Histoire**, 12 Rue de Morat (Tues–Sun 11am–6pm, Thurs until 8pm; Fr.8; Ⓦ www.fr.ch/mahf). Begin on the left in the Ratzé mansion, filled with medieval art and reliquaries; upstairs resides the revolting jewel-bedecked skeleton of St Felix, dating from 1755, with glitter for lips. A tunnel connects to the old abattoir alongside, which now shelters saints' statues and a mournful Tinguely sculpture.

Neuveville and Planche-Supérieure

From the Hôtel de Ville, the ancient cobbled Rue de la Grand-Fontaine heads sharply downhill into **Neuveville**, perhaps the most photogenic area of the city, exemplified by the Escaliers du Court-Chemin (Short-Cut Stairs) which clatter down onto **Rue de la Neuveville**, boasting tinkling fountains and whole rows of original Gothic buildings. A quirky **funicular** (daily 9.30am–7pm; passes valid) runs down from St-Pierre, beside Place Python, to Place du Pertuis at the western end of Rue de la Neuveville: it works by tapping the city's sewers and diverting sewage into a chamber beneath the car at the top to make it heavy enough to haul its partner up the slope. It's the smelliest ride in Switzerland.

A backstreet off Rue de la Neuveville is home to the **Fri-Art** gallery, 22 Petites-Rames (Wed–Fri noon–6pm, Sat & Sun 2–5pm; Fr.6, free on Thurs 6–8pm; Ⓦ www.fri-art.ch), hosting changing exhibitions of contemporary art.

From Neuveville, the triple-arched Pont de St-Jean (1746) crosses the river to the **Planche-Supérieure** square, overlooked by a fountain statue of John the Baptist (1547) and the old **granary** (1708), with zigzagging step gables and chevron-design shutters. Cafés on the square offer incredible afternoon panoramas across the valley to the backs of the Grand'Rue mansions, supported on foundations plunging into the bedrock: they may show seven or more storeys of windows to the valley, but only the uppermost three or four are above street level. Stepped paths climb south to the **Chapelle de Lorette** (1648), an ornate little building on a lofty terrace with spectacular views.

Auge

From the cathedral, Grand'Rue and its parallel neighbours channel traffic down to cross the lofty Pont de Zaehringen, leaving the lower quarter of the Basse-Ville

(Lower Town) – known as **Auge** – mostly to pedestrians. This district, absorbed into the city as early as the 1160s, is the oldest in Fribourg. It's full of atmosphere, with its cobbled streets and Gothic houses still very much lived-in; the sense of community surviving in such ancient surroundings is what marks Fribourg out. The **Place du Petit-St-Jean** is the local hub, ringed by cafés. A little northwest is the **Église des Augustins**, part of a monastery founded in the mid-thirteenth century. The **Pont du Milieu** beetles southwest from the square to Planche-Supérieure, below the mighty precipices cut by the Sarine; beside the bridge is the titchy **Musée de la Marionnette** (Sat & Sun 2–5pm; Fr.5; Ⓦ www .marionnette.ch), with a lovely collection of puppets, face masks and other theatrical paraphernalia.

Northeast from the Place du Petit-St-Jean is the covered wooden **Pont de Berne**, leading to the ancient Rue des Forgerons (Street of the Blacksmiths) on the east bank of the river. The little bridgehead square leads onward left (northwest) to the **Porte de Berne**, a city gate dating from 1270 with its original doors, while riverside Rue des Forgerons – a narrow track – heads right (east) beneath the modern Pont du Gottéron some 60m up into the forested **Gottéron gorge**, past old mills and cottages. An hour's walk east is a crossing point at **Ameismühle**, from where high-level routes to both left and right can bring you back to the Pont de Berne.

Eating and drinking

Fribourg is something of a foodie's town. Fondue is a local speciality, served up in many of Fribourg's cheery **restaurants**, but there's also a good array of other options, including several places in the Old Town for unusually fine dining.

Cafés and café-bars

Belvédère 36 Grand'Rue. Amiable old café, tucked away at the head of the precipitous street Stalden and popular with students and alternative types. The mood is warm, the service friendly, but the appeal of the place is its comfy old armchairs, saggy sofas and bookcase-lined walls. An outside terrace gives eagle-eye views over the river. Also serves good, inexpensive food. Closes around midnight. Closed Mon.

🏃 **Café de la Marionnette** 2 Derrieres-les-Jardins Ⓦ www.cafe-marionnette.ch. Wonderful little hideaway beside the marionnette museum at the foot of the town – think old sofas, red drapes, wood floors, a wind-up gramophone and a piano with a candelabrum – it's got the lot.

Hole up with a slice of cake, or take a light lunch on the enclosed rear terrace. Closed Mon & Tues. **Café Populaire** 9 Rue St-Michel Ⓦ www .cafepopulaire.ch. A popular student café-bar, also offering simple stomach-fillers like bagels, salads and baked potatoes. Closed Sun. **Midi** 25 Rue de Romont Ⓦ www.lemidi.ch. One of the best pavement cafés along this central shopping street, in prime people-watching territory. Also does decent food, including Fribourgeois fondue. **La Spirale** 39 Place du Petit-St-Jean Ⓦ www .laspirale.ch. Cellar bar and venue for live music, with small-scale gigs, DJs and a range of jazzy performers. Wed–Sun 8.30pm–2am.

Restaurants

Aigle Noir 10 Rue des Alpes ☎ 026 322 49 77, Ⓦ www.aiglenoir.ch. Quality French cuisine (from Fr.35) in the heart of the Old Town, with an attractive modern interior and warmly efficient service. Closed Sun & Mon. **Bindella** 38 Rue de Lausanne ☎ 026 322 49 05, Ⓦ www.bindella.ch. Classy Italian in the city centre,

with cosy, warm decor and excellent fresh pastas (*menus* around Fr.25). **L'Eau à la Babouche** 25 Rue de Lausanne ☎ 026 321 36 46. Cheerful Moroccan terrace café-cum-restaurant in the centre of town. Stop in for a mint tea, or go for specialities such as pastilla, tagine or couscous (Fr.25–35).

Fleur-de-Lys 18 Rue des Forgerons ☎026 321 49 40. A gastronome's delight on a medieval lane by the river. A tumbledown exterior preludes a cosy, atmospheric interior and fresh seasonal dishes of the highest quality: plump for the five-course *menu du marché* (Fr.80) or *menu tradition* (Fr.100). Locals love the place. Closed Sat lunch, Sun & Mon.

Gothard 18 Rue du Pont-Muré. A Fribourg institution, beloved of Jean Tinguely, which is just about the last old-fashioned café in town, opened in 1861 and in the hands of the same *patronne* for decades. Equally popular with old-timers at their regular seats sipping a beer as with students downing an espresso before heading off to a party. Posters and ephemera cover the walls under a riot of fairy-light decoration, but the food is solid quality – excellent fondues, and daily *menus* for Fr.18 or so. Closed Wed.

La Grotta 5 Rue d'Or ☎026 322 81 00, ⊛www .lagrotta.ch. Romantic little Italian insinuated into the rocky cliffs of Auge – a low, wood-panelled dining room preludes an even tinier rear cellar, every table laid perfectly with candles. Service is careful and welcoming; pasta and risotto are filled out with notably good fish. *Menus* Fr.60–70. Closed Sat lunch, Sun & Mon.

Manora Grands-Places. The Manor department store houses a good, low-priced self-service restaurant (see p.44), with fifth-floor views. Closed Sun.

Zum Schild 21 Planche-Supérieure ☎026 322 42 25, ⊛www.le-schild.ch. Fine, award-winning restaurant in a sixteenth-century town house, offering refined modern French cuisine in a pleasant, upscale atmosphere. During the hunting season (Oct & Nov) expect a full range of game. Reckon on Fr.50 and above. Closed Wed & Thurs.

Travel details

Full timetables for all trains, buses, trams, boats and cable cars in Switzerland – as well as international connections – are searchable at ⊛www.rail.ch. For details of the boat trip on the River Aare from Solothurn to Biel/Bienne, see ⊛www.bielersee.ch.

Trains

Bern to: Baden (twice hourly; 1hr 10min); Basel (every 30min; 1hr); Biel/Bienne (3 hourly; 30min); Brig (hourly; 1hr 35min); Burgdorf (3 hourly; 15min); Fribourg (every 30min; 20min); Geneva (every 30min; 1hr 45min); Interlaken West & Ost (every 30min; 45min); Langnau (4 hourly; 40min); Lausanne (twice hourly; 1hr 10min); Lucerne (twice hourly; 1hr 5min); Neuchâtel (3 hourly; 35min); Solothurn (every 30min; 40min); Thun (4 hourly; 20min); Zürich (3 hourly; 1hr).

Fribourg to: Bern (every 30min; 20min); Estavayer (hourly; 40min); Lausanne (twice hourly; 45min); Murten/Morat (hourly; 25min); Yverdon (hourly; 55min).
Solothurn to: Bern (every 30min; 40min); Biel/Bienne (3 hourly; 20min); Neuchâtel (twice hourly; 40min); Zürich (twice hourly; 55min).

Buses

Fribourg to: Avenches (8 daily; 25min); Bulle (for Gruyères; hourly; 30min).
Kemmeriboden to: Schangnau (every 2hr; 15min).

Boats

Solothurn to: Biel/Bienne (April–Oct 2–3 daily; 2hr 50min).

6

The Bernese Oberland

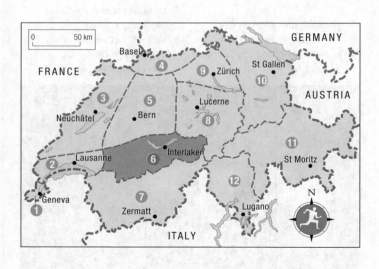

CHAPTER 6 # Highlights

✳ **Interlaken** Bustling resort town at the hub of the region's excellent mountain railway network. See p.233

✳ **Schynige Platte** One of the finest Alpine viewpoints. See p.239

✳ **Lauterbrunnen valley** Breathtaking U-shaped cleft, its high, craggy walls doused by waterfalls such as the Trümmelbach. See p.240

✳ **Wengen and Mürren** Car-free mountain resorts with superb skiing and fine hiking. See p.243

✳ **Schilthorn** The cable-car ride up to this lofty summit is unforgettably dramatic. See p.244

✳ **Grindelwald** Long-acclaimed ski and sports resort at the foot of the mighty Eiger. See p.246

✳ **Jungfraujoch** The train ride up to Europe's highest station is easily done in a day from Interlaken. See p.250

✳ **Gstaad** Legendary Alpine hideaway of the rich and famous, set amidst lovely countryside on the Golden Pass train line. See p.262

▲ Alfresco drinking, Interlaken

The Bernese Oberland

outh of Bern and Lucerne lies the grand Alpine heart of Switzerland, a massively impressive region of classic Swiss scenery – high peaks, sheer valleys and cool lakes – that makes for great hiking and gentle walking, not to mention world-class winter sports. The **BERNESE OBERLAND** (Ⓦwww.berneseoberland.ch) is the most accessible and touristed area, and also the most spectacular, best known for a triple-peaked ridge of Alpine giants at its core: the Eiger, Mönch and Jungfrau, cresting 4000m. On the approaches to the high mountains, **Lake Thun** – or, in German, the Thunersee (with the atmospheric old town of **Thun** at its head) – and **Lake Brienz** or Brienzersee (with **Brienz**) offer Alpine beauty to merit a stop of their own. Between them, the bustling town of **Interlaken** is the main transport hub for the region, but the sheer volume of tourist traffic passing through can make it a less-than-restful place to stay; you'd do better to head straight for the mountains.

Exploring the Bernese Oberland

Rail ticket offices sell the **Bernese Oberland Regional Pass** (Ⓦwww.regiopass -berneroberland.ch), which has a vast area of validity. The **core region** extends from Gstaad to Meiringen, and includes boats and trains between Thun, Interlaken and Brienz, as well as trains, buses, funiculars and cable cars serving Schynige Platte, Lauterbrunnen, Mürren, Stechelberg, Wengen, Grindelwald, First, Kleine Scheidegg and Kandersteg. Core-region transport is free on the days you choose, and half-price the rest of the time. **All other transport** in the region is half-price throughout the pass's validity (aside from a few cable cars which offer only a 25 percent discount): this includes the rides up to the Jungfraujoch and the Schilthorn; trains from Bern to Thun, Lucerne to Brienz, and Montreux to Gstaad; buses over the Grimsel, Furka and Susten passes; and a network of connections further afield.

There are two passes, both available in the summer season only (May–Oct). The **seven-day pass** (Fr.230) covers any three days of free travel in the core region, plus the remaining four days' travel throughout the area at half-price. The **fifteen-day pass** (Fr.277) covers any five days' core-region travel for free, plus the remaining ten days at half-price across the area.

On a visit to the region, and stunned by the natural drama all around, the composer Felix Mendelssohn wrote: "Anyone who has not seen the scenery which surrounds Interlaken does not know Switzerland." Once you've seen it, you'll know what he meant. Arguably the single most captivating place in the entire Alps lies just a short way south of Interlaken – the gorgeous **Lauterbrunnen valley**, with the resorts of **Wengen** and **Mürren** perched on plateaux above providing excellent winter skiing and summer hiking. **Grindelwald** is another bustling resort in its own valley slightly to the east. Both offer access to one of Switzerland's top excursions, the rack-railway journey winding up through spectacular mountain scenery to the ice-bound **Jungfraujoch**, a windswept col nestling at 3454m just below the peak of the Jungfrau itself, and the site of the highest train station in Europe. Further west, the Oberland rolls on through less-visited wooded valleys and pastureland, out to the borders of the German-speaking area, where **Gstaad** sits.

Tourist offices have information on thousands of **chalets** and **private rooms**, many of which close in the quiet off-season. They can also provide details of the region's numerous **mountain huts** (generally open June–Sept), which offer hikers or ski trekkers a bed and simple comforts in the wilds of nature.

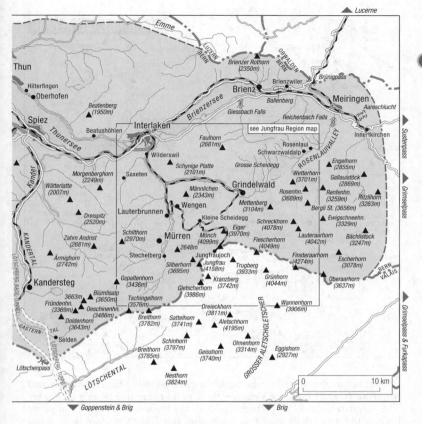

Beware that almost everything in the high resorts – shops, hotels, attractions, walking routes, mountain railways and cable cars – may be **closed during off-season** (mid-April to early June & mid-Oct to mid-Dec); see p.27 for more. We've specified months of opening only when they differ from this pattern.

The Jungfrau region

The **JUNGFRAU REGION** (ⓦ www.jungfrau.ch) lying south of the gateway resort of **Interlaken** is the rather uninspiring title foisted on what is perhaps the most dramatic, certainly the most memorable, mountain scenery in the whole of Switzerland. The quantity and scale of the awesome giants on offer here at close quarters takes your breath away.

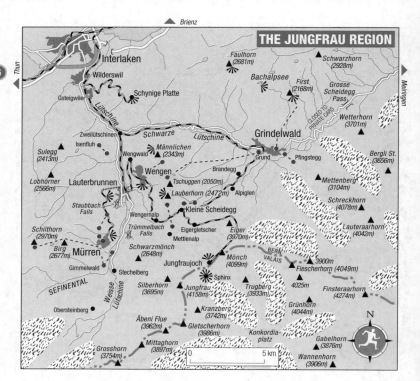

Sightlines are dominated by the mighty triple crest of the **Eiger**, **Mönch and Jungfrau** (Ogre, Monk and Virgin) – three peaks rising side by side to 4000m. The Jungfrau is the focus, partly because it's the highest (at 4158m), and partly because the network of mountain trains from Interlaken Ost culminates at the **Jungfraujoch**, a saddle below the peak that hosts the highest train station in Europe. The ride up – dubbed "Top of Europe" – is touted endlessly in Interlaken and beyond as being the highlight of your holiday; despite the hype, it's not far wrong, although the competing journey up the **Schilthorn**, also accessed from Interlaken Ost, is cheaper, quicker, less crowded and uses cable cars – always more scenic and dramatic than cogwheel trains.

There's plenty of equally stunning scenery to be enjoyed at lower altitudes. The region is centred on two valleys, which divide a few kilometres south of

Exploring the Jungfrau region

All mountain transport in the region comes under the umbrella of the **Jungfraubahnen** (Ⓦ www.jungfraubahn.ch), which takes in BOB trains from Interlaken Ost to Lauterbrunnen and Grindelwald; WAB trains from Lauterbrunnen, Wengen and Grindelwald up to Kleine Scheidegg; JB trains from Kleine Scheidegg to the Jungfraujoch; the SPB line to Schynige Platte; the BLM route from Lauterbrunnen to Mürren; the HB funicular from Interlaken to Harderkulm; a load of cable-car routes (including GGM Grindelwald–Männlichen, LWM Wengen–Männlichen, BGF Grindelwald–First and LGP Grindelwald–Pfingstegg); and Grindelwald's buses

Interlaken. To the west is the **Lauterbrunnen valley**, celebrated as the loveliest mountain valley in Europe, with its car-free resorts of Wengen and Mürren. To the east, the narrow Lütschental widens out on its way to **Grindelwald**, perfectly placed for its many visitors to take advantage of the hiking and skiing possibilities all around. Excellent transport means that you can roam to your heart's content – which, with the quality of natural scenery on offer, may take a while.

Interlaken

Don't be ashamed of being a tourist in **INTERLAKEN** – that's what the place exists for. Interlaken is all that many visitors ever see of Switzerland, whisked through the country on a rapid lakes-and-mountains tour. The town is perfectly positioned as the gateway into the Oberland, linked into main train routes to and from Bern and Zürich, with branch lines feeding out in all directions into the high Alps nearby. It's a pleasant enough place, if commercial, and it's useful for its proximity to the mountains.

The town is situated on the Bödeli, an alluvial neck of land between the twin **lakes** of the Thunersee and Brienzersee. It's one of the oldest resorts in the country, famed for its superb **views** towards the Jungfrau massif, which lies perfectly framed between two hills to the south of town. And that's pretty much the whole story: history, character and tradition take a back seat to the necessities of providing for the millions of trippers who pass through on their way to more dramatic backdrops. Many of the shops which cram the centre of town have prominent signs in Japanese (a quarter of visitors are from Japan).

Arrival and information

Interlaken clusters around its long main street, **Höheweg**, which has a train station at each end. Mainline trains terminate at **Interlaken Ost** station, 1km east of the centre, but those coming from the Bern/Thun direction pass first through **Interlaken West** station, a more useful place to get off since it's closer to the town centre. (Be aware that branch-line trains into the mountains depart only from Ost station.) Both stations are linked by trains and city buses, which run roughly every ten minutes from one to the other.

See the box on p.253 for details of the **boats** which run on the lakes flanking Interlaken; those from Brienz dock directly behind Ost station, those from Thun behind West station.

Interlaken is only one of five communities on the neck of land between the two lakes: to the west is **Unterseen**; to the south are **Matten** and, a little further

as far as the Grosse Scheidegg pass. **Swiss Pass** holders get free travel on all transport as far up as Mürren, Wengen and Grindelwald, and a 25 percent discount on journeys higher than this.

The **Jungfraubahnen Pass** (May–Oct only; Fr.200) is a cheaper but more limited alternative to the Bernese Oberland Regional Pass (see p.229): it is valid for free travel on six consecutive days on all trains, buses, cable cars and gondolas in the region, except the railway line between Eigergletscher and Jungfraujoch, for which you get a fifty percent discount.

For coverage of Interlaken's twin **lakes** of Thun and Brienz, turn to p.252.

out, **Wilderswil**; to the east is **Bönigen**. Although the built-up area is contiguous from one to another, all five retain their individual identity and postal codes: if you go looking for something on Hauptstrasse, be aware that Unterseen's Hauptstrasse is a long way from Matten's Hauptstrasse.

The **tourist office** is in the town centre, on the ground floor of the *Hotel Metropole*, Interlaken's only skyscraper, at Höheweg 37 (June Mon–Fri 8am–6pm, Sat 8am–4pm; July & Aug Mon–Fri 8am–7pm, Sat 8am–5pm, Sun 10am–noon & 5–7pm; Sept Mon–Fri 8am–6pm; Oct–May Mon–Fri 8am–noon & 1.30–6pm, Sat 9am–noon; ☎033 826 53 00, ⓦwww.interlaken.ch).

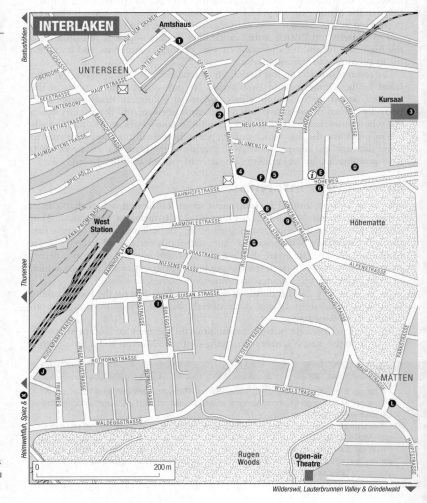

INTERLAKEN

Wilderswil, Lauterbrunnen Valley & Grindelwald ▼

Guests staying overnight are entitled to a free **Interlaken Visitors Card**, giving unlimited use of all local transport. Several operators have mountain and city **bikes for rent**, including at both train stations and several of the hostels.

Accommodation

Interlaken has literally dozens of **accommodation** options. The downside of the town's popularity is that breakfasts can be skimpier, corners dusted less assiduously, and personal service less expansive than in quieter towns. Beware that all accommodation fills up very quickly in the summer season. In winter, when most people stay in the mountains, many places close for a month or two.

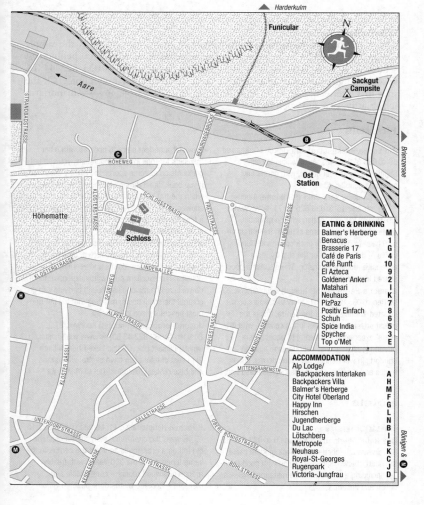

Harderkulm

Funicular

N

Aare

Sackgut
Campsite

Brienzersee

B

HÖHEWEG

C

Ost
Station

SCHLOSSSTRASSE

KLOSTERSTRASSE

FREIESTRASSE

ALLMENDSTRASSE

Höhematte

Schloss

STRANDBADSTRASSE

LINDENALLEE

KLOSTERSTRASSE

H

SPARWEG

ALPENSTRASSE

FREIESTRASSE

ALLMENDSTRASSE

KLOSTER GASSLI

MITTENGRABENSTR.

OELESTRASSE

OBERE BÖNIGSTRASSE

UNTERDORFSTRASSE

M

KESSLERGASSE

RÜTISTRASSE

BÜHLSTRASSE

Bönigen & N

EATING & DRINKING

Balmer's Herberge	M
Benacus	1
Brasserie 17	G
Café de Paris	4
Café Runft	10
El Azteca	9
Goldener Anker	2
Matahari	I
Neuhaus	K
PizPaz	7
Positiv Einfach	8
Schuh	6
Spice India	5
Spycher	3
Top o'Met	E

ACCOMMODATION

Alp Lodge/ Backpackers Interlaken	A
Backpackers Villa	H
Balmer's Herberge	M
City Hotel Oberland	F
Happy Inn	G
Hirschen	L
Jugendherberge	N
Du Lac	B
Lötschberg	I
Metropole	E
Neuhaus	K
Royal-St-Georges	C
Rugenpark	J
Victoria-Jungfrau	D

Open-air Tell

Interlaken is famous throughout Switzerland for its annual staging of Schiller's play **William Tell**, performed every summer since 1912 in an open-air theatre (with covered seating) in the Rugen woods near Matten. The stage is framed by old wooden houses in thirteenth-century style, and backed by the forest – the perfect backdrop for the cast of 250, all sporting Swiss national dress and authentic medieval uniforms, and the several dozen horses, cattle and farm animals which wander around bringing a festive air to the show. The dialogue is in German only, but it's pretty obvious what the plot is (see p.346).

Evening performances run twice weekly from July to September. **Tickets** (Fr.32–48) are available at ⓦ www.tellspiele.ch and from most tourist offices in the region. The Interlaken tourist office has packages comprising accommodation plus tickets, from around Fr.150/250 for one/two nights.

Camping

There are thirteen **campsites** within 4km of town. The closest is the simple *Sackgut* (☏033 822 44 34, ⓦ www.campinginterlaken.ch; May–Oct) behind Ost station. Less than 1km south of the centre is *Jungfraublick* (☏033 822 44 14, ⓦ www.jungfraublick.ch; May–Sept), a more comfortable family choice. Of the sites in Unterseen, lakeside *Manor Farm* (☏033 822 22 64, ⓦ www.manorfarm .ch) is a five-star site open all year.

Hostels

Alp Lodge/Backpackers Interlaken Marktgasse 59 ☏033 822 47 48, ⓦ www.alplodge.com. Slightly down-at-heel hostel, with dorms and adequate doubles. ❶

Backpackers Villa (SB hostel) Alpenstrasse 16 ☏033 826 71 71, ⓦ www.villa .ch. Quality low-cost option with comfortable, spotless dorms and rooms either in the attractive old chalet (rooms at the back command stunning views of the Jungfrau) or the slightly more expensive modern extension. There's also a good shared kitchen. ❶

Balmer's Herberge (SB hostel) Hauptstrasse 23, Matten ☏033 822 19 61, ⓦ www.balmers.com. Located 15min south of the centre, this is the oldest privately run hostel in the country, with fifty years' experience of catering to backpackers, offering kitchen access, laundry, and spartan comforts in well-tended pinewood dorms, quads, triples and doubles. The atmosphere is brash and

convivial, a perfect place to hook up with other travellers for trips into the mountains; you can get discounts on extreme sports and activity excursions if you book direct through the hostel. In summer, when the frat-party atmosphere and queues for the shower and for breakfast get too much, they set up a tent village in a field 800m south, with tents sleeping over a hundred. ❶

Happy Inn (SB hostel) Rosenstrasse 17 ☏033 822 32 25, ⓦ www.happy-inn.com. Clean and centrally located with dorms and very cheap doubles. The excellent pub (with inexpensive food) downstairs is a major plus, though partying can go on until the small hours, meaning that it's not the most peaceful place in town. ❶

Jugendherberge (HI hostel) Aareweg 21, Bönigen ☏033 822 43 53, ⓦ www.youthhostel.ch. Quiet, pleasant place in this Lake Brienz village 2km east of Interlaken town centre, with dorms and bike rental. Closed mid-Oct to March. ❶

Hotels

Inexpensive

City Hotel Oberland Marktgasse 6 ☏033 827 87 87, ⓦ www.city-oberland.ch. Slick modern place in the heart of town, spotlessly clean with good facilities including a trio of in-house restaurants (Swiss, Italian and Indian). ❸–❹

Hirschen Hauptstrasse 11, Matten ☏033 822 15 45, ⓦ www.hirschen-interlaken.ch. Atmospheric old inn on a crossroads south of the centre, in the same family for some 300 years, with freshly redone pinewood rooms – comfortable and pleasant – boosted by the dark-beamed *Stübli* and restaurant. Also has plenty of parking. Closed Nov. ❷–❸

Lötschberg General-Guisanstrasse 31 ☎033 822 25 45, ⓦ www.lotschberg.ch. Characterful family-run hotel in a residential quarter, with inexpensive rooms, plus some keenly priced apartments. There are further excellent-value rooms at the attached *Susi's B&B* guesthouse. Discounts for long stays. Closed Jan. ❸

Rugenpark Rugenparkstrasse 19 ☎033 822 36 61, ⓦ www.rugenpark.ch. Quiet, very friendly family-run little place close to West station, with modest, attractive rooms that are cosily unrenovated – only some are en suite. ❶–❷

Mid-range and expensive

Du Lac Höheweg 225 ☎033 822 29 22, ⓦ www.dulac-interlaken.ch. Comfortable, stylish old house in a perfectly quiet riverside location beside Ost station. In the same family since 1888 (and at one time hosting Field Marshal Montgomery during World War II), it offers bright, light rooms that are a mid-range bargain. ❹–❺

Metropole Höheweg 37 ☎033 828 66 66, ⓦ www.metropole-interlaken.ch. The town's major landmark, and its sole high-rise, soaring above the tourist office. Generic business-class facilities inside, memorable only for the stunning upper-floor views (the fourteenth is top), which are worth paying for. ❺–❼

🏃 **Neuhaus** Seestrasse 121, Neuhaus on the Thunersee ☎033 822 82 82, ⓦ www.hotel-neuhaus.ch. Far and away the most relaxing spot in and around Interlaken, a lone old inn guarding this end of the Thunersee, 4km west of the centre. It styles itself as a golf and beach hotel – stretching the definition on both scores – although, with sailing and watersports on offer, it's a popular weekend draw for locals. You can always find a quiet spot on the lakeside lawns to take in the stunning views over to the Niesen. Reception is in the modern annexe to one side, but ask for a room in the main house (which doubles as a fine restaurant): they're neither big nor modern, but are characterful and wonderfully quiet. The welcome is warm – this is a corner few tourists find – and boosts the feeling of being well out of the Interlaken hubbub. Free parking. ❸–❹

Royal-St-Georges Höheweg 139 ☎033 822 75 75, ⓦ www.royal-stgeorges.ch. Wonderfully stuffy town-centre palace hotel, renovated to prime Victorian-era condition throughout. ❺–❻

🏃 **Victoria-Jungfrau** Höheweg 41 ☎033 828 28 28, ⓦ www.victoria-jungfrau.ch. One of the grandest hotels in the country, dating from 1864–65, which is located perfectly in the town centre and once hosted Mark Twain on his journey around Switzerland. These days it's been entirely restored (although its front rooms still boast sensational views of the Jungfrau) and now incorporates a beautiful, state-of-the-art luxury spa. Staying here is a really special treat. ❾

In and above the town

Interlaken itself is only of passing interest, with precious little to see or do other than a couple of hours of exploratory wanderings, either on foot or from the back of one of the horse-drawn carriages which ply for business outside West station. The large grassy **Höhematte** in the centre of town was where the monks of Interlaken's ancient Augustinian monastery pastured their cattle; on the east side of the park is the **Schloss**, dating from 1747 but incorporating some of the fifteenth-century monastical buildings. Parts of the Gothic church survive in the renovated **Schlosskirche** adjacent, which has also clung onto its old cloister, each window of which, curiously, is of a different design. Strolling west along the River Aare beneath the looming cliffs brings you into pretty **Unterseen**. This atmospheric district houses some of the area's oldest buildings: the square in front of the Amtshaus off Untere Gasse is particularly picturesque.

Interlaken starts to reveal its secrets when you explore further afield. Before you even venture into the mountains, there are a couple of viewpoints above the town to enjoy, both laced with hiking trails. A funicular (May–Oct) rises from behind Ost station through the woods to the **Harderkulm** (1310m), offering vistas over the town, both lakes and a panorama of snowy peaks close enough to touch. Thursday evening sees folk music and dancing at the summit restaurant, with special late trains laid on; book through the tourist office. On the other side of town, some 500m south of West station, is a station for the vintage red funicular (May–Oct) serving the **Heimwehfluh** (669m), a more

Touring the Alpine passes

The configuration of roads over the high Alps means that it's straightforward to put together a looping day-long driving tour of the highest roads in Europe, bringing with it spectacular scenery from every angle. Every one of the passes mentioned below has at least a restaurant on top, and most have some form of inn accommodation as well, making it easy to break your journey.

From Interlaken, lakeside roads run to Brienz and on to Meiringen (see p.258), just beyond which at Innertkirchen is a split of mountain routes. East lies the Susten Pass (see below), while south is the stunning climb to the **Grimsel Pass** (2165m; see p.307), beyond which, at Gletsch, is another choice of routes. You could head down the valley of the young Rhône and branch off near Oberwald over the **Nufenen Pass** (2478m; see p.307), followed by a scenic drive to Airolo and up over the celebrated **Gotthard Pass** (2108m; see p.348) to the Alpine hub town of Andermatt. Alternatively, from Gletsch another hairpin route leads steeply up on a breathtaking drive over the **Furka Pass** (2431m; see p.349) and on down to Andermatt. From Andermatt, continue north through the Reuss gorges to Wassen, where a road climbs west up over the **Susten Pass** (2224m) and back to Meiringen.

The easiest way to go is with one or other of the excellent summer tours by **postbus** (ⓦwww.postbus.ch). The **Four Passes tour** from Meiringen follows the route outlined above, taking in the Grimsel, Nufenen, Gotthard and Susten in a full-day loop. Alternatively, the **"Ticino Route Express"** runs from Andermatt over the Gotthard and Nufenen passes to Oberwald, while the **"Romantic Route Express"** runs from Andermatt over the Furka and Grimsel before following the spectacular narrow route from Meiringen over the **Grosse Scheidegg Pass** (1962m; closed to private cars) to Grindelwald. All transport passes are valid, but you must pay a small surcharge and reserve a seat in advance (see the website).

---

touristic venture, with the summit often crowded with parents taking the kids round the model-train exhibition and the miniature bob-run.

Eating and drinking

Most of Interlaken's **restaurants** offer fairly basic, unadventurous fare. For self-service staples head to *Migros* restaurant opposite West station (closed Sun).

Cafés and café-bars

Balmer's Herberge The sociable travellers' bar attached to this busy hostel (see p.236) serves up cheap beer nightly to its backpacking clientele.

Brasserie 17 Rosenstrasse 17. Loud central pub beneath the *Happy Inn* hostel, with cheap food (sandwiches, snacks and veggie fare) and big beers.

Café de Paris Marktgasse. Sociable café serving up good sandwiches, salads and good-value lunchtime *menus* (around Fr.17). Choose between the perky modern interior or the attractive terrace on the small square outside.

Café Runft Bahnhofplatz 51, opposite West station. A cosy tearoom, snackery and bar open daily until 3am.

Goldener Anker Marktgasse 57 ⓦwww.anker.ch. Local pub crammed most nights with young people hanging out and shooting pool. The food is cheap

and simple (*menus* from Fr.21), and occasional live bands fill out the atmosphere.

Positiv Einfach Centralstrasse 11 ⓦwww .positiv-einfach.ch. Popular and crowded little bar with DJs or live music most nights – anything from jazz to house.

Schuh Höheweg 56 ⓦwww.schuh-interlaken.ch. A tearoom-cum-*chocolatier*-cum-restaurant on the corner of the Höhematte – refinement in the midst of kitsch-souvenir hell. The elegant interior preludes equally elegant tea and cakes or international cuisine (plus veggie options), helped down by the cocktail pianist tinkling away in the corner. Daytime *menus* Fr.20; evening à la carte Fr.20–50.

Top o'Met Top floor of *Hotel Metropole*, Höheweg 37. Fifteenth-floor views out over the town and lakes, with an outdoor terrace.

Restaurants

Benacus Kirchgasse 3, Unterseen ☎ 033 821 20 20, ⓦ www.benacus.ch. Svelte modern wine bar in a nice corner of the Old Town with a small but eclectic menu (steaks, salads, tapas, curries) in the evenings, plus good lunchtime *menus* (from Fr.16). Closed Sun & Mon.

El Azteca Jungfraustrasse 30 ☎ 033 822 71 31, ⓦ www.hotel-blume.ch. Attractive little Mexican place with tasty food (*menus* Fr.22–38) and live mariachi (Fri & Sat). Closed Wed in winter.

Hirschen Hauptstrasse 11, Matten ☎ 033 822 15 45, ⓦ www.hirschen-interlaken.ch. Traditional, rustic old wood-beamed inn serving up huge portions of steaming Swiss fare, with *menus* from Fr.25 or so. Closed Tues.

Matahari *Hotel Lötschberg*, General-Guisanstrasse 31 ☎ 033 823 80 01. Quality Indonesian cuisine, including *rijsttafel*, a sampler of many Indonesian dishes, plus a range of Indian dishes with plenty for vegetarians. *Menus* around Fr.22. Closed Tues & lunch on Wed.

Neuhaus Comfortable old inn (see p.237) situated right on the Thunersee shore, with views across the water from the large waterside terrace. The quality of both cooking and service is high. The speciality is, of course, freshly caught fish (around Fr.30), and there are some excellent vegetarian dishes (Fr.25 or so).

PizPaz Centralplatz ☎ 033 822 25 33. Pleasant modern place serving generic pasta, pizza and fish dishes from around Fr.15. Closed Mon in off-season.

Spice India Postgasse 6 ☎ 033 821 00 91, ⓦ www.spice-india.net. Upmarket Indian dining, with broad range of North Indian meat standards (Fr.29–36) – tandooris, tikkas, kebabs and biryanis – plus an excellent vegetarian selection (Fr.18–22). Closed Mon.

Schynige Platte

The best short trip from Interlaken – and one of the finest mountain excursions in the country – is the ride up to the breathtaking **SCHYNIGE PLATTE** at 2000m, from where you can survey some of the best panoramic views in the entire Alps.

The rack-railway (June–Oct only) up to Schynige Platte starts from the peaceful village of **Wilderswil**, a few kilometres south of Interlaken, reachable from Ost station by train or from West station by bus #5. It's an attractive little place in its own right, full of traditional wooden houses; the main road bypasses the village centre. From Wilderswil, trains coil their way up for fifty minutes through some spectacular scenery to the top station, from where perfect views of the Eiger, Mönch and Jungfrau, ranged high above the valley opposite, open up. A short walk away is the busy restaurant and **hotel** *Schynige Platte* (☎ 033 828 73 73, ⓦ www.schynigeplatte.ch; ❷).

Marked trails branch out in all directions from here. The easy **Panoram-aweg** leads you on a two-hour circuit of the summit ridge above the station, with, at the halfway point, an unforgettable panoramic view taking in the full sweep of Lake Thun, Interlaken and Lake Brienz. The return leg continues in a wide arc through meadows to the **Botanischer Alpengarten** (ⓦ www .alpengarten.ch; free), filled with the local flora, and one of the few places where you can be guaranteed to see a genuine living edelweiss. As a longer alternative, a fine walk leads from Schynige Platte along the crest up to the Faulhorn (2681m), and then down past the tranquil Bachalpsee to First and Grindelwald (roughly 6hr).

The standard **fare** from Interlaken is Fr.65 return (Swiss Pass half-price), or Fr.30 after 2pm; two kids can travel free with a fare-paying adult. Buying a cheaper ticket to the midway station of Breitlauenen and enjoying the views on the walk to the top (1hr 30min) is no hardship.

The Lauterbrunnen valley

It's hard to overstate just how stunning the **LAUTERBRUNNEN VALLEY** is – even hardened Alpinists shrug their shoulders and call it the most beautiful valley in Europe, bar none. An immense U-shaped cleft (the world's deepest) with bluffs on either side rising 1000m sheer, doused by some 72 waterfalls, it is utterly spectacular. Staying in Interlaken or Grindelwald comes a poor second to basing yourself in or above Lauterbrunnen: whether you stay two hours or two weeks, you won't want to leave.

Lauterbrunnen village stands on the valley floor, while the slopes above nurture two of Switzerland's most appealing little resorts. **Mürren** to the west is the transfer point for the dramatic cable-car ride up to the **Schilthorn** peak, while **Wengen** to the east is a stop on the train line up to Kleine Scheidegg and the **Jungfraujoch**. Both of them are car-free, perched on narrow shelves of pasture, and both offer some of the best hiking and skiing to be had in the Alps.

Lauterbrunnen

The road south from Interlaken shadows the train tracks and the River Lütschine through Wilderswil. Cliffs close in either side as you reach **Zweilütschinen**: the Schwarze Lütschine tumbles in from Grindelwald further east, while the road and railway continue south alongside the rushing Weisse

---

Sports and activities in the Jungfrau region

The Jungfrau region offers a vast array of **sports** and **activities**. We've outlined the best summer walks throughout this chapter, and highlighted a week-long trail in the box on p.245.

Winter sports

In winter, resorts like Wengen, Mürren and Grindelwald can offer some of the finest skiing and snowboarding in the Alps: ⓦ**www.jungfrauwinter.ch** has the full rundown. The Jungfrau region is divided into three ski sectors: **Grindelwald-First**, **Kleine Scheidegg-Männlichen** (which includes lifts from both the Grindelwald and Wengen sides) and **Mürren-Schilthorn**. There's skiing and snowboarding for all levels and the season is unusually long: from mid-November through to the end of April. Beginners are best served at **Wengen** and **Grindelwald**, both of which have nursery slopes and plenty of blue runs very close to the village centres. Red pistes run beneath the long Männlichen–Grindelwald gondola line, while there are long blue runs from **Kleine Scheidegg** down to Brandegg and Grindelwald-Grund. **First** (2168m), above Grindelwald, also has a host of blue and red runs. **Mürren** offers some wonderfully scenic skiing, with a chairlift accessing more than half-a-dozen routes down from the Schiltgrat (2145m), and the Allmendhubel funicular linking with a draglift to access lots more pistes-with-a-view.

There are thrilling red and black runs from the **Lauberhorn** down to Wengen, following the course of the famous World Cup downhills and slaloms. At 4km, this is the world's longest competition piste; if you're around in mid-January try and catch a glimpse of the professionals. Black runs around the region are satisfyingly testing, most notably those down to Wengen from the **Eigergletscher** (2320m). The steep "Inferno" piste from the Schilthorn summit (2970m), through difficult mogul fields and the infamous "Gun Barrel" down to Mürren, covers 11km.

The best location for **snowboarding** is the Snowpark at Bärgelegg (2501m), above First, where there's an array of rails, bank jumps, waves and kickers, plus a giant superpipe at Schreckfeld. Plenty of options for **sledging** include from Alpiglen to

Lütschine (named "white" for its foaminess) through a charming wooded gorge. At the point where the valley opens up, sunlit and picturesque, you enter the busy little village of **LAUTERBRUNNEN** (796m). The train station here is the junction point for journeys up to Wengen and on up to the Jungfraujoch.

At the entrance to the village, opposite the train station, a gondola run by BLM ("Mürrenbahn") crests the west wall of the valley to **Grütschalp**, from where a train – one of the most scenic rides in Switzerland – trundles its way along the cliff edge, in full view of the snowy giants across the way, to Mürren (see p.243). You might, instead, fancy the steep path up to Grütschalp (rising 690m in 2hr), in order to take advantage of the panoramic stroll alongside the tracks to Mürren (1hr 10min).

Just before Lauterbrunnen, precipitous roads and footpaths wind up west to **Isenfluh**, an isolated little hamlet on a tiny patch of green, from where little-trod hiking trails fan out and a cable car rises to the Sulwald alp, at the foot of the distinctively jagged Lobhörner crag (2566m).

At the southern end of Lauterbrunnen village, the delicate **Staubbach Falls** – at nearly 300m, the highest in Switzerland – gush out of a sheer cliff, like a lacy decoration on the rugged precipice.

From Lauterbrunnen it's a scenic half-hour walk, or an hourly postbus, 3km up the valley to the hugely enjoyable **Trümmelbach Falls** (daily: July & Aug 8.30am–6pm; April–June & Sept–Oct 9am–5pm; Fr.11; ⓦ www.truemmelbach .ch). These impressively thunderous waterfalls – the runoff from the high

Brandegg in the shadow of the Eiger's North Wall, and a huge 15km run from First round to Bussalp and down to Grindelwald.

Passes are good value. For the Mürren-Schilthorn sector, 1/6 days cost Fr.59/261, for the joint Grindelwald-Wengen sector (covering First, Kleine Scheidegg and Männlichen), 1/6 days cost Fr.96/277. The Jungfrau Region Sportpass, valid in all sectors, is Fr.126 for 2 days, Fr.308 for 6 days. There are **discount** deals for early/late season skiing, as well as **classes**.

Adventure sports

Loads of companies in and around Interlaken run all kinds of adventure sports, many of them year-round. A popular choice is **tandem paragliding** (from about Fr.150), with tandem hang-gliding not far behind: top takeoff spots are the Beatenberg, Schynige Platte, the Niederhorn and even the Schilthorn. **Tandem skydiving** from 4000m or 4600m (around Fr.400) gives you up to a minute of freefall at 200kph. **Bungee jumping** is also hugely popular, from various vantage points around the region (Fr.125 or more), and plenty of operators offer **canyoning** (half-day about Fr.110, full day Fr.170). **Rafting** on the Lütschine, the Simme, the Saane and elsewhere costs around Fr.100. **Rock-climbing** is Fr.90 for half a day. **Horse-trekking** costs around Fr.75 for 2hr.

The biggest operators include **Alpin Raft**, beside *Balmer's Herberge* in Interlaken (☏ 033 823 41 00, ⓦ www.alpinraft.ch), **Alpin Center**, opposite *Balmer's* and at Wilder-swil station (☏ 033 823 55 23, ⓦ www.alpincenter.ch), and **Swissraft**, Jungfraustrasse 72 (☏ 081 911 52 50, ⓦ www.swissraft.ch), but also check out ⓦ www.outdoor -interlaken.ch, www.paragliding-grindelwald.ch, www.paragliding-interlaken.ch and www.skydiveinterlaken.ch. You can generally book at your hotel too. Gunten on the Thunersee is a centre for **windsurfing**, **waterskiing** and **wakeboarding** (ⓦ www .wasserskischule.ch), and there are tons of options for **mountain biking** solo (tourist offices stock maps and route details) or on guided trips (ⓦ www.mtbeer.ch). Meanwhile ⓦ www.swissalpineguides.ch, www.grindelwaldsports.ch and www.be-je.ch, among others, run full- or multi-day **guided treks** in the high mountains.

▲ Lauterbrunnen

mountains – have carved corkscrew channels through the valley walls: a stepped catwalk leads you over the enclosed, boiling cauldrons of rushing water (up to 20,000 litres a second), which throw up plenty of spray and have eroded the rock into weird and wonderful shapes. From the top, above the falls, trails from Mettlenalp connect to paths leading to Wengen and Wengernalp.

Practicalities

Lauterbrunnen's **train station** is at the northernmost end of the village, directly opposite both the gondola station for Mürren and the **tourist office** (daily 9am–noon & 1–6pm; Oct–May closed Sat & Sun; ☎033 856 85 68, ⓦwww .lauterbrunnen.ch).

Lots of places offer dorm **accommodation**. Down by the tracks is the cosy SB *Valley Hostel* (☎033 855 20 08, ⓦwww.valleyhostel.ch; ❶), most of its rooms with balconies. There are two **campsites** at the southern end of the village, including *Jungfrau* (☎033 856 20 10, ⓦwww.camping-jungfrau.ch) on the west bank. Among the **hotels** is jovial, backpacker-ish *Horner* (☎033 855 16 73, ⓦwww.hornerpub.ch; ❶), just beyond the tourist office. Beside the station is the *Steinbock* (☎033 855 12 31, ⓦwww.steinbocklauterbrunnen.ch; ❷), with cosy, uncomplicated rooms and cooking to match. ⚑ *Silberhorn* (☎033 856 22 10, ⓦwww.silberhorn.com; ❸) is up off the main drag but only a minute from the station, with pristinely quiet rooms.

Eating and drinking are best done in the various hotels along the main street: the *Horner* has bargain pizza/pasta meals for under Fr.13, while the friendly restaurant at the *Oberland*, just past the tourist office, has a good range of Swiss and international food (Fr.15–25), and is a nice place for afternoon tea with apple strudel. Slightly further along the main road, the restaurant in *Hotel Schützen* is slightly more upmarket, but still very affordable, with inventive Swiss and Italian dishes (Fr.17–48) plus inexpensive daytime *menus*.

Long-term parking

Since both Wengen and Mürren are car-free, Lauterbrunnen has built for itself a multistorey **car park** directly behind the train station – the community knows the value of its views, and has ensured that the car park doesn't disturb the eye and that it filters most of the traffic away from the village. Parking for 24 hours costs Fr.10 (mid-April to Dec) or Fr.13 (Jan to mid-April); one-week equivalents are Fr.59 and Fr.79. Always try to **reserve in advance** online at ⓦwww.jungfraubahn.ch – at least two weeks ahead ideally. Two other small open-air parking areas within the village cost around Fr.10 per day. Stechelberg has another large parking area at the foot of the Schilthornbahn cable car (Fr.8 per day, Fr.24 per week).

Stechelberg and beyond

The bus from Lauterbrunnen to the Trümmelbach Falls continues to **STECHELBERG** (900m), a peaceful hamlet at the end of the road. It has a minuscule **tourist office** (☎033 855 10 32, ⓦwww.stechelberg.ch), open limited hours. Stechelberg is the starting point for the **cable-car ride** (see overleaf) up to Gimmelwald, Mürren and the Schilthorn; the huge base station complex is 1km before the hamlet. Buses stop here, and terminate at the end of the road in front of the *Hotel Stechelberg* (☎033 855 29 21, ⓦwww.hotel-stechelberg.ch; ❶–❷), a fine old hikers' inn with creaky rooms upstairs. Round the corner, the friendly *Alpenhof* (☎033 855 12 02, ⓦwww.alpenhof-stechelberg.ch; ❶) offers simple but comfy dorms and rooms at bargain rates, and free use of the kitchen.

Beyond Stechelberg, trails continue into the undeveloped and unpopulated upper part of the valley, which forms part of the hiking circuit described in the box on p.245. Only the hardiest folk venture here, but the trails aren't difficult and can offer some of the most rewarding hikes in the region, both for the spectacular views and for the isolation. There are no roads, and a short distance beyond Stechelberg begins a large area of land protected as a **nature reserve**. Three comfortable old **inns** along the main trail, all open May to October only and all requiring advance reservation, might persuade you to stay a night or two. An hour beyond Stechelberg is *Berghaus Trachsellauenen* (☎033 855 12 35; ❶), a pretty half-timbered house set in the woods; an hour and a quarter further is the characterful *Hotel Tschingelhorn* (☎033 855 13 43; ❶), while twenty minutes on up the trail is the *Obersteinberg* (☎033 855 20 33; ❶), a working farm that relies on candlelight and has no showers. Both the latter also have dorm places.

Mürren

The Schilthorn cable car from Stechelberg leaps the valley's west wall to reach the idyllically quiet hamlet of **GIMMELWALD** (1400m; ⓦwww.gimmelwald.ch), a little-visited spot set among meadows ablaze with spring and summer wildflowers. Walking is lovely here, and there's also the attraction of the excellent self-catering *Mountain Hostel* (☎033 855 17 04, ⓦwww.mountainhostel.com; ❶).

You have to switch cable cars at Gimmelwald, rising further to car-free **MÜRREN** (1650m), an eyrie of a village set on an elevated shelf of pasture which has managed to retain its endearing desert-island atmosphere (in the off-season at least). You can also reach Mürren **from Lauterbrunnen** by taking the gondola up to Grütschalp (see p.241) and then the cliff-edge train on to Mürren. From Mürren, the valley floor is 800m straight down, and the **views** of snowy peaks filling the sky are dazzling: you gaze across at the Schwarzmönch, with the great Trümmelbach gorge slicing a wedge of light into the dark rock, while the awesome trio of the Eiger, Mönch and Jungfrau are ranged above and behind in picture-perfect formation.

Mürren was "discovered" by the British in the 1840s, and has a long tradition of winter sports (see p.240): some of the first competition **skiing** in Switzerland was done on the slopes around here. An Englishman, Arnold Lunn, claims to have invented the slalom here in 1922, while the famous "Inferno" amateur downhill race from the Schilthorn peak to Mürren (a descent of 2170m) was held for the first time in 1928, and is still an annual fixture in February.

Midway between the Schilthorn cable-car station and the Mürrenbahn BLM train station, a vintage funicular rises up to the **Allmendhubel** meadow (1907m), from where hiking trails connect to the Blumental (see below) and another trail (3hr 15min) leads up to Marchegg, then down into the rugged Saustal and through the Sprissenwald forest to Grütschalp.

Practicalities

Mürren's sports centre houses the **tourist office** (Mon–Sat 8.30am–7pm, Thurs until 8pm, Sun 8.30am–6pm; shorter hours in spring and autumn; ℡033 856 86 86, Ⓦwww.mymuerren.ch).

Accommodation is excellent. Almost all places close for April and November. Most hotels will arrange to pick you and your bags up from either the cable car or the train station, if you've reserved in advance. The fine four-star *Eiger* (℡033 856 54 54, Ⓦwww.hoteleiger.com; ❺–❻) is opposite the train station, jointly run with the modern, well-equipped *Eiger Guesthouse* next door (℡033 856 54 60, Ⓦwww.eigerguesthouse.com; ❷). The *Regina* (℡033 855 42 42, Ⓦwww.regina-muerren.ch; ❷; closed May, June & Sept–Nov) has well-appointed, Art-Deco-style rooms, while the ⚏ *Alpenruh*, beside the Schilthorn cable car (℡033 856 88 00, Ⓦwww.alpenruh-muerren.ch; ❹), is tops: simply one of the most appealing little hotels in the whole region – cosy, attractive, friendly and with dreamy views.

Eating is a hotel affair, with top billing going to the excellent *Alpenruh*. For an early-morning excursion, a few hotels allow you to defer your breakfast until you reach the Schilthorn summit restaurant – and the food (the cost of which is covered by your hotel deal) is actually pretty good once you get there.

Above Mürren, a short half-hour hike east brings you up to the *Sonnenberg* (℡033 855 11 27, Ⓦwww.muerren.ch/sonnenberg; ❷), a cosy and atmospheric modern inn in the **Blumental** (so-called for its wildflowers). A little further on is the *Suppenalp* (℡033 855 17 26, Ⓦwww.suppenalp.ch; ❷), an older building with simple comforts and simpler rooms.

To the Schilthorn

One of the best mountain excursions in the region is by a series of cable cars from the valley floor at Stechelberg, via Mürren, on a breathtaking ride up to Birg and then the **Schilthorn** summit (2970m; Ⓦwww.schilthorn.ch). The trip's less expensive than the one to the Jungfraujoch, and also less of a tourist merry-go-round, but just as memorable. The exposed top terrace is, if anything, even more dramatic than the Jungfraujoch, with a wraparound vista of icy peaks, from the Eiger to the Matterhorn to Mont Blanc, plus a clear view down to Thun and Bern. You can enjoy the exceptional views and sip cocktails in the revolving *Piz Gloria* summit restaurant, which featured in the James Bond film *On Her Majesty's Secret Service*; a touristy Bond-centred audiovisual show plays in the basement.

As with the Jungfraujoch, it's easy – if you're based in Interlaken, say – to go up one way and down another. The train from Interlaken Ost to Lauterbrunnen connects well with the link to Mürren (by gondola to Grütschalp and then clifftop train), from where the cable car rises to the summit. On the way down, you can descend on the cable car to Stechelberg, and then make your way by bus back down the valley floor to Lauterbrunnen (perhaps via the Trümmelbach falls), from where trains return to Interlaken. This whole trip, with an hour on top to enjoy the views, takes four hours, compared with six for the equivalent ride from Interlaken up the Jungfraujoch (the last 40min of which is climbing inside a dark tunnel).

Fares on the Schilthornbahn are steep, but not outrageous. A round-trip from Interlaken to the top is Fr.117, from Stechelberg Fr.92, from Mürren Fr.66. Swiss Pass holders travel free to Mürren and pay half-price from there upwards.

Wengen

On the opposite side of the valley from Mürren, trains bound for Kleine Scheidegg (see p.251) grind up from Lauterbrunnen to **WENGEN** (1274m), another gorgeous, car-free haven perched on a shelf of tranquil southwest-facing meadow. Wengen is one of Switzerland's best-known ski resorts (see p.240 for winter sports information), most famous for hosting World Cup downhill and slalom races on the Lauberhorn every January. It's slightly bigger and livelier than Mürren but still no more than a chalet-style village, with a long tradition of hospitality. Once the snows have receded, Wengen

---

Walking in the Bernese Alps

Making a loop around the Lauterbrunnen valley, the week-long **Grindelwald Circuit** enjoys magnificent big-mountain scenery without treading glaciers or major screes. The paths are mostly good, but with some very long and steep slopes to negotiate – both in ascent and descent – and you'll need to be fit. Each stage could be shortened or lengthened to suit personal preference. *The Bernese Alps, A Walking Guide* by Kev Reynolds (see "Books", p.512) is an essential companion.

Start by riding the rack railway from **Wilderswil** to the viewpoint of **Schynige Platte** and set out on what many consider to be *the* classic walk of the area, the high route to Grindelwald. Spend a night at the hotel on the **Faulhorn** in order to enjoy sunset and sunrise over the mountains. On day two descend past the tranquil Bachsee lake – there are stunning views to the witch's-peak Finsteraarhorn (4274m) – and from there continue down to **Grindelwald**.

Below Grindelwald head southwest up steep meadows at the foot of the notorious North Face of the Eiger to **Kleine Scheidegg** and one of the nearby inns. Crossing the saddle on day three, a track leads down to Wengernalp and Mettlenalp. Either take the easy way to **Wengen**, and steeply down from there to **Lauterbrunnen**, or tackle a knee-testingly steep path via the little alp of Preech which descends through the **Trümmelbach Gorge** into the Lauterbrunnen valley. Wander upstream to **Stechelberg** and continue into the secluded upper valley where mountain inns provide peaceful lodging.

On day four take the path which climbs steeply above *Berghotel Obersteinberg* to gain the **Busengrat** at an astonishing little meadow known as the Tanzbödeli ("dance floor"). The pasture plunges dizzyingly to great depths on two sides, but a 360° panorama will hold you in its spell. A path descends to the wild Sefinen valley (also with accommodation), then climbs to **Gimmelwald** and **Mürren**. Next day go up into the Blumen valley and follow a gentle trail to **Grütschalp**, and then through forest to the Soustal before tackling a final climb that leads to the **Lobhorn Hut** (☎033 855 30 85) for a privileged view of the Jungfrau. Day six is spent climbing to the Ballehochst viewpoint, then descending to **Saxeten** and finally back down to **Wilderswil**.

sits amidst ideal hiking country, overlooked by the Jungfrau and the distinctive creamy cone of the Silberhorn. Its lofty outlook means it enjoys unrivalled valley sunsets.

Walks thread through the countryside around and above Wengen. Even simple little excursions such as down to **Wengwald** below the village can reveal flower-strewn meadows, romantic footpaths and stunning views out over the great chasm of the Lauterbrunnen valley. Opposite, the horse's tail of the Staubbach falls is clearly visible, while the jagged Lobhörner peak stands out, silhouetted against the sky. The cliff-edge **Mönchblick** viewpoint beyond Wengwald is less than an hour's stroll (120m down) from Wengen. Longer walks lead up to **Wengernalp** (also with a useful train station) and on up to the rail junction at Kleine Scheidegg (3hr total). The LWM cable car from Wengen crests the bluff overlooking the village to the beautiful plateau of **Männlichen** (see p.251); you can, as an alternative, hike the steep three-hour trail, which rises a testing 1070m.

Practicalities

Heading out of the **train station** onto Wengen's main street brings you to the **tourist office** (daily 9am–6pm; April, May & Nov closed Sat & Sun; ☎033 855 14 14, ⓦwww.mywengen.ch). Trains from Lauterbrunnen to Wengen are free to Swiss Pass holders, but beware that they can be crowded; in peak periods there's often standing room only.

Accommodation is plentiful, but watch out for between-season closures and also for the international skiing in January, which can book the village out. Budget places include the cosy *Bären* (☎033 855 14 19, ⓦwww.baeren-wengen.ch; ❸–❹), on the east side of the village, while the *Belvédère* (☎033 856 68 68, ⓦwww.belvedere-wengen.ch; ❸–❺) is a beautiful Jugendstil house from 1912 in a quiet location above the village centre. A handful of grand old palaces, including the superb ⚑ *Regina* (☎033 856 58 58, ⓦwww.hotelregina.ch; ❺–❻), of 1894 vintage, have got the room-with-a-view – plus all the luxury trimmings – package down to perfection.

All these hotels have **restaurants** attached – elsewhere, the popular *Crystal* café-bar, next to the tourist office, does budget food (mains from around Fr.15), while *Da Sina's* is a pleasant little place at the end of the main street with pizzas (Fr.13–24) and steaks (Fr.29–49), and also with a pub attached.

Grindelwald and around

At Zweilütschinen south of Wilderswil, the road and the train tracks divide: one branch heads south to Lauterbrunnen, while the other follows the course of the Schwarze Lütschine torrent east through the Lütschental into broad, open uplands and the hugely popular resort of **GRINDELWALD** (1034m). Unlike Wengen and Mürren nearby, Grindelwald is accessible by car and bus, and thus sees a great deal more tourist traffic than the Lauterbrunnen resorts.

Rural character is to be found out of the village. Nestling under the craggy trio of the Wetterhorn, Mettenberg and Eiger, Grindelwald offers easy access to explore some large glaciers close to, and has a network of cable cars leading up to numerous short- and long-distance trails throughout the region and beyond. Skiing is excellent (see p.240), but there are also plenty of hiking trails which stay as such all winter, making this a top choice for non-skiers on a winter holiday.

▲ Views around Grindelwald

Arrival and information

The village is tiered above the valley floor on a series of long terraces. Trains to and from Interlaken Ost and Kleine Scheidegg (see p.251) arrive at the **station**, at the western end of the centre. Most facilities are strung east from here along the 1km-long main street. The base-station for the GGM gondola to Männlichen (see p.251) is alongside **Grindelwald–Grund station** (also a stop for the Kleine Scheidegg trains), way down on the valley floor – it's a stiff hike (or a shuttle-bus ride) up to the village. At the eastern edge of the village, a cable car rises north to **First**, while a little further east, another rises south to **Pfingstegg**. The **road** into Grindelwald from Interlaken continues east through the village, but a few kilometres on (at a car park near the Oberergletscher) the road is barred to private cars; only **postbuses** go on to cross the Grosse Scheidegg pass to Meiringen.

Grindelwald's friendly **tourist office** (Mon–Sat 8am–noon & 1.30–6pm, Sun 9am–noon & 1.30–5pm; shorter hours in off-season; ☎033 854 12 12, ⓦwww.grindelwald.com) is 200m east of the station, alongside **Grindelwald Sports** (☎033 854 12 80, ⓦwww.grindelwaldsports.ch), which offers bungee jumps, canyon leaps and easy guided ascents. The box on p.241 has more on adventure sports.

Accommodation

There's a wider range of **accommodation** – and kitschy souvenir shops – in Grindelwald than in the Lauterbrunnen resorts, but prices aren't any lower. The nearest **campsite** is *Gletscherdorf* (☎033 853 14 29, ⓦwww.gletscherdorf.ch) near the Pfingstegg cable car.

Hostels

Downtown Lodge ☎033 828 77 30, ⓦwww .downtown-lodge.ch. Bright, cheery and well-equipped hostel right in the heart of the village. ❶

Jugendherberge (HI hostel) ☎033 853 10 09, ⓦwww.youthhostel.ch. A bus from opposite *Hotel Bernerhof* outside the station, or a steep 15min walk north, will get you to

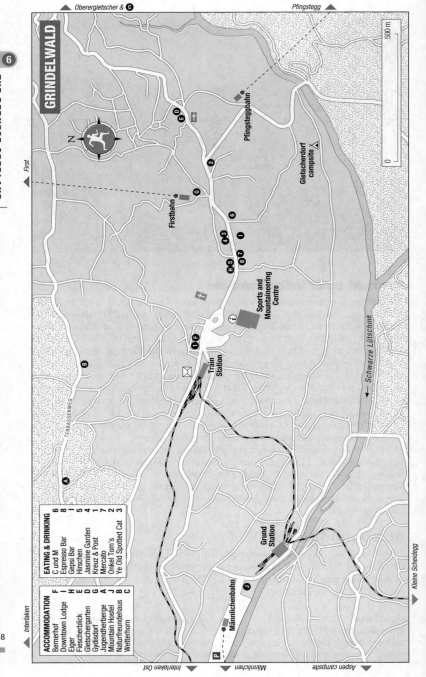

THE BERNESE OBERLAND

6

GRINDELWALD

Oberergietscher & C

Pfingstegg

N

First

500 m

0

Pfingsteggbahn

Gletscherdorf campsite

Schwarze Lütschine

Firstbahn

Sports and Mountaineering Centre

Train Station

TERRASSENWEG

Grund Station

Männlichenbahn

P

Kleine Scheidegg

Aspen campsite

Männlichen

Interlaken Ost

Interlaken

ACCOMMODATION	
Bernerhof	F
Downtown Lodge	I
Eiger	H
Fiescherblick	E
Gletschergarten	D
Gydisdorf	G
Jugendherberge	A
Mountain Hostel	J
Naturfreundehaus	B
Wetterhorn	C

EATING & DRINKING	
C und M	6
Espresso Bar	8
Gepsi Bar	I
Hirschen	5
Jasmine Garden	4
Kreuz & Post	1
Mercato	7
Onkel Tom's	2
Ye Old Spotted Cat	3

Terrassenweg, a quiet lane running on a terrace 100m above the village proper. Up here is this excellent hostel, with a cosy atmosphere, spotless dorms, good facilities and amazing views. Closed mid-April to mid-May & mid-Oct to mid-Dec. ❶

Mountain Hostel (SB hostel) ☎033 854 38 38, ⓦwww.mountainhostel.ch. A lively and well-run hostel on the valley floor beside Grindelwald-Grund station (free shuttle bus from the village on demand). ❶

Naturfreundehaus ☎033 853 13 33, ⓦwww .naturfreunde.ch. Spartan dorms not far from the HI hostel on the same street, Terrassenweg. ❶

Hotels

Bernerhof ☎033 853 10 21, ⓦwww.bernerhof hotel.ch. Reliable three-star in the village centre, with a range of decent, modern rooms, some with Eiger-view balconies. ❸–❹

Eiger ☎033 854 31 31, ⓦwww.eiger -grindelwald.ch. In the heart of the bustle, but with rooms well off the street that remain quiet, this is a chic, contemporary place rather reminiscent of a city business hotel – a breath of fresh, modern design amidst the kitschy chalets. ❼

Fiescherblick ☎033 854 53 53, ⓦwww.fiescher blick.ch. Passable choice east of the village with friendly staff and a superb restaurant. It's worth paying a little extra for the space and pleasant decor of the superior-class rooms. ❸–❺

Gletschergarten ☎033 853 17 21, ⓦwww.hotel -gletschergarten.ch. A wonderful old, rustic, window-box-laden pension next door to the *Fiescherblick*, with a loyal clientele who return year after year. ❺

Gydisdorf ☎033 853 13 03. A comfortable, welcoming hotel at the foot of the First cable car, with a reputation for fine service to complement its pleasant and very reasonably priced rooms. ❷–❸

Wetterhorn ☎033 853 12 18, ⓦwww.hotel -wetterhorn.ch. Comfortable old roadside inn an hour's walk east of the village opposite the Oberergletscher, at the point where private cars must park or turn back. It attracts plenty of hikers, not only for its location and its dorms but also for the hearty portions of Swiss cooking on offer in the restaurant. ❷

Eating and drinking

Eating is mainly a hotel-based activity. There are a couple of obvious **bars** up and down the main street, including the modern (but misleadingly titled) *Espresso Bar* and the more traditional *Gepsi Bar* in the *Hotel Eiger*.

C und M This cool, modern place functions as a café by day – with excellent breakfasts and home-made cakes, plus superb mountain views from the outside terrace – then turns into more of a restaurant in the evenings, with inventive Swiss and Italian food (Fr.18–38).

Hirschen The fish here (around Fr.30), plucked fresh from Lake Thun, is rightly celebrated, and there are also a few fondue and meat options (from Fr.23). Closed Thurs.

Jasmine Garden Passable Chinese cuisine (mains from around Fr.20), including a reasonable range of veggie options. Closed Sat lunch and all day Tues.

Kreuz & Post ☎033 854 54 92, ⓦwww.kreuz -post.ch. Quality Swiss cooking (mains Fr.28–43, *menus* around Fr.45) plus a few cheaper pasta and vegetarian options.

Mercato Good pizzas and pasta for Fr.16–25.

Onkel Tom's Tiny chalet to the east of town (closed Mon) serving up excellent – and enormous – wood-fired pizzas in a cosy ambience. Closed Mon.

Ye Old Spotted Cat *Hotel Bellevue*. Cosy traditional chalet-style restaurant, with affordable pastas and fondues (Fr.18–25), plus pricier Swiss meat and fish options (Fr.28–49). Closed Mon.

First, Pfingstegg and the glaciers

The possibilities for exploring the area are endless. The area around **First** (2168m) has some particularly lovely hiking trails (for skiing, see p.240): the gondola rises in three stages, and from the hotel/restaurant on top relatively easy routes lead off in all directions – to the Schwarzhorn summit (3hr) passing through Schilt, renowned for its population of marmots; or a high-level route over the Grosse Scheidegg pass (2hr or so); or back down to Grindelwald (2hr 30min); or, best of all, on a stunning ridge-top walk to the Bachalpsee lake and on to the **Faulhorn** summit (2hr 30min) with its atmospheric *Berghotel* (☎033 853 27 13, ⓦwww.berghotel-faulhorn.ch; ❷); the stunning sunset and sunrise views from here are one of the high points of a walking tour of Switzerland. Schynige Platte (see p.239) is about the same distance again further on.

The cable car (May–Oct) up to **Pfingstegg** (1391m) and the little café at the top station, with its giant views, make for a pleasant excursion for non-athletic types; an interesting trail leads for a little over an hour from Pfingstegg through varying geological formations on the slopes of the Mettenberg (the Breitlouwina terrace is celebrated for its evidence of glacial action), to the Oberergletscher (see below), from where an easy valley-floor hour's stroll brings you back into Grindelwald.

Grund station is the start for several fine walks, including a two-hour ramble up the sloping pastureland through Brandegg to the *Alpiglen* hotel (☏033 853 11 30, ⓦwww.alpiglen.ch; ❶), a stop at 1616m on the Kleine Scheidegg train line. Starting from here cuts the cost of the ride up to the Jungfraujoch, as would continuing up the Eiger Trail from Alpiglen to the hut alongside Eigergletscher station, a spectacular, but steep, route (3hr) that passes directly beneath the awesome North Face.

The five-hour trail from Grund beneath the gondola line to Männlichen brings you up through meadows and rolling open countryside, also with the towering Eiger a constant presence. From Grund, if you cross the river and head southeast for a few minutes, you'll come to the **Gletscherschlucht** (Glacier gorge; May–Oct daily 9am–6pm; Fr.5), catwalks leading you for 1km or more into a narrow defile above the Lütschine River, with evidence of glacial erosion everywhere, including polished valley walls, corkscrew potholes and lumps of green and pinkish marble in the river bed.

An hourly bus from Grindelwald station (or an hour's walk east) leads you close to the icy caverns of the **Oberergletscher** – from the *Hotel Wetterhorn* bus stop follow the leafy trail down to the river and, on the other side, climb the 890 stairs to the nose of the glacier. There's a missable ice-grotto up there (May–Oct daily 9am–6pm; Fr.5), and, a ten-minute walk further up, a much more dramatic path which runs alongside the glacier itself, giving spectacular views.

To the Jungfraujoch

Switzerland's most popular (and expensive) mountain railway excursion is touted under the shoutline "**Top of Europe**": for once, though, the reality justifies the hype. Trains trundle through lush countryside south from Interlaken before coiling spectacularly up across the high pastures above either Wengen or Grindelwald, breaking the tree line at Kleine Scheidegg and tunnelling clean through the Eiger to emerge at the **JUNGFRAUJOCH**, an icy, windswept col at 3454m, just below the Jungfrau summit. This is the highest train station in Europe, and offers an unforgettable experience of the mountains; you'd be missing out if you decided against shelling out the exorbitant sums necessary to get there.

Trains run all year round, come rain, fog, snow or shine. However, **good weather** is essential for the views: if there's a hint of cloud you'd be wasting your time heading up. Check the pictures from the summit, broadcast live on ⓦwww.jungfrau.ch and on cable TV throughout the region, for an idea of the weather conditions, or ask your hotel or nearest tourist office for the latest forecasts. Remember, too, that it takes two and a half hours to reach the summit from Interlaken, and weather conditions can change rapidly on the journey. You should also bring **sunglasses** with you: the snows never melt up here, and if the sky is blue, the sun's glare and glitter can be painful.

There are two **routes** to the top. BOB trains head southwest from Interlaken Ost along the valley floor to Lauterbrunnen, from where you pick up the WAB mountain line which climbs through Wengen to Kleine Scheidegg. Alternatively, different BOB trains head southeast from Interlaken Ost to Grindelwald, where you change for the climb, arriving at Kleine Scheidegg from the other direction. All trains terminate at Kleine Scheidegg, where you must change for the final pull to Jungfraujoch; the popular practice is to go up one way and down the other.

Currently, the adult round-trip **fare** to Jungfraujoch from Interlaken is a budget-crunching Fr.182. One way to cut costs is to take advantage of the discounted **Good Morning ticket** (Fr.158), valid if you travel up on the first train of the day (6.35am from Interlaken), and leave the summit by noon (Nov–April: first or second train plus later departure permitted).

Walking some sections of the journey, up or down, is perfectly feasible in summer, and can also save plenty, with fares from intermediate points along the route considerably lower. The Good Morning ticket from Lauterbrunnen is Fr.137 (6.59am train), from Grindelwald Fr.138 (7.15am), from Wengen Fr.125 (7.15am) and from Kleine Scheidegg Fr.85 (8am). Excellent transport networks and vista-rich footpaths linking all stations mean that with judicious use of a hiking map and timetable you can see and do a great deal in a day and still get back to Interlaken, or even Bern or Zürich, by bedtime.

Kleine Scheidegg

Trains climbing from Wengen and Grindelwald meet at **KLEINE SCHEIDEGG** (2061m) – four buildings huddled in the most dramatic of locations directly below the soaring Eiger Nordwand, or **North Face of the Eiger**, a sheer wall of rock 2300m high. The settlement (it doesn't even count as a hamlet) throngs with daytime crowds switching trains on their way to or from the Jungfraujoch, but sees virtually nobody staying overnight.

The station building, which doubles as the *Röstizzeria* restaurant and *Mountain Lodge* (℡033 828 78 28, Ⓦwww.bahnhof-scheidegg.ch; ❷), has spartan, comfortable dorms and rooms, while the grand old *Bellevue des Alpes* (℡033 855 12 12, Ⓦwww.scheidegg-hotels.ch; ❼ incl. half-board) – the two large chalets beside the station, focus of the Clint Eastwood film *The Eiger Sanction* – has historically been the base station for worried relatives scanning the Eiger wall to track the progress of loved ones engaged in what's become known as one of the most difficult mountaineering ascents in the world. The hotel decor, all chintzy pelmets, wood panelling and armchairs by the fire, is from another world. Within view behind the hotel is the *Grindelwaldblick* (℡033 855 13 74, Ⓦwww.grindelwaldblick.ch; ❶), a serviceable restaurant with dorms.

Kleine Scheidegg is the trailhead for a wealth of **high-country walks**. Hikes down to Wengen (roughly 2hr) or Grindelwald (roughly 4hr), or up the "back" of the nearby Lauberhorn (1hr), are relatively easy-going. There's a tougher one-hour trail up to the **EIGERGLETSCHER** train station (2320m), overlooking the massive sheet of ice sliding down from the high peaks; the station has well-maintained double and triple rooms (℡033 828 78 88; ❷) alongside husky kennels. A superb two-hour walking trail from here arcs around directly beneath the looming North Face down to Alpiglen.

Männlichen

North from Kleine Scheidegg, away from the Eiger, a picturesque ninety-minute trail to **Männlichen**, perched on a ridge and with one of the best mountain refuges in the region (℡033 853 10 68, Ⓦwww.maennlichen.ch; ❸), is particularly lovely and virtually flat the whole way. From Männlichen, the LWM cable car drops down to Wengen in one direction, while in the other, the GGM gondola glides for an amazing half-hour – the longest gondola line in the world – across the pastures to Grindelwald-Grund (both closed May & Nov).

The Jungfraujoch

Most people at Kleine Scheidegg don't leave the area of the station buildings, only stopping to switch trains for the final leg up to the "Top of Europe". After the short run to the Eigergletscher station, the train enters a long tunnel carved out of the heart of the Eiger. There are five-minute stops at Eigerwand and Eismeer stations, both with viewing galleries out over the frozen landscape, and after forty minutes in the dark, you pull into the **Jungfraujoch** summit station (3454m).

Inevitably, the place is a tourist circus of ice sculptures, husky sleigh rides, glacier walks, a short ski run, dismal restaurants and a post office, all invariably overflowing with tour groups. Nonetheless, panoramic views from the open-air **Sphinx Terrace**, at 3571m, to Germany's Black Forest, the Vosges in France and across a gleaming wasteland to the Italian Alps, are heart-thumping – as is the thin atmosphere up here. Yawning away below the silver-domed weather station on top is the mighty Jungfraufirn glacier, which joins up with several others (including the Aletschgletscher, largest in the Alps) at the resonantly named Konkordiaplatz ice plain 3km southeast.

The best way to avoid being smothered by snap-happy crowds is to travel up on the first train of the day, and on arrival follow the signs quickly straight to the high-speed lift for the Sphinx Terrace – that way, you can snatch five or ten minutes of crisp, undisturbed silence at the loftiest point of all, and be the first of the day to sweep the snow off the railings. Once you've finished at the terrace, it's easy to leave the bustling summit station behind and head out across the snows into solitude and silence, although you must stick to the marked trails (crevasses give no warning).

If you've had experience of snow hiking in the mountains, and you have good boots, a map, sunglasses and proper clothing, let the tourist office in Interlaken know that you want to head out on the simple one-hour trail from the Jungfraujoch around the base of the Mönch to the **Mönchsjochhütte** at 3629m (☎033 971 34 72, ⊛www.moenchsjoch.ch; April–Oct; ❶) – you don't need a guide, and the isolation of the hut offers a night to remember. You should walk at half pace, or you may find yourself dizzy and labouring to catch your breath. A handful of other glacier-bound huts are dotted around the area, but you need a mountain guide and all the professional gear to reach them.

The lakes

Flanking Interlaken in the heart of the Bernese Oberland, **Lake Thun** (the Thunersee) and **Lake Brienz** (the Brienzersee) form the gateway to the region. They are often overlooked by visitors in a hurry to get into the mountains, or returning to the lowlands, but there's something very peaceful about them, poised between the big cities of the north and the high Alps further south. Even the most hurried of Oberland tours should give them a day or two.

> ## Boats on Lake Thun and Lake Brienz
>
> The **BLS** company (named for its main rail route "Bern-Lötschberg-Simplon", between the Swiss capital and Milan; Ⓦ www.bls.ch) runs boat services on both lakes, which are free to Swiss Pass holders.
>
> Lake Thun is the more picturesque of the two, overlooked by the pyramidal Niesen and the Stockhorn to the west, the wooded slopes of the Beatenberg to the east, and with the snowy peaks of the Eiger, Mönch and Jungfrau always in view to the south. There are at least three boats a day in summer (June–Sept) between **Thun** and **Interlaken West** (2hr), stopping at – among other places – Hilterfingen, Oberhofen, Spiez, Beatenbucht and the Beatushöhlen. Service is just as regular on the bleaker, cliff-girt Lake Brienz between **Brienz** and **Interlaken Ost** (1hr 15min). If you're visiting out of season, note that boats run on both lakes at least once daily from April to October, although in winter service is drastically reduced and may be cut altogether. There's also a host of eat-aboard **cruises**, and other special excursions – check the website for details.

Both lakes are well served by transport, with mainline **trains** running between Thun, Spiez, Interlaken West and Ost, Brienz and on to Lucerne, quite often swishing along within metres of the water, plunging in and out of tunnels cut beneath the mountains which ring the shoreline. Unless speed is of the essence, though, you'd do well to take at least one trip by **boat** (see box above).

Around Lake Thun

Lake Thun (the **Thunersee**) is one of the prettiest in the country, a tranquil patch of misty blue loomed over by high shoreline mountains. The presence of the snowy Bernese Alps to the south, ranged above the water in a breathtaking panorama, constantly beckons you on. **Thun**, at the northernmost tip of the lake where the Aare flows out towards Bern, is an attractive overnight stop – much more relaxing than Interlaken – and small, rather twee little lakeside resorts such as **Spiez** can pleasantly break a slow journey.

The Thunersee tourist office (Ⓣ 033 251 00 00, Ⓦ www.thunersee.ch) has devised an easy five-day walking tour around the lake (May–Oct; Ⓦ www.alpavia.ch) for Fr.550 per person, including four nights' half-board and luggage transport.

Thun

Set astride the River Aare on the lake which bears its name, **THUN** (pronounced *toon*) – with its picturesque castle and quaint medieval centre – offers memorable views of the Eiger, Mönch and Jungfrau and, closer at hand, the giant pyramidal Niesen (2362m) and flat-topped Stockhorn (2190m).

Across the river from the station, Thun's low-lying Old Town is renowned for the arcading both of the main street, split-level **Obere Hauptgasse**, and the cobbled **Rathausplatz** at its northwestern end. Steps lead up from various points along the picturesque street to the fairy-tale turreted **castle** which looms above, built in 1190 and occupied by the Bernese in 1386. Its lofty halls now contain a historical **museum** (April–Oct daily 10am–4pm; Feb & March daily 1–4pm; Nov–Jan Sun 1–4pm; Fr.8; Ⓦ www.schlossthun.ch), with the usual

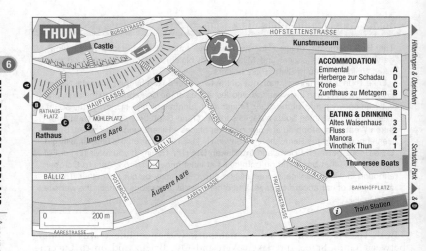

Hilterfingen & Oberhofen

Schadau Park

& D

period furniture and militaria. A short walk east is a grand *belle-époque* lakeside building housing the **Kunstmuseum** (Tues–Sun 10am–5pm, Wed until 9pm; Fr.10, joint ticket with Panorama Fr.13; Ⓦ www.kunstmuseumthun .ch), which stages worthwhile exhibitions of modern Swiss and international art.

At the lakeshore but on the station side of the river is the **Schadau Park**, home to perfectly tended flowerbeds, stunning views across the water to the mountains, and a nineteenth-century folly planted majestically on the waterside. Beside it is an odd cylindrical building housing the **Thun** (or "**Wocher**") **Panorama** (May–Oct Tues–Sun 10am–5pm; Fr.6, joint ticket with Kunstmuseum Fr.13; Ⓦ www.thun-panorama.com), a giant painting – the oldest of its kind in the world – running all the way around the interior wall, which depicts the daily life of Thun circa 1810.

Practicalities

The **train station** is five minutes south of the centre; adjacent is the **tourist office** (July & Aug Mon–Fri 8am–7pm, Sat 9am–noon & 1–4pm; rest of year Mon–Fri 8am–noon & 1–6pm, Sat 9am–noon; Ⓣ033 225 90 00, Ⓦwww .thuntourismus.ch). **Boats** around the lake, and to Interlaken West, depart from outside the station.

For **accommodation**, walk right from the station for the spotless *Herberge zur Schadau* **hostel**, Seestrasse 22 (Ⓣ033 222 52 22, Ⓦwww.herberge.ch; ❶), an old house in a quiet location, well maintained but pricey; or you could plump for a bunk in a metal tubular module at the lakeside **campsite** (Ⓣ033 336 40 67) at Gwatt, a three-kilometre bus ride southwest. Of the **hotels**, quiet *Zunfthaus zu Metzgern* on Rathausplatz (Ⓣ033 222 21 41, Ⓦwww.zumetzgern.ch; ❷) – an inn dating back to 1361 – is most atmospheric, and has exceptionally good-value rooms overlooking the cobbled square. *Emmental*, Bernstrasse 2 (Ⓣ033 222 01 20, Ⓦwww.thunisst.ch; ❸), is a colourful old guesthouse with a handful of pleasant rooms. *Krone* on Rathausplatz (Ⓣ033 227 88 88, Ⓦwww.krone-thun .ch; ❹–❺) is a step up in ambience and quality.

The liveliest place to **eat** and **drink** is the vibrant Mühleplatz, which boasts dozens of cafés and restaurants, with outdoor seating along a pedestrianized riverside promenade. Stand-out options include the swish modern *Vinothek*

Thun wine bar-cum-restaurant (closed Sun & Mon; evenings only except Sat), and the cool *Fluss* riverside bar, with good sushi, plus snacks and other meals (from Fr.18).

On the other side of the river, Bälliz, Thun's central shopping street (with a twice-weekly **market** on Wed & Sat), is lined with pavement cafés, most relaxed of which is the *Altes Waisenhaus* at no. 61, perfect for a beer in the sun, or an inexpensive Swiss *menu* (Fr.15–24). The atmospheric restaurant attached to *Zunfthaus zu Metzgern* (see opposite) serves good Swiss and Italian fare (*menus* Fr.15–18, mains Fr.26–36; closed Mon). For inexpensive self-service meals head to the *Manora* restaurant opposite the station.

Along the northern shore

Visitable castles and stately homes are dotted around the shore of the Thunersee. All are served – and best visited – by boats which stop at or very close to the castles themselves.

Schloss Hünegg at Hilterfingen, 2km southeast of Thun (mid-May to mid-Oct Mon–Sat 2–5pm, Sun 11am–5pm; Fr.8; Ⓦ www.schlosshuenegg .ch), was built in the 1860s in the style of a Loire château. It houses an interior unchanged since 1900, with bedchambers, boudoirs and halls displaying the wealthiest of lifestyles (the owner was a former officer in the Prussian army).

A couple of kilometres further along the lakeshore is the mighty **Schloss Oberhofen** (mid-May to mid-Oct Mon 2–5pm, Tues–Sun 11am–5pm; Fr.10; Ⓦ www.schlossoberhofen.ch), set in its own lush gardens. It dates from the thirteenth century, and houses collections of furnishings from the Bern Historical Museum: a range of restored interiors, a stone-flagged knights' hall, salons furnished in Empire style and even a Turkish *selamlik*, or smoking room, way up under the eaves. The formal waterside **park** (mid-May to Oct daily 10am–sunset; free) is delightful, shaded by trees and planted with all kinds of flowers.

St-Beatus-Höhlen

Beyond the funicular at Beatenbucht – which serves the gently sloping summit of the Niederhorn (Ⓦ www.niederhorn.ch), with walks and show-stopping views to the high Alps – are the **ST-BEATUS-HÖHLEN** (St Beatus Caves; Ⓦ www.beatushoehlen.ch), an impressive set of drippy subterranean chambers filled with stalactites and stalagmites, formerly the residence of the early Christian ascetic St Beatus. The caves are tucked into the cliffs 3km northwest of Interlaken; it's a **walk** of about two hours from Interlaken, or you can take hourly **bus** #21, which runs both ways along the shoreside road between Thun and Interlaken's Ost and West stations. In the summer, about half-a-dozen **boats** a day between Thun and Interlaken West stop at Beatushöhlen-Sundlauenen, ten minutes' walk south of the cave entrance.

Beatus himself reputedly came from Britain. The story goes that having given all his wealth to the poor to follow Christ, he was baptized in Rome by St Peter and sent with a companion, Justus, into the Alps as the first apostle to the heathen Helvetians. (In all probability, though, Beatus was one of the Irish followers of St Columba who brought Christianity to Switzerland in the sixth century.) When Beatus and Justus came to the lake, local people told them of a terrible **dragon** that occupied a cave overlooking the water. Beatus climbed up to the cave alone, and when the dragon emerged, raised his cross and spoke the name of the Holy Trinity, thereby sending the monster over the cliff edge into the water below. Beatus took over its cave, praying and working miracles until his death at the age of 90. A cult of pilgrimage rapidly grew up around him and the cave.

Today, you can visit only on **guided tours**, which depart every half-hour (April to mid-Oct daily 10.30am–5pm; Fr.18; duration 1hr) from the ticket office a short climb above the lakeside road. Note that a visit involves a full two-kilometre walk through the caves (1km each way), which are chilly year-round. You can leave bags at the ticket desk for Fr.1. The guides lead you past the grotto where Beatus reputedly passed his days, and then on into the cool gloom of the cave interior, filled with the noise of rushing underground streams – the best time to visit is springtime, when a wet winter and snowmelt conspire to shoot torrents of water through the corkscrewing channels.

Spiez

On the opposite, southern shore, huddled above and around a small bay 11km south of Thun, **SPIEZ** is a gentle little resort village, dominated by its medieval waterside castle and stunning views over the lake to the high mountains all around. It lies at a major **rail junction**, where the main line from Bern splits: one branch continues to Interlaken, another climbs south into the Kander valley (see p.260) to the Lötschberg Tunnel under the Alps and on to Brig. In addition, trains from Spiez head west to Zweisimmen, Gstaad and Montreux on the celebrated Golden Pass panoramic route (see p.131).

The **train station** is in a modern shopping area high above the Old Town; find your way down on stairs and the descending main Seestrasse. Boats from Thun and Interlaken dock right beside the Old Town. The castle, **Schloss Spiez** (Easter to mid-Oct Mon 2–5pm, Tues–Sun 10am–5pm; July & Aug closes 6pm; Fr.8; ⓦwww.schloss-spiez.ch), dating from the fifteenth and sixteenth centuries but with earlier foundations, was the residence of the Stretlingen family before passing to the Bernese noble dynasties of Von Bubenberg and, from 1516 to 1875, Von Erlach. Inside, don't miss the Baroque banqueting hall. The Romanesque **church** adjacent, with its seventeenth-century spire, has original frescoes in the apse and the crypt. Wandering through the tiny lanes around the castle, and around the bay filled with yachts (Spiez is home to a renowned sailing school), is a good way to get a feel for the town.

Spiez's friendly **tourist office** is on platform 1 of the station (July & Aug Mon–Fri 8am–6.30pm, Sat 10am–1pm & 2–4pm, Sun 9am–noon; rest of year Mon–Fri 8am–noon & 2–6pm; May, June & Sept also Sat 9am–noon; ⓉⒷ033 655 90 00, ⓦwww.spiez.ch). The town's popularity with holidaying German and Swiss-German families leads to some conservatism among the **hotels**. *Bellevue*, Seestrasse 36 (Ⓣ033 654 84 64, ⓦwww.bellevue-spiez.ch; ❷), is a cosy if uninspiring place, while lakefront *Aqua Welle* (Ⓣ033 654 40 44, ⓦwww .aquawelle.ch; ❸) has better views but less character. A few kilometres south at Leissigen is a peaceful HI **hostel** (Ⓣ033 847 12 14, ⓦwww.youthhostel.ch; May–Oct; ❶). Seestrasse holds a clutch of inexpensive tearooms and pizzerias, including the popular *Brasserie 66* at no. 4 (ⓦwww.brasserie66.ch), up near the station.

Lake Brienz and beyond

Stretching east of Interlaken, **Lake Brienz** (the **Brienzersee**) is much vaunted as the cleanest lake in Switzerland, beautifully set in an enclosed bowl amidst forested slopes, streams tumbling down from on high, overlooked to the south by the Faulhorn (2681m) and to the northeast by the Brienzer Rothorn

(2350m), the latter served by a rack railway from the main town of the lake, **Brienz**. East of Brienz, a tortuous road crosses the Brünig Pass on the way to Lucerne, while the main road scoots along the floor of the Haslital, beside the youthful Aare, to **Meiringen**, scene of the "death" of Sherlock Holmes and final staging-post before the major trans-Alpine routes over the Grimsel and Susten passes.

Brienz

At the easternmost tip of its lake, **BRIENZ** has a quiet, community feel; not many people come visiting, and most that do stop for just an hour or two. The town is known as a centre of **woodcarving**, and has many workshops and souvenir shops hawking everything from mass-produced tat to quality hand-tooled items. Brienz also boasts the last steam-driven rack railway in Switzerland, with a fine old beast puffing its way up the flower-strewn slopes for an hour, from the lake at 566m to the **Brienz Rothorn** summit station at 2244m (daily June–Oct; Ⓦwww.brienz-rothorn-bahn.ch). There are plenty of strolls around and about on the top, as well as a tough trail heading northwest through the mountains to Kemmeriboden (see p.215).

Brienz **tourist office**, Hauptstrasse 143 (July & Aug Mon–Fri 8am–6.30pm, Sat 8am–noon & 4–6pm; rest of year Mon–Fri 8am–noon & 2–6pm, May, June & Sept also Sat 8am–noon; Ⓣ033 952 80 80, Ⓦwww.alpenregion.ch), is metres from the jetty where **boats** dock from Interlaken Ost and directly opposite the **train station**. A stone's throw away is the Rothornbahn station, departure point of the vintage locos. **Hotels** include some generic options in the ❷–❸ range along the lakefront, while on the Rothorn summit is the *Rothorn Kulm* hotel (Ⓣ033 951 12 21, Ⓦwww.brienz-rothorn-bahn.ch; ❸), with plain rooms and dorms. Brienz's comfortable HI **hostel** is at Strandweg 10, a fifteen-minute walk east around the head of the lake (Ⓣ033 951 11 52, Ⓦwww.youthhostel .ch; April–Oct; ❶).

Restaurants line the waterfront Hauptstrasse, all offering fresh lake fish: the best is the *Steinbock* chalet, at no. 123 (Ⓣ033 951 40 55; closed Tues), a rather fussy place but with the best fish in town (*menus* from Fr.20).

Just opposite Brienz, reachable by boat or on a scenic lakeside trail from the hamlet of Iseltwald, are the **Giessbach falls**, which tumble over a series of terraces down the cliffside. Above stands the ⚘ *Grandhotel Giessbach* (Ⓣ033 952 25 25, Ⓦwww.giessbach.ch; ❾; April–Oct), carefully restored to its turn-of-the-century elegance.

Ballenberg Open-Air Museum
Near Brienz is the **Ballenberg Open-Air Museum** (Freilichtmuseum; April–Oct daily 10am–5pm; Ⓦwww.ballenberg.ch; Fr.18), 3km east of the town, a huge area of rolling parkland which serves as a living showcase for traditional Swiss architecture and crafts. There are two entrances, the West nearest Brienz and, some 4km away, the East entrance near Brienzwiler; regular postbuses from Brienz station serve both. In between are thirteen separate areas, each containing several examples of traditional houses from different parts of Switzerland, transported here piece by piece from their original settings, reassembled and restored. Within each building are held daily demonstrations of traditional crafts, everything from needlework to faggot binding. The whole place is fascinating, but it's really too big to absorb in one go; you'd do well to select a few areas from the museum map (Fr.2) and aim for them alone – or, alternatively, ask for a discounted two-day pass and spread your visit. There are three restaurants on

site, as well as groceries where you can buy provisions for a barbecue (free firewood provided).

6 Meiringen and around

The creation of meringue and the death of Sherlock Holmes are the two claims to fame of the old town of **MEIRINGEN**. From the way visitors approach the place, though, it seems that many have difficulty deciding which story is real and which invented.

Set at the heart of the Hasliberg hiking region, the town has long been a favourite mountain-walking resort of the English. Sir Arthur Conan Doyle, creator of Sherlock Holmes, stayed in genteel Meiringen many times, and the town's sole attraction is the **Sherlock Holmes Museum** in Conan Doyle Place (May–Sept Tues–Sun 1.30–6pm, Oct Wed–Sun 3–6pm; Fr.4, joint ticket with Reichenbach Falls funicular Fr.10). This interesting little den is in the cellar of the English Church, and includes a life-size replica of the detective's study at 221b Baker Street, complete with taped commentary. The town **church**, north of the centre on Kirchgasse, has a freestanding Romanesque tower with a wooden spire, some fourteenth-century interior frescoes, and remnants below the crypt of the eleventh-century predecessor.

Meiringen's **train station** is in the town centre, with the **tourist office** opposite (July & Aug Mon–Fri 8am–6pm, Sat 8am–noon & 4–6pm, Sept–June Mon–Fri 8am–noon & 2–6pm, Sat 8am–noon & 2.30–4pm; ☏033 972 50 50, ⓦwww.alpenregion.ch). **Hotels** include the smart, modern *Victoria* on Bahnhofplatz (☏033 972 10 40, ⓦwww.victoria-meiringen.ch; ❸–❹), which is

The "death" of Sherlock Holmes

The novelist **Sir Arthur Conan Doyle** chose the Reichenbach falls as the setting for the death of his character Sherlock Holmes. In *The Final Problem* (1891), Conan Doyle wrote of Reichenbach:

> It is, indeed, a fearful place. The torrent, swollen by the melting snow, plunges into a tremendous abyss, from which the spray rolls up like the smoke from a burning house. The shaft into which the river hurls itself is an immense chasm, lined by glistening coal-black rock, and narrowing into a creaming, boiling pit of incalculable depth, which brims over and shoots the stream onward over its jagged lip.

The story goes on to tell of the death of Holmes. On May 4, 1891, the detective met his archenemy Professor Moriarty on a ledge above the falls. The two became locked in a titanic hand-to-hand struggle before both tumbled over the precipice, presumably to their deaths. This neat device was Conan Doyle's way to free himself of the burden of constantly churning out pulpy detective stories and was intended to give himself the freedom to write more elevated literature instead. But he didn't reckon on public opinion. The outcry against the death of such a popular character as Holmes was so great that in 1903 Conan Doyle was forced to give in to the pressure of his fan mail. He resurrected his nemesis by claiming that Holmes had managed to grab a tuft of grass during the fall into the "dreadful cauldron" and so had lived to solve another mystery. Conan Doyle – much to his chagrin – was far more celebrated during his lifetime for his detective stories than for his various expeditions and good works; these days his elevated writings have largely been forgotten, while his Holmes tales are world famous.

Every year on May 4, members of the international Sherlock Holmes Society make a pilgrimage to the falls to commemorate the "death" of their hero.

A sticky end

Odd though it seems for such a delicate creation, **meringue** originated in the rural Bernese Oberland. At some unknown time in the pre-Revolutionary eighteenth century, an Italian baker by the name of Gasparini invented a baked concoction of egg whites, sugar and cream, and named it after Meiringen, the scene of his inspiration. Documented names of the rich dessert include *meiring* (plural *meiringe*) and *meirinken* – until Louis XV took a liking to Gasparini's creation, whereupon the French name "meringue" took over.

Unfortunately, the documentary evidence for Meiringen's noble patrimony went up in smoke long ago during two disastrous town fires. Undaunted, researchers in Frankfurt's Culinary Museum early last century turned up further solid evidence. Meiringen's bigwigs thought their claim to fame was secure, but Allied fighter pilots during World War II had other ideas, and bombed Frankfurt – and the museum – into dust. Nonetheless, the locals are sticking to their story, and patisseries in Meiringen still churn out 1500 top-quality meringues a day to fuel the legend.

excellent value. Conan Doyle's old haunt, the *Parkhotel du Sauvage* (☎033 972 18 80, ⓦ www.sauvage.ch; ❹–❺), is still around: the management undoubtedly benefits by a few francs from associations with fame, but can still come up with the appropriate atmosphere and comforts. **Eating and drinking** is a case of following your nose: the *Victoria* has a decent-ish restaurant, with some veggie options, as does the *Alpin Sherpa* hotel opposite. The best **meringue** in Meiringen, by all accounts, is served at the low-key *Café Brunner*, Bahnhofstrasse 8 – but on careful analysis you may feel that the ones whipped up over the mountains at Kemmeriboden (see p.215) steal a march.

Around Meiringen

Meiringen itself is much less appealing than the countryside all around. The tourist office can supply details of the many hikes in and around the Hasli valley and Hasliberg region, but the most accessible excursion is to the dramatic **Reichenbach Falls**. A wonderful old funicular (mid-May to Sept; Fr.10; joint ticket with Sherlock Holmes Museum Fr.11; joint ticket with Aareschlucht Fr.13; ⓦ www.reichenbachfall.ch) runs from the south of town up to a vantage point below the roaring falls, best visited in spring laden with snowmelt from the glaciers further upstream.

Stepped paths lead up beside the falls through the mossy forests to **Zwirgi** village, at the foot of the dramatic Reichenbach valley. Trails lead on southwest up the valley past the hamlet of Kaltenbrunnen to **Rosenlaui**, where a grand four-storey pile, the atmospheric ⚜ *Rosenlaui Hotel* (☎033 971 29 12, ⓦ www.rosenlaui.ch; mid-May to mid-Oct; ❸), stands overlooking a stream. The hotel was built a hundred years ago; its public rooms are a breath of elegance from a former age. From Rosenlaui, trails head on up to Schwarzwaldalp (beyond which private cars are forbidden) and over the **Grosse Scheidegg** pass to Grindelwald, a route also served by postbuses from Meiringen (June–Sept).

A couple of kilometres east of Meiringen, served by buses to Innertkirchen, is the **Aareschlucht** (Aare Gorge; daily: July & Aug 8am–6pm; April–June, Sept & Oct 9am–5pm; Fr.7.50, joint ticket with Reichenbach Falls Fr.13; ⓦ www .aareschlucht.ch), with a path snaking for 1.4km through the sheer-sided gorge, which is floodlit on summer nights (July & Aug Wed & Fri 9–11pm).

The western valleys

The section of the Bernese Oberland west of Lake Thun, which holds the only route through the mountains towards Lake Geneva, stands in sharp contrast to the rock and ice of the Jungfrau region. Broad, leafy valleys reach between the peaks, sheltering a handful of resorts and quiet country towns. The especially lovely Kander valley runs south from Spiez, climbing to the old-style resort village of **Kandersteg**, while the forested, picture-pretty gorge of the River Simme heads west through a succession of old villages filled with examples of the local heavy-eaved dark wood chalets, some dating from as early as the 1750s. The valley of the **Simmental** curves south into the rural, hilly **Saanenland**, focused around the world-famous ski resort of **Gstaad**. Continuing west, you cross into an outpost of French-speaking Canton Vaud, whereupon the same rolling hills and broad, quiet valleys are re-titled the **Pays d'Enhaut**.

The Kander valley

South of Spiez, the Niesen stands sentinel over the peaceful **Kander valley**, a narrow finger pointing the way south to the wall of high peaks around the mighty Blümlisalp massif (which rises to 3663m). Nestling at the end of the sharply ascending valley, hard up against the mountains in the most idyllic of locations, is the laid-back resort of **Kandersteg**, offering hikers fantastic opportunities to get out in the wild.

Kandersteg

Long a centre for mountaineering, the picturesque, chalet-strewn village of **KANDERSTEG** (1200m) was for centuries the trailhead for travellers crossing the high mountain passes into Canton Valais. In 1912, it was changed forever by the completion of the **Lötschberg Tunnel** (see box below) just

---

The Lötschberg Tunnels

Kandersteg is the north portal of the long-standing **Lötschberg Tunnel**, a rail-only route beneath the Alps to Goppenstein in the Valais (see p.295) that also runs car-carrying trains. For drivers, this is a very handy connection, since without it you'd be forced to drive over the Grimsel Pass or make a detour to Montreux. Regular shuttle trains through the tunnel run year-round, every half-hour between 5am and midnight; in July only, there are hourly shuttles throughout Friday nights. Both termini have drive-on drive-off facilities, and journey time is only fifteen minutes. You can buy your ticket on the spot – Fr.20 for a car (Fri–Sun Fr.25). For more information, check Ⓦ www.bls.ch.

Complementing the Lötschberg Tunnel is the **Lötschberg Base Tunnel**, a mammoth engineering project opened in 2007, comprising a twin-bore rail tunnel 34.5km long at a depth well below that of the original version. The base tunnel runs between Frutigen, north of Kandersteg, and Raron in the Rhône valley, just west of Visp, and is used by high-speed intercity trains which travel at up to 250kph underground, significantly reducing journey times between Bern and Milan.

south of the village, a crucially important rail link between northern and southern Europe – the only one between Geneva and the Gotthard – which created a through route from Bern to Milan. Although the small valley road into the village can get heavy with trans-Alpine traffic, most vehicles are heading for the car-train terminus, situated on the outskirts; once you arrive in Kandersteg itself, all is tranquil. The new **Lötschberg Base Tunnel** has its entrance further north at Frutigen.

The main reason to visit is to explore the countryside. Kandersteg is a fine place to learn how to ski: beginners can test out their snowplough techniques on the easiest and least daunting of slopes, with other beginners all around and not a trace of big-resort swagger. The village itself is strung out along the valley floor for several kilometres, loomed over by the Doldenhorn to the southeast and the First massif to the northwest. Prime hiking and recreation spot above the village is the crag-ringed **Oeschinensee** (Ⓦwww.oeschinensee.ch), a small lake accessed by a chairlift from the eastern edge of the village. From the top station, it's a twenty-minute stroll to the lake itself, warm and glittering in summer and iced over for cross-country skiing in winter. A handful of trails fan out around the area, dotted with mountain refuges (the tourist office in Kandersteg has a complete list, with hiking routes), and the walk back down to Kandersteg is only about an hour. Another lift on the opposite side of the valley accesses the **Allmenalp**.

Practicalities

Head out of the train station and turn left on the main road to reach Kandersteg's **tourist office** (June–Aug & Christmas–Feb Mon–Fri 8am–noon & 1.30–6pm, Sat 8.30am–noon & 3–6pm; rest of year Mon–Fri 8am–noon & 2–5pm; Ⓣ033 675 80 80, Ⓦwww.kandersteg.ch).

Accommodation is of universally good quality. Several places offer **dorms**, including the *Rendezvous*, near the Oeschinen chairlift (Ⓣ033 675 13 54; ❶), beside a good **campsite** (Ⓣ033 675 15 34, Ⓦwww.camping-kandersteg.ch). Standing out among the **hotels** is the fine *Ruedihus* (Ⓣ033 675 81 82, Ⓦwww .ruedihus.ch; ❺), in a meadow off the road south of the *National*. A beautifully restored chalet from 1753, its nine characterful rooms display minute attention to detail, with original rustic furniture and fittings set off by the most spotless of modern en-suite bathrooms. The *Zur Post* (Ⓣ033 675 12 58, Ⓦwww.hotel -zur-post.ch; ❷), in the centre, is a quality lower-end choice. There's a welter of luxury pads, best of which is the central ⚑ *Victoria Ritter* (Ⓣ033 675 80 00, Ⓦwww.hotel-victoria.ch; ❹), a stout old place with a good reputation. The *Waldhotel Doldenhorn* (Ⓣ033 675 81 81, Ⓦwww.doldenhorn-ruedihus.ch; ❺) is out in the countryside, boasting comfort and quiet.

Eating and drinking covers the gamut from the simple but palatable dishes (some veggie) in the cosy little *Bahnhofbuffet* train station diner, up to the gourmet spreads at the luxury hotels. Meals at the *Ruedihus* (see above) are excellent, with a choice between the formal restaurant above and the atmospheric *Stübli* below, serving a range of inexpensive Swiss specialities (from Fr.20). Most of the hotels along the main street serve food, but the *Victoria Ritter* prides itself on its kitchen – justifiably so, with a changing menu of intricately well-presented international cuisine (from Fr.25).

Beyond Kandersteg

At the end of Kandersteg village, beside the rushing Kander torrent, is a small crossroads. To the southwest a tortuous path climbs into the bleak **Üschinental**, which penetrates for 4 or 5km between the summits, and is the scene for some tough mountain-bike trails and tougher hikes up to the Gemmi Pass above the town of Leukerbad (see p.295).

Southeast from the same crossroads, a private road (Fr.10 per car, pay at tourist office) accesses the wild **Gasterntal**; beware that the road is narrow and rocky, and runs on an alternate one-way system. A private bus follows the road in good weather only (June–Sept 2–7 daily; Fr.23 return; reservations essential ☏033 671 11 72). Nobody comes down here apart from local hikers in the know, but this was formerly the main route by foot into the Valais: about an hour-and-a-half's walk from the crossroads into the forgotten valley – the walls of which are laced with waterfalls – you'll come to the hamlet of **SELDEN** (1535m) with a couple of inns, including cosy *Gasthaus Selden* (☏033 675 11 63; ❶). From here, a path cuts south four hours up to the **Lötschen Pass** (2690m), passing another inn, the *Gfelalp* (☏033 675 11 61; ❶), on the ascent. From the basic *Lötschenpasshütte* (☏027 939 19 81, ⓦwww.loetschenpass.ch; June–Sept; ❷) on the summit, three more paths lead down to the villages of the Lötschental on the other side (see p.295). Check with the Kandersteg tourist office before setting out in these remote areas.

Gstaad

GSTAAD – twinned expertly with Cannes – is an odd place. You'd think, from the high profile of its name, that it would be some kind of glittering Geneva-in-the-Alps, a fantastically expensive mountain paradise. Yet although its instant name-recognition may effortlessly attract Europe's royal households, celebrities galore and countless hangers-on, Gstaad is in fact just a one-street village, full of restored weathered-wood chalets and an overabundance of jewellery shops

Sports and activities around Gstaad

There's plenty of **hiking** in the four main valleys surrounding Gstaad. A cable car and trails run up to the nearby **Eggli** (1557m), favoured excursion from the village, with plenty of paths from there across the plateau, and a long high-level route winding past the tranquil Arnensee and down to **Feutersoey**, some 9km further up the Saane. On the opposite, eastern side of Gstaad looms the **Wispile** (1911m), also served by a cable car, with trails of about two and a half hours leading back to Gstaad. It's equally easy to head due east from the village along the **Turbach** valley, through a hamlet or two on the banks of the stream, and then keep heading straight over the low pass at Reulissen to the busy resorts of **Lenk** or **St Stephan**, both on the Simme some 12km east (4hr 30min total) and linked to Zweisimmen by train.

Swiss Adventures (☏0848 161 161, ⓦwww.swissadventures.ch), in Gstaad's Alpinzentrum, offers a host of **adventure activities** from igloo building, sledding and showshoeing in winter through to rafting, canoeing and canyoning in summer. The **skiing**, however, might be a disappointment. None of the lifts around the village rises above 2200m, which means that snow cover is unreliable, although some lifts nearby beyond Gsteig do serve the Diablerets "Glacier 3000" (see p.275), at just under 3000m. Roughly half the pistes in the whole area are rated blue or easy red. There's a complicated system of **lift passes**, covering six very widespread sectors. A one-day pass costs Fr.59 for sector 1 (Zweisimmen, Gstaad, Rougemont); Fr.42 for sector 3 (Château d'Oex); Fr.59 for sector 4 (Diablerets, including the glacier); Fr.30 for sector 5 (Gsteig); and Fr.35 for sector 6 (Lauenen). Four-hour passes are available. For longer periods, you must buy an all-inclusive Top-Card for the whole region, which costs Fr.118/297 for two/six days.

and furriers. But its high-roller status makes it a village like no other: if you fancy being snubbed by the world's richest people, come here for Christmas week, scene of a heady round of sparkling soirées and lavish banquet-style dinner parties all but barred to ordinary mortals.

Gstaad is far more of a place to spend the odd ten grand renting a hillside chalet and sipping champagne around town than somewhere you can get stuck into any serious skiing. Where the area really enters into its own, prosaically enough, is as a centre from which to **hike** the surrounding Saanenland during the summer months.

Arrival and information

Gstaad is on the MOB narrow-gauge "Golden Pass" **train** line (see p.131) between Montreux and Zweisimmen. Arriving by car, a turning from **Saanen** – the village on the main Simmental road some 45km west of Spiez – heads south for 3km to Gstaad. Cars are diverted away from Gstaad centre to parking garages nearby.

The tiny **train station** is just off the main Promenade. Some 100m further south on Promenade, after the railway bridge, is the **tourist office** (July, Aug & Dec–March Mon–Fri 8am–6.30pm, Sat & Sun 9am–noon & 1.30–5pm; rest of year Mon–Fri 8.30am–noon & 1.30–6pm, Sat 10am–noon & 1.30–5pm; ☎033 748 81 81, ⓦwww.gstaad.ch).

Accommodation

As you might expect, the sky's the limit if you choose to **stay** in Gstaad. However, it's not impossible to find inexpensive accommodation. Ten minutes' walk northwest of Saanen is a comfortable, rustic HI **hostel** *Jugendherberge* in the old-style *Chalet Rüblihorn* (☎033 744 13 43, ⓦwww.youthhostel.ch; ❶).

Saanen and neighbouring villages also have the least expensive **hotels**, including the stylish three-star *Kernen* in Schönried (☎033 748 40 20, ⓦwww .hotel-kernen.ch; ❸). Within Gstaad, *Posthotel Rössli* is a cosy mid-range choice (☎033 748 42 42, ⓦwww.posthotelroessli.ch; ❺), the oldest hotel in the village, with renovated pine-decor rooms, while *Olden* (☎033 748 49 50, ⓦwww .hotelolden.com; ❻) is more upmarket but still with plenty of atmosphere. Steps from the station is the *Bernerhof* (☎033 748 88 44, ⓦwww.bernerhof-gstaad .ch; ❺–❻), a huge place with generous rooms and an indoor pool. Towering over the village and visible from all points is the fantasy *Palace Hotel* (☎033 748 50 00, ⓦwww.palace.ch; ❾), laughingly calling itself a "family pension" as it asks up to Fr.1900 for a double room in the winter peak (and half that in the summer) – but then again, with underwater music in the pool, giant bedrooms and lavish dinners on the south-facing terrace, they know their clientele well.

The village

Gstaad's main pedestrian-only street, running north–south through the village, is dubbed **Promenade** – no more than five minutes' walk end to end. Focus of the village centre is an open area just at the point cars are barred, which is used as an ice rink in winter, and in July as the location for the prestigious **Swiss Open** tennis tournament. The world's sporting media and celebs galore descend on the village for the tournament (ⓦwww.allianzsuisseopengstaad .com), part of the international ATP tour, drawing some of the best players in the world. Another glittering event is the **Menuhin Festival** (ⓦwww .menuhinfestivalgstaad.ch), which runs from mid-July until early September.

Founded by the violinist Yehudi Menuhin to serve as a showcase for young talent, it has developed into a cycle of major classical concerts – with stellar performers – staged at a variety of locations in and around town.

Eating and drinking

For **eating and drinking**, check out where the champagne set are gathering in any of half a dozen (often surprisingly unpretentious) terrace cafés and restaurants along Promenade. *Charly's* is perhaps the most famous: a sunny little tearoom with inexpensive light meals and *menus* (Fr.13–27). *Café Pernet* near the chapel is also popular: an inexpensive café-cum-pub with *menus* for around Fr.20 – or head opposite to the more upmarket *Rialto*, which does quality Italian food with prices to match (mains Fr.23–69). The restaurant in *Posthotel Rössli* has good, plain Swiss meals without the fuss (mains Fr.19–26), while *Sporthotel Rütti*, ten minutes' walk south of town, is acclaimed for its tasty Swiss and Italian-style cooking (mains from around Fr.15). At the other end of the scale, *Chesery* (☎033 744 24 51, ⓦwww.chesery.ch) is the place to see and be seen, a lively late-night gourmet eatery and piano bar, with the prices as high as the stilettos (mains Fr.65–98, set *menu* Fr.168; closed Mon & Tues).

The Pays d'Enhaut

Barely 3km west of Saanen you cross the border from Canton Bern into Canton Vaud, and with it the linguistic *Röstigraben*: not 1km further on is the francophone resort of **Rougemont**, a charming little place full of character that is, so far, successfully fending off the encroachment of Gstaad's high rollers. This sliver of mountain territory is known as the **PAYS D'ENHAUT**, or Highlands. The main valley, with its succession of broad, enclosed side valleys set amidst gentle peaks carpeted by lush summer pasture, is separated from Vaud's better-known Alpine resorts such as Leysin and Les Diablerets (see p.275) by the Col des Mosses pass (1445m) further south. West of Rougemont is the largest town of the region, **Château d'Oex**, best known as a centre for hot-air ballooning.

The MOB narrow-gauge **train** line runs along the valley floor from Gstaad through Château d'Oex, shortly afterwards winding its way down alongside the Dent de Jaman to Montreux (see p.131). A branch line from **Montbovon**, some 11km west of Château d'Oex, runs north to Gruyères (see p.111).

Rougemont

About 7km west of Gstaad, **ROUGEMONT** is an attractive, historic village full of the traditional broad-eaved wooden chalets that characterize the region. Its late eleventh-century Romanesque church is especially picturesque, as is the sixteenth-century château behind, although the latter is privately owned. It's a quiet and attractive place to base yourself for hiking or skiing; the village (ⓦwww.rougemont.ch) is included in the Gstaad ski pass and, as well as hosting its own blue and red runs, it's only a short train ride from access to the pistes above Gstaad. Amidst the village's handful of simple **hotels**, *Valrose* (☎026 925 81 46, ⓦwww.valrose.ch; ❷) is a cosy and friendly little place with appealingly home-cooked meals. The **Videmanette cable car** (ⓦwww.videmanette.ch) runs from the village up to a trailhead for high-country walks at 2186m, where you'll find a restaurant and, round the corner, a mountain inn with dorms (☎026 924 64 65; ❶). The pleasant stroll along the valley floor from Rougemont to Saanen takes about an hour and a half.

Château d'Oex

A family ski and sports resort located where the road from the Col des Mosses joins the valley, **CHÂTEAU D'OEX** (pronounced *day*) is a quiet place in a spectacular location. The wide, sloping valley bowl in which it sits generates exactly the right kinds of thermal air currents for perfect **hot-air ballooning**, and the town is acclaimed as one of the world centres for the sport. Every January, the town hosts perhaps the most beautiful sports event in the Swiss calendar, the annual **Hot-Air Ballooning Week** (ⓦwww.festivaldeballons.ch), when eighty or more colourful giants catch the thermals to float peaceably over the hills and valleys. For speedier thrills, the town and its slopes are linked in to the Gstaad ski pass (see p.262): as well as easy and intermediate pistes all around the town, there are a few testing runs down from the La Braye cable car, spanning the valley up to a height of 1630m.

The **station** is in the centre, right opposite the cable-car station. About 100m west is the **tourist office** (Mon–Fri 8am–noon & 2–6pm, Sat 9am–noon & 2–5pm; ☎026 924 25 25, ⓦwww.chateau-doex.ch). They can set you up with a balloon flight, or alternatively you could contact Swissraft in Gstaad (☎033 744 50 80, ⓦwww.swissraft.ch), who charge around Fr.500 for two hours' silent floating.

There's an HI **hostel** *Auberge de Jeunesse* a few minutes' walk downhill from the centre (☎026 924 64 04, ⓦwww.youthhostel.ch; ❶). Of the **hotels**, the *Bon Acceuil* (☎026 924 63 20, ⓦwww.bonacceuil.ch; ❸–❹), set in its own grounds about 1km west of the centre, is the bargain of the region, a small, charming hotel in a restored eighteenth-century light wood chalet overlooking the valley. Attention to detail – and the lightly prepared cuisine in the atmospheric restaurant – mark it out as extra special.

Travel details

Full timetables for all trains, buses, trams, boats and cable cars in Switzerland – as well as international connections – are searchable at ⓦwww.rail.ch. For details of mountain transport in the Jungfrau Region, see ⓦwww.jungfraubahn.ch.

Trains

Gstaad to: Château d'Oex (hourly; 20min); Montreux (hourly; 1hr 20min).

Interlaken Ost to: Bern (1–2 hourly; 50min); Brienz (twice hourly; 10min); Grindelwald (every 30min; 35min); Gstaad (hourly; 1hr 45min–2hr 30min; change at Zweisimmen); Lauterbrunnen (every 30min; 20min); Lucerne (hourly; 2hr); Meiringen (every 30min; 30min); Thun (every 30min; 35min).

Interlaken West to: Bern (every 30min; 45min); Thun (every 30min; 25min).

Lauterbrunnen to: Interlaken Ost (every 30min; 20min); Mürren (every 15min; 25min); Wengen (every 20min; 15min).

Meiringen to: Brienz (twice hourly; 10min); Interlaken Ost (twice hourly; 35–40min); Lucerne (hourly; 1hr 20min).

Thun to: Bern (5 hourly; 20–30min); Interlaken West & Ost (1–2 hourly; 35min); Spiez (3 hourly; 10min).

Buses

Grindelwald to: Meiringen (June–Oct hourly; 1hr 45min; change at Schwarzwaldalp).

Gstaad to: Les Diablerets (5 daily; 50min).

Interlaken Ost & West to: Beatushöhlen (1–2 hourly; 25min).

Lauterbrunnen to: Stechelberg (1–2 hourly; 15min).

6

Meiringen to: Grindelwald (June–Oct hourly; 1hr 45min; change at Schwarzwaldalp).

Boats

Following is a summary of June–Sept summer services; fewer boats run in other months, generally Sat & Sun only, if at all. For details, see ⓦ www.bls.ch.

Brienz to: Interlaken Ost (approx hourly; 1hr 30min).
Interlaken Ost to: Brienz (approx hourly; 1hr 30min).
Interlaken West to: Beatushöhlen (hourly; 35min); Spiez (hourly; 1hr 45min); Thun (hourly; 2hr 25min).
Thun to: Beatushöhlen (hourly; 1hr 45min); Interlaken West (hourly; 2hr 20min); Spiez (hourly; 1hr 15min).

7

Valais

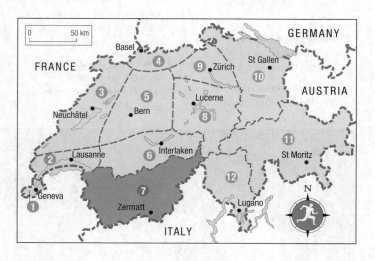

CHAPTER 7

Highlights

* **Fondation Pierre Gianadda, Martigny** Outstanding art gallery in this little-visited crossroads town. See p.280

* **Verbier** One of the Alps's top mountain resorts, offering marvellously scenic skiing and walking. See p.284

* **Sion** Characterful valley-floor town, with a fine old quarter and twin castles. See p.287

* **Sierre** Lovely wine town on the Rhône, sunny and unpretentious. See p.291

* **Crans-Montana** High-glitz resort, with shopping and skiing in the limelight. See p.293

* **Zermatt** Switzerland's most famous mountain resort offers a vast array of skiing and boarding, plus great summer walks – all watched over by the giant Matterhorn. See p.297

* **Saas-Fee** Beautiful village set in an amphitheatre of glaciers, ideal for sunny summer walks and gentle skiing and boarding. See p.304

* **The Goms** Unsung, rarely visited high country: remote, tranquil and sublime. See p.306

▲ The Matterhorn

Valais

The Valais is not so much Mediterranean as Iberian in tone: east of Sion, the cicada begins.

John Russell, *Switzerland* (1950)

The **VALAIS** (Wallis in German; Vallese in Italian; www.valaistourism .ch) is Switzerland's third-largest canton, a diverse swathe of country occupying the valley – hence the name – of the **River Rhône**, from its source in the glaciers of the central Alps to its inflow to Lake Geneva. Fully twenty percent of the canton is covered by glaciers, and yet the region has the driest climate, with the lowest rainfall and the most sunshine, of the whole country. The artificial irrigation system set in place by the valley dwellers in the Middle Ages – a vast network of channels, called *bisses* in French and *Suonen* in Swiss German – still weaves over the foothills of the high mountains, supplemented these days by half-a-dozen of the tallest and highest-altitude dams in the world.

For the Swiss, the Valais somehow represents a piece of common heritage all but lost elsewhere in the country: in the most unlikely corners of Geneva and Zürich, you can find restaurants done up as traditional Valaisian-style dark wood chalets, complete with farm tools as decoration, serving up the local speciality **raclette** (see p.45) under a nameboard "Chalet Valaisanne" or "Walliser Stube". The dryness and sunshine of the valley are ideal vine-growing conditions, and the canton's 22,000 vineyard owners are famous for producing some of the finest **wine** in the country.

The Valais is still a wild and little-known place outside the trio of famous resorts bred by the mountains: **Zermatt**, **Verbier** and **Crans-Montana**. Few outsiders bother to penetrate the deep rural side valleys either side of the single road and rail line that run along the valley floor – though those who do make the effort find plenty of long-distance hiking and adventure sports of all kinds. The only town of any size is the cantonal capital **Sion**, with a low-key, easy-going atmosphere and a handful of sights. In the north-ernmost extremities of the region, an area of Vaud known as **Haut-Léman** occupies the east bank of the Rhône just before it flows into Lake Geneva, where the resorts of the **Alpes Vaudoises** share the mountainous scenery of Valais Romand.

A **Swiss Pass** (see p.35) is valid for free bus and train transport around Valais and free admission to almost all museums reviewed in this book.

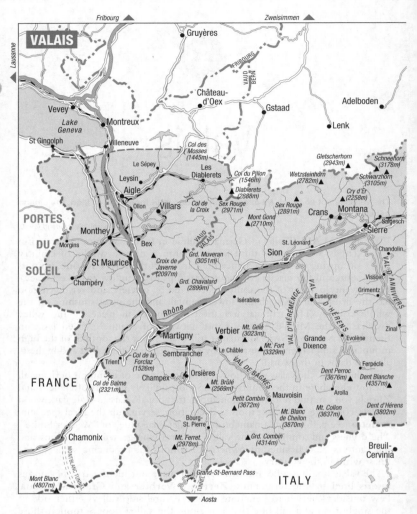

VALAIS

Lausanne

Fribourg ▲

Zweisimmen ▲

Gruyères

Château-
d'Oex

Gstaad

Adelboden

Vevey

Montreux

Lenk

Lake
Geneva

St Gingolph

Villeneuve

Col des
Mosses
(1445m)

Le Sépey

Gletscherhorn
(2943m)

Schneehorn
(3178m)

Leysin

Les
Diablerets

Col du Pillon
(1546m)

Wetzsteinhorn
(2782m)

Schwarzhorn
(3105m)

Aigle

Villars

Diablerets
(2888m)

Sex Rouge
(2891m)

Cry d'Er
(2258m)

Ollon

Col de
la Croix

Sex Rouge
(2971m)

Crans

Montana

PORTES

Monthey

Bex

Mont Gond
(2710m)

St. Léonard

Salgesch

Sierre

DU

Morgins

St Maurice

Grd. Muveran
(3051m)

Sion

Chandolin

Vissoie

SOLEIL

Champéry

Croix de
Javerne
(2097m)

Grd. Chavalard
(2899m)

Isérables

Euseigne

Grimentz

Rhône

Martigny

Verbier

Mt. Gelé
(3023m)

Grande
Dixence

Evolène

Zinal

FRANCE

Col de la
Forclaz
(1526m)

Sembrancher

Le Châble

Mt. Fort
(3329m)

Dent Perroc
(3676m)

Dent Blanche
(4357m)

Trient

Champex

Orsières

Mt. Brûlé
(2569m)

Ferpècle

Col de Balme
(2321m)

Petit Combin
(3672m)

Mauvoisin

Mt. Blanc
de Cheilon
(3870m)

Mt. Collon
(3637m)

Dent d'Hérens
(3802m)

Chamonix

Bourg-
St. Pierre

Mt. Ferret
(2978m)

Grd. Combin
(4314m)

Breuil-
Cervinia

Mont Blanc
(4807m)

Grand-St-Bernard Pass

ITALY

▼ Aosta

Some history

Cut off on all sides by mountains, the Valais has always been a world apart. In the first century BC, a Roman army under **Julius Caesar** conquered the Celtic peoples of the valley, reaching as far as modern-day Sierre. They left behind a legacy of Latin: even today, Sierre is the easternmost French-speaking town in the canton, while beyond it the mother tongue is Swiss German, descended from the language of the unconquered Aleman tribes.

Once the Romans retreated, few outsiders had much success in challenging the peoples of the valley. **Christianity** arrived before the fourth century with the travel of clerics and merchants over the Grand-St-Bernard Pass, but the Reformation never made it any further than Aigle, in neighbouring Canton Vaud, and Valais remains majority Catholic to this day. At times of severe hardship many **Walsers** have chosen to leave their home villages and travel

over the mountains to seek a better life elsewhere. Walser communities survive as far apart as Argentina and Liechtenstein, still nurturing their distinctive dialect and culture.

The Valais remained independent until 1815, when it joined the Swiss Confederation. It's a mark of the social changes taking place over recent years that German-speakers in the east of the canton worry about the encroachment

As well as Canton Valais, this chapter covers parts of Canton Vaud, including towns around **Aigle** and the mountain resorts of the **Alpes Vaudoises** (though not Château d'Oex and Rougemont, which are covered in Chapter 6). For an account of the tiny stretch of Lake Geneva shoreline that falls within Canton Valais, including St-Gingolph, turn to p.124.

of **French** up the valley: with the economic power of the French-speaking lower valley, German-speakers are increasingly finding employment in francophone areas, while francophone firms are expanding into German-speaking communities.

Haut-Léman

Before mainline trains running south from Montreux enter Valais, they first pass through a diverse area of Vaud known as **HAUT-LÉMAN**, extending southeast of Lake Geneva. The Rhône – which here marks the cantonal border between Vaud on the east bank and Valais on the west – meanders between the craggy Dents-du-Midi and the heights of Les Diablerets. The valley floor and west-facing foothills make up the acclaimed wine region of **Chablais**, centred on the fine old town of **Aigle**, with its turreted castle surrounded by vineyards. Above Aigle rise the 3000m-plus peaks of the **Alpes Vaudoises**, centred on a handful of attractive, small-scale resorts such as **Villars** and **Les Diablerets** that offer excellent skiing and a cosy atmosphere well away from the bustle of Verbier and Crans-Montana further south.

   The **Lake Geneva Regional Pass** (see box, p.93) is valid for transport in the whole of Haut-Léman, including routes to Aigle, Leysin, Les Diablerets, Villars and St-Maurice.

Aigle

Although the main valley highway bypasses **AIGLE**, this alluring little town is well worth the small detour for a lazy afternoon of castle exploration and wine-tasting. Aigle is the main town of the Chablais wine region, and its prime

---

The salt mines of Bex

Some 9km south of Aigle and connected by train is the small town of **Bex** (pronounced *bay*), unremarkable but for the fact that it sits beside Switzerland's only working **salt mine**, named Le Bouillet. All through the Middle Ages Switzerland had to rely on expensive imports of salt, mainly from Franche-Comté. Then, in the fifteenth century, legend has it that a shepherd pasturing his flocks above Bex noticed that the animals preferred drinking from two particular springs. He discovered they were salty. This led to further investigation and the mines have been worked ever since. Today a labyrinthine network of galleries burrows for some 50km beneath the mountains, still producing salt for domestic consumption.

   You can visit some parts of the mines on **guided tours** lasting about two hours (June–Sept 4–5 tours daily; Oct Tues–Sun 4 daily; Nov–Christmas Sun 2pm; Fr.18; advance booking recommended at ⓦ www.mines.ch or ☏024 463 03 30). Tours (available in English) begin with an audiovisual show and include a long underground narrow-gauge train ride and plenty of subterranean walking. There are irregular **buses** from Bex station to the mines, or you can walk from Bex in about 45 minutes.

landmark – the fantastical **Château d'Aigle**, a fifteenth-century folly with corner towers and witch's-hat turrets – is home to two museums devoted to wine production.

Along with its near-neighbour Yvorne, Aigle produces what are acclaimed as some of the best **wines** in Switzerland, the gravelly, clay-like soil nurturing especially good, dustily elegant, fruity whites ("It's difficult to find a bad white Aigle," commented wine writer John C. Sloan). *Les Murailles*, from the Badoux winery, and the *Crosex Grillé* Grand Cru are the two best names to ask for. Further south, the nearby towns of Bex and Ollon produce their own tangy, flowery whites: *Philos* is probably the best of them.

The town and château

The station lies west of the centre, at one end of the 300m-long Rue de la Gare; at the other end is the small **tourist office**, 5 Rue Colomb (Mon–Fri 8.30am– noon & 2–6pm; April–Oct also Sat 9am–noon; ☎024 466 30 00, ⓦwww.aigle .ch). Just before it are turnings to the pedestrianized café street of **Rue de Bourg** and, parallel, the cobbled alley **Ruelle de Jérusalem**, so named because the upper floors of its old wooden houses span the street in a style which reminded one nineteenth-century observer of the shaded residential quarters of Middle Eastern cities.

From the central Place du Marché, a ten-minute stroll southeast along Avenue du Cloître reveals the looming turrets of **Château d'Aigle**. Ranged beneath is an attractive little quarter of old houses, among which stands the ancient Église St-Maurice or Église du Cloître, founded in 1143 and renovated over the centuries in a mixture of styles.

Atmospheric cobbled lanes wind up to the **château**, founded by the advancing Savoyards in the thirteenth century. The Bernese burnt the place to the ground in 1475, rebuilding it to serve both a defensive function on the fringes of Bernese power and as a residence for their bailiffs. Following the Vaudois revolution of 1798, the castle reverted to local hands, and remained the town's prison until 1972. At that point, nobody could be found to take on the job of jailer and so all the resident convicts were transferred to Vevey. It is now home to two museums (July & Aug daily 11am–6pm; April–June, Sept & Oct Tues–Sun 11am–6pm; Fr.9; ⓦwww.chateauaigle.ch). The **Musée de la Vigne et du Vin** displays a rustic array of old-fashioned wine-making equipment, including mighty barrels and traditional winepresses, while the **Musée de l'Étiquette** offers a rather sedate display of wine labels from around the world. Better than either is to walk around the ramparts, admiring the frescoes in the watchtowers and – above all – the romantic views over the sea of vines all around.

Practicalities

Aigle's **train station** is the focus of the Transports Publics du Chablais network (ⓦwww.tpc.ch): in addition to mainline CFF trains, it's served by AL (Aigle–Leysin) and ASD (Aigle–Sépey–Diablerets), which both climb into the adjacent hills, as well as AOMC (Aigle–Ollon–Monthey–Champéry), which crosses the Rhône. Just up the valley, the BVB line climbs from Bex to Villars and Bretaye.

Aigle has only a couple of central **hotels**: *Les Messageries*, 19 Rue du Midi (☎024 466 20 60; ②), has plain en-suite and shared-bath rooms; *Hôtel du Nord*, 2 Rue Colomb (☎024 468 10 55, ⓦwww.hoteldunord.ch; ②–③), is slightly more upmarket.

Rue de Bourg is lined with pleasant **restaurants**. The popular *La Croix Blanche*, at no. 40, serves inexpensive pizza and *plats du jour* (Fr.14–28); there's similar fare at *Des Alpes* at no. 29 (closed Wed), which also has a pleasant streetside terrace. Top choice in town is *Pinte du Paradis* within the château's Maison de la Dîme (Tues–Sat 10am–11pm, Sun 10am–6pm; July & Aug also Mon; ⓦ www.reichenbach-paradis-saveurs.ch) for excellent Vaudois cuisine and local Chablais wines. The streets around the château offer plenty of places to sample and buy local **wines**.

The Alpes Vaudoises

The huge peaks east of Aigle and the Rhône valley are collectively dubbed the **Alpes Vaudoises**, sheltering a few attractive, isolated family-oriented ski villages that offer some of the best facilities outside the huge Valaisian resorts further south. Friendly **Villars** leads the bunch, connected by a system of lifts both with its neighbour, Gryon, and with the separate resort of **Les Diablerets**, which is linked to Gstaad's lift pass and is subtitled "Glacier 3000" for its access to year-round glacier skiing and boarding above 3000m. Tiny **Leysin**, tucked away in a valley above Aigle, completes the picture. In summer, all these villages slumber quietly in the sunshine, hosting walkers and those seeking undisturbed Alpine isolation. **Transport** between the three is sporadic; they serve better as places to base yourself rather than as stepping stones around the region.

Villars-Gryon

The neat, unpretentious little resort of **VILLARS** is linked to Bex, down in the valley, by a quaint Edwardian train on the BVB line, and to Aigle by a rather less romantic postbus. It wins few awards for stylishness, but where it does score (and where it *has* won awards) is for its family-oriented service. Winter after winter, Villars and the neighbouring community of **GRYON**, 4km away on the train line, attract scores of families on skiing breaks, while remaining virtually unknown to a wider clientele. The skiing around the town is pretty good (see box opposite), with the added bonuses of direct lift linkage to the Diablerets sector for glacier pistes up to 3000m. Multi-day lift passes are also valid in the Gstaad ski region (see p.262), a bus ride away.

Villars' **station** is in the heart of the village; 50m to the right on the main Avenue Central is the **tourist office** (daily 8am–noon & 1.30–6pm; ☏024 495 32 32, ⓦ www.villars.ch). For **accommodation**, the large *Eurotel Victoria* (☏024 495 31 31, ⓦ www.eurotel-victoria.ch; ⑤–⑥) has spacious, modern rooms, some with balconies. *Alpe Fleurie* (☏024 496 30 70, ⓦ www.alpe-fleurie.com; ④) and *Ecureuil* (☏024 496 37 37, ⓦ www.hotel-ecureuil.ch; ②–③) are old-style chalet-hotels with a long history of catering to families, both conveniently central. A low-end option is the charming *Chalet Martin* **hostel** five minutes' walk above Gryon station (☏079 724 63 74, ⓦ www.gryon.com; no credit cards; ②), a cosy, friendly place run by a Swiss-Australian couple. *Le Vieux-Villars*, on the Route des Hôtels, is a three-storey **restaurant** known for its fondues and raclettes.

The twin resorts of **Château d'Oex** and **Rougemont** – formally part of the Alpes Vaudoises, but cut off from their neighbours by the Col des Mosses pass (1445m) and nearer to Gstaad – are covered on p.264.

Winter sports in the Alpes Vaudoises

There's good **skiing** in the neighbouring areas of Villars-Gryon, Les Diablerets and Leysin. **Diablerets** village has close access to the Col de Pillon gondola serving the "**Glacier 3000**" (Ⓦwww.glacier3000.ch), which slides down from the peaks of Scex Rouge (2970m) and Les Diablerets itself (3209m). Most of the pistes up here are blue and red, even way on top around the Quille du Diable – a jutting natural obelisk up at 3000m. A single hair-raising black run plunges beneath the gondola from **Pierres-Pointes** (2217m) down to the Col du Pillon. From Diablerets village, another gondola serves the slopes of **Isenau** to the north, laced with blue and red runs, while a third rises to **Meilleret**, in the direction of Villars. Les Diablerets also prides itself on its **summer skiing**, with good snow assured even in June and July on the glacier.

From **Villars** village, a gondola rises to the **Roc d'Orsay** (2000m), from where a long blue run delivers you to the hub of the skiing at **Bretaye**, set in a broad bowl and also served by a rack railway from Villars centre. Gentle red pistes abound, and from **Barboleuse** a gondola heads up to Les Chaux (1750m), offering a long and rewarding blue run, as well as a red or two and a long steep black down to Sodoleuvre. It's also easy to work your way over to Les Diablerets – although beware that if the snow at Villars or Gstaad isn't that great, everybody heads up to the glacier, which can sometimes make things a bit overcrowded. From **Leysin** village, lifts and gondolas serve a host of red and blue pistes, as well as a half-pipe for snowboarders below the peak of **La Berneuse** (2048m), where there's a panoramic revolving restaurant.

Lift passes are good value. For a full day, Les Diablerets plus Villars-Gryon (excluding the glacier) is Fr.49, Leysin Fr.45. Otherwise, an all-inclusive pass takes in the above plus the Glacier 3000, Les Mosses and sectors of the Gstaad ski region (see p.262) for Fr.58/277 for one/six days.

Adventure sports are a mainstay of all three resorts. Mountain Evasion (Ⓦwww .mountain-evasion.ch) and Centre Par Adventure (Ⓦwww.swissaventure.ch) are two companies in Les Diablerets organizing canyoning, zorbing, luge, mud-biking, rappelling and more.

Les Diablerets

Snoozing quietly in its peaceful backwater valley, **LES DIABLERETS** really deserves to be left well alone. It's so tranquil that it's almost a shame to mark it on a map – indeed, less than a century ago, it wasn't on any maps, and it was only with the arrival of the railway in 1914 that outsiders noticed the place. These days Les Diablerets has a small but loyal band of guests, who return each year to enjoy the valley's charm.

Regular ASD **trains** run to Les Diablerets from Aigle; **buses** also connect the village with Gstaad via a steep road which winds over the Col du Pillon (1546m), 4km east of Les Diablerets. The tiny switchback road over the Col de la Croix (1778m), 4km south of Les Diablerets, leads to Villars; three buses a day (July–Sept only) shuttle between the two resorts.

The **station** is beside the river, about 100m north of the **tourist office** (July, Aug & Dec–April daily 8.30am–6pm; rest of year Mon–Sat 8.30am–12.30pm & 2.30–6pm, Sun 9am–12.30pm; ☏024 492 33 58, Ⓦwww.diablerets.ch). Les Diablerets hosts the International **Alpine Film Festival** in August (Ⓦwww.fifad.ch).

Most accommodation is in chalets, but of the **hotels**, the *Auberge de la Poste* (☏024 492 31 24, Ⓦwww.aubergedelaposte.ch; ❹–❺), a 200-year-old inn that claims to have hosted Victor Hugo, Stravinsky and Lenin, is pleasantly rustic. Top place in town is the lovely *Hôtel des Diablerets* (☏024 492 09 09,

The devils of Les Diablerets

The mountain communities of the Alpes Vaudoises love their legends and **folk tales**, and Les Diablerets – its name meaning "abode of devils" – is no exception. To the south and east of the village loom the two glaciers of Diablerets and **Tsanfleuron**. Legend has it that the latter ("Field of Flowers" in the local dialect) was a beautiful sunny meadow until the arrival, long ago, of demons and devils in the mountains. Soon after, as the devils played their games of skill, trying to hit a natural obelisk, the **Quille du Diable** (Devil's Skittle), the shepherds of Tsanfleuron began to be bombarded by rocks bouncing down from on high. Fearing for the safety of their flocks and themselves, they moved away from the area, which lost its vitality and beauty and turned into the icy wasteland it remains today.

Other tales abound of **lost souls** seen at night, drifting with lanterns alone or in groups through the woods, pastures and rocky defiles of the mountain; local people attested to seeing their lantern lights and hearing their moans just before the two terrible landslides of 1714 and 1740. The meadows and hills are also said to be inhabited by elves, goblins and a local brand of **imp** named a *servan*, one of whom, it is said, once mischievously turned himself into a fox and was seen sitting at night in a hay loft knitting with the hair of his own tail.

Ⓦ www.hoteldesdiablerets.ch; ❺–❻). There are two mountain inns with **dorms** above the village, including the *Cabane des Diablerets* (☏ 024 492 21 02, Ⓦ www.cabanesdesdiablerets.ch; mid-June to mid-Sept; ❶), at 2525m overlooking the glacier. **Eating** is mainly a hotel option, with the inexpensive restaurants at the *Auberge de la Poste* and *Hôtel Les Lilas* worth a look.

Leysin

The road from Aigle up into the mountains divides at Le Sépey: Les Diablerets is east, the Col des Mosses leading to Château d'Oex is north, while buses follow a tiny winding road west to the beautifully located little village of **LEYSIN**, once a centre for the treatment of respiratory diseases, but now transformed into a popular and well-maintained Alpine resort. For **accommodation**, the warmest welcome can be found at the excellent SB hostel *Hiking Sheep*, in the Villa La Joux (☏ 024 494 35 35, Ⓦ www.hikingsheep.com; ❶), which has some twin rooms and good dorms. Satellite TV, a large cosy lounge, dining rooms with log fires, kitchen use, balconies with perfect views and switched-on multilingual staff add to the attraction (as do reductions for long stays). The beauty of the surroundings, and relative isolation, make Leysin a perfect place for a quiet getaway.

Valais Romand

Tacked seamlessly south of Haut-Léman, **VALAIS ROMAND**, or the French-speaking part of Valais, comprises the westernmost portions of the canton. Occupying the broad Rhône valley floor and the most accessible foothills just above, it's more populated and livelier than the wilder German-speaking east. Mountain passes aside, the road and train line from Montreux are the sole routes in and out: the mountains flanking the Rhône are cut through with a handful of dead-end valleys, ideal for long-distance hiking, but only the high pass roads over the **Grand-St-Bernard** to Aosta (Italy) and the Col de la Forclaz to Chamonix (France) give access from outside. These two roads join the valley at **Martigny**, a rather unprepossessing place overshadowed in style and appeal by the cantonal capital **Sion** and its neighbour **Sierre**. The vapid resort towns of **Verbier** near Martigny, and **Crans-Montana** above Sierre, are two of the best-known ski resorts in the world, offering the combination of groomed pistes and chic après-ski that Switzerland is famous for.

South to Martigny

Roads and train tracks cross west across the broad Rhône at Aigle and Bex to a slice of Valais holding the small resort of **Champéry**, where you can ski the **Portes du Soleil** region, straddling the French border. Main roads head on south towards Martigny, crossing the Vaud–Valais frontier at the ancient town of **St-Maurice**.

The Portes du Soleil

Spreading across a mountainous region west of the Rhône valley, in the shadow of the Dents du Midi range, is the huge **Portes du Soleil** ski area (Ⓦwww .portesdusoleil.com), comprising twelve linked Swiss and French resorts. It's a very popular ski destination, but, in truth, is too low to have consistently good snow cover: its top height is only around 2400m and, if snow is poor lower down, the bottlenecks to reach higher pistes can be terrible. On the French side, the key resort – with good snowboarding and the notorious "Wall" black run – is **Avoriaz**, a collection of 1960s apartment blocks on a cliffside above overcrowded **Morzine**.

On the Swiss side, access is via a couple of small villages. From the gateway town of **Monthey**, just across from Bex, roads and a train line from Aigle penetrate the narrow, steep Val d'Illiez to **CHAMPÉRY**, an attractive Alpine tourist resort that's been in business since the 1850s and boasts large-capacity cable cars up to Croix de Culet. A **tourist office** (daily 8am–noon & 2–6pm; ☎024 479 20 20, Ⓦwww.champery.ch) has information on the whole area. *Hôtel Suisse* (☎024 479 07 07, Ⓦwww.hotel-champery.ch; ❹–❺) retains old-fashioned character; *Pension Souvenir* (☎024 479 13 40; ❷) is a good downmarket option. A lift pass for the Portes du Soleil costs Fr.60/308 for one/six days, or Fr.43 for a day on the CLCF sector around Champéry only.

St-Maurice

About 3km south of Bex, at the point where the narrowing of the Rhône prompted the Romans to build a bridge, is **ST-MAURICE**, named after the warrior-saint Maurice who is purported to have been martyred nearby. Maurice was ordered in 287 AD by Emperor Maximian to serve against his fellow Christians on campaigns in Gaul, but refused, according to a later chronicler, with the words: "We are your soldiers, O Emperor… To you is due military obedience, but to God, justice… We cannot take up arms to strike pious men." Maximian duly had the whole legion slaughtered.

A shrine grew up around the supposed tomb of the saint, hard up against a rocky cliff on the banks of the Rhône, as early as 390, replaced by a monastery in 515; this is still in existence as the oldest surviving abbey north of the Alps. Pilgrims have come to the **abbey church** for over 1500 years, bringing with them items of gold and silver as homage: the church **treasury** holds many exquisitely beautiful pieces, including a Roman sardonyx vase, the intricate gold cloisonné Casket of Teuderic, an embossed silver bust of St Candidus and filigreed silver Arm of St Bernard. Although the church is open at any time, you must visit the treasury on **guided tours**, available in English (Tues–Sun: July & Aug 10.30am not Sun, 2pm & 3.15pm; May, June, Sept & Oct 10.30am not Sun, 3pm & 4.30pm; Nov–April 3pm; Fr.10; ⓦ www.abbaye-stmaurice.ch).

Heading straight ahead out of the **train station** along Avenue de la Gare will bring you after 100m to the **tourist office** (Mon 3–6pm, Tues–Fri 9am–noon & 3–6pm; June–Oct also Sat 9am–noon; ⓣ024 485 40 40, ⓦ www.st-maurice .ch). The ancient Grand-Rue runs through the centre of town with the abbey church to your left. The small **hotel** *Dent-du-Midi*, set in gardens at 1 Avenue du Simplon, near the station (ⓣ024 485 12 09, ⓦ www.torrente.ch; ❷), is comfortable and modern. For **eating**, there are a dozen attractive little cafés along Grand-Rue. The *Dent-du-Midi* serves up Valaisian specialities, while *La Croix Fédérale*, 45 Grand-Rue (closed Sun), has good fondue.

Martigny

There are few more dramatically sited cities in Switzerland than **MARTIGNY**. Set down on the broad valley floor, with wooded heights soaring on all sides, it's positioned at a natural crossroads. The Rhône suddenly makes a sharp right-angled turn at Martigny, heading off to Lake Geneva; elevated points within the town give yawning views along both valleys, east and north. The major attraction is the **Fondation Pierre Gianadda**, one of the country's most prestigious art galleries. Roman ruins add more interest, and the small, cobbled Old Town, or

Valaisian cowfighting

One of the oddest of the Valais' peculiar local traditions is **cowfighting**. Utterly unlike Spanish bullfighting, bloodless Valaisian cowfighting stems from village get-togethers to see whose cow was best suited to lead the herds up to the summer Alpine pastures. The cattle all come from the local Hérens breed – bright-eyed with short legs and powerful chests – who naturally pick fights with each other in the open meadows: originally, farmers merely corralled them together to see who would win the squabbles. These days, the winner of the annual cowfighting championship can be assured a head price in the tens of thousands of francs.

Farmers feed up the most bullish of their cows on an extra-rich diet to improve (or worsen) the temper, occasionally allowing her a bucket of wine as a tonic and coaching her in sparring contests amongst the herd. Come the day of battle, farmers tie a huge cowbell around their champion's neck, lead her into the field, and introduce her to her opponent. There's never any gore, and the winner is generally deemed to be the cow who has intimidated her opponent into submission.

Local contests are held on Sundays once or twice a month in various towns from late March to September, accompanied by much revelry. Two events stand out: the **cantonal championships** are held in Aproz, just outside Sion, in mid-May, with the winners going on to Martigny for the **Combats des Reines**, held in the 5000-seater Roman amphitheatre in early October. It's here that the supreme champion is crowned Queen of the Herd.

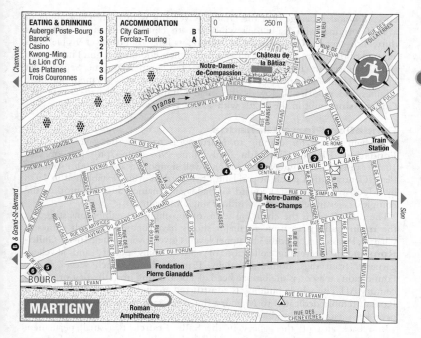

Bourg, makes for some attractive wandering. Martigny is not unpleasant, but there's just not much going on, and – even worse – not many characterful places to sit and watch life go by.

See ⓦ www.momc.ch for details of the **Mont Blanc Express** and **St-Bernard Express**, two scenic Alpine train rides that begin in Martigny.

Arrival, information and accommodation

Martigny's **station** is at the northeastern end of Avenue de la Gare, which cuts a broad swathe through town, passing the **tourist office** at no. 6 (July & Aug Mon–Fri 9am–6.30pm, Sat 9am–5pm, Sun 10am–12.30pm & 3–5pm, May, June, Sept & Oct Mon–Sat 9am–noon & 1.30–6.30pm, Sat closes 4.30pm, shorter hours in winter; ☎027 720 49 49, ⓦ www.martigny.com). They're well equipped with information and maps for the whole area. Just beyond the tourist office is the main **Place Centrale**.

There's a handful of town **hotels**, many unromantically planted on the busy Avenue du Grand-St-Bernard as sleepover motels to catch traffic heading for the Alpine passes. Other, better, options include *City Garni*, 7 Place St-Michel (☎027 723 36 00; ②), clean and modern if generic, and the slicker three-star *Forclaz-Touring*, 15 Rue du Léman (☎027 722 27 01, ⓦ www.hotelforclaztouring.ch; ②), with comfortable en-suite rooms near the station.

The Town

Just behind Place Centrale is the **Église Notre-Dame-des-Champs**, completed in 1687, with magnificent carved doors but a modest interior. From Place Centrale, if you follow Rue Marc-Morand north, you'll come to an old covered wooden bridge over the Dranse River; this is an 1818 replacement of a 1350 original, and leads to a winding path climbing to the semi-ruined thirteenth-century **Château de la Bâtiaz**, its lofty round tower visible from all parts of the town, and especially dramatic when floodlit at night. The château (July & Aug Mon–Thurs 2–6pm, Fri–Sun 11am–6pm; May, June, Sept & Oct Fri–Sun 11am–6pm; free; ⓦwww.batiaz.ch) has a display of medieval siege engines and pillories. Below is the small **Chapelle de Notre-Dame-de-Compassion**, built in the 1620s with a later, Rococo, altar.

Fondation Pierre Gianadda

The main reason for coming to Martigny is to visit the galleries of the **Fondation Pierre Gianadda** (daily: June–Nov 9am–7pm; rest of year 10am–6pm; Fr.20; ⓦwww.gianadda.ch), well signposted about 500m south of Place Centrale on a patch of parkland off Rue du Forum. Established in 1978 by a local philanthropist, Léonard Gianadda, and named after his brother, the complex takes in several areas within a single museum.

The main focus is the changing series of top-flight art exhibitions staged in the **main gallery** area: recent major shows have focused on such names as Chagall, Picasso and Rodin. The upper level is given over to the **Musée Gallo-Romain**, an interesting collection of statues, coins, pottery and jewellery garnered from digs around Martigny. Prime exhibit, which serves as the Foundation's mascot, is the bronze head of a bull, dating from the first or second century AD. The whole building is constructed around the remains of a Gallo-Roman temple dedicated to Mercury, the inner-sanctum walls of which have been left intact in the middle of the museum's floor space.

In a back area off the gallery, in the **Salle Franck**, is a small permanent exhibition of ten modernist works, which includes Picasso's blue-period *Nu aux jambes croisées* (1903). Further along the corridor, the smell of motor oil and rubber preludes the subterranean **Musée de l'Auto**, displaying fifty-odd vintage cars including a Model T Ford (1912) and dashing Lagonda (1936). Outside is the **Parc des Sculptures**, an open area of green overlooked by Martigny's wooded slopes and dotted with works by – among many others – Rodin, Moore and Miró, as well as Brancusi's celebrated *Le Grand Coq* (1949), a striking zigzag of gleaming metal. Here, too, is the **Cour Chagall**, devoted to a monumental mosaic by the artist (1964). By the café at the rear of the park is the **Vieil Arsenal**, which houses excellent temporary art shows.

The museum also stages a prestigious cycle of **classical music concerts**, around fifteen a year, which give the unique opportunity to see stellar names at close quarters in the intimate gallery space: Cecilia Bartoli is a regular performer. Tickets (roughly Fr.50–200) are very limited.

Within a few hundred metres of the museum, to the south beyond the train tracks, lies Martigny's Roman **amphitheatre**, dating from the second to fourth centuries AD and now restored to seat 5000 spectators. It comes into its own as the venue for the annual cowfighting championships in early October (see box, p.278).

Eating and drinking

Place Centrale is where it happens in Martigny – though "it" covers little more than sitting around under the plane trees at pleasant terrace cafés eating plates of chips and drinking beer. The sociable *Les Platanes* does a good range of local specialities, plus salads and crêpes (Fr.18–39), while the street-side terrace of the adjacent *Barock* is a nice place for a drink. Down in the Bourg, the *Auberge Poste-Bourg*,

81 Avenue du Grand-Saint-Bernard, offers inexpensive Valaisian dishes (around Fr.16), while *Hôtel des Trois Couronnes*, 8 Place du Bourg (closed Sun & Mon), is an old, traditional-style auberge from 1609 serving quality French menus at Fr.22 and upwards – go for the house speciality of kidneys in garlic. Near Place Centrale, *Le Lion d'Or*, 1 Avenue du Grand-St-Bernard (closed Sun & Mon), makes its own fresh pasta, and has Italian favourites such as *osso bucco*. *Kwong-Ming*, Place de Rome (℡027 722 45 15; closed June), serves up well-judged Chinese dishes in a calm, dark wood interior or *al fresco* beside the interior garden; *menus* can be Fr.20 at lunch, double that in the evening. Along Avenue de la Gare, the *Casino* cinema has a fairly civilized **bar**.

West of Martigny: Col de la Forclaz

A dramatic road climbs west of Martigny through the mountains via the **Col de la Forclaz** to the French border. The well-maintained highway passes through the villages of La Fontaine and Le Fays before hairpinning up to the top of the pass, trailhead for a number of fine walks, including to the foot of the extensive Glacier du Trient, and base for a scenic chair-lift rising to the summit of Mont de l'Arpille (2089m). On the pass, *Hôtel Col de la Forclaz* (℡027 722 26 88, Ⓦwww.coldelaforclaz.ch; ❶) offers rooms, dorms and a cosy **restaurant**. The road continues down to the border, and then on to the French resort of **CHAMONIX**, with superb views of **Mont Blanc** en route.

The narrow-gauge **Mont Blanc Express** (Ⓦwww.momc.ch) train follows a spectacular alternative route to the border through the heavily forested Trient valley, a few kilometres to the north, before descending alongside the road for the final stretch down to Chamonix.

Pays du St-Bernard

South of Martigny, the **Pays du St-Bernard** (Ⓦwww.saint-bernard.ch) comprises wild valleys hemmed in by the giant Pennine Alps marking the Italian border. Branch-line trains from Martigny station follow the Dranse valley and divide; one branch serves **Le Châble**, tucked beneath the ski resort of Verbier (see p.284), while the other is the gateway to the Val d'Entremont, leading south to the **Grand–St-Bernard Pass**, beyond which is Italy. The Martigny tourist office stocks good maps and guides to the area.

Trains, and the road, from Martigny divide at **Sembrancher**, long a staging post on the route up to the pass. It's an attractive, medieval village, with a Baroque church and street fountains flowing with water that is unusually high in natural fluoride. About 6km south is **ORSIÈRES** (820m), notable for the beautiful Gothic bell-tower alongside its relatively modern church. Trains terminate here, replaced by buses. A branch road from Orsières penetrates the lonesome **Val Ferret**, an excellent birdwatching zone, extending for some 20km between towering peaks.

On a zigzagging side road above Orsières lies the little resort of **CHAMPEX** (1470m), ranged around a lakelet and renowned as a mountaineering centre and trailhead, including for the famous Circuit of Mont Blanc. Two **hotels** stand out, both country inns in idyllic woodland settings: down-to-earth *Belvédère* (℡027 783 11 14, Ⓦwww.le-belvedere.ch; ❸) is renowned for its organic, home-produced cuisine, while *Au Vieux-Champex* (℡027 783 12 16, Ⓦwww.champex-immobilier.com; ❷) has comfortable apartments and a fine gourmet restaurant.

History of the Grand-St-Bernard Pass

The **Grand-St-Bernard Pass** is the oldest of Alpine pass routes, in use at least since the Bronze Age (about 800 BC). Tribes and armies have tramped their way to and fro for millennia – in 390 BC, a Gaulish army crossed to defeat Rome – and from the earliest times ordinary people used the pass to trade goods between northern Europe and Italy. In 57 BC, **Julius Caesar** crossed the *Summa Poenina*, as it was known, to conquer the pagan peoples of Martigny. Shortly after, Emperor **Augustus** built a road across the pass.

In the early 900s, Huns and Saracens swept through the region, raping, pillaging and destroying churches: to keep them quiet, Hugh of Provence, King of Italy, granted them guardianship of the pass, whereupon they began to terrorize travellers and demand payment. Deeply concerned at the disruption caused to merchants and pilgrims Europe-wide, King Canute of Denmark had a quiet word with King Rudolf III of Burgundy, and together they ejected the heathens. The archdeacon of Aosta, one **Bernard of Menthon**, then oversaw the construction of a hospice on the pass. Bernard himself travelled around the area spreading the word of God, and was beatified shortly after his death in the 1080s – and named patron saint of the Alps in 1923.

Throughout the Middle Ages, the hospice provided free shelter and food to pilgrims, clerics and travellers – a welcome point of safety on an extremely dangerous route. In 1800, **Napoleon** led 40,000 troops this way into Italy, en route consuming 21,724 bottles of wine, a tonne and a half of cheese, 800kg of meat, and more, running up a bill with the hospice of Fr.40,000 before departing with a wave of his hand. The monks had to wait until 1984 for a token gesture of account-settling from French president François Mitterrand.

First mention of the famous **St Bernard dogs** – product of an unknown cross between a mastiff, Great Dane and/or Newfoundland – was in 1708. Since then, these heavy-set, jowly beasts, with a little flask tied to their collar (supposedly holding brandy, though milk is more likely), have come to stand as icons of the mountains. The hospice still keeps a kennel for them on the pass.

With the construction of the Simplon Tunnel further east in 1905, train travel rapidly superseded the road journey over the Grand-St-Bernard, and in 1964 a motorway **tunnel** (@www.letunnel.com) opened beneath the pass to safeguard traffic flow year-round. These days the hospice spends the summer crowded with visitors and hikers, and the winter receiving people climbing up from below to spend a few days or weeks on a snowbound spiritual retreat.

The main road from Orsières climbs amidst increasingly spectacular scenery to the village of **Bourg-St-Pierre** (1632m), residence from the eighth century of the guardians of the pass; the old church, rebuilt in 1739, has at its northeastern corner a Roman milestone dating from about 310 AD. Shortly afterwards, traffic shoots into the Grand-St-Bernard tunnel, emerging 5.9km on in Italy, but a tiny winding road to one side continues up the mountainside, past a ski lift serving the small Super-St-Bernard peak (part of the Four Valleys ski area – see p.285 – with a couple of red runs and a lonesome black), before it eventually arrives at the **Grand-St-Bernard Pass**.

Col du Grand-St-Bernard

The **Col du Grand-St-Bernard** (2470m; see box above) is the oldest Alpine pass route, protected for almost a millennium by monks inhabiting the **hospice** on top. The views aren't outstanding, and the souvenir stalls are an eyesore, but the sense of history is what draws you in: for centuries, this was the only road between northern Europe and southern Europe for hundreds of kilometres on either flank, and countless travellers have arrived to the same view of the little summit lake backed by the same mountain panorama. The interesting **museum** (June–Sept daily 10am–6pm; Fr.8, **⊛** www.gsbernard.net) documents the history of the pass, and includes several quaking accounts of fatal or near-fatal crossings. The two buildings which make up the hospice, exposed to winter storms which have been known to bring 25m of snow and temperatures of -30°C, date from 1560 and 1898; the older one contains a Baroque **church**. If you walk down from the hospice, the Italian frontier guards will let you cross the international border to explore the area; around the **statue** of St Bernard atop its round pillar (1905) you'll find traces of the Roman road cut into the bedrock.

In summer, it's possible to **stay** in the 🏠 hospice (**☎**027 787 12 36, **⊛** www .gsbernard.ch; **❶**), which is still a functioning religious community, either in plain, cosy rooms or dorms; the cooking is suitably hearty and the atmosphere jovial. During the winter months (Nov–June) and over Easter, you can arrange an individual retreat, to take advantage of the solitude for personal reflection.

Walking from Chamonix to Zermatt

The west-to-east **Walker's Haute Route** which begins in **Chamonix** (France) below Mont Blanc and ends in Zermatt at the foot of the Matterhorn, is one of the most beautiful and scenically rewarding of Europe's long walks. It's a demanding **two-week trek**, but there are no glaciers or permanent snowfields to cross, and overnight accommodation is plentiful. You can also easily join the route partway along for a few days' hiking: the Val de Bagnes, Arolla and Zinal, for instance, are all served by public transport from main Valais towns. Along with good maps, take *Chamonix to Zermatt, the Walker's Haute Route* by Kev Reynolds (see "Books", p.512).

With a long climb out of the Chamonix valley, the Haute Route enters Switzerland by way of Col de Balme and descends to **Trient**. On day three there are two routes to choose from: either the formidable but non-technical Fenêtre d'Arpette alongside the Trient Glacier, or the more pedestrian Alp Bovine route to **Champex**. From here, an easy valley walk leads to **Le Châble** in Val de Bagnes, from where the route makes a 1600m climb to **Mont-Fort**, with stunning views to Mont Blanc. Next day, an airy balcony walk takes you along the Sentier des Chamois, with the Grand Combin (4314m) a mighty presence across the valley, then over Col de Louvie to skirt below the Grand Désert glacier. A short climb to Col des Roux reveals the tranquil Lac des Dix below. Beyond, the way crosses either Col de Riedmatten (2919m) or the neighbouring Pas de Chèvres before a very pleasant descent through pastures to **Arolla**.

Day eight is easy, taking you down to Les Haudères and up to **La Sage**, while on day nine Col de Torrent (2919m) leads you into the Moiry glen, overlooking a cascading icefall. Col de Sorebois is next, with the descent from there to **Zinal** in Val d'Anniviers allowing you to make the acquaintance of the hugely impressive **Weisshorn** (4505m). On day eleven, you head north from Zinal on another balcony path, then cross the Meidpass (2790m) to **Gruben** in the Turtmanntal, a truly forgotten little corner. The penultimate stage (day thirteen) crosses the 2894m **Augstbordpass** into the Mattertal, the valley which leads to Zermatt and the Matterhorn; an hour and a half below the pass the trail turns a spur to confront you with the most amazing of panoramas. Across the unseen depths of the Mattertal soars the **Dom** (4545m), the highest mountain located entirely in Switzerland; at the head of the valley far away a long crest of snow and ice stretches from Monte Rosa to the Breithorn, while the Weisshorn dominates the right-hand wall. An hour below that viewpoint lies Jungen, a summer alp hamlet clinging to the near-vertical hillside. Day fourteen offers a mere wander up the valley from St Niklaus to **Zermatt**, in order to make your final pilgrimage to the **Matterhorn**.

Verbier

It's the skiing that put **VERBIER** on the map: few places in the world offer such breadth of possibilities with such awe-inspiring scenery as a backdrop. Before 1910, the plateau on which Verbier sits was an empty summer pasture; the first hotel opened in 1934, and even by 1950 the place was still a tiny village. No more. Following the 1960s ski boom, Verbier now sprawls, characterized by apartment blocks and modern housing. It's not particularly charming or endearing, but with this quality of skiing on offer, it doesn't have to be. European high society flocks to the resort in season, when the mood of the place can get brash, but still the slopes hold sway. Fully half of the million annual visitors are Swiss, many scooting over from Lausanne and Geneva for a weekend in their apartments or chalets; it's a feature of Verbier that chalet accommodation outnumbers hotel beds ten-to-one, making it much more advisable to visit on a ski-chalet package booked from home than to arrive independently without a hotel reservation.

Arrival and information

Branch-line **trains** from Martigny split at Sembrancher: one half terminates at Orsières, the other at **Le Châble**, the valley community at the foot of Verbier's hill. From Le Châble, a gondola runs every fifteen minutes up to Verbier, arriving at the huge Médran station at the east end of the resort. Postbuses also do the run from Le Châble, climbing first through "Verbier-Village" (the locals' town) before terminating in "Verbier-Station" (the resort), at the central post office just off Place Centrale.

Orientation around the resort is straightforward. The Rue de Médran climbs southeast from Place Centrale to the **Médran** lift station, arrival point for gondolas up from Le Châble, and departure point for gondolas and a chairlift continuing up to Les Ruinettes, main access point for the pistes. It's along Rue de Médran, and

▲ Skier on the slopes

Sports and activities at Verbier

Winter sports

Verbier is the main resort of the **Four Valleys** ski area (ⓦ www.4vallees.ch), covering some 400km of piste at all levels of difficulty, stretching from Thyon, Veysonnaz and Nendaz in the west, through the central Savoleyres and Mont-Fort areas and down to La Tzoumaz. The **Verbier** sector covers lifts to Les Ruinettes, Attelas and Mont-Gelé (but not Mont-Fort); the **Savoleyres** sector is accessed both from Verbier village and La Tzoumaz; and the family-friendly **Bruson** sector faces Verbier across the valley, accessed from Le Châble.

Aside from a handful of blues at Bruson, beginners have a dedicated "**Station**" sub-sector, comprising nursery slopes in and just above Verbier village itself. There's a host of red runs from **Savoleyres** (2354m), and the Médran lifts take you up to **Les Ruinettes** (2200m), with its own cat's cradle of reds and a steep black run, in addition to some carving. Large-capacity gondolas connect to **Attelas** (2727m), with blacks and reds, and on either to the **Mont-Gelé** summit (3023m), or by chairlift over to **Tortin** (2050m) from where reds or a fiendishly difficult black connect to the Siviez and Thyon ski areas. From **La Chaux** (2260m) above Ruinettes, one of Switzerland's largest cable cars, the Jumbo, scoops 150 people at a time up to the glacier slopes of **Mont-Fort** (3330m). This is prime territory for snowboarders, with half-pipes and excellent facilities at Gentianes on Mont-Fort and at "BoarderX" at La Chaux itself (2260–2845m), where there's also a snow park, as well as at Savoleyres.

A **lift pass** for one/six days on the Verbier sector is Fr.58/301, on Savoleyres/Tzoumaz Fr.52/267, on Bruson Fr.37/189, and for the entire Four Valleys region Fr.65/337. Discounted part-day and advance-purchase passes, and other deals, are available (ⓦ www.verbierbooking.com).

Adventure sports and extreme events

Verbier is a mecca for **adventure** addicts, with a host of companies competing with each other to come up with the thrill of the season. **Verbier Sports** (ⓣ 027 775 33 63, ⓦ www.verbierbooking.com) is home to official ski and snowboarding schools and the mountain guides office, and has a huge range of activities, including heli-skiing and heli-boarding, snow-shoeing, ice-climbing, guided high-altitude walking, and more, as well as summer canyoning, rafting and caving. Paragliding centres include Centre Parapente (ⓣ 027 771 68 18, ⓦ www.flyverbier.ch), Fly Time (ⓣ 027 776 12 22, ⓦ www.fly-time.ch) and Verbier Summits (ⓣ 027 776 11 34, ⓦ www.verbier-summits .com). **La Fantastique** (ⓣ 027 771 41 41, ⓦ www.lafantastique.com) and **Adrenaline** (ⓣ 027 771 74 59, ⓦ www.adrenaline-verbier.ch) are ski and snowboard schools also offering heli-skiing, guides for off-piste (Fr.500 per day) and long-distance ski-safaris.

Xtreme Verbier (ⓦ www.xtremeverbier.com), one of the top international showcases of freeride snowboarding, is held each March, when some of the world's best boarders do their thing at Bec des Rosses (3222m), way up on the mountainside at Gentianes, with 55° gradients, broad expanses of powder and plenty of obstacles. **Verbier Ride** (ⓦ www.verbierride.com) is an exhibition showcase of free-style skiing, held in early March. The **Patrouille des Glaciers** (ⓦ www.pdg.ch) is a long-distance endurance test across the 53km of glaciers, summits and passes from Zermatt to Verbier, dubbed "Paris–Dakar on skis". In August, Verbier also hosts the world's longest mountain-bike race, the **Grand Raid** (ⓦ www.grand-raid.ch), a one-day race across six valleys (rising at one point to 2792m) on a 121km route to Grimentz.

in the surrounding area, that most of the resort's après–ski happens. Verbier's other gondola rises from the **Savoleyres** station, best part of a kilometre north of Place Centrale. West of Place Centrale is the massive Centre Sportif with, below and south of it, workaday Verbier Village. **Free buses** link all of these throughout the winter season (Dec–April daily 8am–7pm).

The efficient **tourist office** is on Place Centrale (July & Aug Mon–Sat 8am–noon & 2–6.30pm, Sun 9am–noon & 3–6.30pm, May, June & Sept–Nov Mon–Fri 8am–noon & 1.30–6pm, Sat 9am–noon & 4–6.30pm; Sun 9am–noon; Dec–April Mon–Fri 8am–noon & 2–6.30pm, Sat 8.30am–7pm, Sun 9am–noon & 3–6.30pm; ℡ 027 775 38 88, Ⓦ www.verbier.ch).

Late July sees one of Switzerland's most prestigious classical music events, the **Verbier Festival** (Ⓦ www.verbierfestival.com). For two weeks, the resort plays host to top-flight soloists and conductors, performing and leading masterclasses. Tickets for individual concerts go for Fr.35–130.

Accommodation

Verbier is tricky when it comes to **hotels**: there just aren't that many of them, and in season most won't accept bookings for fewer than seven days. In the April/May and October/November between-seasons many places close; summer and between-season prices can be up to a third cheaper than winter. Accommodation is least expensive in the handful of private rooms on offer through the tourist office, or in any of the thousands of chalets, which must be booked months in advance.

Bristol ℡ 027 771 65 77, Ⓦ www.bristol-verbier .ch. Friendly, cosy and quiet, and very central, but watch out for that peak-season price hike. ❸–❻
Ermitage ℡ 027 771 64 77, Ⓦ www.ermitage -verbier.ch. Well-run and very convenient place on Place Centrale, delivering unexpected value for money. ❸–❻
Garbo ℡ 027 771 62 72, Ⓦ www.hotelgarbo.com. Central spot, midway between Place Centrale and the Médran lifts. Open winter only, when it's one of the cheapest places in the village. ❹

Les Touristes ℡ 027 771 21 47, Ⓦ www .hoteltouristes-verbier.ch. One of the best ways to avoid Verbier's high prices and uninspiring anonymity: it's on a street corner in Verbier-Village, linked to the lifts by bus, with spartan, TV-free rooms, most with shared bathrooms. The quiet restaurant and chic-free atmosphere are a breath of fresh air. ❷–❸

Eating and drinking

There are dozens of **eating** options. Wander your way up Rue de Médran from Place Centrale until you see something you fancy: there's a handful of pizzerias – the *Fer à Cheval* is one of the better ones (Ⓦ www.feracheval.ch), with a lively après-ski scene, or there's the *Garbo* close at hand, which also shakes a leg. As you emerge from the Médran station, *Au Vieux Valais* is within view, a cosy traditional-style place for raclette, fondue and other belly-warmers.

Heading in the other direction from Place Centrale, the cosy modern *Chez Martin*, just down the hill on Route de Verbier-Station, also serves up a good range of inexpensive and unpretentious fare. The gourmet choice is the Michelin-starred *Le Table d'Adrien* (℡ 027 771 62 00, Ⓦ www.chalet-adrien .com) at the *Chalet d'Adrien* hotel next to Savoleyres station, which has superb modern French-Italian cuisine and one of the village's nicest terraces. There's also slightly more affordable fine dining at the *Montpelier* hotel restaurant (℡ 027 771 61 31, Ⓦ www.hotelmontpelier.ch) on the west side of town, with an innovative take on classic French dishes.

The resort's most colourful place to **drink** is the raucous *Pub Mont Fort* (Ⓦ www.pubmontfort.com), near the Médran station. The *Nelson*, off Place Centrale, is another good option, while the *Farm Club* (Ⓦ www.kingsverbier .ch), west of the centre in the *Nevaï* hotel, is the best place for a spot of celeb- and royal-watching.

Val de Bagnes

From **Le Châble**, a peaceful, rural community tucked on the valley floor below Verbier, the long **Val de Bagnes** runs southeast into the high mountains. Buses run twice a day (July–Sept only) from Le Châble, the capital of the Bagnes commune, up to the impressive **Mauvoisin Dam**, a giant 250m-high wall blocking the end of the valley. At 1961m, it's one of the highest-altitude dams in the world. A **hotel** at the base (℡027 778 11 30, Ⓦwww.mauvoisin.ch; ❷) has rooms and dorms – handy for an overnight stay either after a walk up from Fionnay or Lourtier villages in the valley, or before taking a full day to hike back to Le Châble.

Sion

SION (pronounced *see-ohh*), known as Sitten in German, is the capital of Valais, an alluring and attractive town of 27,000 with an exceptionally long history: archeological evidence points to the site having been inhabited during Neolithic times. What attracted settlement, no doubt, was the incongruous presence, on the otherwise flat valley floor, of two jutting rocky hills, visible from afar and now adorned with the medieval castles **Valère** and **Tourbillon**. They're an odd and slightly sinister sight, which matches the common Swiss notion that the locals (named Sédunois, after the town's Latin name Sedunum, meaning Place of Castles) are themselves a bit odd, impenetrably taciturn and clannish. Prejudice aside, Sion enjoys a simply glorious **climate**, dry, mild and consistently clear; afternoons are bathed in bright sunshine. Its **wines** (see p.46) are outstanding.

Arrival and information

Sion's **train station** is at the southern end of the long, straight Avenue de la Gare, with the **postbus station** to one side. Some 500m north along Avenue de la Gare is the concrete **Place de la Planta**, on which stands the **tourist office** (July & Aug Mon–Fri 9am–6pm, Sat 9.30am–4pm; rest of year Mon–Fri 9am–noon & 2–5.30pm, Sat 9am–12.30pm; ℡027 327 77 27, Ⓦwww.siontourism.ch). They have a brochure detailing a self-guided **walking tour** of the town. Sion's tiny **airport** (℡027 329 06 00, Ⓦwww.sionairport.ch) is 5km west of the centre.

Aside from the annual **cowfighting** championship held in May at nearby Aproz (see p.278), Sion plays host to a prestigious **International Music Festival** (Ⓦwww.sion-festival.ch), which runs in August and September at venues around Valais. Running concurrently in July and August are the **Académie de Musique de Tibor Varga** (Ⓦwww.amsion.ch), a cycle of masterclasses given by international soloists, and the **Festival International de l'Orgue Ancien**, centred on the world's oldest organ, still playable in the town's Château de Valère.

Accommodation

Of Sion's **hotels**, the ⚞ *Elite*, 6 Avenue du Midi (℡027 322 03 27, Ⓦwww.hotelelite-sion.ch; ❷–❸), doesn't look like much, but it's been tastefully renovated inside and is a good choice, or head for the slightly more upmarket *Du Rhône*, 10 Rue du Scex (℡027 322 82 91, Ⓦwww.bestwestern.ch; ❸). Sion's best is *Europa*, a business hotel out towards the airfield, at 19 Rue de l'Envoi (℡027 322 24 23, Ⓦwww.zghotels.ch; ❹).

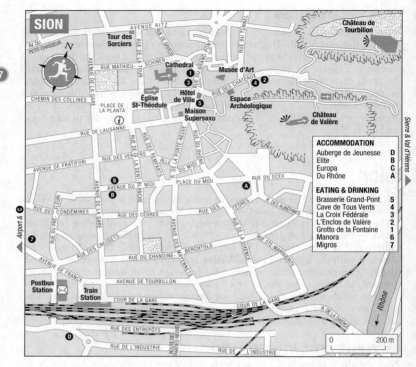

SION

ACCOMMODATION
Auberge de Jeunesse	D
Elite	B
Europa	C
Du Rhône	A

EATING & DRINKING
Brasserie Grand-Pont	5
Cave de Tous Vents	4
La Croix Fédérale	3
L'Enclos de Valère	2
Grotto de la Fontaine	1
Manora	6
Migros	7

0   200 m

The good HI **hostel** *Auberge de Jeunesse*, 2 Rue de l'Industrie (☎027 323 74 70, ⓦwww.youthhostel.ch; closed Dec & Jan; ❶), is just behind the station – modern, clean and well run, while the nearest and best **campsite** is *Les Iles* (☎027 346 43 47, ⓦwww.campingtcs.ch), 4km west on Route d'Aproz.

The Town

Sion's Old Town is interesting: a slow wander through the cobbled alleys, with their old inns and sixteenth-century shuttered town houses, can fill an atmospheric afternoon. Just northeast of Place de la Planta is the small **Église St-Théodule**, dating from the sixteenth century and with some fine vaulting in the choir. Just beside it is the **Cathédrale Notre-Dame du Glarier** (Our Lady of the Gravel – referring to the ground on which the cathedral was built). The main building is fifteenth century, with elements of earlier Romanesque and Gothic structures incorporated within it, including a fine belfry. Its most noticeable feature, though, is the bells, which strike every quarter-hour in a near-exact copy of the sound of Big Ben in London, although the bass bell's slightly higher pitch gives the ensemble an inescapably mournful tone. Some 100m to the south is Rue Supersaxo, with the **Maison Supersaxo** (Mon–Fri 8am–noon & 2–6pm; free) tucked into the tiny Passage Supersaxo off the street. This lavish residence was built in 1505 by the local governor, Georges Supersaxo, to show the town's bishop who was boss: climb the Gothic staircase inside to a hall on the upper floor with a magnificent carved and painted ceiling. Two minutes north on Rue de la

Tour brings you to the witch's-hat **Tour des Sorciers**, part of the town's medieval fortifications.

Beside the imposing **Hôtel de Ville** on Rue du Grand-Pont, lanes and back alleys cut east to Rue des Châteaux, which climbs steeply towards the twin hills of Tourbillon and Valère. Before you get there, though, after 150m you'll pass on the left the **Musée d'Art**, Place de la Majorie (Tues–Sun 1–5pm; Fr.5, free on 1st Sun of month; ⓦwww.musees-valais.ch). Located in the impressive thirteenth-century Château de la Majorie, the museum houses an extensive collection of works by artists associated with the Valais, ranging from eighteenth-century mountain landscapes to contemporary abstracts. Opposite is the **Espace Archéologique** (Tues–Sun 1–5pm, June–Sept until 6pm; Fr.4, free on 1st Sun of month), with an impressive collection of mainly Roman bits and pieces, as well as Bronze Age steles and prehistoric dolmens.

Valère and Tourbillon

Rue des Châteaux climbs to a parking area in the groove between the twin castles of Sion. From here, paths divide up the dry, scrubby hillsides – left (north) to Tourbillon, right (south) to Valère.

Château de Valère is the more interesting of the two, and the more complete. The hike up brings you past the tiny fourteenth-century Chapelle de Tous-les-Saints and massive Roman foundation walls to the castle-church. As it stands, the château dates from the thirteenth century, but elements survive of earlier buildings, and the whole thing may well stand on the ruins of a Roman temple. The most notable features of the church interior (daily 10am–5pm; Oct–May closed Mon; Fr.3) are the oldest playable **organ** in the world, high on the back wall, dating from 1390, and the faded murals of the chancel and adjoining chapel.

The **Château de Tourbillon** on the opposite hill dates from 1294, but was ruined by fire in 1788 and today, aside from the external walls, little is left. These days, it's open for scrambling (Tues–Sun 11am–6pm, Oct–May closes 5pm; free) and yields excellent views along the valley and over the town.

Eating and drinking

There are a surprising number of good places to **eat and drink** for such a small city as Sion. The basics are taken care of at various **self-service** restaurants, including a *Manora* on Avenue du Midi, and a huge *Migros* west of the station on Avenue de France.

Rue du Grand-Pont in the Old Town is lined with attractive little corners for a bite. *Grotto de la Fontaine*, at no. 21 (closed Tues & Wed), is a Ticinese-style inn serving fresh pastas, stews and risottos (Fr.25–40); *La Croix Fédérale*, at no. 13 (☏027 322 16 95; closed Mon), offers an extensive menu specializing in mouthwatering fish dishes (around Fr.30), while the *Brasserie du Grand-Pont*, at no. 6 (closed Sun), has an unusually wide-ranging menu of international dishes for around Fr.30, plus lower-priced *plats du jour*.

To the east, on steep, cobbled Rue des Châteaux, there are two excellent options very close to each other: ⚒ *L'Enclos de Valère*, at no. 18 (☏027 323 32 30, ⓦwww.enclosdevalere.ch; Oct–April closed Sun eve & Mon), has a big shaded terrace on which to enjoy its classic gourmet cuisine (*menus* around Fr.40), while just about next door is the ⚒ *Cave de Tous Vents* (☏027 322 46 84; evening only, closed Sun & Mon; ⓦwww.cave-tous-vents.ch), an atmospheric vaulted cellar in a thirteenth-century building that serves quality cheese-based dishes ranging from fondues to *mets au fromage*, accompanied by a long list of local wines (*menus* Fr.16–42).

Val d'Hérens

Branching southeast from Sion, the **VAL D'HÉRENS**, a world apart from the main valley, gives a fascinating glimpse of traditional rural life. Even people from Sion can barely understand the odd guttural patois spoken in the valley – which strikes city folk as being a little like Arabic. Unsubstantiated supposition brings out the idea that the generally dark-skinned, dark-eyed people of the Val d'Hérens may be descended from the conquering Saracen armies who swept through the area after the Battle of Poitiers in 732. Having planted that idea, Sédunois will then tell you about the people of Isérables, a town west of Sion, who have been called *Les Bedjuis* for as long as anyone can remember – a nickname remarkably close to "Bedouin". The Allalinhorn peak near Saas-Fee is another clue, its name apparently derived from "Allah".

One of the sights of the valley can be found near the village of Euseigne, where the road passes beneath the **Pyramides d'Euseigne**, a bizarre geological outcrop of glacial moraines. Whereas erosion flattened the area all around, these stone jags were protected by hard rock caps. Today, they're hard to believe – a wall of unnaturally bare and pointed stalagmites in the open wooded valley, each crag crowned by a dark boulder balanced on a needle point.

Some 15km south is **Evolène**, a quaint village now bypassed by the main road, which has preserved along its main street traditional wooden houses and an air of rural tranquillity. The locals have cheerfully capitalized on this by deciding to wear traditional dress – only partly, it seems, in a self-conscious bid for tourist appeal. A handful of cafés and simple inns cater to hikers and day-trippers.

Arolla

South of the hamlet of **Les Haudères** beyond Evolène, you begin to penetrate the wild countryside. One road branches east over the crest to Ferpècle, while another climbs west up and over into the tranquil hidden **Val d'Arolla**, terminating some 12km south after a series of nerve-racking tunnels at the pristine hamlet of **AROLLA** (1998m). This tiny, outdoorsy place is one of the stops on the Walkers' Haute Route between Chamonix and Zermatt (see p.283), and offers a wealth of half- and full-day hikes all around. There's a handful of blue and red ski-pistes served by lifts rising from the village; passes are Fr.34/155 for one/six days. Four or five **hotels** offer quality retreats, including the sleek *Hôtel du Pigne* (☎027 283 71 00, ⓦ www.hoteldupigne.ch; ❸). Half-a-dozen places offer dorms; the **tourist office** (☎027 283 10 83, ⓦ www.arolla.com) has information. Amazingly, in January ski-passes are **half-price** and all hotels slash their rates by a third or more, giving seven nights amidst the deep snow for under Fr.580 half-board in a double room at *Hôtel du Pigne*, as little as Fr.200 in a pension.

Walking in the Val d'Hérens

Sion tourist office has an all-inclusive deal for a self-guided **walking tour** right around the Val d'Hérens. Starting from Sion, this involves 5–7 hours of walking a day: from Thyon to the Dixence dam; from the Lac des Dix over the passes to Arolla; a valley-floor stroll to Evolène; and finally on a scenic path high up the valley side to Becs de Bosson and down to Nax. Included are six nights' half-board accommodation and five picnic lunches, postbuses to and from Sion, transport of one bag per person from hotel to hotel, documentation and a 1:25,000 map. This all-in deal costs Fr.634 per person (sharing a double room). Check details at ⓦ www.coeurduvalais.ch.

St-Léonard

On the road from Sion east to Sierre, the small village of **ST-LÉONARD** sits alongside one of the largest **underground lakes** in Europe (mid-March to mid-Oct daily 9am–5pm; Fr.10). Frequent buses drop off either in the village or at the car park beneath the ticket office. Tours of the lake, by large rowing boats with everyone crowded in side by side, take about thirty minutes – and it's cold down there, so bring a jumper. The cave entrance is just a gap in the mountainside, but as you launch off onto the inky water, the illuminated, otherworldly cavern stretching out ahead of you is very impressive. The guides, who do the rowing, have a nice line in multilingual patter, regaling you with all kinds of stories and details about the lake and its geology.

Sierre

Hardly any foreigners come to **SIERRE** (Siders in German) unless they're catching the funicular up to the ski resorts of Crans and Montana on the hillside above. Which is all to the good, because it leaves this idyllic little valley-floor town quiet, perfect for a day or two of strolling and wine-tasting in the vineyards all around.

Sierre lies almost exactly on the French–German language border, which is marked by the tiny Raspille stream a couple of kilometres east of the town. The road east from Sierre to the sleepy village of **Salgesch** (Salquenen in

---

Into the Val d'Anniviers

The people and history of Sierre are inextricably linked with the **Val d'Anniviers**, which opens at a narrow chink in the mountain high up opposite Sierre to the south but broadens out to extend southwards for some 40km, terminating in the hiking trailhead of **Zinal**.

The residents of the Anniviers (the name means "seasonal") were the last people in Switzerland to follow a genuinely **nomadic** lifestyle. Up until a few decades ago, people would arrive in Sierre from the Anniviers in spring, each community bringing with it flocks, a schoolteacher and a priest. For a few months everyone would stay and work on the vineyards before departing in mid-June to pasture their flocks on the heights above Sierre. In mid-September, everybody would drift down again for the grape harvest before dispersing back to their villages in the Anniviers valley for the winter. This carries on today in lesser form, but families no longer have to bring bag and baggage when they come to work in Sierre, and tend also to keep their children in school in one place or the other.

The valley is acclaimed by walkers and climbers as one of the finest in the whole region. Sierre tourist office has put together a self-guided **Tour pédestre du Val d'Anniviers** (W www.sierre-anniviers.ch/touranniviers) – a perfect way to explore this beautiful, isolated landscape. It runs in summer (mid-June to mid-Oct) and takes six nights, staying in two- and three-star hotels with all meals (including picnic lunches), postbus connections, baggage transport and a map included, for Fr.860 per person. If that sounds like too much hard work, aim instead for the picturesque mid-valley hamlet of **St-Luc** – up a series of switchbacks from the valley floor – then take a funicular (W www.rma.ch) up the flanks of Mt Bella Tola to **Tignousa** (2186m) and continue on foot (1hr) to the majestically situated *Hotel Weisshorn* (T 027 475 11 06, W www.weisshorn.ch; ❺ including half board), perched at 2300m and retaining much character from its origins in the 1880s. Hole up here for as long as you can afford.

French) begins as the Rue de la Gemmi and ends five minutes later as the Gemmistrasse; Sierre sits alongside the Rhône, while in Salgesch the same river is dubbed the Rotten. **Wine** is what fuels both communities, and there are plenty of trails through and between the vineyards, with equally numerous opportunities to stop and sample a glass or two. Sierre is the driest town in Switzerland, and gets an average of almost seven and a half hours of sunshine daily from May to October (and a total of 330 sunny days a year), helping it to produce excellent Fendant whites; Salgesch, meanwhile, is renowned for its Pinot Noir reds. Not for nothing did the Romans call the place *Sirrum amoenum*, Sierre the agreeable.

The Town

If you turn left (west) from the train station and then aim northwest up Avenue du Marché, you'll come into the little-visited old quarters of Sierre. At the top of Rue de Villa, alongside a vineyard, stands the **Château de Villa**, one half of Sierre-Salgesch's modest **Musée Valaisan de la Vigne et du Vin** (April–Nov Tues–Sun 2–5pm; Fr.5 for both museums; Ⓦwww.museevalaisanduvin.ch). The Sierre half focuses on the wine itself, with interesting displays (in French and German) on grape varieties and the history of cultivation and some old presses. In the same building are a restaurant and wine-bar (see opposite). From here, a six-kilometre Vineyard Walk (*Sentier Viticole/Rebweg*) runs for a couple of hours through quiet, shuttered lanes and out through the open hillside vineyards to the other half of the wine museum, in the creaky old **Zumofenhaus** in the heart of Salgesch. Displays are more scholarly here, on the technical aspects of viticulture, cultivation methods and history, but the enthusiastic guardian will be happy to give you a rundown in English on what's what. Trains or buses can run you back to Sierre.

An interesting detour from the Wine Path is to the small **Musée Charles-Clos Olsommer**, signposted in Veyras (July–Sept Wed–Sun 2–5pm; Oct–June Sat & Sun 2–5pm; Fr.5; Ⓦwww.musee-olsommer.ch). Olsommer, born in Neuchâtel in 1883, studied in Munich at the same time as Klee and Kandinsky, but unlike them became fixated with a Klimt-like style rooted in symbolism. He lived in Sierre from 1912 until his death in 1966, painting moody scenes of women praying in the wilderness or surrounded by psychedelic patterns.

Back in the town centre at 30 Rue du Bourg, the **Musée Rilke** (April–Sept Tues–Sun 3–7pm; Fr.6; Ⓦwww.fondationrilke.ch) celebrates Sierre's most famous resident, the Prague-born poet Rainer Maria Rilke, who wrote his celebrated *Sonnets to Orpheus* in Sierre. Rilke suffered from leukaemia, and died in 1926 after pricking his finger on a rose-thorn.

A fifteen-minute walk east of Sierre stands a pristine pine forest, the **Forêt de Finges/Pfynwald** (both terms derived from the Latin *fines*, or border; this was the ancient limit of Roman control; Ⓦwww.pfyn-finges.ch), fringed by marshes on the Rhône banks. Protected but not developed, it's perfect for long walks and peaceful picnics.

Practicalities

Sierre's **station** houses the **tourist office** (Mon–Fri 8.30am–6pm, Sat 9am–5.30pm, Sun 9am–1pm; ☎027 455 85 35, Ⓦwww.sierre-salgesch.ch). The longest **funicular** in Switzerland (4.2km) heads up to Montana from the SMC station two minutes' walk away, left onto the main Avenue Général-Guisan outside the station.

Near the station, **hotel** *La Poste*, 22 Rue du Bourg (☎027 456 57 60, Ⓦwww.hotel-sierre.ch; ④), has smart modern rooms, cheery decor and a nice restaurant.

Opposite the station, ⚜ *Le Terminus* (☎027 455 13 51, Ⓦ www.hotel-terminus
.ch; ❹) has a chic, modern style and boasts the excellent *Didier de Courten* fine-
dining **restaurant**, offering Swiss haute cuisine accompanied by an extensive
wine list (*menu* Fr.140; closed Sun & Mon). The restaurant in the Château de Villa
(see opposite; ☎027 455 18 96) is one of the more prestigious places to sample
Valaisian specialities, and its "oenotheque" (daily 10.30am–1pm & 4.30–8.30pm)
stocks more than 600 of the region's wines. South of town next to the small Lac
de Géronde (aka "Grand Lac") is the pleasant ⚜ *La Grotte* (☎027 455 46 46), a
terrace restaurant known only to the locals, serving very good fish (*menus* around
Fr.30), and with fourteen comfortable, characterful rooms upstairs (❷).

Crans-Montana

CRANS-MONTANA is another of Switzerland's big, world-famous ski
resorts, occupying what is claimed to be the sunniest plateau in the Alps, facing
south over the Rhône valley with a spectacular panorama of peaks yawning
beyond. Along with Verbier and St Moritz, it's also one of the glitziest, with
what the tourist office likes to call the finest shopping in the Alps.

The resort actually comprises three villages, **Crans-sur-Sierre** (pronounced
crawh), **Montana** and, out on a limb, **Aminona**; the agglomeration sprawls for
more than 2km between Crans, to the west, and Montana, to the east, with
nothing to mark the shift from one to another. Traffic is permanently heavy: in
high season, village-to-village gridlock is not unknown. The **skiing**, rather
unfairly dubbed "irretrievably intermediate" by some sports writers, takes
second place to the wining and dining of Crans-Montana's affluent socialites
– although the resort does have the advantage of access to year-round skiing on
the Plaine Morte glacier, way up above 3000m.

Skiing aside, the place is best known for hosting the **European Masters golf**
tournament every September (Ⓦ www.omegaeuropeanmasters.com), second
only on the European circuit to the British Open for prestige and top names.
Crans' scenic course – "the most spectacular tournament site in the world"
according to Greg Norman – was redesigned by Seve Ballesteros, and now
boasts fiendishly complex upturned-saucer greens.

Arrival and information

The SMC **funicular** from Sierre arrives at **Vermala station** at the eastern end
of Montana. There are also free **buses** (Ⓦ www.cie-smc.ch) running up from

---

Winter sports at Crans-Montana

Access to the pistes (Ⓦ www.mycma.ch), almost all of which are relatively straightforward blues and reds – if beautifully scenic – is via five gondolas ranged along the
base of the mountain. From west to east, these are **Chetseron** and **Crans** (both
within Crans village), **Grand Signal** in Montana, **Violettes** near the Montana funicular
station, and **Aminona**. The woods above Montana are crisscrossed by red runs
winding between the trees, while **Cry d'Err** above Crans has a host of lifts serving
blues galore down to the village. Violettes gives access to the **Plaine Morte** top
station (3000m), with some exciting blues, and the start of a long meandering red
back to the village. **Lift passes** valid in all four sectors (Crans, Montana, Violettes and
Aminona) for one/six days cost Fr.63/292.

Sierre along different routes – check with Sierre tourist office for details. In addition, a bus runs up to Crans from Sion.

Montana tourist office (July & Aug daily 8.30am–6pm; rest of year Mon–Fri 8.30am–noon & 2–6pm, Sat 8.30am–noon; ☎027 485 04 04, ⓦwww .crans-montana.ch) is 100m west (left) of the Vermala funicular station, in the post office. The village centre is another 200m west, focused around the Ycoor ice-skating rink. Just beyond is the small **Lac Grenon**; running along its northern shore is the Route de Rawyl – always busy with cars – which, some 800m west, feeds into Rue Centrale in Crans, site of the **Crans tourist office** (same hours; ☎027 485 08 00). More or less opposite is the **Étang Long** lakelet, which backs onto the championship golf course.

Accommodation

A host of basic **hotels** offer inexpensive rooms: *Central* in Crans (☎027 481 36 65, ⓦwww.3963.ch/central; ❸) and *Olympic* in Montana (☎027 481 29 85, ⓦwww.amadays.ch; ❷) are two examples, both in the centre of their villages, and both tidy and well kept. The slightly more expensive *Robinson* (☎027 481 13 53, ⓦwww.valaisonline.com/robinson; ❸–❹) is an uncomplicated option beside the two Crans gondolas, while the more upmarket *Art de Vivre* (☎027 481 33 12, ⓦwww.art-vivre.ch; ❹–❻) is a smart, modern family-run four-star with a well-equipped spa, set in a quiet location within easy reach of the lifts. The *Lac Moubra* **campsite** in Montana (☎027 481 28 51; closed mid-Oct to Dec) has basic **dorms**.

Eating and drinking

Eating wins no prizes for invention or quality. Body and soul are kept together by simple diners such as *Café du Centre* beside the church. The *Auberge de la Diligence* (☎027 485 99 85), 500m east of Montana's Vermala station, is Lebanese-run, and serves up quality Middle Eastern food (*menus* Fr.22); it also has affordable rooms (❷). Next door, the *Hôtel de la Forêt* (☎027 480 21 31, ⓦwww.delaforet.ch) caters specifically for vegetarians. *Café-Bar 1900* is the place to hang out in the centre of Crans, just round the corner from the Rue du Prado with all the big, glitzy designer names – Vuitton, Gucci, Hermès and all.

Oberwallis

East of Sierre stretches the German-speaking portion of Valais – or **Wallis**, as it officially becomes. To mark it out from the Lower Valais to the west, this is known as Upper Valais, or **Oberwallis**. The main town of the region, **Brig**, is an important road and rail junction, but is otherwise of limited interest; the concealed **Lötschen valley** is a more worthwhile detour. The reason that everybody passes through the area is to make a pilgrimage to the little mountain village of **Zermatt**, in order to lay eyes upon the **Matterhorn**, the most famous (if not actually the highest) of all Switzerland's mountains. In a side valley nearby sits the equally alluring resort of **Saas-Fee**, while east of Brig, the remote **Goms** region follows the Rhône to its glacial source.

East of Sierre

Heading **east of Sierre**, traffic on the valley-floor road starts to build up as you approach the Lötschberg Tunnel, the turn-offs to Zermatt and Saas-Fee and the Simplon Pass route into Italy. A couple of diversions bring you out of the crush. Just beyond the French–German language border is a turning to the ancient village of **Leuk**, with the spa resort of **Leukerbad** further up; while beyond the Lötschberg Tunnel terminus at Goppenstein, a minor road penetrates between the high rocky walls into the lovely **Lötschental**.

Leuk and Leukerbad

Perched above the valley floor, **LEUK** (Loèche in French; Ⓦ www.leuk.ch) is remarkably good-looking, with an array of photogenic ancient buildings, including a fine Rathaus and medieval Bischofsschloss. Beyond, the road winds up to **LEUKERBAD** (Loèche-les-Bains), Europe's highest spa, at 1411m. Above the village, amidst some good winter skiing, is the pedestrian-only Gemmi Pass, one end of a tough hiking trail from Kandersteg (see p.260), from where cable cars bring you down to the village. Soothe your tired muscles at either of the main public spa complexes. The Burgerbad (daily 8am–8pm; Fr.26; Ⓦ www.burgerbad.ch) has outdoor and indoor thermal pools as well as steam baths, plunge pools and exercise rooms; the Lindner Alpentherme (same hours; Fr.30; Ⓦ www.alpentherme.ch) is a more refined affair – indulge in the works at their Roman-Irish bath. The **tourist office** (Ⓣ 027 472 71 71, Ⓦ www .leukerbad.ch) has details of the many discount deals and all-in packages offered by spa hotels.

The Lötschental

A short distance east, above the villages of Steg and Gampel, is the valley of the River Lonza. A narrow road switchbacks up from the valley floor; traffic remains heavy until the village of **Goppenstein**, at the southern exit of the Lötschberg Tunnel from Kandersteg (see box, p.260), used by car-carrying trains that shuttle continuously beneath the Alps. Ignore the bustle of this most incongruous rail station, towered over by rocky crags, and head on. You emerge into the stunningly beautiful **LÖTSCHENTAL**, comprising half-a-dozen tranquil communities strung along 10km of the valley floor and overlooked on both sides by Alpine ridges topping 3300m. The huge glaciers sliding down from the Konkordiaplatz (see p.252) are a constant presence at the head of the valley. There are few more impressive scenes in the Alps.

Trails from Kandersteg via the **Lötschen Pass** (see p.262) drop down to the valley floor at the first village, **Ferden** (1389m). Just 2km on, past the photogenic hamlet of **Kippel**, the main valley community is **Wiler**, home both of the tourist office (Ⓣ 027 938 88 88, Ⓦ www.loetschental.ch) and a cable car up to the **Lauchernalp**. This is the focus of skiing in winter, with access to pistes up to 3111m on the looming Hockenhorn (a one/six-day pass is Fr.49/253). The valley-floor road trickles on amidst increasingly wild and beautiful scenery past **Blatten** to end at the hamlet of **Fafleralp** (1788m), a scant 4km from the nose of the massive Langgletscher glacier. The Lötschental is known for its tradition of mask-making, displayed to full effect in the week before Ash Wednesday for the extraordinary **Roitschäggättä**, when locals don grotesque, shaggy masks for a series of night-time parades through the villages in an ancient Lenten ceremony.

Hotels and hikers' inns are dotted along the valley. The grand but inexpensive *Lötschberg* at Kippel (℡027 939 13 09, ⓦwww.hotel-loetschberg.ch; ❷) has been around since 1902; the *Sporting* at Wiler (℡027 939 13 77, ⓦwww.rhone .ch/sporting; ❷) and welcoming *Fafleralp* (℡027 939 14 51, ⓦwww.fafleralp .ch; ❷–❸) are also good bets. The biggest of half a dozen **campsites** is *Lonza-strand* (℡027 939 14 16).

Brig and the Simplon

By virtue of its location, you may find yourself spending a night in the graceful old town of **BRIG** (Brigue in French; Briga in Italian). It's the fulcrum for a dizzying series of major road and rail routes: southeast through the Simplon train tunnel into Italy; southwest to Zermatt at the foot of the Matterhorn, and Saas-Fee; west to Lake Geneva; north through the Lötschberg Base Tunnel towards Bern; and northeast to the high Alpine passes.

The huge train station stands at the northern edge of the town, connected to Brig's broad cobbled central square – the focus of the Old Town and called in its various sectors **Stadtplatz**, **Marktplatz** and **Sebastiansplatz** – by the main shopping street of Bahnhofstrasse. Overlooking the square is the tiny **Sebastian-skapelle**, built by local bigwig Stockalper (see below) in 1637, with a network of picturesque alleys winding behind and around it.

Lanes off the southeast corner of the square lead along Alte Simplonstrasse past many fine patrician town houses dating from the seventeenth and eighteenth centuries to the **Schloss Stockalper**. This grandiose Italianate palace dominates the otherwise simple town. It was completed in 1678 to serve as the home of Kaspar Jodok von Stockalper, a merchant from Brig who first made a mint controlling the trade in silk over the Simplon Pass to Lyon, moved on to make another killing organizing mail transport between Milan and Geneva, and finally gained the monopoly in trading salt over the pass. You can stroll from the street into the triple-arcaded interior courtyard. Rearing up overhead are three giant corner towers topped by the onion domes that are visible from much of the town. **Entry** to the few rooms open to the public is by guided tour only (May–Oct Tues–Sun 9.30am, 10.30am, 1.30, 2.30 & 3.30pm, June–Sept also 4.30pm; Fr.5).

Practicalities

Brig's **tourist office** is in the train station (July–Sept Mon–Fri 8.30am–noon & 1.30–6pm, Sat 9am–6pm, Sun 9am–1pm; rest of year Sat closes 1pm, closed Sun; ℡027 921 60 30, ⓦwww.brig-belalp.ch). From the forecourt of Brig station, MGB **trains** depart on two routes: to Zermatt, and to Andermatt (see p.345) via Oberwald and the tunnel beneath the Furka Pass. "Glacier Express" panoramic trains (see p.34) use the latter line to reach Chur, Davos and St Moritz. For details of the Lötschberg Tunnel car-carrying train, see p.260.

Hotels in Brig are all moderately priced. The *De Londres Schweizerhof*, Bahnhof-strasse 17 (℡027 922 93 93, ⓦwww.hotel-delondres.ch; ❷), is a comfortable old place, with pleasant rooms overlooking the main square. The graceful *Schlosshotel Art Furrer*, Schlosspark (℡027 922 95 95, ⓦwww.schlosshotel.ch; ❷), has bright and attractive rooms overlooking the Schloss Stockalper.

All the **cafés and restaurants** around the main square set tables outside during summer: pick of the bunch is *Zum Eidgenossen*, which offers fondues and meaty Walliser fare in a traditional atmosphere from around Fr.20. Nearby on Alte Simplonstrasse is the pleasant local bistro *Matza*, serving up pizzas and simple meals from Fr.15. Down by the station you'll find the *Hotel Victoria*, which offers good brasserie-style food, with some veggie options (around Fr.20), as well as a self-service *Migros*.

The Simplon Pass and Tunnel

The road over the **Simplon Pass** (2005m), southwest of Brig, was built by Napoleon as a military through-route between 1800 and 1808, immediately after he'd successfully crossed the Grand-St-Bernard with an army (see p.282). These days the old pass road is a modern, Swiss-engineered highway, and the pass itself isn't really worth a specific journey, with views nowhere near as impressive as those from the other great Alpine passes. What *is* worthwhile, though, is to explore the cobbled alleys and picturesque old houses of **Simplon-Dorf** on the other side – still in Switzerland – as well as, down towards the Italian border, the terrifyingly steep and narrow gorge leading to the frontier hamlet of **Gondo**; there are few places where the cliff walls feel so high and you feel so small. A stone next to the road commemorates the victims of a torrential mud slide which swept half the village away in 2000. An energetic two- or three-day **hike** covers the 35-kilometre Stockalper Road, from Brig to Gondo; this is the mule track completed by Stockalper for transport of goods between Italy and the Valais, and has inns aplenty dotted along its route, which is mostly away from the highway.

While you're standing on the pass heights, give a thought for those careering at speed on trains through the **Simplon Tunnel**, some 2400m beneath the Wasenhorn peak just to the east. This was once the longest rail tunnel in the world, entered just after leaving Brig station and emerging 19.8km later in Italy for the short run to Domodossola (from where Swiss trains connect on the Centovalli line to Locarno; see p.479), and on south to Milan. The completion of the tunnel in 1905 opened up an entirely new train route from London and Paris to Istanbul – the so-called **Venice–Simplon Orient Express** – which in turn led to a whole new era in pan-European travel.

The Simplon Pass road is kept open year-round, and offers an easy short-cut if you're driving to Ticino. From the Italian border at Gondo, it's 22km to the town of **Domodossola** (see p.480); signage there is poor, but if you aim for Masera, you'll pick up the road heading east towards **Santa Maria Maggiore** in the Val Vigezzo, which leads on to the Swiss border at Cámedo (roughly 26km from Domodossola). From Cámedo, the road continues through the Centovalli (see p.479) to Locarno.

Zermatt

St Moritz may have the glamour, Verbier may have the cool, Wengen may have the pistes, but **ZERMATT** beats them all – Zermatt has the **Matterhorn**. No other natural or human structure in the whole country is so immediately recognizable; indeed, in most people's minds the Matterhorn stands for Switzerland like the Eiffel Tower stands for France.

Part of the reason the Matterhorn is so famous is that it stands alone, its impossibly pointy shape sticking up from an otherwise uncrowded horizon above

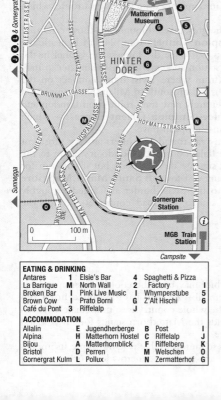

EATING & DRINKING

Antares	1	Elsie's Bar	4	Spaghetti & Pizza		
La Barrique	M	North Wall	2	Factory	I	
Broken Bar	I	Pink Live Music	I	Whymperstube	5	
Brown Cow	I	Prato Borni	G	Z'Alt Hischi	6	
Café du Pont	3	Riffelalp	J			

ACCOMMODATION

Allalin	E	Jugendherberge	B	Post	I	
Alpina	H	Matterhorn Hostel	C	Riffelalp	I J	
Bijou	A	Matterhornblick	F	Riffelberg	J K	
Bristol	D	Perren	M	Welschen	O	
Gornergrat Kulm	L	Pollux	N	Zermatterhof	G	

Zermatt village. But you get the feeling that it would be famous even if it stood within a chain of peaks: there's just something about it that's bizarrely mesmerizing.

Emerging from Zermatt station is an experience in itself: this one little village (at 1620m) – which has managed, much to its credit, to cling onto its old brown chalets and atmospheric twisting alleys – welcomes everybody, regardless of financial status, and the station square is where all worlds collide. Backpackers and hikers rub shoulders with high-society glitterati amidst a fluster of tour groups, electric taxis and horse-drawn carriages. Everyone has come to see the mountain. Zermatt has no off-season – it's busy year-round – yet the crowds never seem to matter. You may have to shoulder your way down the main street, but the terrain all around is expansive enough that with a little effort you could vanish into the wilderness, leaving everyone else behind.

The small area around Zermatt features 36 mountains over 4000m, a statistic as enticing to summer hikers as to winter skiers. As early as the 1820s, British climbers adopted the isolated hamlet as a base camp from which to scale the nearby peaks. The first hotel opened in 1838. All through the nineteenth century, word of the place spread, and the local community quickly saw the potential: grand hotels went up and public funds were diverted into construction of the Gornergrat rack railway at the turn of the century. The skiing boom of the 1960s saw the hamlet double in size, but today it's still acceptably small and low-key, rooted to the valley floor in a natural bowl open to the south. The Gornergrat railway lifts you up to a spectacular vantage point overlooking the

Monte Rosa massif, with its summit the **Dufourspitze** (4634m) – the highest point in Switzerland. The skiing is superb, but in many ways the hiking is better, with some of the most scenic mountain walks in the whole country within easy reach of the village.

Arrival, orientation and information

The Matterhorn Gotthard Bahn (Ⓦwww.mgbahn.ch) operates the **trains** from Brig and Visp to Zermatt; they're free to Swiss Pass holders. Although **Brig** is the starting point for MGB trains, mainline trains from the west (from Lake Geneva and Sion) are quite often timed to make the connection at **Visp** instead (Viège in French); check the timetable carefully. At Brig station, MGB trains run on tracks laid in the street outside the front of the station, not from the usual platforms.

South of Visp, trains climb to **Stalden** (departure point for buses to Saas-Fee) and then enter the picturesque Mattertal, clinging precariously above the ravine as they rise past a series of villages. A minor **road** also runs along the valley: it's possible to drive as far as the village of **TÄSCH**, where vast car parks (see box below) take care of all motorized transport, with everybody bundling onto trains (and extra Pendelzüge shuttles) for the final twelve-minute pull into Zermatt.

Zermatt's **train station** is a large, bustling place at the northern end of the village's main street. The square outside is generally full of little **electric taxis**, which cost about Fr.15 for up to four people (more including luggage) to anywhere within the village. There are also **electric buses**, free with a ski-pass (or around Fr.3), which serve all points. The **GGB Gornergrat-Bahn** station is directly opposite the main station, while the underground funicular to **Sunnegga** leaves from the opposite bank (head east from the station beside the Gornergrat tracks and over the river, then cut left for 100m).

Zermatt's super-friendly **tourist office** is beside the station (mid-June to Sept daily 8.30am–6pm; rest of year Mon–Sat 8.30am–noon & 1.30–6pm, Sun 9.30am–noon & 4–6pm; ☎027 966 81 00, Ⓦwww.zermatt.ch). The **Zermatt Festival** (Ⓦwww.zermattfestival.com), held every September, features classical music concerts, film screenings and exhibitions.

Accommodation

Accommodation in Zermatt is almost universally excellent. The village is so used to tourists – in fact, there *is* no village without the tourists – that service has been fine-tuned and facilities across all price brackets are good. There are dozens of hotels, so you shouldn't have any problem finding somewhere to suit. Book well in advance for the winter and summer high seasons. It must be said,

---

Driving to Zermatt

Zermatt is **car-free** – private vehicles are permitted no closer than **Täsch**, 6km away, from where trains, electric taxis and horse-drawn carriages shuttle people into Zermatt. There are a dozen large parking areas in Täsch, including the giant Matterhorn Terminal (Fr.13.50 per day; Ⓦwww.matterhornterminal.ch). Shuttle **trains** from Täsch to Zermatt run from 6am to 1am, every 20min during the day (Thurs–Sat nights also hourly 2–5am). They are free to Swiss Pass holders; otherwise Fr.15.20 return. Plenty of **taxi** companies also operate from Täsch, most offering discounts on parking if you use them to reach Zermatt. All the villages along the road from Visp to Zermatt either charge for parking or happily ticket offenders for parking illegally.

▲ Zermatt village centre

too, that **Matterhorn views** from your balcony or window are truly worth paying extra for.

Apartments or **chalets** should also be booked well in advance (some places are reserved a year ahead). The standard rental period is a Saturday-to-Saturday week; only a handful of owners are willing to rent for less, and then only in the low season for a minimum three days.

Campsite

Matterhorn ☎027 967 39 21. Good site located just north of the train station. June–Sept.

Hostels

Jugendherberge (HI hostel) ☎027 967 23 20, ⓦwww.youthhostel.ch. Large hostel, a 10min walk from the centre, with expensive dorm beds and rooms, many with enticing Matterhorn views and private rooms. Closed May & Nov. ❷–❹
Matterhorn Hostel (SB hostel) ☎027 968 19 19, ⓦwww.matterhornhostel.com. In the same quarter as the HI hostel, but on the riverbank, with decent dorms. ❶

Inexpensive hotels

Alpina ☎027 967 10 50, ⓦwww.alpina-zermatt .ch. Down in the Hinterdorf, with amiable staff and a calm atmosphere. ❸–❹
Matterhornblick ☎027 967 20 17, ⓦwww.matter hornblick.ch. A modern place beside the church, drenched in light pine but living up to its name (*blick* means view), with mountain views out back. ❸–❹
🏃 **Post** ☎027 967 19 31, ⓦwww.hotelpost .ch. Lively main-drag institution, with a

popular bar and restaurant topped by a selection of comfortable, individually styled rooms. ❹–❻
🏃 **Welschen** ☎027 967 54 22, ⓦwww .reconline.ch/welschen. A real find, up on a hill beside the Sunnegga station, small, pleasant, atmospheric and family-run. ❸–❹

Mid-range hotels

🏃 **Allalin** ☎027 966 82 66, ⓦwww.hotel -allalin.ch. Acclaimed "garni" hotel beside the church, with modern decor and plenty of comforts. Service is outstanding, and there are balconies in all rooms (including ones facing south to the Matterhorn). ❹
Bijou ☎027 966 51 51, ⓦwww.hotel-bijou.ch. Far away from the centre on a slope just next to the Matterhorn cable car, this is a small, family-run place with some nice, cosy touches in the rooms. ❹–❻
Bristol ☎027 966 33 66, ⓦwww.hotel-bristol .ch. Excellent mid-range choice, with efficient, friendly service and cosy rooms – those facing south with picture-postcard views (go for the upper floors). ❹–❼
🏃 **Gornergrat Kulm** ☎027 966 64 00, ⓦwww.zermatt.ch/gornergrat.kulm. Solidly

Skiing and snowboarding

There are three ski and board sectors, all connected but each accessed by its own transport route: pistes from **Sunnegga/Rothorn** link to the adjacent **Gornergrat/ Stockhorn**, while the **Schwarzsee/Klein Matterhorn** sector, rising to 3900m, connects to the Italian resort of Cervinia. All of them offer satisfying runs at most levels of ability, with a healthy dose of blues and reds around **Blauherd** above Sunnegga, and some good, scenic blues and reds at **Gifthittli** above Riffelberg; from here, long, leg-stretching reds take you down to **Gant** in the valley, which has lifts on both sides up to more choice runs. The spectacular "**Triftji Bumps**", from Hohtälli above Gornergrat, is one of the most famous black runs in the Alps, but it also has a separate, less challenging red twin that meets it at the bottom.

Top destination has got to be the network of pistes and lifts above **Furi**, with some airy red and black runs around Schwarzsee and **Trockener Steg**, and a long blue dubbed **Gandegg**. The high-level red runs around **Testa Grigia** and the Klein Matterhorn station, well above 3800m, are superb, and there are plenty of options to ski down from here to **Cervinia** (passport needed). Up here on the Theodul glacier is also where you'll find **Gravity Park**, one of Europe's biggest snow parks, with a 200m super-pipe, half-pipe, kickers, rails and plenty more to keep boarders happy. These pistes also offer memorable **summer skiing** and **boarding**, in a sweeping area from the Klein Matterhorn at 3900m down to Trockener Steg at 2900m. A **ski-pass** for universal access at Zermatt and Cervinia is Fr.82/405 for one/six days. A pass for Zermatt's lifts only is Fr.73/350.

Schools include **Stoked** (Ⓦwww.stoked.ch), perhaps the best of Switzerland's new wave of ski and board academies; also check out Ⓦwww.skischulezermatt.ch and Ⓦwww.matterhornskiwochen.ch. Zermatt comes into its own with the array of heli-skiing (around Fr.300) and off-piste possibilities all around the area; schools and the Snow & Alpine Center (see below) can advise.

Extreme sports, climbing and trekking

Zermatt's **Snow and Alpine Center** (Ⓣ027 966 24 60, Ⓦwww.alpincenter-zermatt .ch), on the main street, can provide advice and guides for extreme sports all year round. In addition to canyoning, ice-climbing, snowshoeing, heli-skiing and more, they run regular guided **climbs** up some of the nearby peaks. The Matterhorn itself is out unless you have mountaineering experience, a week for special training and about Fr.1200 in fees. However, they run daily guided excursions for Fr.100–200 that are suitable for beginners, including a four-hour trek from Klein Matterhorn across glaciers to Trockener Steg, an easy ascent to a 4000m peak such as the Breithorn, or a basic climbing course on the Riffelhorn. For something a bit more family-friendly, **Forest Fun Park** (daily March–Oct; Fr.31; Ⓦwww.zermatt-fun.ch), on the south side of town, comprises three adventure circuits of varying difficulty, with ziplines and bridges strung between the trees.

One of the best **long-distance walks** – aside from the Haute Route to Zermatt from Chamonix (see p.283) – is the **Matterhorn Tour**. This comprises a 34-stage circular walk around the mountain, mostly on Alpine paths, crossing from the Mattertal into the Val d'Anniviers and Val d'Hérens, as well as into Italy; you'll need to hire a guide for two short stages, across the glacier-bound Theodul Pass and, further round, across a glacier above Arolla. It takes ten days to do in full, or you can select certain half- or full-day stages. The tourist office has a map and full details. The **Zermatt Marathon** (Ⓦwww.zermatt-marathon.ch) is held in July on a fiendish 42km course from St Niklaus (1085m) up to the Gornergrat peak (3010m).

built mountain hotel alongside the terminus of the Gornergrat railway from Zermatt – currently the highest hotel in the Alps, at 3100m above sea level. It's a popular spot for day-trippers to gawp at the Matterhorn from the hotel terrace, or eat in the restaurant, but in the evening, after most of the crowds have departed, this can be a uniquely atmospheric place to spend the night. 45min by Gornergrat train from Zermatt. ⑥ inc. half board

Perren ⊕ 027 966 52 00, ⓦ www.hotel-perren.ch. Graceful, modern hotel on the riverbank, with an appealing stylishness to its well-appointed rooms. A bargain. ⑤–⑥

Pollux ⊕ 027 966 40 00, ⓦ www.reconline.ch /pollux. Modern glitzy place bang on the main drag, with plenty of style and comfortable rooms, some facing off the street. ⑤–⑥

Riffelberg ⊕ 027 966 65 00, ⓦ www.zermatt.ch /riffelberg. Another 10min up the Gornergrat train line past *Riffelalp* (see below) – a fairly standard three-star mountain hotel at 2585m, with cosy, comfortable rooms, priced high for the great location. ⑤–⑥

Expensive hotels

Riffelalp ⊕ 027 966 05 55, ⓦ www.riffelalp.com. Superbly renovated mountain hotel, way up at 2222m on the slopes above the village – for decades a rather down-at-heel mountain inn, now a full-blown luxury resort, with spacious, stylish rooms and suites, and some outstanding Matterhorn views. 20min by Gornergrat train from Zermatt. ⑧–⑨

Zermatterhof ⊕ 027 966 66 00, ⓦ www.zermatt .ch/zermatterhof. The grandest hotel in the canton, and one of the finest in the country, built well over a century ago but glitteringly up to date inside. Manages to be effortlessly luxurious without a hint of tasteless resort swagger. ⑧–⑨

In and around the village

Zermatt's narrow main street, although picturesque, is packed all the way down with shops, hotels, restaurants and – for most of the year – people. To the east, alleys run down into **Hinterdorf**, an attractive old quarter by the river, full of weathered-wood chalets and traditional *mazots* (barns raised on stone discs to protect against mice). Some 400m south of the station is the **church**, another main landmark, its riverside cemetery filled with memorials to attempts on the Matterhorn and other peaks gone wrong. From here a street doglegs east over the river to the district of **Steinmatte** on the opposite bank. The cable-car station up to **Trockener Steg** and Klein Matterhorn is 500m south of the church.

Opposite the church is the subterranean **Matterhorn Museum** (June–Sept daily 11am–6pm; Easter–June & Oct daily 2–6pm; mid-Dec to Easter 3–7pm; Fr.10), featuring films, interactive displays and a reconstructed nineteenth-century village house. There's also an interesting collection of mountaineering bits and bobs, including exhibits related to Edward Whymper, the English climber who led the first ascent of the Matterhorn on July 14, 1865, only for his rope to snap during the descent – four of his party of seven went over a precipice.

The Gornergrat railway

In summer, the slopes above Zermatt hold some of the country's most scenic hiking trails. The ever-popular GGB **Gornergrat Bahn** (2–3 hourly; 45min; ⓦ www.ggb.ch) leads up from the village across the meadows of the Riffelalp to the **Gornergrat** itself (3130m) – sit on the right-hand side for magical Matterhorn vistas. The Gornergrat is the first point on a ridge that runs out to the Hohtälligrat (3286m) and, amidst a sea of ice, the **Stockhorn** (3407m), all linked by cable car from Gornergrat. The view from any of these peaks is terrific, with the entire Monte Rosa massif laid out in front of you, the vast Gornergletscher at your feet, and the Matterhorn itself in isolation away to one side. At your back is the Rothorn (3103m), behind it the Dom (4545m), and behind the Dom the whole sweep of the Pennine Alps.

Hikes between the various stations on the Gornergrat railway are all very rewarding, with, for example, three good trails leading out from the grand hotel alongside the station at **Riffelalp** (see "Accommodation"), easiest of which is the pleasant one-hour walk up to the **Riffelberg** hotel, on a spectacular exposed platform overlooking the valley. In summer (mid-June to mid-Sept), there are once-weekly dawn trains up to the Gornergrat so you can catch an awe-inspiring sunrise break on the Matterhorn.

Other mountain routes above Zermatt

From Zermatt village, an underground funicular tunnels up to **Sunnegga** (2300m), also on a plateau and linked to the **Rothorn** summit by gondola. Walks from Sunnegga are beautiful, weaving for a comfortable hour or two between the tiny lakelets of the Leisee, Moosjesee, Grindjisee and Stellisee out to **Fluhalp** (2616m).

From the south end of Zermatt village, cable cars run to **Furi** and on up to **Trockener Steg** (2939m), overlooking the gigantic Theodulgletscher, which slides over the Italian border at the foot of the Matterhorn. From Trockener Steg, another cable car runs up to the crest of the **Klein Matterhorn** – at 3820m, the highest cable-car station in Europe, boasting the inevitable restaurant, shop and an ice pavilion. From Furi, the cable car up to the little **Schwarzsee** gives access to high-level walks that include some memorable Matterhorn viewpoints, as well as a long, easy trail (7hr) back down into Zermatt village.

Eating and drinking

Considering the prices in some of Zermatt's hundred-plus **restaurants**, opting for picnic fare from the Co-op supermarket opposite the train station is a prudent move if you're on a tight budget. A fair bit of Zermatt's **nightlife** happens in the assorted bars and lounges squirrelled away inside the *Hotel Post*, although there's a number of other bars and pubs dotted around the village.

Cafés and restaurants

Antares ⓦ www.hotel-antares.ch. On the far side of the river, serving quality fish dishes in its plush carved-wood dining room for upwards of Fr.35.

La Barrique ⓦ www.hotel-perren.ch. Peaceful and attractive modern restaurant – mainly Swiss, with fine-dining pretensions, but at quite reasonable prices. Three-course *menus* for Fr.40, or mains from Fr.25.

Café du Pont ⓦ www.dupont-zermatt.ch. Peaceful and cosy little restaurant serving simple, inexpensive Swiss fare including *Röstis* and fondues, plus set *menus*, all for under Fr.30.

Prato Borni ⓦ www.zermatterhof.ch. A haven of fine dining in one of Zermatt's most opulent grand hotels, with international menus from Fr.105. Closed May–July.

Riffelalp ⓦ www.riffelalp.com. Partway up the Gornergrat line, this five-star mountain resort boasts three excellent restaurants – the Italian *Al Bosco*, the Swiss *Walliser Keller* and the fine-dining *Alexandre* (the last two only open evenings only) – plus sensational views.

Spaghetti & Pizza Factory ⓦ www .hotelpost.ch. Despite the name, this is a chic modern Italian restaurant occupying a beautifully restored wooden chalet, with pizza and pasta from Fr.20, plus more expensive meat dishes.

Whymperstube ⓦ www.whymper-stube.ch. Cosy little wood-panelled basement restaurant, offering no less than nine different kinds of fondue plus assorted Swiss-style meat dishes. Mains Fr.21–45.

Bars

Broken Bar ⓦ www.hotelpost.ch. Occupying an atmospherically poky little stone-walled cellar, this bar-cum-disco is the oldest tourist haunt in Zermatt, opened in 1958 and still going strong, attracting an eclectic crowd of international revellers. For something quieter, the Loft Club and Papa Caesar lounge bar, upstairs in the same hotel, offer a more sedate form of nightlife. Open from 10pm.

Brown Cow ⓦ www.hotelpost.ch. Cosy and sociable pub, with low-priced beer, sports TV and inexpensive pub food.

Elsie's Bar ⓦ www.elsiebar.ch. Cosy little nook opposite the church that is an après-ski institution, although a little over-glitzy in season. Light snacks to help your cocktail go down include spaghetti with caviar and the house special: a dozen oysters. Open from 4pm.

North Wall ⓦ www.northwallbar.com. Popular backpacker hangout on the far side of the river south of the Bristol, with pizzas from around Fr.15 plus cheap draught beer. Daily from 5pm.

Pink Live Music Bar ⓦ www.hotelpost.ch. Zermatt's only live music venue, with bands nightly in the winter season (Dec–April).

Z'Alt Hischi ⓦ www.hischibar.ch. Nice place for a quiet beer down in Hinterdorf.

Saas-Fee

Lying in the next-door valley to Zermatt, **SAAS-FEE** (1800m) is sometimes overlooked, perhaps because it doesn't have any train access. However, were it not for the Matterhorn next door, the array of peaks around Saas-Fee would take centre-stage on any Alpine itinerary: the village is perched on a shelf of pasture at the base of a horseshoe of thirteen 4000m-plus peaks. Oozing out from between them is the giant Feegletscher ("Fairy Glacier"), trickling its meltwater down through the village, and active enough in its various sectors to limit what would otherwise be spectacular skiing. (The danger of falling down a glacial crevasse if you stray beyond piste-markings is more pronounced in Saas-Fee than in most other resorts.) The village is heavily touristed, but can lay claim to unrivalled Alpine views and landscapes.

Saas-Fee is one of four linked villages at the end of the Saastal. **Buses** from Brig pass through Visp and then **Stalden** (both on the train line) before

---

Sports and activities at Saas-Fee

With a preponderance of blue and red pistes, Saas-Fee is ideal territory for beginners or intermediates, and its snowboarding facilities have made it one of Switzerland's top boarding destinations. The focus of attention is the "Alpin Express" lifts serving the **Felskinn** (3000m); from here, there are plenty of good blue and red runs coming down the side of the huge glacial bowl that towers all around, plus a snowboarding half-pipe. From Felskinn, the "Metro Alpin" takes over, the highest underground funicular system in the world, which tunnels up to the **Mittelallalin** station (3500m), below the mighty Allalinhorn summit (4027m). Up here are the world's highest revolving restaurant (ⓦ www.drehrestaurant-allalin.ch) and ice pavilion (ⓦ www.eispavillon.ch), as well as a half-pipe, a hatful of scenic red runs on the Feegletscher and a long, exhilarating blue all the way down to **Längfluh** (2870m), which is served by its own lifts from the village via Spielboden. An alternative is the lift to **Plattjen** (2570m), from where red and another long blue wind back down to Saas-Fee. There's also **summer skiing** from the Mittelallalin. The **Hannig** (2350m) is barred to skiers, but has good sledge runs and winter walking trails.

Lift passes for one/six days cost Fr.66/336 for Saas-Fee alone, or Fr.71/366 for additional access to the limited runs above Saas-Grund and Saas-Almagell (ski bus included). Good discount deals for families are available. In addition to the official ski and snowboard school (ⓦ www.skischule-saas-fee.ch), check out ⓦ www.eskimos.ch. The **Mountain Guides** office (ⓦ www.mountain-life.ch) runs a host of adventure excursions, including husky tours, snowshoe trekking, snow-tubing, ice-climbing and more.

Hiking routes abound, both in summer, with long treks finding a way between the peaks into the Mattertal, and in winter, when some 30km of trails above the village remain open. The summer seven-day **hiking pass** (Fr.179, family Fr.362) covers all mountain transport in the Saastal and the Stalden–Saas-Fee postbus.

branching off into the Saastal itself, passing first through **Saas–Balen**, then **Saas–Grund**, the main village on the valley floor. From Saas-Grund a road branches up to Saas-Fee – which is car-free – while a few kilometres on down the valley is **Saas–Almagell**.

Arrival and information

From the entrance to Saas-Fee, several quaint lanes flanked by dozens of old-fashioned *mazots* (wooden barns) propped up on stone discs lead down (southwest) into the heart of the village, which is packed with shops and boutiques.

Saas-Fee is car-free, and there is a huge **parking** area at the entrance to the village (Fr.12 per day, discounted with a visitor card issued by your hotel); parking at the base of the gondola in Saas-Grund, or at Saas-Almagell, is only slightly cheaper. Electro-taxis shuttle around all points in the village for Fr.12–18 or so. The **bus station** is beside the car park; note that you're meant to reserve your seat for the return journey back down the valley two hours in advance. Beside the bus station is the **tourist office** (Mon–Fri 8.30am–noon & 2–6pm, Sat 8am–7pm, Sun 9am–noon & 3–6pm; ☎027 958 18 58, ⓦwww .saas-fee.ch). There's also a tourist office in Saas-Grund (Mon–Sat 8.30am–noon & 2–6pm, Sun 8.30–11am & 3.30–6pm; ☎027 958 66 66, ⓦwww.saastal.ch), and smaller offices along the valley.

Accommodation

The tourist office has an **accommodation** booking line (☎027 958 18 68, ⓔto@saas-fee.ch) that can reserve a room at any of the resort's hotels. Saas-Grund has several **campsites**, but only the simple *Bergheimat* site (☎027 957 20 66) stays open year-round.

Hotels

Dolomit ☎027 957 24 89, ⓦwww.dolomit.ch. Well-run sports hotel, with modern, no-fuss rooms and low prices. Runs guided hikes, mountain-bike rides, climbs and ski-tours. ❸

Ferienart ☎027 958 19 00, ⓦwww.ferienart.ch. Top-rated five-star hotel bang in the heart of the village, with spa, sauna and solarium in addition to spacious, elegant rooms (many with a jacuzzi) and superbly luxurious suites. ❽–❾

Hotel Burgener ☎027 958 92 80, ⓦwww.hotel -burgener.ch. Charming little hotel near the lifts, with the quiet *Skihütte* restaurant adjoining. ❹–❺

Jägerhof ☎027 957 13 10, ⓦwww.saas-fee.ch /jaegerhof. Fine mid-range option in a tranquil location right on the edge of the village – in winter, you can ski to the door. ❹–❻

Romantik-Hotel Beau Site ☎027 958 15 60, ⓦwww.beausite.org. Superb, central

"wellness" hotel, with onsite spa and health centre. A fixture in the village for more than 100 years, with uniquely characterful rooms and attentive service. ❹–❼

Saaserhof ☎027 957 35 51, ⓦwww.saaserhof .ch. Modern, reliably accomplished and comfortable four-star hotel, very convenient for the lifts and right beside the slopes. ❻–❽

Tenne ☎027 957 12 12, ⓦwww.hotel-tenne.ch. Family hotel in a good, central location, with an upmarket restaurant and fresh, light-pine rooms. ❸–❺

Zur Mühle ☎027 957 26 76, ⓦwww.moulin -saas-fee.ch. Small, excellent-value place in an old burnt-wood chalet, with all rooms facing south and balconied. 500m southwest of the tourist office, close to all the lifts and on the riverbank. ❸

Eating and drinking

Choosing somewhere to eat or drink is a case of wandering until your stomach, or your eyes, tell you to stop. In the centre, *Boccalino* does decent pizza, pasta and risotto for Fr.15–25. The restaurant attached to *Hotel Zur Mühle* is a reliable proposition for inexpensive local cuisine – mainly fondues and raclettes.

Grab a table on the terrace of the *Skihütte* restaurant, attached to *Hotel Burgener*, for good local cooking and superb views. *Restaurant La Ferme*, in the *Romantik Hotel Beau-Site*, is a step up in quality, with good *menus* from Fr.25. The sky's the limit for gourmet cuisine at two temples to the art: the *Fletschhorn Waldhotel* (☎027 957 21 31, ⓦwww.fletschhorn.ch), out in the woods north of the village, and the *Cäsar Ritz* restaurant within the *Ferienart* hotel (evenings only; ☎027 958 19 00, ⓦwww.ferienart.ch), in the centre with six-course set *menus* for around Fr.90. Alternatively, the *Vernissage* restaurant downstairs in the same hotel offers a more relaxed gourmet experience in less stuffy surroundings, with fine meat and fish dishes for around Fr.50.

The Goms

The upper part of the Rhône valley, stretching from Brig to the high Alpine passes, is known as the **Goms** (ⓦwww.goms.ch). Winter sees thick snow covering the whole region, perfect for cross-country skiing at all levels. Traffic, at least in the warmer months, is often heavy on the valley road (which accesses the Furka, Grimsel and Nufenen passes), but drivers generally prefer to keep their foot down, zipping straight past the pine forests, wide-open meadows and the picturesque villages of traditional dark wood chalets without stopping. If you've got a car, it's worth taking a break at a couple of places on the long drive up the valley. Buses and local trains from Brig stop at all villages.

About 8km out of Brig you'll pass **Mörel**, with signs for cable cars rising west to **RIEDERALP** and, a little further on, **Betten**, with cable cars to **BETTMERALP**. Both these car-free resorts are perched on ridge-top plateaux, with lifts serving the unspoilt **Aletschwald**, one of the highest pine forests in Europe, which in turn overlooks the **Aletsch Glacier**, a mammoth ice sheet – longest in the Alps, and a UNESCO World Natural Heritage Site – which winds its way down 23km from the base of the Jungfrau. There are hiking possibilities galore around here, and **tourist offices** in Riederalp (ⓦwww.riederalp.ch) and Bettmeralp (ⓦwww.bettmeralp.ch) can provide details. **Fiesch**, the next main town along the valley, has lifts up to the vantage point of the **Eggishorn**, above the hamlet of Kuhboden, offering the finest views of the glacier.

Above Fiesch, the Rhône is little more than a fast-flowing mountain brook, and the villages become smaller and more rural. Some 9km past Fiesch is the little community of **MÜNSTER**. Away from the main road, the tranquil village is characterized by the traditional Valaisian-style chalets, all clustered together higgledy-piggledy, burnt a rich dark brown and decorated with pretty geranium window boxes. At their centre is a striking white church with a wood-panelled barrel-vault ceiling and florid Baroque interior. The handful of **hotels** in the village is worth passing over in favour of the ⚜*Croix d'Or et Poste* beside the main road (☎027 974 15 15, ⓦwww.hotel-postmuenster.ch; ❸), a marvellous old building dating from 1620. Up to 1900 or so it was the residence of the noble family of prince-bishops Von Riedmatten; these days, it's every bit as atmospheric as that sounds, its public rooms festooned with Victorian bric-a-brac. Value for money extends to the cooking as well, with superb *menus* for around Fr.25.

The high Alpine passes

Above Münster, you enter the **Obergoms** (Upper Goms) region, and begin to approach the high Alpine passes. The guaranteed snow up here, and breathtaking scenery, make for some outstanding cross-country skiing. Ulrichen, 4km on, has a turning southeast along the Agenetal to the **Nufenen Pass**, or Passo della Novena (2478m), which crosses into Ticino and the Val Bedretto (see p.472). The main road continues through **Oberwald** (1368m), where the Obergoms tourist office is located (☎027 973 32 32, ⓦwww.obergoms.ch), and then immediately begins to climb in a series of great looping switchbacks.

Way above Oberwald is the junction point of **GLETSCH** (1759m) – not really even a hamlet, but with a hotel, *Glacier du Rhône* (☎027 973 15 15, ⓦwww.glacier-du-rhone.ch; June–Sept; ❷), from which to enjoy the spectacular views. In summer, DFB (ⓦwww.furka-bergstrecke.ch) runs an antique **steam train** on a cogwheel track through spectacular scenery up to the Furka Pass via a short tunnel at Muttbach, heading on to Realp (see p.349). The round trip costs Fr.93. By the time you read this, a long-awaited rail link from Oberwald to Gletsch is expected to be running.

To the Furka Pass

Northeast from Gletsch, heading up to the Furka Pass, the road sidewinds its way up the cliffside, coiling around the landmark **Hotel Belvédère** on the way (2300m; ⓦwww.gletscher.ch). In season, this once-grand edifice is swamped by the traffic swarming up the road; it's not worth staying here, but it is worth stopping to explore the **Rhône Glacier**, which fills the head of the valley to the north. This is the source of the Rhône itself, which you can see spouting out as meltwater from beneath the glacier's eaves. Owners of a souvenir stall in the *Belvédère*'s car park have cashed in on the glacier's appeal – and its proximity to the road – by carving, fresh each year, a tunnel deep into the blueish ice for their many customers to walk along (June–Oct daily 8am–6pm; Fr.5). By the end of the summer, about a third of the tunnel's length has melted, as the glacier shifts by some 30m each year.

A short climb further is the **Furka Pass** itself (2431m; full account on p.349), beyond which lie Realp and Andermatt.

To the Grimsel Pass

The other road from Gletsch climbs west in ever tighter curves up to the **Grimsel Pass** (2165m), which marks the border between Valais and Canton Bern. There are three hotels on the top, and this is an extraordinarily dramatic place to spend the night, with the bare, snow-patched rocks rising all around, the summit Totensee ("Dead Lake") icy all summer, and stunning sunset views down over the Grimselsee just below. The ⚴ *Grimselblick* (☎027 973 11 77, ⓦwww.grimselpass.ch; ❶) is the best on offer, a cosy place once the daytime tour buses have departed, with a particularly enticing en-suite double room, complete with four-poster bed, that's worth asking for. On the other side of the lake is the simpler *Alpenrösli* (☎033 973 12 91; ❶). Three buses a day (July–Sept) run from Oberwald to Meiringen (see p.258) via the Grimsel Pass.

Travel details

Full timetables for all trains, buses, trams, boats and cable cars in Switzerland – as well as international connections – are searchable at Ⓦ www.rail .ch. For details of trains to Zermatt, and from Brig over the Furka and Oberalp passes, see Ⓦ www .mgbahn.ch. For the route from Bern through the Lötschberg Base Tunnel to Brig and on into Italy, see Ⓦ www.bls.ch.

Trains

Aigle to: Bex (hourly; 5min); Geneva (twice hourly; 1hr 20min); Les Diablerets (hourly; 50min); Leysin (hourly; 25min); Martigny (every 30min; 20min); St-Maurice (hourly; 10min); Sion (every 30min; 30min).
Bex to: Villars (hourly; 40min).
Brig to: Andermatt (hourly; 2hr 5min); Bern (every 30min; 1hr 5min); Domodossola, Italy (1–2 hourly; 35min); Geneva (twice hourly; 2hr 30min); Martigny (twice hourly; 50min); Sion (3–4 hourly; 30–45min); Zermatt (twice hourly; 1hr 30min); Zürich (hourly; 2hr 10min).
Martigny to: Aigle (every 30min; 20min); Brig (twice hourly; 50min); Orsières (hourly; 25min); St-Maurice (twice hourly; 15min); Sierre (2–3 hourly; 15–25min); Sion (2–3 hourly; 12–25min).

Sion to: Aigle (every 30min; 30min); Brig (3–4 hourly; 30–45min); Geneva (twice hourly; 1hr 45min–2hr); Martigny (2–3 hourly; 15–25min); Sierre (3 hourly; 10min); Zermatt (twice hourly; 2hr; change at Visp).
Zermatt to: Brig (twice hourly; 1hr 25min).

Buses

Aigle to: Villars (every 2hr; 35min).
Brig to: Saas-Fee (twice hourly; 1hr 20min).
Le Châble to: Verbier (hourly; 25min).
Crans to: Montana (continuously; 5min); Sierre (every 30min; 40–50min); Sion (hourly; 45min);.
Les Diablerets to: Gstaad (7 daily; 50min).
Martigny to: Chamonix, France (hourly; 1hr 30min); Grand-St-Bernard Pass (1 daily; 1hr 30min; change at Orsières).
Saas-Fee to: Brig (hourly; 1hr 10min); Stalden (hourly; 40min).
Sierre to: Crans (every 30min; 40–50min); Montana (every 30min; 40–50min); Sion (hourly; 30min).
Sion to: Crans (hourly; 45min).
Villars to: Aigle (every 2hr; 35min).
Visp to: Saas-Fee (every 30min; 55min).

Lucerne and
Central Switzerland

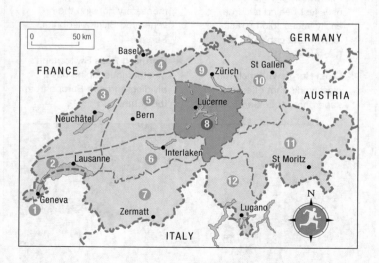

CHAPTER 8

Highlights

* **Vierwaldstättersee**
Experience beautiful Lake Lucerne from the deck of an old-time steamer. See p.315

* **Luzerner Fasnacht**
The biggest carnival in Switzerland. See p.320

* **Sammlung Rosengart**
Gallery of modern art in central Lucerne, focusing on Picasso and Klee. See p.323

* **Pilatus** Craggy giant that rises just behind Lucerne, easily accessible by rack railway and cable car. See p.323

* **Glasi Hergiswil** Small-town glassworks that offers a superb free tour. See p.330

* **Weg der Schweiz** Scenic lakeside walking route in William Tell country. See p.331

* **Titlis** Year-round skiing and snowboarding above the village of Engelberg. See p.335

* **Rigi** With three routes up, this is a popular way to take in the views from 2000m. See p.336

* **Einsiedeln** Benedictine monastery housing the venerated Black Madonna. See p.342

* **Gotthard Pass** Switzerland's most famous Alpine pass, dividing northern Europe from the south. See p.348

▲ Lucerne

Lucerne and
Central Switzerland

The oddly shaped **Lake Lucerne** (in German, *Vierwaldstättersee*, the "Lake of the Four Forest Cantons") lies at the geographical and spiritual heart of Switzerland. It's the country's most beautiful and dramatic body of water by far, thickly wooded slopes rising sheer from misty wavelets, bays and peninsulas giving constantly changing views from the decks of the steamers which ply to and fro. At the lake's western tip, **Lucerne** (in German, **Luzern**) is an attractive town steeped in history and a natural gateway to the diverse region of **Central Switzerland** (Zentralschweiz).

Zentralschweiz – or as it is often dubbed, Innerschweiz – is a land of tradition. Here, in the tidy villages of Switzerland's core, is where the founding myths of the country are nurtured. In the Middle Ages, the communities of the four so-called "forest cantons" dotted around the lake – **Uri**, **Schwyz**, **Nidwalden** and **Obwalden** (the last two often conflated into one as "**Unterwalden**") – guarded the approaches to the **Gotthard Pass**, key to the newly opened road between northern and southern Europe. When Habsburg overlords tried to encroach on their privileges, the communities formed an alliance at the lakeside Rütli Meadow in 1291 which was to prove the beginning of the Swiss Confederation. Lucerne, as the principal market town for the region, was drawn into the bond shortly after, and tales soon began to circulate of a legendary figure from the Uri countryside named **William Tell**, who had pitted his wits against the local Habsburg tyrant and won. Today, the clifftop paths and shoreline trails of this region are trod less by foreigners than by a tide of Swiss tourists who make the journey from their suburban homes to walk in the footsteps of William Tell and the semi-mystical founders of the nation.

Transport links around the region are excellent, with the fleet of lake steamers from Lucerne running throughout the year, serving shoreside villages and small resorts tucked against the sugarloaf cliffs that have limited or no road access. In addition, a handful of rack railways serve mountain tops around the lake (most famously the **Pilatus** and the **Rigi**), and plenty of easy short- and long-distance hiking trails can get you well off the beaten path. Central Switzerland's long-standing tradition of tourism means that every hamlet has its choice of hotels and restaurants. The array of sights, excursions, museums and activities makes this one of the densest, and most rewarding, areas of the country to explore.

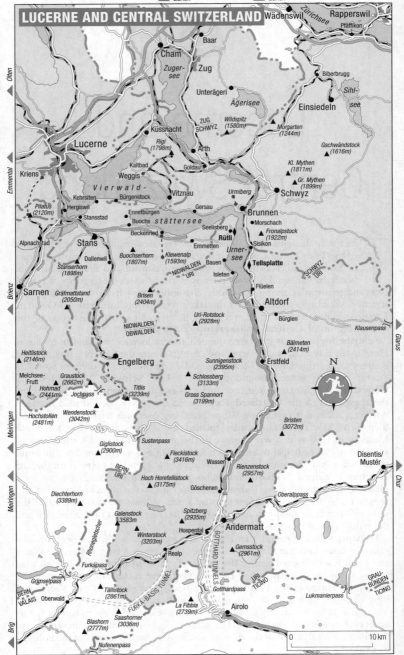

Zürich Zürich Wädenswil Zürichsee Rapperswil
Pfäffikon

Olten

Baar

Cham Zug

Zugersee

Unterägeri Ägerisee Einsiedeln Sihlsee

Biberbrugg

ZUG Wildspitz Morgarten Gschwändstock
SCHWYZ (1580m) (1244m) (1616m)

Küssnacht Arth Kl. Mythen
(1811m)

Emmental Rigi Goldau Gr. Mythen
(1798m) (1899m)

Lucerne Kaltbad Schwyz

Kriens Weggis

Vierwald- Urmiberg

Pilatus Kehrsiten Vitznau Brunnen
(2120m) Hergiswil Bürgenstock Gersau Morschach Fronalpstock
Stansstad Ennetbürgen stättersee (1922m)

Brienz Alpnachstad Buochs Seelisberg Rütli Sisikon
Beckenried Emmetten SCHWYZ
Stans Urner- URI
Dallenwil Buochserhorn Bauen see Tellsplatte
Stanserhorn (1807m) Klewenalp
(1898m) (1593m) NIDWALDEN Isleten
Sarnen Gräfmattstand URI
(2050m) Brisen Flüelen
(2404m)
Altdorf
NIDWALDEN Uri-Rotstock Bürglen
OBWALDEN (2928m) Klausenpass

Heitlistock Bälmeten
(2146m) (2414m)

Melchsee- Graustock Sunnigenstock Erstfeld
Frutt (2662m) (2395m)
Hohmad Engelberg Schlossberg
(2441m) Jochpass Titlis (3133m)
Hochstollen (3239m) Gross Spannort
(2481m) Wendenstock (3199m)
(3042m)

Meiringen Giglistock Sustenpass Bristen
(2900m) Fleckistock (3072m)
BERN (3416m) Wassen
URI Rienzenstock
Diechterhorn Hoch Horefellistock (2957m) Disentis/
(3389m) (3175m) Göschenen Mustér

Oberalppass Chur

Galenstock Spitzberg
3583m (2935m)
Winterstock Hospental Andermatt
(3203m) GRAU-
Realp Gemsstock BÜNDEN
Furkapass (2961m) TICINO

Grimselpass URI Gotthardpass
BERN Tällistock TICINO Lukmanierpass
VALAIS Oberwald (2861m) FURKA-BASIS TUNNEL GOTTHARD TUNNELS

Brig Blashorn Saashorner La Fibbia
(2777m) (3036m) (2739m) Airolo

Nufenenpass 0 10 km

Bellinzona

N

Lucerne

An hour south of Basel and Zürich, and boasting invigorating mountain views, lake cruises and a picturesque old quarter, **Luzern** (**LUCERNE** in French and English, Lucerna in Italian) has long been one of Europe's most heavily touristed towns. When Queen Victoria came for a long holiday in August 1868 (checking in under the pseudonym of the "Countess of Kent"), the town was already well known; these days five million admirers pass through annually. Tourism is the leading source of income, which in recent years has led, in some quarters, to a rather blasé attitude towards visitors: although the city has retained a good deal of charm, the same can't be said of all its restaurant waiters and hotel staff.

The **River Reuss** splits the town, flowing rapidly out of the northwestern end of the lake. Both banks are clustered with medieval squares, frescoed houses, ancient guildhalls, churches and chapels, and filled with a commercially minded liveliness that belies the city's age. Aside from using Lucerne as a base to explore the region, it would be easy to spend at least a couple of days taking in some of its quality museums – the outstanding **Sammlung Rosengart** or the impressive **Verkehrshaus** – in between walking on the medieval **battlements**, and exploring cobbled alleys and hidden garden courtyards.

But Lucerne is no museum piece; the city's large population of young people love their café culture, and at midnight on a weekend night, the main Pilatusstrasse boulevard has the buzz of any European capital.

Some history

Lucerne's founding is lost in history. The town's name probably derives from the Celtic word *lozzeria*, meaning "a settlement on marshy ground", and that's more or less all Lucerne was in the mid-eighth century when the small Benedictine **monastery** which existed here is thought to have come under the control of the Alsatian Abbey of Murbach. Nothing concrete is known about Lucerne until 1178, when an abbot established a lay order at the Kapellkirche (now St Peter's Chapel), indicating that quite a substantial settlement must have existed in the area. Around 1220, the opening of the **Gotthard Pass** further south created new impetus for growth, with merchants and travellers setting sail from Lucerne for the long trans-Alpine journey (the first lakeside road was built only in 1865).

Eyeing the prosperity flowing into the communities on the northern side of the new pass, Rudolf of Habsburg bought Lucerne outright from Murbach in 1291, intending to subdue it and channel its profits into the imperial coffers. At the same time, though, the peasant farmers of Uri, Schwyz and Unterwalden on the eastern shores of the lake had formed a pact of mutual defence at **Rütli** (see box, p.331) against the Austrian threat, and after some instability, Lucerne joined them in 1332, the first major city to do so. This pact was the beginning of the Swiss Confederation, which survives today. The defeat of Austrian forces in the **Battle of Sempach** in 1386 severed the Habsburg claim to Lucerne, and the city's elders reinforced their independence by building the Musegg fortifications, which are still standing.

Lucerne remained Catholic throughout the Reformation and, like much of the country, was ruled by patrician families up until the late eighteenth-century revolutions. The early nineteenth-century quarrels in politics and religion led to civil war, with Lucerne at the heart of the Catholic rebel **Sonderbund**

8

(see p.501) – an association which, after Confederate forces had reasserted their control in 1847, led to Lucerne being passed over for the choice of federal capital.

By this time, though, **tourism** to Switzerland had already begun, and with the cessation of hostilities Lucerne became a focus for the increasing tide of foreign visitors, both for its own lakeside location, and as the gateway to the high Alps. In the 1830s parts of the medieval Old Town were torn down in favour of redeveloping the city centre and creating new lakeside promenades. The railway arrived in 1859, and over the following fifty years, Lucerne's population quadrupled to forty thousand, with tourism, then as now, the mainstay of the city's economy.

All through the twentieth century, Lucerne has clung tight onto its conservative, traditional roots: these days, the city is renowned as the heartland of Switzerland's SVP, an extreme right-wing political party with a strident and increasingly successful set of anti-immigration, anti-EU policies.

Arrival, information and lake transport

Lucerne's giant modern **train station** is on the south bank of the Reuss, exactly at the point where the lake narrows into the river. Broad **Pilatusstrasse** runs southwest from Bahnhofplatz into the main shopping and commercial districts of the modern city. From the busy bus stops outside the station, the main Seebrücke takes traffic over the Reuss alongside the ancient **Kapellbrücke**, the latter marked by the distinctive stone Wasserturm (water tower). The pedestrian-only alleys of the Old Town occupy the northern bank, with the city walls ranged on the slopes above, as well as a small part of the southern bank.

If you're **driving**, try to arrange parking with your hotel or leave your vehicle in the suburbs: Lucerne is just about the most car-hostile city in Switzerland, with a fiendish one-way system woven tightly around the pedestrianized Old Town. There's little chance of finding a parking space on the street and the few, expensive parking garages are often full (Ⓦ www.parking-luzern.ch).

Lucerne's festivals

Lucerne's two biggest festivals come from opposite ends of the cultural spectrum. February's **carnival** (see box, p.320) features the biggest celebrations in the country, with six days and nights of continuous drinking and raucous partying. The city also plays host to one of Europe's most prestigious classical music events, the **Lucerne Festival** (Ⓦ www.lucernefestival.ch), inaugurated in 1938 with a concert conducted by Arturo Toscanini in the grounds of Wagner's lakeside house at Tribschen. The festival comprises three separate elements. The "Sommer" event, in August and September, is the main one, a concert cycle held in venues ranging from the stunning KKL concert hall to town churches and even the Löwendenkmal that draws the world's finest soloists and orchestras. Smaller offshoots – "Ostern" at Easter, with a mix of classic and contemporary, sacred and secular music; and "Piano" in November, focusing on keyboard soloists in jazz and the classics – fill out the annual programme. Lucerne also has an array of other music festivals, most notably the **Blue Balls Festival** (Ⓦ www.blueballs.ch), held during the second half of July at venues around the lake and featuring some big-name pop, rock, jazz and world music acts. The fourth Saturday in June is the day of the **Luzernerfest** (formerly known as the Altstadtfest; Ⓦ www.altstadtfest-luzern.ch) – the Old Town filled with oompah bands and food and beer stalls – while July sees prestigious international **rowing** regattas held on the Rotsee, a long, narrow lake 2km north of town.

Information

The **tourist office** has entrances on platform 3 of the train station and at Zentralstrasse 5 (mid-June to mid-Sept Mon–Fri 8.30am–7.30pm, Sat & Sun 9am–7.30pm; May to mid-June & mid-Sept to Oct daily closes 7pm; Nov–April Mon–Fri 8.30am–5.30pm, Sat & Sun 9am–1pm; ☎041 227 17 17, ⓦwww.luzern.org). With the vast quantity of tourists tramping through the city, staff are well used to answering questions, and have stacks of information to impart – but you should be prepared to queue at peak times. Their **Lucerne Card** (Fr.19/27/33 for 1/2/3 days) offers unlimited use of the city's public transport (except boats) and half-price entrance to museums. There's an array of **walking tours**, including a self-guided option using downloadable GPS data (see website for details).

Lake transport

The Vierwaldstättersee, or **Lake Lucerne**, is crossed year-round by the fine old boats of the SGV (☎041 367 67 67, ⓦwww.lakelucerne.ch), free to Swiss Pass holders. All SGV boats – including their half-dozen paddle steamers and a catamaran – depart from the quay directly outside the station, stopping at places on both shores: **Alpnachstad** gives access to the Pilatus summit; **Weggis** and **Vitznau** to Mount Rigi; **Kehrsiten** to Bürgenstock, and from there to the Hammetschwand summit; and **Beckenried** to Klewenalp. All of these have limited road and rail connections, but at the far eastern end of the lake, **Brunnen** (close to Schwyz) and **Flüelen** (close to Altdorf) are less than an hour's train journey from Lucerne on the Zürich–Lugano main line, making it easy to construct half- and full-day round-trips by boat and train.

In summer (June–Sept), at least seven boats daily make the full run from Lucerne to Flüelen, with several more serving intermediate points. In autumn (Oct) and spring (April & May), service is slightly curtailed in the evenings. Winter (Nov–March) sees two boats a day as far as Brunnen, with Flüelen served only by Sunday services. SGV also runs **cruises** and eat-aboard trips, including a three-hour summer sunset excursion.

Accommodation

Accommodation covers the gamut from dorms to palaces. Summer is especially busy, with double-room prices in many hotels rising by almost fifty percent: an establishment we've listed at ❺ to reflect high-season prices might charge ❸ prices between October and April. Booking ahead is a priority across all price brackets.

Campsite

Lido Lidostrasse 8 ☎041 370 21 46, ⓦwww .camping-international.ch. Right by the Verkehrshaus, also with some dorm beds. Open all year.

Hostels

Backpackers (SB hostel) Alpenquai 42 ☎041 360 04 20, ⓦwww.backpackerslucerne.ch. Friendly former student house on the lakeshore 800m southeast of the station; take bus #6, #7 or

#8 to Weinbergli, then head left for 150m. Pleasant dorms and basic doubles. ❶
Jugendherberge (HI hostel) Sedelstrasse 12 ☎041 420 88 00, ⓦwww.youthhostel.ch. Quality hostel 1km northwest of town near the Rotsee lake; bus #18 to "Jugendherberge". ❶

Inexpensive hotels

Des Alpes Furrengasse 3 ☎041 417 20 60, ⓦwww.desalpes-luzern.ch. Comfortable rooms,

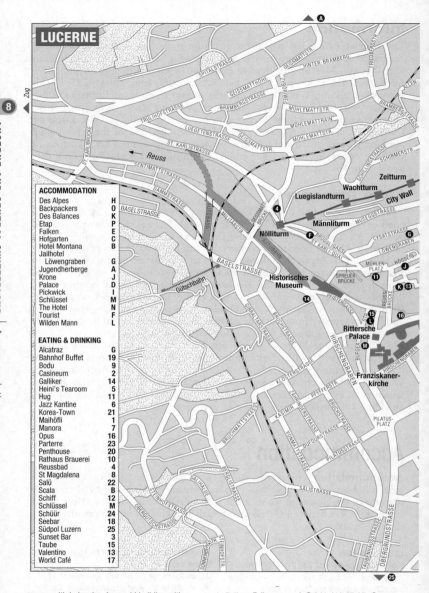

LUCERNE

ACCOMMODATION

Des Alpes	H
Backpackers	O
Des Balances	K
Etap	P
Falken	E
Hofgarten	C
Hotel Montana	B
Jailhotel	
Löwengraben	G
Jugendherberge	A
Krone	J
Palace	D
Pickwick	I
Schlüssel	M
The Hotel	N
Tourist	F
Wilden Mann	L

EATING & DRINKING

Alcatraz	G
Bahnhof Buffet	19
Bodu	9
Casineum	2
Galliker	14
Heini's Tearoom	5
Hug	11
Jazz Kantine	6
Korea-Town	21
Maihöfli	1
Manora	7
Opus	16
Parterre	23
Penthouse	20
Rathaus Brauerei	10
Reussbad	4
St Magdalena	8
Salü	22
Scala	B
Schiff	12
Schlüssel	M
Schüür	24
Seebar	18
Südpol Luzern	25
Sunset Bar	3
Taube	15
Valentino	13
World Café	17

some with balconies, in an old building with a
picturesque waterfront setting and a good
restaurant. ❸–❹

Etap Kellerstrasse 6 ☎041 367 80 00, ⓦwww
.etaphotel.com. Chain hotel, about 1km south of
the centre, with attractive modern rooms at bargain
prices. Bus #7 or #8. ❶

Falken Falkengasse 6 ☎041 410 37 37, ⓦwww
.hotel-falken.ch. Recently renovated and upgraded
small hotel with comfortable modern rooms in a
very central location. ❸

🏃 **Jailhotel Löwengraben** Löwengraben 18
☎041 410 78 30, ⓦwww.jailhotel.ch.
Lucerne's Old Town prison from 1862 to 1998, now

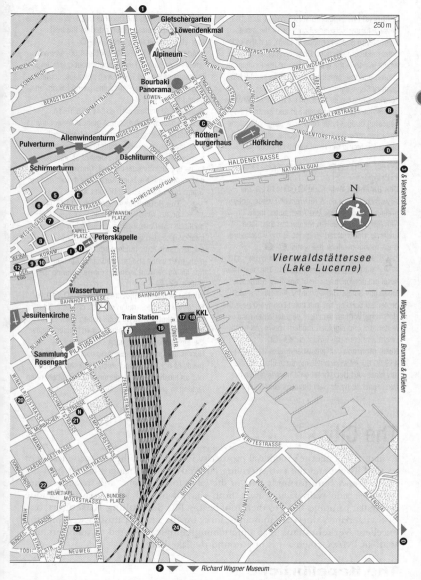

0   250 m

Gletschergarten
Löwendenkmal
Alpineum
Bourbaki
Panorama
Allenwindenturm
Pulverturm
Dächliturm
Schirmerturm
Rothen-
burgerhaus
Hofkirche

St
Peterskapelle

*Vierwaldstättersee
(Lake Lucerne)*

N

Wasserturm

Jesuitenkirche
Train Station   KKL

Sammlung
Rosengart

Richard Wagner Museum

converted into a surprisingly classy budget hotel, with a lively atmosphere. The refurbished cells are inevitably poky, but complete with en-suite shower cubicles and barred windows. Of the larger rooms, go for the panelled Director's Suite, the former prison governor's office or the Falling Waters Suite, once the visiting room. ❸

Pickwick Rathausquai 6 ☎ 041 410 59 27, ⓦ www.hotelpickwick.ch. In spartan contrast to *Des Alpes* next door, a raucous English-style pub with rooms above, sharing the excellent views but not the welcoming management style of its neighbour. No breakfast served. ❸

Schlüssel Franziskanerplatz 12 ☎041 210 10 61, ⓦwww.luzern-schluessel.ch. One of the most characterful budget options in town, and the oldest hotel in Lucerne to boot. Only ten rooms, some of which overlook the quiet square of the Franciscan church and the formal gardens of the eighteenth-century Segesser mansion. ❷–❸

Tourist St Karliquai 12 ☎041 410 24 74, ⓦwww .touristhotel.ch. Clean, well-run and central (though peaceful) budget hotel offering a range of options including renovated modern rooms with suntrap balconies facing the river. Excellent value. ❸

Mid-range and expensive hotels

Des Balances Weinmarkt ☎041 418 28 28, ⓦwww.balances.ch. A reverentially white lobby preludes a super-chic Old Town hotel, more reminiscent of midtown Manhattan than little Lucerne. Understated elegance is the watchword. Back rooms overlook the water. ❻–❽

🏃 **Hofgarten** Stadthofstrasse 14 ☎041 410 88 88, ⓦwww.hofgarten.ch. The best-value hotel in Lucerne, and one of the most attractive small city hotels in the country. A centuries-old protected building set in a quiet courtyard near the Hofkirche, with an excellent vegetarian terrace restaurant and eighteen modern rooms, all fresh, bright and carefully furnished. ❺–❻

Hotel Montana Adligenswilerstrasse 22 ☎041 419 00 00, ⓦwww.hotel-montana.ch. Exceptionally classy Art Deco hotel on a hillside above the lake, reached by its own funicular and boasting

spectacular views. The decor is faultless and rooms are generously sized. Often rated as the best four-star hotel in the country. ❻–❽

Krone Weinmarkt 12 ☎041 419 44 00, ⓦwww .krone-luzern.ch. Friendly, bright boutique hotel in the heart of the Old Town, with spacious, contemporary styled rooms – crisp linen, wood floors and muted tones. ❺

Palace Haldenstrasse 10 ☎041 416 16 16, ⓦwww.palace-luzern.com. A giant *belle-époque* landmark catering to the ritziest of traditional five-star tastes, revelling both in wide-open views across the lake and the grandest of appointments to the broad, lofty guest rooms. Dominates the city waterfront with the huge *Kursaal* next door and the *Grand Hotel National* just beyond. ❾

🏃 **The Hotel** Sempacherstrasse 14 ☎041 226 86 86, ⓦwww.the-hotel.ch. Outstanding boutique hotel overlooking a quiet city-centre park, interior-designed by architect Jean Nouvel and featuring chic, modern suites decorated in dark, matt tones and brushed steel. Each bedroom has an image from a classic movie covering the ceiling. ❼–❾

Wilden Mann Bahnhofstrasse 30 ☎041 210 16 66, ⓦwww.wilden-mann.ch. Fine choice in this price bracket, a historic hotel dating back to 1517 that occupies seven adjoining town houses amidst the atmospheric south bank Old Town lanes. Rooms are generous, tastefully decorated with plenty of rich wood, and quiet, while the service has an elusive blend of alertness and subtlety often lacking in grander places. ❻–❽

The City

Evidence of Lucerne's medieval prosperity is manifest in the frescoed facades of its **Old Town** and the two surviving covered wooden bridges which span the River Reuss, both formerly part of the city's fortifications (and so with higher defensive side walls facing away from the town) and both boasting unique triangular paintings fixed to their roof beams. The **Sammlung Rosengart**, one of Switzerland's finest art museums, lurks on the busy Pilatusstrasse, while the excellent **Verkehrshaus** – an entertaining complex devoted to transport, also with an IMAX cinema – is just around the lakeshore.

The Kapellbrücke

Any tour of Lucerne must begin with the fourteenth-century covered **Kapell-brücke** (Chapel Bridge), the oldest road bridge in Europe, angled around the octagonal mid-river **Wasserturm**. In deference to the fact that the city's development arose largely from defence of this bridge, its distinctive Wasserturm (formerly a lighthouse, a prison, a treasury and today serving as a meeting house) has come to stand as the symbol of Lucerne. Disaster struck in the early hours of August 18, 1993, when a small boat moored alongside the bridge

▲ The Wasserturm

caught fire and the flames rapidly spread to engulf the whole structure. By dawn, virtually the entire bridge had been destroyed, with only the bridgeheads on both banks surviving. The authorities set about reconstruction, and an identical replacement was completed nine months later; today, it's easy to see where the old wood meets the new.

Before the fire, the principal historical interest of the bridge lay in its collection of double-sided triangular **roof panels**, painted in the seventeenth century with scenes from the city's past and present. Of the 111 panels, 65 were entirely ruined and had to be replaced with facsimiles, 30 were restored, and the remainder are still charred and impossible to make out. Each is numbered, and captioned with rhyming couplets, the idiosyncratic local dialect written out in obscure medieval Gothic script. The most distinctive image is panel no. 31, which shows **William Tell** shooting the apple from his son's head, but it's fun to work your way slowly along. Panel no. 1 shows a giant, the first Luzerner; no. 3 Lucerne in the earliest times, with the Hofkirche separated from the town by a bridged inlet; no. 4 the foundation of Lucerne's monastery; no. 6 the town around 1600; no. 15 St Beatus (see p.255); no. 16 Einsiedeln (see p.342); no. 17 Lucerne's Franciscan church; no. 26 local hero Winkelried slaying a dragon; no. 32 the Rütli oath; no. 38 the great fire of Lucerne in 1340; and no. 58 the 1476 Battle of Grandson (see p.148).

Just downstream, the **Spreuerbrücke** is also worth a look for its macabre "Dance of Death" roof panels. These begin at the northern bankside with a little verse:

> *All living things that fly or leap*
> *Or crawl or swim or run or creep*
> *Fear Death, yet can they find no spot*
> *In all the world where Death is not.*

The succession of images shows a grinning skeleton leading kings, gallant princes, lawmen, nuns, merchants, prostitutes, peasants and maidens alike to

Carnival!

Lucerne's infamously raucous six-day all-in **carnival** (ⓦwww.luzerner-fasnacht.ch), ending on Mardi Gras night, is the biggest and best in Switzerland, a genuinely participatory event which knocks Basel's stand-and-watch parades into a cocked hat. It's worth going out of your way to visit, even though the streets of the Old Town get more and more crammed with revellers year on year.

Celebrations are focused around three "official" carnival days. The Thursday before Mardi Gras is dubbed **Schmotzig Donnschtig**, or Dirty Thursday; the following Monday is **Güdis Määntig**, or Fat Monday; while Mardi Gras itself (Fat Tuesday) is **Güdis Ziischtig**. *Güdis* comes from the dialect word *Güdel*, meaning belly, while *Schmotzig*, or dirty, has its roots in the word for grease or fat: carnival was traditionally a time for excess, to lay in some high-calorie *Fasnachtsküechli*, fried sweet layered pastry, before Lenten fasting.

Lucerne's carnival is centred on the figure of **Fritschi**, mentioned as early as 1443 and later subsumed into the legends surrounding a victory at the Battle of Ragaz on March 6, 1446. (March 6 was the day of Fridolin, patron saint of Glarus, and Fritschi is a diminutive of Fridolin.) Originally Fritschi was a lifesize straw doll carried through Lucerne accompanied by **Fritschene**, his "wife"; these days a costumed couple take their place. Around the middle of the eighteenth century, the two were joined on parade by a nanny, a jester named Bajazzo and some musicians.

To this day, Fritschi begins Lucerne's carnival at 5am on the morning of Dirty Thursday, when he and his entourage lean out of an upper window of the **Rathaus** on Kornmarkt as a cannon signals the start of festivities. From breakfast time onwards, bands of masked and costumed musicians, dancers and acrobats roam the Old Town streets, some performing **Guggenmusig** – comical oompah played on a handful of dented trombones and percussion – while others set up stages to give impromptu gigs to the promenading costumed crowds. The highlight of the day is the evening **Fritschi parade**, where Fritschi, Fritschene and the rest are paraded through the Old Town and around Löwenplatz, all the while flinging oranges out to carousing onlookers.

Friday, Saturday and Sunday aren't official carnival days, but nonetheless see plenty of activity: there are parties around the town on Friday and Saturday nights, with bars open late and lots of live music in the streets and clubs. **Fat Monday** is when carnival really takes off, with strolling musicians and *commedia dell'arte* pantomime players roaming the cafés and restaurants, and all the Old Town squares taken over by exuberant mass dancing. Monday night's raucously chaotic parade is broadcast live on Swiss TV, and Old Town bars are given special all-night licences in preparation for **Fat Tuesday**, Mardi Gras itself. The climax of carnival is a **Monsterkonzert**, the grand finale of all the bands performing together throughout the Old Town on the Tuesday night, accompanied by plenty of eating, drinking and merrymaking, a mighty blowout which lasts until 4am. Two hours later, street cleaners arrive to restore order, and respectably groomed and suited businesspeople return to Lucerne's early-morning cafés to begin real life again amidst the exhausted revellers of the night before.

their inevitable fate. The final panel, predictably enough, shows a majestic Christ vanquishing bony Death.

The Old Town

The north bank of the Reuss is home to the **Old Town**'s most atmospheric cluster of medieval houses, with Mühlenplatz, Weinmarkt, Hirschenplatz and Kornmarkt forming a compact ensemble of cobbled, fountained squares ringed by colourful facades. Modern commerce is definitely the motive force of the place these days, and it takes some imagination to conjure up the Middle Ages amidst the welter of shoppers and familiar brand names.

Kapellplatz, at the bridgehead of the Kapellbrücke, encircles the tiny eighteenth-century **St-Peterskapelle**, built over a predecessor dating from as early as 1178. Some 150m west is **Kornmarkt**, site of the medieval public marketplace. On one side, overlooking the riverside market area of Unter der Egg, is the huge **Rathaus**, completed in 1606 in Italian Renaissance style but crowned with an incongruous Emmentaler-style roof. The market survives today, with vegetable, fish and flower stalls doing a roaring trade every Tuesday and Saturday morning. Kornmarktgasse runs west to the atmospheric frescoed **Weinmarkt**, where Passion Plays were staged in the late Middle Ages.

The battlements walk

A short stroll west from Weinmarkt along riverside St Karli-quai past the sophisticated-looking hydroelectric turbines on the Reuss brings you to the **Nölliturm**, a fortified gate marking the southwestern extent of a lengthy stretch of the surviving fourteenth-century town walls. Pass through the gate and head right up the hill to gain access to the Musegg **battlements** (Easter–Sept daily 8am–7pm) and their impressive views. This is an oddly rustic corner of Lucerne, cut off from the city behind the walls, and you may come across a cow or two quietly grazing back here. Stairs rise to the top of both the **Männliturm** and, further along, the **Luegislandturm**, but the battlements walk proper starts at the **Wachtturm**. From here, you can follow the parapets along to the **Zytturm**, with the oldest clock in Lucerne (granted the honour of chiming one minute before all the others in the town). The rooftop walk continues to the adjacent **Schirmerturm**, gutted by an arsonist in 1994 and still bearing smoke-blackened stones. This is where the battlements walk runs out, but you can descend to follow the road through the Schirmerturm gate and down tranquil Museggstrasse through another breach in the old wall to the traffic-choked Löwenplatz.

Löwenplatz and around

Just northeast of Löwenplatz is one of the highlights of Lucerne, the terribly sad **Löwendenkmal** (Lion Monument). This wounded beast – dubbed "the Dying Lion of Lucerne" – draped over his shield, with a broken spear sticking out of his flank, was hewn out of a cliff face in 1821 to commemorate the 700 Swiss mercenaries killed in Paris in 1792. On August 10 that year, French revolutionaries stormed the royal palace, the Tuileries; in the face of the mob, the Swiss palace guards were ordered to lay down their arms by Louis XVI and so were massacred. This would be a movingly tranquil spot, with its foliage and gently rippling pool in front, were it not for the fact that it's the single most touristed place in the entire city.

Adjacent are a handful of nineteenth-century tourist attractions, quaint and rather old-fashioned today. A joint ticket for all three costs Fr.17. The **Gletschergarten**, Denkmalstrasse 4 (Glacier Garden; daily: April–Oct 9am–6pm; Nov–March 10am–5pm; Fr.12; ⓦ www.gletschergarten.ch), holds within its grounds a fusty museum of old relief maps, a wonderful Mirror Maze (built in 1896 and restored in mock-Moorish style) and a set of geological potholes telling of the subtropical ocean beach that was Lucerne twenty million years ago. The **Alpineum** opposite (April–Oct daily 9am–12.30pm & 1.30–6pm; Fr.5; ⓦ www.alpineum.ch) is a relic from a bygone age with static models of Alpine scenes behind glass. More impressive is the **Bourbaki Panorama** (April–Oct Mon 1–6pm, Tues–Sun 9am–6pm; Nov–March Mon

1–5pm, Tues–Sun 10am–5pm; Fr.8; ⓦ www.bourbakipanorama.ch), a giant 110m-by-10m circular mural housed in a glass building on Löwenplatz; it depicts the retreat into Switzerland of the French Eastern Army under General Bourbaki during the Franco-Prussian War of 1870–71. Sound effects and good background information go some way to hold your attention.

The Hofkirche

Busy Löwenstrasse runs south from Löwenplatz to the riverside; just before you reach the Schweizerhofquai, the arrow-straight St-Leodegarstrasse cuts east to broad steps leading up to the **Hofkirche** (Sat–Thurs 10am–noon & 2–5pm). This grand structure sits on the site of the first monastery of Lucerne, which dated from the mid-eighth century and was dedicated to St Leodegar (St Leger). The Romanesque church which replaced the monastery in the late twelfth century was burned to the ground on Easter Sunday 1633, the blaze reputedly sparked by the verger's careless shooting at birds. Only its twin **towers** escaped, and they survive today either side of a bizarrely incongruous Renaissance gable. The impressive main doors are carved with the two patron saints of Lucerne: on the left is **St Leger**, a French bishop who was blinded with a drill (which he is holding), and on the right is **St Maurice**, a martyred Roman soldier-saint.

The interior design and furniture are almost wholly original Renaissance from the 1630s and 1640s, a unity rarely found in Swiss or European churches. On the right, elaborate **pews** divided into individual seats were reserved for city councillors; plainer pews on the left were for the rank and file. Beyond the exceptionally fine **choir screen** – one of the earliest examples of strong three-dimensional perspective used to draw the congregation's attention forward – is the **high altar** in black marble, flanked by statues of the two patron saints. Above the Italianate depiction of the Agony at Gethsemane is a half-length figure of God. The carved choir stalls, as well as the beautiful pulpit, are the work of Niklaus Geissler. Against the north wall (left) is the lavish **Death of the Virgin altar**, showing Mary on a bed surrounded by disciples: dating from around 1500, this was the only relic to survive the 1633 fire. The mighty **organ**, bedecked in ornament, features 2826 pipes, along with a machine to mimic the sound of rain and a special register for thunder and hail.

The church is set amidst a lovely Italianate **cloister**, lined with the graves of Luzerner patrician families (who continue to be buried here to this day). Just west of the church is the ancient **Rothenburgerhaus**, a teetering pile claimed to be one of the oldest wooden town houses in the country, dating from about 1500. On the slopes north of the church is the old cemetery, now a public park, while about 500m further north on the hilltop is the Capuchin monastery of **Wesemlin**, founded in 1584 and still functioning as the principal seat of the order in Switzerland.

The south bank

The Old Town extends to the **south bank** of the Reuss, comprising a triangular area known as the Kleinstadt, originally walled. Facing Unter der Egg is the huge **Jesuitenkirche**, dominating the riverside with its twin onion-domed towers. Completed in 1673, its interior is a frothy Rococo concoction of gilt stucco and marble. Among the profusion of frescoes is one on the ceiling that, intriguingly, depicts the church exterior as it was 300 years ago. A few steps west is the **Rittersche Palace**, built in 1557 in Florentine Renaissance style as a private mansion but now the seat of Lucerne's cantonal government. Behind it to the south is the **Franziskanerkirche**, the oldest building in

Lucerne, dating from 1270 (though much restored). It's unusually richly decorated for a Franciscan church, with Renaissance choir stalls and battle standards lining the walls – copies of those looted from battlefields through the centuries. Continuing west, peaceful Pfistergasse curves to meet the south side of the Spreuerbrücke, where you'll spot the stout, sixteenth-century town arsenal, now home to the **Historisches Museum** (Tues–Sun 10am–5pm; Fr.10; Ⓦ www.hmluzern.ch), filled with arms and armour, restored interiors, costumes and crafts telling the history of Lucerne.

Sammlung Rosengart

Busy, traffic-heavy Pilatusstrasse, lined with shops, cafés and banks, storms southwest from the station, defining the limits of the Old Town. About 100m along is a solid Neoclassical building from 1923 – formerly the Lucerne headquarters of the Swiss National Bank, and now renovated to house the outstanding **Sammlung Rosengart** (Rosengart Collection; daily: April–Oct 10am–6pm; Nov–March 11am–5pm; Fr.15; Ⓦ www.rosengart.ch). Art dealers Siegfried Rosengart and his daughter Angela – the latter born in Lucerne in 1932 and still a resident – built up over forty years a collection of more than two hundred key twentieth-century works.

The **ground floor** is devoted to a magnificent overview of **Picasso**'s art, from early paintings – including a statuesque *Portrait Alice Derain* dated 1905, when Picasso was 24 – through to works full of light and space painted in Cannes in the mid-1950s, and five exuberant canvases dated 1967–69, a few years before the artist's death.

There are further Picassos on the **upper floor**, mainly late drawings and aquatints, including a series of six tender portraits of Angela Rosengart, as well as nearly two hundred intimate and often brilliant photographs of the artist's

---

Above Lucerne – Mount Pilatus

The giant mountain looming above Lucerne to the southwest is **Mount Pilatus** (2132m; Ⓦ www.pilatus.com), an odd name supposedly deriving from the myth that the corpse of Pontius Pilate was flung into a lake on the mountain, his spirit forever after haunting the summit and certain to bring tempest and damnation onto Lucerne if disturbed. (More prosaically, it's probably derived from the Latin *pileatus*, meaning "capped" – ie with clouds.) There are two means of transport to the top, making it easy to do a half- or full-day round-trip from Lucerne – simpler than in 1868, when Queen Victoria made the excursion on muleback.

Boats and local trains run from Lucerne to **Alpnachstad**, from where the **steepest rack-railway in the world** runs at a gradient touching 48 percent directly to the top of the mountain – the journey up is half an hour, while the journey down takes a careful forty minutes. The second route up the mountain starts at **Kriens** (connected to Lucerne's city centre by bus #1); from here a gondola rises to Krienseregg and Fräkmüntegg, and then a cable car to the summit (total 30min). The Kriens–Pilatus route runs year-round, while the Alpnachstad–Pilatus railway is summer only (mid-June to mid-Nov). Most tour groups follow a circuit going up from Kriens – so you might want to go up from Alpnachstad instead, to avoid the crush.

On the top are two hotels, the *Bellevue* and *Kulm*, but if you're looking for an overnight mountain-top stay, you'd do better on the nearby Rigi (see p.337). The walk to the highest point of the mountain, the Tomlishorn, takes less than thirty minutes from the top station, with expansive views the whole way along the clifftop path. It's also easy to walk back to Lucerne from Fräkmüntegg (2hr 30min), or to make your way down from the summit to Alpnachstad or Hergiswil (3hr) or Kriens (3hr 30min).

private life taken by American photographer David Douglas Duncan from 1956 until Picasso's death in 1973. Also here is a creatively assembled array of Impressionist and Modernist works, including a fine array of Chagalls – among them *Le soir à la fenêtre* (*Evening at the window*; 1950), a distinctive scene of blissful lovers looking out over a sleeping town – two fine Monets, and works by Renoir, Matisse, Miró and others.

The **basement** holds one of the broadest collections of works by **Paul Klee** in private hands, a seamless chronological record showing the development of Klee's fluent and compelling fantasy world. In the first room – ahead at the bottom of the stairs – Klee's visit to Tunisia is reflected in a number of colourful North African landscapes and the many works with Arab and Jewish elements. His expressive imagination takes hold in the second room, which includes the unsettling *Ironic Fairytale* (#69), featuring two jesters on the edge of a nebulous wood beneath a furious moon. One of the most characteristic (and memorable) sketches is *Little X* (#117), in the third room – a dozen simple brushstrokes that create a universe of childhood experience, lost in a bigger, more serious adult world.

The KKL

On a plum waterfront site beside the station and alongside the quays stands Lucerne's pride and joy, the multifunctional *Kultur- und Kongresszentrum Luzern*, known as the **KKL** (pronounced "kaka-el"; Ⓦ www.kkl-luzern.ch). Within such a traditional-looking and -thinking city, Jean Nouvel's landmark architecture in glass and steel is a revelation. Reflecting pools all around draw the lake into the building, as an immense cantilevered roof floats high above. The atmosphere of the place changes according to the weather conditions: standing on the lakeside apron during a storm – exposed yet protected by the roof – is quite an experience. Parts of the building may be taken up with conferences when you visit, and the concert halls are off-limits, but there's nothing to stop you exploring the public areas, which are well signed.

On the station side rises a huge, glazed block, fenced in by an all-enveloping steel cage and penetrating deep beneath the dark roof; this is the **Kongresszentrum** wing, with a bistro at ground level and the Kunstmuseum on the top floor. Beside it, at the centre of the complex, is the **Luzernersaal**, a small hall used for concerts or meetings. The easterly third of the complex is the **Konzertsaal**, one of the world's most acoustically advanced concert halls, and the principal venue for the Lucerne Festival. Adjoining it at ground level is the trendy *Seebar* (see p.327).

On the top floor of the KKL's Kongresszentrum wing – from the train station, take the exit by platform 15 and cross the street – is the **Kunstmuseum** (Tues–Sun 10am–6pm, Tues & Wed until 8pm; longer hours during Lucerne Festival; Fr.12; Ⓦ www.kunstmuseumluzern.ch). Lifts take you up to the ticket desk (press button "K"). The permanent collection – less-than-stunning canvases by Swiss artists of the nineteenth and early twentieth centuries, displayed in the first half-dozen rooms – is overshadowed both by the ground-breaking exhibitions of avant-garde contemporary art held in the rooms beyond, and by the breathtaking architecture: more than once you cross between galleries on slender catwalks high up in the building's interior, bathed in light with the reflecting pools far below.

Out of the centre

Although many of Lucerne's sights are packed close together in the city centre, there are a few incentives to venture further afield. Facing each other across the lake roughly 2km out of the centre are the **Verkehrshaus** (Transport Museum) on the northern shore, and the **Richard Wagner museum**, the composer's former home, on the southern shore. Buses run close to both, but the way to get there in style is by **boat**.

The Verkehrshaus

One of the main draws of Lucerne is the **Verkehrshaus**, 2km east of the centre at Lidostrasse 5 (Transport Museum; daily 10am–6pm, Nov–March closes 5pm; Fr.27, joint ticket including one IMAX film Fr.37; discounts available for families and rail-pass holders; Ⓦ www.verkehrshaus.ch). If you're not arriving by boat, hop on bus #6 or #8, or take the pleasant twenty-minute stroll around the lakeshore.

This vast complex is devoted to Swiss engineering and could keep you amused all day: you'll need the free plan to navigate your way around. It's divided into several large areas, taking in Road Transport, Rail Transport, Aviation and Space Travel, Cableways and Tourism, and so on. Everything is in English, and "hands-on" is a rule, not an exception. Particular highlights include the **train** section, with dozens of giant locomotives (complete with evocative oily smell) and a well-presented walk-through account of the digging of the Gotthard tunnel. The airplane section has flight simulators, a mock-up of an airport control tower and the **Cosmorama**, an interactive tour of the asteroid belt. The tourism section has the **Swissarena**, a composite aerial photograph of the entire country covering the floor of a 200-square-metre hall. There's also a huge section devoted to communications, an excellent **Planetarium** and a separate giant building housing an **IMAX cinema** (regular showings throughout the day for an extra Fr.18; Ⓦ www.imax.ch).

The Hans Erni Museum

In an entirely different vein, a far-flung building on the edge of the Verkehrshaus site – regrettably overlooked by most visitors – houses a fine museum dedicated to the Luzerner artist **Hans Erni** (same hours as Verkehrshaus; admission included with Verkehrshaus ticket, or Fr.12 for Hans Erni Museum only; Ⓦ www.hanserni.ch). Erni, born in 1909, has spent his long career producing art that is wonderfully warm and human, full of a fluidity of figures and geometries. His concern for human dignity in the face of modern technology stands more as a healthy counterpoint to all those displays of engineering skill. Erni is not well known outside Switzerland, but this museum – displaying 300 works – merits a special visit. Particularly outstanding are the lithographs, made as illustrations for limited-edition books.

The Richard Wagner museum

Southeast of the city centre, in an idyllic location on a headland named Tribschen, is a villa that was **Richard Wagner**'s home from 1866 to 1872, and is now a **museum** to him (mid-March to Nov Tues–Sun 10am–noon & 2–5pm; Fr.6; boat to Tribschen; bus #6, #7 or #8 to Wartegg, then 5min walk; or a pleasant 30min lakeside walk from the station; Ⓦ www.richard-wagner-museum.ch). After many visits to Switzerland, the composer and his partner Cosima – Franz Liszt's daughter – spotted the derelict Tribschen villa in early 1866, made arrangements to rent it for an extended period, and moved in. "Nobody will get me out of here again," Wagner said, and it's generally agreed that this was the happiest and most productive time of his life, not least because Cosima's long-dead marriage was finally dissolved in 1870 and the couple were able to marry. It was here that Wagner completed *Die Meistersinger von Nürnberg* and composed parts of the *Ring* cycle, as well as the *Siegfried Idyll*, which was first performed at the villa in 1870. The tranquillity of the lakeside house is still tangible today, as you wander through the rooms laid out with Wagneriana of all kinds – letters, pictures, original furniture, instruments and even his death mask – with Wagner compositions playing in the background.

Eating, drinking and nightlife

Lucerne has a fine range of **eating and drinking** venues covering all budgets: the crowded, generic places that are in plain view tend to be least interesting, but a small amount of backstreet searching will turn up plenty of more rewarding options.

Local specialities to keep an eye out for are led by the celebrated *Luzerner Kügelipastete* – spelled by many Old Town restaurant menus in dialect, along the lines of *Lozärner Chögalipaschtetli*, also often prefixed by *ächti* ("authentic"). This stomach-lining dish is a glorified vol-au-vent, a large puff-pastry shell filled with a super-rich concoction of diced veal and mushrooms in a creamy sauce. Otherwise, fish is the thing, in endless varieties: you'll see *Forellen* (trout), *Egli* (perch), *Felchen* (a kind of white fish) and *Hecht* (pike) on most menus. Wash it all down either with a *Kaffee fertig*, a coffee laced with Schnapps, or a *Kafi Luz*, traditionally seen in Canton Lucerne outside the city but nowadays easy to find in the Old Town cafés. The right way to make one is to put a five-franc coin in a vase-shaped glass, pour hot coffee in until you can't see the coin, then add Schnapps until the coin becomes visible again. Stir in two large spoons of sugar, and you have the perfect farmers' pick-me-up.

Cafés and café-bars

Cafés and **café-bars** crowd the waterfront and the Old Town squares, and do a roaring trade amongst the flood of tour groups passing through the town. Better places, frequented by locals, abound in less-trod corners, such as Helvetiaplatz. The pocket guide *Luzerner Barführer* (⊛ www.barfuehrer.ch), available free from the tourist office, appraises dozens of establishments.

North of the river

Alcatraz Löwengraben 18. Chic café-bar within the *Jailhotel Löwengraben* (see "Accommodation"). Also serves moderately priced meals.
Heini's Tearoom Falkenplatz ⊛ www.heini.ch. Perfect place for cakes and pastries on a broad, people-watching corner in the Old Town.
Hug Mühlenplatz. Superb breakfast café, open from 7am, with warm fresh bread and croissants, that also does quality inexpensive lunch *menus* (around Fr.18). Closed Sun.
Jazz Kantine Grabenstrasse 8. Buzzing Old Town hub, open during the day for coffee and beers, and on into the late night as a lively bar and meeting point, with DJs and live music downstairs.
Sunset Bar Seeburgstrasse 61 ⊛ www.sunsetbar .ch. Perfect lakeside café-bar opposite *Hotel*

Seeburg, with just the right tone for summer lazing: deckchairs, music, spacious lawns, home-made iced tea, dreamy views and its own landing stage. Beware, though: the sharp-dressed regulars crowd in after 6pm. April–Oct only.

South of the river

Opus Bahnhofstrasse 16 ⊛ www .restaurant-opus.ch. Fine waterside café, restaurant and wine-bar, with a lovely terrace outside. The Italian-leaning menu features plenty of pasta and salads (mains Fr.20–38). Daily until midnight (Fri & Sat 1.30am).
Parterre Mythenstrasse 7 ⊛ www.parterre.ch. Relaxed and inexpensive locals' hangout, open daily from breakfast until after midnight, with quality lunchtime *menus* (Fr.16–19). Try their

English breakfast – it's satisfyingly filling, even if a little lacking in authenticity.
Penthouse In the *Astoria* hotel, Pilatusstrasse 29. Rooftop bar with big views and bigger sofas.
Salü Helvetiaplatz. French-style café, complete with *citron pressé* and *pain au chocolat* plus soups, sandwiches and salads. One of several options on this little square. Open until 8pm; closed Sun.

Seebar In the KKL complex. Pleasant daytime hangout, with waterfront views, snacks and sandwiches. Stays open into the night as a DJ-bar.
World Café In the KKL complex. Bustling, airy place that does a rapid round of salads, light meals and drinks from breakfast until late.

Restaurants

There are hundreds of **restaurants** in Lucerne, plenty of which need do nothing more than occupy a panelled dining room and churn out a handful of traditional dishes to gone-tomorrow tourists in order to make money. A little searching can turn up more worthwhile eateries.

North of the river
Bodu Kornmarkt 5 ☎041 410 01 77, ⓦwww .bordeauxwine.ch. Acclaimed French brasserie with superb meat and fish dishes (mains Fr.35–45). Decor is pleasant, service attentive and the wine superb – but the location, with a fine river view, is the clincher.

Maihöfli Maihofstrasse 70 ☎041 420 60 60, ⓦwww.maihoefli.ch. Marvellously relaxed and friendly little all-wood place 1km north of the centre – comfortable, cosy and atmospheric. The cuisine is fresh and modern, with a light, inventive touch, expertly presented. Mains Fr.25–42. Closed Sun.
Manora Weggisgasse 5. Good, inexpensive self-service restaurant. Mon–Wed 9am–6pm, Thurs & Fri 9am–9pm, Sat 8am–4pm.
Reussbad Brüggligasse 19 ☎041 240 54 23, ⓦwww.reussbad.ch. Easy-going riverside joint featuring a renowned range of fresh fish (from around Fr.40), plus lots of salads and assorted *menus* at around Fr.15–24. Closed Mon; winter also closed Sun evening.
Scala *Hotel Montana*, Adligenswilerstrasse 22. Shamelessly romantic restaurant in the superb *Hotel Montana* (see p.318), serving up top-notch modern Italian-cum-international fish and meat creations; sit either in the plush dining room or on the terrace outside, with superb views over lake, mountains and city. Mains Fr.38–50.
Schiff Unter der Egg 8 ☎041 418 52 52, ⓦwww .hotel-schiff-luzern.ch. Wonderful old wood-panelled hotel restaurant on the riverside, celebrated for three things: top-quality *Wurst*, huge portions of *Chögelipastetli* and *Hacktschli Gross-mutterart* ("Granny's home-made pork meatballs"). Summer sees tables set under the arcades directly on the waterfront. *Menus* are around Fr.25–35.
Valentino Weinmarkt. Inexpensive Italian joint in the city centre, with pasta, pizza and risotto (Fr.16–25) plus more expensive fish and meat mains. Closed Sun.

South of the river
Bahnhof Buffet Top floor of the train station ⓦwww.brl.ch. A low-budget gem. This greasy-table diner – replete with smoking schoolchildren and boozy businessmen – charges budget prices for food which has been prepared next door in the kitchen of the adjacent *Au Premier* gourmet restaurant. A meal which might cost you Fr.100 in *Au Premier* may set you back a third of that in the *Bahnhof Buffet* – if you can stand the ambience, that is. Mains Fr.18–36; *menus* Fr.18.
Galliker Schützenstrasse 1, at Kasernenplatz ☎041 240 10 02. Hearty, meat-heavy Swiss specialities in a tavern-like setting crammed with people, noise and smoke. The food is consistently excellent, with quality *Chögelipastetli* joined by *cordon bleu* (veal steak slathered with cheese and ham). Mains are Fr.30–40, not much more than lunchtime *menus*. Closed Sun & Mon, and Aug.
Korea-Town Hirschmattstrasse 23. Pleasant ambience and a good choice mark this Korean place out as something a little more worthwhile than average, with midday buffets for Fr.18 and a range of *menus* (veggie and not) from Fr.17.
Schlüssel Franziskanerplatz (see "Accommodation"). Tiny old hotel offering a wide range of bargain two-course lunch *menus* for Fr.15–24.
Taube Burgerstrasse 3 ☎041 210 07 47, ⓦwww.taube-luzern.ch. Excellent traditional Swiss home cooking, featuring dishes like *Härdöpfelschtock ond Gmües* (beef rolls in smoked bacon), served either on the pleasant outdoor terrace or in the intimate, cellar-like restaurant within. *Menus* around Fr.20; mains Fr.25–33. Closed Sun.

Nightlife and entertainment

Lucerne's **nightlife** scene is active, with plenty of arts centres and music venues around the Old Town and the rest of the city. The Panorama building on Löwenplatz houses the arthouse **Stattkino** (W www.stattkino.ch), where you can pick up listings magazines (also stocked at the tourist office).

Bars, clubs and music venues

Casineum Grand Casino, Haldenstrasse 6 W www.casineum.ch. Generally reckoned the best club in Lucerne, attracting a 20/30-something crowd thanks to its good party atmosphere. Fri & Sat from 11pm (plus occasional special events on other nights). Entrance Fr.15–25.

Jazz Kantine Grabenstrasse 8 W www.jsl.ch/kantine.htm. Happening Old Town café-bar beside Lucerne's jazz school, with DJs and live music (not only jazz) in the basement (usually Thurs & Fri).

Rathaus Brauerei Unter der Egg W www.rathausbrauerei.ch. Wonderful echoing cross-vaulted terrace bar below the arches of the Rathaus, where young enthusiastic drinkers come to sample a range of powerful beers brewed on site.

Schüür Tribschenstrasse 1 W www.schuur.ch. Daytime bar with cheap weekday lunches, which after dark becomes a frenetic venue for excellent live music (Fri & Sat until 4am).

Seebar Within the KKL complex. Swanky modern bar which stays open till late.

St Magdalena Eisengasse 5 W www.magdalena.ch. Universally known as the Magdi-Bar, with a crowded ground-floor bar and a more sociable upstairs, although everything gets more and more raucous as the night goes on.

Südpol Luzern Arsenalstrasse 28 T 041 318 00 40, W www.suedpol.ch. This funky new performing arts venue hosts a range of musical acts, along with dance and theatre.

Listings

Bike and skate rental In the station (June–Sept daily 7am–7.45pm; Oct–May Mon–Sat 7am–7.45pm, Sun 9.30am–7pm).

Boat rental SNG, Alpenquai 11 (T 041 368 08 08, W www.sng.ch), has pedalos and rowing-boats (about Fr.25 per hr) and motorboats (about Fr.45 per hr) for rent, all requiring a deposit (Fr.20–100). Prices rise after 7pm. Two competitors are Bucher at Luzernerhof (T 041 410 20 55) and Herzog at Nationalquai (T 041 410 43 33).

Markets Every Tuesday and Saturday morning, large and colourful food markets spill over both banks of the Reuss and under the arcades, with a supplementary fish market every Friday. There's a flea market every Saturday (May–Oct) on the south bank, and a monthly crafts market (April–Dec, first Sat of month) on Weinmarkt. In the modern part of town, Moosstrasse/Helvetiaplatz hosts a relaxed Saturday-morning farmers' market of cheeses, organic vegetables, home-made jams and more.

Medical facilities 24hr emergency room at Permanence Medical Centre (T 041 211 14 44) beneath the train station.

Post Main office is across from the station (Mon–Fri 7.30am–6.30pm, Sat 8am–noon).

Central Switzerland

Zentralschweiz (Central Switzerland) is one of the most rewarding areas of the country in which to travel, with a host of different attractions to draw you off the beaten path. For details of the **boats** which crisscross Lake Lucerne year-round – often the most convenient method of transport – see p.315.

The southern shore is quiet, characterized by country towns such as **Stans**, and offers clifftop hikes. The excursion south to the once-grand resort of **Engelberg**, base station for the trip up to the summit of the **Titlis**, matches more famous rides for drama and natural beauty. The northern shore of the lake is studded by the lofty presence of the **Rigi**, with the old town of **Zug** behind; its easternmost finger, oriented north–south and dubbed the **Urnersee** (Lake Uri), channels the Föhn wind down from the high Alps, and so is a prime windsurfing spot. This is one of the country's most historically resonant areas, its wild and rocky shores the setting both for the legend of **William Tell** and for an ancient pact of mutual defence signed on a lakeside meadow – the **Rütli** – which laid the foundations for the Swiss Confederation as it survives today.

The southern lakeshore

The south shore of the lake – **Vierwaldstättersee–Süd** in German – is a land of broad green meadows and lush valleys interspersed with high forested plateau towering over the water. Once you gain some height, the views are magnificent, out across the whole shimmering expanse of blue. The shore forms part of the ancient canton of Unterwalden, divided for as long as anyone can remember into two small half-cantons, **Nidwalden** (the Lower Forest) and **Obwalden** (the Upper Forest). It's a perfect area for hiking and cycling, and it's easy to base yourself either in Lucerne or in the main town of the region, tiny **Stans**.

Exploring Central Switzerland

The **Tellpass** (April–Oct only; ⓦ www.tell-pass.ch) is the regional pass for Central Switzerland – but you'll need to cover plenty of ground to make it pay. The core region covers all boats on the lake, all routes to the Rigi and Pilatus, the train from Lucerne to Engelberg, and cable cars from Engelberg up to Trübsee and the Jochpass. With a **seven-day** Tellpass (Fr.158), you get two days free and five days at half price; a **fifteen-day** Tellpass (Fr.210) buys five days free plus ten at half price. You can buy the pass from tourist offices and train stations throughout the region.

Adventure sports

Central Switzerland is one of the country's top **adventure sports** destinations. **Outventure** (ⓣ041 611 14 41, ⓦ www.outventure.ch) is the leading local operator offering all manner of activities including bungee-jumps out of the Titlis cable car, white-water rafting, mountaineering and glacier walks. One winter highlight, aside from snowshoe trekking and tobogganing, is a two-day **igloo package** where you build your own igloo then sleep in it.

Another operator is the highly acclaimed **Trekking Team** (ⓣ041 390 40 40, ⓦ www .trekking.ch) – with a branch in Ticino (see p.477) – which also offers trekking, river rafting, canyoning and paragliding plus winter snowshoe trekking, ice-climbing and igloo-building. Their main draw is access to the vast **Hölloch caves** near Schwyz, 190km long and one of the largest such systems in the world; they run various excursions from short tours (90min) to overnighting below ground.

Windsurfing Urnersee (ⓣ041 870 92 22, ⓦ www.windsurfing-urnersee.ch) offers windsurfing, kitesurfing, wakeboarding and kayaking. Brunnen's Touch And Go (ⓣ041 820 54 31, ⓦ www.paragliding.ch) is a respected operator running tandem **paragliding** flights from the Urmiberg (see p.340).

Stans

The highest peak in the area is the beautiful Stanserhorn, rising to 1900m above the old village of **STANS**, capital of Nidwalden and on a direct train link with Lucerne. The centre of the village lies behind the station. The hub, Dorfplatz, is overlooked by the large **Pfarrkirche St Peter und Paul**. From the Middle Ages onwards this was the sole house of worship in the canton, and so was expanded time and time again to accommodate the increasing population until it was completely renovated in 1647; the early Baroque building remains crowned by a Romanesque bell tower. The alleys surrounding Dorfplatz are worth a wander; east is quiet Schmiedgasse, while to the west is Altes Postplatz and the **Höfli**, or **Rosenburg House**, a medieval turreted building with a rear courtyard overlooked by beautiful Italianate loggias.

A couple of minutes beyond the Höfli is the station for the old-time cog railway up to the summit of the green and pleasant **Stanserhorn** (mid-April to Nov; Ⓦ www.stanserhorn.ch), with views from the *Rondorama* revolving restaurant on top and the many trails on the summit taking in ten lakes as well as the close-at-hand high mountains around the Titlis. The zigzag walk back down to Stans takes about three and a half hours, or alternatively, you can head down the side of the mountain to Wirzweli (in 2hr 30min), from where a cable car deposits you at the village of **Dallenwil** for the bus ride back to Stans.

The **tourist office** for the region (Mon–Fri 9am–noon & 2–5pm; ☎041 610 88 33, Ⓦ www.lakeluzern.ch) is in the train station, where there are bikes for rent. There are two pleasant **hotels** on Dorfplatz: the *Engel* (☎041 619 10 10, Ⓦ www.engelstans.ch; ❸), with a fresh, contemporary style, and the more traditional *Linde* (☎041 619 09 30, Ⓦ www.hotel-linde.ch; ❸). Both have good **restaurants**, or you could plump for the *Wilhelm Tell* restaurant just off the square on Engelbergstrasse (*menus* from Fr.15). Stans's top eating choice is the fine restaurant within the Höfli (*menus* around Fr.35; closed Mon & Tues; Ⓦ www.rosenburg-stans.ch).

Hergiswil and beyond

On the train line midway between Lucerne and Stans is the small lakeside community of **HERGISWIL**, for centuries a fishing village until it rose to fame for the **Glasi Hergiswil** glassworks, founded in 1817. For over a hundred years, the glassworks was one of the busiest in the country, yet by 1975 it was hopelessly obsolete, with no chance of matching the automated methods of more modern competitors. The "Glasi" would have closed altogether but for Roberto Niederer, a Ticinese glass designer who, backed by local people, bought it up and changed its products and its target market. Niederer's rejuvenation, continued today by his son, enabled the plant – and the village economy – to survive: it's a remarkable success story. The visitor-friendly Glasi now employs a hundred people, producing hand-blown pieces for sale as well as serving as a workshop for artists from around the world to design and work with glass using traditional craft techniques. The onsite **museum** (Mon–Fri 9am–6pm, Sat 9am–4pm; free; Ⓦ www.glasi.ch) is excellent, focused around an audiovisual walk-through history of glassmaking and the Glasi. The story ends as a door opens onto a gallery above the blazing-hot **factory floor**, where you can watch a team of glass-blowers do their stuff.

Bürgenstock

East of Hergiswil rises a grand plateau, atop which is the private luxury resort of **BÜRGENSTOCK**, an odd little enclave owned by the handful of

The Rütli meadow and Swiss Path

On the western shore of Lake Lucerne's "Urnersee" branch – visible from Brunnen, across the water – is a flapping Swiss flag planted in the **Rütli meadow**, a sloping patch of grass that holds almost mystical significance for the Swiss. Legend and national pride says it was here, on August 1, 1291, that representatives from the three forest cantons around the lake (Uri, Schwyz and Unterwalden) met amidst continuing Habsburg repression to sign a pact of eternal mutual defence, thereby laying the foundation of the Swiss Confederation as it stands today. Nowadays, 1291 is taken as the birthdate of the nation, and August 1 is the official Swiss national holiday.

And yet, despite the crowds of parents who bring their children here to tell them the story of William Tell (see box, p.346) and the birth of Switzerland, many historians doubt that anything very much happened at Rütli at all. Some suggest that the Swiss Confederation developed organically, and that there was either no movement of resistance against the Habsburgs in 1291 at all, or that the Rütli oath was merely one in an array of other equally "eternal" or "perpetual" alliances between valley communities that came and went over the centuries. Nothing is certain, but most ordinary people have little truck with such trifling details: the story has come to represent much more than its bare facts might suggest. The **Charter of Confederation**, as the Rütli document came to be known, has become as potently symbolic for the Swiss as the Declaration of Independence is for Americans, and the meadow itself has become a place of patriotic pilgrimage, focus of the country's national celebrations every August.

Weg der Schweiz (Swiss Path)

Rütli is the starting point for the long-distance **Weg der Schweiz** (Swiss Path) walking route, inaugurated in 1991 as part of the 700th anniversary celebrations of the founding of the Swiss Confederation.

The scenic trail, which circumnavigates the Urnersee to **Brunnen** (see p.340), is almost 35km long, walkable in two days of roughly six hours each (with a midway overnight stop in **Flüelen** or **Altdorf**; see p.344), or is easily dividable into smaller chunks. Sections are: **Rütli to Bauen** (11km up and down; 3hr 30min); **Bauen to Flüelen** (a flat 10km; 2hr 45min); **Flüelen to Sisikon** (reasonably flat 8km; 2hr); and **Sisikon to Brunnen** (climbing and dropping 8km; 3hr). Distinctive yellow route markers – a Swiss cross incorporating an arrow – show the way (ignore whichever way the stylized arrow faces and follow the signpost's directional finger instead). **Boats** shuttle between Rütli, Bauen, Isleten, Flüelen, Sisikon and Brunnen, and **trains** run between Flüelen, Sisikon and Brunnen, enabling you to pick and choose which sections you fancy. Tourist offices stock English guides to the route.

The idea behind the path is to provide a lasting reminder of the state of the nation in 1991. Marked stones identify the 26 cantons in the order in which they joined the Confederation, with each canton allotted a length of the path proportionate to its population: every 5mm represents a single Swiss citizen. So the initial climb from the Rütli takes care of Uri, Schwyz, Nidwalden and Obwalden (who were co-founders in 1291, and are all lightly populated); then there's a section of 1.6km representing Lucerne (which joined in 1332); then 6.1km, the longest section for the most populous canton, Zürich (1351), and so on. It's a magnificent walk through classic Swiss scenery.

business-oriented hotels that occupy it, themselves mostly owned by a single family. Buses from Stans stop short at Obbürgen (from where a private toll road serves the resort), and the only way to access the area directly is by **boat** from Lucerne to Kehrsiten, way down on the lake; from there, a **funicular** rises to Bürgenstock itself – Sophia Loren's summer getaway for many years, and a renowned setting for diplomatic negotiations and all kinds of

▲ A section of the Swiss Path at Lake Uri

international politicking. If you want to stay here, or eat here, or play golf here, you'll need a packet of money (double rooms start around Fr.360; Ⓦwww.buergenstock-hotels.ch), but it doesn't cost anything to enjoy the views. Strike out east on the Felsenweg path for a scenic twenty-minute clifftop walk to Europe's fastest outdoor elevator, which swishes you in seconds to the **Hammetschwand** summit (1128m), complete with a more affordable restaurant and stunning lake vistas. You can return to Bürgenstock via a steeper path zigzagging down the back of the Hammetschwand (35min), from where another path cuts down to the Kehrsiten boat station; or follow a four-hour trail east across the wooded hilltops down to Ennetbürgen and Beckenried, which gives expansive views over the lake and south to the high mountains.

Beckenried and Klewenalp

Just round the lakeshore from Kehrsiten, and accessible by bus from Stans (or boat), is **Beckenried**, from where a gondola rises to **Klewenalp** (1593m; Ⓦwww.klewenalp.ch) and plenty more walking routes. This is touted strongly as **mountain-bike** territory, and you can rent at the gondola station, and from many outlets in Beckenried, Dallenwil and Seelisberg – around Fr.25 for a half-day. Two easy bike routes link Dallenwil and Beckenried (10km), and Emmetten and Seelisberg (7km), with harder ones climbing to Klewenalp and beyond to various mountain inns. One option is to rent from Beckenried, cycle to Seelisberg (about 12km) and then catch a boat from Treib, Seelisberg's boat station, back to Beckenried. You can **camp** west of Beckenried near Buochs (Ⓣ041 620 34 74; April–Sept).

Seelisberg and Treib

Beyond Beckenried, the main road enters a long tunnel beneath the cliffs and forests of the Seelisberg peninsula, emerging close to Flüelen (see p.344). Buses from Stans follow a minor road up onto the plateau, leading past spectacular views to little **SEELISBERG**. A funicular (Ⓦwww.seelisberg.com) shadows the steep path coiling down the cliff to the lakeside inn and boat station of **Treib** below, directly opposite Brunnen. Below the top funicular station, on the short path which ends up at the Rütli meadow (see p.331), you'll find an HI **hostel** (℡041 820 52 32, Ⓦwww.youthhostel.ch; April–Oct; ❶). Seelisberg has some inexpensive **hotels**, as well as the plusher *Bellevue* (℡041 825 66 66, Ⓦwww.bellevue-seelisberg.ch; ❸).

Engelberg

Situated at the southern end of the valley road and rail line from Stans in an enclave of Canton Obwalden, the top-quality ski resort of **ENGELBERG** (1050m) boasts an excursion to the highest point in central Switzerland – a station at 3028m, just below the distinctive crest-of-a-wave summit of the **Titlis** mountain (3239m). This, along with the village's huge Benedictine Kloster (monastery) and the faded grandeur of its hotel architecture, makes Engelberg well worth a visit.

Arrival, information and accommodation

After a picturesque valley-floor ride, the Lucerne–Stans–Engelberg (LSE) **train** pulls into the station in the middle of the village. Turn left on Bahnhofstrasse, and right onto the main central Dorfstrasse for the **tourist office**, in a sports complex at Klosterstrasse 3 (July–Oct & Dec–April Mon–Sat 8am–6.30pm, Sun 8am–6pm; rest of year Mon–Fri 8am–6pm, Sat 8am–5pm; ℡041 639 77 77, Ⓦwww.engelberg.ch). Dozens of **hotels** are dotted throughout the town and surrounding slopes.

Campsite

Eienwäldli ℡041 637 19 49, Ⓦwww.eienwaeldli .ch. Five-star site on the southeastern edge of the village, about half-an-hour's walk from the centre. Closed Nov.

Hostel

Jugendherberge (HI hostel) Dorfstrasse 80 ℡041 637 12 92, Ⓦwww.youthhostel.ch. Located 500m west of the station, with dorms, rooms and excellent meals. Closed May & Nov. ❶

Hotels

Bänklialp Bänklialpweg 25 ℡041 639 73 73, Ⓦwww.baenklialp.ch. Good, straightforward, high-quality holiday hotel, in a useful location, with plenty of services and comfortable, functional rooms. ❸

Bellevue Bahnhofplatz ℡041 639 68 68, Ⓦwww .bellevue-engelberg.ch. Characterful old hotel with a grand lobby and comfortable old-fashioned rooms. All a bit shabby around the edges, but renovations are planned. Excellent value at current rates. ❹

Bollywood in the Alps

Engelberg stands at the centre of the biggest story in Swiss tourism in years: **Bollywood**. With ongoing conflict in Kashmir making location-shoots with a mountain backdrop impossible, directors from India's film industry (centred on Mumbai, formerly Bombay – hence the name) have been discovering that it's easier and cheaper to fly cast and crew out to the Alps than it is to battle with bureaucrats for permits to film in the Himalaya. Engelberg – less than two hours from Zürich airport, and with guaranteed snow cover on the Titlis all year round – is a top-choice destination. Wealthy film buffs back home have been reading the credits closely, and these days India is one of Swiss tourism's biggest growth markets, dozens of tour groups visiting Engelberg and other Alpine film locations to tread in the footsteps of the famous.

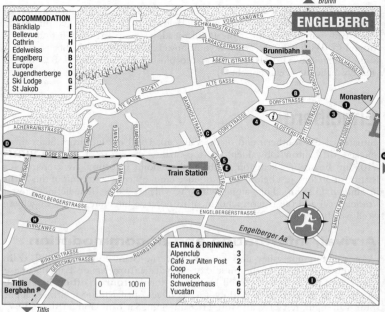

Cathrin Birrenweg 22 ☏ 041 637 44 66, ⓦ www
.cathrin-engelberg.ch. Pleasant, quiet place near
the Titlis cable car, away from the bustle. ❸–❹
Edelweiss Terracestrasse 10 ☏ 041 639 78 78,
ⓦ www.edelweissengelberg.ch. Charming Art
Nouveau hotel above the village, dating from 1901,
with stylish, spotless rooms and broad valley
views backed up by excellent, welcoming
service. ❹–❺
Engelberg Dorfstrasse 14 ☏ 041 639 79 79,
ⓦ www.hotel-engelberg.ch. Comfortable place on
the pedestrianized main street, with warm, cosy
rooms and a good restaurant. ❹
Europe Dorfstrasse 40 ☏ 041 639 75 75, ⓦ www
.hoteleurope.ch. Grandiose village-centre pile

dating from 1905. Most of the bright, attractive
rooms boast original wrought-iron balconies,
chandeliers and fittings from an age of tourism
long past. ❹
Ski Lodge Erlenweg 36 ☏ 078 675 33 66,
ⓦ www.skilodgeengelberg.com. Attractive
modern hotel run by a ski-crazy Swedish couple
who can give outdoor enthusiasts the lowdown
on all local activities. Also home to one of the
village's livelier bars, plus a Swedish sauna in
the garden outside. ❸–❹
St Jakob Engelbergerstrasse ☏ 041 637 13 88,
ⓦ www.st-jakobpension.ch. Small, simple family
pension on the road west of the centre, also with
dorms. ❸

In and around the village

Dominating the village is a huge Benedictine **monastery**. The first monks
arrived in the valley around 1120, and during the Middle Ages the monastery
was key to the expansion of ascetic mysticism in Germany and Switzerland.
The buildings as they stand today date from a rebuilding after a fire in 1729.
Until 1798, when French troops arrived in force, the monks ruled the whole
valley, which was independent of the Swiss Confederation and answered only
to the pope; the Revolution changed all that, and the monastery first joined
Canton Nidwalden in 1803, then changed its mind and switched to
Obwalden twelve years later. These days, the thirty or so monks teach high
school and further education courses. The Rococo **church**, dating from 1730,

Sports and activities at Engelberg

Engelberg's skiing and boarding is focused on the **Titlis** (Ⓦ www.titlis.ch), specifically the area above **Gerschnialp**: on lower slopes there's a network of fine blue runs, while further up, from the **Klein Titlis** station all the way down past **Stand** to the **Trübsee**, are plenty of red runs. There's excellent cross-country skiing around Trübsee as well, plus sledding at Gerschnialp. Klein Titlis benefits from summer skiing and snowboarding while the **Jochpass** has its own boarder park. On the other side of the valley, the smaller **Brunni** sector (Ⓦ www.brunni.ch) features a cable car up to **Ristis**, from where a chairlift reaches the **Brunnihütte** (1860m), which offers idyllic summer walks along the hillside meadows and down through forests to the village. In winter, a handful of blue ski runs swish you down almost to the valley floor. The guest card gives discounts on **lift passes**, which are otherwise Fr.59/274 (one/six days), or Fr.41/176 for Brunni only. The two local schools are Ⓦ www.skischule-engelberg.ch and Ⓦ www.prime-engelberg.ch.

Engelberg has an excellent reputation for **adventure sports**, with top operators Outventure (see box, p.329) and Adventure Engelberg (Ⓦ www.adventure-engelberg .ch) organizing bungee-jumping, crevasse abseiling, canyoning, snowshoeing, igloo-building, ice-climbing, rafting, kayaking and more. Don't miss the Devil Bike, a huge, fat-tyred contraption which makes short work of the scenic downhill bike run from Jochpass to Trübsee.

---

is stunning – a vast, elegant space with eleven altars. A riot of ornamental stucco leads you through to the dramatic high altar, framing a luminescent painting of the Assumption. Guided **tours** (some in English) of the whole complex, including the church and several impressive halls within the monastery, run year-round (June–Oct daily 4pm, also Mon–Fri 10am; fewer in off-season; Fr.8; Ⓦ www.kloster-engelberg.ch).

To the Titlis

The monastery aside, Engelberg's attractions are all in the hills. The main excursion, well worthwhile if the weather's clear, is the four-stage journey to the **Titlis** (Ⓦ www.titlis.ch). The first ascent crests a plateau to **Gerschnialp**, from where walking routes depart on both sides back to the village and another lift brings you to the ridge above the small picturesque **Trübsee**. From the Trübsee station, you can detour on an easy stroll around the lake to the base station of a different cable car serving the **Jochpass** and **Engstlen**, a little-frequented corner. Back at Trübsee, a gondola rises on a breathtakingly exposed journey over the lake to **Stand**, perched way above the valley at 2428m, with its own sun terrace and restaurant. From here, you switch onto the "Rotair", the world's first revolving gondola; the broad cabin begins to rotate shortly after starting the ascent, and on the five-minute journey to the top station turns completely round once, giving you a 360° panorama of the ride over the vast and impressive Titlis Glacier. On top, you'll find the standard circus of souvenir shops and ice grottoes, but the views more than compensate.

The full return **fare** Engelberg–Titlis is Fr.82 (although various passes offer discounts), but as usual, walking some sections – notably from the Trübsee back down to the village (2hr) – can save plenty.

Eating and drinking

The *Coop* supermarket opposite the tourist office on Klosterstrasse has a budget self-service **restaurant** for daytime eating. Otherwise, there are plenty of places

to fuel up along Dorfstrasse and through the centre. The *Alpenclub* (Ⓦwww
.alpenclub.ch) has a fine mountain-facing outdoor terrace and a wide-ranging
menu featuring good pizzas, fondues and more expensive Swiss meat and fish
mains. Further west along Dorfstrasse, the simple little *Café zur Alten Post* (open
until 6.30pm; closed Wed) has salads plus basic stomach-filling *menus* from
around Fr.15. For more upmarket fare, head to the *Schweizerhaus* hotel, about
fifteen minutes' walk east of the village, which has superb Swiss-style fine dining
(mains Fr.30–45), plus cheaper lunchtime *menus*.

There are plenty of options for late-night après-ski partying, including the
Yucatan **bar** (Ⓦwww.yucatan.ch), which also offers good Mexican and international food (mains Fr.15–30), and the bars at the *Hoheneck* and *Ski Lodge*
hotels, while the *Spindle* bar-cum-disco (Ⓦwww.spindle.ch), within the
Alpenclub on Dorfstrasse, is the place for late-night drinking and dancing.

Routes to the Rigi

The titanic chunk of the **Rigi** (Ⓦwww.rigi.ch), which rises to 1798m between
the lakes of Lucerne and Zug, has long been famous as a majestic viewpoint. By
itself it's actually rather scrubby, a steep-scarped grassy ridge with several
summits, but it stands alone dividing the two lakes, and offers wonderful views
south to the Alps.

There are several transport options up the mountain. **Vitznau** – where a
rack-railway begins – has the bonus of accessibility from Lucerne by boat, but
Arth-Goldau (base station for a separate rack-railway line) benefits from being
a major junction-point on the Zürich–Gotthard mainline train route. Red
trains from Vitznau and blue ones from Goldau converge at Staffel near the
summit for the final pull to **Rigi-Kulm** at the very top. A third route up the
mountain, a cable car from picturesque **Weggis**, also on Lake Lucerne, rises to
connect with the Vitznau trains at an intermediate stop named Rigi-Kaltbad. If

▲ Train en route to the Rigi

you're hiking to the summit, reckon on four hours for the trek up from Weggis. It's easy to make the Rigi a **day-trip from Lucerne**; or you could spend a night on the summit to enjoy the sunrise over the Alps.

Weggis

On a sheltered, south-facing bay, protected from cold northerly weather by the Rigi itself, **WEGGIS** basks in its own subtropical microclimate – the palm trees, figs and magnolias grow naturally. It looks out over the lake and across to the Bürgenstock cliffs, and has been a popular summer resort for a couple of centuries, with a dedicated older clientele returning year after year to soak up the sun.

The **tourist office** for Weggis, the Rigi region and the whole north shore of the lake is right beside the boat station, at Seestrasse 5 (May–Sept Mon–Fri 8am–noon & 1–5pm, Sat & Sun 9.30am–1.30pm; Dec–April Mon–Fri 9am–5pm; ☎041 390 11 55, ⓦwww.wvrt.ch). There's no shortage of **accommodation**. Least pricey is the well-kept *Budget Hotel*, in a residential district a stiff walk uphill and west from the boat station (☎041 390 11 31, ⓦwww.budgethotel.ch; ❷). A couple of minutes east of the landing stage is the *Seehof Hotel du Lac* (☎041 390 11 51, ⓦwww.hotel-du-lac.ch; closed Nov & Dec; ❸–❹), a charming, quiet family-run place of some quality – it's worth splashing out for the lakeview rooms with balconies. Just beside it is the classy *Beau-Rivage* (☎041 392 79 00, ⓦwww.beaurivage-weggis.ch; April–Sept; ❼), with plenty of creature comforts and an enclosed lakeside lawn for sunny lounging. The cable-car station for Rigi-Kaltbad is northeast of the landing stage, well signposted.

Vitznau and Gersau

A couple of hours' stroll east from Weggis is the small village of **VITZNAU**, base station for Europe's oldest rack railway (inaugurated in 1871) running up to the Rigi-Kulm from the main station. Whereas Weggis can seem a trifle twee, tranquil Vitznau – set in a sheltered west-facing bay close to the narrowest strait of the lake – has plenty of character, despite the hordes of day-trippers in the village centre. The train station for the Rigi is right opposite the boat station, with the **tourist office** beside it (May–Sept Mon–Fri 8.30am–noon & 1.30–5.30pm, Sat 9am–1pm; Oct–April Mon–Fri 9am–noon & 1.30–5pm; ☎041 398 00 35, ⓦwww.wvrt.ch). Vitznau's top **hotel** address is the *Park Hotel* (☎041 399 60 60, ⓦwww.parkhotel-vitznau .ch; ❾), a palatial *belle-époque* vision, with vast rooms, two gourmet restaurants, sauna, tennis courts and more. In the village itself, opposite the tourist office, the *Rigi* (☎041 399 85 85, ⓦwww.rigi-vitznau.ch; ❸) is an attractive shuttered old house with renovated rooms.

Less than two hours' walk east of Vitznau is **GERSAU**, a patch of meadow that was, from 1390 until 1798, the smallest independent free republic in Europe. Midway between Vitznau and Gersau is an HI **hostel**, *Jugendherberge Rotschuo* (☎041 828 12 77, ⓦwww.youthhostel.ch; March–Nov; ❶). Buses connect Weggis, Vitznau and Gersau with Brunnen.

The Rigi

There are hiking routes all over the Rigi, most starting from **Rigi-Kaltbad** (1453m) or **Rigi-Klösterli** (1315m), the first accessible from both Weggis and Vitznau, the second a midway stop on the Arth-Goldau train line. Kaltbad is a peaceful traffic-free resort on a terrace of pastureland high above Weggis; there's a handful of hotels here, as well as relatively easy two- or three-hour hiking routes through the pine trees out to the Känzeli viewpoint, up onto the ridge at First, or to the Rotstock peak above Kaltbad (1659m). Red trains from Vitznau and blue ones from Arth-Goldau meet at Staffel for the final stretch to **Rigi-Kulm**, home of the *Hotel Rigi-Kulm* (T041 880 18 88, W www.rigikulm .ch; ❹), an unromantic 1950s creation offering a superb sunrise over the Alps. The summit is a 200-metre stroll from the hotel, and gives bird's-eye views over Lucerne and the Vierwaldstättersee on one side, and Zug and the Zugersee on the other.

Zug

The town of **ZUG** (pronounced *tsoogk*), 22km from Lucerne on the north side of the Rigi, is the richest place in Switzerland, which makes it very rich indeed. Tiny Canton Zug has some of the lowest tax rates in the country – about half the national average – which attracts flocks of multinational corporations pushing average *per capita* net income up to an incredible Fr.70,000 (roughly £40,000) a year. Zug's modern, business-driven existence proceeds without pomp amidst the glittering offices and malls of the new town, a world away from the picturesque medieval churches and cobbled waterfront lanes of the compact Old Town adjacent. The town's location on the crystal-blue Zugersee is very attractive, framed by the high wooded plateau of the Zugerberg rising 600m to the east and the peak of the Rigi (see p.337) on its southwest shores.

Arrival, information and accommodation

The ultra-modern **station** – with light installations by artist James Turrell – is about 400m north of the lakeshore, and the same amount again north of the Old Town, which ranges down the eastern shore of the lake. Zug is a rail junction, where a line from Lucerne in the west meets the main north–south route running from Zürich via Flüelen and the Gotthard Tunnel to Ticino. You emerge from the station at the head of Alpenstrasse, leading down (south) to the lake. Within the station is the **tourist office** (Mon–Fri 9am–7pm, Sat 9am–4pm, Sun 9am–3pm; T041 723 68 00, W www.zug-tourismus.ch); they run guided walking tours of the Old Town (Sat 10am; Fr.5).

SGZ **boats** (W www.zugersee-info.ch) tour the Zugersee from the Bahnhofsteg, at the foot of Alpenstrasse; check their posted timetable, which also has details of their numerous eat-aboard trips – everything from winter brunches to music-accompanied starlit dinners.

Zug's high business profile, its proximity to both Lucerne and Zürich and its chronic shortage of **accommodation** means that hotels can overcharge and still be rewarded with enviably high occupancy rates. Booking ahead is vital.

Campsite
Zugersee Chamer Fussweg 36 T041 741 84 22. Located 2km west of Zug on the lakeshore – take bus #4 from Bundesplatz to Brüggli (direction Hünenberg).

Hostel
Jugendherberge (HI hostel) Allmendstrasse 8 T041 711 53 54, W www.youthhostel.ch. Walk west along the lakefront Chamerstrasse, follow Allmendstrasse north under a railway bridge, and the hostel is to the right behind a petrol station. ❶

Hotels
Guggital Zugerbergstrasse 46 T041 728 74 17, W www.hotel-guggital.ch. Up on the slopes overlooking the town from the south: for the views and the service, the best mid-range choice. All

rooms are modern and renovated, and virtually all face the lake for gorgeous sunsets (pay more for a balcony). Bus #11 stops outside. ③—④

Ibis Bahnhofstrasse 15, Baar ☎041 766 76 00, ⓦwww.hotelibis.com. Of the many motels and travel lodges off the Gotthard motorway near Zug, this is the most reliable – located at Baar train station, with parking. ①—②

Löwen am See Landsgemeindeplatz ☎041 725 22 22, ⓦwww.loewen-zug.ch. Attractive,

renovated hotel in a car-free location on the main Old Town square, just a stone's throw from the water. ⑤

Ochsen Kolinplatz 11 ☎041 729 32 32, ⓦwww .ochsen-zug.ch. A sixteenth-century gabled exterior and plush reception belie the rather less characterful rooms – the best are high up at the back overlooking rooftops and an internal courtyard. Prices drop at weekends. ④—⑤

The Town

Alpenstrasse leads from the station past Bundesplatz straight down to the lakeshore jetty, from where there are splendid views of the Rigi and Pilatus. Vorstadt follows the eastern lakeshore to **Postplatz**, on the edge of Zug's tiny Old Town.

From Postplatz, shop-lined Neugasse leads south to **Kolinplatz** and the striped-roof **Zytturm**, at 52m the Old Town's tallest building. Built in the mid-thirteenth century as a watchtower, it was renovated in 1557 and endowed with a clock in 1574. The shields below the clock face are those of the eight Swiss cantons at the time of the tower's construction. There's a host of tiny details on the tower, including a painting of a rat made by medieval watchmen as a device to scare away the rodents that stole their food during long nights on duty.

Heading beneath the Zytturm brings you into the most atmospheric part of the Old Town, cobbled lanes lined with medieval gabled, balconied and often frescoed houses. Just behind the Zytturm is Zug's **Rathaus**, dating from 1509 and retaining much of its original woodwork, and a few steps north is the waterside **Landsgemeindeplatz**. From the Rathaus, the streets Unteraltstadt and Oberaltstadt both lead south to the sturdy **Liebfrauenkapelle**, dating from 1266 but boasting a Baroque interior.

If you follow the alleys uphill from the chapel, and cross the main Grabenstrasse, you'll spot St Oswaldsgasse leading left to the **Kirche St Oswald**, built between 1478 and 1545 and dedicated to St Oswald of Northumbria (605–642). Inside you'll find another lavish Baroque interior and a nineteenth-century mural; as you leave, look above the double portal to see a beautiful carved statue of Mary flanked by St Oswald and St Michael. Follow Kirchenstrasse up the hill to the **Kunsthaus**, with usually very good temporary art exhibitions. If you head along Dorfstrasse, and across the main Ägeristrasse, you'll spot a set of quiet, concealed steps leading up to the **chapel** of a Capuchin convent (1597), with an adjacent, well-tended walled cemetery. Tranquil covered steps bring you down close to the old **mint**, with Postplatz ahead of you.

Top attraction in the surrounding countryside is the lofty **Zugerberg** (take bus #11 from the station, followed by a short cable-car ride), from where there are wonderful views and some 80km of hiking trails.

Eating and drinking

The best concentration of places to **eat and drink** is on Landsgemeindeplatz: on sunny days there are tables out on the waterfront square, and there's also plenty of choice in the surrounding alleys, particularly on nearby Fischmarkt, as well as a few more places further north along the lakeside Vorstadt.

Zug is famous around Switzerland for its cherries, which give rise both to many varieties of local **Kirsch** (cherry brandy) and to **Zuger Kirschtorte**, a delectably buttery almond tart saturated with Kirsch but, oddly, without a single fruit adorning it. *Kirschtorte* is on offer all over town – the best is made fresh daily at *Konditorei Meier* (Ⓦwww.diezugerkirschtorte.ch) in front of the station at Alpenstrasse 16.

Liguria Fischmarkt 2 ☎041 710 24 24, Ⓦwww .liguria-zg.ch. Outstanding Italian restaurant occupying a historic lakefront building with quality fish dishes (around Fr.50) and various truffle-based specialities plus lunchtime *menus* from around Fr.20.

Rathauskeller Oberaltstadt 1 ☎041 711 00 58, Ⓦwww.rathauskeller.ch. One of Canton Zug's top restaurants, housed in the historic Rathaus. Upstairs is the highest of *haute cuisine*, with a six-course evening *menu* around Fr.150, but the ground-floor bistro serves simpler, more affordable dishes from the same kitchen. Closed Sun & Mon.

Schiff Graben 2. Popular but tiny terrace bar above the *Schiff* restaurant, in a lovely Old Town house

with lakeside views. You'll need to arrive early to bag a seat, however.

Speck Alpenstrasse 12 Ⓦwww.speck.ch. Pleasant little café with good *Kirschtorte* plus lots of salads, sandwiches and inexpensive *menus* (Fr.15). Mon–Fri 6.30am–7pm, Sat 7am–5pm, Sun 8am–noon.

🏃 **Widder** Landsgemeindeplatz 12 ☎041 711 03 16, Ⓦwww.gasthaus-widder.ch. Excellent Old Town choice, with terrace seating in summer and an unusually extensive menu featuring South African ostrich, kudu and biltong, plus spicy Sri Lankan curries, along with a good spread of Swiss specialities and fresh lake fish. Mains Fr.20–40.

Schwyzerland

Occupying the picturesque northeastern corner of Lake Lucerne and extending north to the wild hills bordering the Zürichsee, unsung **Schwyzerland** takes in a series of broad, lush valleys enclosed between Alpine foothills and overlooked by the twin peaks of the Mythen. The gentle resort of **Brunnen** lies on the lake, while a short distance inland is the cantonal capital **Schwyz**, an old and graceful town. To the north, the ancient monastery church at **Einsiedeln** draws pilgrims from around the world to pay homage to the icon of the Black Madonna.

Brunnen

Of all the resort towns on the lake, **BRUNNEN** is perhaps most dramatically located, snug in a right-angled corner between the crests of the Rigi and the scarps of the Fronalpstock. Vistas from its jetty are stupendous, looking the length of the Urnersee south to the snowy peaks around the Gotthard; directly across to the misty cliffs of Seelisberg, with the Uri-Rotstock and Titlis behind; and east the length of the Vierwaldstättersee to far-distant Lucerne. Brunnen basks at the head of a wind tunnel which draws the warm Föhn north from the Mediterranean, frequently turning the Urnersee choppy and stormy. Mad King Ludwig of Bavaria took a real shine to Brunnen in 1865; one of his favourite pastimes was ordering a team of alphorn-blowers to play to him while he sat in a small boat on the lake at midnight.

The easiest excursion from Brunnen is to the **Urmiberg** peak nearby (1140m; Ⓦwww.urmiberg.ch), with stunning views both on the way up in the tiny cable car and from the summit itself. Hiking trails from the top include a steep path back down to Brunnen (1hr 30min; a gentler descent adds 1hr), and other trails down to Gersau or Goldau (both 3hr). There's a summit restaurant, and also the opportunity to take off on a **tandem paragliding** flight, courtesy

of the local adventure operator Touch And Go (☏041 820 54 31, ⓦwww
.paragliding.ch; from Fr.150).

Practicalities

Brunnen's **train station** is set back from the lakeshore jetty, about ten minutes'
walk inland on the main Bahnhofstrasse: you should allow plenty of time if
you're switching from a boat to a train, or vice versa (switching at Flüelen is
easier). Before you get to the station, you'll pass the **tourist office**, a short way
from the jetty at Bahnhofstrasse 15 (June–Sept Mon–Fri 8.30am–6pm, Sat
9am–1pm; July & Aug also Sun 9am–3pm; Oct–May Mon–Fri 8.30am–noon
& 1.30–5.30pm; ☏041 825 00 40, ⓦwww.brunnentourismus.ch).

Top choice of lakefront **hotels** is *Waldstätterhof* (☏041 825 06 06, ⓦwww
.waldstaetterhof.ch; ❻), an elegant, good-value, five-star palace. Lakefront
Bellevue (☏041 820 13 18, ⓦwww.bellevue-brunnen.ch; ❸–❹) has comfortable
modern rooms behind ornate wrought-iron balconies. On the main street in
the village is the seventeenth-century *Weisses Rössli* (☏041 825 13 00, ⓦwww
.weisses-roessli-brunnen.ch; ❸–❹), Ludwig's old haunt, which has reinvented
itself as a smart contemporary hotel with slick but moderately priced rooms
behind its traditional pink facade.

Eating is mainly focused around the hotels. The *Rôtisserie* in the *Waldstätterhof*
has moderately priced seasonal cuisine (mains Fr.25–48), while the restaurant at
the *Weisses Rössli* specializes in solid Swiss-German fare (mains Fr.18–44). *Bacco*,
at Gersauerstrasse 21 (the street opposite the *Weisses Rössli*), has a good spread
of Italian dishes, including inexpensive pizza and pasta (Fr.18–25). There's a
handful of lively **café-bars**, with cocktails and pricey food, while the lakeside
terrace at the *Waldstätterhof* is the perfect venue for afternoon coffee and cake,
with expansive views across the waters.

Schwyz

A small but characterful town 5km northeast of Brunnen, **SCHWYZ**
(pronounced *shveets*) is capital of its canton. After the combined confederate forces
won a famous victory against the Habsburgs at nearby Morgarten in 1315, they
became collectively dubbed "Schwyzers", while the whole country – formerly
Helvetia – became known as Schwyz (or Schweiz in modern High German), a
name that stuck as the country grew. Throughout the Middle Ages and after, the
men of Schwyz were sought-after as particularly accomplished mercenaries, and
many were able to return to their home town with fat wallets to build for
themselves the fine town houses which characterize the old centre today.

Cutting a dash

In 1884, an impoverished young man, Carl Elsener, founded the Swiss Cutlers'
Association in order to supply knives and blades to the Swiss army, patenting them
in 1897. The knives grew in popularity, and Swiss army officers began to ask for them
specifically. Elsener had originally named his factory after his mother Victoria, but
when stainless steel was invented in 1921 and given the international designation
INOX, Elsener devised a new combination word linking the two. **Victorinox** knives
(ⓦwww.victorinox.ch) gained official backing from the Swiss Army and, after World
War II, from the US Army too. Today, tens of thousands are churned out in myriad
varieties by the same factory in Ibach, about ten minutes' walk south of Schwyz town
centre at Schmiedgasse 57. Its onsite **shop** sells the complete range of knives at
discount prices (Mon–Fri 7.30am–noon & 1.15–6pm, Sat 8am–3pm).

Schwyz is best known for being the repository of the ancient documents embodying the history of the Confederation, on display in the **Bundesbrief-museum**, Bahnhofstrasse 20 in the town centre (Museum of Federal Charters; May–Oct Tues–Fri 9–11.30am & 1.30–5pm, Sat & Sun 9am–5pm; Nov–April Tues–Fri same hours, Sat & Sun 1.30–5pm; Fr.4; Ⓦwww.bundesbriefmuseum .ch). A museum pass, valid for all three of Schwyz's museums, costs Fr.10. This small, beautifully simple 1936 building, with a garden and a cloister of attractive arches, houses banners, flags, coins and documents recording events in Swiss history – ask for the excellent English notes at the desk. The main treasure is upstairs, in a great hall lined with flags taken from various battlefields over the centuries. At the far end, lying alone in its own display case, is a small rectangular piece of parchment covered in close lines of text. This is the original **Charter of Confederation**, dating from 1291 (see p.331); the wax seals of Uri and Nidwalden still dangle from it, but the seal of Schwyz was lost long ago.

The historical theme is continued in the **Forum der Schweizer Geschichte** (Forum of Swiss History), a branch of the Swiss National Museum, in the town centre beside the bus station (Tues–Sun 10am–5pm; Fr.10; Ⓦwww.musee-suisse .com), offering videos and interactive displays on Switzerland's social history.

The central Hauptplatz square is a few steps east of the museum, dominated by two great buildings, both rebuilt after a town fire in 1642: on a terrace above is the large parish church of **St Martin**, with an ornate interior, while the **Rathaus** sits on the square itself, its facade decorated with frescoes painted in 1891 to celebrate the 600th anniversary of the Rütli oath. Alleys to the northwest bring you to the **Ital–Reding Haus** (May–Oct Tues–Fri 2–5pm, Sat & Sun 10am–noon & 2–5pm; Fr.5; Ⓦwww.irh.ch), a splendid early seventeenth-century manor house set in its own gardens and with a magnificent interior, its upper rooms bedecked with skilfully carved panelling on wall and ceiling. Across the garden – and within the same complex – is the ancient **Haus Bethlehem**, the oldest wooden house in the country, dating from 1287. Squeezing through its minuscule rooms makes you feel a bit like Alice.

Practicalities

Schwyz is rather awkward both to get to and to stay in, and you'd probably do better spending the night in Brunnen down the road. It's a **bus**-oriented town, with the main central bus station ("Schwyz-Post") handling arrivals from Brunnen. The **train station** is in the suburb of Seewen, some 2km west of Schwyz centre; buses run from outside to Schwyz-Post. The small **tourist office** is by the bus station at Bahnhofstrasse 4 (Mon–Fri 6.30am–6.30pm, Sat 7.30am– noon; ☏041 810 19 91, Ⓦwww.info-schwyz.ch & www.schwyz-tourismus.ch).

Hotels include *Hirschen*, Hinterdorfstrasse 14 (☏041 811 12 76, Ⓦwww .hirschen-schwyz.ch; ❶), a cosy old place also with dorms, and the classier *Wysses Rössli*, Hauptplatz 3 (☏041 811 19 22, Ⓦwww.roessli-schwyz.ch; ❹), with large pleasant rooms and an excellent **restaurant** (*mains* from Fr.21). *Ratskeller*, Strehlgasse 3, just off the main square behind the Rathaus (☏041 811 10 87, Ⓦwww.ratskeller.ch; closed Sat lunch, Sun & Mon), is another quality restaurant, with a less expensive bistro area to one side (*menus* around Fr.20). The *Schwyzer Stubli*, just north of Hauptplatz at Riedstrasse 3, is a good place for Swiss *menus* at around Fr.22 (☏041 811 10 66, Ⓦwww.schwyzer-stubli.ch; closed Sat lunch & Sun).

Einsiedeln

The small village of **EINSIEDELN** (900m), in the hills of northern Schwyz 25km northeast of Brunnen, has been Switzerland's most important site of pilgrimage for a thousand years, and still draws a quarter of a million devout believers every year. The village itself is unremarkable, but the mighty Benedictine **Kloster** (monastery) which dominates it is exceptional, and worth a detour whether you're drawn by faith or curiosity.

Einsiedeln means hermitage, and is named for **St Meginrat**, who withdrew to what was then wild forest in about 828 AD. After his death in 861, hermits maintained Meginrat's self-built altar, forming a **Benedictine** community in 934 at the behest of a provost of Strasbourg cathedral, who invited the Bishop of Konstanz to perform the consecration of a new church on the site – the bishop was about to do so, when a voice was heard ringing through the church, insisting three times over that Christ himself had already consecrated the church. The pope declared this to be a **miracle**, and issued a papal bull blessing the pilgrimage to Einsiedeln.

From then on, the monastery enjoyed special privilege, with large royal grants and positions of honour for the abbots. By 1286 the Chapel of Our Lady, built over the remains of Meginrat's cell, was already a focal point; it was adorned after a destructive fire in 1468 with a statuette of Mary with the infant Christ, carved in wood some time before 1440. It is this figure which became the focus for pilgrimage as the Black Madonna.

The church

The monastery complex was rebuilt from 1704 to 1726 in the most lavish of late-Baroque styles. As you emerge from the cluster of the village centre, the vast **Klosterplatz** opens out in front. The rather plain sandstone front of the church, with its twin towers rising from an immense 140m-long facade, is framed by unusual semicircular sunken arcades. The ornate **Well of Our Lady** in the square taps the water of Meginrat's spring – pilgrims traditionally drink from each of the fourteen spouts in turn on their approach to the church.

The interior, designed by Kaspar Moosbrugger, one of the monks, is breathtaking. The nave is decorated with detailed **frescoes** by Cosmas Damian Asam, and every part of the lofty white interior is detailed in lavish gold. An intricate wrought-iron choir screen gives into the stunning pink Rococo **choir**, its ceiling bedecked with animated sculptures of angels. However, the focus of all the pilgrims' attention is the black marble **Chapel of Our Lady**, positioned in a huge octagonal bay just inside the main portal. The invading French destroyed the chapel in 1798 (although the monks had already removed the Black Madonna to the Tyrol for safekeeping), and the present chapel building dates from a Neoclassical reconstruction in 1817. The **Black Madonna** itself, a little over 1m tall and usually dressed in a jewelled and tasselled golden dress donated by Canton Uri in 1734, stands illuminated within.

Einsiedeln remains a fully functioning monastic community (ⓦ www.kloster -einsiedeln.ch), with around a hundred priests and brothers. **Mass** is celebrated several times a day. Of the many annual **pilgrimage festivals**, the most colourful is the Feast of the Miraculous Dedication on September 14, which culminates in a candlelit procession around the square.

Practicalities

Trains run every hour from Lucerne to Biberbrugg, where you have to change for the climb to Einsiedeln; trains from Brunnen and Zug require an extra change at Arth-Goldau. Einsiedeln's **train station** is a five-minute walk from the church: cross Dorfplatz and head east along Hauptstrasse. The **tourist office** is just off Klosterplatz at Hauptstrasse 85 (Mon–Fri 9am–5pm, Sat 9am–4pm, Sun 10am–1pm; ☏ 055 418 44 88, ⓦ www.einsiedeln.ch). Almost every building in sight of the church is a **hotel**: on the square, *Linde* (☎055 418 48 48, ⓦwww.linde-einsiedeln.ch; ❸–❹) is a good mid-range choice, with a surprisingly classy restaurant, tucked away just off the square, while *Storchen*, close by at Hauptstrasse 79 (☎055 412 37 60, ⓦwww.hotel-storchen.ch; ❸), is a comfortable place with simple rooms and another good restaurant. There are plenty of places to **eat** – ranging from the quality restaurants on and near Klosterplatz (such as *St Georg*) through to various less formal options along Hauptstrasse, including *La Fontanella* at no. 48, with inexpensive pizza and pasta, and *Muang Thai*, on the first floor of no. 73 (closed Mon), with lunchtime buffets for Fr.20.

Every few years, the monastery stages a mass **open-air** production of the *Great World Theatre* – a religious drama by Pedro Calderón de la Barca that was premiered at the Spanish court in 1685. Some six hundred villagers take part, coached by the monks themselves. Check ⓦwww.welttheater.ch for details of the next production.

Uri and the Alpine passes

The mountainous **Canton Uri** occupies the land between Lake Lucerne and the barrier of the high Alps. Although Uri shares borders with Bern, Valais, Ticino, Graubünden and Glarus, it is cut off from them all by 2000m-plus mountain passes, and the only cantons with which it has easy exchange of influence are its old partners from the 1291 Rütli oath, Schwyz and Nidwalden. It's no coincidence that Uri is the setting for the medieval legend of **William Tell** (see box, p.347), absorbed into Swiss consciousness as near fact and serving to define the essence of Swissness to the rest of the world. The small cantonal capital **Altdorf** was where Tell did his apple-shooting.

Uri also holds the keys to the great trans-Alpine **Gotthard** route, one of the main Alpine passes. For centuries, people and traffic have followed the ancient road up and over the mountains, although these days massively long tunnels draw trains and most of the cars swiftly to and from Ticino and Italy. **Andermatt**, on the south side of the Gotthard, is uniquely located at an Alpine crossroads, with six high-level routes passing through or near the town.

Flüelen, Altdorf and Bürglen

FLÜELEN is the farthest point of the Vierwaldstättersee from Lucerne, a picturesque little town with the train station right beside the landing stage. Fast trains from Flüelen serve both Lucerne and Zürich (with alternate services requiring a change at Arth-Goldau), as well as heading south through the Gotthard to Ticino. It's also the southern terminus of the **Axenstrasse**, the narrow road which clings below the cliffs of the eastern shore of the Urnersee south from Brunnen. The road was only completed in 1865, and enabled travellers to approach the Gotthard for the first time by land, instead of forcing them to take ship from Lucerne or Brunnen. Some 3km north of Flüelen – and accessible only by car, boat or on foot (no buses use the Axenstrasse) – is the **Tellsplatte**, a flat rock onto which William Tell is purported to have leapt to escape the clutches of Gessler (see box, p.347). Beside it is a restaurant and, beautifully framed amidst the trees, the **Tellskapelle**, a tiny monument built in 1880 with arched loggia featuring vivid frescoes depicting the story of Tell. Boats serving this point from Brunnen also pass the **Schillerstein**, a 25m high natural obelisk near the Rütli which was inscribed in 1859: "To Friedrich Schiller, the Chronicler of Tell". For details of the **Weg der Schweiz** (Swiss Path) walking route which passes by Flüelen, see p.331.

Buses from Flüelen station run into central **ALTDORF**, some 3km south (Altdorf's own train station is inconveniently located 1km west of the centre). At the traffic-bound heart of Altdorf is the Rathausplatz, dominated by the impressive **Telldenkmal** (Tell Monument) – a much-photographed icon erected in 1895. This square is reputedly the scene of the apple-shooting event itself. Nearby alleys have retained plenty of character, but if the Tell bug has bitten you, grab a bus (from the square, or from Altdorf-Post, 100m south on Bahnhofstrasse) to **BÜRGLEN**, a village 2km northeast on the Klausen road, which is celebrated as Tell's birthplace. The **chapel** which sits beside Bürglen's village church on the site of Tell's house was dedicated as early as 1582, with interior frescoes depicting the legend dating from the 1750s. Around the corner from the 1786 Tell fountain out front is the **Tell Museum** (daily: July & Aug 10am–5pm; late May, June, Sept & early Oct 10–11.30am & 1.30–5pm; Fr.5; Ⓦ www.tellmuseum.ch), a worthwhile little place crammed with Tell curiosities; ask them to set up the informative twenty-minute slide-show (in English) on the history of the legend.

The road through Bürglen continues up on a spectacular drive – followed by buses in summer – to the **Klausen Pass** (see also p.413) and over to Linthal in Canton Glarus. This is one of the most scenic pass routes in the country, with dizzy views constantly distracting you from the business of keeping on the narrow road.

Practicalities

Altdorf's **tourist office**, with information on the whole canton, is just off the main square at Schützengasse 11 (Mon–Fri 9–11.30am & 1.30–5.30pm, Sat 9–11.30am; Ⓣ 041 874 80 00, Ⓦ www.altdorftourismus.ch).

For accommodation in **Flüelen**, aim for the serviceable *Weisses Kreuz*, opposite the landing stage at Axenstrasse 2 (Ⓣ 041 870 17 17, Ⓦ www.weisseskreuz-fluelen .ch; ❷). The campsite (Ⓣ 041 870 92 22, Ⓦ www.windsurfing-urnersee.ch), fifteen minutes' walk from the station, doubles as a windsurfing centre.

The best-value hotel in **Altdorf** is the *Schwarzen Löwen*, Tellsgasse 8 (Ⓣ 041 874 80 80, Ⓦ www.hotelloewen-altdorf.ch; ❸), which has pleasant renovated rooms (choose one off the street) – one room has retained the original furniture from when Goethe stopped by in the 1770s.

Best of the lot is the ⚘ *Gasthaus Adler* in the centre of **Bürglen** (Ⓣ 041 870 11 33; ❶), a fine old sixteenth-century roadhouse inn, with wooden eaves bedecked in ivy and twelve alluringly creaky guest rooms above a traditional restaurant.

Andermatt and around

If you're travelling south by fast train, you're likely to miss the small town of **ANDERMATT** (1444m), surrounded by the high Alps on all sides, since it lies beyond the entrance to the Gotthard Tunnel at **Göschenen** (see p.348). This once-great staging post for four major Alpine crossings is now bypassed by the motorway, which plunges into its own tunnel, also at Göschenen. However, as the hub of many long-distance hiking routes, Andermatt still sees plenty of visitors in the short Alpine summer (June–Sept), and equal numbers in the winter skiing season, with red and black runs galore off the nearby **Gemsstock** summit (2963m), and an abundance of cross-country

The legend of William Tell

The legend of **William Tell** is the central defining myth in Swiss national consciousness. Most schoolchildren, whether in Switzerland or elsewhere in the West, know at least the bare bones of the story, but whereas in most cultures it is little more than a folk tale, in Switzerland it has come to embody the very essence of Swissness.

The story

At a time soon after the opening of the Gotthard Pass in the thirteenth century, when the Habsburg emperors of Vienna sought to control Uri and thus control trans-Alpine trade, a new bailiff, **Hermann Gessler**, was despatched to Altdorf. The proud mountain folk of Uri had already joined with their Schwyzer and Nidwaldner neighbours at Rütli in pledging to resist the Austrians, and when Gessler raised a pole in the central square of Altdorf and perched his hat on the top, commanding all who passed before it to bow in respect, it was the last straw. **William Tell**, a countryman from nearby Bürglen, either hadn't heard about Gessler's command or chose to ignore it; whichever, he walked past the hat without bowing. Gessler seized Tell, who was well known as a marksman, and set him a challenge. He ordered him to shoot an apple off his son's head with his crossbow; if Tell was successful, he would be released, but if he failed or refused, both he and his son would die.

The boy's hands were tied. Tell put one arrow in his quiver and another in his crossbow, took aim, and shot the apple clean off his son's head. Gessler was impressed and infuriated – and then asked what the second arrow was for. Tell looked the tyrant in the eye and replied that if the first arrow had struck the child, the second would have been for Gessler. For such impertinence, Tell was arrested and sentenced to lifelong imprisonment in the dungeons of Gessler's castle at Küssnacht, northeast of Lucerne. During the long boat journey when a violent storm arose, and the oarsmen – unfamiliar with the lake – begged with Gessler to release Tell so that he could steer them to safety. Gessler acceded, and Tell cannily manoeuvred the boat close to the shore, then leapt to freedom, landing on a flat rock (the **Tellsplatte**) and simultaneously pushing the boat back into the stormy waters.

Determined to see his task through and use the second arrow, Tell hurried to Küssnacht. As Gessler and his party walked along on a dark lane called Hohlegasse on their way to the castle, Tell leapt out, shot a bolt into the tyrant's heart and melted back into the woods to return to Uri. His comrades were inspired by Tell's act of bravery to throw off the yoke of Habsburg oppression in their homeland, and to remain forever free.

The legend

Walter Dettwiler, in his book *William Tell: Portrait of a Legend* (1991, see p.512), outlines the impact of the Tell legend over the centuries. The basis of the story – a

routes. The Gemsstock is also the best summer viewpoint in the area, since the town is too close to the valley sides to offer any panoramas of its own. Andermatt serves as the Swiss Army's principal Alpine training centre, and will shortly take on new importance: Orascom, a global investment group, is pouring money into creating an environmentally sustainable mountain resort here, with apartments, villas, six luxury hotels, Alpine golf and more, due for opening in 2014.

Andermatt's **train station** is 400m north of the town centre. Turn left outside for the **tourist office**, in the same building as the postbus booking centre (Mon–Fri 9am–noon & 1.30–5pm, high season also Sat & Sun 10am–4pm; ☏041 888 71 00, ⊚www.andermatt.ch). **Accommodation** is clustered around the picturesque main Gotthardstrasse, which can get crowded in summer: *Sonne*, marksman forced by an overlord to shoot an object from the head of a loved one – first appears in **Scandinavian sagas** written centuries before the Swiss version was first committed to paper in the fifteenth century. It was an epic song, however, composed in 1477 about the founding of the Swiss Confederation and including a section on the story of Tell, which accounted for the widespread circulation of the legend. During the **French Revolution**, the popularity of Tell rose to a peak: he was viewed as a freedom fighter in the noblest of traditions and the tale was held up as a justification for the killing of Louis XVI – all the more so because Tell and the French revolutionary armies shared a common enemy, the Austrian Habsburgs. In the 1770s and 1780s, the German poet Goethe had travelled extensively throughout Switzerland, later telling his friend, the playwright **Friedrich Schiller**, of his journeyings. Schiller's famous play *Wilhelm Tell* (1804) drew from Goethe's first-hand accounts as well as from ancient Swiss chronicles to set the Tell legend in stone, and over subsequent decades, to broadcast the story to a wide European public. **Rossini**'s opera *Guillaume Tell*, which premiered in Paris in 1829, did for the Romance-language countries of Europe what Schiller's play had done for the Teutonic.

With the final unification of Switzerland in 1848 after half a century of war, a mood of national liberation and communal purpose became crystallized around the enduring significance of William Tell, who began to be portrayed with increasing idealism, notably in the **Tell monument** in Altdorf, which was unveiled in 1895. **Ferdinand Hodler**, most famous of Swiss artists, drew directly on this monument for his seminal portrait of Tell as a godlike figure, emerging from a gap in the clouds with arm outstretched (see p.217). Throughout **World War II**, the image and notion of a deeply moral, fervently nationalistic Tell hardened the resolve of ordinary Swiss to resist domination by Nazi Germany, and contributed to Switzerland's self-imposed exclusion from the co-operative international organizations – specifically the United Nations and the European Union – which arose after 1945.

However, the **700th anniversary** of the Confederation, celebrated in 1991, brought dissenting voices to the fore for the first time, with revisionist historians searching for more pragmatic reasons for the survival of Swiss culture than the doings of a single male hero. The annual retelling of Schiller's drama on an open stage in touristic Interlaken (see p.236) to an audience increasingly made up of foreigners is, too, beginning to ring hollow, and popular perception has become increasingly cynical over the continuing appropriateness of William Tell as an icon for a 21st-century Switzerland.

at no. 76 (☎041 887 12 26, ⓦwww.hotelsonneandermatt.ch; ❸), is a cosy old wooden place, while the *Drei Könige & Post*, at no. 69 (☎041 887 00 01, ⓦwww.3koenige.ch; ❸–❺), has modern, comfortable rooms. The **restaurant** *Di Alt Apotheke* (☎041 887 00 25), attached to the *River House* hotel at Gotthardstrasse 58, is a cut above the rest on this busy stretch, with well-prepared regional cuisine (mains from Fr.30).

The high passes all around offer possibilities for spectacular round-trip **driving tours** – you can follow the route from Andermatt over the Gotthard, Nufenen and Furka passes by postbus in summer; or it's equally possible to strike out with your own transport over the Susten, Grimsel and Furka passes, with an intermediate stop for lunch in Meiringen (see p.258). To the east, the Oberalp Pass leads to Disentis/Mustér (see p.436).

The most famous of all the Alpine passes, the **St Gotthard** or **San Gottardo** (2108m) is also the most memorable to visit. The turbulent Schöllenen Gorge, a few kilometres north of Andermatt, was first bridged in the thirteenth century, allowing traffic to penetrate up the full length of the Reuss valley from Flüelen to the pass itself, from where a continuation road followed the valley of the River Ticino all the way south to Bellinzona and Milan. Today, three daily buses (July–Sept only) follow the new road from Andermatt up to the pass and on down to Airolo. The old cobbled road, which branches off partway up, is much quieter and more picturesque. Both meet on top, where you'll find a wild windswept spot with a handful of buildings clustered around a small lake that's become an unfortunately popular picnicking spot for day-tripping families. The pass is one of Europe's watersheds: rain or snowmelt on the north side ultimately ends up in the Rhine and the North Sea, while moisture on the south side flows into the Po and the Mediterranean.

The old **hospice** beside the road now houses the engaging **Museo Nazionale del San Gottardo** (June–Oct daily 9am–6pm; Fr.9), which outlines the history of the pass with models, reliefs, paintings and audiovisual slide-shows.

Across the road, there are simple modern rooms available at the often-busy ⚐ *Albergo San Gottardo* (☎091 869 12 35, ⓦwww.gotthard-hospiz.ch; ❷; May–Oct). From the pass, most traffic follows the new road down to Airolo, but the old cobbled road that snakes down behind the *albergo* off the back of the pass into Ticino is truly spectacular, with views all the way down into the Val Tremolo ("Valley of Trembling"). If you're **hiking**, it's a three-hour walk to Airolo this way, or six hours by an off-road route through Val Canaria; on the north side, Andermatt is three hours away via the small village of Hospental, or six by a more scenic route through the deserted valleys around Maighels.

The Gotthard tunnels

Foot traffic has used the Gotthard Pass since about 1200, and the first carriage crossed in 1775. Less than a century later, in 1872, after decades of debate over routes and costs, work began on a **rail tunnel** beneath the pass. Over seven years and 277 lives later, the bores which had begun simultaneously from Göschenen and Airolo met midway on February 29, 1880. The first trains ran through the 15km-long tunnel in 1882.

This line is still a vital north–south artery, carrying at peak times an average of one train every six minutes – with five million passengers and 25 million tonnes of freight carried to and fro each year. The Gotthard journey is one of Switzerland's great train rides, not so much for the long stretch of blackness as you swoosh beneath the Alps, but for the spectacular approach. South of Flüelen, you climb slowly and dramatically up the wild valley, passing through dozens of straight tunnels and, around **Wassen**, a series of tightly spiralled tunnels, which gain maximum altitude at minimum gradients. Wassen's little onion-domed church, prominent on its rock, is a famous landmark: you'll pass it three times, first high above you, then on a level, and finally far below you before you're plunged into darkness shortly afterwards at **Göschenen**. Trains emerge at Airolo (see p.472) for the long journey down to Bellinzona.

The 16.3-kilometre Gotthard **road tunnel**, completed in 1980, which runs in parallel from Göschenen to Airolo, was the longest road tunnel in the world until a Norwegian project overtook it in 2000. Although prone to hideous kilometres-long jams on both approaches, it remains open year-round, while the pass road above is impassable in winter.

Work is now well under way on the new **Gotthard Base Tunnel**, part of an ambitious project to upgrade high-speed train routes beneath the Alps in order to take freight off the roads and shorten long-distance rail journeys. When the tunnel opens in 2017, trains will enter at Erstfeld, a few kilometres south of Altdorf, speeding through the deep tunnel to the exit at Bodio, 58km south. Avoiding the long climb up to Göschenen and the long descent from Airolo will cut a full hour off Zürich–Milan journey times. Legislation is also in place to force pan-European road freight onto the new line, thus clearing the N2 highway in the upper Reuss and upper Ticino of its appalling traffic jams and easing environmental degradation. Full information and progress reports are at Ⓦ www.alptransit.ch.

The Furka Pass

Summer postbuses from Andermatt cross the **Furka Pass** (2431m; see also p.307) westwards into Canton Valais, while mainline passenger and car-carrying trains use the year-round Furka-Basis Tunnel beneath the pass. Buses aside, the main draw on the Uri side is a volunteer-run antique mountain **steam train**, the DFB (Ⓦ www.furka-bergstrecke.ch), which in summer puffs its way from **Realp** – a hamlet an easy hour-and-three-quarter walk from Andermatt – up to a station near the pass and on through the short Muttbach tunnel to Gletsch. The round trip costs Fr.93.

Between Realp and the pass is *Hotel Tiefenbach* (Ⓣ041 887 13 22, Ⓦ www .hotel-tiefenbach.ch; ➋), with quality dorms from Fr.42, also open in winter as base camp for some fine cross-country skiing. On the pass sits the historic *Furkablick* (Ⓣ041 887 07 17; June–Sept; ➋), a fine old inn bought in the 1990s by gallery-owner Marc Hostettler, who has preserved much of the charm and many features of the century-old interior – not least the library, now crammed with books on contemporary art. Dutch architect Rem Koolhaas worked on part of the renovations.

The Oberalp Pass

Directly east of Andermatt is the **Oberalp Pass** (2044m) into Canton Graubünden, open to trains year-round. This is the route of the famous Glacier Express (see p.34) between Zermatt and St Moritz, which runs via the Furka-Basis Tunnel, Andermatt and the Oberalp on its way to Chur. Local trains from Andermatt to Disentis/Mustér (see p.436) can drop you on the pass itself, trailhead for a host of high-country summer hikes. Two scenic routes run through the bleak and invigorating high country down to Andermatt, one via the Lolenpass (5hr 30min), the other via the Maighelspass (6hr 30min), while an easier one heads out to Fellilücke, and from there to Nätschen and Andermatt (5hr).

Car-carrying trains: the Furka and Oberalp passes

If you're heading west into Valais and would prefer to avoid the climb over the Furka Pass, note that **car-carrying trains** run daily year-round from Realp (near Andermatt) through the **Furka-Basis Tunnel** (15.4km) to Oberwald, at least every hour (6am–9pm); a one-way fare is Fr.25 (Oct–May Fr.30). Journey time is 15min. You can also avoid the climb eastwards over the **Oberalp Pass** into Graubünden by loading your car onto a train at Andermatt for the hour-long pull to Sedrun (4 daily; Fr.65). Full information on both routes is at Ⓦ www.mgbahn.ch.

Travel details

Full timetables for all trains, buses, trams, boats and cable cars in Switzerland – as well as international connections – are searchable at ⓦ www.rail .ch. For details of trains from Andermatt over the Furka and Oberalp passes, see ⓦ www.mgbahn.ch.

Trains

Andermatt to: Brig (hourly; 1hr 30min); Disentis/Mustér (4 daily; 1hr 10min); Flüelen (hourly; 50min; change at Göschenen); Oberalppass (hourly; 20min).

Brunnen to: Altdorf (hourly; 15min); Flüelen (every 30min; 15min); Lucerne (hourly; 45min); Zug (1–2 hourly; 30min).

Flüelen to: Andermatt (hourly; 45min; change at Göschenen); Brunnen (every 30min; 10min); Lucerne (every 30min; 55min; some change at Arth-Goldau); Lugano (hourly; 2hr 10min); Schwyz (every 30min; 15min); Zürich (every 30min; 1hr 10min; some change at Arth-Goldau).

Lucerne to: Basel (every 30min; 1hr 10min); Bellinzona (hourly; 2hr 5min); Bern (hourly; 1hr); Brienz (hourly; 1hr 40min); Brunnen (twice hourly; 45min; some change at Arth-Goldau); Einsiedeln (hourly; 1hr; change at Biberbrugg); Engelberg (hourly; 1hr 5min); Flüelen (every 30min; 55min; some change at Arth-Goldau); Hergiswil (4 hourly; 10min); Interlaken Ost (hourly; 1hr 55min); Lugano (hourly; 2hr 30min; some change at Arth-Goldau); Stans (every 30min; 20min); Zug (3–4 hourly; 20min); Zürich (twice hourly; 45min).

Zug to: Brunnen (every 30min; 30min); Lucerne (3–4 hourly; 20min); Lugano (hourly; 2hr 15min); Zürich (twice hourly; 25min).

Buses

Altdorf to: Bürglen (twice hourly; 5min); Flüelen (every 15min; 10min).

Flüelen to: Altdorf (every 15min; 10min); Linthal via Klausenpass (July–Sept 1 daily; 2hr 25min).

Schwyz to: Brunnen (every 10–20min; 25min).

Stans to: Beckenried (twice hourly; 25min); Seelisberg (hourly; 50min).

Weggis to: Gersau (hourly; 25min); Vitznau (hourly; 15min).

Boats

Following is a summary of April–Oct services on Lake Lucerne; fewer boats run in other months, quite often only on Sun, if at all. Full details are at ⓦ www.lakelucerne.ch.

Brunnen to: Lucerne (hourly; 2hr 15min); Vitznau (hourly; 1hr 10min).

Flüelen to: Lucerne (hourly; 3hr).

Lucerne to: Alpnachstad (hourly; 1hr 40min); Beckenried (hourly; 1hr 30min); Brunnen (hourly; 2hr 15min); Flüelen (hourly; 3hr); Kehrsiten-Bürgenstock (6 daily; 35min); Vitznau (hourly; 1hr); Weggis (hourly; 50min).

Vitznau to: Brunnen (hourly; 1hr 10min); Lucerne (hourly; 1hr).

9

Zürich

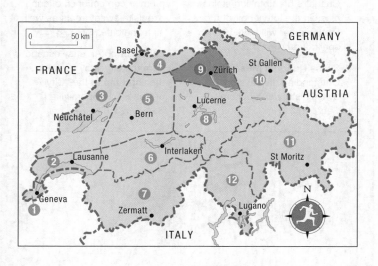

CHAPTER 9

Highlights

* **Grossmünster** Zürich's "Great Minster", from where Zwingli preached the Reformation. See p.367

* **Kunsthaus** World-class gallery of art, unmissable if only for the vast array of works by Alberto Giacometti. See p.369

* **Chagall windows** Marc Chagall's breathtaking stained glass in the lofty choir of the Fraumünster will have you spellbound. See p.371

* **Swiss National Museum** Outstanding displays on Swiss history and culture. See p.372

* **Uetliberg** Steep-sided ridge rising above the city, with stunning views and wooded walking trails. See p.373

* **Zürich West** Hotbed of the city's counterculture, centred on the buzzing Langstrasse. See p.374

* **Confiserie Sprüngli** Zürich's premier confectioner, offering exquisite sweet treats as well as a fine café. See p.376

* **Lake Zürich** An easy escape from the city is by boat for the short trip to the "City of Roses", Rapperswil. See p.383

▲ The Grossmünster

Zürich

Zürich's relationship to the world is not of the spirit, but of commerce.

C.G. Jung

Not so long ago, **ZÜRICH** was famed chiefly for being the cleanest, most icily efficient city in Europe – prim, but devoid of soul. Things have changed. Switzerland's largest city (population 380,000) has shaken off its reputation as Europe's sourpuss and you'll find its still pristinely clean streets abuzz with newfound confidence on the back of global recognition: Zürich consistently rates at or near the top of annual surveys judging cities worldwide for their quality of life. These days it qualifies as a metropolis with style – and even a touch of glamour.

Zürich is still best known, though, as a city to do business. After World War II, the city's foreign exchange speculators had become so powerful and secretive that exasperated British ministers, amidst the 1964 sterling crisis, spoke of them as gnomes, scurrying about in the corridors of their private banks forever counting their gold. Their reference to "**the gnomes of Zürich**" stuck, and journalists reporting on Switzerland's banking and finance industries still reach for the phrase today. Aptly, Zürich now hosts the world's most important market for trading **gold** and precious metals, and boasts the fourth-largest stock market, after New York, London and Tokyo. Exceptional affluence tends to define the area these days, and yet, despite its wealth and status, Zürich is not a flashy place at all. The city's ingrained Protestant work ethic bears the stamp of the Bible-thumping Reformer Huldrych Zwingli – yet it's the freedom of thought that Zwingli encouraged which continually bubbles to the surface. Wry Zürchers like to make much of how apt it is that you have to tut, purse your lips and clear your throat just to say the city's name (*tsoorikh* in dialect), but they're deliberately pandering to a long-outdated stereotype.

You're likely to find plenty to keep you occupied in this good-looking city, poised astride the River Limmat, adorned with over a thousand medieval and modern fountains, and turned towards the **Zürichsee** (**Lake Zürich**), so crystal-clear the Swiss authorities have certified its water safe to drink. In recent years the city has undergone a boom in arts and popular culture, expressed most tangibly in a host of innovative restaurants and clubs. The medieval **Old Town**, characterized by the steep, cobbled alleys and attractive, small-scale architecture of the **Niederdorf** district, comprises a substantial part of the city centre and is perfect for exploratory wanderings. With a handful of medieval churches to take in, including the mighty **Grossmünster** and graceful **Fraumünster**, the superb **Kunsthaus** art gallery and the most engaging café culture in German-speaking Switzerland, you could easily spend days here.

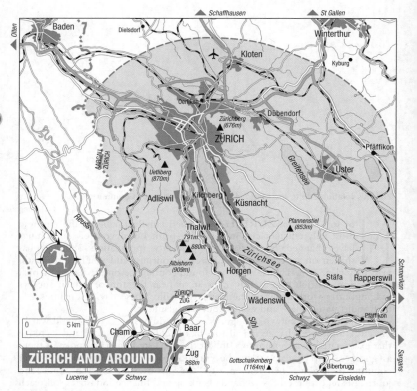

ZÜRICH AND AROUND

Some history

The **Romans** were the first to fortify the area, creating a customs post on the Lindenhof in the first century BC and naming it *Turicum*. The legend of the city's foundation dates from the martyrdom of **Felix and Regula**, deserters from a Roman legion based in Valais.

During the eleventh and twelfth centuries, Zürich's traders built up fabulous wealth, mainly from textiles such as wool and silk – but in 1336 a visionary burgomaster, **Rudolf Brun**, shuffled the merchant nobility out of power, handing control instead to workers' guilds (which were to keep a hold on the city until the nineteenth century). Shortly after, still under Brun's direction, Zürich joined the nascent Swiss Confederation.

The thriving city experienced its zenith of power and prestige in the sixteenth century, when it became the first Swiss city to embrace the **Reformation**. The city's spiritual father, Huldrych **Zwingli** (see box, p.368), preached in the Grossmünster from 1519 until his death in 1531. With the abolition of the Catholic Mass in 1525, Zürich became a centre for dissident intellectuals from all over Europe. After 1549, when Calvinist doctrine was adopted over Zwinglian, the city experienced a slow fading in its fortunes. The French Revolution of 1789 sparked **pro-libertarian** demonstrations at Stäfa, south of Zürich, but the city itself remained a backwater.

A late nineteenth-century city councillor, **Alfred Escher**, is credited with reinventing Zürich as the economic capital of Switzerland, his legislative

Too rich!

Political activism within Zürich's youth movement during the 1970s culminated in major riots in 1980–81 and the police closure of the city's autonomous youth centre. The counterculture regrouped around two large community **squats**, the activities of which have passed into the city's collective memory. The first, known as **Wohlgroth**, took over an empty commercial building next to the train tracks on Zollstrasse; the squatters immediately erected a placard on the roof to greet trains rolling into the city with a huge imitation SBB station sign reading not "Zürich" but "*Zu reich*" ("Too rich"). At a stroke, this guaranteed them fame – wry chuckles mixing equally with establishment fury. The Wohlgroth developed into a thriving centre for arts, music and alternative culture, and such was its popularity that, after some years of hand-wringing at the loss of rent on such a prime site, the chief executive of the corporation which owned the building personally came visiting with the offer to donate another, less embarrassingly visible building to the collective. His offer, needless to say, was rejected, and shortly afterwards, in 1993, the police evicted the place with tear gas and water cannon. Perhaps the greatest legacy of the Wohlgroth, aside from their classic *Zu reich* prank, is that the neighbourhood has now become the heart of the city's new subculture.

The second big squat of the early 1980s was of the **Rote Fabrik**, a former silk mill in a beautiful lakeside location south of the city, owned by the municipality. Whereas similar city-owned places squatted in Bern and Geneva have remained illegal and on the radical fringes of city life to this day, it's a mark of discreet Zürcher pragmatism that in 1987 the Rote Fabrik collective voted to apply for legal status and an arts subsidy from the city council. This was granted, millions of francs flowing into their coffers shortly after. These days, although its alternative heart still beats, the Rote Fabrik is able to develop and stage avant-garde dance and drama worthy of attention from the *Neue Zürcher Zeitung*, the city's most conservative newspaper. The flipside, of course, is that a mere mention of the place makes the committed radicals in Bern roll their eyes and start muttering about a sell-out.

innovations boosting tourism, banking and local manufacturing industry. Strict neutrality during World War I again made Zürich a refuge for dissidents, and for some months in 1916 and 1917 the city was home to **Lenin**, mulling over the future Russian Revolution, **James Joyce**, holed up near the university writing *Ulysses*, and a band of émigré artists calling themselves "Dada", who spent their evenings lampooning Western culture at the famous **Cabaret Voltaire**.

Zürich's exact role during and after **World War II** remains murky, but the city emerged postwar to flourish, becoming one of the world's leading financial centres. More recently, following a relaxation of licensing laws, Zürich is discovering a new will to party. Alongside all its sights and its lakeside beauty, Zürich is reinventing itself again, and a gritty and engaging subculture – centred in the up-and-coming district of **Zürich West** – is thriving beneath the city's slick, monied surface.

Arrival

Zürich's **airport** (W www.zurich-airport.com) is 11km northeast in Kloten. Its subterranean **train station** is clearly signed. Trains depart roughly every ten minutes for the city's main station, Zürich HB (takes 10min); some go nonstop, others have an intermediate halt at Zürich-Oerlikon. Beware that a few stop at suburban stations but not at Zürich HB – check the departure boards carefully. Swiss Pass holders travel free; others should buy a ticket from the machines (Fr.6.20; press the red button), but note that if you intend to stay a day or two in Zürich, it may be more economical to get a ZürichCARD (see box below) from a staffed counter.

Frequent fast trains also go direct from Zürich airport to points all over the country – major destinations like Basel, Bern, Lucerne, Interlaken, Lausanne and Geneva, as well as other cities including Baden, Winterthur, St Gallen, Fribourg and Brig (for Zermatt), cutting out the need to change at Zürich HB. Check timetables at Ⓦ **www.rail.ch**.

Some Zürich **hotels** will pick you up at Arrivals and drive you to the door – ask about this service (which is often free) when you book your room. A **taxi** into the city centre costs Fr.60 or more.

By train

Zürich's main station, or **Hauptbahnhof** (HB), has trains arriving continuously from all corners of Switzerland and around Europe. It's a massive beehive of a place located in the heart of the city, extending three storeys below ground and taking in a shopping mall, supermarket and some good restaurants. Most trains arrive at **street level** (platforms 3–18), where the echoing station concourse is home to a scattering of fast-food stalls and cafés, a post office and, at the far end beyond the giant clock, the tourist office (see opposite). Out of sight behind the travel bureau are the bike rental office and left-luggage counter.

One level down you'll find luggage lockers, while going down again brings you to the **shopping level**, with a warren of echoing subterranean passageways stretching off in all directions. **S-Bahn** suburban trains leave from the lowest level (platforms 1–2 and, separately, 21–24) to local destinations such as Uetliberg and Adliswil; the huge information boards on the street-level concourse list S-Bahn departures separately from mainline departures (*Fernverkehr*). Some S-Bahn trains depart from platforms 51–54, located at street level halfway along platform 3. S-Bahn services to nearby towns such as Winterthur and Baden are slower than mainline trains, but go more frequently.

By car and bus

Parking is difficult and expensive. All of the Old Town, plus chunks of the central commercial district, are off-limits to cars, and although there are nine parking garages in the centre, pinpointed at Ⓦ www.parking.ch, they can be prohibitively expensive, often more than Fr.30 a day. It's a good idea to ask your hotel in advance about parking: some can reserve free or discounted spaces for guests. International **buses** arrive at the open bus park on Sihlquai opposite the *Walhalla* hotel, 50m behind the station.

The ZürichCARD

If you haven't already got a Swiss transport pass, the **ZürichCARD** represents excellent value (Fr.19 for 24hr; Fr.38 for 72hr). It is available at the tourist office, train stations (including the airport station) or at hotels, and is valid for **free public transport** by train, bus, tram, boat or funicular throughout the city centre (extending as far as the airport, Uetliberg and short trips on the lake), **free admission** to over forty museums, and a host of **discounts**. In addition, it gets you a **free drink** at lunch or dinner at twenty restaurants around the city. The **ZürichCARD PLUS** (Fr.36 for 24hr) covers a wider area of validity.

▲ Zürich city centre

Information

On the street-level concourse of the city's main train station, Zürich HB, sits the well-equipped **tourist office** (May–Oct Mon–Sat 8am–8.30pm, Sun 8.30am–6.30pm; Nov–April Mon–Sat 8.30am–7pm, Sun 9am–6pm; ☎044 215 40 00, Ⓦwww.zuerich.com). Staff can book you onto a two-hour **guided walk** through the Old Town in English (April–Oct Mon–Fri 3pm, Sat & Sun 11am & 3pm; Nov–March Wed, Sat & Sun 11am; Fr.20), or a two-hour **city tour** on a bus done up as a vintage trolley-bus, where you listen to a headphone commentary (daily 9.45am, noon & 2pm; Fr.33). There's a host of other tours available by bike, bus and/or boat, generally costing Fr.40–50. The tourist office stocks, for free, *Züritipp* (Ⓦwww.zueritipp.ch), the best weekly **what's–on** paper, in German only.

City transport

One of the great advantages of Zürich is that you can enjoy all the buzz of big city life in a compact setting that's no larger than a single *arrondissement* of Paris: covering the city **on foot** is perfectly feasible. The main Bahnhofstrasse, which extends from the station to Bürkliplatz, is only a little over 1km long. Nonetheless, Zürich's **city transport** system is legendary for its efficiency, punctuality and convenience.

The main mode of transport is **tram**: cars are being eased off the city-centre streets. **S-Bahn** suburban trains, most originating from or passing through the main station, add another dimension, linking to Zug and Einsiedeln in the south and Winterthur, Schaffhausen and Stein-am-Rhein in the north, as well as

A **Swiss Pass** (see p.35) is valid for free city transport in Zürich and free admission to almost all museums reviewed in this book.

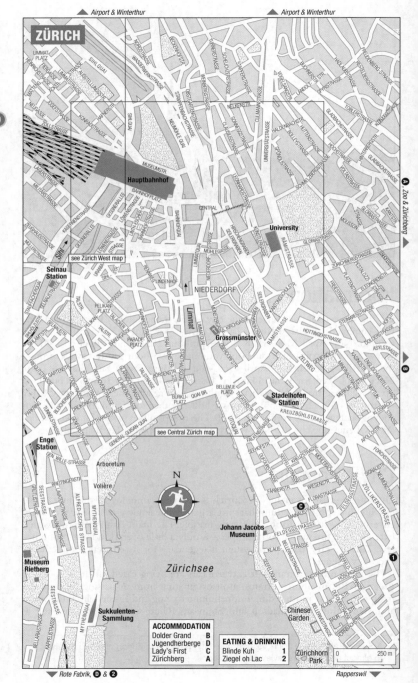

serving the nearby Uetliberg summit. **Boats** crisscross their way up and down Lake Zürich. There's even a **free bike-rental** scheme (see p.383).

Taxis, in a city where even millionaire bankers use the tram, are expensive and largely unnecessary: expect a Fr.6 flagfall plus Fr.3.80 per kilometre. Grab one at a rank, or order from, for example, Taxi 444 (☎044 444 44 44) or Alpha Taxi (☎044 777 77 77).

Ticketing and fares

Ticketing is organized by zone, with the city centre covered by Zone 10 (the airport is in neighbouring Zone 21; Uetliberg in Zone 55). All tickets can be used for all transport – both land- and water-based – within each zone, with unlimited changes permitted. Full information is at ⓦwww.vbz.ch.

If you hold a **Swiss Pass** (see p.35) or a **ZürichCARD** (see box, p.356), all public transport in the city is **free**.

Otherwise, of the tickets buyable with coins from the machines at all tram and bus stops, the most useful ticket is the Fr.8 **Tageskarte** (press the green button), valid for 24 hours' travel in Zone 10. The blue "**Stadt Zürich**" button gives a Zone 10 ticket valid for an hour (Fr.4). If you hold a Swiss Card, press "1/2" to get your discount. The **9-Uhr Tagespass** (9 o'Clock Day Pass, valid Mon–Fri after 9am, Sat & Sun all day; Fr.23) is good for an off-peak day-trip, valid throughout the whole region north to Winterthur (Zone 20) and the Rhine falls (Zone 16) and south to Rapperswil (Zone 80); to get one, key ★141 on any ticket machine. Several other passes and combi-tickets are available.

Boats

Zürich has plenty of **boat** trips. The tourist office has full information, as does the Lake Zürich Shipping Company (ZSG; ☎044 487 13 33, ⓦwww.zsg.ch). Full timetables are posted at the company office at **Bürkliplatz**, from where almost all boats depart. Note that most of the trips mentioned below operate only in summer (April–Oct); in winter, service is reduced and is dependent on good weather. If you hold a **Swiss Pass** (see p.35), boat travel is **free**. The **ZürichCARD** (see box, p.356) is valid for free travel on shorter routes only.

There's a host of **pleasure cruises**, including circular sightseeing trips (*Rundfahrten*) from and to Zürich-Bürkliplatz without stopping (*Kleine* 1hr 30min Fr.8; *Mittlere* 2hr 30min Fr.20; *Grosse* 4hr Fr.23). **Eat-aboard cruises** – in daylight and after dark – are also popular. Meanwhile, regular boats ply the length of the lake from Zürich to **Rapperswil** (see p.384; 1hr 45min) and beyond, stopping at just about every shoreside town on the way.

One of the best short trips is on the **Limmat-Schiff**, which departs from the Landesmuseum for the scenic upriver journey through the heart of the city, including a short trip on the lake and the return journey down the Limmat again. Departures are every half-hour (July & Aug daily 10am–9pm; May, June & Sept Mon–Fri 1–9pm, Sat & Sun 10am–9pm; shorter hours in April & Oct; takes 55min; Fr.4).

Accommodation

Zürich has a full range of **accommodation** and – despite its being one of the most expensive cities in the world – if you book ahead you'll have a strong chance of finding somewhere good within your price range. Prices at the higher-end places, though, can be frightful, and some mid-range hoteliers take this as carte blanche to overcharge: ask what you'll be getting for your money

Easy day-trips from Zürich by train

Braunwald p.413. Car-free Alpine hideaway for rapid battery-recharge. Change at Ziegelbrücke and Linthal. 1hr 45min.

Einsiedeln monastery p.342. Centuries-old site of pilgrimage up in the hills. Change at Wädenswil. 45min.

Lucerne p.313. Exquisite Old Town plus breathtaking lake-and-mountains scenery. Direct. 45min. Either train back, or boat Lucerne–Flüelen then train Flüelen–Zürich.

Rapperswil p.384. Gentle, easy-going town on Lake Zürich, perfect for a lazy afternoon. Direct. 35min (or 1hr 45min by boat).

Rhine falls p.398. Europe's biggest waterfall. Change at Winterthur for Schloss Laufen or Neuhausen. 50min.

Rigi p.336. A popular ride up the nearest high mountain to Zürich (1798m). Change at Arth-Goldau. 1hr 40min.

Schaffhausen p.394. Fascinating, little-visited Old Town; combine it with a river trip to Stein-am-Rhein. Direct. 55min.

Uetliberg p.373. Zürich's "home mountain", with a network of easy walking routes. Direct. 20min.

Winterthur p.390. Relaxed city with high-quality art museums. Direct. 25min.

before you check in. Nearby **Baden** (see p.184) and **Winterthur** (see p.390) offer equally characterful accommodation at more affordable prices. It's worth checking with the tourist office about any weekend or off-season promotions, which can slash walk-in rates.

All these establishments are **keyed on the maps** – either of the city (p.358), the central area (p.364) or Zürich West (p.374).

Camping and hostels

The one **campsite** within easy reach is *Seebucht*, Seestrasse 559 (℡044 482 16 12, ⓦwww.camping-zurich.ch; May–Sept); take bus #161 or #165 from Bürkliplatz south along the western shore of the lake to Stadtgrenze.

Hostels

City Backpacker/Hotel Biber (SB hostel)
Niederdorfstrasse 5 ℡044 251 90 15, ⓦwww
.city-backpacker.ch. A good atmosphere, central
location in the Old Town and super-friendly
management. Dorms, singles and doubles are
available, along with free kitchen use, laundry
service and other services. ❶

Jugendherberge (HI hostel) Mutschellenstrasse
114 ℡043 399 78 00, ⓦwww.youthhostel.ch. A
rather institutional hostel, awkwardly situated in a
humdrum southwestern suburb. Take tram #7
(direction Wollishofen) to Morgental, then walk
5min (follow the signs). ❶

Hotels

The greatest concentration of **inexpensive hotels** is in the Old Town's Niederdorf district. None is more than ten minutes' walk from the station, or you could hop on tram #4 (direction Tiefenbrunnen): it runs south down Limmatquai, stopping at Central, each of the three river bridges and Bellevue. To reach Zürich West, tram #3 from the station (direction Albisrieden) stops at Bezirksgebäude, at the southern end of Langstrasse, while tram #13 (direction Frankental) stops at Limmatplatz and Escher-Wyss-Platz.

Mid-range hotels in Niederdorf are generally quiet and characterful, although often pricey, while those elsewhere in the city tend to offer better value but have noisier or more mundane surroundings. Withdrawing to one of the good-value hotels in the wooded hills to east and west is a sound ploy.

Zürich has any number of **expensive hotels**, chain- and private-owned palaces catering chiefly to executives and glitterati who demand luxury at any price.

Inexpensive hotels

Niederdorf

G Marktgasse 14 ☏ 044 250 70 80, ⓦ www .g-hotel.ch. Excellent value, with an easy-going atmosphere. This is the only hotel in Zürich which makes a selling-point of its gay- and lesbian-friendliness. The comfortable rooms are large, bright, individually decorated and inexpensive, but you should insist on the fifth floor to avoid noise from the bars and nightclub at street level. They also have quality apartments for around Fr.250. ❸–❹

Limmathof Limmatquai 142 ☏ 044 267 60 40, ⓦ www.limmathof.com. A two-star that is one of the cheaper options overlooking the river; eschew the noisy river-view rooms for the newer, quieter ones at the back. Either way, you may have problems swinging a cat. Has two restaurants on site, one of which (the *Pot au Vert*) is vegetarian. ❸

Martahaus Zähringerstrasse 36 ☏ 044 251 45 50, ⓦ www.martahaus.ch. Budget hotel in a slightly dodgy neighbourhood, but a safe, clean and thoroughly respectable place to rest your head. Was closed at the time of writing for complete renovation: by the time you read this it should have reopened with brand-new interiors. ❷–❸

🏃 **Otter** Oberdorfstrasse 7 ☏ 044 251 22 07, ⓦ www.hotelotter.ch. Best in this bracket by miles for character and value, with a relaxed, friendly vibe and an unconventional, arty clientele. Colourful rooms, all with plump, comfy beds, are decked in murals, drapes and plants; ones higher up have lovely rooftop views. Shower and toilet are shared between the three rooms on each floor. A good indication of the mood of the place is that breakfast only happens from 9am (10am weekend). The top-floor apartment, for Fr.200, feels like home. ❸

Splendid Rosengasse 5 ☏ 044 252 58 50, ⓦ www.hotelsplendid.ch. Old-fashioned little one-star hotel on a central alley, with few facilities but a friendly welcome. ❷

Zic-Zac Marktgasse 17 ☏ 044 261 21 81, ⓦ www.ziczac.ch. Ordinary cheapie which has taken some marketing advice and reinvented itself as a "rock hotel", dubbing their modestly sized but brightly painted rooms the "Bryan Adams" or the "Pink Floyd". Lively atmosphere in the bar. ❷–❸

Zürich West

EasyHotel Zwinglistrasse 14 ☏ 0900 327 994, ⓦ www.easyhotel.com. Reliably good-value budget chain hotel. You get a tiny room with a double bed, a shower, toilet and washbasin, and one towel per person; everything else, including food, drinks, TV and housekeeping, costs extra. The neighbourhood is fascinating: on a short stroll you'll pass Indian and Thai restaurants, a Haitian bar, a Vietnamese takeaway, and more. ❶

Etap Technoparkstrasse 2 ☏ 044 276 20 00, ⓦ www.etaphotel.com. Budget international chain. Generic, functional rooms in the heart of the old industrial quarter, priced identically – and very low. Located alongside the *Ibis* and *Novotel* hotels, just behind the trendy Schiffbau arts centre. ❶

Rothaus Sihlhallenstrasse 1 ☏ 044 322 10 50, ⓦ www.hotelrothaus.ch. Decent two-star, newly renovated, with good facilities and a great location on a busy corner of the honky-tonk Langstrasse. Some larger rooms have balconies – and the top (fifth) floor includes a very affordable suite under the eaves with private terrace. ❷

Walhalla Limmatstrasse 5 ☏ 044 446 54 00, ⓦ www.walhalla-hotel.ch. Reasonable value in a useful but unromantic location, 50m behind the train station, with large, pleasantly decorated rooms. Cheaper rooms available in a nearby annexe. ❸–❹

X-tra Limmatstrasse 118 ☏ 044 448 15 95, ⓦ www.x-tra.ch. In the same building as the popular *X-tra* bar and nightclub (see p.382), just off the Limmatplatz in a young and lively part of town. Rooms are compact, but come with postmodern decor and all facilities. ❸

Mid-range hotels

In town

🏃 **Adler** Rosengasse 10 ☏ 044 266 96 96, ⓦ www.hotel-adler.ch. Fresh, light and pleasant three-star, offering hand-decorated rooms set right in the heart of the Niederdorf buzz above a famous restaurant. Service is good, the pastel interior is modern, and rates undercut similar places on the west bank. Weekend discounts. ❹

Altstadt Kirchgasse 4 ☎044 250 53 53, ⓦwww
.hotel-altstadt.ch. Appealingly simple rooms in a
decent small hotel in the Old Town lanes. Interiors
feature design and decor by a range of artists and
poets, and both the welcome and the facilities
match up. ④–⑤

Franziskaner Niederdorfstrasse 1 ☎044 250 53
00, ⓦwww.hotel-franziskaner.ch. Charming small
city hotel in classic style, with dark-wood decor
and a popular outdoor terrace on a square in the
heart of the Old Town. A little pricey for what you
get, but the top-floor rooms, sharing a spacious
rooftop terrace, are delightful. ⑤

Helmhaus Schifflände 30 ☎044 266 95 95,
ⓦwww.helmhaus.ch. Fine boutique-style four-star,
with a contemporary feel, insinuated into a historic
building by the river. Unfussy rooms, compact but
comfortable, are quiet, calm and pleasant. ⑤–⑥

Lady's First Mainaustrasse 24 ☎044 380 80 10,
ⓦwww.ladysfirst.ch. Upmarket designer hotel near
the lake south of the Opera House, with spacious,
airy singles and doubles displaying style and a good
attention to detail. Billed as "for dynamic women
and modern men". Spa, sauna and solarium; also
cosmetic and massage treatments. ⑤–⑥

Limmatblick Limmatquai 136 ☎044 254 60 00,
ⓦwww.limmatblick.ch. Small hotel directly on the
riverfront close to Central, with airy, contemporary-
styled rooms (some with balconies) that are good
value despite some traffic noise. ④

Rössli Rössligasse 7 ☎044 256 70 50, ⓦwww
.hotelroessli.ch. Super-chic choice on a quiet
Niederdorf lane. The spartan wood-and-stone
rooms with crisp white styling are spotless, and
service is friendly and attentive. ⑤

Seidenhof Sihlstrasse 9 ☎044 228 75 00,
ⓦwww.seidenhof.ch. Stylish three-star-superior

hotel in the shopping streets behind Bahnhofstrasse. Its days as a trading centre for silk (Seide
in German) have passed, but the rooms are airy
and uncluttered, and both the central location and
good onsite restaurant *Mishio* (see p.378) are
pluses. ⑤

Du Theatre Seilergraben 69 ☎044 267 26 70,
ⓦwww.hotel-du-theatre.ch. Rather elegant,
well-run design hotel with a sense of style, in a
convenient location just behind the main Central
square at the head of the Niederdorf. ④

Out of town

Uto Kulm Uetliberg ☎044 457 66 66, ⓦwww
.utokulm.ch. Hotel and restaurant atop the forested
Uetliberg ridge (see p.373), towering over the city
and lake from the west. Its chic, contemporary
rooms offer better value for money than similar
city-centre hotels, especially when you throw in the
tranquillity, the Alpine vistas and walking paths
nearby. Eight romantic suites feature oversized
circular bathtubs, balconies and – in the Tower
Suite – a separate conservatory. No cars: take the
train to Uetliberg, from where the hotel is a short
walk (luggage collection on request). ⑤–⑥

🏃 **Zürichberg** Orellistrasse 21 ☎044 268 35
35, ⓦwww.zuerichberg.ch. Comfortable,
attractive four-star, opened in 1899 in the wooded
hills east of the city. Now renovated with bright,
spacious rooms, most with balconies and all with
full facilities. Alongside is a low, curved annexe
sheathed in wood which has attracted much architectural acclaim; accessed only by a subterranean
corridor from the main building, it's designed
around an airy atrium and a cool, Guggenheim-
style elliptical interior ramp. All its rooms have
private balconies. Tram #6 to Zoo. ⑤–⑥

Expensive hotels

Baur au Lac Talstrasse 1 ☎044 220 50 20,
ⓦwww.bauraulac.ch. One of Zürich's oldest hotels,
in the same family since 1844, and recently
completely renovated. Set in a private park on the
lakeshore adjacent to Bahnhofstrasse, it fairly
shimmers with opulent grandeur. ⑨

Dolder Grand Kurhausstrasse 65 ☎044 456 60
00, ⓦwww.thedoldergrand.com. Zürich's most
famous luxury hotel – a nineteenth-century
turreted palace perched atop a hill overlooking the
city and newly expanded with a jaw-dropping
contemporary wing designed by Norman Foster.
Rooms, whether in the old building or the new,
breathe world-class elegance. ⑨

Kindli Pfalzgasse 1 ☎043 888 76 76, ⓦwww
.kindli.ch. A building dating from the sixteenth

century that has provided lodging since (at least)
1774, in a tranquil location on the steep cobbled
lanes below the Lindenhof. These days it's one of
Zürich's most charming small hotels, renovated
throughout. Rooms are not spacious (it only has a
three-star rating), but are full of character. ⑧

🏃 **Park Hyatt** Beethovenstrasse 21 ☎043
883 12 34, ⓦwww.hyatt.com. Zürich has
many upmarket hotels, but for all-round appeal this
classy hideaway is hard to beat. Occupying an
entire block in the heart of the city centre, midway
between Paradeplatz and the lake, the hotel wows
with contemporary-styled interiors, public areas
adorned with original art by Sol LeWitt (among
others), state-of-the-art technology and spacious,
amenity-packed rooms. ⑨

Storchen Weinplatz 2 ☏044 227 27 27, ⓦwww
.storchen.ch. A Zürich landmark – the only hotel
located directly on the riverfront, in the heart of the
Old Town. This is a romantic place to hole up, with
traditionally styled interiors, classic old-fashioned
service and stunning views of the Grossmünster
towers across the water. ❾

Widder Rennweg 7 ☏044 224 25 26, ⓦwww
.widderhotel.ch. On a quiet Old Town street, a row
of eight medieval houses has been gutted – at
a cost of Fr.100m – to make this innovative,
effortlessly classy hotel. The attention to detail,
both architecturally and in the interior decor, is
meticulous, and the array of several hundred single
malt whiskies in the bar – which also stages live
jazz – adds to the appeal. A great choice for its
cool elegance and contemporary design. ❾

The City

Because the River Limmat divides the **Old Town** into two distinct halves, it
makes more sense to consider the two banks of the river separately rather than
concentrate on a New Town/Old Town split.

The alleys of the east bank – known as **Niederdorf** or the "Dörfli" – are full
of cafés and small shops, with the enormous twin towers of the **Grossmünster**
as a centrepiece. The slender spire to the north belongs to the Predigerkirche
with, above it on a hill to the east, the grandiose architecture of the university.

Opposite, the **west bank** is the oldest part of the city, centred around the
raised platform of the **Lindenhof** and characterized by expensive fashion
outlets and offices. Nearby rise the graceful spires both of **St Peter's**, featuring
the largest clock face in Europe, and the **Fraumünster**, a medieval church
decorated in the last century with beautiful stained glass by Marc Chagall. The
long, curving **Bahnhofstrasse** follows the ancient course of the western city
wall, and is now one of Europe's most prestigious shopping streets, packed with
jewellers and designer boutiques.

The best of the city's clutch of **museums** are the Kunsthaus on the fringes of
the Niederdorf, and the Schweizerisches Landesmuseum (Swiss National
Museum) in a park on the west bank.

Zürich's festivals

Zürich's biggest party is August's massive **Street-Parade** (ⓦwww.street-parade.ch),
a tumultuous long weekend of floats, costumes, dancing in the streets and general
hedonism.

The **Sechseläuten** (ⓦwww.sechselaeuten.ch) is Zürich's spring festival, held on
the third Monday in April: the highlight is a costumed parade by the city's guilds. The
festival culminates with the burning of the Böögg – an effigy stuffed with fireworks
– on Sechseläutenplatz next to Bellevue, to symbolize the end of winter. Not long
after, Sechseläutenplatz is taken over by the regular month-long May residency of the
Swiss National Circus, **Circus Knie** (ⓦwww.knie.ch).

Zürich's February **Fasnacht** (Carnival) is a boisterous affair, fun if you happen to be
in the city. The July **Züri Fäscht** (ⓦwww.zuerifaescht.ch), held every three years (next
in 2010 and 2013), is worth making a diversion for, with the whole city throwing itself
into fairground revelry. The annual **Festspiele** (ⓦwww.zuercher-festspiele.ch) is a
festival of theatre, opera, music and art, held from late June into mid-July, with special
productions, concerts and exhibitions all over the city. Late August's **Theater-
spektakel** (ⓦwww.theaterspektakel.ch) packs out the city's stages. One evening in the
week before Christmas sees the **Lichterschwimmen**, a tradition of launching floating
candles from the Rathausbrücke onto the river, to the accompaniment of gingerbread
and *glühwein*.

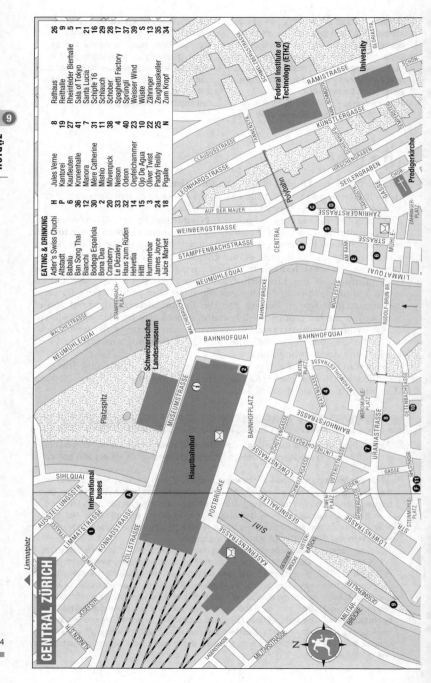

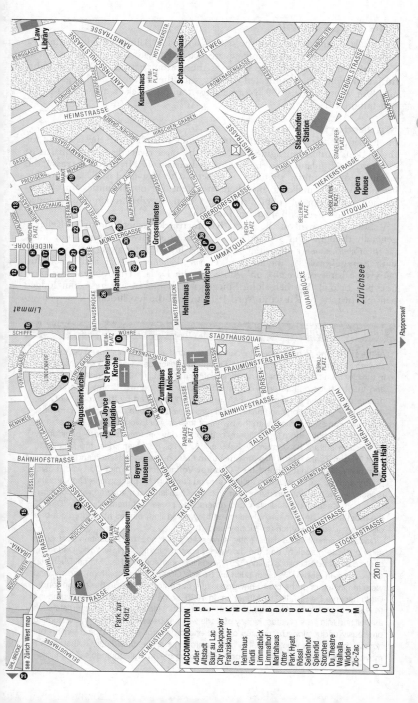

▶ Rapperswil

Limmat

Zürichsee

Law Library

Kunsthaus

Schauspielhaus

Stadelhofen Station

Opera House

Grossmünster

Rathaus

Helmhaus

Wasserkirche

St Peters-Kirche

Augustinerkirche

James Joyce Foundation

Zunfthaus zur Meisen

Fraumünster

Beyer Museum

Völkerkundemuseum

Tonhalle Concert Hall

Park zur Katz

see Zürich West map

ACCOMMODATION

Adler	H
Altstadt	P
Baur au Lac	T
City Backpacker	I
Franziskaner	K
G	N
Helmhaus	Q
Kindli	L
Limmatblick	E
Limmathof	B
Martahaus	D
Otter	S
Park Hyatt	U
Rössli	R
Seidenhof	F
Splendid	G
Storchen	O
Du Theatre	C
Walhalla	A
Widder	J
Zic-Zac	M

200 m

The east bank

It's a walk of only 100m from the station across the Bahnhofbrücke to the east bank of the Limmat and a large square bedecked with tram wires, known as **Central**. On one side of the square is the bottom station of the **Polybahn funicular**, which has connected the city with the university buildings on the hill 40m above since 1889. Normal city transport tickets are valid for the two-minute ride.

Niederdorf

From Central, the **Niederdorf** district stretches south along the riverside for about 1km. A more engaging walk than the busy riverside Limmatquai is to fork one block inland onto the narrow pedestrianized **Niederdorfstrasse**; the tackiness of its initial stretches – replete with fast-food stalls and lowlife beerhalls – soon mellows, and there are plenty of opportunities for absent-minded exploration of cobbled side-alleys, many of which open onto secluded courtyards adorned with medieval fountains.

A short way down on the left is **Rindermarkt**, where Gottfried Keller – generally thought of as Switzerland's national poet – lived (at no. 9) and drank (at the *Oepfelchammer* opposite; see p.380). A little further along, on the corner with **Spiegelgasse**, is the updated *Cabaret Voltaire* café–bar and arts centre (ⓦ www.cabaretvoltaire.ch), on whose site the Dada art movement was born (see box below). Further along Spiegelgasse is no. 14, where Lenin lodged before returning to Russia in April 1917 to lead the revolution.

Dada in Zürich

At the same time as both a pre-Revolution Lenin and a *Ulysses*-obsessed Joyce were staying in Zürich, a group of maverick European intellectuals was also seeking refuge in the city from the bloodshed and misery of World War I. In 1915, **Hugo Ball**, a writer and theatre director, had arrived from Munich with his partner **Emmy Hennings**, a dancer and singer. It seemed to them, as to many horrified by the brutality of war, that Western civilization had finally lost all reason; with a group of like-minded friends, they made an arrangement with the owner of the *Meierei* tavern at Spiegelgasse 1 to use the pub's back room for a "literary cabaret" to demonstrate the moral bankruptcy of Western culture. On Saturday, February 3, 1916, Ball, Hennings, the Romanian poet **Tristan Tzara**, **Hans Arp** (an artist from Franco-German Alsace), and a handful of other émigrés inaugurated the "Cabaret Voltaire" with a night of wild music, poetry and dance, intended to satirize art and literature by placing unreason against reason, anti-art against art. Later that year they published a magazine with contributions from Kandinsky, Modigliani and others, and presented themselves as "**Dada**", the most significantly meaningless name they could find, picked at random out of a dictionary (*dada* is French for "hobby-horse").

Dada's poignant absurdities aptly expressed the mood of dislocation and crisis seizing Western society, and the movement spread rapidly. In **New York**, Dada was centred at Alfred Stieglitz's gallery "291", meeting point for Man Ray, Marcel Duchamp and others. In **Berlin**, Dadaists such as George Grosz lampooned high society, and were the initiators of the brand-new technique of photomontage. In **the Netherlands**, Dada became *De Stijl*, led by Mondrian. In 1920, some of the Zürich Dadaists moved to **Paris** and there formed the Surrealist movement, which later attracted artists such as Dalí and Miró. The greatest legacy of Dada was its liberating influence in overturning previously unquestioned strictures of style and order, not only in art and writing but across society as a whole. What is both appropriate and extraordinary is that such a movement should have emerged from – of all places – neutral, bourgeois Zürich.

Niederdorfstrasse, which becomes **Münstergasse**, leads on to the **Grossmünster** and beyond, as Oberdorfstrasse, out to the open **Bellevueplatz**, dominated on its south side by the lavish opera house. A short distance up the hill to the left – by the main Rämistrasse or any of the back alleys (tiny **Trittligasse** is the most alluring) – lies the Kunsthaus (see p.369), while a pleasant walk south along the lake brings you after 1km to the Zürichhorn park.

The Grossmünster

With its distinctive twin sugar-loafed towers, and a venerable history at the heart of the Swiss-German Reformation, the **Grossmünster**, or Great Minster (daily 9am–6pm; Nov–Feb 10am–5pm; ⓦ www.kirche-zh.ch), dominates Zürich's skyline. In a tight-packed city of generally modest, small-scale architecture, it is dauntingly gigantic; and yet, caught half a millennium ago in the eye of a tight-lipped theological hurricane, its interior has been denuded of virtually all its decorative grandeur. Today it's as bare as a cellar inside, but the beauty – as the Reformers would have wanted – is all in its lofty austerity, and its associations. In twelve years preaching from the Grossmünster's pulpit in the sixteenth century, **Huldrych Zwingli**, a contemporary of Luther's and the initiator of the Reformation in Switzerland (see box, p.368), transformed Zürich from a sparsely populated hinterland town into a religious centre attracting students and theologians from around Europe. The sense of history in the church is compelling.

After its foundation by **Charlemagne** in the ninth century on a site of long-established religious significance (excavations suggest the existence of a **Roman** cemetery), the church was constructed in its present form between 1100 and 1230. At that time, the north tower was higher than its twin, since it held, and still holds, the bells. In the fifteenth century, the south tower was brought up to the same height and adorned on its south side with a statue of a seated Charlemagne. After a **fire** in 1763, the spires and upper sections of the towers were demolished, and reconstruction shortly after produced the Gothic belfries, watchrooms and octagonal cupolae which survive today. The fire also prompted **Baroque** alteration to the church interior; later centuries saw its original Romanesque character restored.

The building is skewed from the river bank, its broad front facing northwest. The most impressive approach is across paved **Zwingliplatz**, with the main North Portal featuring capitals adorned with animals, birds and, on the extreme left, a fiddle player. To the right, at the base of the North Tower, is a modern statue of Heinrich Bullinger, Zwingli's successor.

Inside, the overriding impression is of the loftiness of the galleried space and its austerity; aside from some **capitals** decorated with battle scenes – and, on the third pillar on the north side, Charlemagne's discovery of the graves of Felix and Regula – almost no decoration survives. The altar paintings were removed in 1524 at Zwingli's behest, as were the church treasures. Most decorative elements which survive today are replacements, including the pulpit (1851) and the organ (1960). The **stained-glass** windows were made in 1933 by Augusto Giacometti. It's worth ducking into the **crypt**, a long triple-aisled hall, the largest of its kind in Switzerland, dominated by the fifteenth-century statue of Charlemagne taken from the South Tower (the one up there now is a replica) and also featuring some well-preserved brush wall drawings dating from 1500. You can **climb** the 187 steps of the 62-metre South Tower for a spectacular view over the city (Mon–Sat 9.15am–5pm, Sun 12.30–5.30pm; Nov–March Mon–Sat 10am–4.30pm, Sun 12.30–4.30pm; Fr.2).

Huldrych Zwingli

At the vanguard of the Reformation, **Huldrych** (or Ulrich) **Zwingli** (1484–1531) is one of the most radical anti-establishment figures in European history, a dedicated and eloquent humanist who developed a passion for the liberty of individuals to decide the course of their lives free from the strictures of the past. He used his position of authority to undermine and reinvent the church's power structures, and died at 47 fighting for his cause.

Like his contemporary, **Martin Luther**, Zwingli came to his personal revolution through education, studying in Basel, Bern, Vienna and possibly Paris, and absorbing the humanist ideas of the Dutch philosopher Erasmus. After ten years as a pastor, his study of scripture led Zwingli to begin questioning the teachings of the Catholic Church; after 1518, when he was appointed to the Grossmünster, he began to develop his controversial ideas from the pulpit, proclaiming the sole authority of the word of God as revealed in the Bible and preaching against church practices. Zürich's congregation, democratically inclined and politically autonomous, was receptive. Barely a year had passed since Luther had nailed his 95 theses to the door of the Wittenberg church.

In 1523, with mounting tension fuelled by an increasingly vocal opposition to clerical celibacy, monasticism, the observance of Lent and the whole structure of papal control, Zwingli was summoned to a public disputation in Zürich with a papal representative. It says a great deal for Zwingli's powers of persuasion (and the city council's courage!) that Zürich's councillors came down on the side of their preacher. The papal representative returned to Rome the loser, and Mass was celebrated at the Grossmünster for the last time in 1525.

Zwingli's ideas spread rapidly, and by 1529 Bern, Basel and St Gallen had all embraced the Reformation. Opposition came from two sides: the Anabaptists, who wanted even more radical reform, and the Swiss "Forest Cantons" around Lake Lucerne that had taken up arms in loyalty to Rome. War broke out in 1531; Zwingli went into battle and was killed at Kappel.

Zwingli's lead in Zürich was followed by his son-in-law **Heinrich Bullinger**, but after 1536 the impetus for reform in Switzerland passed to **Jean Calvin**, a young preacher working in Geneva. Calvin initially followed Zwingli's doctrine, but then developed his own strict theology. Today, thanks in no small measure to the voyages of Calvinist Puritans to the New World, Calvin is much better-known than his predecessor, but it was the unsung Zwingli who paved the way, forging ideas of personal liberty, and using them to strike at the very heart of the institutionalized hierarchy that had been taken for granted throughout Europe for centuries.

To the right as you leave the Grossmünster onto Zwingliplatz is a door set into the wall of what was once the chapterhouse, now the university's Theological Institute. This gives into the atmospheric **cloister**, originally built in 1170–80, partly demolished in 1848 and renovated in the 1960s. Aside from strolling through the vaulted bays around a central garden, it's worth visiting to see the twelfth-century capitals and spandrels of the arched windows, decorated with grotesque faces, monkeys, dragons and centaurs.

The Wasserkirche and Helmhaus

Near the Grossmünster, down on the riverside, stands the beautiful late Gothic **Wasserkirche** (Wed 2–5pm, Sat noon–5pm), site of the martyrdom of Zürich's patron saints, Felix and Regula, but still used mostly for services. Alongside is the Baroque **Helmhaus** (guildhall), Limmatquai 31 (Tues–Sun 10am–6pm, Thurs until 8pm; free; Ⓦ www.helmhaus.org), now converted to an art gallery, staging temporary exhibits of mainly Swiss painting. This marks the Münsterbrücke, which leads across the river directly to the **Fraumünster** (see p.371).

The Kunsthaus

Five minutes' walk east up the hill from Bellevue is a square formally dubbed Heimplatz but known to every Zürcher as "Pfauen" (Peacocks), after the peacock statue over the famous Schauspielhaus theatre. The adjacent café was for decades known as the Pfauen Café, and was James Joyce's favourite watering hole; it still has a peacock as its inn sign.

Dominating the square is the **Kunsthaus**, Switzerland's finest gallery (Tues–Sun 10am–6pm, Wed–Fri until 8pm; Fr.14, free on Wed, temporary exhibits Fr.13–18 extra, but joint tickets are available, audioguide Fr.6; Ⓦwww .kunsthaus.ch). As well as a large permanent collection, the Kunsthaus hosts a continuous flow of top-flight temporary exhibitions.

The collection begins even before you get inside: beside the main door is **Rodin**'s vivid *Gate of Hell*, while sculptures by **Moore**, Maillol and others dot the grounds. Inside, most of the ground-floor galleries house whatever temporary exhibit is on, aside from one whole wing of the ground floor which is given over to a permanent display of the widest array of Alberto **Giacometti**'s sculpture in the world.

Elsewhere, you'll find Dutch and Flemish painting represented by **Rubens**, **Rembrandt**, **Hals** and others, the Venetian room showing **Canaletto** and **El Greco**, and canvases from the Italian and Dutch Baroque. There's a complex of rooms devoted mainly to Swiss artists of the nineteenth century, including many works by Anker, Böcklin, Segantini and **Füssli**, who lived and worked for many years in London. Only a tiny fraction of the massive **Graphische Sammlung**, comprising 80,000 graphic works, is on display at any one time.

The collection of twentieth-century art is stunning. A broad selection of pop, concrete and abstract expressionist art is headed by a number of works by **Warhol**, a **Rothko**, a gigantic wall-sized installation by Baselitz, geometric constructivist sculpture and works by Bacon and Twombly. A collection of French sculpture since Rodin is dominated, unusually, by **Matisse**. Cubism, Fauvism and **Dada** are all represented, and works by Miró, Dalí and De Chirico head an impressive **Surrealist** overview. **Picasso**, **Chagall** and **Kandinsky** are all represented, there are two of **Monet**'s most beautiful water-lily canvases, while **Van Gogh**, Gauguin, Cézanne and the largest **Munch** collection outside Scandinavia top an extraordinary journey. Last but not least is the rare chance to revel in the powerful, mystical landscapes of Alps and lakes by the Swiss painter Ferdinand **Hodler**.

At the university

If you follow Rämistrasse uphill from the Kunsthaus, you'll soon come to the university quarter. At Rämistrasse 73 is the **Archäologische Sammlung** (Archeological Collection; Tues–Fri 1–6pm, Sat & Sun 11am–5pm; free; Ⓦwww.archinst.uzh.ch), with a range of impressive pieces. Aside from the wealth of Etruscan ware, the most interesting artefacts come from the Middle East, with an entire case devoted to the stunning Egyptian Fayoum portraits from the first centuries BC–AD, wall-sized steles from ninth-century BC Nimrud (in modern Iraq), dozens of statuettes of ancient Egyptian deities and many Roman and Hellenic pieces. Close by, the **Graphische Sammlung der ETH**, Rämistrasse 101 (entrance on Karl Schmid-Strasse; Mon–Fri 10am–5pm, Wed until 7pm; free; Ⓦwww.gs.ethz.ch), houses thousands of woodcuts, etchings and engravings from all periods, particularly strong on Dürer, Rembrandt, Goya and Picasso.

Before you reach these, partway up Rämistrasse at the junction with Zürichbergstrasse stands the **university's law library** (Rechtswissenschaftliches

Institut; Ⓦwww.rwi.uzh.ch/bibliothek; Mon–Fri 8am–9pm, Sat 8am–5pm), at no. 74. Unremarkable from the street, it boasts a stunning modern interior, designed by architect **Santiago Calatrava** – a vast, six-storey interior atrium encircled by smooth curves and flooded with natural light. It is a cathedral-like space, hugely impressive to explore.

South to the Zürichhorn

The lakeside promenades running south from Bellevue are crowded with people all summer long, blading, strolling and chatting in the sunshine. Following them south brings you past the **Johann Jacobs Museum**, Seefeldquai 17 (Fri 2–7pm, Sat 2–5pm, Sun 10am–5pm; free; Ⓦwww.johann-jacobs-museum.ch), a mildly diverting place in an elegant lakeside villa, devoted to the cultural history of coffee. Selections of Rococo and Neoclassical porcelain ware, silver coffeepots, painting, prints and drawings are fleshed out by videos of TV coffee ads – and free coffee to drink.

Just beyond is the **Zürichhorn** park, a popular place for soaking up some sunshine that also boasts the fine *Heureka* sculpture by Jean Tinguely and a visually striking, but underwhelming, walled **Chinese garden** (April–Oct daily 11am–6pm; Ⓦwww.chinagarten-zuerich.ch), a gift from Zürich's twin city of Kunming, featuring a traditional zigzag bridge and pavilions, and the three symbolic species of pine, bamboo and cherry. The grand Zürichhorn Casino building has a popular terrace café for refreshments, and a jetty from where boats shuttle to and from Bürkliplatz. A couple of blocks inland from the Zürichhorn is the pleasant, open **Botanischer Garten**, Zollikerstrasse 107 (Mon–Fri 7am–7pm, Sat & Sun 8am–6pm; shorter hours in winter; tram #2 or #4 to Höschgasse; free; Ⓦwww.bguz.uzh.ch), a riot of colour in spring and summer, with three tropical planthouses and a café.

The west bank

Emerging on the south side of the station into hectic Bahnhofplatz, you're met by a statue of Alfred Escher, a prominent nineteenth-century politician and industrialist who is credited with single-handedly leading Zürich into the modern business age. In an inspired piece of statue placement, he gazes down **Bahnhofstrasse** (Ⓦwww.bahnhofstrasse-zuerich.ch), one of the most prestigious shopping streets in Europe and a fascinating counterpoint to the quaintness of the Niederdorf alleys. This is where all of Zürich comes to walk, snack and shop, whether to browse at the inexpensive department stores that crowd the first third of the street, or to sign away thousands on a Rolex watch or a Vuitton handbag at the understated super-chic boutiques further south. At no. 31, below the Beyer watch and jewellery shop, is the **Beyer Museum** (Mon–Fri 2–6pm; Fr.5; Ⓦwww.beyer-ch.com), filled with examples of timekeeping, from sundials and an ancient Egyptian water-clock onwards.

Two-thirds of the way along the boulevard is **Paradeplatz**, a tram-packed little square offering some of the best people-watching in the city. It's around here that the frippery retreats and Zürich's serious money begins: the streets off Paradeplatz are home to more financial institutions, insurance companies and top-name designer outlets than you could shake a stick at, as well as the headquarters of many Swiss banks.

Bahnhofstrasse ends at the unromantic, paved **Bürkliplatz**, departure point for all boat trips on the lake and boasting a fabulous view of Lake Zürich and its eastern "Gold Coast", named for the mansions and grandiose public buildings lining the shore that bask all summer long in the afternoon sunshine.

Around the Lindenhof

Between Bahnhofstrasse and the river lies the western portion of the Old Town; there are many picturesque alleys to explore here. Rennweg branches off Bahnhofstrasse, and a short walk left from it up the hill brings you to the **Lindenhof**, the oldest part of Zürich and site of a Roman customs post. The broad space is quiet now, occupied mostly by chess-playing old-timers, and gives a fine panorama over the rooftops. Down below, on the riverside, is the old quarter of **Schipfe**, once the centre of Zürich's silk industry, now known for artisans' shops and quiet little cafés. On the Lindenhof's other side, **Pfalzgasse** descends steeply into a dense network of cobbled lanes, where **Augustinergasse**, with its romantic oriel-windowed houses, leads to tiny Münzplatz overlooked by the beautiful **Augustinerkirche**, dating from 1274. Spare and simple inside, the church was secularized during the Reformation in 1524 and became the town's mint, but it was renovated and re-dedicated in the nineteenth century and is now used by the Christ Catholic Church (see p.200).

Nearby, the top floor of the Strauhof literary museum is home to the **James Joyce Foundation**, Augustinergasse 9 (Mon–Fri 10am–5pm; free; ⓦ www .joycefoundation.ch), which has a creaking library and reading room crammed with Joyceana. Joyce wrote *Ulysses* during his wartime exile in Zürich (1915–19); he returned in 1940, and died on January 13, 1941, laid to rest in Fluntern cemetery near the zoo, where there is now a statue of him. The Foundation can direct you to his various haunts around town, and they also hold regular open readings – free to all – from *Ulysses* (Tues 5.30–7pm) and *Finnegans Wake* (Thurs 4.30–6pm & 7–8.30pm).

Augustinergasse leads on to the **St Peters Kirche** (Mon–Fri 8am–6pm, Sat 10am–4pm, Sun 11am–5pm; ⓦ www.st-peter-zh.ch), dating from the thirteenth century but much altered in 1705. The fact that it boasts the largest clock face in Europe (8.7m in diameter; 1534) is less interesting than the unusual sight, above the pulpit amidst Baroque bas-relief, of the name of God in Hebrew lettering, legacy of the Reformers' desire to reclaim the fundamental sources of Christianity. A stepped alley adjacent to the church, **Thermengasse**, has a catwalk taking you over an excavated Roman baths. A short distance south is the Münsterhof, overlooked by the grand Baroque **Zunfthaus zur Meisen**.

The Fraumünster

The Münsterhof is dominated by the graceful, slender-spired **Fraumünster** (daily 10am–6pm, Nov–March closes 4pm; ⓦ www.fraumuenster.ch), a beautiful church boasting a breathtaking series of stained-glass windows by Marc Chagall and Augusto Giacometti that should not be missed.

It's not known when the church was founded, but on July 21, 853, King Ludwig the German signed over to his daughter Hildegard a convent which already stood on the site. In 874, Hildegard's sister Bertha consecrated what was probably a simple, towerless basilica, and built a crypt beneath to house the relics of **Felix and Regula**, Roman Christians and the patron saints of Zürich. During the eleventh century, the convent abbesses gained considerable rights, and the present structure was built during the thirteenth century. The convent was suppressed under Zwingli's Reformation, and in 1524 all the icons, ornaments and the organ were destroyed. During the following centuries, the minster became a place of worship for Veltliner and Huguenot refugees, was temporarily a Russian Orthodox church, and – between 1833 and 1844 – hosted both Catholic and Protestant services. There was much renovation during the twentieth century, and in 1967, **Marc Chagall** – then 80 – accepted the commission to make new stained glass for the five 10m-high windows of the Romanesque choir. The stunning artistry of the work he produced makes them one of the highlights of Zürich.

The Chagall windows

Entrance is into the transept through the small east door beneath the spire. The Romanesque **choir** dates from 1250–70; it is extremely high (18m) and has a simplicity of design that would make it a magical place even without its windows.

Chagall's blood-red "**Prophets**" window, on the north wall (left), features Elisha at the bottom watching Elijah mount to heaven in a chariot of fire; above, drenched in a divine blue, sits Jeremiah. The "**Law**" window, on the opposite wall, has Moses looking down upon the disobedience and suffering of the people, who are following a horseman into war. Below is Isaiah in the arms of a seraph, preparing to proclaim his message of peace to the world.

Of the three main windows, the left, known as the "**Jacob**" window, shows the patriarch's struggle with the angel and his dream of a ladder to heaven. The yellow "**Zion**" window on the right shows an angel trumpeting the beginning of eternity and the descent of New Jerusalem from the heavens; below are a radiant King David and Bathsheba. Finally, the central "**Christ**" window shows Joseph standing at the bottom beside a huge tree – the tree of life, and the family tree of Christ. Floating in its upper branches is a vision of Mary holding the baby Jesus with the Lamb of God at her feet. Scenes from Jesus' life and parables culminate in an associative depiction of the crucifixion; a cross is barely visible, and Christ is already floating free of the world.

Giacometti's 1940s work in the 9m-high window in the north transept, visible as you head out, is equally stunning. Were it not for the Chagall windows, this vision of God and Christ, with eight prophets below, and Matthew, Mark, Luke and John framed by ten angels, would take pride of place; as it is, it's doomed to play second fiddle.

West of Bahnhofstrasse

The shopping streets to the west, between Bahnhofstrasse and the River Sihl, hold little interest. Very near Pelikanplatz, in the **Park zur Katz** (Mon–Fri 7am–7pm, Sat & Sun 7am–6pm; shorter hours in winter) – once the city's botanical garden, and still boasting an octagonal glasshouse – is the **Völkerkundemuseum**, Pelikanstrasse 40 (Tues–Fri 10am–1pm & 2–5pm, Sat 2–5pm, Sun 11am–5pm; free; ⓦwww.musethno.uzh.ch), a highly acclaimed museum of non-European cultures. Not far away, at Selnaustrasse 25, the **Haus Konstruktiv** (Tues–Fri noon–6pm, Wed until 8pm, Sat & Sun 11am–6pm; Fr.14; ⓦwww.hauskonstruktiv.ch) hosts changing exhibits of concrete and constructivist art.

Swiss National Museum

Behind the train station, housed in a purpose-built mock-Gothic castle, is the **Schweizerisches Landesmuseum** (Swiss National Museum: Tues–Sun 10am–5pm, Thurs until 7pm; Fr.10; ⓦwww.musee-suisse.com). This massive building has a varied collection covering the range of Swiss history, though an ongoing programme of renovation work (due to last until 2013) means that various parts of the building may be off-limits when you visit.

Superbly presented, state-of-the-art displays on the history of Switzerland – divided into thematic areas, such as migration and religious history – as well as a "collections gallery" form the core of the permanent exhibitions: expect a welter of **sacred art** from the ninth to the sixteenth centuries, medieval **stained glass**, antique watches and clocks, fashion and design, many items of **militaria** and much more. In the **archeological collections**, one major highlight is a display of Roman gold treasure buried around 260 AD at Lunnern in the Zürich countryside and unearthed 1500 years later, including beautiful jewellery, figures and a stunning embossed golden bowl. But as much of a draw as the permanent displays are the continuing series of temporary shows – generally focused on Swiss themes and often innovative and absorbing.

Stretching behind the museum, the small, shady **Platzspitz** park (daily 6am–9pm), where the Sihl meets the Limmat, is a pleasant spot for a wander between the two rivers.

Museum Rietberg

The impressive **Museum Rietberg** (Tues–Sun 10am–5pm, Wed & Thurs until 8pm; Fr.12, plus about Fr.4 for any special exhibits; ⓦ www.rietberg.ch), set in a lush park southwest of the centre, houses a splendid collection of non-European art. Signs from the Rietberg stop on tram #7 direct you up into the park. Take the right-hand fork to reach the **Smaragd** (Emerald) building, a new wing in greenish glass; start downstairs with the Chinese and Japanese collections, including a splendid Han-dynasty bronze horse (room 2), colourful glazed figures from the eighth-century Tan dynasty (room 4) and a series of sixteenth-century Noh theatre masks (room 11). Opposite stands the grandiose **Villa Wesendonck**, where the composer Richard Wagner lived for a time in 1857, housing Buddhist art from India and Pakistan, including a stunning four-armed dancing Shiva in bronze, surrounded by a ring of fire (room 28). Indian painting and a small Persian collection – including exquisite calligraphy – is displayed in the **Park-Villa Rieter**, a smaller building that lies a short walk away across the park.

Above Zürich – Uetliberg

One of the best short trips out of the city is to the hill of **Uetliberg**, a twenty-minute train ride away and a favoured getaway for the locals to do a spot of sledding (winter) or picnicking (summer). Uetliberg is also one end of a popular hiking route, running about two hours south along a forested ridge overlooking the lake to Felsenegg, from where a cable car can deliver you 300m down to Adliswil village to catch a train back to Zürich. Swiss Pass and ZürichCARD holders travel free; otherwise, press *131 on the ticket machine for an all-inclusive day-pass ("AlbisTageskarte") or 8138 for a ticket to Uetliberg only.

From Zürich HB, S-Bahn **trains** depart at least every half-hour to Uetliberg. At the tiny end station, an information hut stocks a free hiking map of the area identifying plenty of short and long trails. The trail which begins at Uetliberg station is dubbed the *Planetenweg* (Planet Path), and features models of the planets on a scale of 1:1 billion, with the distances between them also to scale. From the station, it's about a ten-minute walk uphill to the **summit**, passing the Sun, Mercury, Venus, Earth and Mars on the way; Pluto is about 5km away at Felsenegg.

From the top of the summit's 30m viewing tower, which boosts your altitude to 900m, there are terrific 360-degree views over Zürich, the whole curve of the lake and, on a clear day, east into Austria and as far southwest as the Jungfrau. Also on the summit is the *Uto Kulm* hotel (see p.362) and **restaurant**, a handy spot for refreshment. The panoramic walking route from *Uto Kulm* to Felsenegg and beyond passes another couple of restaurants. A **cable car** (daily: May–Sept 8am–10pm; Oct–April 9am–8pm) runs every fifteen minutes between Felsenegg and Adliswil, from where it's a short walk to Adliswil train station.

Zürich West

For a clean break from the sometimes overly packaged Zürich of cobbled alleys, medieval guildhalls and glitzy shopping, you need to head west. The new home of the city's underground is the residential and post-industrial area comprising the postal districts of 8004 (*Kreis 4*) and 8005 (*Kreis 5*), together known as **Zürich West**.

The north–south artery of **Langstrasse** is where the daily dramas are played out, a sometimes seedy but absorbing 1.5-kilometre-long strip of designer bars, independent cinemas, clubwear outlets and cheap eateries. Trams #2 or #3 to Bezirksgebäude deliver you to the southern end of Langstrasse around **Helvetiaplatz**, relaxed home of the *Xenix* bar and cinema. Strolling north, the street narrows and the mood changes. This was once Zürich's red-light

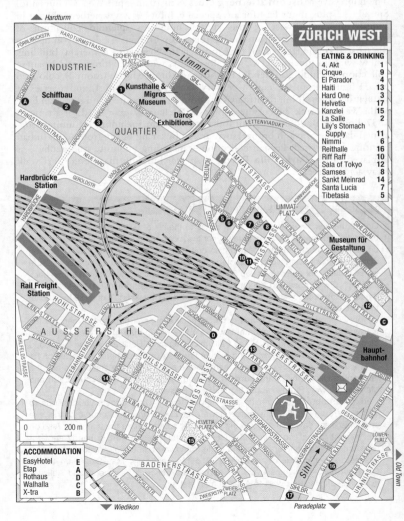

▲ Hardturm

ZÜRICH WEST

INDUSTRIE-

Schiffbau

Kunsthalle & Migros Museum

Daros Exhibitions

QUARTIER

Hardbrücke Station

Rail Freight Station

AUSSERSIHL

Museum für Gestaltung

Haupt-bahnhof

EATING & DRINKING

4. Akt	1
Cinque	9
El Parador	4
Haiti	13
Hard One	3
Helvetia	17
Kanzlei	15
La Salle	2
Lily's Stomach Supply	11
Nimmi	6
Reithalle	16
Riff Raff	10
Sala of Tokyo	12
Samses	8
Sankt Meinrad	14
Santa Lucia	7
Tibetasia	5

ACCOMMODATION

EasyHotel	E
Etap	A
Rothaus	D
Walhalla	C
X-tra	B

0   200 m

N

▼ Wiedikon

Paradeplatz ▼

Old Town ▲

district; the unpleasantness has departed and in its place has developed a downmarket ethnic and social mix that is a universe away from the homogeneous collection of expensive suits and fur coats parading the Bahnhofstrasse not 1km east: lowlife bars rub shoulders with avant-garde galleries, smells of greasy kebabs mix with wood-fired pizza and marijuana, and the whole street is a mingle of Swiss-German voices with French-African, Portuguese, Turkish, Balkan, Latin American, Haitian and more.

Two-thirds of the way along, Langstrasse dips beneath the train tracks; the style north of the underpass is different again, with residential side-streets increasingly attracting artists and creative types who have, in turn, spawned plenty of hip bars, high-quality restaurants and designer boutiques on and off the stretch leading to the major **Limmatplatz** junction (served by trams #4 and #13). A short walk east, set amongst streets packed with independent galleries and design studios, is the **Museum für Gestaltung**, Ausstellungsstrasse 60 (Design Museum; Tues–Thurs 10am–8pm, Fri–Sun 10am–5pm; Fr.12; Ⓦwww.museum-gestaltung.ch), with exhibits relating to design, the visual arts, advertising and the media.

The Industrie-quartier

More interest lies in wandering the streets west of Limmatplatz; from here all the way out to the football stadium at Hardturm is the old **industrial quarter**, still largely unreclaimed. Trains and heavy traffic pass on viaducts way above the roofs of working depots, old factories and business parks, while in between thrives a lively subculture focused on industrial spaces reclaimed as galleries and restaurants, and anonymous-looking bunkers that double as some of Zürich's best clubs.

West of the rail viaduct off Ottostrasse stands the old Löwenbräu brewery, a vast brick building at Limmatstrasse 268–270, that now houses, aside from five small galleries and an art bookshop, the acclaimed contemporary-art shows of the **Kunsthalle** (Tues–Fri noon–6pm, Sat & Sun 11am–5pm; Fr.8; Ⓦwww.kunsthallezurich.ch), the **Migros Museum für Gegenwartskunst** (Contemporary Art; same hours; Fr.8; Ⓦwww.migrosmuseum.ch) and **Daros Exhibitions** (Thurs–Sun noon–6pm; Fr.8; Ⓦwww.daros.ch).

Close by is the busy **Escher-Wyss-Platz**, its swirl of cars, bikes, buses and trams smothered by a traffic overpass: high overhead, stressed-out city-centre workers speed home to the suburbs, while down at street level locals relax in the clutch of trendy bars and cafés on and off Hardstrasse. Signed just off the street is perhaps the city's most impressive architectural space, the **Schiffbau**, a huge plant which once produced ship parts; now, with bare concrete largely left unadorned and heavy machinery still hanging in the ceiling, it houses, in its various sectors, two drama stages of the Schauspielhaus, *Moods* jazz club and *LaSalle*, one of the city's best restaurants. It's open for exploration throughout the day.

You can get back to Zürich HB either on tram #4 or #13 from Escher-Wyss-Platz, or by train from Hardbrücke station, located 300m south of the Schiffbau.

Eating and drinking

As you might expect from a city like Zürich, there's a wealth of **eating and drinking** possibilities, with as much available citywide at the bottom end of the market as at the top.

All the places reviewed here are **keyed on the maps** – either of the city (p.358), the central area (p.364) or Zürich West (opposite).

Cafés

Zürich has an enormous variety of **cafés**, with any number of places all through the **Niederdorf** alleys where you can sit and watch the world go by over a coffee or glass of beer. Don't stick – as many visitors do – to the slightly seedy cafés along Niederdorfstrasse itself; Zürich's most alluring café culture takes place further south, at the pavement cafés along the riverside Limmatquai and the cobbled squares, such as Hechtplatz and Schiffländeplatz, that open onto it.

The west bank of the river, **around Bahnhofstrasse**, is less of a draw, not least because this is shopping territory: long expanses of shop windows don't make the streets especially amble-friendly, although a bit of poking around in the old-town alleys between Bahnhofstrasse and the river can turn up trumps.

Niederdorf

Altstadt Kirchgasse 4 ⓦ www.hotel-altstadt.ch. Cool, jazzy café-bar, open from breakfast time onwards, that's gaining a reputation as an Old Town meeting point.

Odeon Limmatquai 2 ⓦ www.odeon.ch. Compact café-bar on Bellevueplatz, where Lenin once sat and watched the world go by. There's little sign of revolutionary activity these days – although the bar prices would spark a popular uprising anywhere other than Zürich.

Rathaus In the Rathaus on Limmatquai. Pleasant place with comfy chairs and sofas on an outside terrace alongside the old Town Hall, sandwiched neatly between the river and the Limmatquai trams.

Schlauch Münstergasse 20 (upstairs). Quiet, friendly and relaxed diner-bar, perfect to catch your breath after the Niederdorf scrum. Sizeable plates of organic, health-conscious food (veggie and not), and a snooker hall adjacent, attract a young, vaguely alternative crowd. Closed Sun & Mon.

Schober Napfgasse 4. A very popular confectioner's and café, famous for its hot chocolate but also serving coffee and cakey creations throughout the day.

Zähringer Zähringerplatz 11 ⓦ www.cafe -zaehringer.ch. Long-standing cooperative-run bastion of Zürcher counterculture, attracting an alternative clientele for snacks, herbal teas and beer. Mon 6pm–midnight, Tues–Sun 9am–midnight.

Around Bahnhofstrasse

Juice Market Augustinergasse 42. Pleasant little café on a quiet alley off the main shopping streets around Bahnhofstrasse – perfect for a reviving juice, coffee or light bite. Unusually it stays open late, morphing on Fridays and Saturdays after 8pm into a champagne bar with a DJ.

Mövenpick Paradeplatz 4. Perfect people-watching café, with a great selection of teas and coffees from around the world, plus snacks and full meals all day long.

Schipfe 16 Schipfe 16. Attractive little terrace café gazing out across the river (and, intriguingly, run by the city council as a way to help unemployed people back into work). Stop by for a coffee or a beer, or fill up on a light lunch of well-prepared, inexpensive home cooking.

Sprüngli Bahnhofstrasse 21 ⓦ www .confiserie-spruengli.ch. Main branch of the world-famous confectioner's, in this location since 1859, displaying cabinets full of exquisite chocolates and cakes, plus their own speciality, *Luxemburgerli*, cream-filled pastry bites that are truly drool-worthy. Enjoy it all in the upstairs café-patisserie overlooking Paradeplatz, the city's most atmospheric tearoom, where Zürich's ladies come to gossip discreetly over coffee and cake. Free chocolate with every espresso.

Restaurants

Traditional Zürich cuisine is rich and heavy with meat, epitomized in the city's trademark dish *Züri Gschnetzlets* – diced veal in a creamy mushroom sauce, generally served alongside *Rösti*. There's a host of good-quality **restaurants** in every corner of the city that can do you a filling lunch for Fr.20, or a full evening meal for roughly twice that; Niederdorf is shoulder to shoulder with them. As a general rule, the area around Bahnhofstrasse is livelier than Niederdorf at lunch time, while in the evening the reverse is true. There's also no shortage of expensive places, where you'd be lucky to come away with change from Fr.75 per person, and are probably looking at almost twice that for a full meal.

Mountain excursions

Although it barely needs saying, the Swiss mountains are sensationally beautiful. Few visitors leave without journeying to at least one summit during their stay – and, fortunately, peaks all across the country are easily accessible to non-mountaineers, thanks to a network of mountain railways and cable cars.

The Cardada cable car, Locarno ▲

Piz Gloria restaurant at the Schilthorn summit ▼

Descending funicular, Muottas Muragl ▼

Wherever you start from, it's rarely more than a couple of hours' journey to the mountains. Almost all regions have some means of getting to the top of at least one local peak, and even relatively unsung Swiss summits can offer breathtaking panoramic views.

The experience of being effortlessly lifted out of everyday life into the high mountains – a world of fresh air and bright colour, clear sunlight pouring from saturated blue skies, pure, cool lakes and the uncluttered landscapes above the tree line – is powerful and extraordinary. You might find that it's the most memorable part of your trip. And with the smoothness and efficiency of Swiss public transport, the journey is often as good as the destination.

Most mountains that can be accessed by public transport also feature at least one summit restaurant or terrace café; often, there are several to choose from. These tend to be popular getaways: if you're seeking solitude and tranquillity, you generally have to hike away from the summit station, or choose a mountain where the only means of reaching the top is shanks's pony.

Timetable practicalities

The online timetable Ⓦwww.rail.ch gives timings for every train, bus, boat, funicular, cable car, gondola and chairlift in the country, displaying detailed information on connections between each.

Fares – except on the flagship tourist routes such as to the Jungfraujoch or the Titlis – aren't excessive, and are usually discounted if you hold a Swiss travel pass: 25–50 percent is common.

Where printed timetables or station noticeboards don't show exact timings (often because cable cars or chairlifts run continuously), they at least note the first ascent (Bergfahrt, montée, salita) in the morning, the frequency of service throughout the day, and the final descent (Talfahrt, descente, discesa) in the evening.

On the highest peaks you may have to leave the top station in mid-afternoon, say 3–4pm, if you want to reach the valley without having to hike or ski part or all of the way down.

▲ View of Lauterbrunnen in the Bernese Oberland

▼ Walking near the Matterhorn

▼ Igloo village, Gornergrat

Ten classic mountain excursions

The following is a selection of ten of the best mountain journeys Switzerland has to offer. Most of these journeys do not operate outside high season – for details, see p.27. Some advice about planning walks in the mountains is given on p.49, while p.508 has information on Alpine flora and fauna.

The Albula railway p.432. This incredibly well-engineered section of track – also followed by the Glacier Express panoramic train – links St Moritz with the gorges and ravines of central Graubünden via a high pass route.

The Bernina railway p.421. Another superb train ride from St Moritz, over the ice-bound Bernina Pass and down into Italy.

Cardada p.476. Mountain station above Locarno: within minutes, you can leave the lakeside bustle behind for the cool pine forests on the slopes above.

Gornergrat p.302. A rack-railway from Zermatt that crawls its way up impossible slopes to view the Alpine giants close-up.

Jungfraujoch p.250. Flagship tourist route from Interlaken up to Europe's highest train station, at 3454m.

Klausen Pass p.413. Unsung pass road (open summer only) between Uri and

View around Mürren, in the Bernese Oberland ▲

Glarus, above Lake Lucerne, which offers a magnificent drive through classic Swiss scenery.

Klein Matterhorn p.301. Perhaps Switzerland's best cable car; a heart-stopping ride in several stages above Zermatt, ending at a fairy-tale razor-edge peak at 3900m – Europe's highest cable-car station, set opposite the mesmeric Matterhorn.

Muottas Muragl p.454. Of the many high-altitude rides above St Moritz, this is perhaps the best – a viewpoint lower than most, but with inch-perfect positioning on a crag facing directly along the funnel of the beautiful Engadine valley, threaded with lakes and forests and flanked by the tallest peaks in the eastern Alps.

Schilthorn p.244. Superbly scenic cable-car trip above Interlaken – quicker, cheaper and more spectacular than the Jungfraujoch.

Schynige Platte p.239. Another outstanding route from Interlaken, by rack-railway up to all-round panoramic views over lakes, towns and mountains.

Mountain transport terms

▶▶ **Cable car** Seilbahn or Luftseilbahn, téléphérique, funivia.
▶▶ **Chairlift** Sesselbahn, télésiège, seggiovia.
▶▶ **Draglift** Schlepplift, téléski, sciovia.
▶▶ **Funicular** Standseilbahn, funiculaire, funicolare.
▶▶ **Gondola** Gondelbahn, télécabine, cabinovia.
▶▶ **Mountain transport network** Bergbahnen, remontées mécaniques, impianti di risalita.
▶▶ **Rack-railway** Zahnradbahn, chemin de fer à crémaillère, ferrovia della cremagliera.

Niederdorf and east bank

Adler's Swiss Chuchi Rosengasse 10
☎044 266 96 96, ⓦwww.hotel-adler.ch.
Landmark Swiss restaurant on Niederdorf's main
drag below the *Adler* hotel, freshly renovated in
bright, modern style. Good-value fondue or raclette
(around Fr.30) are what to go for; the bargain lunch
specials have a careful, home-cooked touch as
well, but cheese is the thing – you'll sniff the place
before you see it. Booking essential.

Ban Song Thai Kirchgasse 6 ☎044 252 33 31,
ⓦwww.bansongthai.ch. One of the city's better
Thais, small and pleasant with a varied menu.
Lunch specials start from Fr.18, evening meals
more than twice that. Closed Sat lunch & Sun.

Blinde Kuh (literally "Blind Cow", German for Blind
Man's Buff), Mühlebachstrasse 148 ☎044 421 50
50, ⓦwww.blindekuh.ch. Remarkable restaurant
offering the unique experience of dining in
darkness: after the foyer (there are lights here and
in the toilets), you're led into the pitch-dark dining
room where you literally can't see a thing. The
business is run as a way for sighted folk to sample
the experience of losing their sight for a couple of
hours. The menus (one meat, one fish and one
vegetarian, all moderately priced) change each
week. All the waiters are blind or partially sighted.
It's a popular place: book well ahead. Open every
evening; also Wed–Fri for lunch.

Bodega Española Münstergasse 15 ☎044 251
23 10. Small dark-wood place, dripping with
atmosphere, that's been here since 1892,
concealed from the street behind its attached wine
shop. Upstairs is the restaurant, with a long menu
ranging from *tortilla catalana* to an unmissable
paella (around Fr.45 for two). The buzzing tapas bar
downstairs is also outstanding, with a huge range
from about Fr.5.

Le Dézaley Römergasse 7 ☎044 251 61 29,
ⓦwww.le-dezaley.ch. Excellent Swiss-French
restaurant nestling in a quiet alley at the foot of
the Grossmünster's north tower. House specialities
are pricey Vaudois dishes such as *fondue
bourguignonne* (with a cellarful of Vaudois wines
to boot), but there are many inexpensive options
available. Interior decor is attractive, and there's
also a lovely little courtyard garden. Closed Sun.

Kantorei Neumarkt 2 ☎044 252 27 27, ⓦwww
.restaurant-kantorei.ch. Pleasant, award-winning
lounge-style restaurant, occupying a 600-year-old
building in a little-visited part of the Old Town and
serving unpretentious, but excellently prepared,
modern Swiss cuisine. Doubles as a tranquil café
between mealtimes.

Mère Catherine Nägelihof 3 ☎044 250 59 40,
ⓦwww.commercio.ch. Pleasant little place in a
hard-to-find courtyard below the Grossmünster,
brightly done up and touting itself as *"un peu
provençal"* – salads and seafood are the main
draw, with especially good *bouillabaisse*. Menus
change monthly.

Santa Lucia Marktgasse 21 ☎044 262 36 26,
ⓦwww.santalucia.ch. Simple Niederdorf Italian with
a wide selection of good-value pasta and pizza, plus
the bonus of late-night service until 2am.

Spaghetti Factory Niederdorfstrasse 5 ☎044 251
94 00, ⓦwww.spaghettifactory.ch. Straightforward
pasta restaurant in the heart of the Niederdorf
buzz, good and cheap. Daily until after midnight.
Also at Schifflände 6, behind Hechtplatz.

Weisser Wind Oberdorfstrasse 20 ☎044 251 18
45, ⓦwww.weisserwind.ch. Comfortable, traditional setting for Italian and Swiss specialities, with
plenty of vegetarian options, for around Fr.25–35. A
beerhall in all but name. Closed Sat lunch & Sun.

Around Bahnhofstrasse

Bona Dea Bahnhofplatz 15 ☎044 217 15 15,
ⓦwww.bona-dea.ch. Fine vegetarian buffet restaurant attached to the main train station, with a wide

---

Cheap eats

Zürich offers a wealth of places to **eat cheaply** and reasonably well. *Manora*, on the
fifth floor of the Manor department store at Bahnhofstrasse 75 (Mon–Fri 9am–8pm,
Sat 9am–5pm), has good, balanced self-service meals of all kinds from Fr.13
upwards. All along Niederdorfstrasse are dozens of hole-in-the-wall snack joints
churning out kebabs, falafels, sausages, noodles and/or chips, from about Fr.10; you
can often do better with the daily special (around Fr.14) at one of the beerhalls on the
same street. In the train station, in addition to the good-value *Nordsee* fish diner
opposite the tourist office (full meals from Fr.14; take-away available; ⓦwww
.nordsee.de), check out the stand-up *Suan Long*, on the lower shopping level (daily
11am–9.30pm), which does filling Asian dishes, veggie and otherwise, for Fr.14–18.

9

ZÜRICH | Eating and drinking

www.roughguides.com

choice of dishes. Note that, despite the location, this is a dainty, upmarket kind of place (and priced accordingly: expect Fr.40 and upwards).

Hiltl Sihlstrasse 28 ☎044 227 70 00, ⓦwww.hiltl.ch. Top-quality vegetarian restaurant, a city institution since 1898 but now completely renovated with bright decor, calm, friendly service and excellent food. Sample the à la carte options, or plump for the expansive and great-value hot and cold buffet; even if you don't eat, this is a great, buzzy place to bag a corner table for a spot of people-watching over a cappuccino.

Mishio Sihlstrasse 9 ☎044 228 76 76, ⓦwww .mishio.ch. Their shoutline says it all: "Casual Asian Dining". This is a great find – a simple, bright, informal restaurant serving fresh-cooked Asian food for business people (and shoppers) in a hurry: think satay and spring rolls, simple wok stir-fries, green curry, pad Thai, chow mein – everything fresh, well spiced, delicious and not expensive (mains Fr.22–30). Closed Sun.

Ojo De Agua Oetenbachgasse 13 ☎044 210 47 00, ⓦwww.ojodeagua.ch. Another great find – an atmospheric little wood-floored wine-bar, selling only Argentinian wines, which doubles as a tiny restaurant, setting out six tables at which to tuck into prime organic Argentinian beef – roast, tartar, carpaccio, entrecôte, you name it. Red meat, red wine and red-blooded tango to accompany: an unbeatable combination. Closed Sat eve & Sun.

Zeughauskeller Bahnhofstrasse 28a at Paradeplatz ☎044 211 26 90, ⓦwww .zeughauskeller.ch. A wood-ceilinged room dating from the fifteenth century, that's now the city's top beerhall, a sometimes chaotic place serving hearty meat dishes and plenty of the amber nectar. One of the most extensive sausage menus around – over a dozen different varieties, served with onion sauce and fresh potato salad – is crowned by a one-metre giant (around Fr.85) that should keep four people occupied for some time. Although the menu is in English (and ten other languages), this place is still very popular with Zürchers of a certain bank balance – a long way from the rough-and-ready beerhalls of Niederdorf.

Zum Kropf In Gassen 16 ☎044 221 18 05, ⓦwww.zumkropf.ch. An atmospheric listed building, boasting a frescoed interior which dates from its conversion into a restaurant in 1888, and which stands a little askance with the solid *bürgerliche* cooking on offer: Bacchic revels may be erupting all around, but only in picture form on the ceiling. Meat, potatoes and dumplings in various forms, along with tripe, are staples, and yet standards are high and the food is never dull. Closed Sun.

Zürich West

Cinque Langstrasse 215 ☎044 272 46 30, ⓦwww.restaurant-cinque.ch. Upmarket local Italian restaurant on a busy corner. A cosy place – think wood panelling and bookshelves – in which to sample excellent pastas, *ossobuco*, grilled cuttlefish and the like. Expect well over Fr.60 a head. Closed Sat lunch & Sun.

El Parador Luisenstrasse 43 ☎043 366 88 85, ⓦwww.elparador.ch. Acclaimed Spanish restaurant in a residential area, on the quiet corner with Heinrichstrasse, with a small, select menu of authentic dishes. Food is expertly prepared – the *paella* and *crema catalana* are both spot on – but don't expect to pay less than about Fr.60 a head. Closed Sat lunch & Sun.

Lily's Stomach Supply Langstrasse 197 ☎044 440 18 85, ⓦwww.lilys.ch. Clean, modern place in the heart of the Langstrasse district, always busy, churning out authentic Asian dishes fresh-cooked in the open kitchen – anything from Tamil chicken curry or Pakistani *panji renga* to Japanese *yaki soba*, Thai noodles or *hong shao tofu* (mains around Fr.19–23), washed down with Filipino beer. Seating is at long, communal tables with benches. Closed Sun lunch.

Nimmi Josefstrasse 137. Friendly neighbourhood Sri Lankan/South Indian café and curry house, in a residential quarter: stop in for utterly authentic veg and non-veg curries of all kinds, including *dosa* and delectable *Kottu Rotti* – bread and meat fried with onions and chillies. Prices are low: Fr.20 will cover it.

Reithalle Gessnerallee 8 ☎044 212 07 66, ⓦwww.restaurant-reithalle.ch. Formerly the military riding school, this complex of buildings along the Sihl has been turned into a theatre and centre for performing arts, with one long stone-floored hall serving as a combination bar and restaurant. It attracts a lively and eclectic crowd of twenty-somethings with a varied menu of light, modern dishes (many vegetarian), and a relaxed, share-a-table attitude. On Saturday nights they crank up the music for late-night dancing.

Samses Langstrasse 231 ☎044 440 13 13, ⓦwww.samses.ch. Rather trendy vegetarian café-restaurant, sporting crimson walls and candles on the tables. The food is fresh and delicious – pasta staples filled out with wild rice salads, tofu and a daily veggie buffet priced around Fr.4 per 100g (they weigh your plate at the till). Closed Sat lunch & Sun.

Sankt Meinrad Stauffacherstrasse 163 ☎043 534 82 77, ⓦwww.sanktmeinrad.ch. A fine, innovative young team is busy working wonders at this small

restaurant devoted to Swiss specialities with a contemporary twist – beef with lavender, ravioli of Alpine cheese with mushroom foam, venison smoked over birch chips, and so on. A seven-course set menu comes in at Fr.130; otherwise, mains are roughly Fr.55–65. Not easy to find, hidden away in a residential neighbourhood (tram #8 to Bäckeranlage) – but well worth hunting down. Closed Sat lunch, all day Sun & Mon, and Tues lunch.
Santa Lucia Luisenstrasse 31, corner Josefstrasse ⊕044 272 58 93, ⓦwww.santalucia.ch. Bright,

airy Italian on a quiet residential street, with a wood-fired pizza oven and excellent fresh pasta. The friendly, accommodating service makes it popular with the locals. Daily until midnight.
Tibetasia Quellenstrasse 6 ⊕044 271 20 30, ⓦwww.tibetasia.ch. Authentic, much-loved Tibetan restaurant in residential Zürich West, offering mid-priced specialities such as *Yak Momo* (dumplings filled with yak meat and tomato chutney), in amongst more familiar Thai dishes. Closed Sat lunch, Sun, Mon evening.

Expensive restaurants

Bianchi Limmatquai 82 ⊕044 262 98 44, ⓦwww.ristorante-bianchi.ch. A busy, rather posh Italian – prices reflect the high quality of the food. Seafood is a speciality: plump for *risotto ai frutti di mare, gamberoni, spaghetti alle vongole* or fish – both sea fish and local catch-of-the-day. Expect a meal to remember, but a bill over Fr.70 a head.
Haus zum Rüden Limmatquai 42 ⊕044 261 95 66, ⓦwww.hauszumrueden.ch. Splendid thirteenth-century riverside *Zunfthaus* (guildhall), complete with vaulted ceiling and late Gothic decor; book in advance for a window table. The food covers most of the standard Zürich bases – plenty of meat and rich sauces, including the famous *Züri Gschnetzlets*, prepared with care and skill. Bank on Fr.100 a head. Closed Sat & Sun.
Hummerbar In *Hotel St Gotthard*, Bahnhofstrasse 87 ⊕044 227 76 21, ⓦwww.hummerbar.ch. A romantic place for *Hummer* (lobster) and a host of other seafood (including Iranian caviar), all flown in fresh daily and prepared in pristine style for consumption amidst a formal, *fin-de-siècle* setting. Prices – compared with others under this heading – are reasonable, but who's counting when you're contemplating fresh oysters? Lobster and seafood speciality mains are around Fr.90. Closed Sun & Mon.
Kronenhalle Rämistrasse 4 ⊕044 262 99 00, ⓦwww.kronenhalle.com. Despite the impressive array of the twentieth century's great and good who've licked their chops appreciatively here, the ambience of this classically grand place, bedecked with original Picassos, Matisses and Braques, remains amiable rather than stiff. (With at least one hors d'oeuvre on the menu over Fr.100, they can afford to be amiable.) The cuisine is outstanding but undramatic – there's little on the menu that you won't have seen before – but where the place scores is in its down-to-earth attitude to those who decide to spurn the champagne and truffles in favour of enjoying the atmosphere over a sausage and a glass of beer instead. A classic Zürich restaurant: discreet and hearty.

LaSalle In Schiffbau building, off Hardstrasse ⊕044 258 70 71, ⓦwww.lasalle-restaurant.ch. Amazing place set within a huge glass cube on the factory floor of the old Schiffbau (see p.375); you eat beneath a giant glowing Murano chandelier suspended on high. It's far from downmarket, though – all white table-cloths and silver service – and is a breath of fresh air after the stuffiness of traditional city-centre restaurants. The modern European cuisine is outstanding (Fr.70 or so per head), but the surroundings are just as alluring as the food. Unmissable, whether you come to gawp or dine. Closed Sat & Sun lunch.
Sala of Tokyo Limmatstrasse 29 ⊕044 271 52 90, ⓦwww.sala-of-tokyo.ch. You'd never know it, but this dowdy, anonymous building at the station end of a busy traffic street hides one of Switzerland's best Japanese restaurants. Prices are very high (roughly Fr.90 for lunch, Fr.150 in the evening), but the quality of the traditional cuisine, using the freshest of ingredients, is outstanding. Closed Sat lunch, Sun & Mon; also late July to early Aug.

Out of town

Petermann's Kunststuben Seestrasse 160, Küsnacht ⊕044 910 07 15, ⓦwww.kunststuben.com. Universally acclaimed as one of Switzerland's top five restaurants, replete with two Michelin stars, several international awards (including the title "Best Restaurant in Europe", as assessed by 8250 diners for Zagat) and pages of gushing reportage from foodie journalists. To cut to the chase: if you're prepared to invest Fr.100 per head for lunch, or twice that in the evening – plus the cost of getting to and from Küsnacht, 8km south of town – then you'll get a meal to remember for years to come. The dining-room setting is classy, sophisticated with a light, arty touch, and chef Horst Petermann is constantly at work refining his menu. You'll need to book several weeks ahead. Closed Sun & Mon, also early Sept and late Feb.

Bars and pubs

Niederdorf

Babalu Schmidgasse 6 ⓦ www.babalubar.ch. Tiny postmodern-style bar, its chic denizens quaffing bottled beers and cocktails amidst an onslaught of deep beats.

Oepfelchammer Rindermarkt 12 ⓦ www .oepfelchammer.ch. A 200-year-old building, all creaking timbers and lop-sided ceilings, famous for its association with the city's literary son, Gottfried Keller. The reason to visit is for beer in the tiny low-beamed upper front room, which is invariably packed. Legend has it that if you can swing up and wriggle your way through the gap between beam and ceiling, your beers are on the house: Keller may have done it, but few have succeeded since. Closed Sun & Mon.

Oliver Twist Rindermarkt 6 ⓦ www.pickwick.ch. Snug little pub on a Niederdorf back alley, a mecca for expats and Anglophiles in search of pints, English conversation and football on the telly.

Pigalle Marktgasse 14 ⓦ www.pigalle.ch. Legendary little campy bar filled with the elegantly wasted, or at least those who are aspiring.

Rheinfelder Bierhalle Niederdorfstrasse 76 ⓦ www.rheinfelder.ch. Best of the many beerhalls at the northern end of the street. With wooden benches, zero decoration and bright lights, this is a place to get shamelessly, sociably drunk, laugh loudly and clap strangers on the back. The food is cheap and hearty: daily specials for around Fr.13 are padded out by their infamous "Jumbo Jumbo Cordon Bleu" – a slab of deep-fried cheese-slathered meat so big it dangles off the plate on both sides. Closed Sun.

Wüste Oberdorfstrasse 7 ⓦ www.wueste.ch. Mellow, comfortable street-level bar of the *Otter* hotel, located on a quiet lane in the Old Town – opposite are a florist and an antiquarian bookseller. The hippyish interior is done up in vaguely ethnic style, dotted with candles.

Around Bahnhofstrasse

Helvetia Stauffacherquai 1 ⓦ www.hotel-helvetia .ch. Loud and jovial locals' haunt – nicknamed the Helvti-Bar – just across the Sihl. Open late during the week, it closes at 2am on Fridays and Saturdays, when it is the only bar in town offering full table service after midnight. Very civilized for a nightcap or three.

James Joyce Pelikanstrasse 8 ⓦ www .jamesjoyce.ch. For many years this pub comprised the original nineteenth-century "Antique Bar" of Dublin's *Jury Hotel*, saved from developers in the 1970s, transported here piece by piece and reassembled to stand as a relic of a bygone age. Its location – in the heart of the financial district – let it down, but it retained the ring of authenticity. Tragically, new management has now installed black leather seats, shiny metal tables and generally tarted the place up to be just another wine-bar. Barely a shred of atmosphere remains. Go, if only to weep into your Zinfandel. Closed Sat evening and all day Sun.

Jules Verne Access through *Brasserie Lipp*, Uraniastrasse 9 ⓣ 043 888 66 66, ⓦ www.jules -verne.ch. Intimate little city-centre bar in the stubby-domed observatory building, done up with canvas decor to mimic the basket of a hot-air balloon and boasting panoramic views across the rooftops and steeples – worth the price of refreshment. Phone ahead to reserve a table facing south towards the mountains for twilight. Take the lift to the tenth floor, and then climb another 17 steps. Closes midnight Mon–Thurs, 1am Fri & Sat, 11pm Sun.

Kaufleuten Pelikanstrasse 18 ⓦ www.kaufleuten .com. Modish venue for mixing with Zürich's burgeoning "in" scene. Designers, musicians, bankers and the idle rich flock here, and to the club next door. A pricey beer is worth it for the buzz.

Nelson Beatengasse 11 ⓦ www.thenelsonpub .com. Massive, noisy pub seconds from the station, crammed on weekend nights with Zürich's sizeable contingent of teenage au pairs and exchange students on the pull. Cheap beer, late opening, live music, DJs and TV sport make for a heady, if predictable, brew. Sun–Wed until 2am, Thurs–Sat until 3 or 4am.

Paddy Reilly Talacker 43/Talstrasse 82 ⓦ www .paddys.ch. Good beer, good service and a talkative atmosphere make this cramped mock-Irish pub – with doors front and back – hugely popular with locals and expats alike.

Zürich West and south

4. Akt Heinrichstrasse 262 ⓦ www.4akt.ch. Deeply cool bar at the Hardstrasse junction, with plenty of outside tables, a good, up-to-date music selection, and a small food menu (about Fr.22).

Haiti Militärstrasse 91. If you fancy a full-on slice of local Zürich West life, drop into this Haitian corner bar, open daily from mid-afternoon until 3am or so. As well as the vibe, the booze and the many dodgy characters, this is one of the few places in Switzerland to sample Creole-style grilled tilapia fish, or shrimps in a tomato salsa (around Fr.30).

Hard One Hardstrasse 260 ⓦ www.hardone.ch. Fresh, cool and buzzy club, bar and lounge, open

▲ Ziegel oh Lac bar and restaurant

from breakfast until the small hours – the street-level lounge with sofas and terrace seating, dubbed Aya, is a perfect place for a sociable cocktail ahead of a busy evening.

Kanzlei Kanzleistrasse 56 Ⓦ www.kanzlei.ch. Friendly, informal bar just off Helvetiaplatz at the southern end of Langstrasse – a great place to plug into the atmosphere and buzz of Zürich West.

Riff Raff Neugasse 57 Ⓦ www.riffraff.ch. Small cinema attached to a trendy bar, a few steps off Langstrasse. The building has a longer history than it seems; it showed silent movies back in

the early days, and has now been taken over by a cooperative dedicated to restoring its reputation and promoting independent film-making. The walls, like the clientele, are floor-to-ceiling matt black, and the bar stands between two small auditoria.

Ziegel oh Lac At the Rote Fabrik arts centre, Seestrasse 395 Ⓦ www.ziegelohlac.ch. One of Zürich's more appealing bar/restaurant spaces, with a light, open interior and waterside seating in summer. Located way south of the centre, far from the crush. Closed Mon.

Nightlife and entertainment

For a city that's a minnow in world terms, Zürich has a surprisingly wide range of **nightlife and entertainment**. Live rock and jazz – although easy to find most nights of the week – take second place to the city's dynamic club scene, which covers the gamut from techno to salsa. Zürich is also home to a top-flight orchestra, a world-famous opera company, and one of the German-speaking world's premier theatres. You can find complete what's-on **listings** for the week ahead in *ZüriTipp* (Ⓦ www.zueritipp.ch), the Friday supplement to the *Tages Anzeiger* newspaper, available free at the tourist office.

Clubs and live music

Zürich's **club** and **music** scene has skyrocketed recently, helped by legislation permitting some all-night opening: you'll find the city's dance venues heaving with a new-found energy lacking in most European cities. At the heart of the new subculture are the cosmopolitan bars, chic bistros and crowded alternative hangouts of **Zürich West** – particularly on and off Langstrasse and Hardstrasse

Zürich has a thriving **gay and lesbian** scene, probably the best established and most diverse in the country. No hotel will turn a gay or lesbian couple away; however, the *G* hotel (see p.361) is the only one to make a selling point of its gay- and lesbian-friendliness; handily enough, it occupies the same building as *T&M* (Ⓦwww.gaybar .ch), one of the best gay bar/cabaret/disco venues in the city. The huge *Barfüsser*, Spitalgasse 14 (Ⓦwww.barfuesser.ch), is Europe's longest-running gay bar, established in 1956 – and now also serves good sushi. *Cranberry*, Metzgergasse 3 (Ⓦwww.cranberry.ch), is a sociable cocktail bar. For more **information**, check Ⓦwww.zuerigay.ch or www.csdzurich.ch.

– although you'll find that the northern half of **Niederdorf**, bang in the city centre, has some of the same vibe. The **industrial quarter** northwest of Langstrasse is where the best underground clubs hide themselves; venues move, nights change and new places open virtually every month. Check flyers at the bars up and down Langstrasse.

Bands and DJs

Abart Manessestrasse 170 Ⓦwww.abart.ch. Eclectic programme of local and foreign bands, plus dance parties.

Dynamo Wasserwerkstrasse 21 Ⓦwww.dynamo .ch. Bills itself as a "youth culture centre" and, as well as a disco and jazz school, hosts live bands with an alternative, punkish bias. Also excellent club nights.

Kanzlei Kanzleistrasse 56 at Helvetiaplatz Ⓦwww .kanzlei.ch. Groovy lounge bar and club just off Langstrasse, with a full programme of DJ events.

Kaufleuten Pelikanstrasse 18 Ⓦwww.kaufleuten .com. Plush city-centre nightspot, its housey beats drawing an unusual blend of hardcore clubbers and work-to-play young professionals. Voted one of the world's best party venues by the *Wall Street Journal* (which says it all). Dress to impress.

Oxa Andreasstrasse 70 Ⓦwww.oxa.com. Premier venue for trance and house, with two dancefloors, a garden and even a restaurant; famous for its after-hours parties (Sun 5–11am).

Rohstofflager Duttweilerstrasse, corner Pfingst-weidstrasse Ⓦwww.rohstofflager.ch. Lively mix of DJs and live bands.

Rote Fabrik Seestrasse 395 Ⓦwww.rotefabrik .ch. Alternative-style arts complex, in old graffitied industrial buildings on the lakeshore some 5km southwest of town, hosting a continuous flow of bands famous and unknown from all musical genres, as well as big-name DJs. Bus #161 or #165 from Bürkliplatz (last bus returns after midnight).

Toni Molkerei Förrlibuckstrasse 109 Ⓦwww .tonimolkerei.com. Eclectic, highly acclaimed and popular house club and relaxed DJ-bar occupying a vast 3000-square-metre industrial space. As well as a great vibe, it has the unique attribute of high-quality bar food as well.

X-tra Limmatstrasse 118 Ⓦwww.x-tra.ch. Hugely popular multipurpose venue just off Limmatplatz, with triphop and funky sounds entertaining a youngish crowd. Bar and restaurant adjacent, and hotel upstairs.

Live jazz

Casa Bar Münstergasse 20 Ⓦwww.casabar.ch. Zürich's longest-running jazz venue, still featuring live music nightly in the Niederdorf.

Moods In Schiffbau building, off Hardstrasse Ⓦwww.moods.ch. The city's premier jazz club, with a good restaurant attached, pulling in top-flight names.

Classical music, opera and ballet

The acoustically superb **Tonhalle** concert hall, Claridenstrasse 7 (Ⓦwww .tonhalle.ch), inaugurated by Brahms in 1895, has a programme of world-class **classical music** of all kinds from both the resident Tonhalle and Zürich Chamber orchestras and guest performers. Many of Zürich's **churches** – principally the Grossmünster, Fraumünster, Predigerkirche and St Peter's – host regular concerts of organ, choral and chamber music, as does the Kunsthaus. The city's majestic **Opera House** (ⓦ www.opernhaus.ch) has an impressive programme of both **opera and ballet** – performances sell out quickly.

Listings

Bike rental The station has the usual paid bike-rental facilities (daily 6am–10.50pm), but you can also take advantage of the *Züri-Rollt* scheme (ⓦ www.zuerirollt.ch), a free bike-rental scheme to help unemployed people get back to work. There are pick-up points around the city (all daily 7.30am–9.30pm): the main one is "Velogate" at the train station, next to platform 18 (open year-round). You must leave your passport and Fr.20 as a deposit; various machines are available, from multigeared city bikes to mountain bikes, electric bikes, scooters and skateboards.

Books Zürich's best English bookshop – complete with Rough Guides – is Orell Füssli, Bahnhofstrasse 70. The Travel Bookshop, Rindermarkt 20, is another good source.

Consulates Ireland, Claridenstrasse 25 ☏ 044 289 25 15; UK, Hegibachstrasse 47 ☏ 044 383 65 60; USA, Dufourstrasse 101 ☏ 043 499 29 60.

Otherwise turn to p.211 for details of embassies in Bern.

Flights Zürich-Kloten airport flight enquiries ☏ 0900 300 313, ⓦ www.zurich-airport.com. For a train ticket to the airport from the city centre, press 8058 on the ticket machines.

Medical facilities Most convenient is the Permanence Medical Centre at Bahnhofplatz 15 (daily 7am–11pm, but with a 24hr emergency room; ☏ 044 215 44 44). Alongside it is the Bahnhof Apotheke pharmacy (daily 7am–midnight).

Police Headquarters is at Bahnhofquai 3 ☏ 044 216 71 11.

Post office Zürich's main post office is beside the main station at Kasernenstrasse 95 (Mon–Fri 6.30am–10.30pm, Sat 6.30am–8pm, Sun 10am–10.30pm). There's also a post office within the station.

Around Lake Zürich

A pleasant day-trip leads out of the city around the long, slender **ZÜRICHSEE** (**Lake Zürich**), which nestles between the parallel ridges of the Uetliberg to the west and the Pfannenstiel opposite. The best way to go is by **boat** – ZSG ferries (see p.359) stop at every lakeside town in summer – while picturesque S-Bahn **train** lines run the length of both shores.

Heading along the **eastern shore**, you leave the city and plunge directly into a comfortable, leafy world of trimmed hedges and car dealerships. The unremarkable suburb of **KÜSNACHT**, 7km south, is made significant by some excellent restaurants, including *Petermann's Kunststuben* (see p.379). Some 15km south lies **STÄFA**, a mildly picturesque village clustered at the foot of the Pfannenstiel, in the largest vine-growing region in the canton. From Stäfa, Rapperswil is 12km southeast.

Lying 6km from Bürkliplatz along the **western shore** is the dormitory town of **KILCHBERG**, unremarkable but for the fragrant presence of the huge Lindt & Sprüngli **chocolate factory**, which has a shop selling the full range (Mon–Fri 10am–5pm). As you head south, suburbia fades away, replaced by evidence of a more down-to-earth, rural existence that feels a long way from the Zürich hubbub. Past the old warehouses of Wädenswil, from where trains branch off into the hills to Einsiedeln (see p.342), is **PFÄFFIKON**, 23km south of Kilchberg in an outpost of Canton Schwyz (and so-named on timetables as "Pfäffikon SZ" to differentiate it from another Pfäffikon nearby). Here sits the popular **Alpamare waterpark** (daily 9/10am–10/11pm; day-pass Fr.49, other tickets and family passes available; ⓦ www.alpamare.ch), replete with slides, flumes, heated wave pools and saunas. Rapperswil is a short distance across the lake by road or rail.

Rapperswil

Lying 37km south of Zürich, the small lakefront town of **RAPPERSWIL** repays a gentle afternoon's exploration. Avoid the modern part of town and lose yourself in the quiet Old Town alleys, which weave around and between a succession of plazas. Prettiest is **Fischmarktplatz**, open to the lake and lined with terrace cafés. A lane or two back is a Capuchin monastery dating from 1597, with, beside the main gate, a delightful walled **rose-garden** – one of a handful around town that support Rapperswil's moniker "City of Roses". Alleys climb to the dour thirteenth-century **castle**. The lake beyond Rapperswil is known as the **Obersee**, served by boats and trains as far as Schmerikon.

The **train station** stands on the edge of the Old Town; head left and cross the road to reach Fischmarktplatz, behind which, at Hintergasse 16, is the **tourist office** (Mon–Fri 8.30am–noon & 1.30–5pm; ☏0848 811 500, ⓦwww .zuerichsee.ch). The most characterful **hotel** is the attractive *Hirschen*, Fischmark-tplatz 7 (☏055 220 61 80, ⓦwww.hirschen-rapperswil.ch; ❸), not far from the pleasant, easy-going *Jakob*, Hauptplatz 11 (☏055 220 00 50, ⓦwww.jakob-hotel .ch; ❸). A little way inland near Jona is an HI **hostel**, *Jugendherberge Busskirch*, Hessenhofweg 10 (☏055 210 99 27, ⓦwww.youthhostel.ch).

Best **restaurant** is *Schloss Rapperswil* (☏055 210 18 28, ⓦwww.schloss -restaurant.ch), with a fine location within the castle and outstanding fish and seafood that has won it a Michelin star; *menus* range from Fr.70 to Fr.135. *Marsala/San Marco*, Marktgasse 21 (☏055 211 22 24, ⓦwww.san-marco-rappi .ch), is a good, mid-priced Italian with a modern ambience, or you could opt for the convivial bistro within the *Jakob* hotel.

Travel details

Full timetables for all trains, buses, trams, boats and cable cars in Switzerland – as well as international connections – are searchable at ⓦwww.rail.ch. Details of the boat service on Lake Zürich are at ⓦwww.zsg.ch.

Trains

Zürich HB to: airport (4–7 hourly; 10min); Baden (every 30min; 15min); Basel (every 15min; 55min); Bern (3 hourly; 1hr); Biel/Bienne (twice hourly; 1hr 10min); Chur (twice hourly; 1hr 15min); Einsiedeln (every 30min; 45min – change at Wädenswil); Flughafen/Airport (4–7 hourly; 10min); Fribourg (every 30min; 1hr 25min); Geneva (every 30min; 2hr 45min); Interlaken Ost (twice hourly; 2hr 5min); Lausanne (twice hourly; 2hr 10min); Lucerne (twice hourly; 45min); Lugano (hourly; 2hr 55min); Neuchâtel (3 hourly; 1hr 35min); St Gallen (every 30min; 1hr 5min); Sargans (twice hourly; 55min); Schaffhausen (twice hourly; 40min); Solothurn (twice hourly; 55min); Uetliberg (every 30min; 20min); Winterthur (4 hourly; 20min); Zug (twice hourly; 25min); Zürich airport (4–7 hourly; 10min).

Boats

Zürich (Bürkliplatz) to: Rapperswil (hourly; 1hr 45min).

Northeast Switzerland

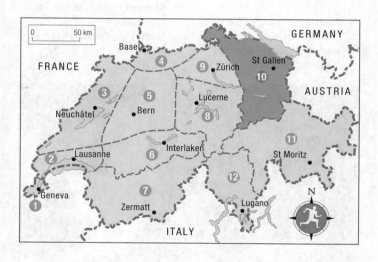

* **Winterthur** Easy-going city with an array of world-class art museums. See p.390

* **Schaffhausen** Beautiful but little-visited market town, crammed with superb medieval architecture. See p.394

* **Rhine falls** The Wagnerian spectacle of Europe's largest waterfall. See p.398

* **Stein-am-Rhein** Switzerland's most picturesque village square, ringed by frescoed facades. See p.399

* **Abbey library, St Gallen** A splendid Rococo interior, lined with books from floor to ceiling. See p.407

* **Appenzell** Quiet, rustic village set amidst the craggy Alpstein range. See p.410

* **Braunwald** Remote car-free mountain hideaway. See p.413

* **Klausen Pass** Spectacular pass road, one of the country's most scenic drives. See p.413

▲ The Rhine falls

Northeast Switzerland

Rural **NORTHEAST SWITZERLAND** – known as **Ostschweiz** – is one of the least celebrated areas of the country, and is often sidelined by tourists anxious to get to the famous Alpine regions further south. Which, of course, means that you can enjoy the mountains and lakes, medieval town centres and verdant countryside in relative peace, free from hard-sell tourism and the glitz and glamour of big-name resorts. Most visitors haven't even heard of the main city of the northeast, **St Gallen**, and yet its magnificent Baroque cathedral and well-preserved medieval town centre make it a major cultural landmark. Just to the west, **Winterthur** has a set of excellent museums to complement its urban neighbour, Zürich.

Immediately south of St Gallen lies the hilly backcountry of **Appenzell**, sheltering a close-knit community of farmers and craftspeople occupying the foothills of the Alpstein range. The Säntis peak tops 2500m – mediocre in Swiss terms, but still tall enough to enjoy plenty of snow, vistas stretching to the horizon and quality hiking in the web of valleys beneath it. Further south, walled in by Alpine giants, is isolated **Glarnerland**.

The River Rhine, which bulges out into the huge **Bodensee** (**Lake Constance**) in Switzerland's northeast corner, throws a protective loop around this part of Switzerland, forming international frontiers with Germany to the north, and Austria and the tiny independent statelet of **Liechtenstein** to the east. At the westernmost tip of the lake, the cosmopolitan German city of **Konstanz** is divided from its Swiss twin of **Kreuzlingen** only by an arbitrary frontier between buildings. The beautiful river journey west from Kreuzlingen

Exploring Northeast Switzerland

Local Swiss, German and Austrian tourist boards market the Ostschweiz region strongly, focusing chiefly on the Bodensee. Several different passes give discounts to attractions all round the lake. Best is the **Bodensee Erlebniskarte** (April–Oct only; Ⓦ www.bodensee.eu), which comes in different varieties, most comprehensive of which is the *Seebärenkarte* (Fr.109/142/194 for 3/7/14 days, less for children). This gives free transport on all boats on the lake and the Rhine; free admission to Insel Mainau, the St Gallen abbey library, museums in Appenzell and Stein-am-Rhein, and dozens more attractions; free travel up the Säntis and other mountains; and so on. It's available from tourist offices. Alternatives worth investigating, with complex zone networks and tariffs, are the four-country **EuRegio Tageskarte** (Ⓦ www.euregiokarte .com) and the Switzerland-only **Ostwind Tageskarte** (Ⓦ www.ostwind.ch). For information on the whole region (which excludes Winterthur), contact **Ostschweiz Tourismus** (Ⓣ 071 227 37 37, Ⓦ www.ostschweiz.ch).

THE NORTHEAST &
LIECHTENSTEIN

Innsbruck

Stuttgart

Stuttgart

Basel

Baden

ZÜRICH

GERMANY

Bodensee

St Gallen

Bregenz
Lindau
Langenargen
Friedrichshafen
Immenstaad
Hagnau
Meersburg
Überlingen
Mainau
Reichenau
Radolfzell
Singen
Steckborn
Stein-am-Rhein
Herblingen
Büsingen
Dachsen
Schaffhausen
Neuhausen
Rhine Falls
Stühlingen
Hallau
Andelfingen
Rhine
Wettingen
Dietikon

Überlingersee
Untersee
Konstanz
Kreuzlingen
Münsterlingen
Kesswil
Romanshorn
Arbon
Horn
Rorschach
Heiden
St Margrethen
Altstätten
Trogen
Gais
Gäbris
(1247m)
App. A.R.
App. I.R.
Appenzell
Stein
Gonten
Herisau
Gossau
Weinfelden
Wil
Lichtensteig
Thur
THURGAU
ST GALLEN
Frauenfeld
Warth
Kartause
Ittingen
Winterthur

N

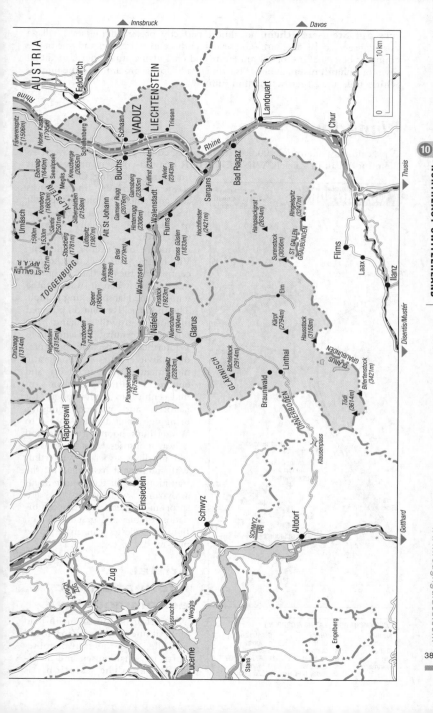

runs past **Stein-am-Rhein**, an almost perfectly preserved medieval village boasting spectacular sixteenth- and seventeenth-century frescoes and one of the country's best small historical museums, and ends at the atmospheric medieval town of **Schaffhausen**, dubbed "Rheinfallstadt" for its proximity to the mighty **Rhine falls**, the largest waterfall in Europe.

Winterthur

A peaceful city of around 100,000, set in rolling countryside on the River Töss 25km northeast of Zürich, **WINTERTHUR** boasts a volley of impressive art museums, displaying Old Masters, classic Modernists, Impressionists and contemporary photography. It lies in Canton Zürich, slightly west of what is usually termed Ostschweiz.

Evidence of a nearby settlement, Vitudurum, goes back to the first century, but the city dates its history from 1264, when it was granted status by the Habsburg king Rudolf. The Industrial Revolution powered meteoric growth during the nineteenth century, and after 1848 Winterthur also became the centre of Switzerland's democratic movement. Local architects and engineers visited England in mid-century to study designs for factories and workers' housing, bringing English ideas back to Winterthur's booming textile and railway industries. Most Swiss today still indelibly associate Winterthur with industry: it has pulled off the transition into hi-tech, and remains a dynamic, wealthy city. It's also surprisingly green, and the combination of bicycles, green hills and fine art galleries can make for a pleasant day or two.

Arrival, information and accommodation

Winterthur lies on the main road and rail lines between Zürich and St Gallen, at a junction of routes north to Schaffhausen and Stein-am-Rhein. The **station** is

WINTERTHUR

Sammlung
Oskar Reinhart
Am Römerholz

Schaffhausen & Frauenfeld

Sulzer-Areal & 10

St Gallen & 6

Kunstmuseum

Museum Oskar
Reinhart Am
Stadtgarten

Kunsthalle

Train
Station

Stadtkirche

0   250 m

ACCOMMODATION		EATING & DRINKING			
Albani	C	Albani	C	Strauss	2
Grüntal	E	Gleis 11	A	Tibits	3
Krone	B	Gotthard	6	Trübli	7
Loge	D	Kraftfeld	10	Wagamama	4
Wartmann	A	Obergass	8	Widder	9
		Paddy O'Brien's	1	Zur Sonne	5

Travel between Winterthur and Zürich

Winterthur is viable as an alternative base for exploring Zürich – cheaper, smaller and quieter than its neighbour. Travel between the two cities is straightforward: **trains** run roughly every ten minutes all day on a variety of routes. The quickest is S-Bahn **S12**, which takes just sixteen minutes to reach **Zürich Stadelhofen** station (centrally located near Bellevueplatz) and another three minutes into **Zürich HB**. Otherwise **S8** trains go a slightly longer way round into Zürich HB (27min); **S7** and **S16** take twenty-eight minutes to reach **Zürich Hardbrücke** (for Zürich West) and another two minutes into HB; and so on – all interspersed with several intercity trains each hour (which stop midway at **Zürich Airport**; 15min). The **last train** back from Zürich HB to Winterthur departs around 12.20am.

centrally located, and hosts the helpful **tourist office** (Mon–Fri 8.30am–6.30pm, Sat 8.30am–4pm; ☎052 267 67 00, ⓦwww.winterthurtourism.ch) – ask them for details of **walking tours** (which have variable dates), or check ⓦwww.citystroll.ch to join an innovative guided evening walk around the Old Town (May–Sept Thurs 6pm; Fr.25 incl. two drinks). Weekly food **markets** are held in Steinberggasse (Tues & Fri 6–11am). **Accommodation** is geared largely towards business people, though prices are still lower than Zürich. You should always book ahead.

Hotels

Albani Steinberggasse 16 ☎052 212 69 96, ⓦwww.albani.ch. Budget hotel above the famous Old Town club and music venue just south of Kirchplatz. The adequate rooms are big and well kept, but aren't en suite and there's no breakfast. Free entry for gigs downstairs. Don't bother phoning before 3pm. ❷

Grüntal Im Grüntal 1 ☎052 232 25 52, ⓦwww .restaurant-gruental.ch. Solid country inn at a quiet crossroads 4.5km southeast of town, with hospitality, good service, basic, pleasant rooms and free parking. Bus #3 to Grüntal. Phone ahead, as it's closed for walk-in arrivals Tues & Wed. ❸

Krone Marktgasse 49 ☎052 208 18 18, ⓦwww.kronewinterthur.ch. Historic building in the Old Town, renovated to a high standard, with stylish and comfortable three-star-superior rooms. Significant weekend discounts. ❹–❺

Loge Graben 6 ☎052 268 12 00, ⓦwww .hotelloge.ch. Modern, quiet three-star Old Town hotel – excellent value. Go for the light, top-floor rooms with panoramic balcony. Onsite parking. ❹

Wartmann Rudolfstrasse 15 ☎052 260 07 07, ⓦwww.wartmann.ch. Quality business hotel in a renovated building dating from 1894, just behind the train station. Two standards of rooms; prices on both drop at weekends. ❸–❹

The Town

Winterthur's main draw is its excellent **museums**, principally the two separate Oskar Reinhart art collections – one housed in the town centre ("Am Stadtgarten"), the other on a hill near the town ("Am Römerholz") – and the Kunstmuseum. The Fotomuseum and Villa Flora are close runners-up. A Museumspass (see box, 393) grants free admission. Note that all Winterthur's museums are **closed on Mondays**.

The pedestrianized Old Town has some charm once you get off the main shopping streets – the elegant medieval Stadtkirche, for example, with its kitschy modern murals, is worth a look. If Victorian industrial architecture lights your fire, head southwest under the tracks into the **Sulzer-Areal** district, where hulking brick-built factories are being reclaimed as atmospheric theatre spaces, bars and skating arenas.

Winterthur's festivals

The most popular event is the **Albanifäscht** (🌐www.albanifest.ch), a weekend of live rock music in late June. The August **Kyburgiade** (🌐www.kyburgiade.ch) is an international chamber music festival in the romantic setting of Kyburg castle, outside town. The **Musikfestwochen** (🌐www.musikfestwochen.ch), in late August, see Winterthur's Old Town taken over for live music of all kinds. Whitsun is celebrated in Winterthur as **Afro-Pfingsten** (🌐www.afro-pfingsten.ch), a mini-carnival of African music, dance and food.

The Oskar Reinhart museums

Oskar Reinhart was born into a local trading family in 1885. Aged 41, he withdrew from business and moved into the hilltop villa "Am Römerholz" to devote himself to his passion for art. When he died in 1965, part of his collection – one of the leading private art collections assembled in Europe in the twentieth century – passed to the municipality (and is now housed in the Stadtgarten museum), and the remaining 200 paintings and his villa at Römerholz were bequeathed to the nation.

By the time you read this, renovation work at the **Sammlung Oskar Reinhart "Am Römerholz"**, Haldenstrasse 95 (formerly Tues–Sun 10am–5pm, Wed until 8pm; Fr.10, joint ticket with "Am Stadtgarten" Fr.12; 🌐www.roemerholz.ch), will be complete. This fine museum forms an idiosyncratic mingling of styles and periods. There are works from fifteenth- and sixteenth-century German masters, including Matthias Grünewald, Lukas Cranach the Elder and Hans Holbein the Younger; a small group of Italian and Spanish works, including by El Greco and Goya; and fifteenth- to seventeenth-century Dutch and Flemish painting dominated by Brueghel, Rubens, Hals and Rembrandt. Works by French Baroque, Neoclassical and Romantic artists – including some of Delacroix's best portraits – lead on to Reinhart's marvellous Impressionist collection, covering Renoir, Manet, Degas and many more. The museum has a lovely sunny café.

Back in town, the **Museum Oskar Reinhart "Am Stadtgarten"**, Stadthausstrasse 6 (Tues 10am–8pm, Wed–Sun 10am–5pm; Fr.8; 🌐www.museumoskarreinhart.ch), concentrates on German, Swiss and Austrian artists from the eighteenth to the twentieth centuries, including portraits by local artists including Graff and Füssli, Romantic Swiss landscapes, fine studies of children by the Swiss artist Albert Anker and works by Hodler, Segantini and Giovanni Giacometti.

Other museums

Also newly renovated when you visit, with a modern wing opened in 2010, will be the **Kunstmuseum**, Museumstrasse 52 (formerly Tues 10am–8pm, Wed–Sun 10am–5pm; Fr.10; 🌐www.kmw.ch), with a splendid collection covering international art over the last century, led by Van Gogh, Monet, Rousseau and sculpture by Picasso and Rodin. Hodler and Cubist works lead on to a Surrealist collection topped by Miró and a rare self-portrait by De Chirico, with works also featured by Brancusi, Mondrian, American artists and sculpture by Alberto Giacometti. The **Kunsthalle**, nearby at Marktgasse 25 (Wed–Fri noon–6pm, Sat & Sun noon–4pm; free; 🌐www.kunsthallewinterthur.ch), stages changing shows of contemporary art.

The critic Paul Graham has called Winterthur's **Fotomuseum**, Grüzenstrasse 44 (Tues–Sun 11am–6pm, Wed until 8pm; Fr.9; 🌐www.fotomuseum.ch), "the most beautiful museum of photography in Europe", and it's easy to see why. Housed in a brick-built renovated former warehouse, it's light, bright and open, and benefits further from its policy of staging five or six top-notch annual exhibitions each year. It lies a walkable 400m southeast from the Old Town, off Tösstalstrasse (or bus #2 to Fotozentrum).

Nearby is the **Villa Flora**, Tösstalstrasse 44 (Tues–Sat 2–5pm, Sun 11am–3pm; Fr.12.50; Ⓦ www.villaflora.ch), which houses the private collection of Hedy Hahnloser, built up between 1907 and 1930. It comprises a small but high-quality selection – on continuous rotation – of French Post-Impressionism, Fauvist and Nabi works (Bonnard, Matisse, Vallotton and more) fleshed out with earlier works by Cézanne, Van Gogh and others.

Eating, drinking and nightlife

You'll have no trouble finding places in the Old Town to **eat and drink**. **Nightlife** can be surprisingly good, with the excellent *Albani* bar and venue, plus some lively music bars on Neumarkt.

Restaurants and cafés

Gleis 11 At *Hotel Wartmann*, Rudolfstrasse 15 ☏052 260 07 07, Ⓦ www.wartmann.ch. Stylish hotel restaurant, with warm, contemporary decor and a pleasant atmosphere. Great-value mid-priced lunch buffets of salads and hot mains.

Obergass Schulgasse 1, corner Obergasse. Quiet easy-going café to eat, read and drink in, with a wide range of food, veggie and not, for Fr.15–25. Closed Sun.

Strauss Stadthausstrasse 8 ☏052 212 29 70, Ⓦ www.strauss-winterthur.ch. Contemporary Mediterranean cuisine at this sociable, friendly restaurant set back from the street beside the city's main theatre – gazpacho and tapas feature alongside fish and sushi, with relaxed service and artful presentation. Reckon on Fr.40–50. Closed Sun.

Tibits Oberer Graben 48 Ⓦ www.tibits.ch. Local branch of the excellent Swiss chain of chic, stylish eateries – loads of buffet salads, sandwiches, soup and light bites, plus fresh-squeezed juices, gourmet coffees and more. Open daily from breakfast time to around midnight.

Trübli Bosshardengässchen 2 ☏052 212 55 36, Ⓦ www.truebli-winterthur.ch. Located on an alley just off Neumarkt square, this fine old restaurant is a popular after-work stop for local business folk, now also serving swanky international cuisine in a low-key interior. Closed Sun & Mon.

Wagamama Marktgasse 7 Ⓦ www.wagamama .ch. The familiar international chain of fast-paced Japanese eateries comes to Winterthur, with soups, stir-fries and noodles for around Fr.20–25. Closed Sun.

Widder Metzggasse 9 Ⓦ www.gasthofzumwidder .ch. Subculture Old Town café-bar, with long wooden tables and loud music. Good cheap food, well prepared and in massive portions, for around Fr.15.

Zur Sonne Marktgasse 15 ☏052 213 00 50, Ⓦ www.zur-sonne.ch. Charming, cosy restaurant in congenial Swiss style, with excellent, mid-priced *Rösti*, fondues and other belt-bulgers.

Bars and clubs

Albani Steinberggasse 16 Ⓦ www.albani.ch. Smallish Old Town bar and venue well able to draw

Zürchers out into the sticks with a quality programme of DJs and live music – previous headliners have included Pearl Jam and Sheryl Crow. Weekend nights are packed. Fr.15 or so for bands.

Gotthard 1900 Untertor 34, opposite station Ⓦ www.gotthard1900.ch. Switzerland's first ever 24hr bar, a young, friendly joint that's a peaceful café during the day; at night it attracts a few lowlifes but avoids the sleaze of its Bahnhofplatz neighbours.

Kraftfeld Lagerplatz 18, off Tössfeldstrasse in Sulzer-Areal industrial quarter, 100m beyond Brockenhalle junk shop Ⓦ www.kraftfeld.ch.

Alternative artists' community which lays on excellent DJ nights featuring experimental drum'n'bass, plus bands, films and other events. Wandering around the nearby streets will turn up similar post-industrial venues: the design-conscious *Plan B Bar* (Ⓦ www.planb-bar.ch), the Aussie-styled *Outback Lodge* bar/BBQ-diner (Ⓦ www.outback-lodge.ch), and others.

Paddy O'Brien's Merkurstrasse 25 Ⓦ www .paddyobriens.ch. Quality Irish pub 5min north of the station to warm your jaded cockles, with 12 beers on tap, televised football and enough of a reputation to pull in The Dubliners for a gig now and again. Daily 3pm–2am.

Schaffhausen and around

Capital of the northernmost Swiss canton of the same name, **SCHAFF-HAUSEN** can boast one of the most captivating medieval town centres in the whole of Switzerland as well as, 4km downriver, the mighty **Rhine falls** – and yet it remains uncelebrated, as if too far north to be of concern to most visitors. (For the record, trains from Zürich take just 38 minutes.) Adding to the allure is the splendid medieval village of **Stein-am-Rhein**, within easy reach upriver.

A bankside docking point had already developed into the thriving market town of Scafusun by 1045 (the name of the town probably derives from its many riverside boathouses). It grew rapidly, handling salt and grain from Bavaria and the Tyrol and joining the Swiss Confederation in 1501. The town maintained steady growth, its eighteenth-century merchants indulging in the fashion for adding ornate **oriel windows** to the Gothic or Renaissance buildings, both to demonstrate their wealth and good taste, and also to give people inside a clear view up and down the street. With 170-odd examples on show, Schaffhausen's nickname *Erkerstadt* ("City of Oriel Windows") is well-earned. Hydroelectric works, built to exploit the flow of the Rhine, brought the area into the industrial age and Schaffhausen capitalized on its position to act as a commercial and cultural bridge between Germany and Switzerland. In recent years it has absorbed a high number of Sri Lankan immigrants and asylum seekers, leading to an unusually broad ethnic mix on the streets.

Arrival, information and accommodation

Schaffhausen's **train station** is at the northwestern edge of the compact Old Town, served by both Swiss SBB and German DB trains. One block east is bustling Fronwagplatz. Just south at Herrenacker 15 is the **tourist office** (June–Sept Mon–Fri 9.30am–6pm, Sat 9.30am–4pm, July & Aug also Sun 9.30am–2pm, Oct–May Mon–Fri 9.30am–5pm, Sat 9.30am–2pm; ☎ 052 632 40 20, Ⓦ www.schaffhauserland.ch), which offers a guided **walking tour** of the Old Town (May–Oct Tues 10am & Sat 2pm, also on some summer Sundays; Fr.14; 75min).

The best way to arrive is **by boat** from further up the Rhine. At least three boats a day (May–Sept; see p.401) make the beautiful journey along the river from Kreuzlingen via Stein-am-Rhein, a peaceful ride between wooded banks. They dock at Freier Platz, at the southeastern corner of the Old Town.

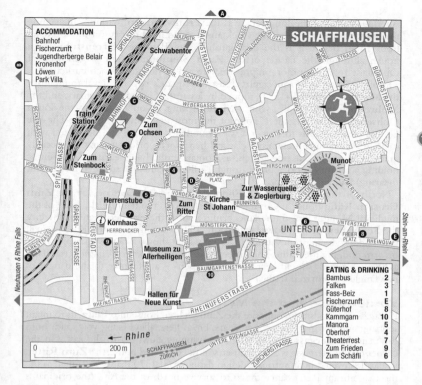

Hostel

Jugendherberge Belair (HI hostel)
Randenstrasse 65 ☎052 625 88 00, ⊛www
.youthhostel.ch. Award-winning hostel, housed in
a sixteenth-century manor house 1km northwest
of the station, which featured in Hermann
Hesse's 1914 novel *Rosshalde*. March–Nov. See
p.398 for details of a hostel at Neuhausen, by the
Rhine Falls. **❶**

Hotels

Bahnhof Bahnhofstrasse 46 ☎052 630 35 35,
⊛www.hotelbahnhof.ch. Decent business hotel
opposite the station, with good facilities. **❺**
Fischerzunft Rheinquai 8 ☎052 632 05 05,
⊛www.fischerzunft.ch. A modern Relais &
Châteaux hotel on the riverfront. Its ten rooms have
been done up in a rather flouncy style, with Asian

touches; it's worth plumping for one of the more
restrained, tasteful suites. **❻**
Kronenhof Kirchhofplatz 7 ☎052 635 75 75,
⊛www.kronenhof.ch. Slick, modern three-star
rooms in a central location, also with some good,
spacious suites. **❹**
Löwen Im Höfli 2 ☎052 643 22 08, ⊛www
.loewen-sh.ch. Comfortable old guesthouse in the
suburb of Herblingen, 3km north (bus #5), with
modern, renovated rooms. **❷**

🏃 **Park Villa** Parkstrasse 18 ☎052 635 60
60, ⊛www.parkvilla.ch. Atmospheric old
mansion on the edge of Schaffhausen's Old Town,
with 25 individually decorated rooms, complete
with chandeliers and Persian carpets. Splash out
on the Royal Suite for the rooftop balcony and fine,
wood-panelled bedchamber with four-poster bed,
or dine in the wonderful Louis XVI salon. **❸–❹**

The Town

Schaffhausen's beautiful riverside Old Town is crammed full of well-preserved
architecture, lending the cobbled streets considerable charm. A good place to
begin is the central **Fronwagplatz**, the town's marketplace during the Middle

Ages. Dominating the long square is the **Fronwagturm**, within which hung the market's massive scales; the clock and astronomical device on the top dates from 1564. Beside it is the distinguished, late Baroque **Herrenstube** town house, although the facade of the **Zum Steinbock** house, 100m west at Oberstadt 16, is even more impressive, covered in stucco Rococo curlicues.

Strolling north on Fronwagplatz, past the square's two medieval fountains – the **Metzgerbrunnen** (1524), topped by a statue of a Swiss mercenary, and the **Mohrenbrunnen** (1535), with a Moorish king – you'll come to the **Zum Ochsen** house at Vorstadt 17, one of the most grandiose in the city. The late Gothic facade of this former inn was remodelled in 1608 and decorated with striking Renaissance frescoes of classical heroes. The oriel window is especially graceful: it shows, in five panels, a woman embodying each of the senses: holding a mirror (sight), a glove (touch), a flower (smell), a stringed instrument (hearing) and a cake (taste).

North of the Zum Ochsen, a short detour past the frescoes of the **Zum Grossen Käfig** house at Vorstadt 43, which shows the triumphal parade of the medieval Mongol king Tamerlane, brings you to the northern gate of the city, the **Schwabentor**. The tower dates from 1370, but on the outer face is a small panel added during renovations in 1933, which shows a boy with a pig under his arm dodging the traffic. The dialect inscription *Lappi tue d'Augen uf* translates as "Knuckleheads should keep their eyes open" – a reference to the danger of newfangled motorized traffic.

Vordergasse and the Munot

Karstgässchen leads from opposite the Zum Ochsen house into **Platz**, its fountain sporting another grim-faced mercenary. From here, alleys bring you south onto the main **Vordergasse**, a shopping street sloping downhill to the east. On the corner of Münstergasse is Schaffhausen's most celebrated house, the **Zum Ritter**, its facade covered in an intricate design dating from 1570 that is acclaimed as the most significant Renaissance fresco to survive north of the Alps (the original is now preserved in the town museum; this is a 1930s copy). The fresco depicts, over three storeys, various elements of knightly virtues (*Ritter* means "knight"): the central panel shows Odysseus in the Land of the Lotus-Eaters, tempted by a voluptuous woman, while above is a Roman knight who sacrificed himself for the glory of his country. Below is a trusting girl, symbolizing virtue, protected by a king (the government) and a woman holding a mitre (the church). From the Zum Ritter, alleys head southwest to another of Schaffhausen's broad, open squares, **Herrenacker**, surrounded by tall, dignified facades and, on the west side, the massive **Kornhaus** (1679).

From the Zum Ritter house, Vordergasse continues east to the Gothic, five-naved **Kirche St Johann** (Mon–Sat 9am–6pm, Oct–March 10am–5pm), expanded six times since it was begun in the eleventh century. A few steps east, in front of a fountain statue of William Tell, is the magnificent double-fronted Rococo mansion **Zur Wasserquelle und Zieglerburg**.

Some 50m north is a footbridge over the main Bachstrasse road, which brings you onto steps climbing the hill to the **Munot**. This is Schaffhausen's trademark circular fortress, built by forced labour in 1564 after the religious wars of the Reformation. The interior (daily 8am–8pm, Oct–April 9am–5pm; Ⓦwww.munot.ch) is gloomy, with massive stone vaulting strong enough to support the 40,000-tonne superstructure. An internal spiral ramp leads up to the circular roof of the bastion, with good views over the town. A different door exits onto stairs running through the vines planted on the Munot hill, down to the small riverside quarter known as **Unterstadt**; Schaffhausen's annual Old Town shindig, held on a weekend in late June, still passes on alternate years between the salt-of-the-earth folk of the Unterstadt and their toffee-nosed neighbours of the town centre further west.

Münster zu Allerheiligen

Schaffhausen's lofty **Münster zu Allerheiligen** (All Saints' Minster; Tues–Sun 10am–noon & 2–5pm; ⊕www.muenster-schaffhausen.ch) is the focus of the Old Town. The first church on the site dated from 1049, replaced in 1103 by the building which still stands today. The beautifully restored Romanesque tower gives a hint of the interior, in which twelve huge columns of Rorschach sandstone line the austere nave. Beside the cathedral, the Romanesque-Gothic **cloister** is the largest in Switzerland, a lovely broad walkway circling the Junkernfriedhof (noblemen's cemetery). In the cathedral courtyard sits the huge **Schiller Bell**, cast in 1486; the German poet Friedrich Schiller never set foot in Schaffhausen, but was inspired to compose his *Song of the Clock* by Goethe's record of this bell's Latin inscription: *vivos voco, mortuos plango, fulgura frango* ("I call on the living, lament the dead, shatter the lightning"). Just beyond is an atmospheric little herb garden.

In the same complex is the vast **Museum zu Allerheiligen** (Tues–Sun 11am–5pm; Fr.9; ⊕www.allerheiligen.ch). The archeological collections on the ground floor have no English notes, but the upstairs galleries devoted to the history of Schaffhausen are better presented, with touch-screens and English translations. Room 15 holds a massive set of cast-iron scales, used on Schaffhausen's riverside wharves in the 1750s, room 17 displays exquisite medieval stained glass, while room 25 and its neighbours hold meticulous reconstructions of seventeenth- and eighteenth-century interiors. Restoration of the museum is still ongoing.

Hallen für Neue Kunst

Baumgartenstrasse marks the southern boundary of the cathedral quarter. In a giant old textile factory at no. 23 is the outstanding **Hallen für Neue Kunst** (New Art Spaces; Sat 3–5pm, Sun 11am–5pm; Fr.14; ⊕www.modern-art.ch). This impressive gallery focuses on American and European art from the 1960s to the 1990s, spread over several vast floors. Particularly striking in such airy surroundings are the geometrical games in two and three dimensions of Robert Mangold, and Sol LeWitt's dazzling cube installations.

Eating and drinking

Schaffhausen has a good range of places to **eat**, from the *Manora* self-service diner (just off Fronwagplatz) upwards. Cafés and **bars** line all the Old Town squares.

Bambus Vorstadt 9 ☎052 624 09 05, ⊕www
.bambus.sh. Informal Thai restaurant above a WWF
shop, offering good food (including veggie *menus*)
for around Fr.15. Closed Sun lunch, Mon & Tues.
Falken Vorstadt 5. Quality Swiss food in this
congenial Old Town café-restaurant for around
Fr.20. Daily from breakfast until around midnight.
　Fass-Beiz Webergasse 13 ⊕www
.fassbeiz.ch. Easy-going cooperative-run
café-bar, set back from the street in a concealed
interior courtyard behind a bookshop, which offers
the best budget dining in town: plenty of

wholesome, home-cooked veggie dishes for under
Fr.15. Closed Sun.
Fischerzunft (see "Hotels"). One of Switzerland's
top half-dozen restaurants – a Rhineside dining
room decorated creatively with luxurious fabrics,
also with an open terrace. The cuisine is sensational, a unique blend of French and East Asian
elements. *Menus* range from Fr.200 up to the
five-course Menu Yin/Yang, at Fr.285 (including a
different wine with each dish). Closed Mon & Tues.
Güterhof Freier Platz 10 ☎052 630 40 40,
⊕www.gueterhof.ch. Historic dockside building

with a lazy suntrap terrace on the river and a large, busy interior propped up by heavy wooden beams. Come for a coffee or a beer, or take in the pricey Asian fusion-style cuisine – saddle of lamb with mango, tenderloin with tiger prawns – for Fr.75 per head and upwards. DJs play on weekend nights. Frequently booked solid.

Kammgarn Baumgartenstrasse 19 @www .kammgarn.ch. Easy-going arts centre that also has a sociable café-bar, offering drinks and excellent, uncomplicated food for around Fr.20. Closed Sun & Mon.

Oberhof Stadthausgasse 15 @www.oberhof -schaffhausen.ch. Fresh, young, funky little place with a lounge bar on street level and a contemporary-styled restaurant up above, with *menus* for Fr.45–50. Come for the choice of excellent Saturday brunches, including muffins, eggs sunny-side-up, bagels, toast and muesli (under Fr.20). Closed Sun.

Theaterrestaurant Herrenacker 23 ☏052 625 05 58, @www.theaterrestaurant.ch. An informal

bistro at ground level, serving salads and light meals for moderate prices in cool, pleasant surroundings. Upstairs, the fine-dining restaurant has classic dishes such as fillet of perch, veal or steak (expect around Fr.80 a head) in an attractive, modern, pastel-toned dining room. The wines – many from in and around Schaffhausen – are outstanding. Closed Sun & Mon; restaurant also closed Sat lunch.

Zum Frieden Herrenacker 11 ☏052 625 47 15, @www.wirtschaft-frieden.ch. An atmospheric tavern-style place with a good-value *Stübli* at ground-floor level – including a lovely secluded back garden – and a pricier formal restaurant upstairs serving Frenchified mains for around Fr.40. Closed Sun lunch & Tues.

Zum Schäfli Unterstadt 21. Typical of the cheerful, inexpensive places on Unterstadt that are generally full of hearty locals; *menus* of standard Swiss fare cost from Fr.18.

The Rhine falls

Schaffhausen's best excursion is the short trip westwards to the **Rhine falls** (@www.rheinfall.ch), Europe's largest waterfalls. They are truly magnificent, not so much for their height (a mere 23m) as for their impressive breadth (150m) and the sheer drama of the place, with the spray rising in a cloud of rainbows above the forested banks. The turreted castle, **Schloss Laufen**, on a cliff directly above the falls to the south completes the spectacle. August 1 – the Swiss National Day – sees a mighty fireworks display staged on the riverside.

The four-kilometre riverside **walk** from Schaffhausen to the suburban town of **NEUHAUSEN**, where the falls are located, takes about 45 minutes; or you could take city **bus** #1 or #6 to Neuhausen Zentrum, from where the well-signposted falls are five minutes' walk away. Schloss Laufen has a **train** station (April–Oct only), served by hourly trains between Schaffhausen and Winterthur, but Neuhausen's own station is awkwardly far away.

Once you're within sight of the falls, you're inevitably brought down to earth by the hordes of tourists crowding both banks in search of the best camera angle, and by the circus of souvenir stalls and dismal restaurants all around. The worst of it is on the north (right) bank; crossing by the arched footbridge over to the south (left) bank – which can still get crowded – at least means you can experience the power of the falls at close quarters. Damp **steps** lead down from the souvenir shop at Schloss Laufen to various vantage points overlooking the falls, where the roaring waters tumble centimetres from your nose.

Another great view can be had from one of the daredevil **boats** which scurry around in the spray; their top excursion, termed a *Felsenfahrt*, docks at the craggy rock in the centre of the cataract. Both Rhyfall Mändli (@www.maendli.ch) and Schiff Mändli (@www.schiffmaendli.ch) run trips continuously all day (May–Sept) for as little as Fr.7. Boats depart from easy-to-spot jetties on both banks.

If you fancy staying here, instead of in Schaffhausen, opt for the **HI hostel** *Jugendherberge Dachsen*, located in an annexe of Schloss Laufen (☏052 659 61 52, @www.youthhostel.ch; March–Oct; ❶).

Stein-am-Rhein

Positioned on the Rhine 20km east of Schaffhausen, little **STEIN-AM-RHEIN** is an almost perfectly preserved medieval village, famed for the intricacy of the sixteenth-century **frescoes** which adorn houses in the village. It's well worth a visit, but sees so many tour buses during the frantic summer season – about a million people pass through annually – that to enjoy the place you should stay overnight: it's only after 5pm and before 10am that there's much peace.

From the Schiffländi quay, if you head east and then cut north on tiny Schwarzhorngasse, you'll come in a minute's stroll to the **Rathausplatz**, often acclaimed as the most picturesque square in Switzerland, ringed by medieval half-timbered buildings vying with each other for the lavishness of their **frescoes** and the gracefulness of their oriels. Standing alone at the head of the square is the Rathaus, built in 1539–42: the half-timbered top storeys are original, the middle floor dates from a 1745 renovation, and the ground floor facade and entranceway were added in 1865. The line of facades along the south side of the square is dazzling, each one sporting a fresco illustrating the house name: these are, from left to right, the *Hirschen* (stag), *Krone* (crown), *Vordere Krone* (foremost crown, which sports an especially lofty gable), *Roter Ochsen* (red ox, the town's oldest tavern, with a Gothic facade), *Steinerner Trauben* (stony grapes), *Sonne* (sun, the oldest hotel in the village but with twentieth-century frescoes) and the *Schwarzer Horn* (black horn). Opposite are the *Adler* (eagle) and, most impressive of all, the *Weisser Adler* (white eagle), bedecked in the town's oldest frescoes, a Holbein-esque series painted in 1520–25.

The rest of the village pales in comparison, but there are plenty of picturesque narrow lanes and alleys to explore, ignored by most visitors. A manor house at Understadt 18, dating from 1279 and renovated in 1819, has been converted into the **Museum Lindwurm** (March–Oct 10am–5pm, closed Tues; Fr.5; Ⓦ www.museum-lindwurm.ch), with surprisingly interesting displays on Stein-am-Rhein's bourgeois and agricultural life in the nineteenth century.

Arrival, information and accommodation

At least six **boats** a day in summer arrive at Stein-am-Rhein, three from Kreuzlingen upriver and three from Schaffhausen downriver. The **train station** is on the southern bank of the Rhine, a couple of minutes' walk from the bridge. The tiny **tourist office** is at Oberstadt 9 (Mon–Fri 9.30am–noon & 1.30–5pm, May–Sept also Sat & Sun 9.30am–noon & 1.30–4pm; ☏ 052 742 20 90, Ⓦ www.steinamrhein.ch). **Accommodation** is varied.

Hostel

Schwanen Charregass 5 ☏ 052 741 50 00, Ⓦ www.schwanen-hotel.ch. Simple little hotel occupying an old building by the bridge between the station and the Old Town. Aside from a few plain singles and doubles, it concentrates on its budget-priced dorms, large and small. ❶–❷

Hotels

Adler Rathausplatz ☏ 052 742 61 61, Ⓦ www .adlersteinamrhein.ch. Directly on Rathausplatz, with a brilliantly decorated facade sheltering pine-decor rooms which are surprisingly ordinary, though comfortable enough. ❸

Chlosterhof Oehningerstrasse 2 ☏ 052 742 42 42, Ⓦ www.chlosterhof.ch. An unattractively modern building just to the east of the village centre which has spacious rooms, tastefully decorated in contemporary style – many with balconies over the Rhine. Weekend discounts. ❺–❻

Rheinfels Rhigass 8 ☏ 052 741 21 44, Ⓦ www .rheinfels.ch. Fine old Rhineside inn, dating from the sixteenth century, with atmospheric public areas and sixteen comfortable, modernized rooms, all with a river view. Closed Jan & Feb. ❸–❹

Rheingerbe Schifflände 5 ☏ 052 741 29 91, Ⓦ www.rheingerbe.ch. Old wood-beamed inn with some rooms overlooking the Rhine. ❸

Eating and drinking

The village is crammed with **eating** places. There's an inexpensive crêperie at Understadt 10, while the historic *Rheinfels* inn (see "Hotels") has an atmospheric all-wood dining room (Sept–June closed Wed) specializing in excellent fish; *menus* are around Fr.40. The gorgeous interior of the *Rother Ochsen* wine-bar on Rathausplatz (℡052 741 23 28, ⓦwww.rotherochsen.ch; closed Sun evening, Tues & Wed) suits its outstanding Swiss food, made from only local ingredients. Another good choice on Rathausplatz is the *Adler* (see "Hotels"; closed Mon), with creative Swiss and international cuisine at mid-range prices.

Kartause Ittingen

A fine detour with picnic possibilities is to the **KARTAUSE ITTINGEN** (ⓦwww.kartause.ch), a former Charterhouse (Carthusian monastery) set amidst hop fields and open farmland 6km south of Stein-am-Rhein over a hilly ridge.

From 1461 until 1868, the old buildings, arrayed around a large, peaceful courtyard, were home to a community of between twelve and fifteen monks; today, the **Ittinger Museum** (daily 11am–6pm, Oct–April Mon–Fri 2–5pm, Sat & Sun 11am–5pm; Fr.10) sheds light on the life of the order. The monks lived a life of extreme austerity, taking all meals except Sunday lunch alone in their cell and remaining committed by oath to silence. The Rococo **church** has a long nave, divided into four and flanked by intricate choir stalls carved around 1700, and a dramatic high altarpiece depicting St Bruno, founder of the order. There's no organ, since the Carthusian Mass is sung without accompaniment. Beside the church is the **Little Cloister**, prelude to a series of decorated and partly furnished rooms once used by the monks, including the Refectory (room 4), with seventeenth-century portraits ringing the walls. The fifteen monks' cells lie off the **Great Cloister**. Upstairs rooms include a tiny **prison** with barred window, and an unusual upper-level gallery in the church. Some rooms are given over to a local art museum (ⓦwww.kunstmuseum.ch), showing twentieth-century Swiss art.

The onsite **restaurant**, *Zur Mühle*, has quality, affordable modern cuisine (*menus* about Fr.20–25), but the farmland all around is prime picnic territory; pick up some home-made goodies from the little **shop**, which sells vegetables, fresh-baked bread, fragrant *eaux-de-vie* and bottles of lip-smacking Klosterbräu beer, brewed from hand-picked hops. Part of the Kartause has been renovated as a modern conference-style **hotel** (℡052 748 44 11; ❹–❺) – all exposed brick and bright, functional comforts. The *Herberge* section adjacent has simpler shared-bath rooms (❷). The Kartause hosts an internationally renowned **festival of chamber music** every Whitsun.

From Stein-am-Rhein take a bus to **Warth**, fifteen minutes' walk (or a two-minute bus ride) from the Kartause. From Winterthur or Zürich take a train to **Frauenfeld**, from where several buses a day run direct to the Kartause; alternatively, you could rent bikes from Frauenfeld station for the ride 4km north to the monastery – the station tourist office (Mon–Fri 9am–noon & 2–6pm, Sat 9am–noon; ℡052 721 31 28, ⓦwww.regiofrauenfeld.ch) has maps and information.

Lake Constance (Bodensee)

Forming a natural border between Switzerland and Germany, the long **Bodensee** – often anglicized to **Lake Constance** – is a huge bulge in the course of the Rhine, some 67km from end to end. Unlike most of the Swiss lakes, it doesn't have the benefit of shoreline mountains, and so is exposed to

Boats on Lake Constance (Bodensee)

All three countries' **boat operators** have formed a joint body, the VSU (ⓦwww .vsu-online.info). The Swiss partners are **Untersee & Rhein** (ⓦwww.urh.ch), operating between Kreuzlingen, Stein-am-Rhein and Schaffhausen; and **SBS** (ⓦwww.sbsag.ch), with one section based in Romanshorn running boats between Kreuzlingen and Rorschach, and another based in Rorschach for short trips to Rheineck. The German shore is served by BSB (ⓦwww.bsb-online.com), while Austrian Railways also runs a fleet (ⓦwww.bodenseeschifffahrt.at).

There are dozens of **excursion cruises** all round the lake during the summer season (April–Oct), most of them round-trips and many with refreshments on board. In the peak season (June to mid-Sept), it's possible to spend **a day on the lake**, leaving Rorschach at 10.45am for the two-hour cruise to Kreuzlingen, where you have a short break before departing at 2pm on the leisurely journey down the Rhine to Schaffhausen, arriving at 5.45pm. The other way, going upstream, takes from 9.10am to 4.35pm. You can eat lunch on board. In addition to the numerous passenger services, year-round **car ferries** run between Romanshorn and Friedrichshafen, and between Konstanz and Meersburg. You'll need to show your **passport** on international ferries. **Swiss Pass** holders travel free. See p.387 for details of regional passes.

winds year-round and can experience rough winter weather. If there is heavy rain further south in the Alps combined with rapid snowmelt, the Bodensee's lakeside towns are the first to feel the effects: spring and summer floods have been an increasingly common event in recent years.

Three countries border the Bodensee. The head of the lake, at its southeastern corner, is **Austrian**, focused around the genteel town of **Bregenz**. The largest settlement on the northern, **German** shore is the cosmopolitan city of **Konstanz**, separated from its contiguous Swiss suburb of **Kreuzlingen** only by an arbitrary international frontier. The lake is one of the main summer destinations for holidaying German families; this rubs off on the southern, **Swiss** shore, too, where the scattering of soporific little resorts such as **Rorschach** and **Arbon** have a strong Teutonic air about them.

Kreuzlingen and around

At the northwestern corner of the Bodensee, the small Swiss town of **KREUZLINGEN** is an anomaly, nothing more than a southern suburb of the historic German city of **Konstanz**; the international frontier separating them runs arbitrarily between buildings. Kreuzlingen is like border towns everywhere, full of traffic streaming through without stopping and imbued with a feeling that the exciting stuff is happening elsewhere, just out of sight. It has little history of its own, but is worth stopping in for the **Kirche St Ulrich**, 150m south of the centre on Hauptstrasse. This Baroque church houses the remarkable Ölbergkapelle, containing a 1780 wood carving of the Passion comprising around three hundred individual figures; the sculpture is teeming with intricate detail, and is surmounted by a fifteenth-century cross (*Kreuz* in German) which has survived three major fires. The church itself is no less dazzling, with an ornate choir screen in green and gilt.

Kreuzlingen's main station, the **Hauptbahnhof**, is 150m south of the international border; head east (left) out of the station to reach the traffic lights on

There is a **map** of Lake Constance on p.388.

Hauptstrasse. The **tourist office** is 50m away, just behind Hauptstrasse at Sonnenstrasse 4 (Mon–Fri 10am–12.30pm & 1.30–5/6pm; May–Sept also Sat 10am–12.30pm; ℡071 672 38 40, Ⓦwww.kreuzlingen-tourismus.ch). From these traffic lights, Hafenstrasse continues east to the lakeshore, where you'll find the harbour and the **Hafenbahnhof** train station. Nearby is the old Villa Hörnliberg, housing an HI **hostel**, Promenadenstrasse 7 (℡071 688 26 63, Ⓦwww.youthhostel.ch; March–Nov; ❶). South along the lakeshore is the *Fischerhaus* **campsite** (℡071 688 49 03, Ⓦwww.camping-fischerhaus.ch; April–Oct). Opposite the Hauptbahnhof, friendly *Bahnhof-Post* **hotel**, Nationalstrasse 2 (℡071 672 79 72, Ⓦwww.hotel-bahnhof-post.ch; ❷), has pleasant en-suite rooms. *Zapfenzieher*, Hauptstrasse 44, is an amiable **café-bar** with terrace (closed Sun eve), while *Seegarten*, Promenadenstrasse 40 (℡071 688 28 77, Ⓦwww.seegarten.ch; closed Mon, Sept–May also closed Tues), is a high-class **restaurant** at the marina; expect Fr.50 and up.

Konstanz and Insel Mainau

The main point of coming to Kreuzlingen is to visit **KONSTANZ** just over the German frontier. This ancient city straddling the Rhine has been an important ecclesiastical hub for centuries: the Council of Konstanz (1414–18), which tried and failed to heal divisions within the Church, met in the huge **Münster**, originally a Romanesque basilica, set amidst a web of characterful alleys now lively with students from the city's university. The **tourist office** beside the station (April–Oct Mon–Fri 9am–6.30pm, Sat 9am–4pm, Sun 10am–1pm; rest of year Mon–Fri 9.30am–12.30pm & 2–6pm; ℡0049 7531 133030, Ⓦwww.konstanz.de) has English information about a self-guided walking tour. **Trains** take three minutes from Kreuzlingen's main station, but it's no hardship to walk the fifteen minutes or so; either way, you'll need to show your **passport**.

Just 8km north in Germany – accessible by direct ferry from Swiss and German ports – is **INSEL MAINAU** (daily sunrise–sunset; April–Oct €14.90, Nov–March €7; Ⓦwww.mainau.de), a forested island occupied by a Baroque castle and beautiful gardens.

Münsterlingen

About 2km east of Kreuzlingen lies the village of **Münsterlingen**, worth stopping in to visit its sixteenth-century Baroque church, originally part of a Benedictine convent. The interior is beautifully decorated, with a lavish altarpiece flanked by twisted gilt and turquoise columns, and a cupola overhead painted with a *trompe l'oeil* fresco: the abbess of the convent in the 1680s was related to master sculptor Christof Daniel Schenck from Konstanz, and brought him in to do some of the decoration and to sculpt the wood figures still on display in the church. An altar curtain dating from 1565, used during Lent to hide the glory of the altar, hangs to one side.

The church's most interesting tale begins in the sixteenth century when the lake froze solid six or seven times. One winter a church official from **Hagnau**, on the German bank opposite, walked across the frozen lake to Münsterlingen, saved a statuette of John the Baptist from being destroyed by Protestant Reformers and took it back to Hagnau for safekeeping. When the lake froze again some years later, he brought it back. Since then, a freezing of the lake has precipitated a solemn procession to carry the statuette to the opposite shore. In 1830, villagers delivered it to Hagnau, where it remained until the harsh winter of 1963, when the ice was solid enough to return it to Münsterlingen church. There it still sits, in the crypt (a copy is on display), awaiting the next icy spell.

Romanshorn and around

Along the shore is **Romanshorn**, a run-of-the-mill lakeside resort, arrival point for boats from **Friedrichshafen** on the German bank opposite. About 7km east is the ancient village of **ARBON**, reputedly the point at which Columba and Gallus (see p.404) stepped ashore. Walk left from the station for about ten minutes to reach the tranquil centre, marked by the spire of the **Kirche St Martin**, with, in its grounds, the tiny eleventh-century Galluskapelle. Adjacent is the sixteenth-century **Schloss Arbon**, housing a pleasant little restaurant (Ⓦ www.zumschloss.ch; closed Sat & Sun). The old streets nearby hold a number of half-timbered buildings, most seventeenth- or eighteenth-century; on Kapell-gasse is a chapel built in 1390, but deconsecrated in 1777.

Rorschach

A couple of hours' walk southeast of Arbon, the pleasant lakeside resort of **RORSCHACH** occupies a bay below the grassy Rorschacherberg, 9km from St Gallen. It has three train stations. The main Rorschach-HB (Hauptbahnhof) is awkwardly located 1km east of the harbour and town centre. Coming from St Gallen, trains stop first at **Rorschach-Stadt**, a short walk above the harbour. Trains from Romanshorn, though, stop first at **Rorschach-Hafen** (harbour), directly on the lakefront alongside the old **Kornhaus**, emblem of a once-thriving grain trade between St Gallen and Germany. From the Hafenbahnhof, **Hauptstrasse** heads east, flanked by fine sixteenth- to eighteenth-century houses with attractive oriel windows. The **Kolumbanskirche** just off the street is a broad, white, late Baroque church dedicated to the Irish monk Columba, with much gilded glitter inside. A rack railway (Ⓦ www.ar-bergbahnen.ch) winds up from the Hafenbahnhof to the hill resort of **Heiden**, which offers views and hiking trails. As well as regular Bodensee ferries, the local boat operator (Ⓦ www.sbsag.ch) runs short pleasure trips to Rheineck, on the Austrian border just east of town.

Rorschach's **tourist office** is opposite the Hafenbahnhof, Hauptstrasse 63 (Mon–Fri 8.30am–noon & 1.30–6pm, May–Sept also Sat 9am–1.30pm; ☎071 841 70 34, Ⓦ www.tourist-rorschach.ch). There's a pleasant HI **hostel** on the lake, Churerstrasse 4 (☎071 844 97 12, Ⓦ www.youthhostel.ch; ❶; April–Sept). The lakefront **hotel** *Mozart*, 150m west of the Hafenbahnhof (☎071 844 47 47, Ⓦ www.mozart-rorschach.ch; ❸), has comfortable, renovated rooms and an excellent **restaurant** for mid-priced daily *menus* and convivial Sunday brunches.

As a footnote, the famous **Rorschach Ink-Blot Test**, in which a subject under therapy is asked to describe the images they see in the random shape of a blot, was named after its deviser, Swiss psychologist Hermann Rorschach (1884–1922), rather than after the town.

Friedrichshafen airport

Friedrichshafen airport (☎0049 7541 28401, Ⓦ www.bodenseeairport.eu) is a few kilometres inland from the town. Taxis (€12) and hourly trains shuttle from the airport through the city (Stadt) to the harbourside (Hafen) train station (€1.80; takes 11min; last train to harbour 7.40pm, to city 11.20pm; Ⓦ www.bob-fn.de). From Friedrichshafen harbour, ferries run hourly to **Romanshorn** (40min; last ferry 8.40pm, July & Aug Fri & Sat 10.40pm; Ⓦ www.sbsag.ch), where trains depart regularly from the main station near the dock to destinations all over Switzerland. The last train to Zürich is 10.30pm, to St Gallen 11.30pm.

St Gallen

The main urban centre of eastern Switzerland, **ST GALLEN** is a relaxed provincial city set amidst rolling countryside between the Appenzell hills and the Bodensee, with a busy modern centre and a beautiful Old Town. The centrepiece is its extraordinarily lavish Baroque abbey, declared a UNESCO World Heritage Site: the cathedral is impressive enough alone, but the **abbey library** is celebrated as Switzerland's finest secular Rococo interior and contains a world-class collection of ancient books and manuscripts.

Some history

St Gallen owes its existence to the religious community which remains at its core. In around 612, the Irish monk **Gallus** – a follower of Columba – was travelling south from the Bodensee into the forest. Legend has it that he either fell over, or stumbled into a briar patch, or told a bear to fetch some firewood whereupon it obeyed; whichever, Gallus felt he had received a sign from God, and so chose that spot to build his hermitage. In the eighth century, a follower named **Otmar** established a monastic community around Gallus's cell, and founded a school of scribes and translators. In the 830s, Abbot Gozbert established the great **library**, and St Gallen's reputation as a centre of culture and learning grew. By the thirteenth century, St Gallen had become an important market town and its reputation as a centre of learning was being superseded by its reputation as a producer and exporter of high-quality **linen**. By the end of the Middle Ages, it was the only Swiss town to have trade representatives

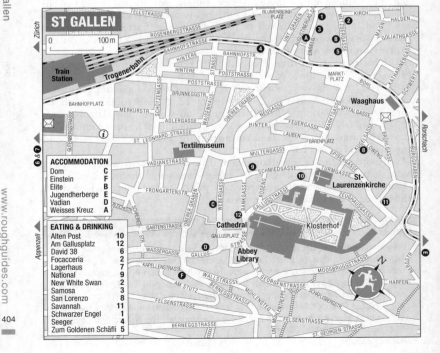

ST GALLEN

0 — 100 m

Train Station

ACCOMMODATION
Dom	C
Einstein	F
Elite	B
Jugendherberge	E
Vadian	D
Weisses Kreuz	A

EATING & DRINKING
Alten Post	10
Am Gallusplatz	12
David 38	6
Focacceria	2
Lagerhaus	7
National	9
New White Swan	2
Samosa	3
San Lorenzo	8
Savannah	11
Schwarzer Engel	1
Seeger	4
Zum Goldenen Schäfli	5

Textilmuseum

Waaghaus

St-Laurenzenkirche

Cathedral

Klosterhof

Abbey Library

resident in foreign cities, and was linked by stagecoach to centres of textile processing in Nuremberg and Lyon.

In 1529, Joachim von Watt – known as **Vadian** – introduced the Reformation, sparking iconoclastic riots which forced the monks temporarily to flee; the abbey survived, however, as a walled Catholic enclave within the Protestant city.

In the eighteenth century, St Gallen's weavers switched to the new fashion for **hand-embroidery**: by 1790, some 40,000 women were working from home to embroider cotton and muslin for export – notably to the young United States. By 1913, embroidery was Switzerland's largest export industry, with St Gallen accounting for around half of the entire world production of textiles. These days, that figure is down to just 0.5 percent, but Swiss embroidery remains a highly valued, luxury commodity, with small, highly specialized companies supplying designs and finished products to *haute couture* fashion houses: Lacoste's famous crocodile logo, for instance, is Swiss-embroidered. Nonetheless, St Gallen's embroidery industry – now almost entirely computerized – still relies on two thousand local women working from home, hand-sewing detailing that is impossible to achieve by machine.

Arrival, information and accommodation

St Gallen's **train station** is 200m southwest of the Old Town. The **tourist office** is on the far side of the square, Bahnhofplatz 1a (Mon–Fri 9am–6pm, Sat 10am–3pm; Nov–April Sat closes 1pm; ☎071 227 37 37, Ⓦ www.st.gallen-bodensee .ch). Staff can supply information on the whole Ostschweiz region, and they run an excellent two-hour guided **walking tour** (May–Oct Mon & Wed–Sat 2pm, July & Aug also Tues & Sun 2pm, Jan–April & Nov Sat 11am; Fr.18). The **OpenAir** pop festival (Ⓦ www.openairsg.ch), in late June, pulls in international performers from Van Morrison to Metallica. **Accommodation** includes a clutch of business hotels at the station, and a few more characterful choices.

Hostel

Jugendherberge (HI hostel) Jüchstrasse 25 ☎071 245 47 77, Ⓦ www.youthhostel.ch. Take the Trogenerbahn narrow-gauge train from St Gallen station (platforms 11–14, accessed from platform 1A) to the Schülerhaus stop, and walk up the hill. March–Nov. ➊

Hotels

Dom Webergasse 22 ☎071 227 71 71, Ⓦ www .hoteldom.ch. Pleasant little hotel on an Old Town lane, with good, modern rooms decorated with original works of *art brut*, or naïve art. Parking on site. ➋–➌
Einstein Berneggstrasse 2 ☎071 227 55 55, Ⓦ www.einstein.ch. The city's top choice, a grand old hotel housed in a former textile factory, with generously appointed rooms and quality service. ➐
Elite Metzgergasse 9 ☎071 222 12 36, Ⓦ www .hotel-elite.ch. Plain and serviceable rooms in a

lively neighbourhood near Marktplatz, both en suite and not. ➋
Vadian Gallusstrasse 36 ☎071 228 18 78, Ⓦ www.hotel-vadian.com. House-proud little two-star on a quiet street near the cathedral, with pleasantly renovated rooms, some en suite. ➌
Weisses Kreuz Engelgasse 9 ☎071 223 28 43. Nice little family-run hotel, unprepossessing from the outside, sleek and modern within. ➋

Out of town

Null Stern Teufen ☎071 330 01 63, Ⓦ www .nullsternhotel.ch. The world's first "zero-star" hotel opened in 2008 in this village outside St Gallen. You sleep in a former nuclear bunker, sharing the windowless space with others in beds alongside, and the zero-star concept extends to the complimentary breakfast – which comprises tea or coffee. It's an experience. Teufen lies on the narrow-gauge train line from St Gallen towards Appenzell. ➊

The City

From the tourist office, as you head east along Vadianstrasse into the roughly circular Old Town, you'll pass the **Textilmuseum**, Vadianstrasse 2 (daily

▲ St Gallen's Old Town

10am–5pm; Fr.10; Ⓦwww.textilmuseum.ch), which has an interesting and well-presented collection, focusing on handmade embroidery and lace. Before you get there, diverting a block south to Bleichestrasse brings you into the **Stadtlounge** (Ⓦwww.stadtlounge.ch), where the artist Pipilotti Rist has created a public lounge space featuring red (solid) sofas ranged on little plazas paved in red concrete, beneath giant bubble-like shapes that glow after dark. It's all rather odd.

Once you cross Oberer Graben, you enter the Old Town proper. These attractive streets and alleys are adorned with 111 elaborate **oriels**, or small projecting bay windows, most of which are younger than the houses to which they're attached: a fashion for them in the eighteenth century meant that many were carved from wood, painted, and then stuck onto the stone facade to satisfy the whim of the nouveau-riche merchant who lived within. Some of the finest can be found at Schmiedgasse 15 (House of the Pelican) and 21 (House of Strength); Kugelgasse 8 (House of the Ball) and 10 (House of the Swan); Hinterlauben 10 (House of the Deep Cellar); and Spisergasse 22 (the Camel Oriel). Along **Gallusstrasse** you'll also find half-timbered cottages from the Middle Ages rubbing shoulders with Baroque town houses and grand nineteenth-century dwellings put up during St Gallen's golden age of textile production.

The tall, steepled **St-Laurenzenkirche** on Marktgasse (Mon 9.30–11.30am & 2–4pm, Tues–Sat 9.30am–4pm) dates from the ninth century, and originally stood within the monastic enclosure of the cathedral and abbey. Renovated in neo-Gothic style in the mid-nineteenth century, it has a narrow, lofty nave flanked by Gothic pointed side arches.

The cathedral

St Gallen's giant Baroque **cathedral** (Mon–Sat 9am–6pm, Sun 12.15–5.30pm) is unmissable, its twin towers visible from most points. Designed by one Peter Thumb from Bregenz, it was completed in 1767 after just twelve years' work. Easiest access is through the west door on Gallusstrasse, although it's worth

Schoggi Land chocolate factory

A short way west of St Gallen is the **Maestrani chocolate factory** – dubbed "**Schoggi Land**", Toggenburgerstrasse 41, Flawil (Mon–Fri 9am–noon & 2–6pm, Sat 9am–noon; ☎071 228 38 88, ⓦwww.schoggi-land.ch). Displays highlight the history of Maestrani (one of the oldest Swiss chocolate firms, founded in 1852), and you're allowed onto a gallery above the factory floor to watch the production lines running. There's also a shop. To **get there**, take a train to **FLAWIL** from St Gallen (14min) or Zürich (59min), then switch to a bus (direction Lütisburg, Ganterschwil or Bütschwil) for the five-minute ride to the factory's own "Flawil Maestrani" bus stop. By car, take the Uzwil exit off the A1 (Zürich–St Gallen); the factory lies between Flawil and Wattwil.

10

making your way through the church and out into the enclosed Klosterhof, at the heart of the complex, where you can gaze up at the soaring **east facade**. To the left is the palace wing, still the residence of the Bishop of St Gallen.

The **interior** is vast, a broad, brightly lit white basilica with a triple-aisled nave and central cupola. Although not especially high, it has a sense of huge depth and breadth thanks to its accomplished architecture: from the sandstone of the floor and wood of the pews, fanciful light-green stuccowork – characteristic of churches in the Konstanz region – draws your eye up the massive double-width pillars to the array of frescoes on the ceiling, which are almost entirely the work of one artist, Josef Wannenmacher. Above the western end of the nave is a panel showing Mary surrounded by angels. The central cupola shows paradise, with the Holy Trinity, apostles and saints. Details throughout the rest of the cathedral are splendid: the lavish, mock-tasselled pulpit; the ornate choir screen; the richly carved walnut-wood confessionals; the intricate choir stalls; and, far away at the back of the choir, the high altar flanked by black marble columns with gold trim. The south altar features a bell brought by Gallus on his seventh-century journey from Ireland, one of the three oldest surviving bells in Europe.

The abbey library (Stiftsbibliothek)

Within the same complex of buildings as the cathedral, and just adjacent to it, is the **abbey library** (Mon–Sat 10am–5pm, Sun 10am–4pm, closed for three weeks in late Nov; Fr.10; ⓦwww.stibi.ch), one of the oldest libraries in Europe, and famous both for its superb Baroque interior and for its huge collection of rare and unique medieval books and manuscripts. You enter beneath a sign reading YUCHS IATREION (*psyches iatreion*, Greek for "Pharmacy of the Soul"). Ranged beside are dozens of oversized felt slippers; slip your shoed feet into a pair, to save the inlaid wooden floor of the library from scuffing.

The 28-by-10-metre room is acclaimed as Switzerland's finest example of a Baroque secular interior, and the first glimpse of it as you enter is dizzying. Designed by the same Peter Thumb who worked on the cathedral, the library dates from slightly later: its orthodox Baroque architecture is overlaid with the opulent decoration of the Rococo period which then held sway. The four **ceiling frescoes** by Josef Wannenmacher depict with bold *trompe l'oeil* perspectives the early Christian theological councils of Nicaea, Constantinople, Ephesus and Chalcedon. Amongst the wealth of smaller frescoes set amongst the ceiling stucco, in the corner directly above the entrance door you'll spot **The Venerable Bede**, a seventh-century English monk from Northumbria who wrote one of the first histories of England: he is shown as a scholar, with, beside him, a magic number square. This four-by-four sequence, where the numbers add up to 34 horizontally, vertically, diagonally and from the four corners, is thought to have been invented by Pythagoras in ancient Greece, but took on a new mystical power for early Christians who believed Christ to have died at 34 years of age.

The **books** are ranged on floor-to-ceiling shelves all around, originally organized by subject (indicated by the cherubs at the head of capitals around the library), but now arranged alphabetically. This is still an ordinary lending library and study centre, with some 140,000 volumes focused on the Middle Ages. Its list of cultural treasures is extraordinary. There are more **Irish manuscripts** in St Gallen than there are in Dublin, fifteen handwritten examples including a Latin manuscript of the Gospels dating from 750. Other works include an astronomical textbook written in 300 BC; copies made in the fifth century of works by Virgil, Horace and other classical authors; texts written by Bede in his original Northumbrian language; and the oldest book to have survived in German, dating from the eighth century. Various of these and other treasures of the library's upstairs manuscript room (no public access) are displayed in glass cases dotted around the main library area. An ancient Egyptian **mummy** in the library dates from 700 BC and was a gift to the mayor of St Gallen in the early nineteenth century; unsure of what to do with the thing, he plonked it in this corner, where it has sat incongruously ever since.

Eating and drinking

St Gallen has a good range of **eating and drinking** places. Look out for stalls selling St Gallen's famous pale Olma sausage, eaten ketchup- and mustard-free in a *Bürli*, or bread roll. A feature of St Gallen dining is the handful of traditional tavern-restaurants on the upper floor of old town houses, while a cluster of streets north of Marktplatz holds livelier, more alternative cafés and restaurants.

Cafés and café-bars

Focacceria Metzgergasse 22 ⓦ www.focacceria .ch. Tucked-away little nook offering fresh focaccia, panini and other light bites – a nice place for a cosy chinwag. Closed Sun & Mon.

National Schmiedgasse 30. An atmospheric half-timbered house in the Old Town offering eight varieties of home-brewed beer and local snacks such as *Weisswürste* (veal sausage) and *Chäschüechli* (cheese pie). Closed Sat lunch & Sun.

Schwarzer Engel Engelgasse 22 ⓦ www .schwarzerengel.ch. Popular, unpretentious cooperative-run café-bar, with good beer, a sociable atmosphere and inexpensive food (Fr.20–25), both veggie and not. Closed Tues eve & Sat lunch.

Seeger Oberer Graben 2 ⓦ www.seeger-restaurants .ch. Elegant big-windowed lounge café with inexpensive food, playing easy music to a twenty-something crowd relaxing on the leather sofas inside, or at tables on the pavement terrace. Stays open till midnight or later.

Restaurants

Alten Post Gallusstrasse 4 ⓣ 071 222 66 01, ⓦ www.apost.ch. Tiny, much-loved traditional

restaurant, in an Old Town building dating from 1552. Market-fresh ingredients go into its hearty international cuisine – steak, rack of lamb, fresh lake fish and the like. Reckon on Fr.60–80. Closed Sun & Mon.

Am Gallusplatz Gallusstrasse 24 ⓣ 071 223 33 30, ⓦ www.gallusplatz.ch. The city's leading restaurant, serving high-quality French cuisine amidst suitably stout decor. Your best option is to come for lunch, when *menus* are lighter in tone and cost less (Fr.25–30). In the evening, expect Fr.70-plus. Closed Sat lunch & Mon.

David 38 Davidstrasse 38 ⓣ 071 230 28 38, ⓦ www.david38.ch. Located 5min walk west of the Old Town, this quiet, chic restaurant – white linens, art on the walls, parquet floors, black ceiling – offers excellent Asian fusion cuisine on a range of *menus* from Fr.72 (three courses) up to Fr.192 (seven courses including wine). Closed Sat lunch & Sun.

🏃 **Lagerhaus** Davidstrasse 42 ⓣ 071 223 70 07, ⓦ www.restaurantlagerhaus.ch. After a day amid the tourist maelstrom of the abbey district, plug into a slice of local St Gallen life at this wonderfully relaxed hideaway 250m west of the Old Town. A post-industrial space dotted with candelabra and exposed pipework, it offers light, simple food – fish, pasta, salads and the like – from a well-priced menu to twenty- and thirty-somethings out to enjoy a bottle of wine with friends. Closed Sat lunch, Sun & Mon.

New White Swan Metzgergasse 24. Fast-paced little diner serving up huge portions of steaming Asian-style stomach fillers to students and others on tight budgets.

Samosa Engelgasse 20 ⓦwww.samosa.ch. Authentic backstreet curry house, offering lunchtime all-you-can-eat buffets (Fr.14–17) and a wide range of dishes, both veggie and meat. Closed Sun (Sept–May open Sun eve).

San Lorenzo Kugelgasse 7 ⓣ071 222 11 70. Lively, uncomplicated pizza and pasta joint, invariably crowded, with a good-sized menu and rapid service.

Zum Goldenen Schäfli Metzgergasse 5 ⓣ071 223 37 37, ⓦwww.zumgoldenenschaefli.ch. Best known of St Gallen's upper-floor restaurants, with low ceilings, wood panelling all around and creaking floors. The food is all hearty local fare, with plenty of offal on the menu – the house speciality is calf's liver – and other local dishes such as sautéed lake fish. *Menus* start from a reasonable Fr.40 or so. Closed Sun.

Appenzellerland

The residents of **Appenzellerland** are the butt of many a Swiss joke, regarded by cosmopolitan urbanites as country bumpkins and mercilessly mocked for their folksy ways. Yet although a sophisticated Lausannois or Basler might chortle to hear it, this rustic region is something of a sensuous delight: as you cross the verdant hills south from St Gallen, the pungent smells of cows and cheese assault your nose; on a wander through the villages, busy embroidery and the fussily net-curtained windows of wooden houses delight the eye; and local cooking, particularly rich with butter and cream, has a delicious silkiness on the tongue. Yet it remains virtually unknown: 85 percent of tourists to the region are Swiss, with another 13 percent from nearby areas in Germany.

Encircled by rolling hills, with the snowy peaks of the Alpstein ridges to the south, Appenzell has for centuries been a land apart. Monks from St Gallen colonized the area in the tenth century, calling it *Abtszell* ("Abbey Cell"), but the fiercely independent local peasantry threw off ecclesiastical control in a series of wars in the fourteenth century. Although surrounded by St Gallen's territory, Appenzell joined the Swiss Confederation in 1513, long before its more powerful neighbour. Shortly afterwards it split into two tiny autonomous half-cantons – Protestant **Appenzell Ausserrhoden** (abbreviated to "AR"), and Catholic **Appenzell Innerrhoden** ("AI"). For touristic purposes, the two half-cantons are together dubbed "Appenzellerland", but the divisions between them remain to this day, with Ausserrhoden's dynamic economy based on manufacturing industry and Innerrhoden's slower one based on tourism and the preservation of traditional culture.

Appenzell village, capital of Innerrhoden, the least populous Swiss canton, is the main draw for its quaint, traditional air – preserved even amidst the high-season day-trippers. Other than **Stein**'s museum and show-dairy, surrounding

Exploring Appenzell

If you book to stay in the region for three nights or more, you receive, free of charge from your hotel, the **Appenzeller Ferienkarte** or Appenzell Card (ⓦwww.appenzell.ch), which covers transport on local buses and trains (including to and from St Gallen), as well as cable cars, admission to museums, a cheese-tasting session at the Stein show-dairy and other benefits.

villages hold few attractions, but there's plenty of good **hill-walking**, with routes crossing the velvety slopes towards the rocky peaks of the Alpstein and its highest point, the snowy **Säntis** (2502m).

Appenzell

The main street of **APPENZELL**, 20km south of St Gallen, is car-free Hauptgasse, running from a bridge over the River Sitter at the entrance to the village west for 300m or so to the broad, open **Landsgemeindeplatz**; wander along to admire the intricately painted old wooden houses – notably *Löwen Drogerie*, a pharmacy at no. 20 – with their rows of small, closely packed windows. During the nineteenth century, the embroidery industry of nearby St Gallen relied upon thousands of women working by hand from home, with the intricate work of Appenzell particularly highly prized: the upstairs rooms in these buildings, flooded by daylight through the lines of windows, were used as workshops.

In the same building as the tourist office is the **Appenzell Museum**, Hauptgasse 4 (April–Oct daily 10am–noon & 2–5pm, Nov–March Tues–Sun 2–5pm; Fr.7; ⓦ www.museum.ai.ch). This interesting exhibition of local crafts is spread out over six floors: highlights include many examples of Appenzell hand-embroidery, as well as militaria from Clanx Castle, the ruins of which are visible on a nearby hilltop. Don't miss the short videos shown on demand in a viewing room on the ground floor: the one on local musical traditions is especially good. A few steps away is the Baroque church of **St Mauritius**, much more ornate than you would expect for a country village, its high altar flanked by gold figures.

Museum Liner stands on the edge of the village, Unterrainstrasse 5 (April–Oct Tues–Fri 10am–noon & 2–5pm, Sat & Sun 11am–5pm; Nov–March Tues–Sat 2–5pm, Sun 11am–5pm; Fr.9; ⓦ www.museumliner.ch). This gallery, devoted to the work of father-and-son local artists Carl August Liner and Carl Walter Liner, is interesting mainly for its boldly conceived design in steel by the Zürich partnership of Annette Gigon and Mike Guyer. Exhibitions of the Liners' uninspiring modernistic art are made more appealing by additional exhibits of Swiss contemporary works.

Arrival, information and accommodation

Appenzeller Bahnen's narrow-gauge **train** to Appenzell (free to Swiss Pass holders; ⓦ www.appenzellerbahnen.ch) starts from platforms 11–14 of St Gallen station, which are separate from the main platforms, accessed via a path beside platform 1A. Trains arrive at Appenzell's **station**, 200m south of the centre. The friendly **tourist office** is at Hauptgasse 4 (Mon–Fri 9am–noon & 1.30–6pm, Sat & Sun 10am–noon & 2–5pm, Nov–March Mon–Fri 9am–noon & 2–5pm, Sat & Sun 2–5pm; ☎ 071 788 96 41, ⓦ www.appenzell.ch).

Appenzell's **accommodation** is neat, quiet and characterful, to suit the village. Not many people seem to stay, but it's definitely worth doing so, not least because the village is set on a sloping patch of meadow tipped westwards towards low hills, and on clear summer evenings the tranquil streets are filled with lingering twilight until 10pm.

Adler Adlerplatz/Hauptgasse 1 ☎ 071 787 13 89, ⓦ www.adlerhotel.ch. Attractive, well-run family hotel overlooking the river, with a range of quality rooms both modern and traditionally styled. ❸

Appenzell Landsgemeindeplatz ☎ 071 788 15 15, ⓦ www.hotel-appenzell.ch. Characterful, heavily gabled old building on the upper (south) side of the square, with chunky wooden beds in spacious and comfortable rooms, and fine, friendly service. ❹

Freudenberg Riedstrasse 57 ☎ 071 787 12 40, ⓦ www.hotel-freudenberg.ch. It's worth making your way up the hill behind the station to find this place, not so much for the rooms, which are pleasant but unremarkable, but for the views from the balconies over the village and surrounding countryside. Closed Nov. ❸

Säntis Landsgemeindeplatz ☎071 788 11 11, ⓦ www.saentis-appenzell.ch. Another big old traditional building, on the north (lower) side of the main square, and a member of the prestigious Romantik group. Some rooms feature canopied or four-poster beds and there's polished wood everywhere; smaller attic rooms are priced attractively. ❹–❺

Eating and drinking

Of all the local specialities – including *Chäshörnli* (cheese-and-potato mini-dumplings), *Birnebrot* (pear bread), a sweet liqueur named *Alpenbitter*, and a fragrant herb-based Schnapps dubbed *Kräuter* – the most ubiquitous is ripe, spicy **Appenzeller cheese**. It's powerful stuff: if you buy some, take the shopkeeper's advice and have it vacuum-sealed, otherwise you'll find the pong seeping its way into everything else in your bag.

Many hotels offer quality **eating and drinking**. The best value is *Appenzell*: go through the *confiserie* shop into the restaurant behind. *Menus* start from about Fr.20, excellently prepared with a light touch; the house speciality is a range of fresh vegetarian and health-conscious food. Elsewhere, traditional fare abounds, relying heavily on pork, potatoes and creamy sauces. The bustling old-fashioned restaurant in *Gasthaus Hof*, Engelgasse 4 (ⓦ www.gasthaus-hof.ch), concentrates on a host of excellent cheese dishes, including *Käseschnitte* (cheese on toast). The *Säntis* hotel has the swankiest dining in town, although the ground-floor *Stübli* and terrace is considerably cheaper and much less formal than the upstairs restaurant with its Gallic-accented menu.

Around Appenzell

Walking in the pretty countryside **around Appenzell** can be rewarding, with inns and guesthouses dotting the landscape – so many that you could walk for

---

Appenzell traditions

Appenzell has clung on to its many rural **traditions** as modern, living elements of local culture: although you may be tempted to dismiss demonstrations of local crafts or evenings of folkloric music as phoney touristic kitsch, in fact such events are put on as much for the benefit of locals as for visitors. Weddings, dances and celebrations of all kinds count as excuses for locals to don **traditional dress**, with the women in stiff-winged caps and lace-edged dresses, and the men in elaborate embroidered scarlet waistcoats, with tight black trousers and a silver earring dangling from their right ear.

The village of **Urnäsch**, 10km west of Appenzell, celebrates New Year's Eve (Silvesterklausen) twice, once on December 31 and again, in order to keep faith with the long-abandoned Julian calendar, on January 13. Even the ornate silver **pipes** smoked by Appenzeller old-timers are idiosyncratic, curving down at the end instead of up, with the tobacco kept in place by a little sliding lid.

In politics, too, Appenzell stands alone. It was only in 1990 that the men of Ausserrhoden finally, and reluctantly, allowed **women** to have the vote in cantonal affairs. Innerrhoden held out for another year, and remains one of the last Swiss cantons to use the **Landsgemeinde**, the ancient embodiment of Swiss direct democracy (Glarus – see p.413 – is the only other), in which citizens gather in traditional dress once a year in the town square of the cantonal capital to vote by brandishing a short sword (the badge of citizenship) in response to a series of shouted yay-or-nay questions. It takes place on the last Sunday in April and is a nationally televised event.

days from inn to inn without encountering a town and without having to carry food. The Appenzell tourist office has plenty of maps, trail guides and mountain-bike routes, including details of *Barfuss durchs Appenzellerland*, a trail which you can follow **barefoot** through grassy meadows from Appenzell village up to **Gonten**, a couple of hours west, scene of June's cantonal Schwingen (traditional wrestling) championships.

Most hiking trails are crammed into and around the narrow valleys sandwiched between the three great rock walls of the **Alpstein** range. The small village of **Wasserauen**, a short train ride or a couple of hours' walk south of Appenzell, is the base station for a cable car running up to **EBENALP** (ⓦwww.ebenalp.ch; 1640m), from where a high-level route takes you five hours along the ridge to the Säntis. Another route from Wasserauen runs up for an hour into the narrow valley of the beautiful **SEEALPSEE** (1141m). This isolated tarn hosts the attractive lakeside *Berggasthaus Forelle* (ⓣ071 799 11 88, ⓦwww.gasthausforelle.ch; April–Oct; ❶), with comfort-able, traditional-style rooms as well as dorms, as well as the simpler *Berggasthaus Seealpsee* (ⓣ071 799 11 40, ⓦwww.seealpsee.ch; April–Oct; ❶). Both have terrace tables at which to enjoy succulently prepared lake fish. Beyond Seealpsee, a two-hour trail hairpins its way steeply up to tranquil **MEGLISALP** (1517m), with its own rustic *Berggasthaus Meglisalp* (ⓣ071 799 11 28, ⓦwww.meglisalp.ch; May–Oct; ❶).

Appenzell's most famous peak is the **Säntis** (2502m), well below the proportions of the Alps but nonetheless the highest point for many kilometres around. Trains run from Appenzell to the small town of **Urnäsch**, departure point for hourly buses which follow a winding road up to **Schwägalp**, from where a cable car (Fr.41 return; ⓦwww.saentisbahn.ch) rises to the Säntis summit. This is a popular day-trip, especially in summer: if you're staying for lunch, you'd do best to aim for the atmospheric *Berggasthaus* on top (ⓦwww.berggasthaus-saentis.ch), rather than the newer canteen-style diner – both, though, have terraces offering spectacular panoramas. From the summit, it's an easy three-and-a-half-hour hike along to Ebenalp, from where there's transport back to Appenzell.

Stein

Herisau, capital of the half-canton Appenzell Ausserrhoden (AR), and connected to Appenzell village by train, is a workaday town, handy for its bus link to St Gallen via the backcountry village of **Stein** (often dubbed "Stein AR"; not to be confused with Stein-am-Rhein). Stein hosts the engaging **Appenzeller Volkskunde Museum** (Folklore Museum; Tues–Sun 10am–5pm; Fr.7; ⓦwww.avm-stein.ch). The highlight is on the top floor, which is devoted to Appenzell's **folk art**, made by nineteenth-century farmers who decorated furniture, milk pails and other implements with ornate designs, painting scenes from daily life on canvas and wood. Johannes Müller is the most prolific of these uncelebrated artists; he lived all his 91 years in Stein as a clockmaker, and his simple paintings are characterized by vibrantly green hills crisscrossed by long lines of cattle led by herders in traditional dress.

Next door is the **Appenzeller Schaukäserei** (Show Dairy; daily 8.30am–6.30pm; Nov–April closes 5.30pm; free; ⓦwww.showcheese.ch), where you can watch the various processes of cheesemaking from a gallery above the huge vats and churns – try to time your visit to coincide with the main cheesemaking procedures (which stop at 5pm). Cheese-lovers won't want to miss the Sunday-morning all-you-can-eat breakfast buffet (8.30–11am; Fr.23).

Glarnerland

Switzerland's least-known and hardest-to-reach region is **Glarnerland**, centred on Canton Glarus, a tract of mountain territory featuring just a handful of widely spaced settlements and very low-key tourism. Its isolation is its main attraction: this is a place to turn your back on the crowds and head for the wilderness.

The slender, cliff-girt **Walensee** is pretty much bypassed by both the N3 autobahn and Zürich–Chur trains. **Ziegelbrücke**, at the lake's western tip, marks the start of routes squeezing southwards. The main **tourist office** is on the autobahn, near Ziegelbrücke at the Niederurnen rest-stop (July & Aug daily 8am–6pm; rest of year Mon–Fri 8.15am–noon & 1.30–5.30pm, Sat 8am–5.30pm, Sun 8am–1pm; ☎055 610 21 25, ⓦwww.glarnerland.ch); their wide range of outdoorsy deals includes two days' all-in hill-trekking on horseback (Fr.135). **GLARUS**, the picturesque little capital, lies 12km south, dwarfed by the looming Glärnisch massif; there's little reason to stay, unless you're here on the first Sunday in May for the **Landsgemeinde**, a traditional form of direct democracy when cantonal affairs are decided by public voting in the main square.

The main road continues south to scenic **Linthal**, base station for a short funicular ride up to the unsung gem of the region – the car-free mountain resort of **BRAUNWALD**; there are few quieter, more refreshing places to rest up, take in the Alpine views and get out into nature. As you emerge from the top station, you'll see map-boards of the village and its surrounds; the **tourist office** (July–Oct & Christmas–Easter Mon–Fri 8am–5pm, Sat 8am–2pm; rest of year Mon–Fri 9am–noon & 2–4pm; ☎055 653 65 65, ⓦwww.braunwald .ch) can advise on routes: there are lifts to higher slopes as well as a host of walks around Braunwald's plateau. **Hotels** all have balconies and sun-terraces; the *Waldhaus* (☎055 653 54 55, ⓦwww.klausen-resort.ch; ❸) is conveniently beside the funicular station, and there's a good **SB hostel**, *Adrenalin* (☎079 347 29 05, ⓦwww.adrenalin.gl; ❶).

The Klausen Pass

Beyond Linthal, the road climbs west over the **Klausen Pass** (1948m) towards Lake Lucerne. This is a simply stunning drive through breathtaking scenery, but is little used: the road is only open in summer (June–Oct) and is mostly very narrow – just about two car-widths between the cliff and the ravine. Tortuous hairpin bends mean that you should reckon on at least an hour and a half to cover the 47km to **Altdorf** (see p.345).

After some steep climbing out of Linthal, you emerge into the lovely, high, enclosed valley of **URNERBODEN**, dotted with a few farms and dozens of wandering cows; to the left is the Clariden (3268m), to the right the cliffs of the Ortstock (2717m). The road meanders its way past a couple of inns, including the sturdy *Urnerboden* (☎055 643 14 16, ⓦwww.gasthaus-urnerboden.ch; ❷), which is open year-round – in winter there's some fine cross-country skiing up here. Faced by a sheer cliff at the head of the valley, the road somehow jinks its way up and around to the pass itself, where there's a refreshment kiosk; 1km down the other side – just before the truly awesome scenery kicks in – is the century-old *Hotel Klausenpasshöhe* (☎041 879 11 64, ⓦwww.klausenpasshoehe. ch; May–Oct; ❶), with unrenovated rooms. The route from here all the way down to Altdorf is a battle: you'll constantly have to drag your eyes away from the spectacular views to concentrate on the road.

Postbuses run both ways on the "Historic Route Express" between Linthal and Altdorf in summer (June–Sept; reserve on ☎041 870 21 36, ⓦwww .postbus.ch), and from Linthal up to Urnerboden all year round.

Liechtenstein

The Principality of **LIECHTENSTEIN** (*Fürstentum Liechtenstein*, abbreviated to "**FL**") is the world's sixth-smallest country, a chip of green squeezed between the Rhine and the Austrian Alps. It's a quiet, unassuming place, home to 35,000 mostly Catholic Liechtensteiners, who take an impressive 22 days' public holiday a year, sing their own German words to the tune of "God Save the Queen" as the national anthem, and regard themselves as entirely separate from the Swiss, with whom neighbourly relations only began in 1923. This said, you won't notice many differences and, inevitably, the main reason to visit is the novelty value. There are some rustic spots to enjoy outside the toy-town capital **Vaduz**, as well as lonely walks and family-friendly skiing in the craggy mountains.

Regular **postbuses** run to Vaduz from **Sargans** and **Buchs**, both of them on the main SBB train line between St Gallen and Chur. Austrian Railways (ÖBB, or OeBB) operates a few **trains** a day between Buchs and Feldkirch (Austria) which stop at Schaan, 3km north of Vaduz, from where buses shuttle into the capital. The principality's biggest event is **Staatsfeiertag** (National Holiday; Ⓦ www.staatsfeiertag.li), on August 15.

Some history

Liechtenstein is the only country in the world to have been named after the person who bought it. After the Romans came through in 15 BC, the area was passed from pillar to post until 1699, when Johann Adam Andreas of the **Von Liechtenstein** family of Vienna purchased the Lordship of Schellenberg, and then in 1712 the County of Vaduz, in order to get a seat for himself in the imperial German Diet of Princes. Shortly after, the little patch was renamed after him. Liechtenstein won independence in 1866, the Prince taking an active political role within a so-called **democratic monarchy** linked to Austria-Hungary. After that empire's war defeat, Liechtenstein negotiated a customs treaty with Switzerland in 1923, since when borders between the two neighbours have been open and unmarked. The next milestone was 1984, when women got the vote.

The current head of state is His Serene Highness **Prince Hans Adam II von und zu Liechtenstein**, although in 2004 he placed his son, **Crown Prince Alois**, in charge of day-to-day affairs. Although tiny, Liechtenstein has often gone its own way, joining the United Nations in 1990 and the sub-EU European Economic Area in 1995, both of which created a gulf in relations with more reticent Switzerland. Then, in 2003, the people voted in a referendum to hand the prince significant new powers to appoint judges, veto parliamentary decisions and dismiss the government, effectively creating Europe's only absolute monarchy. The bitterly divisive campaign which led up to the vote exposed serious fault-lines in Liechtensteiner society: shortly afterwards, in an unprecedented snub to the entrenched power of the Catholic Church, the people voted in another referendum to legalize abortion.

Meanwhile, the principality gets on with what it does best: making **money**. Around 75,000 international companies are nominally headquartered in

---

Exploring Liechtenstein

Buses (Ⓦ www.lba.li) serve all points. Swiss Pass holders travel free; otherwise opt for a one-day national bus pass (Fr.7) or the **Erlebnispass** (Ⓦ www.erlebnispass.li), which covers unlimited bus transport, a city-train tour in Vaduz, the Malbun chairlift, admission to all museums, wine-tasting and other attractions for Fr.25/45 (two/six days).

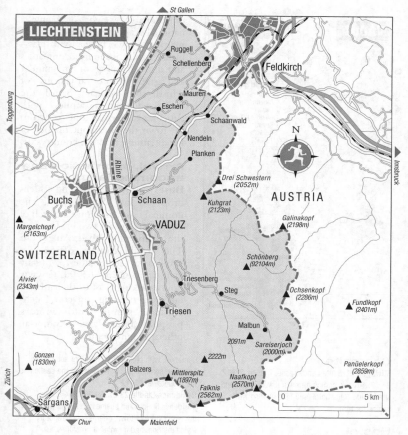

Liechtenstein, purely to take advantage of the favourable tax regime. The **banks** – which hold assets of Fr.80 billion or more – were part-reformed in 2000 in a bid to limit money-laundering by organized crime, but still persist with their system of anonymous numbered accounts: in 2008 Liechtenstein was deemed an "uncooperative tax haven". High finance aside, the principality has also made a mint from producing highly collectable **postage stamps**, as well as false teeth. Liechtensteiner villages have a neat, bourgeois atmosphere about them, rather disappointing if you've come expecting to see signs of an ancient monarchy stuck somewhere in the Middle Ages.

Vaduz

Whereas quiet, provincial towns on the Swiss side of the Rhine such as Sargans and Buchs slumber, on the opposite bank **VADUZ** labours under the

Although Liechtenstein uses Swiss francs, it has its own telephone country code ☏423, completely separate from the Swiss phone system. More information is on p.56.

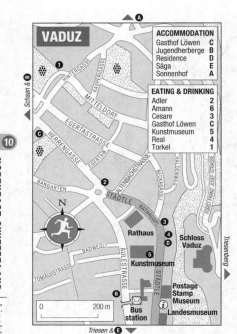

Triesen & **E** ▼

unreasonable weight of being a national capital. The spick-and-span little town bulges with glass-plated banks, insurance companies and all the trappings of government and state, while squadrons of whistle-stop visitors patrol the pint-sized squares, aimless with anticlimax. Take an hour or two in the town, then head out: the best of Liechtenstein is in the countryside.

Arrival, information and accommodation

Buses from Sargans and Buchs drop off at "Vaduz-Post", the nominal bus station (just a clutch of bus stops) beneath two bridges over the main traffic road, Äulestrasse. The helpful **tourist office** is a stroll away at Städtle 37 (daily 9am–5pm; ☎239 63 00, Ⓦwww .tourismus.li). Most of their time is taken up banging souvenir Liechtenstein stamps into visitors' passports (Fr.2) – a novelty, not an official requirement.

Campsite

Mittagsspitze Alte Landstrasse, Triesen ☎392 36 77, Ⓦwww.campingtriesen.li. Well-equipped site beside *Säga* hotel (see below), also with cabins for rent.

Hostel

Jugendherberge Untere Rüttigasse 6, Schaan ☎232 50 22, Ⓦwww.youthhostel.ch. Good HI hostel 2km north of Vaduz, near the neighbouring town of Schaan, a short walk from the Mühleholz bus stop. March–Oct. ❶

Hotels

Löwen Herrengasse 35 ☎238 11 44, Ⓦwww .hotel-loewen.li. Liechtenstein's oldest hotel, in business since 1380. The style is comfortably

upmarket, with characterful interiors and period furniture; some rooms have views of the castle and the mountains. ❻–❼

Residence Städtle 23 ☎239 20 20, Ⓦwww .residence.li. Splendid business-oriented hotel in the very centre of town, offering contemporary styled interiors and a range of amenities. ❻

Säga Alte Landstrasse 17, Triesen ☎392 43 77, Ⓦwww.saega.li. Spotless, family-run hotel in the countryside 6km south of Vaduz, with nine plain, comfortable rooms. Bus to Triesen Säga. ❸

Sonnenhof Mareestrasse 29 ☎239 02 02, Ⓦwww.sonnenhof.li. Probably the finest hotel in the country, a small, romantic Relais & Châteaux property set in its own grounds on the edge of Vaduz. ❽

The Town

Everything in Vaduz happens along **Städtle**, the pedestrianized main street, lined with cafés, souvenir shops and hotels. Occupying a sleek, dark building in the middle of the action is the ultra-modern **Kunstmuseum** (Tues–Sun 10am–5pm, Thurs until 8pm; Fr.12, joint ticket with Landesmuseum Fr.15; Ⓦwww.kunstmuseum.li). Extracts from its collection embrace modern and contemporary art, particularly strong on sculpture: you may find a Courbet landscape alongside a Giacometti bronze opposite a spindly Arte Povera installation. Running simultaneously are shows of contemporary art as well as exhibits taken from the private collection inherited and added to by the Prince, which includes works by Rubens, Van Dyck, Rembrandt and others. The juxtaposition is particularly engaging, played out in such a well-designed space.

A stroll away on Städtle is the **Landesmuseum** (National Museum; Tues–Sun 10am–5pm, Wed until 8pm; Fr.8, joint ticket with Kunstmuseum Fr.15; ⓦ www .landesmuseum.li), with interesting themed displays covering archeology, history, contemporary life and more. Notes are in German, but there's a free audioguide in English. Five minutes' stroll south on Städtle brings you past the parliament building on its little plaza to the spire of the attractive nineteenth-century **St Florinskirche**, a modest parish church known as Vaduz Cathedral.

Wandering the older streets north of the centre leads to the signposted **Hofkellerei des Fürsten von Liechtenstein**, the Prince's vineyards and cellars (ⓦ www.hofkellerei.li). Groups can book ahead for a tour; otherwise anyone can drop into the onsite shop to taste any of the wines for free (Mon–Fri 8am–noon & 1.30–6pm, Sat 9am–1pm). The Prince's photogenic restored sixteenth-century **Schloss Vaduz** perches picturesquely on the forested hillside above Vaduz, visible from all over town. Knots of people gather at the castle gates to admire the towers and turrets, but entry is forbidden.

Eating and drinking

Nothing is cheap in Vaduz, and that applies to **restaurant** food in particular: expect good quality but high prices. In this devoutly Catholic country, almost everywhere is closed on Sunday.

Adler Herrengasse 2 ☎ 232 21 31, ⓦ www.adler.li. Family-run restaurant just off Städtle, with an informal, cheery atmosphere and mid-priced international cuisine. Closed Sat & Sun.

Amann Äulestrasse 56. Incognito locals' café on the main road, with basic, good-value meals and a touch of atmosphere. Closed Sun.

Cesare Städtle 15 ⓦ www.adler.li. Decent little Italian with good *menus* from Fr.35 or so. Closed Sat & Sun.

Kunstmuseum Städtle 32 ⓦ www.kunstmuseum.li. The museum café is a lovely place to sit, serving salads, light bites and sushi, even when the museum itself isn't open. Daily 9am–6pm, Wed–Fri until 11pm.

Löwen (see "Hotels"). Lovely restaurant set amid its own vineyards a stroll away from Städtle, serving seasonal cuisine in a tasteful, upmarket setting. Closed Sat & Sun.

Real Städtle 21 ☎ 232 22 22, ⓦ www.hotel-real.li. Top address in Vaduz, a classic top-class hotel with a restaurant to match, serving an arty, creative take on traditional Liechtensteiner cuisine. Presentation is superb and quality is exceptional.

Torkel Hintergasse 9 ☎ 232 44 10, ⓦ www.torkel .li. Fine old-fashioned restaurant amid the prince's vineyards, serving high-priced Swiss and Austrian specialities. Closed Sun.

Around Vaduz

Attractions around the principality are low-key, and aside from the mountain resort of Malbun, almost entirely untouristed. North of Schaan is the Unterland region, with some pleasant walks through the rolling countryside and dark woods. From **Nendeln**, a path climbs for an hour through the forest to **Planken**, Liechtenstein's smallest village (pop. 370), from where a steep two-hour route takes you up to spectacular views at the **Gafadurahütte** at 1428m (☎ 262 89 27, ⓦ www.alpen verein.li). Further north is tiny **SCHELLENBERG**, overlooked by the ruins of the medieval Obere Burg castle set amidst lush forest. Its sole hotel is the simple, cosy *Krone* (☎ 373 11 68, ⓦ www.hotelkrone.li; ❷), where children get a discount.

South of Vaduz is the Liechtensteiner Oberland, with workaday Triesen overshadowed by pretty **TRIESENBERG**, perched on a sunny hillside above the Rhine and best known as the adopted home of a community of Walser people, who left their homes in Wallis (German-speaking Valais) in the thirteenth century to spread out across central Europe. Many of the houses are old wooden chalets built in the Walser style. The modern, well-presented **Walsermuseum** (Mon–Fri 8am–noon & 2–6pm, Sat 8–11am & 1.30–5pm; Fr.2) documents the community's history and culture. A fine, scenic walk leads from Triesenberg through Gnalp and Masescha and back (3hr), while the **views** from here – a stupendous panorama over the Rhine valley and the Alps – merit a night at the chalet-style **hotel** *Kulm* in the village centre (☎237 79 79, ⊛www.hotelkulm.com; ❸–❹): book ahead for its comfortable balconied rooms facing over the valley.

Malbun

From Triesenberg, a back-country road climbs through a tunnel beneath an Alpine ridge to **Steg** and on to **MALBUN**. This quiet hamlet at 1600m is Liechtenstein's only ski resort, with half-a-dozen little lifts (⊛www.bergbahnen.li) and a handful of gentle runs. Steg is the trailhead for a web of **cross-country ski** routes through the Valüna valley to the south. In summer, the area has a wealth of lonesome high-country **hikes**: a classic full-day mountain trek from Steg rises south through the Valüna valley up to the Naafkopf (2570m), before returning via the Augstenberg and Malbun. From Malbun, a rewarding three- or four-hour hike begins with a journey up the Sareis chairlift and then heads south along the Austrian border to the scenically positioned **Pfälzerhütte** at 2108m (☎263 36 79).

Malbun has a little **tourist office** (June–Oct & mid-Dec to mid-April Mon–Sat 9am–noon & 1.30–5pm; ☎263 65 77). A congenial **place to stay** is *Berggasthaus Sücka* near Steg (☎263 25 79, ⊛www.suecka.li; ❶), also with dorms and good food. Malbun makes a selling-point of its family-friendliness: *Hotel Gorfion* (☎265 90 00, ⊛www.gorfion.li; ❷–❹) is a great place to bring the kids, with comfortable rooms and good amenities. The *Galina* hotel (☎265 34 24, ⊛www.galina.li; ❸) – another good choice – works with a local falconer Norman Vögeli, who gives regular falconry shows in this magnificent Alpine setting: check the website for details. **Eating and drinking** is at the handful of hotel restaurants, or at the top station (2000m) of the Sareis chairlift (⊛www.bergrestaurant-sareis.li) – otherwise an hour's hike up from Malbun – which has a scenic terrace and hearty Swiss nosh.

Travel details

Full timetables for all trains, buses, trams, boats and cable cars in Switzerland – as well as international connections – are searchable at ⊛www.rail .ch. Details of boats on Lake Constance (Bodensee) are at ⊛www.vsu-online.info.

Trains

Appenzell to: St Gallen (every 30min; 45min).
St Gallen to: Appenzell (every 30min; 45min); Chur (hourly; 1hr 35min); Rorschach (3 hourly; 15min); Sargans (hourly; 1hr 10min); Schaffhausen (3 hourly; 1hr 30min; some change in Winterthur); Stein-am-Rhein (hourly; 1hr 25min); Winterthur (3 hourly; 35min); Zürich (3 hourly; 1hr).
Schaffhausen to: Kreuzlingen (hourly; 55min); Schloss Laufen (twice hourly; 5min); Stein-am-Rhein (every 30min; 25min); Winterthur (3 hourly; 25min); Zürich (twice hourly; 40min).

Stein-am-Rhein to: St Gallen (hourly; 1hr 25min): Schaffhausen (every 30min; 25min).
Winterthur to: St Gallen (3 hourly; 35min); Schaffhausen (3 hourly; 25min); Zürich (6 hourly; 20min).

Buses

Vaduz to: Buchs (every 20min; 15min); Malbun (hourly; 30min); Sargans (every 20min; 30min).

Boats

(Following is a summary of May–Sept services.)
Kreuzlingen to: Romanshorn (at least 2 daily; 1hr 15min); Schaffhausen (at least 3 daily; 3hr 45min); Stein-am-Rhein (at least 3 daily; 2hr 25min).
Schaffhausen to: Kreuzlingen (at least 3 daily; 4hr 45min); Stein-am-Rhein (at least 3 daily; 2hr).

Graubünden

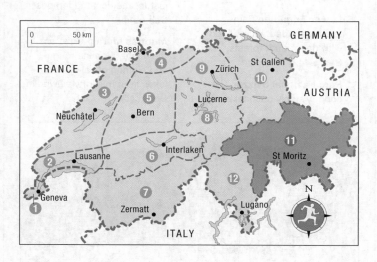

CHAPTER 11 # Highlights

* **Rhätische Bahn** The local train company has a superbly scenic network. See p.421

* **Arosa** Outstanding small resort, high in the mountains above Chur. See p.427

* **Flims-Laax** Top destination for snowboarders. See p.434

* **Davos and Klosters** Two of the biggest names in the Alps. See p.437

* **Lower Engadine** Fairy-tale high-sided valley, lined with deep, dark forests. See p.442

* **Parc Naziunal Svizzer** The country's only national park,

with a network of fine walking trails. See p.445

* **Müstair** Remote village huddled round a frescoed abbey. See p.446

* **Upper Engadine** Perhaps the most beautiful valley in the Alps, with over 320 days of sunshine a year. See p.447

* **St Moritz** One of Europe's best-known ski resorts, not just for the rich and famous. See p.448

* **Muottas Muragl** Gaze on the mighty Bernina range and a string of valley-floor lakes from this lofty viewpoint. See p.454

▲ A Rhätische Bahn train climbing to St Moritz

Graubünden

GRAUBÜNDEN (Ⓦ www.graubuenden.ch), Switzerland's largest canton, occupies the entire southeast of the country, encompassing a sparsely populated area that borders Austria to the north and Italy to the east and south. Its folded landscape of deep, isolated valleys, sheer, rocky summits and thick pine forests makes it the wildest and loneliest part of Switzerland, with some of the finest scenery in the Alps. Glaciers launch two

---

Exploring Graubünden

Graubünden's **Rhätische Bahn** (RhB; Ⓦ www.rhb.ch) has one of the most scenic train networks in the world, with tracks spanning deep valleys on soaring viaducts and crossing several mountain passes. Many of the most dramatic routes are marketed as attractions in their own right (see p.34), but are all served by regular, scheduled trains at **standard fares**. The only extra costs are seat reservations (always advisable, for a few francs), surcharges to sit in panoramic coaches, upgrades to first class and/or reservations for the dining car that often accompanies longer journeys. Otherwise, all RhB trains are **free** to Swiss Pass holders.

The RhB **Graubündenpass** – on sale at all stations – covers all public transport within the canton for Fr.125 (3 days' travel in a week) or Fr.155 (five days' travel in two weeks).

Despite the excellent train service, if you want to cover a lot of ground independently, Graubünden merits **renting a car**. Buses penetrate to the most remote valleys and hamlets, but often only every two hours, and journeys can be long and tortuous.

Special train journeys

Although the following are headline routes, it's easy to cherry-pick the most attractive or convenient bits of any of them to construct your own itinerary. Full details are at Ⓦ www.rhb.ch. The **Glacier Express** runs from St Moritz and Davos to Chur and then west over the Alps to Zermatt. The **Bernina Express** runs from Chur over the Albula Pass to St Moritz, then over the high Bernina Pass to Tirano, switching to a postbus for the journey around Lake Como to Lugano; the Albula and Bernina sections are listed as UNESCO World Heritage. The **Aqualino** runs from Landquart through Klosters to Scuol, tying in with day packages at the Bogn Engiadina spa. The **Arosa Express** does the run from Chur to Arosa.

On selected days in summer, the RhB also runs its own **Pullman** coaches on various scenic full-day routes, as well as similar outings pulled by **steam-engines**. There are **full-moon** train trips into the mountains on selected nights during the year, the chance to ride on the footplate with the driver on certain routes, and – perhaps the most fun of the lot – the **Railrider**, a roofless train completely open to the elements, which shuttles the forty minutes between Filisur and Preda on the steep, dramatic Albula route every Sunday from late June to early September (Fr.17 one-way; no reservation needed).

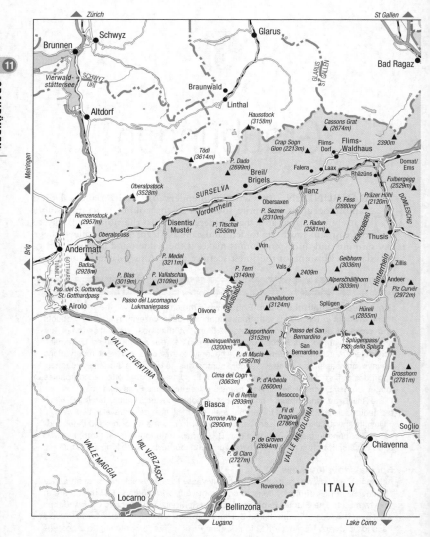

of Europe's great rivers – the Rhine and the Inn – on their long journeys to the North Sea and the Black Sea respectively, while two smaller rivers water pomegranates, figs and chestnuts en route to the Po and the Adriatic.

The canton – once the Roman province of Rhaetia Prima – is officially **trilingual**, known as Graubünden in German, Grigioni in Italian and Grischun in **Romansh**, the last of these a direct descendant of Latin which has survived locked away in the mountain fastnesses far from the capital **Chur**. You'll also come across the canton's French name of **Grisons**, although there are no French-speaking communities.

Until the nineteenth century, **Rhaetia** was entirely separate from its western neighbour of Helvetia. As Helvetia began to experience stirrings towards

independence in the thirteenth and fourteenth centuries, the population of Rhaetia also began to organize themselves. The 1367 League of the House of God was the first of these popular associations, soon followed by the **Grey League** in 1395 (formed by a band of highland shepherds dubbed "the grey farmers" for their woollen cloth). With the spur of the Reformation, the united "**Graubünden**", or Grey Leagues, seized political power from the nobility. Since then the people have been free, and they relish the fact more than most other Swiss. It was only in 1803 that they assented to join the Swiss Confederation, and to this day Bündners consistently vote in large numbers against joining the EU.

The canton's resorts – headed by **St Moritz**, **Klosters** and **Davos** – are some of the most famous names in the Alps and offer world-class skiing and top-quality hiking, but they're far from the whole story. The beautiful **Engadine valley** runs for almost 100km along a southern terrace of the Alps, bathed in glittering sunlight for well over 300 days a year. This is the heartland of Romansh culture, with its own language, style and architecture. South of the Alps, three of the canton's most enticing valleys – **Bregaglia** and **Poschiavo** in particular – are Italian-speaking, filled with a Mediterranean lushness in their flora and cuisine.

Chur and around

Sitting in a deep valley carved by the Rhine, **CHUR** (pronounced *koor*), the lively cantonal capital, is much overlooked: it has a characterful Old Town, full of medieval cobbled alleys, secret courtyards and solid, foursquare town houses, that is dominated by a huge **cathedral** symbolizing the rule of the bishop-princes of years gone by. Chur serves as the linchpin of transport routes, with buses and trains sneaking their way through the high, narrow valleys of Central Graubünden to Davos and St Moritz, and west through Surselva to the high Alps around Andermatt. In a mountain fastness southeast of the town sits the picturesque resort of **Arosa**, while the gentler foothills to the northeast are cloyingly dubbed "**Heidiland**".

Chur is the oldest continuously inhabited city north of the Alps, with archeological finds dating back to 11,000 BC. Situated on prime north–south routes of commerce and communication, Curia Rhaetorium was founded by the **Romans** after their conquest of 15 BC. **St Luzius**, a missionary, is reputed to

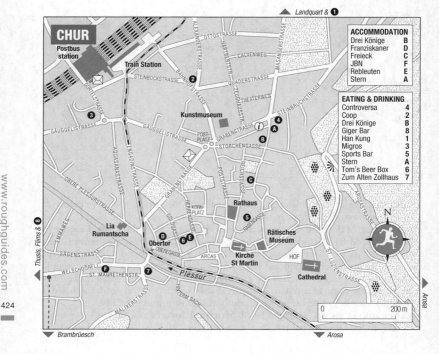

have brought Christianity to the region in the fourth century, and the first **bishop** of Chur to be positively documented was Asinio, in the year 451. A few centuries on, the bishop had become a powerful political ruler, enjoying the patronage of Holy Roman Emperors, and by 1170 the post was officially recognized as a Prince-Bishopric. When the **Reformation** took hold in 1526, Chur's wealthy merchants and craftsworkers took over all significant political decision-making for themselves. Today, from his palace beside the cathedral, the bishop of Chur still controls a diocese covering Graubünden, all the central Swiss cantons and Zürich, and students flock to the adjacent St Luzi theological seminary to train for the priesthood.

Arrival, information and accommodation

Chur's **train** and **postbus station** – resplendent beneath a vast, fully glazed arching roof, reminiscent of nineteenth-century railway architecture – is at the head of Bahnhofstrasse, five minutes northwest of the Old Town. The **tourist office** is beneath the station (Mon–Fri 7.30am–8pm, Sat & Sun 8am–6pm; ☎081 252 18 18, @www.churtourismus.ch). They have an audioguide for a self-guided walk around town (Fr.9 plus Fr.50 deposit; or you can download the MP3 files from their website).

Hostel

JBN Just Be Nice (SB hostel) Welschdörfli 19 ☎ 081 284 10 10, @www.justbenice.ch. Sparklingly clean and modern hostel in a conveniently central location on a lively (if slightly seedy) street, with a range of rooms (some en suite) and dorms. ❷

Hotels

Drei Könige Reichsgasse 18 ☎081 354 90 90, @www.dreikoenige.ch. A 200-year-old inn in the Old Town, characterful and pleasant with a range of rooms. ❷–❸

Franziskaner Kupfergasse 18 ☎081 252 12 61, @www.hotelfranziskaner.ch. Freshly renovated rooms in the heart of the Old Town, both en suite and with shared bath. ❷

Freieck Reichsgasse 44 ☎081 255 15 15, @www.freieck.ch. Comfortable mid-range place spread across a couple of old renovated buildings, with some good rooms updated in pine and pastel. ❸–❹

Rebleuten Pfisterplatz 1 ☎081 255 11 44, @www.rebleuten.ch. Lovely guildhouse dating from 1483, with elaborate scrollwork on its facade, an excellent restaurant, cosy bar and attractive rooms. Superb value. ❸

Stern Reichsgasse 11 ☎081 258 57 57, @www.stern-chur.ch. Poshest hotel in town. An historic inn and member of the Romantik group, with top-quality service, modern, wood-beamed rooms and parking, plus an excellent restaurant. ❹–❺

The Town

Chur's picturesque Old Town nestles in the shadow of the cathedral, which looms on high ground to the southeast. The alleys and fountained squares are characterized by their terraces of old houses, traditionally built without shutters and fronted

Above Chur: Brambrüesch and the Dreibündenstein

Chur is proud of the fact that it's the only Swiss city with its own hiking and winter-sports area accessible directly from the city centre. The **Brambrüesch** (@www.brambruesch.ch) rises immediately southwest of the Old Town: its cable-car station is on Kasernenstrasse, five minutes' walk west of the Obertor. Brambrüesch (1600m) is one of the three peaks of the **Dreibündenstein** (2174m), and has plenty of summer hiking routes, as well as paragliding and a summer toboggan run. In winter, a **ski pass** (Fr.33/41 half/full day) also covers chairlifts above Brambrüesch, giving access to easy pistes and tobogganing.

in rather dour, greyish Scalära stone. The main north–south thoroughfare **Poststrasse** bisects the Old Town; at its northern end is busy Postplatz, overlooked by a large villa housing the **Bündner Kunstmuseum** (Tues–Sun 10am–5pm, Thurs until 8pm; Fr.12; Ⓦwww.buendner-kunstmuseum.ch), featuring paintings by Graubünden artists Angelika Kauffmann and Giovanni and Alberto Giacometti. Something of a feminist icon during her lifetime and afterwards, Kauffmann was born in Chur in 1741, and moved to London at the age of 25. She quickly established a solid reputation there, becoming one of the most popular artists of the time, and was one of the founding members of the Royal Academy in 1768. Although she was best known in her day for the kind of dramatic narrative painting exemplified in *Hector and Paris* (1770), viewable here, art historians now tend to reject such works as overly sentimental and favour instead her portraits, of which there are also plenty on show, not least a graceful self-portrait (1780). The museum also stages high-quality temporary exhibitions.

Following Poststrasse 100m south brings you to the arcaded courtyard of the fifteenth-century **Rathaus**. One street to the east is Reichsgasse, an atmospheric old alley with, at no. 57, a plaque commemorating Angelika Kauffmann's birthplace. Reichsgasse ends in the attractive open square of Arcas, dominated by the Gothic **Kirche St Martin**, dating from 1491 and now sporting three beautiful stained-glass windows by Alberto Giacometti. Arcas hosts the lively Gänggelimarkt flea market (1st Sat of month). Opposite the church, bustling Oberegasse – site of a weekly food market (May–Oct Sat morning) – runs west to the **Obertor** gate, a remnant of Chur's medieval fortifications. Behind the church rises the cathedral hill; just to the left, in a quiet courtyard, stands the impressive **Rätisches Museum** (Tues–Sun 10am–5pm; Fr.6; Ⓦwww.rm.gr.ch), devoted to local history.

The cathedral

Chur is dominated by its **cathedral** (daily 6am–7pm; Ⓦwww.bistum-chur.ch), constructed between 1151 and 1272 in late Romanesque and Gothic styles. Still hived off from the town by a thick gated wall, which reflects the bitterness of the disputes that flared around the Reformation, the cathedral is the focus of the **Hof**, a complex of eighteenth-century buildings in the heart of the city protecting Chur's religious elite from contact with the mob.

The **interior** is modestly proportioned but richly decorated, with finely carved Romanesque capitals above the massive columns and colourfully painted aisle ceilings. High up opposite the Baroque **pulpit** is a tiny gallery: this is one end of a "secret" passage from the bishop's palace next door, allowing the bishop to enter the House of God at a suitably lofty altitude and without soiling his shoes on the courtyard outside. The **choir** is raised at an unusual height above the nave to accommodate the crypt, and is dominated by a superb fifteenth-century high altar.

Eating and drinking

Chur's Old Town has a good range of places to **eat**, many of them offering the classic regional dish of *Bündnerfleisch*, prime air-dried beef served sliced paper-thin to adorn a *Bündnerteller* – a carefully presented plate of cold meats. *Bündnerfleisch* also takes centre stage in *Bündner Gerstensuppe*, a creamy barley soup with vegetables. Hunting is still popular in the countryside, and you'll see game on autumn menus, including stews of deer or chamois. Another local speciality is Passugger **mineral water**, bottled in Passugg 2km south; however, it's not worth paying for, since the same stuff flows out of every tap and street fountain in town. Student **bars** cluster near the Obertor.

Restaurants

Controversa Steinbruchstrasse 2. Classy, modern restaurant with a small menu of upmarket Italian fare (mains from Fr.28). Closed Sat lunch, Sun & Mon.

Drei Könige (see "Hotels"). Attractive wood-panelled dining room that draws a fair range of locals thanks to its hearty, well-priced Swiss cuisine (mains from Fr.18).

Han Kung Masansterstrasse 44 ☎081 252 24 58, ⓦ www.han-kung.ch. Good Chinese housed in a comfortable old manor house 400m north of the centre, with mains from around Fr.20. Closed Sun lunch & Mon.

Migros Gäuggelistrasse 28. Big self-service diner in front of the station. Closed Sun.

🏃 **Rebleuten** Pfisterplatz 1 ☎081 257 13 57, ⓦ www.rebleuten.ch. Excellent regional cooking (daytime mains Fr.16–18; evening Fr.21–32) amidst the medieval surroundings of a pair of formal, wood-panelled dining rooms. Closed Sun.

Stern Reichsgasse 11 ☎081 252 35 55, ⓦ www .stern-chur.ch. Top-choice hotel restaurant for characteristically meaty Bündner specialities, with a cosy, intimate atmosphere. *Menus* around Fr.20.

Zum Alten Zollhaus Malixerstrasse 1 ☎081 252 33 98. Cosy wood-panelled *Stübli* opposite the Obertor, offering a mix of light meals (from Fr.18) – anything from *Rösti* to banana curry – plus more elaborate Swiss dishes (Fr.36–44). The attached

Pizzeria Verdi downstairs dishes up good, moderately priced pizza and pasta (from Fr.15) and other Italian dishes.

Bars

Controvini In *Controversa* restaurant, Steinbruchstrasse 2. Chur's first wine-bar and still a chic, popular spot offering over thirty wines by the glass.

Giger Bar Comercialstrasse 23 ⓦ www.hrgiger .com. A blank cube tucked between office buildings 1.5km west of the Old Town in a business zone of furniture showrooms and petrol stations, much vaunted for its owner and designer, the Swiss-born, Oscar-winning, special-effects supremo H.R. Giger (see p.112). The interior is kitted out in the style of Giger's greatest creation, *Alien*, with sleek, sci-fi power-chairs, jet-black decor and a limbless, writhing female torso hoisted above the bar. Oddly enough, despite the movie-set decor, it's an utterly ordinary after-work bar for local business folk, with its radio tuned to a light-melodies channel. Brad Pitt did stop by once, though. Mon–Thurs 8am–8pm, Fri & Sat 8am–midnight; bus #1 to Agip.

Sports Bar Rabengasse 7. Convivial joint for familiar beers and TV sport. Closed Sun.

Toms Beer Box Unteregasse 11 ⓦ www.toms.ch. Hole-in-the-wall joint (entrance on Goldgasse) which stocks 140 bottled beers from around the world. There's no sign – look for the crowds of drinkers in the street outside.

Arosa

AROSA was discovered by the outside world in 1883 when Dr Otto Herwig-Hold came across the remote hamlet on a skiing tour – a perfect location for his new tuberculosis sanatorium. The chest patients have long since given way to sports enthusiasts, and Arosa has developed into one of Graubünden's finest resorts, yet it's still small enough to have retained its atmosphere and lacks even a trace of the hotshot swagger of Davos or St Moritz.

Arosa lies at the end of a single, spectacular mountain road which cuts its way up into a sheer and narrow valley southeast of Chur, passing through a succession of terraced villages and offering vistas breathtaking enough to make you want to stop and gape every three minutes – which you could do, but for the fact that in the 32-kilometre journey, there's a total of 244 switchbacks. It's somewhat more relaxing to take the **Arosa Express** train, which departs from the forecourt of Chur station and shadows the road all the way up.

Beware that many hotels, restaurants and shops are **closed during off-season** (mid-April to mid-June & mid-Oct to mid-Dec). We've specified months of opening only when they differ from this pattern.

Arrival, information and accommodation

The town consists of two areas: the main resort is **Ausserarosa**, clustered around the train station and the Obersee lakelet, while the older village at the upper end of the valley, about 3km distant, is dubbed **Innerarosa**. The **train station**

Children of the Road

The story of the Swiss gypsy people, known as the **Jenisch** (or Yenish), and how they have been treated over the last century by the Swiss authorities, exposes a calculated policy of Nazi-style eugenics carried out behind closed doors well into the 1970s. For almost fifty years, the Swiss government funded the wholesale kidnapping of Jenisch children, separating more than six hundred babies and toddlers from their families in a determined attempt to wipe out Jenisch culture. Ghosts have not been put to rest and the scandal remains a source of anger and national shame.

The Jenisch are one of the three main groups of central European gypsies, along with the Sinti and the Roma. During and after the great waves of gypsy migration in the seventeenth and eighteenth centuries, many arrived in Graubünden, where they lived a generally quiet, if socially ostracized, life. Following the tide of nationalism that swept through Europe after World War I, the science of **eugenics** gained widespread credibility, with its notion of "cleansing" the racial gene pool by forcibly removing from society those with mental illnesses, physical disabilities and other characteristics seen as aberrant. Along with Jews and homosexuals, people with a lifestyle centred on travelling were singled out for special treatment. In 1926, the Swiss government approved a project set up by the children's charity Pro Juventute intended to eliminate vagrancy. Entitled **Kinder der Landstrasse** ("Children of the Road"), it effectively sanctioned child abduction: police seized Jenisch infants and carted them off to orphanages run by Pro Juventute. Some children were handed on to foster parents, effectively to vanish into society; others ended up shunted from pillar to post until their adulthood. Large numbers of children were consigned to mental institutions, one of the most notorious of which was the Waldhaus clinic in Chur. Parents were actively barred from making inquiries into their children's whereabouts.

Kinder der Landstrasse was founded and directed by **Alfred Siegfried**. One of the aims of the project, according to Siegfried's own admission, was to eliminate the Jenisch: "We must say that we have already achieved much if these people do not start a family, do not reproduce without restraint and bring new generations of degenerate and abnormal children into the world." As late as 1964 Siegfried was writing, "Nomadism, like certain dangerous diseases, is primarily transmitted by women...

---

borders the Obersee, with the **tourist office** five minutes' walk away, uphill on Arosa's only proper road, Poststrasse (Mon–Fri 8am–noon & 1.30–6pm, July, Aug & Dec–April also Sat 9am–1pm & 2–4pm, Sun 9am–noon; ☎081 378 70 20, ⓦ www.arosa.ch). All buses within the village are free, and private cars are banned between midnight and 6am (except to arrive or depart). Some **hotels** charge extra if you stay fewer than three nights, especially in the winter season – but summer sees discounts of up to fifty percent as well as the free **Arosa Card**, which grants unlimited use of all local cable cars for the duration of your stay.

Campsite

Arosa Ausserarosa ☎081 377 17 45. Tranquil site below the main resort, on a path winding down from the tourist office.

Hostel

Backpackers Arosa ☎081 378 84 23, ⓦ www .backpackers-arosa.ch. Offers a range of two- to 12-bed rooms in two separate hostels: the central, well-equipped "Downtown" hostel is on Seewaldweg in Ausserarosa – from the tourist

office, turn off partway down the main road – while the "Mountain Lodge" (open Dec to mid-April only) is up on the slopes. ❶

Hotels

Allegra Isla Neubachstrasse 30 ☎081 377 12 13, ⓦ www.allegra-isla.ch. Pleasant, efficient three-star place on a quiet street between the Obersee and its lower twin, the Untersee, on the edge of the forest. Go for the superb corner room. ❹–❺

Anyone wishing to combat nomadism must aim to destroy the travellers' communal existence. We must put an end to their family community. There is no other way." Under Siegfried's guidance, boys were forced into apprenticeships or onto farms as cheap labour, and girls were often either sent to convents or simply kept under lock and key: **Uschi Waser**, chair of **Naschet Jenische** (Ⓦ www.naschet-jenische.ch), a foundation set up to campaign for Jenisch rights, was placed in 23 different institutions in 18 years. Jenisch were imprisoned for attempting to marry other Jenisch. **Mariella Mehr**, a Jenisch writer (Ⓦ www.mariellamehr.com), described her treatment at the hands of the scientists: "When I was three years old, they realised I didn't want to talk. They decided to force me. They used a kind of bath-tub…The patients were made to lie in the tub and covered with a plank so they couldn't get out. Only their heads were above water. They were kept there in freezing-cold water for up to twenty hours."

In 1972, the Swiss weekly *Der Schweizerischer Beobachter* exposed the Kinder der Landstrasse project, to universal public outrage. Pro Juventute closed down the operation a year later, and yet, according to official reports, there were about a hundred victims still incarcerated in clinics and institutions in 1988, after the Swiss state had formally acknowledged its moral, political and financial responsibility for the abductions and apologized to the Jenisch. Although Pro Juventute's own summations of individual cases remain under a 100-year embargo, the findings of an **official report** into the whole affair were published in 1998, prompting Ruth Dreyfuss, then Swiss president, to admit: "Kinder der Landstrasse is a tragic example of discrimination and persecution."

Meanwhile, about 5000 of Switzerland's 35,000 Jenisch still head out on the road each summer, working as antique dealers or craftspeople, handing on their skills and the Jenisch language to new generations. They have been assigned caravan grounds all over the country, and their children can even study while on the road with correspondence courses offered by many Swiss schools for the purpose. The majority of Jenisch however – often light-skinned and fluent in Swiss German – live a settled life in mostly low-income housing on the edge of many Swiss cities. Pro Juventute, though it dissociates itself from the Kinder der Landstrasse project these days, remains in operation.

Arosa Kulm Innerarosa ☏ 081 378 88 88, Ⓦ www.arosakulm.ch. Palace hotel at the top of town, on the edge of the slopes. Facilities are excellent, with a range of formal restaurants and rooms boasting picture windows and balconies. ❾

Arve Central Hubelstrasse 252 ☏ 081 378 52 52, Ⓦ www.arve-central.ch. Unusually open all year round, offering cut-price bargains in spring, summer and autumn. Friendly staff, a couple of good restaurants and attractive rooms (go for the south-facing ones). ❸–❺

Eden Ausserarosa ☏ 081 378 71 00, Ⓦ www.edenarosa.ch. The most characterful hotel in town, on a quiet street close to the station, with an array of individually decorated rooms, including arty, 1970s-retro hideaways on the top floor. A handful of "normal" rooms are cheaper, but this place is worth a splash. There's also a pair of in-house restaurants plus regular live music and DJs in the Kitchen Bar. ❺–❻

Prätschli ☏ 081 378 80 80, Ⓦ www.praetschli.ch. If you're here to enjoy the winter snows, this is the place to be – a romantic old winter hotel in a unique location on the slopes high above the Obersee, with road access but truly out in the wilds. ❻

Sonnenhalde Innerarosa ☏ 081 378 44 44, Ⓦ www.sonnenhalde-arosa.ch. Good-quality inexpensive hotel near the skating rink, excellently located for the winter-only Carmenna and Tschuggen lifts, with super-friendly service and surprisingly well-appointed rooms. Open all year. ❸

Suveran ☏ 081 377 19 69, Ⓦ www.suveran.ch. Quiet, simple pension on a street above the Catholic church, with shared-bath rooms and low prices. ❶–❷

Tschuggen Grand Innerarosa ☏ 081 378 99 99, Ⓦ www.tschuggen.ch. One of the finest luxury hotels in the Alps, with world-class service and facilities including an architect-designed spa complex, stylishly contemporary interiors and the highest 18-hole golf course in Europe. ❾

Sports and activities in Arosa

Arosa occupies the broad sunny bowl of the Schanfigg, surrounded by snowy peaks. The **Weisshorn** (2653m) is the main focus, due west of the resort, along with the **Hörnli** (2512m) to the south and **Brüggerhorn** (2401m) to the north.

The **skiing** is small-scale but high-quality, with over 70km of mostly blue and red pistes sidewinding down the gentle sunny slopes. There's also 25km of cross-country pistes and a **snowboard** halfpipe up above 2000m. Lifts and a gondola rise from the Obersee to the Weisshorn (with a chairlift branching over to the Brüggerhorn), and at the top of the village in Innerarosa there's another gondola connecting to the Hörnli. A pass for one/six days costs Fr.58/270. For lessons, try ⓦwww.sssa.ch.

Summer hosts several good high-country hikes: from the Weisshorn summit, a scenic four-hour trail heads over the Carmenna Pass and through the lonely Urden valley to Tschiertschen, connected to Chur by postbus; or you could head across the meadows from the Weisshorn middle station to Alpenblick and the tranquil Schwellisee before returning to Arosa (3hr). Another fine route leads off the back of the Hörnli summit and across the peaks to the Parpaner Rothorn (2861m), from where cable cars run down to Lenzerheide, near Valbella 12km south of Chur, and connected to Chur by bus. You can rent **mountain bikes** from the station to tackle any of the five marked MTB trails, which include circular routes as well as downhill runs.

Eating and drinking

In general, **eating and drinking** options are down-to-earth to suit the majority of Arosa's clientele, with a handful of simple diners around the Obersee and the lower reaches of Poststrasse, including *Orelli's* (closed Wed), where you can fill up on fish dishes, *Rösti* or veggie meals for under Fr.20. *Pizzeria Grottino*, just down the road from it, has quality pizza/pasta staples from Fr.20. Otherwise aim for hotel dining: *Hold*, up near the Hörnli cable car, is a popular, traditional place offering *menus* (around Fr.20) and a wide choice of inexpensive dishes; *Quellenhof* (closed Sun & Mon), near the tourist office, is in similar vein. For something more upmarket, aim for *Arosa Kulm*, with a handful of top-rated dining options, including the excellent *Ahaan* Thai restaurant (Wed–Sat eves only), or the super-luxurious dining options within the *Tschuggen Grand* hotel.

Heidiland

The Rhine valley north of Chur winds through lush meadowland to the small industrial town of **Landquart** – an important rail junction for the line to Davos – and on to the spa resort of **Bad Ragaz**. The hills above Bad Ragaz are where the tourist-friendly **Heidiland** region got its name (ⓦwww.heidiland.com): Swiss author Johanna Spyri set her wholesome classic of children's literature *Heidi* in and around the village of **MAIENFELD**, and the place milks its claim to fame mercilessly.

A gentle half-day trail leads from Maienfeld station past the pretty central square and the **tourist office** (Mon–Fri 10am–noon & 1.30–5pm, Sat closes 4pm; ☎081 302 58 58), which stocks plenty of Heidi kitsch, and then on up the hill to the hamlet of Oberrofels, now cruelly renamed **Heididorf** (ⓦwww.heididorf.ch). Despite the lack of evidence linking Spyri's story with any particular house, one old chalet near the execrable *Heidihof Hotel* has been reborn as "the original **Heidi's House**". A scenic and, thankfully, rarely tramped trail leads from Heididorf further up into the high pastures, past another lone chalet designated Peter the Goatherd's Hut, up to **Heidi Alp** and down through lush meadows to the village of Jenins, and back to Heididorf.

The Bündner Herrschaft

The east bank of the Rhine around Maienfeld, taking in the adjacent villages of Fläsch, Jenins and Malans, is one of Switzerland's more unusual winemaking areas, dubbed the **Bündner Herrschaft** (@ www.graubuendenwein.ch). Pinot Noir (Blauburgunder) grapes – introduced in the seventeenth century by the Duc de Rohan – prosper only thanks to the warm southerly Föhn wind, which can sometimes raise summer temperatures well above 25°C. The villages are linked by footpaths, generally quiet once you're out of the range of Heidi-seekers, and have good rustic inns at which to enjoy a carafe of local wine alongside a square meal. Schloss Brandis, a medieval castle on the edge of Maienfeld (T 081 302 24 23, @ www.schlossbrandis.ch), has a renowned **restaurant** and an impressive cellar, and the *Landhaus* in Fläsch (closed Mon & Tues), *Alter Torkel* in Jenins (@ www.torkel.ch) and *Zum Ochsen* in Malans (closed Mon & Tues; @ www.donatsch-malans.ch) all concentrate on their wines as much as on their mid-priced *menus*.

Central Graubünden

The **Central Graubünden** region south of Chur is the canton's wildest area, characterized by deep, narrow valleys, ancient forests, mountain torrents and a succession of old villages that have stayed fairly quiet since the Romans came this way over the **Julier** and **Splügen** passes. Aside from simple inns in most villages and a couple of family-oriented Alpine resorts – Valbella/Lenzerheide is one, Savognin another – there are few facilities for tourists. The most convenient way to experience the area is through the window of a train or a postbus, both of which offer scenic rides through different valleys – notably the sensational ride up to the **Albula** pass by train, now listed as UNESCO World Heritage. Note that, in winter, the Albula road is closed above Preda, but the Julier pass road is kept clear.

Thusis and Tiefencastel

The train from Chur to St Moritz heads west to the road and rail junction of **Reichenau** before cutting south into the Hinterrhein valley to the village of **RHÄZÜNS**. On a forested rise down by the river, ten minutes' walk north of Rhäzüns, is the isolated Carolingian chapel of **Sogn Gieri** (St George; @ www .kirchgemeinde-rhaezuens.ch), its interior covered with amazingly fresh fifteenth-century frescoes (chapel kept locked; key and map at Rhäzüns station). Further south, the valley sides close in, opening out again beyond Rothenbrunnen below the sharp ridges of the **Domleschg** to the east that crest 2500m, and the gentler slopes of the **Heinzenberg** to the west.

Some 12km south of Rhäzüns is the town of **THUSIS**, loomed over by precipitous mountains and thick forest. From here, the main road continues south via the **San Bernardino Pass** and tunnel (see p.433). Another road swings east towards Tiefencastel, shadowed by the train line; an alternative route, followed by postbuses, is via the **Julier Pass**.

Roads and the rail line meet at the small valley-bottom crossroads town of **TIEFENCASTEL**, its prominent white church saving it from being lost altogether in the thick pine forests on all sides. Aside from Thusis, 12km west, every route from Tiefencastel is up: north 35km to Chur, south to the Julier Pass, southeast to the Albula Pass, and northeast 37km to Davos. About ten minutes east of Tiefencastel by train, you pass over what must be the most photographed bridge in Switzerland, the elegant, six-arched **Landwasser Viaduct**, which carries the curving track a soaring 65m above the valley floor into the Landwasser Tunnel, drilled out partway up the sheer cliff face. From the train window you see the vertiginous drop; if you're driving, stop on a bend on the main Davos road, between Alvaneu and Schmitten villages, where you can stand below the viaduct for the full, photogenic effect.

The Albula route

Trains towards St Moritz branch off to climb south into the beautiful **Albula** valley (ⓦwww.albula.ch), marked by the little station at **FILISUR** (1084m). The line from here up to Preda (1792m) is renowned for its extraordinary engineering: the line gains over 700m in a distance, as the crow flies, of around 13km. The road, which runs alongside, is extremely steep, while the rail track coils around on itself in a series of tight hairpins, especially pronounced after **BERGÜN**, a pretty little village clustered around a photogenic central square. Above Bergün the track switchbacks eight times in a series of tunnels, crossing five viaducts; the engineering achievement is mind-boggling. At **PREDA**, little more than a hamlet, the train enters the highest rail tunnel in the Alps – at 1820m – emerging in the Val Bever for the short ride down to **Samedan**, in the Engadine Valley. The road, however, continues above Preda, breaking the tree line to the 2312-metre **Albula Pass** (June–Oct) – which has a restaurant on top – before coiling sharply down to the valley floor at La Punt.

Bergün **tourist office** (ⓣ081 407 11 52, ⓦwww.berguen.ch), on the main street, has details of local walking routes and information about one of Switzerland's most famous winter **toboggan runs**: you rent wooden sleds from Preda station for the rapid five-kilometre slide down to Bergün, from where trains cart you back up to Preda for another go (Fr.35 for a day ticket). Trains run late into the evening, so you can sled the illuminated route by night (not Mon).

The Julier route

On a different, train-free route, south of Tiefencastel, a dramatic road climbs in a series of broad plateaux – each more beautiful than the last – towards the Julier Pass, an often-busy route favoured by trucks. The major resort, just beyond Cunter, is Romansh-speaking **SAVOGNIN**, a family-friendly spot in the broad, sunny Surses valley. Its chairlift up to Somtgant (2112m) gives access to a "Veia Panorama" trail (2hr 30min) to Radons and down to the chairlift mid-station of Tigignas. Mountain-bike routes abound, as well as, in winter, some very scenic blue and red ski runs down from Piz Martegnas (2670m), plus tobogganing, boarding and snowshoeing. The **tourist office**, on the main road Stradung (ⓣ081 659 16 16, ⓦwww.savognin.ch), has full details.

Car-carrying trains: the Albula Tunnel

The road over the Albula Pass is only open in summer, and, although the parallel Julier Pass road remains open all winter, it's not an easy drive, often requiring snow-chains. The RhB (ⓦwww.rhb.ch) runs drive-on drive-off **car-carrying trains** from **Thusis** directly to **Samedan**, cutting out the difficult driving and letting you enjoy one of Switzerland's great railway journeys (Filisur–Preda). Departures run daily all year round (approx hourly 8am–8pm; takes 1hr 35min; car Fr.145, passengers Fr.25 each; book online or by phone: from Thusis ⓣ081 288 47 16, from Samedan ⓣ081 288 55 11).

Further up at 1769m, past the startlingly beautiful Lai da Marmorera set amongst the pines and rocky crags, lies **BIVIO**, the only settlement north of the Alps with an Italian-speaking majority – although in true Swiss style this little village also has Romansh- and German-speakers and Catholic and Protestant churches. Bivio sits near the tree line amidst dramatic upland country, and has plenty of outdoorsy activities: the little **tourist office** (Mon–Fri 8.30–11am & 3–5.30pm; ☎081 684 53 23, Ⓦwww.bivio.ch), within the Banca Cantonale, can advise. The cosy **hotel** *Solaria* (☎081 684 51 07, Ⓦwww.hotel solariabivio.ch; ❸–❹) is known for its summer **horseriding** packages, which include a guided ride over the isolated Septimer Pass (2310m), including full board and baggage transport (Fr.530/650 for two/three days).

About 10km south is the **Julier Pass** (Pass dal Güglia; 2284m), the heights of which are still marked by the column stumps of a long-demolished Roman temple. Silvaplana (see p.456) lies on the other side.

The San Bernardino route

Some 5km south of Thusis, the main road plunges into a narrow ravine, with sheer rock walls rising some 500m from the bed of the foaming Hinterrhein. This **Via Mala** (Evil Road) was first constructed in 1473, various improvements since then resulting in a web of bridges spanning the gorge. At one point, you can descend 321 steps to the valley floor to see both the ancient original road and the bridges lined up way overhead (daily: May–Sept 8am–7pm, April & Oct 9am–6pm; Fr.5; Ⓦwww.viamala.ch). See also Ⓦwww.viaspluga.com for details of hikes in the area.

The gorge opens up 3km further at the farming village of **ZILLIS** (Ziràn in Romansh), whose small **Kirche St Martin** (Baselgia Sontg Martegn; Ⓦwww .zillis-st-martin.ch) has a remarkable twelfth-century wooden ceiling, divided into 153 painted panels (there's a stack of mirrors by the door to save you cricking your neck). Around the edge runs a depiction of the sea, with angels in the corners representing the four winds. The interior panels feature stories from the life of Christ, which start at the east (choir) end and run row by row to the west (door). Christ crowned with thorns is the last of the biblical scenes; the final row is devoted to scenes from the life of St Martin.

The main road bends west 6km south of Zillis. From **Andeer**, a lonely road penetrates some 25km up the remote Val Ferrera, flanked by 3000m-plus peaks. After a handful of waterfalls and widely spaced hamlets comes **Juf**, a cluster of farmhouses which, at 2126m, claims the title of the highest permanently occupied village in Europe. Tough full-day hiking routes lead over the mountains to Bivio.

Splügen and the San Bernardino Pass

The road from Zillis heads through the deep Rheinwald forest to the dourly picturesque village of **SPLÜGEN**, with a jumble of traditional slate-roofed houses, a **tourist office** (☎081 650 90 30, Ⓦwww.splugen.ch), a year-round **campsite** (☎081 664 14 76) and four **hotels**, including the *Pratigiana*, an old smugglers' haunt (☎081 664 11 10; ❷). There are several long-distance hikes that pass this way. The **Splügen Pass** (2113m), 10km south of the village and reached via a twisting minor road, marks the Italian border; postbuses head on to **Chiavenna**, 30km south, from where different buses run back into Switzerland up the Val Bregaglia (see p.457) to St Moritz.

From Splügen, the main road climbs west in the shadow of the giant Zapport-gletscher, one of the sources of the Rhine, to the **San Bernardino Pass** (2065m). The pass route (closed in winter) is undercut by a road tunnel (open year-round), which feeds south into the long, Italian-speaking Valle Mesolcina on the route to Bellinzona (see p.465): once you're out of the mountains, vines, fig trees and chestnut forests spring up all around, giving a hint of the lushness of Ticino spreading out below.

Surselva

A straight road west from Chur shadows the train line into the broad, wooded valley of the River Vorderrhein, a patch of countryside known in Romansh as **Surselva**, the High Forests. The linked ski and sports resorts of **Flims-Laax-Falera** are within easy reach of Chur. Further west, a handful of quiet towns is capped at the end of the valley by a Benedictine abbey at **Disentis/Mustér**, staging post for journeys south into Ticino over the Lukmanier Pass (Lucomagno), and west towards Andermatt via the Oberalp Pass.

Flims-Laax-Falera

On a hillside above the Rhine 18km west of Chur, the three attractive villages of **FLIMS**, **LAAX** and **FALERA** – together forming a single Alpine resort (Ⓦ www.flimslaaxfalera.ch) – are well known to the Swiss, who consistently pack the place out every season, but much less known abroad. Snowboarders in particular will find outstanding facilities. Very confusingly, the local tourism authorities market the whole area as "Laax" in winter (Ⓦ www.laax.com) and "Flims" in summer (Ⓦ www.flims.com), despite the fact that all three villages are open for business year-round. Having two names, two identities and two websites for the same destination is, apparently, a "strategy".

To add to the confusion, Flims has two parts: **Flims-Dorf** is the older, original village with most amenities and the base station for the ski lifts, while on a slightly higher elevation 1km south is **Flims-Waldhaus**, a newer, quieter area with most of the hotels. Some 5km south is the village of **Laax**, with tiny **Falera** up a three-kilometre branch road.

Sports and activities in Flims-Laax-Falera

Flims-Laax-Falera boasts a huge winter-sports area, the largest in Graubünden, with access from all three villages. From Laax-Murschetg, on the edge of Laax village, there's the choice of a cable car to the **Crap Sogn Gion** summit (2228m), or a gondola to the halfway point of Curnius (also accessed from Falera), from where a chairlift continues to the top. From there, a cable car continues to **Crap Masegn** (2477m) and on up to the **Vorab** (2570m), a glacier region with year-round skiing and snowboarding courtesy of T-bars rising to 3018m. From Flims-Dorf a combination of chairlifts and a cable car serve various points on the adjacent **Cassons Grat** (2634m). Aside from the host of blue and reasonably testing red ski runs all over the mountain – and a huge fourteen-kilometre run from Vorab all the way down to Flims – there's plenty for freeriders, with 40km of marked but unprepared runs, and superb facilities for **snowboarders**, with seven halfpipes and boarderparks, including ones way up at 3000m and, allegedly, the world's largest halfpipe (up to 6.7m height). Passes cost Fr.67/315 for one/six days.

In **summer**, the hiking network is extensive, plenty of trails winding their way through the forest. Alternatively, take the chairlift up to the broad, level plateau atop the Cassons Grat, where there's a pleasant three-hour circular walk offering Alpine panoramas. The three-hour trek from Falera up to Crap Sogn Gion, and 3.5km along the crest to Crap Masegn, is especially beautiful too. Swissraft (Ⓦ www.swissraft.ch) runs **white-water rafting** trips between Ilanz and Reichenau.

Practicalities

No trains pass this way, but Flims is served by regular postbuses from Chur. The main **tourist office** is in Flims-Dorf (July, Aug & Dec–April Mon–Fri 8am–6pm, Sat & Sun 8am–noon; shorter hours in off-season; ☎081 920 92 00), with branch offices in Laax and Falera. All local transport is free with the Guest Card, given to you when you check in.

Best reason to **stay** is to experience perhaps the coolest hotel in the Swiss Alps – the stunning ⚐ **Riders Palace** (☎081 927 97 00, ⓦwww.riderspalace .com; ❸–❺), near the Murschetg base station in Laax. The building juxtaposes untreated larch wood and glittering walls of glass to give floor-to-ceiling panoramic views over the forest and slopes. Choose from a budget-priced dorm, a room or a Starck-designed suite. Everything is geared to a young, sporty clientele: room rates include a lift pass, there are sound systems and games consoles, while most weekends in the winter season the basement club hosts international DJs – anything from Asian Dub Foundation to Busta Rhymes. Nearby in Laax-Murschetg, the *Signina* (☎081 927 90 00, ⓦwww.signinahotel .com; ❻) extends the design concept, with tastefully minimalist interiors.

Less trendy options include the modern *Uaul Pign* in Waldhaus (☎081 911 13 39, ⓦwww.kpage.ch/garni.htm; ❷), in a tranquil location well away from the road, its ten balconied rooms looking into the forest; and, in Laax, the quiet *Bellaval* (☎081 921 47 00, ⓦwww.hotelbellaval.ch; ❸–❹), with pleasant, well-appointed rooms. There are also plenty of dorm places, including the SB **hostel** *Backpacker Deluxe/Capricorn* in Laax (☎081 921 21 20, ⓦwww.caprilounge.ch; ❷) and the *Mountain Hostel* in an unbeatable location on the Crap Sogn Gion slopes (☎081 927 73 73, ⓦwww.laax.com/mountainhostel; ❷).

West towards Disentis

Some 5km west of Laax is **ILANZ**, known in Romansh as **Glion**. Set amid the town's stately sixteenth- and seventeenth-century town houses is the unassuming **hotel** *Rätia*, Via Centrala 5 by the bridge (☎081 925 23 93, ⓦwww.hotel -raetia.ch; ❷), with a nice little restaurant serving regional cuisine. A minor road from Ilanz heads south between high valley walls to the spa village of

▲ The Therme Vals spa

VALS (1252m), where Swiss architect Peter Zumthor has built the spectacular ⚲ **Therme Vals** complex (☎081 926 80 80, ⓦwww.therme-vals.ch; closed May & Nov). The building – composed of 60,000 bonded slabs of local quartzite – is effortlessly sleek and sensuous, all water, natural light, wood and polished stone. The **spa** (daily 11am–8pm; Fr.40) has every facility, including therapy treatments. Guests at the stylish attached **hotel** (④–⑦) benefit from extended hours and discounts.

Heading west from Ilanz towards the high Alps, after 28km you'll see the white abbey of **DISENTIS** (also known by its Romansh name **MUSTÉR**). A Benedictine community was founded here, at the foot of Alpine pass roads, in the eighth century, only to be sacked by a Saracen army in 940. The white interior of the current Baroque **abbey church** (ⓦwww.kloster-disentis.ch) is covered in gilt and ornate stucco. An internal passageway in the west wall signposts the way upstairs to the silent Marienkirche, its triple apse dating from before the Saracen attack.

From Disentis, the road and rail line climb west to **Sedrun** and over the **Oberalp Pass** (2033m; see p.349) to Andermatt, while a branch road cuts south from Disentis to cross the **Lukmanier Pass** (1914m; see p.471) to Olivone.

Sports and activities in Davos and Klosters

The options for outdoors activity are almost limitless: the best advice is to check ⓦ**www.davosklosters.ch** for up-to-date details. Look out for good-value winter and summer package deals at hotels, which often include a free lift pass.

Winter

The **skiing** is outstanding. Although the two resorts are quite far apart, they share the same ski area and lift pass; the prime attraction is being able to swoosh down broad, well-tended pistes which go on and on, for more than 10km in many cases from mountaintop to valley bottom. There are 99 downhill pistes, totalling an impressive 321km – half of them intermediate (red), a third beginner (blue) and the rest expert (black).

The big focus of attention is the **Parsenn** ski area on the north side of Davos and the west side of Klosters, centred on the Weissfluh summit. It has only three methods of access. The **Parsennbahn** funicular starts from Davos-Dorf and rises to the Weissfluhjoch saddle just below the summit; the little **Schatzalpbahn** funicular (ⓦwww .schatzalp.ch) from Davos-Platz takes you to a broad snow shelf, from where you must switch to chairlifts and gondolas for the journey further up; and the **Gotschnagrat** cable car rises from Klosters station to a ridge just east of the Weissfluh. On the mountain are plenty of draglifts serving dozens of blue and red runs, including giant, weaving pistes from the summit down through the trees to hamlets such as Küblis, Saas and Serneus. For more testing runs, you could attempt the notorious Gotschnawang or a handful of black runs on the lower, steep slopes above Davos-Dorf and Wolfgang.

Moving onto one of the four other ski sectors can take you away from the crowds. From Davos-Platz, cable cars rise to the **Jakobshorn**, with a hatful of scenic blues and reds. Bus #1 from Davos-Dorf serves the base station of the cable car up to **Pischa**, while a gondola from Davos-Glaris (bus #7) rises to the **Rinerhorn**, which has lifts going higher to access blues, reds and a testing black run. A gondola from Klosters-Dorf climbs east to **Madrisa**, also with plenty of long, exciting reds on pistes which hug the Austrian border. **Snowboarders** should aim principally for the Parsenn, although the Jakobshorn is the focus of a hip boarding fraternity and there's scope for experimentation on the Madrisa as well.

Davos and Klosters

From the junction point of **Landquart**, north of Chur, roads and rail lines meander up the Prättigau ("Meadow Valley") to two of the most famous names in the Alps, enjoying some of the best skiing in the world: first **Klosters**, then, beyond the Wolfgang Pass, **Davos**. Walser migrants arrived in the valley in the thirteenth century, and the area – surrounded on three sides by Romansh – remains German-speaking today. The focus is fair and square on outdoorsiness: skiing and snowboarding in the winter, hiking and mountain-biking in the summer.

During the summer, visitors staying overnight in either resort receive the useful **Davos Klosters Inclusive Card**, which gives free use of all local transport plus a range of other discounts.

Beware that almost everything in both resorts – shops, hotels, attractions, walking routes – is **closed during off-season** (mid-April to mid-June & mid-Oct to mid-Dec). We've specified months of opening only when they differ from this pattern.

Passes, considering the range on offer, are excellent value. A RegionPass for all areas (excluding use of Schatzalpbahn) for 3/6 days is Fr.180/300. Day passes (as well as part-day and selected-day tickets) are available for the Parsenn and Gotschna (Fr.64), Jakobshorn (Fr.59), Madrisa (Fr.50), Pischa (Fr.47) or Rinerhorn (Fr.49). **Schools** include, in Davos ⓦwww.ssd.ch and ⓦwww.topsecretdavos.ch; in Klosters ⓦwww.sssk.ch and ⓦwww.adventure-skiing.ch.

Both resorts have tons of other diversions, including indoor swimming, ice-skating, tobogganing and snowshoe-trekking. Tandem **paragliding** flights cost around Fr.175 at ⓦwww.luftchraft.ch or ⓦwww.fs-grischa.ch.

Summer

Both tourist offices run full-day guided **walks**, free with a Guest Card, that cover some difficult territory – over the Vereina pass, for instance – but it's easy to strike out alone. From the Weissfluhjoch, accessed by the Parsennbahn (or a 3–4hr walk up), the views of Piz Buin and beyond are spectacular, even better from the Weissfluhgipfel summit, served by a cable car from the funicular top station. Invigorating walks head down to Davos (2hr) or Klosters (4hr), or there's a testing route over to Arosa (6hr). From the Gotschnagrat, a fairly tough hike leads to Casanna Alp, then Serneuser Schwendi and on down to Klosters (3hr). Easier walks abound, not least in the meadows and woods around the little Davosersee. A stroll from the top of the Schatzalpbahn brings you to the **Alpinum**, a hillside botanical garden (mid-May to mid-Nov daily 9am–6pm; Fr.5). There are some leg-stretching trails from the Pischa and Jakobshorn summits back to Davos (2–3hr). Top choice from Klosters is the **Madrisa Rundtour**, a two/three-day walk into Austria and back; the price (from Fr.94) includes B&B and cable cars.

There are plenty of **mountain-bike** routes around Davos, including several routes along the valley floor west as far as Wiesen (31km round trip), and a classic 20km run from the Weissfluhjoch down to Küblis; ⓦwww.bike-erlebnis.ch has more. Other activities include tandem paragliding, inline skating, sailing, volleyball, windsurfing, golf, horseriding, mule- or llama-trekking and tons more.

Davos

Twinned in a touristic masterstroke with Aspen, Colorado, **DAVOS** (1560m) is the antithesis of a peaceful Alpine ski village. It's a bustling, sometimes impatient town, famous for its toothpaste-fresh air and its consistently excellent snow cover. It has been attracting **skiers** for generations and has gained new life through the **snowboarding** cognoscenti. In summer, the snows recede to reveal a surrounding of lush countryside and the town takes on a new lease of life – not least because hotel prices plummet. The location, in a high, narrow valley between two lines of peaks, is stunning.

Davos achieved fame as a **health resort**, its high altitude and long hours of sunshine easing the suffering of tuberculosis patients: by 1900, ten years after the railway arrived, there were 700,000 overnight visitors a year. The consumptive Robert Louis Stevenson completed *Treasure Island* here in 1882; Sir Arthur Conan Doyle stayed in 1894–95 and was the first person in Davos to ski; and in 1912 Thomas Mann was inspired while visiting Davos to write *The Magic Mountain*. Even today a few clinics remain: modern science has confirmed the beneficial effects of high altitude on respiratory and dermatological complaints. Davos also has one of the world's top **high-altitude sports training** facilities, used by international athletes to improve fitness and stamina.

Another hat worn by Davos is that of a major **conference** venue: in the last week of January each year, global leaders and assorted mega-suits meet here at the World Economic Forum under the gaze of the world's media to set the financial agenda for the year ahead, regularly sparking anti-capitalist demonstrations in the process.

Arrival, information and accommodation

The two contiguous halves of the town, **Davos-Platz** and **Davos-Dorf**, are strung along a four-kilometre ribbon of low-key development in the Landwasser valley. Approaching from Klosters, you'll pass the picturesque little Davosersee

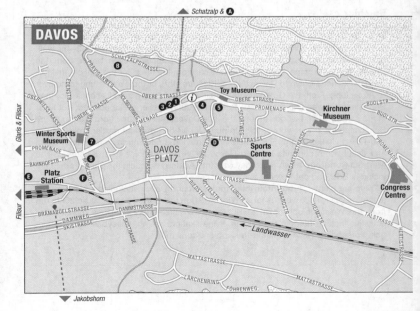

before arriving at Dorf, generally the quieter district. The main street, **Promenade**, lined with shops and hotels, feeds traffic one-way from Dorf past the huge Congress Centre to bustling Platz, home to most of the nightlife; parallel one block downhill (south) is quieter **Talstrasse**, which is one-way from Platz to Dorf. The Weissfluh (2844m) rises immediately to the north, flanked by the Strelagrat (2545m) and Schwarzhorn (2670m). The Jakobshorn (2590m) looms on the other, south, side of the town. Davos lies at the far end of a circular **train** line from Chur: the eastern half runs from Landquart through Klosters, the western half from Filisur. Service is half-hourly but almost always requires a change: the only through trains are the Glacier Express and Bernina Express. **Davos-Platz** is the main terminus, although all trains to and from Klosters/Landquart also stop at Davos-Dorf. **Postbuses** run direct from Chur.

There are two branches of the **tourist office** – the main one is in the Sports Centre at Talstrasse 41 (Mon–Fri 8.30am–6.30pm, Sat 9am–5.30pm; April to mid-June & mid-Oct to Nov Sat closes noon; Dec–March also Sun 10am–noon & 3–5.30pm; ☎081 415 21 21, Ⓦwww.davos.ch), and there's a branch office at Dorf station (slightly curtailed hours). VBD **city buses** (free with a Guest Card) stop at all points of interest, and also run out to Wolfgang, Glaris, the Pischa base station, Laret and Klosters. **Accommodation** is spread between Dorf and Platz, though the latter tends to hold more possibilities.

Hostel

Jugendherberge "Youth Palace" (HI hostel)
Horlaubenstrasse 27, Dorf ☎081 410 19 20,
Ⓦwww.youthhostel.ch. Huge former sanatorium sleeping 250 in a range of small dorms. ❶

Hotels

Alte Post Berglistutz 4, Platz ☎081 417 67 77,
Ⓦwww.mountainhotels.ch. Serviceable little

two-star place beside Platz station; good value in summer. ❸

Bahnhof-Terminus Talstrasse 3, Platz ☎081 414 97 97, Ⓦwww.bahnhof-terminus.ch. A Best Western chain hotel with large, airy rooms and private parking directly opposite Platz station. ❸–❹

Berghotel Schatzalp On Schatzalp above Platz ☎081 415 51 51, Ⓦwww.schatzalp.ch. This old Jugendstil sanatorium is the most characterful

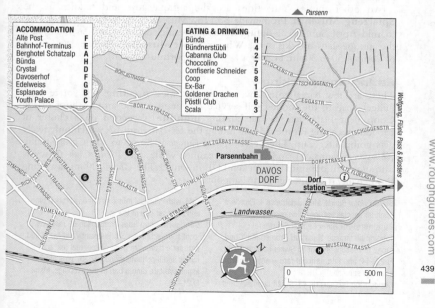

▲ Parsenn

ACCOMMODATION
Alte Post	F
Bahnhof-Terminus	E
Berghotel Schatzalp	A
Bünda	H
Crystal	D
Davoserhof	F
Edelweiss	G
Esplanade	B
Youth Palace	C

EATING & DRINKING
Bünda	H
Bündnerstübli	4
Cabanna Club	2
Choccolino	7
Confiserie Schneider	5
Coop	8
Ex-Bar	1
Goldener Drachen	E
Pöstli Club	6
Scala	3

Wolfgang, Flüela Pass & Klosters

DAVOS DORF

Dorf station

Parsennbahn

Landwasser

MUSEUMSTRASSE

0   500 m

accommodation around, perched on a tranquil terrace 300m above the town and only accessible by funicular. Views over the Jakobshorn and beyond from the ranks of balconied rooms – which boast up to four more hours of sunshine per day than the town – are well worth paying extra for. ❹–❻

🏃 **Bünda** Museumstrasse 4, Dorf ☎081 417 18 19, Ⓦ www.buendadavos.ch. Outstanding three-star a short walk from the Parsennbahn at the foot of the slopes in a perfectly peaceful location. Service is friendly and helpful, and the rooms are characterful and well equipped. ❸–❹

Crystal Eisbahnstrasse 2, Platz ☎081 414 01 01, Ⓦ www.crystal-davos.ch. Central but quiet

three-star with cosy decor and a good in-house restaurant. ❹

Davoserhof Berglistutz 2, Platz ☎081 417 67 77, Ⓦ www.mountainhotels.ch. Comfortable, well-appointed three-star alongside Platz station offering a well-managed blend of luxury with a rustic, country atmosphere. ❹

Edelweiss Rossweidstrasse 9, Platz ☎081 416 10 33, Ⓦ www.edelweiss-davos.ch. One of the cheapest places in town, with private parking and a welcoming, comfortable atmosphere. ❸

Esplanade Strelastrasse 2, Platz ☎081 415 50 50, Ⓦ www.hotel-esplanade.ch. Pleasant, quiet hotel, way up above Platz (with a free shuttle bus up to the ski slopes) with airy and spacious rooms. ❹–❺

The Town

Prime attraction for non-sports fans is the **Kirchner Museum**, Promenade 82 (Tues–Sun: July–Sept & Christmas–Easter 10am–6pm; rest of year 2–6pm; Fr.12; Ⓦ www.kirchnermuseum.ch). This well-designed modern building houses a vibrant collection of artworks by the German Expressionist painter Ernst Ludwig Kirchner. Born in 1880, Kirchner moved to Berlin in 1911, but after an intensive period of work his health deteriorated rapidly. He emigrated to Davos in 1917 and lived in shacks out in the countryside, where he painted prodigiously. In 1936, his work was tagged "degenerate" by the Nazis and two years later in Davos, in a deep depression, he committed suicide. The museum displays work from all periods of Kirchner's life, including starkly stylish woodcuts and sketches from his time in Berlin and dozens of expressive, colourful works painted in Davos.

Two other modest attractions are the antique toys and teddies of the **Spielzeug Museum**, Promenade 83 (Toy Museum; June to mid-Oct & Dec to mid-April Sun–Fri 2–6pm; Fr.6; Ⓦ www.spielzeugmuseum-davos.ch), and the antique sleds and skis of the **Winter Sport Museum**, Promenade 43 (Tues & Thurs 4.30–6.30pm; Fr.5; Ⓦ www.wintersportmuseum.ch).

Eating and drinking

There are few bargains in Davos when it comes to **eating** – if you're on a budget head to the modest self-service restaurant on the ground floor of the Coop, near Platz station. The buzzing **nightlife** is centred on a cluster of bar-lounges along Promenade, including the *Ex-Bar*, at no. 63, which only really gets going after 2am. The nearby *Hotel Europe* is home to the *Cabanna* club (Ⓦ www.cabanna.ch) and a swanky casino, while the *Pöstli Club* (Ⓦ www .morosani.ch) opposite has weekend DJs in winter. The *Chämi*, 200m east along Promenade, is another popular hangout.

Bünda *Hotel Bünda*, Museumstrasse 4. Excellent Bündner specialities, including game.

Bundnerstübli *Hotel Central Sporthotel*, Tobelmühlestrasse 1, just off Promenade. Good range of reasonably priced Swiss cuisine (mains Fr.22–44) and international fare – anything from snails to samosas.

Choccolino Promenade 45. Swish *confiserie* and

café, with classical music at Sunday brunch time and a proper cup of tea.

Confiserie Schneider Promenade 68 (Ⓦ www .confiserie-schneider.ch). Pleasantly old-fashioned patisserie café, with good coffee, real tea, light meals and lunchtime *menus* (Fr.23), plus more expensive fare (and a bar) in the evenings. Mains Fr.21–38.

Goldener Drachen *Hotel Bahnhof-Terminus*, opposite Davos Platz station. The best Chinese in town, serving authentic cuisine for around Fr.25.

Scala *Hotel Europe*, Promenade 63. Bright modern restaurant, with inexpensive pizzas and pastas (Fr.15–25), more expensive meat and fish options.

Klosters

Instantly recognizable to Britons as being the favoured winter getaway of Prince Charles and his family, little **KLOSTERS** (1190m) – about 9km northeast of Davos, below the Wolfgang Pass – steals quite a march on its neighbour in terms of ambience. Where Davos has traffic, bright lights, street bustle and concrete multistorey hotels, Klosters has peace and quiet, an appealing huddle of dark-wood chalets and a village atmosphere. It's linked to Davos's Parsenn ski slopes, and the two share a lift pass covering each other's pistes and mountain transport: in choosing a base, you could do worse than shun Davos altogether. Details of sports and activities are on p.436.

Klosters Platz is the centre of things, and has the main train station; the smaller, quieter **Klosters Dorf** sits 2km north, with its own station. Both are on the Landquart–Davos line, and are also linked by town buses, which are free with the **Davos Klosters Inclusive Card** (see p.437).

Practicalities

The main **tourist office** is a few minutes' walk from Platz station in the village centre, Alte Bahnhofstrasse 6 (Mon–Fri 8.30am–6pm, Sat & Sun 8.30am–4pm, shorter hours in off-season; ☏081 410 20 20, ⓦwww.klosters.ch). There's a branch office at Albeina Sport in Dorf, keeping similar hours.

Klosters has many far better hotels than Davos, with a greater proportion of upmarket properties. The cosy HI **hostel** *Soldanella Jugendherberge* is at Talstrasse 73, a fifteen-minute climb above Platz (☏081 422 13 16, ⓦwww .youthhostel.ch; ❶). The weathered-wood *Sonne*, Landstrasse 155 (☏081 422 13 49, ⓦwww.sonne-klosters.ch; ❷), is one of the best low-end **hotels**, with simple shared-bath rooms, some with balconies. The family-run *Silvapina*, on the edge of Dorf near the Madrisabahn, Silvapinaweg 6 (☏081 422 14 68, ⓦwww.silvapina.ch; ❷–❹), is a fine choice, with attractive guest rooms and good service. *Chesa Grischuna* in Platz (☏081 422 22 22, ⓦwww.chesagrischuna.ch; ❺–❼), may look like a rustic chalet from the outside, but is one of the liveliest and trendiest places in town, with a good deal of style and character. Prince Charles's establishment of choice is the *Walserhof*, Landstrasse 141 (☏081 410 29 29, ⓦwww.walserhof .ch; ❻–❽), a relatively small, cosy Relais & Châteaux hotel that displays superb attention to detail.

Most of the hotels listed above have **restaurants** attached: the *Sonne* (closed Mon & Tues) is a good budget choice, with regional *menus* starting from around Fr.20. For inexpensive Italian fare head for the cosy *Pizzeria Fellini* in the heart of Platz, while the modest *Wynegg*, Landstrasse 205 (☏081 422 13 40; winter only), enjoys royal patronage, serving hearty but surprisingly affordable meals. For more upmarket dining, the chichi *Chesa Grischuna* (see above) has finely crafted modern European cuisine including good vegetarian dishes (mains Fr.30–60). The *Walserhof* restaurant also offers outstanding cuisine and service, with lunch *menus* around Fr.50, or the full *dégustation* experience approaching Fr.150.

The Lower Engadine

Beyond the mountains, in the farthest corner of Switzerland, is the **Lower Engadine** (Engiadina Bassa in Romansh, Unterengadin in German). Remote from Chur, let alone from the rest of the country, this attractive valley nurtures a quite distinct, thoroughly Romansh culture. The succession of hamlets which cling to the banks of the foaming **River Inn** (**En** in Romansh), tumbling its

Romansh

Romansh is the fourth language of Switzerland and the principal everyday tongue of some 70,000 people in Graubünden. In the smaller countryside towns, in particular, you'll find signs to the *staziun* pointing along Via Principala, and hear people greeting each other with "Allegra!" or "Bun di!" in what sounds like Italian with a Swiss-German accent.

History

Romansh can trace its roots directly back to Latin, fountainhead for all the Romance languages of Europe. After the Roman conquests, so-called **Vulgar Latin**, spoken by soldiers, merchants and officials, slowly merged with the pre-existing languages of conquered areas, giving rise to four main linguistic groups: Ibero-Romance, including Spanish and Portuguese; Gallo-Romance, mainly French; Italian; and **Rhaeto-Romance**, comprising Friulian and Ladin, two languages spoken by around 750,000 people in the extreme north of Italy, and Romansh, spoken only in Graubünden. The first significant inroads made by outsiders into the isolated Romansh-speaking mountain communities was in the thirteenth century, when German-speaking Walsers from Canton Valais settled in some of the high valleys; their legacy survives to this day, with Davos still majority Swiss-German, and German-speaking communities clustered together in otherwise Romansh Surselva. In 1464, the arrival of craftspeople from the north to rebuild Chur after a fire virtually erased the town's Romansh culture.

In the mid-nineteenth century Romansh was still counted as the native tongue of over half the population of Graubünden, but the development of roads and railways led to greater and greater erosion. With schools, churches and communes slowly switching over to German, a conscious effort began to preserve Romansh, with cultural groups promoting the language nationwide. In 1938, an amendment to the Swiss Constitution confirmed the status of Romansh as a **national language**. In 1996 a second constitutional amendment elevated Romansh to the status of a **semi-official language**, thereby preserving its status amongst Romansh communities, guaranteeing its appearance on official documents and in legislation affecting Romansh areas, and eliminating the requirement for Romansh-speakers to use any other language.

Dialects

Romansh has several dialects. The word for "cup", for example, in German is *Tasse*, in Italian *tazza*, but in the **Sursilvan** dialect of Romansh, spoken west of Chur, it is *scadiola*; in the **Sutsilvan** of the Hinterrhein valley, *scariola*; in the **Surmiran** of the Julier and Albula valleys, *cuppegn*; in **Putèr**, spoken in the Upper Engadine, *coppa*; and in **Vallader**, spoken in the Lower Engadine, *cuppina*. In 1980, the **Lia Rumantscha**, a leading Romansh cultural organization (Ⓦwww.liarumantscha.ch), put forward a proposal to regularize this mishmash. The result was the creation of **Rumantsch Grischun** ("Graubünden Romansh"), a composite written language formed by averaging out words across all five dialects. (Under this new system, "cup" became *cuppin*.) There was some resistance to forming a hybrid in this way and people stick to their own dialect in everyday life. For more info, go to Ⓦ**www.mypledari.ch**. There is a glossary of Romansh words and phrases on p.528.

way towards Innsbruck and eventually the Black Sea, show their Latin origins as much as the language of their inhabitants does: thick-walled houses with small, deep-set windows and scarlet geraniums sprouting from every windowbox are reminiscent of Mediterranean village architecture found much further south. Everywhere you'll see the characteristic *sgraffiti* decoration: ornate, curlicued designs etched into the white stuccoed facade of a house to reveal a darker layer beneath. The beautifully decorated cottages and quaint cobbled squares, set against a tremendous backdrop of dark pine forests and looming mountains, combine to give the valley a uniquely fairy-tale air.

Scuol is the main town, prefaced by a succession of charming cliffside villages such as Guarda and Ftan. **Zernez** serves as the gateway for exploration of the **Parc Naziunal Svizzer**, the sole national park, a vast chunk of highland wilderness. Beyond the park in tiny **Müstair** village is one of Switzerland's greatest cultural treasures, a Carolingian church sporting perfectly preserved medieval frescoes.

Transport isn't easy. Trains from Landquart and Klosters run through the Vereina tunnel to the terminus at Scuol, while others from Pontresina or St Moritz (changing at Samedan) serve Zernez. To reach the Austrian border or Müstair, you're reliant on postbuses – but timetables can leave you hanging around for hours. Driving is the transport of choice, allowing you to enjoy the sunset in Müstair and still make it to St Moritz by bedtime.

East from Susch to Ftan

The dramatic road from Davos over the icy Flüela Pass drops down into the Engadine at **SUSCH**, a perfect introduction to the valley, its cobbled alleys filled with the rushing noise of the River Inn. Set picturesquely amidst its *sgraffitied* houses is the Baselgia San Jon, with one tower Romanesque, the other late Gothic. To the east, beyond the ruined hilltop castle of Chaschinas, rears the giant Piz Arpiglias (3027m).

The road to Scuol continues through tremendous scenery between the high, wooded valley walls, past a string of alluring little villages. Some 7km northeast

▲ Traditional buildings in the Lower Engadine

of Susch on a lofty perch above the river, **GUARDA** is especially attractive, its architecture and traditional *sgraffiti* meriting a federal order of protection. It's also home to the attractively rustic *Piz Buin* hotel (☎081 861 30 00, ⓦwww .pizbuin.ch; ❷–❹), at the edge of the village. A lovely walk into the Val Tuoi (2hr 30min) leads to the *Chamanna Tuoi* hut (☎081 862 23 22) below Piz Buin; strong walkers could continue across the right-hand ridge at the 2735-metre Furcletta and descend through Val Tasna to Ardez (total 7hr 30min).

Just beyond Guarda, **ARDEZ** and **FTAN** are both equally worthy of a stop. Ftan has a pair of good hotels: the charming *Engiadina* (☎081 864 04 34, ⓦwww.engiadina-ftan.ch; ❹–❺); and the superb, modern-styled *Paradies* (☎081 861 08 08, ⓦwww.paradieshotel.ch; ❽). Both have outstanding restaurants, the latter with two Michelin stars.

Scuol and around

Some 22km east of Susch, the lively town of **SCUOL** (pronounced *shkwol*), known as Schuls in German, is beautifully located in a sunny, open part of the valley at the end of the train line. Its reputation is built on its history as a spa town, and the main draw today is the pristine, modern **Bogn Engiadina** complex in the centre of town (Engadine Spa; daily 9am–10pm; ⓦwww.cseb .ch; Fr.25). Opt for the works: warm and hot rooms, vapour baths, massages, mineral plunge pools and a heavenly two-hour session in the Roman-Irish baths (reserve one day ahead; Fr.66). Behind the spa, quiet streets head down into Scuol's pretty **Old Town**, filled with traditional houses, tinkling fountains and a photogenic village square. The Motta Naluns **ski** area (2146m, with lifts up to 2800m) offers easy and intermediate runs, including long reds from Piz Champatsch 12km back down to Scuol, and plenty for snowboarders. Behind Scuol to the south, **walking** paths lead up Val S-charl to **S-CHARL**, a summer-only hamlet at a confluence of glens. From here, you could cross Fuorcla Funtana da S-charl to the Ofen Pass/Pass dal Fuorn (3hr 30min); the Pass da Costainas to Santa Maria in Val Müstair (5hr); or take an easy stroll (1hr)

Customs in the Lower Engadine

The communities of the Lower Engadine keep alive many ancient local **customs** as an expression of their Romansh heritage. In Ramosch and Tschlin, two hamlets 10km east of Scuol, the **Mattinadas**, held on January 2, can overshadow even Christmas and New Year. During the day, the local children parade a decorated sledge through the village collecting home-made sweets and candy (*mattinadas*); after a communal feast, everyone then embarks on an evening of dancing, whereupon the kids sit down to another banquet, this time of traditional butter biscuits smothered in whipped cream. The whole procedure is then repeated either the next day, or on the Saturday following, by the young men of the village. Epiphany celebrations (Jan 6) take the form of **Bavania** or **Buania**. In the afternoon, the village girls gather together and draw lots to choose a lover; they then visit their allotted man and, to mark their conquest and Fate's irrevocable decision, they tie a red ribbon round his neck. Later that night, at the village dance, the girls are chaperoned by their ribboned partner... presumably happily ever after. In Scuol, the first Saturday in February sees the ceremonial torching of the **Hom d'strom** ("Man of Straw") in front of the court building, probably as a symbolic banishment of the winter. On March 1 many villages stage the children's festival of **Chalandamarz** or **Calonda mars**. This originates in the Roman New Year celebration *Calendae Martii*, which these days takes the form of a colourful spring parade with cowbell-ringing and traditional songs.

to Alp Sesvenna among streams and pastures that are full of Alpine flowers in early summer.

Practicalities

From Scuol's **train station**, it's a ten-minute downhill walk (or a short bus ride) 1km east into town. The **tourist office** is on Stradun (June–Oct Mon–Fri 8am–6.30pm, Sat 9am–noon & 1.30–5.30pm, Sun 9am–noon, rest of year shorter hours; ☎081 861 22 22, ⓦwww.scuol.ch). Scuol's main drag has plenty of ordinary **hotels**, but there are a couple of traditional *sgraffitied* gems just up the hill from Plaz, the old village square, including the rambling old *Gabriel*, Rablüzza 159a (☎081 864 11 52, ⓦwww.hotel-gabriel.ch; ❷–❹), or head to boutique *Guardaval* (☎081 861 09 09, ⓦwww.guardaval-scuol.ch; ❹–❺), occupying a restored seventeenth-century building with a nineteenth-century annexe over the road. Some 6km east of Scuol is Sent, location of the ultimate in tranquil **campsites**, *Sur En* (☎081 866 35 44, ⓦwww.sur-en.ch), open year-round.

Scuol has a few good **eating** options. For inexpensive traditional Engadine fare, try the cosy *Hotel Crusch Alba* at the far (east) end of Stradun, which has a good range plus *Rösti* and pasta (Fr.17–23). Down near Plaz, hotel *Gabriel* (see above) has a beautiful terrace and tasty local dishes (mains Fr.16–25), while the elegant restaurant at *Guardaval* (see above; closed Mon & Tues) offers daily changing *menus* (Fr.65–90) of inventive modern European cuisine.

Samnaun

East of Scuol, postbuses head across the Austrian border to Landeck. Just before the frontier, a minor road curls back to climb into an isolated side-valley, at the end of which sits German-speaking **SAMNAUN** (1840m), a duty-free area crammed with shops and cut-price petrol stations, all open long hours. In winter, Samnaun's snow facilities link to the Austrian resort of **Ischgl** on the other side of a wall of 3000-metre peaks, taking in Europe's single largest snowboarding area; a six-day VIP pass valid on both resorts' lifts is Fr.298. Samnaun-Dorf **tourist office** (☎081 868 58 58, ⓦwww.samnaun.ch) has full details. The best of the summer hikes from Samnaun is a tough, multi-day trail to Ischgl over the Zeblasjoch Pass.

Parc Naziunal Svizzer

Some 6km south of Susch sits **ZERNEZ**, the slender white steeple of its church marking a junction of valleys: north is the Lower Engadine, south is the Upper Engadine, while to the east, a road leads through the **PARC NAZIUNAL SVIZZER** – an Alpine wilderness stretching for 169 square kilometres either side of the road – to the Ofenpass/Pass dal Fuorn and on into the Val Müstair.

Established in 1914, the park's credo is to leave nature well alone: absolutely everything, from the tiniest lichen to the breeding pairs of golden eagles, is protected. Forest fires are monitored but allowed to burn; injured animals are left to their own devices; and roaming wardens will impose fines should you so much as pick a flower. You're allowed to **walk** in the park (provided you don't step off the marked trails), but prominent noticeboards publish stringent **regulations** – as a result, the park remains pristine. Red and roe deer, ibex and chamois roam freely, as do hares, foxes and huge numbers of marmots. Aside from the golden eagles, there are also bearded vultures, kestrels, ravens, various woodpeckers, grouse, partridge and skylarks. The venomous northern viper or adder is also around (but you'd have to tiptoe to come upon one unawares). Pine and larch forests grow up to 2300m, beyond which Alpine meadows are carpeted in springtime with edelweiss, gentians and a host of other high-altitude flowers. Further up still are bare rocky areas and permafrost.

Access, information and accommodation

Entry to the park is free. If you're **driving**, head along the main road to any one of ten free parking areas, from all of which long and short trails twist out to north and south. **Postbuses** running hourly between Zernez and Müstair also stop at six of the parking areas. Cycling is prohibited in the park.

The **National Park Centre** (May–Oct and Dec–March daily 8.30am–6pm, rest of year Mon–Fri 9am–noon & 2–5pm; Fr.7; ℡081 851 41 41, ⓦwww .nationalpark.ch), in a swanky new edifice in the middle of Zernez, has displays on the park's flora and fauna, while in the same building, staff at the **tourist office** (Mon–Sat 8.30am–noon & 1–6pm; ℡081 856 13 00, ⓦwww.zernez.ch) can help with practical information, including maps and guides.

There are only two **places to stay** within the National Park, both of which need reserving in advance. *Hotel Parc Naziunal Il Fuorn*, beside Parking 6 (℡081 856 12 26, ⓦwww.ilfuorn.ch; ❷–❸; mid-May to mid-Oct), is a comfortable old lodge with a newer wing with en-suite rooms. In the middle of the park, at the junction of several trails, is *Chamanna/Blockhaus Cluozza* (℡081 856 12 35; June–Oct), a simple hut with dorm beds.

In Zernez, the **campsite** *Cul* is 500m behind the station (℡081 856 14 62, ⓦwww.camping-cul.ch; May to mid-Oct), and there are plenty of **hotels**: *Spöl* (℡081 856 12 79, ⓦwww.hotel-spoel.ch; ❷) is a characterful low-end choice within ten minutes' walk of the park entrance. About 7km beyond Zernez just outside the park boundary before Parking 1 is *Naturfreundehaus Ova Spin* (℡081 852 31 42, ⓦwww.nfhouse.org; June–Oct; ❶), with dorms.

Walks in the National Park

There are 21 marked **walking** trails in and around the park, ranging from full-day mountain ascents to brief roadside strolls. The following are some of the more straightforward scenic routes that have easy access at either end; always check on trail conditions at the National Park House before you start. (Note that, on high-summer weekends in particular, paths can get crowded.) **Trail 7** (3hr) leads from Zernez into the Cluozza gorge to the *Chamanna Cluozza* (see above), from where **trail 8** (3hr 30min) brings you out on a different route via a steep ascent to Praspöl, emerging at Parking 3 ("Vallun Chafuol"). Both these can be done in reverse. The circular **trail 9** (2hr) leads from Parking 3 through heather and pine forest to Margun Grimmels and back. The tougher **trail 15** (5hr) leads from Buffalora (1968m), just outside the boundary at Parking 10, on a simple ascent of Munt la Schera (2091m) and down to *Hotel Il Fuorn* at Parking 6.

Three of the simpler routes (marked as suitable for children) include **trail 1** (2hr 30min), a circular walk from Parking 1 ("Champlönch"), taking in the view from Alp Grimmels; **trail 13** (2hr), leading from Parking 1 on an easy countryside path to *Hotel Il Fuorn* at Parking 6; and **trail 10** (3hr 30min), a riverside forest walk that loops from Parking 3 through the tranquil Spöltal to Parking 4 ("Punt la Drossa").

Val Müstair

As you crest the Ofenpass/Pass dal Fuorn 20km south of Zernez, spread out in front is the idyllic **Val Müstair** (Münstertal in German), a lush, peaceful valley pointing the way south into Italy. This finger of Switzerland, cut off by the mountains from the rest of Graubünden and entirely surrounded by Italy, is determinedly Romansh in language and culture. Half a dozen hamlets dot the green slopes on the eight-kilometres descent to **Santa Maria**, the main village of the valley, with a Gothic church just off its narrow main street. However, the chief attraction is **MÜSTAIR** (pronounced *moosh-tire*), 4km further, where virtually the last buildings before the Italian frontier are a Carolingian monastery and church, the **Claustra Son Jon**, or Klosterkirche St Johann (daily 8am–7pm; ⓦwww.muestair.ch). This functioning Benedictine convent was reputedly founded by Charlemagne himself around 800 AD, and has been named a UNESCO World Heritage Site for the array of brilliantly coloured Romanesque frescoes adorning the interior of its monastery church. The style and detail of the frescoes, which depict stories such as the stoning of St Stephen and the Dance of Salome, are breathtaking, and the atmosphere of the church, its adjacent cemetery and cobbled courtyard make the journey well worthwhile.

Müstair **tourist office** (May–Oct Mon–Sat 9am–noon & 1.30–5pm, Sun 1.30–5pm, Nov–April Mon–Sat 10am–noon & 1.30–4.30pm, Sun 1.30–4.30pm; ⓣ081 858 58 58, ⓦwww.val-muestair.ch) has information on the valley. In Santa Maria is a characterful HI **hostel**, *Chasa Plaz* (ⓣ081 858 56 61, ⓦwww .youthhostel.ch, ❶; closed April, May, Oct & Nov), while Müstair has the good-value *Landgasthof Münsterhof* (ⓣ081 858 55 41, ⓦwww.muensterhof.ch; ❸), its old rooms filled with antiques.

The Upper Engadine

"I have never seen light as it is up here: it's fantastic!"

Ferdinand Hodler, Swiss painter

The **Upper Engadine** (Engiadin'Ota in Romansh, Oberengadin in German) is one of the most scenic valleys in Switzerland, a heart-stoppingly beautiful array of forests, snowy mountains and silvery lakes, raised high at 1800m and looking southwest directly into the crispest and clearest sunshine in the Alps. The long, straight 55-kilometre run southwest from Zernez takes in a handful of attractive little resorts such as **Pontresina**, **Celerina** and **Silvaplana** – all of them overshadowed by **St Moritz**, which holds court in mid-valley.

Crossing the two major mountain passes that lead on from St Moritz delivers you into small valleys sticking out into Italy that are entirely unlike the rest of Graubünden. To the southwest, the **Maloja Pass** heralds the deep and lush **Val Bregaglia**, while to the southeast, a road and rail line cross the icy **Bernina Pass** into the idyllic **Val Poschiavo**. Both are thoroughly Italian, in language, culture and flora – a breath of fresh air after the rustic ambience of the high mountains.

If you're keen to avoid difficult mountain driving, winter or summer, see p.432 regarding **car-carrying trains** on the Albula pass route. Beware that almost everything – shops, hotels, attractions, walking routes – is **closed during off-season** (mid-April to mid-June & mid-Oct to mid-Dec). We've specified months of opening only when they differ from this pattern.

Don't be misled into thinking that the Upper Engadine is all St Moritz-style glamour: there's a vast range of sports and activities that takes advantage of the valley's natural beauty. Check Ⓦ **www.bergbahnenengadin.ch**.

Winter

There are four main ski and snowboard sectors. On the north side of the valley is the sunny, south-facing **Corviglia–Piz Nair**, with three access routes. From St Moritz-Bad, a cable car rises to Signal, with chairlifts up to the Munt da San Murezzan (2659m). From St Moritz-Dorf a funicular runs via Chantarella to Corviglia itself (2486m), from where a cable car continues to the soaring Piz Nair summit (3057m). A gondola from nearby Celerina rises to **Marguns** (2278m), which gives access to testing runs off Las Trais Fluors and Piz Glüna, as well as linking directly by chairlift to Corviglia. Across the valley is **Corvatsch–Furtschellas**: a cable car from Surlej, 3km south of St Moritz-Bad, arrives at Murtèl (2702m), from where a gondola rises to Piz Corvatsch (3451m). Again, long sweeping reds are plentiful, while dropping through the trees is the testing eight-kilometre Hahnensee black run. A cable car from Sils Maria 4km south of Surlej serves Furtschellas (2800m), linked by chairlifts to Murtèl. Some 12km south of St Moritz – with easy access from Pontresina – is **Diavolezza–Lagalb**, with some steep, difficult runs, including the Minor black run and a fine ten-kilometre-long red along the glacier. Finally, **Zuoz**, around 10km north of St Moritz, hosts the Kinderland child-friendly ski area (including a child-secure chairlift) plus a selection of excellent cross-country ski trails and a handful of reds and blacks.

A peak-season **pass**, valid for 3/6 days in all areas, is Fr.200/355. A half/full day pass for Corvatsch or Corviglia is Fr.58/71, Diavolezza Fr.50/60, Zuoz Fr.42/50. Discounts apply out of peak season, and selected-day and afternoon-only passes are available. **Schools** include Ⓦ www.skischool.ch.

There are some legendary bob and toboggan runs, including an exhilarating 4.2-kilometre toboggan from **Muottas Muragl**, a vertical drop of 700m. Fr.250 buys you an adrenalin-fuelled "taxi ride" down the 1.6-kilometre **Olympia bob run** (Ⓦ www .olympia-bobrun.ch), the world's only natural-ice bobsleigh run, between St Moritz and Celerina, while for Fr.450 you can do five skeleton runs in a season (Christmas–Feb) on the most famous luge course in the world, the death-defying 1.2-kilometre **Cresta Run** (Ⓦ www.cresta-run.com) – which, for no good reason, is barred to women. See p.432 for details of the inexpensive **Preda–Bergün** toboggan run. Ⓦ www.boarders-valley.com is a good local **snowboarding** site.

Other attractions include skiing by moonlight, kite-surfing on ice, skating, curling, paragliding, hang-gliding and winter walking. Ⓦ www.bergsteiger-pontresina.ch offers a range of tough, long-distance guided skiing excursions, and Ⓦ www.govertical.ch has exhilarating back-country boarding for experts. **Horse-drawn sleighs** wait for business beside the Catholic church in St Moritz-Bad; their route crosses the frozen lake into the forest (Fr.95 per hr). Winter events held on the lake include polo, "White Turf" horse races

St Moritz

ST MORITZ is all you expect and more – a brassy, in-your-face reminder of the hotshot world beyond the high valley walls. For a century or more, it's been the prime winter retreat of social high-flyers, minor European royalty and the international jet set, who've sparked the creation of a mini-Mayfair of Vuitton and Armani in this stunningly romantic setting of forest, lake and mountains. When the tourist office trumpets the "champagne climate", they don't neces-sarily mean the sparkling sunshine – although there's plenty of that as well, an unbeatable 322 days of it a year on average.

and cricket. The **Engadin Ski Marathon** in early March (ⓦwww.engadin-skimarathon .ch), 42km down the valley from Maloja to S-chanf, attracts over ten thousand competitors.

Summer

One of the best round-trip summer **walks** starts from **Muottas Muragl** (2453m). A Höhenweg (high-level route) leads across Val Muragl and then splits: a steep path heads up to the Segantini Hütte (2731m), where the painter died, and then comes down to meet the easier path – which has stayed fairly flat – at Unterer Schafberg (2231m) before continuing to the restaurant at Alp Languard (2325m; total 2hr 30min), where a chairlift takes you down to Pontresina. Above St Moritz, **Marguns**, **Signal** and **Corviglia** are hubs for a network of trails, including a panoramic route from Corviglia to the isolated Chamanna Saluver hut and on down to Samedan (3hr 30min). A fairly easy trail runs from Marguns to Corviglia and down via Alp Giop to Signal, or via Alp Nova to Chantarella (1hr 30min); from either, it's a further hour down to St Moritz. A quieter route to the valley floor runs from Marguns to Alp Laret and then into the cool **God da Blais forest** to Celerina (1hr 30min) – or you can detour from Alp Laret to St Moritz. Top long-distance route is the **Via Engiadina**, a reasonably flat high-level trail across the whole region; simplest access is at Marguns or Corviglia, from where you walk for six full hours above the spectacular lake scenery to Maloja (19km). A testing alternative is the full-day trail from Piz Nair down to the **Suvrettasee** and on via the Suvretta Pass into Val Bever, ending at Spinas train station; an alternative leads up from the Suvrettasee around the south face of Piz Nair back to Corviglia (2hr). A lovely half-day walk leads from the **Furtschellas** top station to Marmorè, from where two routes lead back to Sils Maria; the direct option is 1hr 30min, but if you divert down to Curtins, you can trace a path through the meadows of the **Val Fex** to Sils Maria via the frescoed chapel at Fex-Crasta (2hr 30min). There are plenty of easy walks from Murtèl, including a circuit to and from the restaurant at **Fuorcla Surlej** (1hr); a tougher trail leads from there into the Val Roseg to Pontresina (3hr 30min), while another heads down to St Moritz-Bad via the Hahnensee (3hr). At **Diavolezza**, the best route involves a two-hour round trip from the top station up to the spectacular **Munt Pers** (3207m), overlooking the Morteratsch glacier.

There are tons of other activities. ⓦwww.stmoritz-experience.ch runs canyoning, glacier walking and multisports, including abseiling, flying fox, sailing, tubing and more, as well as rock climbing and multi-day **trekking** itineraries. There's also rafting, horse-riding and go-karting in Celerina. The whole area offers superb **mountain-biking routes** with around 400km of trails including a spectacular ride from Lagalb (2893m) way down 22km to Poschiavo (1000m); bikes are permitted in the cable car to Corviglia. The Innline Engadina is a marked **inline skating** and **cycling** off-road path that follows the river 8.6km from La Punt to S-chanf. Silvaplana is known for its **windsurfing** (ⓦwww .windsurfing-silvaplana.ch) and **kitesurfing** (ⓦwww.kitesailing.ch).

Not unlike its twin, Vail, Colorado, this can be the kind of town to give money a bad name. It's neither cosmopolitan, characterful nor especially attractive. And yet its name glisters better than gold, enough for the tourist board to make "St Moritz" a patented registered trademark. All winter long an endless round of banquets, celebrations and spectacles is staged on or near the frozen lake. Summer is downtime, when the hoi polloi arrive to hike and relax in the sunshine.

There's been a spa here since the Bronze Age, although the tale really begins in 1864, when local hotelier Johannes Badrutt laid down a challenge to a party of English summer regulars: spend a winter here, he said, and I'll foot the bill.

▲ Celerina   Chur ▲   ▲ Pontresina & Bernina Pass

ST MORITZ

----- Bob/Luge run

Cresta Run

ST MORITZ-DORF

Corviglia & ❶

Train Station

VIA MAISTRA

VIA BRATTAS

VIA STREDA

VIA SERLAS

VIA SERLAS

VIA VEGLIA

VIA MAISTRA

VIA QUADRELLAS

PL DA SCOLA

VIA GREVAS

2 **3**

1 ❷

4

5

Berry Museum

Design Gallery escalator

St Moritzersee

Lej da San Murezzan /

Engadiner Museum

VIA GREVAS

VIA ARONA

VIA DAL BAGN

VIA SOMPLA

Giovanni Segantini Museum

St Moritz-Bad

VIA LUDAINS

VIA GREVAS

VIA DAL BAGN

VIA SALET

VIA SOMPLAZ

SEGANTINI

VIA MEZDI

VIA SURPUNT

VIA SELA

VIA TEGIATSCHA

VIA ROSATSCH

VIA SAN GIAN

VIA GIOVANNI

VIA MEZDI

VIA MEZDI

❻ **❼**

H

❽

❾

J

L

I

K

N

0   250 m

▲ Signal & Munt da San Murezzan

www.roughguides.com/www.roughguides.com

Maloja Pass ▲   ▲ ❽ ❻ ❾ ▼   Chapter & ▼

ACCOMMODATION

Badrutt's Palace	C
Bellaval	E
Corvatsch	H
Jugendherberge	L
Kempinski Grand	K
Languard	B
La Margna	D
Nolda	I
Steffani	A
Stille	J
Suvretta House	G
Waldhaus am See	F

EATING & DRINKING

Bobby's Pub	5
Boccalino	7
Corvatsch	H
Devil's Place	F
Engiadina	2
Hauser	4
Jöhri's Talvo	8
Laudinella	9
Mathis	1
La Stalla	3
Veltlinerkeller	6

They came, brought their friends the year after, and since then Badrutt has been quids in (the family's hotel is still the most expensive in town).

Arrival, information and accommodation

The town spans two villages: when people refer to St Moritz, they're talking about **St Moritz-Dorf**, a cluster of hotels, restaurants and boutiques on the hillside above the lake. **St Moritz-Bad**, far removed from the glitz 2km southwest down on the lakeshore, is a less attractive mini-sprawl of apartment blocks and sports halls. Via dal Bagn connects the two. The **train station** is located below Dorf, on the opposite side of the lake from Bad. Via Serlas winds up from the station past the **postbus station** to the linked central squares of Dorf. The **tourist office** is signposted 100m east at Via Maistra 12 (late June to mid-Sept & mid-Dec to mid-April Mon–Fri 9am–6.30pm, Sat 9am–12.30pm & 1.30–6pm, Sun 4–6pm; rest of year Mon–Fri 9am–noon & 2–6pm, Sat 9am–noon; ☎ 081 837 33 33, ⓦ www.engadin.stmoritz.ch). Summer visitors staying two nights or more are entitled to a **free transport card**, valid on all local trains, buses, cable cars and funiculars.

Few bargains come wrapped with the St Moritz name, and **accommodation** is no exception: prices are high across the board, and during the winter season they go stratospheric. There are more affordable alternatives at neighbouring Celerina, Pontresina and Silvaplana, as well as up at the Muottas Muragl *Berghotel* (see p.454).

Campsite

Olympiaschanze ☎ 081 833 40 90, ⓦ www .campingtcs.ch. Good site about 1km southwest of Bad. Mid-May to Sept.

Hostel

Jugendherberge Stille (HI hostel) Via Surpunt 60, Bad ☎ 081 833 39 69, ⓦ www.youthhostel.ch. Excellent quality, but beds cost a Moritzy Fr.50 and up. Open year-round. ❶

Inexpensive and mid-range hotels

Bellaval Via Grevas 55, Dorf ☎ 081 833 32 45, ⓦ www.bellaval-stmoritz.ch. Squeezed in between the station and the lake, this is one of the best bargains in Dorf, with modest but pleasant rooms plus free parking. Especially good value in winter. Open year-round. ❷–❸

🏃 **Corvatsch** Via Tegiatscha 1, Bad ☎ 081 837 57 57, ⓦ www.hotel-corvatsch.ch. Excellent family-run hotel, located out of the hustle in peaceful Bad (with parking); an unromantic exterior preludes very pleasant, well-kept rooms with handcarved wooden furniture. Back rooms have views of the lake and mountains. Service is outstanding, and the onsite restaurant is a bonus. ❹–❺

Languard Via Veglia 14, Dorf ☎ 081 833 31 37, ⓦ www.languard-stmoritz.ch. Comfortable, friendly little family hotel with some of the most competitive rates in the centre of Dorf. ❸–❹

Nolda Via Crasta 3, Bad ☎ 081 833 05 75, ⓦ www.nolda.ch. Pleasant enough pack-'em-in hotel next to the Signal cable car and *River Inn*, with pine-clad rooms that do the job. Also has a nearby, more upmarket *Noldapark* annexe. ❹–❻

Stille Beside the hostel in Bad ☎ 081 833 69 48, ⓦ www.hotelstille.ch. Quiet, modern, well-run sports hotel, popular with skiers and snowboarders, who crowd out its no-frills rooms. ❷

Waldhaus am See Via Dim Lej 6 ☎ 081 836 60 00, ⓦ www.waldhaus-am-see.ch. Large, quiet lodge in an idyllic location, just 5min walk from the station and slightly above the lakeshore, but far enough away from the road to be quiet. It's a modern, bustling, three-star establishment, so the atmosphere inside is more holiday-hotel than country-retreat – but if you choose one of the six spacious double-view corner rooms, with superb panoramas over the whole lake and forest, you won't care. Add in the fact that the bar has the widest choice of whiskies in the world – more than 2500 varieties – and you may decide to hole up here for the winter (or summer). ❹–❺

Expensive hotels

Badrutt's Palace Via Serlas 27, Dorf ☎ 081 837 10 00, ⓦ www.badruttspalace.com. Legendary five-star behemoth, one of Switzerland's – and Europe's – swankiest hotels. You may not even get past the flunkey on the door: men must wear a jacket just to stand in the lobby after 7.30pm. If you do get in, make the most of it – this is the haunt of film stars, princesses (real and wannabe) and more fur coats than live in the forest. Staying here involves tossing zeros around like confetti. **9**

Kempinski Grand Hôtel des Bains Via Mezdi 27, Bad ☎081 838 38 38, Ⓦwww.kempinski-stmoritz .ch. Sensational five-star hotel in traditional style down at the spa complex in St Moritz-Bad, entirely fitted out from scratch within the shell of the original 1864 grand hotel. Rooms are spacious and modern, many with balconies or terraces. **7–9**

🏃 **La Margna** Via Serlas 5, Dorf ☎081 836 66 00, Ⓦwww.lamargna.ch. Fine old stalwart hotel, built in 1907, just above the station, with good views over the lake and mountains. Rooms are spacious and solidly comfortable,

service is warm and efficient and the lounge offers stout, wing-backed armchairs arranged around the stone fireplace, with picture windows facing south. Fine, traditional quality. **6**

Steffani Plazza da la Posta Veglia 1, Dorf ☎081 836 96 96, Ⓦwww.steffani.ch. Very comfortable, bustling hotel on the central square, with a few airs and graces but efficient and welcoming nonetheless. Open year-round. **6–8**

Suvretta House Via Chasellas 1, Suvretta ☎081 836 36 36, Ⓦwww.suvrettahouse.ch. Vast luxury hotel located amidst the forests west of St Moritz itself, with uniquely elegant, understated guest rooms and an exquisite attention to detail. Service is formal, but not stiff. **9**

The Town

St Moritz's town museums are worth making time for – although beware their different closing days. About 1km west of Dorf on Via Somplaz, the terrace road, is the domed, church-like **Giovanni Segantini Museum** (mid-May to mid-Oct & mid-Dec to mid-April Tues–Sun 10am–noon & 2–6pm; Fr.10; Ⓦwww.segantini-museum.ch), displaying the beautiful work of this largely self-taught Symbolist. Segantini (1858–99) spent the twelve years before his sudden death at the age of 41 working to portray the clear mountain light of the Upper Engadine. The museum's highlight is the Alpine Triptych, shown upstairs in the circular domed room designed for the purpose. This sequence of vast, luminous canvases, each between 3 and 4m long, covers *Birth*, *Life* and *Death*. Segantini had studiously sketched all three in entirety as preparation (the sketches are also displayed), and was working on the final touches of the complete painted triptych when he died.

On the terrace below is the **Engadiner Museum**, Via dal Bagn 39 (Sun–Fri 10am–noon & 2–5pm; closed May & Nov; Fr.6; Ⓦwww.engadiner-museum .ch), housed in a solid *sgraffitied* building that's one of the few surviving pieces of vernacular architecture in the town. Inside are reconstructed interiors of farmhouses and patrician mansions, along with interesting displays on the history of the spa and Engadine culture.

Just off the central square, the **Berry Museum**, Via Arona 32 (Mon & Wed–Sun 10am–1pm & 4–7pm; Fr.15; Ⓦwww.berrymuseum.com), is devoted to the painter and doctor Peter Robert Berry (1864–1942), housed in the family's former home. The excellent audioguide gives background to Berry's paintings, which were very much influenced by Segantini. Berry spent many winters in the mountains painting, and the best of his work captures the light and ethereal nature of the Alpine landscapes. Look out, particularly, for *The Great Silent Glow* (1910), a panoramic view over the Bernina Pass.

The **St Moritz Design Gallery** is the grandiose name for a long covered escalator (open 24hr; free) between the lakefront and Via Serlas up in the centre, which is lined with changing exhibitions of posters and photos. The real beauty of the thing is that it provides an energy-saving alternative to the tedious hike along the main road between the station and town.

Eating and drinking

You'll find few bargains **eating and drinking** in St Moritz. The big hotels all have super-swanky dining rooms – exclusive, expensive and cloying to a fault.

More down-to-earth establishments might take a bit of sniffing out. Die-hard romantics shouldn't miss the chance to book ahead for a window table at the *Muottas Muragl* restaurant (see p.454).

Many of the **bars**, clubs and lounges are upmarket retreats, either for members only, shielded by sky-high entry fees, or simply dull and expensive. The *Roo Bar*, at *Hotel Hauser*, on Dorf's main square, is an exception, as is *Bobby's Pub*, Via dal Bagn 52, and the chic little *American Bar* next door. Alternatively, you could settle in at the eye-popping *Devil's Place*, the bar of *Hotel Waldhaus am See*, Via Dim Lej 6 (daily 4pm–12.30am), which holds the world's largest selection of **whiskies**.

Restaurants

Boccalino Via dal Bagn 6 ☎081 832 11 11. Lively, bustling place with a range of quality wood-fired pizzas for around Fr.20, as well as pasta dishes and home-made tiramisu.

Corvatsch (see "Accommodation"). Down-to-earth, cosy restaurant, well out of the chic part of town, but with well-presented local cuisine plus wines to match.

Engiadina Plazza da Scuola 10 ☎081 833 32 65. Popular place in the middle of Dorf that concentrates on fondue (Fr.30–46), including the house special with champagne. Closed Sun.

🏃 **Hauser** Via Traunter Plazzas 7 ☎081 837 50 50, ⓦwww.hotelhauser.ch. Occupying a perfect location in the middle of Dorf, on the central square, with a lovely terrace: if it's sunny you can eat lunch outside in shirtsleeves, even if the thermometer reads well below freezing. The food is good, too, with a choice of *Rösti* – including one with smoked salmon and sour cream – kangaroo, buffalo and horse steaks (or the veggie tofu equivalent) grilled on hot stones at your table.

Jöhri's Talvo Via Gunels 15, Champfèr ☎081 833 44 55, ⓦwww.talvo.ch. Perhaps the finest restaurant in the valley, 3km west of St Moritz in neighbouring Champfèr, specializing in superb fish and lobster dishes and also offering classic, elegant takes on heavier local cuisine. Be prepared to pay hundreds of francs for the privilege.

Laudinella Via Tegiatscha 17 ☎081 836 00 00, ⓦwww.laudinella.ch. This suave modern hotel is home to no fewer than eight restaurants and bars, including *Le Carnotzet* (fondues and raclette; winter only), the smart *Pizzeria Caruso* and *Siam Wind* (dinner only), specializing in Thai and Japanese.

Mathis Food Affairs Corviglia funicular top station ☎081 833 63 55, ⓦwww.mathisfood.ch. Book well ahead for a meal to remember at the *Marmite* restaurant, high above town on the Corviglia slopes – think caviar and truffles at 2500m.

La Stalla Plazza dal Mulin 2 ☎081 837 58 59. Pleasant modern Italian restaurant above a newsagent, kitted out to look like a stable (hence the name), with a small range of inexpensive pasta dishes (all under Fr.20) and other mains, plus good-value lunchtime *menus* for Fr.20. Closed Sat lunch & Sun.

Veltlinerkeller Via dal Bagn 11 ☎081 833 40 09. A perennial favourite; ignore the hunting trophies on the walls, and concentrate on the quality, lightly prepared food in front of you: excellent pastas and grilled meats start from Fr.20.

Celerina and around

Just 2km – a half-hour walk – east of St Moritz is **CELERINA** (Schlarigna in Romansh). This pleasant small town on the banks of the Inn, base station for a gondola rising to the ski slopes of Corviglia, has an atmospheric old cobbled quarter of traditional Engadine architecture. It's also the end point of both the infamous Cresta Run skeleton course and the Olympia Bob-Run (for both, see p.448). On a grassy knoll 1km east of the centre is the isolated **Baselgia San Gian**, with a Romanesque choir and a painted wooden ceiling dating from 1478 (mid-June to mid-Oct Mon, Wed & Fri 2–4pm, Dec–March Wed 2–3.30pm; free).

Beware that there are **two train stations**: the main one, on the St Moritz–Samedan line, is on the north side of the centre; the other (dubbed "Celerina Staz"; trains only stop here on request) is on the St Moritz–Pontresina line, 700m south, just over the river. The straight Via da la Staziun links the two. The **tourist office** is at the main station (Mon–Fri 8.30am–6.30pm, Sat 9am–noon & 2–6pm, Sun 4–6pm, May, June & Nov Mon–Fri 8.30am–noon & 2–6.30pm;

☎081 830 00 11, Ⓦwww.celerina.ch). The most characterful **accommodation** is at *Chesa Rosatsch*, a 350-year-old riverside inn (☎081 837 01 01, Ⓦwww.rosatsch.ch; ❻).

Muottas Muragl

Across from Celerina rises the ridge of **MUOTTAS MURAGL** (2456m), accessed by a steep **funicular** from **Punt Muragl**, which is on the Celerina–Pontresina road, connected to St Moritz by buses and trains. The funicular runs every half-hour until 11pm throughout the season (Fr.30 return). The panoramic view from the top, some 700m above the valley, is unmissable summer or winter, offering an uninterrupted gaze southwest up the length of the Engadine, its string of lakes glittering in the sunlight between high peaks. The summit *Berghotel* has reinvented itself as a fine ⚜ **restaurant** (☎081 842 82 32, Ⓦwww.muottasmuragl.ch), with an excellent menu of regional and international cuisine complemented by an outstanding wine list and spectacular views: book in advance for a window table. At lunchtime, mains are Fr.17–30, rising to around Fr.55 in the evening. The spotlessly clean, fresh but simple shared-bath **rooms** are a bargain (❸, including unlimited use of the funicular), while there are some great walks nearby and a winter toboggan run.

Pontresina and beyond

Less than 2km up the Bernina Pass road from Punt Muragl is the swish resort of **PONTRESINA**, lying in a privileged, wind-sheltered position on a southwest-facing terrace amidst meadows and fragrant pine and larch woods. Access to the Diavolezza slopes is easy from here, and the scenery of high rocky peaks to east and west interspersed with glaciers – most notably the huge **Morteratsch glacier**, sidling down from Piz Bernina (4049m) – is impressive; the town stares directly across to the **Val Roseg**, complete with its own glacier. Pontresina is curiously split between its St-Moritzy aspirations, with half a dozen luxury palace hotels and a glitteringly modern main street, and its tough reputation as the best place in the area for adventure sports and hiking; the local mountaineering school is the largest in Switzerland.

Walkers should ask at the tourist office for routes to the *Coaz Hut* (☎081 842 62 78, Ⓦwww.coaz.ch) and/or neighbouring *Tschierva Hut* (☎081 842 63 91), the first in four and a half hours, the second in an hour less: both give close views of glaciers and their icefalls. The *Boval Hut* (☎081 842 64 03) is another unmissable three-and-a-half-hour walk, giving stupendous high mountain and glacier scenery for much of the way. The easy but steep ascent of the 3262-metre Piz Languard directly above Pontresina (up to 4hr) is the best place to enjoy an Alpine sunrise or sunset.

Walks and skiing aside, the most enjoyable excursion (June–Oct only) is by **horse-drawn carriage** from the station for an hour to the tastefully renovated *Hotel Roseg Gletscher* (☎081 842 64 45, Ⓦwww.roseggletscher.ch; ❷–❸), 7km up the car-free Val Roseg at the foot of the glacier. There is a scheduled timetable – up to five carriages a day (Fr.26 return) – but booking is essential (Luigi Costa Carriages ☎081 842 60 57). Otherwise, it's an easy, scenic **walk** (2hr). The views from the hotel (which also offers dorms) are stunning, and plenty of high-level trails lead on deeper into the mountains.

Practicalities

From the station, it's a short walk across the river and up to the **tourist office** (Mon–Fri 8.30am–6pm, Sat 8.30am–noon & 3–6pm, Sun 4–6pm; shorter hours in off-season; ☎081 838 83 00, ⓦwww.pontresina.ch), housed in the landmark Rondo conference centre on Via Maistra, the main road through town. This main thoroughfare slopes upwards into the centre, location of most **hotels**, including simple *Pensione Valtellina* (☎081 842 64 06; ❷), but you'll find more character in the narrow lanes of the Old Town, the other direction on Via Maistra. Here are the *Grand Hotel Kronenhof* (☎081 830 30 30, ⓦwww .kronenhof.com; ❼–❾), a Baroque-style palace set around its own courtyard with luxurious guest rooms; and the delightful *Saratz* (☎081 839 40 00, ⓦwww.saratz.ch; ❼–❾), a similarly grand hotel updated with tasteful contemporary decor. Down by the station is the basic *Hotel Station* (☎081 838 80 00, ⓦwww.station-pontresina.ch; ❷), alongside the HI **hostel** *Jugendherberge Tolais* (☎081 842 72 23, ⓦwww.youthhostel.ch; ❷), where you can get advice on hikes and adventure sports. The **campsite** *Plauns/Morteratsch* (☎081 842 62 85, ⓦwww.campingplauns.ch; closed mid-April to end May & mid-Oct to mid-Dec) is in a lovely countryside location, a couple of stops along the train line at Morteratsch (or a 90min walk).

Val Poschiavo

From Pontresina, the high **Bernina Pass** (2328m) is about 15km southeast. This route is served by ordinary trains as well as the Bernina Express (see p.34), an excursion in panoramic carriages from Chur, Davos and St Moritz into the idyllic **Val Poschiavo** and down to the Italian border town of Tirano, from where you switch onto a postbus around the shores of Lake Como, ending up back in Switzerland at Lugano. However you travel in the valley, it's still gorgeous. A classic vantage point is **Alp Grüm**, on the train line but not the road; a short walk away, the *Belvedere* inn (☎081 844 03 14, ⓦwww .belvedere-engadin.ch; May–Oct; ❷–❸) provides refreshment.

After the **Bernina Pass**, which has its own inn (ⓦwww.bernina-hospiz.ch), the railway joins the road again at the village of **San Carlo**, watched over by its ancient church tower, and heads on 2km to **POSCHIAVO** (pronounced *poss-KYA-vo*). The difference between this laid-back, photogenic Italianate town (Puschlav in German) and the huddled Alpine resort of Pontresina the same distance north of the pass couldn't be more striking. Poschiavo's tranquil old quarter, across the river from the train station, is filled with tall, eighteenth-century shuttered mansions in various shades of pastel, overlooking stone-paved plazas ringed with terrace cafés. The place is perfect for soaking up some sunshine – of which there's plenty – swapping fondue for risotto, and savouring a carafe of Italian Valtellina wine. On the north side of the central Piazza Comunale is the seventeenth-century Protestant church of **Sant'Ignazio**, while the Catholic **San Vittore**, dating from the fifteenth century, remains a powerful presence 200m away on the south side of the square. The same square holds the **tourist office** (Mon–Fri 8am–noon & 2–6pm, July & Aug also Sat 9am–noon & 2–5pm; ☎081 844 05 71, ⓦwww.valposchiavo.ch). Of the **hotels**, *Croce Bianca*, a five-minute walk south (☎081 844 01 44, ⓦwww.croce-bianca.ch; ❸), and *Suisse*, on Via da Mez (☎081 844 07 88, ⓦwww.suisse-poschiavo.ch; ❷–❸), are both long-standing fixtures, with decent rooms.

Beyond Lake Poschiavo and the village of **Brusio** – with its much-photographed circular viaduct bringing trains gently down to the valley floor – is the Italian border at **Campocologno**, 16km south of Poschiavo. Some 4km further is **TIRANO**, terminus of Swiss trains. The Swiss station and its Italian counterpart (with trains to Milan roughly every 2hr) sit beside each other, separated by passport control. Swiss **postbuses** to Lugano – the second leg of the Bernina Express – depart from round the corner (signposted). Tirano's residential

Old Town, dead ahead on the west bank of the river, has cobbled, arcaded court-yards and tiny sloping lanes leading up to the medieval Porta Bormina. The pilgrimage church of **Madonna di Tirano**, commemorating an appearance of the Virgin in 1504, lies 1km northwest of the centre, its shrine focused around a statue of Mary dressed in a silk and gold robe donated by local people in 1746.

Silvaplana and beyond

The Engadine continues to rise gently for 16km beyond St Moritz, past little **Champfèr** to the village of **SILVAPLANA**, on a bulge of land between the diminutive Lej da Champfèr and the grand Lej da Silvaplauna (Silvaplanersee in German). Due to a particular feature of the local summer climate – in which morning thermals rise more quickly than in neighbouring St Moritz or Sils, thus creating the consistently strong, warm "Malojawind" that sweeps across the surface of the lake during the day – Silvaplana is home to some outstanding watersports: it has hosted the windsurfing and kiteboarding world champion-ships. Opposite the village is tiny **Surlej**, base station for the cable car up to Piz Corvatsch.

In the centre of Silvaplana – on the main road up to the Julier Pass (see p.432) – is the **tourist office** (Mon–Fri 8.30am–noon & 1.30–6pm, Sat 9am–noon & 4–6pm; Dec–March also Sun 4–6pm; ℡081 838 60 00, ⑩www.silvaplana .ch). Of the **hotels**, youthful *Julier Palace* (℡081 828 96 44, ⑩www.julierpalace .com; ❸–❹) has a lively atmosphere and an excellent bar. Champfèr's four-star *Chesa Guardalej* (℡081 836 63 00, ⑩www.chesa-guardalej.ch; ❺–❻) has perks like a free ski bus and free parking but also stands out for its good-value summer rates. The acclaimed *Landgasthof Bellavista* (℡081 838 60 50, ⑩www .bellavista.ch; ❺–❼) is in a peaceful location near the Surlej cable car, with a stunning view and a fine restaurant.

Sils and Maloja

Beyond the Lej da Silvaplauna lies the quiet village of **SILS** (Segl in Romansh), with an alluring, rural atmosphere lacking in either Silvaplana or St Moritz: **Sils Baselgia** offers ethereally beautiful views over the Lej da Segl, acclaimed by a century of artistic and literary visitors – not least Hermann Hesse, Marc Chagall and Richard Strauss – while 200m south, **Sils Maria** was the summer home of the philosopher Friedrich Nietzsche for eight creative years. His modest house has been turned into the **Nietzsche–Haus** museum (Tues–Sun 3–6pm; closed May & Nov; Fr.6; ⑩www.nietzschehaus.ch), where you can see manuscripts, photos, death masks and the room where Nietzsche wrote his most celebrated work, *Also Sprach Zarathustra*.

In the Chesa Cumünela on the nearby village square is the well-equipped **tourist office** (Mon–Fri 9am–noon & 1–6pm, Sat 9am–noon & 2–6pm, Sun 3–6pm; shorter hours in off-season; ℡081 838 50 50, ⑩www.sils.ch). Traffic is barred from circulating between Maria and Baselgia: there's a large under-ground car park in Maria and, in winter, free local buses which also serve the base-station of the Furtschellas cable car. A handful of grand **hotels** include the Art Nouveau *Edelweiss* (℡081 838 42 42, ⑩www.hotel-edelweiss.ch; ❻–❽), Sils's oldest hotel, with a renowned restaurant.

From Sils Maria, horse-drawn "buses" run on a schedule into the car-free **Val Fex** (June–Oct at least 2 daily; from Fr.25 return; reserve on ℡081 826 52 86) to the peaceful *Hotel Fex* at the end of the valley (℡081 826 53 55, ⑩www .hotelfex.ch; ❸). A belvedere path above the entrance to the valley makes a high traverse round to St Moritz (5hr).

In summer, a small **motorboat** – dubbed "Europe's highest ferry" (July–Sept; 3–4 daily; takes 40min; Fr.23 return; reserve on ℡081 826 53 43) – chugs around the Lej da Segl, 1800m above sea level, stopping a few times on its way to the village of **MALOJA**, whose church cemetery holds the grave of painter Giovanni Segantini. Rewarding **walks** lead up to the lovely hamlets of Grevasalvas and Blaunca (1hr), above which a path climbs to Piz Lunghin (2780m) in three and a half hours from Maloja. The Lunghin Pass is a rare triple watershed: from this point, the Inn flows into the Danube and the Black Sea; the Julier flows via the Rhine to the North Sea; and the Maira flows into the Po and the Mediterranean.

Val Bregaglia

From the **Maloja Pass** (1815m), the road suddenly tumbles off the cliff edge and down in a series of concertina switchbacks into the beautiful **Val Bregaglia** (Bergell in German), one of Graubünden's three Italian-speaking valleys (along with Mesolcina and Poschiavo). Suddenly, everything is different: the crisp air of the Alps is replaced by the warm breezes of the south, pine forests and rocky, snowy crags by lush, green vegetation, and *sgraffitied* bungalows by flinty cottages. Roughly 14km from the pass is the main village, **Vicosoprano**, an attractive, quiet place bypassed by the main road which heads on south through tiny **Stampa**, birthplace of the painter Augusto Giacometti and his better-known son, the sculptor Alberto, and home to the valley's **tourist office** (℡081 822 15 55, Ⓦwww.bregaglia.ch). The road shadows the river, coiling on down the valley past ruined hilltop castles and isolated, crumbling roadside churches.

From **Promontogno**, 3km west of Stampa and about the same distance east of the border village Castasegna, hourly postbuses follow a narrow branch road which climbs the north wall of the valley to **SOGLIO**. This eyrie of a hamlet, its narrow, cobbled alleys lined with close-set stone buildings, offers tremendous panoramic views: its lofty terrace sits opposite the Pizzo Badile (3300m), and is backed by the equally lofty Piz dal Märc and Piz Duan. The village is the focus of a wealth of mountain walks, easy ones following a valley-side route down to Stampa (2hr), as well as longer high-level hikes back to Vicosoprano, or up through the tree line behind the village to Alp Tombal and on to Pass da Cam and Pass Düana for the most breathtaking views.

But there are lazier reasons to spend a day or three in Soglio: the ⚶ *Palazzo Salis* in the village (℡081 822 12 08, Ⓦwww.palazzosalis.ch; ❸–❺) is one of Switzerland's most extraordinary **hotels**. Soglio was the seat of the Von Salis family long before 1630, when the *palazzo* was constructed, and the hotel is still owned by the same family today. The whole place is an eye-opening experience, from the echoing vaulted hall, crammed with antique furniture, open fireplaces and suits of armour, to its grand guest rooms (some en suite), stone-floored down below, wood-floored above, complete with four-poster beds and antique stoves.

Travel details

Full timetables for all trains, buses, trams, boats and cable cars in Switzerland – as well as international connections – are searchable at Ⓦwww.rail .ch. For details of the Rhätische Bahn's panoramic routes, see Ⓦwww.rhb.ch.

Trains

Chur to: Arosa (hourly; 1hr); Davos Dorf & Platz (twice hourly; 1hr 30min; change in Landquart or Filisur); Klosters (hourly; 1hr 10min); Maienfeld (twice hourly; 15min); St Gallen (hourly; 1hr 35min); St Moritz (hourly; 2hr); Zürich (twice hourly; 1hr 15–30min).

Davos (Platz & Dorf) to: Chur (hourly; 1hr 30min; change in Landquart or Filisur); Klosters (hourly; 25min).

Klosters to: Chur (hourly; 1hr 15min); Davos Dorf & Platz (hourly; 25min); Scuol (hourly; 45min).

St Moritz to: Pontresina (hourly; 10min); Poschiavo (hourly; 1hr 45min); Zernez (hourly; 45min; change at Samedan).

Buses

Chur to: Bellinzona via San Bernardino Tunnel (hourly; 2hr 5min); Flims (twice hourly; 25–35min); Splügen (hourly; 55min); St Moritz via Julier Pass (1–2 daily; 2hr 40min); Zillis (every 2hr; 40min).

Davos (Platz & Dorf) to: Zernez via Flüela Pass (July–Oct every 2hr; 1hr 15min).

St Moritz to: Lugano via Chiavenna, Italy (1 daily; 4hr).

Zernez to: Davos via Flüela Pass (July–Oct every 1–2hr; 1hr 15min); Müstair via Pass dal Fuorn (hourly; 1hr).

Ticino

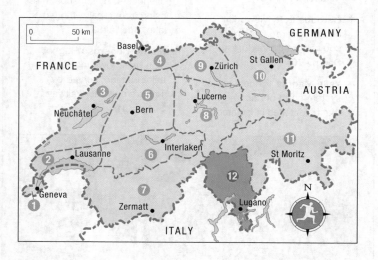

CHAPTER 12 # Highlights

* **Bellinzona** Atmospheric, often-bypassed town, dominated by its three castles. See p.465

* **Alto Ticino** There's some excellent walking on offer in these remote high valleys. See p.469

* **Locarno** Ticino's most stylish lakeside resort – a hint of the Mediterranean. See p.472

* **Cardada** Lofty viewpoint above Locarno, set amidst cool, fragrant pine forests. See p.476

* **Valle Maggia** Tortuous valley system north of Locarno that culminates in isolated

trailheads and a serene Alpine chapel at Mogno. See p.478

* **Centovalli** Highly memorable train ride, winding above a ravine west of Locarno. See p.479

* **Isole di Brissago** Two tiny dots of green in the glittering Lake Maggiore. See p.482

* **Lugano** Chic lakeside city, overlooked by sugarloaf hills rising from a palm-fringed lake. See p.483

* **Monte Generoso** Rugged high peak towering above Lake Lugano, served by Ticino's only rack railway. See p.491

▲ Market in Bellinzona's Old Town

Ticino

It is strange how different the sun-dried, ancient, southern slopes of the world are, from the northern slopes. It is as if the god Pan really had his home among these sunbleached stones and tough, sun-dark trees. So I was content, coming down into Airolo...

D.H. Lawrence

The Italian-speaking canton of **TICINO** (*Tessin* in German and French) occupies the balmy, lake-laced southern foothills of the Alps. It's radically different from the rest of Switzerland: culture, food, architecture, attitude and driving style owe more to Milan than Zürich.

The place is irresistible: a short train ride under the Alps and you emerge to a tiny corner of the Italian Mediterranean that is forever Switzerland, peopled by expressive, stylish, hot-blooded folk as different from the stolid farmers of the north as they could possibly be. As an ethnic and linguistic minority of eight percent in their own country – and nothing more than a quaint irrelevance to the urban hotshots of Milan next door – the Ticinesi have plenty to get hot-blooded about.

The glamour of their canton, and its stunning natural beauty – lushly wooded hills rising from azure water, palm trees swaying against deep blue skies, red roofs framed by purple bougainvillea – often seem to blind outsiders with romance. It takes just three hours from the grey streets of suburban Zürich to the fragrant gardens of Lugano: German Swiss visit in their thousands to sit beneath vine-shaded outdoor terraces of simple *grotti* or *osterie* (rustic local taverns), choose polenta or risotto from Italian–German menus, sample a carafe of Merlot del Ticino, and still pay with francs at the end.

Ticino is divided topographically in two by the **Monte Ceneri** range (1961m), two-thirds of the way down: the area to the north is the **Sopraceneri**

Exploring Ticino

Ticino's hinterland is best accessed by public transport: **trains** serve the major towns and **buses** penetrate to the remotest hamlet. Two regional passes (ⓦwww.utpt.ch) take advantage, obtainable from train stations, hotels and tourist offices. The **Lugano Regional Pass** gives free travel on trains, buses and boats on and around Lake Lugano, with half-price discounts around Locarno; and the **Locarno Regional Pass** does the same in reverse: free travel on trains, buses and boats on and around Lake Maggiore, with half-price discounts around Lugano. Either costs Fr.92/108 for three/ seven days. **Ticino Turismo** (ⓦwww.ticino.ch) has more details. **Swiss Pass** holders travel free anyway (except on Lake Maggiore boats).

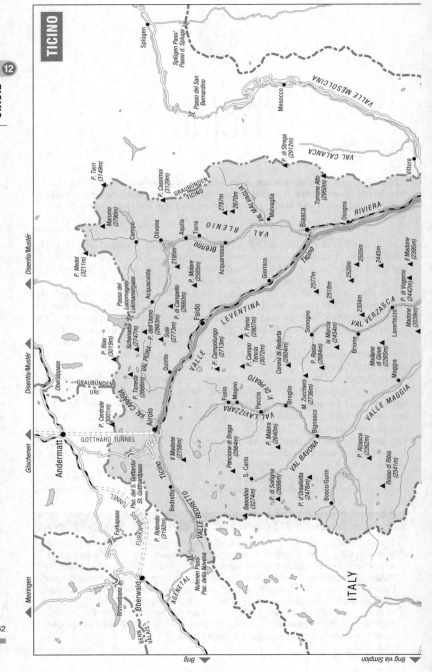

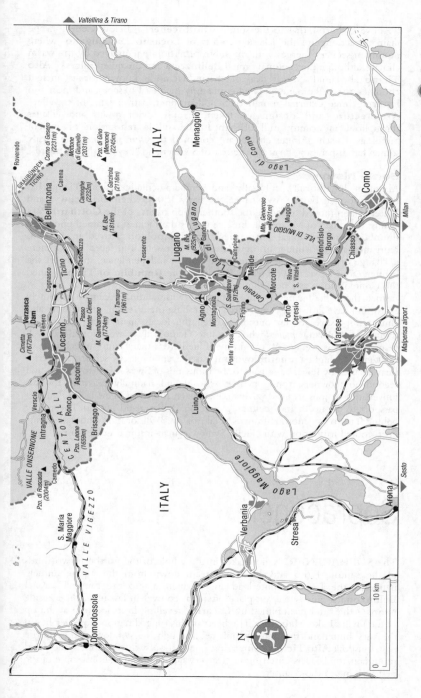

("Above Ceneri"), that to the south is **Sottoceneri** ("Below Ceneri"). The main attractions are the lakeside resorts of **Locarno** and **Lugano**, where mountain scenery merges with the subtropical flora encouraged by the warm climate, although the cantonal capital **Bellinzona** and the quiet valleys of **Alto Ticino** also hold a great deal of charm. Ticino is known for its ancient churches, many Romanesque and containing medieval frescoes, and most also featuring huge external murals of St Christopher, patron saint of travellers. **Architecture and design** are taken seriously, with towns and villages throughout the canton full of sympathetic, subtle restoration of ancient buildings. Kitschy Alpine chalets are confined to *Oltre Gottardo*, the locals' somewhat disparaging term for the rest of Switzerland "beyond the Gotthard".

Some history

Although linguistically, culturally and temperamentally Italian, Ticino has been controlled by the Swiss since the early 1500s, when Uri, Schwyz and Unterwalden moved to secure the southern approaches of the **Gotthard Pass** against the dukes of Milan. For three centuries the Ticinesi remained under the thumb of the tyrannical northerners, until **Napoleon** arrived in 1798 to reorganize the area under his new Cisalpine Republic. But faced with a mere exchange of overlords, the Ticinesi held out for independence, and under the banner *Liberi e Svizzeri!* ("Free and Swiss!"), the **Republic of Ticino** joined the Confederation as a new canton in 1803.

Since then, the Ticinesi – appearances notwithstanding – remain resolutely Swiss, and have little truck with foreigners calling them Italian, although it's also almost impossible for an outsider to tell the locals apart from the tens of thousands of Italian *frontalieri* who cross into Ticino daily to work for salaries well below the Swiss average. A cruel irony of life here is that Ticino suffers some of Switzerland's highest **unemployment** rates even while its service industries thrive, staffed by Italians and paid for by thousands of Swiss-German tourists and second-homeowners. Young people, who would naturally gravitate towards universities or jobs in nearby Milan, have been forced by their lack of an EU passport to go north into culturally "foreign" Switzerland instead. The reality behind Ticino's glamorous front is a tale of social dislocation and a draining, deep-rooted frustration with chiefly Swiss-German-inspired isolationism.

Sopraceneri

The **SOPRACENERI** region takes in the whole of the northern two-thirds of the canton. Road and rail lines stream down from the Alpine tunnels, bypassing the Ticinese hinterland and funnelling into the cantonal capital **Bellinzona**, a quietly elegant place often passed over in favour of the lakeside resorts – the latter exemplified by **Locarno**, revelling in its location at the tip of the idyllic **Lake Maggiore**. The heart of this rugged region, however, lies in the very hinterland that most people see through the window as they hurtle past. Unspoilt **Alto Ticino**, comprising a network of wild, Prealpine valleys and mountain-top lakelets glittering in clear, crystalline sunshine, holds some of the best walking in the country.

Bellinzona

Few people bother with **BELLINZONA** – their loss, since this graceful and beautiful old town is the perfect place to draw breath before hitting the lakeside glitz further south.

A fortress since **Roman** times, Bellinzona occupies a prime valley-floor position, controlling the great Alpine passes of the Novena (Nufenen), Gottardo (Gotthard), Lucomagno (Lukmanier) and San Bernardino. In 1242 it was bought by the Visconti family, dukes of Milan, who built a new **castle** atop the hill in the middle of the valley; their allies, the Rusconi family of Como, built another castle slightly up the hillside. In the fourteenth century, the Swiss confederates north of the Gotthard Pass, who had thrown off Habsburg rule, looked to secure their position by conquering the territory on the south side of the pass. They began a campaign against the Milanese in the 1420s, which spurred the Sforza dynasty then in the ascendant to reinforce the two existing castles and build a third, even higher up the hillside. A massive chain of fortifications cut right across the Ticino valley at Bellinzona, but to no avail, since the Swiss won the town under the Treaty of Arona in 1503. Three centuries of oppression followed, with Swiss overlords posted to Bellinzona to keep control of the peasantry until Ticino won its **independence** in 1803.

Bellinzona lacks a lake, but it also lacks the pace, the crowds and the touristic sheen of its bigger neighbours. This gentle town is blessed with medieval architecture and picturesque churches, with its trio of castles – **Castelgrande**, **Montebello** and **Sasso Corbaro** – listed as a UNESCO World Heritage Site.

Arrival, information and accommodation

Bellinzona's **train station** is 500m northeast of the Old Town. The cobbled streets of the Old Town, from the post office south to Piazza Indipendenza, are banned to private vehicles from 7.30pm to 6am.

The **tourist office** is in the Palazzo Civico on Piazza Nosetto (Mon–Fri 9am–6.30pm, Sat 9am–noon; ☎091 825 21 31, ⒲www.bellinzonaturismo.ch). They have good information on architecture as well as walking routes and driving itineraries in the higher valleys. You can take a self-guided **walking tour** with the ArtKey **audioguide** (Fr.7), available from the tourist office and all three castles and usable by two people at the same time.

Bellinzona's Saturday market

It's worth making a special trip to Bellinzona for the colourful, atmospheric **Saturday market** of breads, local cheeses, wines, fruit and veg and handicrafts, held in the alleys of the Old Town (7.30am–1pm). Many local restaurants take the opportunity to offer polenta or risotto for a civilized Saturday lunch al fresco. Also don't miss the annual cheese market in early October, where all the Ticinese Alpine producers parade their wares.

Bellinzona's festivals

Bellinzona's February carnival, known as **Rabadan** (⒲www.rabadan.ch), takes in a masked parade and festivities, starting on the Thursday before Mardi Gras and continuing all weekend. Early June sees the **Spada nella Rocca** (⒲www.laspadanellarocca .ch), a medieval festival at Montebello. The town also hosts several music festivals, including **Piazza Blues** (⒲www.piazzablues.ch) in late June; past performers include such big names as Albert Collins and Screamin' Jay Hawkins.

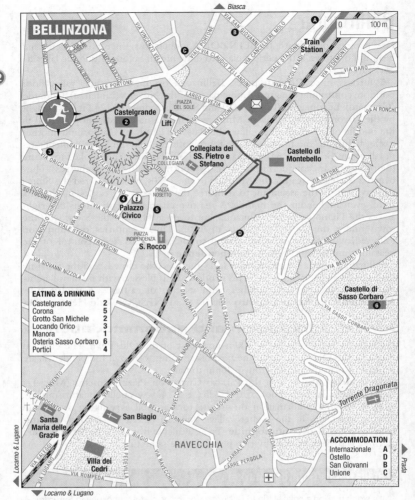

Bellinzona's **hotels** aren't up to much. You'd do better to head out of town: set amidst hillside vineyards on a minor road between Sementina and Gudo, ten minutes south, is the charming ⚘ *Fattoria l'Amorosa* agriturismo (☎091 840 29 50, ⓦwww.amorosa.ch; ❺). Choose between the eight rooms in the main building, presented with taste in a rustic Tuscan style, or the separate cottage "Isabella", where the kids can sleep on a platform under the eaves, and there's a private panoramic terrace and granite bathroom. Balconies and picture windows take advantage of the views.

Otherwise, in town, *San Giovanni*, Via San Giovanni 7 (☎091 825 19 19; ❷), has a few well-kept rooms above a restaurant, while *Unione*, Via Generale Guisan 1 (☎091 825 55 77, ⓦwww.hotel-unione.ch; ❹), is a decent three-star, with efficient service. By the time you visit, *Internazionale*, Piazza Stazione 35 (☎091 825 43 33, ⓦwww.hotel-internazionale.ch), will have reopened as a modern three-star business hotel by the station. The HI **hostel** *Ostello/ Jugendherberge* is in the grand Villa Montebello, Via Nocca 4 (☎091 825 15 22, ⓦ www.youthhostel.ch; ❶).

The Town

The elegant Renaissance buildings of **Piazza Collegiata** mark the centre of the Old Town, dominated by the Collegiata church, built by the same architect who worked on Como's cathedral and decorated with Baroque frescoes and stucco. Narrow lanes branch out all around: arcaded **Piazza Nosetto** is just south, with the Cà Rossa house on the way featuring a striking red terracotta facade – a style fashionable in early nineteenth-century Milan. From Piazza Nosetto, a gateway leads into the courtyard of the **Palazzo Civico** or **Palazzo del Comune**, rebuilt in the 1920s in Renaissance style, with loggias winding attractively around both upper floors.

Castelgrande

High on Bellinzona's central rock rise the massive towers and walls of **Castelgrande** (daily 10am–6pm; free), most impressive of the town's three medieval castles. Known to have been occupied as far back as the Neolithic age, the hill was fortified first by the Romans and then again by Milan in the thirteenth century. For three centuries between the Swiss conquest and Ticinese independence, Castelgrande was known as the Castello di Uri after its trans-Alpine occupiers (Montebello was the Castello di Svitto – Schwyz – while Sasso Corbaro was the Castello di Untervaldo). Just to confuse things further, the rock on which the castle sits is known as **Monte San Michele**.

The hilltop complex has been imaginatively and sympathetically restored by architect Aurelio Galfetti. He added a free public **lift** that is dramatically recessed deep into the bedrock of the hill behind the central **Piazza del Sole** and emerges at a purpose-built modern fortification on an upper terrace of the castle.

The castle grounds are serene, overlooked by the slender thirteenth-century **White Tower**, with two upper windows on all four faces, and the fourteenth-century **Black Tower**, with three windows on its longer side. Despite their names, both, like the castle itself, are grey granite, and between them run lines of distinctive Lombard-style **swallow-tail battlements**, which you'll see on castles all over Ticino.

Off Castelgrande's central lawns is an entrance to the **Museo Storico** (Fr.5; see box below for pass details). The archeology section offers a tour through Bellinzona's ancient past, including an excellent audiovisual show (in English) presenting the history of the town. The prize exhibit is a set of murals made in 1470 to decorate the wooden ceiling of a villa in the town, depicting a complex set of allegorical themes dealing with love, faith and virtue.

Steps wind down the hillside from Castelgrande to Piazza Collegiata.

Montebello and Sasso Corbaro

Behind the Collegiata church, on the eastern side of Piazza Collegiata, a path rises to the picturesque **Castello di Montebello** (March–Nov daily

Bellinzona has two **museum passes** with overlapping validities. A combi-ticket for admission to all three castles is Fr.10. Alternatively, the **CulturaPass Bellinzona** grants admission to the three castles plus the Villa dei Cedri art gallery, for Fr.14. Both are buyable at any of the museums or the tourist office. **Swiss Pass** holders have free admission to all four attractions.

10am–6pm; free), some 90m higher in elevation than Castelgrande, with fine views of the town. From a vantage point on the lofty ramparts, it's easy to trace the line of defensive fortifications which link the two castles across the width of the Ticino valley. The castle itself is impressive, with a fifteenth-century courtyard and residential palace surrounding an older central portion dating from the thirteenth century, the latter now housing the modern **Museo Archeologico e Civico** (Fr.5; see box, p.467 for pass details).

A stiff 45-minute climb further up will bring you to **Castello di Sasso Corbaro** (March–Nov daily 10am–6pm; free), some 230m above Bellinzona, designed and built in six months in 1479 by a military engineer brought in from Florence after the Swiss defeat of Milanese troops at the Battle of Giornico. It shelters a particularly welcome vine-shaded courtyard *osteria* and has a spectacular rampart panorama; its **museum** (Fr.5; see box, p.467 for pass details) includes a gallery showing changing exhibits by contemporary Ticinese artists.

To avoid the climb, catch bus #4 from the centre to Artore, near Castello di Sasso Corbaro, and then wend your own path back down the hillside.

South to the Villa dei Cedri

Peaceful **Piazza Indipendenza** is 100m south of the tourist office and sports a 1903 obelisk commemorating the first century of Ticinese independence. On the east side of the square is the small, atmospheric church of **San Rocco**, built in 1330 and renovated in 1478.

Following Via Lugano south from Piazza Indipendenza for 600m brings you to Piazza San Biagio and the gates of the **Villa dei Cedri** art gallery (Tues–Fri 2–6pm, Sat & Sun 11am–6pm; Fr.8; see box, p.467 for pass details; @www .villacedri.ch), set in beautiful grounds. The modest collection focuses on nineteenth- and twentieth-century Swiss and Lombard art. Beside the villa, the frescoed church of **San Biagio** dates from the twelfth century and has a mural of St Christopher beside the door. Beside a disused convent 100m west across the tracks is **Santa Maria delle Grazie**, with an enormous late fifteenth-century interior fresco of the Crucifixion.

Eating and drinking

The **restaurant** of the *Fattoria l'Amorosa* agriturismo (see "Accommodation") is a great choice, with *menus* of refined local cuisine around Fr.50 – plus a choice of top-rated wines (and balsamic vinegars) produced on site. In town, aim for Castelgrande: you can eat well for Fr.27 at the ☆ *Grotto San Michele* (☎091 826 23 53, @www.castelgrande.ch), which spreads itself over the castle terrace and is recommended by the "SlowFood" guide for its authentic ingredients and

Walks around Bellinzona

There are plenty of picturesque **walks** near Bellinzona which could fill a pleasant afternoon. One of the best begins in nearby **Roveredo** (served by postbuses from Bellinzona), from where an old cart track on the "quiet" side of the river heads through tiny San Giulio and into the woods opposite San Vittore, before crossing the river at a little bridge in Lumino and heading on through the forest to Arbedo on the outskirts of Bellinzona. You'll come across plenty of peaceful shady *grotti* on the way. Side roads off the main Via San Gottardo lead through Arbedo and under the tracks to the picturesque Chiesa Rossa, an ancient red-washed church sitting lost and forgotten beside industrial warehouses on Via del Carmagnola backing onto the tracks (total 2hr walking). Buses can run you the final 1.5km south into Bellinzona centre.

preparation; while the formal *Castelgrande* restaurant (same contacts), full of black leather and tubular steel furniture, is a snootier affair – you'll get little change from Fr.70 for its modern, Ticino-inspired cuisine. The atmospheric *Osteria Sasso Corbaro*, in Bellinzona's topmost castle (⊤091 825 55 32; closed Mon & Nov–March), serves up authentic Ticinese fare at stone tables in the shady castle courtyard, or in a great hall within; *menus* are around Fr.27.

Down in the town, *Locando Orico*, Via Orico 13 (⊤091 825 15 18, ⓦwww .locandaorico.ch; closed Sun & Mon), is a fine gourmet restaurant in an atmospheric old wood-beamed house, with a lunch *menu* for Fr.45 and a six-course *menu degustazione* for Fr.110 (excluding wine). *Portici*, a pleasant *osteria*/pizzeria in the Old Town at Vicolo Muggiasca 4 (closed Sun lunch & Mon), serves palatable food in its shady courtyard to a young, easy crowd of regulars for Fr.22 or less. Cheap self-service nosh is at *Manora* on Viale Stazione. *Corona*, Via Camminata 5 (ⓦwww.ristorantecorona.ch; closed Sun), is an atmospheric café-bar fronting a good restaurant in the back, with *menus* around Fr.25. Pavement **café-bars** abound, especially around Via Codeborgo.

Alto Ticino

The most pristine part of this sometimes tiresomely touristic canton is **ALTO TICINO** (Upper Ticino), north of Bellinzona – a region of wild, lonesome valleys cutting into the landscape on the approach to the high Alps, dotted with rustic stone-built hamlets teetering on steep slopes. If getting off the beaten path is your aim, Alto Ticino is a perfect choice. **Biasca** is the gateway to the region, a small town at the junction of the scenic **Val Blenio** – which heads north from Biasca up to **Olivone**, then cuts over to the Lucomagno Pass – and the main **Valle Leventina**, which bends northwest up to the foot of the Gottardo Pass and the quiet town of Airolo, where the rural Val Bedretto splits off west to the Novena Pass.

Check your plans with the tourist office in Bellinzona before you set off: although information and maps are much the same wherever you go, staff in the regional offices are less likely to be fluent in English.

Biasca

The small town of **BIASCA** sits in a grand location at the junction of three valleys: the Valle Leventina, the Val Blenio, and to the south towards Bellinzona a part of the Ticino valley called the **Riviera**, which crams in a motorway, a main road, a minor road, a train line and several footpaths, all snaking side by side between wooded mountains rising 1500m above your head. High above the town to the southeast, commanding an eagle's-eye view of all routes in and out, is the imposing church of **San Pietro e Paolo**, with a sixteenth-century portico tacked on to its Romanesque facade. Collect the key from the newer parish church halfway up the hillside. Inside, the irregular floor plan – architects seem to have struggled with the sloping bedrock – is original, as are the medieval frescoes.

Biasca's **train station** is 750m south of the centre. The **tourist office** is just off Piazza Centrale on Piazzetta Cavalier Pellanda (Mon–Fri 8.30am–noon & 2–6pm, May–Oct also Sat 8.30–11.30am; ⊤091 862 33 27, ⓦwww.biascaturismo.ch). Steps behind the tourist office rise directly to the church. *Al Giardinetto*, Via Pini 21 (⊤091 862 17 71, ⓦwww.algiardinetto.ch; ➌), is a modern **hotel** in the centre. Look out for the regular Saturday **market**, showcasing fresh produce from the upper valleys.

Val Blenio

Quiet **Val Blenio** heads north from Biasca, away from the main Leventina routes, a broad open valley that basks in generous sunshine. The valley floor is dotted with villages, themselves marked by *rustici*, stone-built peasant dwellings, sometimes little more than shacks, that are topped with rough slate roofs. A lot of these are now renovated as holiday cottages: peace, quiet and unspoilt natural beauty reign supreme. Oddly enough, the Bleniesi have been known throughout Europe for centuries as culinary entrepreneurs, a skill probably picked up in Milan sometime in the Middle Ages and passed on through the generations. In 1600 one Signor Bianchini from the valley was head chef to the King of Spain; in 1849, a Signor Baggi won an award for selling the best ice cream in France; while the Gatti family – also from the Blenio – owned and managed 230 restaurants and cafés throughout late Victorian England.

The Sentiero Basso is the main valley-floor path: the walk from Biasca to **Acquarossa** on the west bank of the river is a gently rising 13km, taking a little under four hours. On the east bank just north of Biasca is **Malvaglia**, whose village church boasts a huge fresco of St Christopher; from here a tortuous branch road climbs in a series of hairpins into the lonesome **Val Malvaglia** amidst tremendous scenery of steep wooded slopes dropping away into a seemingly bottomless ravine. From a point on the road, it's possible to park and walk across a bridge spanning the valley, on the other side of which a dramatic mule track penetrates for a couple of hours' walk to **Dagro**, a hamlet on the northern side of the valley with broad views.

As you rise into the Blenio, the lush green slopes begin to close in. The main town at the head of the valley, below the sharp-peaked Sosto on one side and

A walking tour of Alto Ticino

A two-week walking **Tour of Ticino** explores the most remote landscapes in the upper part of the canton. The granite massifs of the Lepontine Alps, as these mountains are known, are among the least visited of any in Switzerland: you can wander for hours and see no one. Numerous tarns add a sparkle to the crags. Pack a decent **map** as well as *Walking in Ticino* by Kev Reynolds (see "Books", p.512).

The tour begins either in **Torre** or **Dangio**, two adjacent villages in the upper Valle di Blenio. The route heads through Val Soi to Val Carassina, then down to **Olivone** before following a mule track through a defile into Val Camadra. Next day you continue up to Passo di Gana Negra, cross Valle Santa Maria and make a steady ascent to Passo Colombe. An enjoyable descent from there takes the route into gentle Val Piora, then across Bochetta di Cadlimo to Val Canaria and down to **Airolo**. On the south side of Valle Leventina the way resumes on a belvedere trail known as the Strada degli Alpi Bedretto, but on reaching the alp hutments of Piano di Pesciüm it cuts into Val Torta and climbs to make a crossing of the wild, rocky Cristallina massif.

On day eight, an easy walk descends through Val Bavona to **Bignasco** at the head of the Valle Maggia. It's a glorious walk leading past tiny hamlets and feathery waterfalls to a confluence of valleys. You pass through Val Cocco and over Passo del Cocco before negotiating Bochetta di Mugaia in the south ridge of Monte Zucchero and descending 1600m to **Sonogno**. Day eleven crosses Passo di Redorta (2181m) to Val di Pertüs, whose stark walls plunge into the depths of a gorge. Val di Pertüs feeds into Val di Prato, and this in turn spills into Val Lavizzara where you spend the night in **Prato-Sornico**. The tour heads north to **Fusio**, then the final (thirteenth) day's walk leads back to Valle Leventina via Passo Campolungo, more than 1000m above Fusio: the descent to **Rodi-Fiesso** is a steep 1300m, but there are consistently fine views on both sides.

the Töira on the other, is **OLIVONE**, a little place 24km north of Biasca that reflects the valley's once-noble pretensions in its array of grandiose, if worn, eighteenth- and nineteenth-century mansions – rather out of place amidst the orchards and increasingly wild scenery. The **tourist office** (☎091 872 14 87, ⓦ www.blenio.com) has information on the valley. Up in the village is the *Osteria Centrale* (☎091 872 11 07, ⓦ www.osteriacentraleolivone.ch; ❶), which serves tasty home-cooked fare and has a few simple rooms. Down a short hill beside the main road is the post office and bus stop with, alongside, the *Albergo San Martino* (☎091 872 15 21; ❷), also with traditional food and pizzas plus a choice of rooms.

A five-hour walk from Olivone climbs to the **Lucomagno Pass** (1914m). The road over the pass from Olivone to **Disentis/Mustér** in Graubünden (see p.436) is perhaps the most scenic route in and out of Ticino.

Valle Leventina

From Biasca, the motorway, the main road and rail line all blaze a trail northwest into the **Valle Leventina**, heading for the **Passo del Gottardo** (Gotthard Pass) and tunnels (see p.348) at the end. There's no doubt that this is a spectacular route, whether heading north or south, but its heavy usage is its downfall: hemmed in by the high valley walls, the hiss and rumble of traffic noise from the motorway can seem obtrusively loud to valley-floor walkers and cyclists. This situation will change in 2017, with the opening of the **Gotthard Base Tunnel** (see p.349; ⓦ www.alptransit.ch): most of the road and rail traffic will enter the new tunnel at **Bodio**, just north of Biasca, thereby restoring peace and quiet to the upper Leventina.

Giornico

Make time for **GIORNICO**, a small town 9km northwest of Biasca. It was here in 1478 that a Swiss force numbering 600 defeated a 10,000-strong Milanese army, thereby linking Ticino's subsequent history to Switzerland rather than Italy. Giornico is lovely, a typical Ticinese village built on the gentle slopes either side of the tumbling River Ticino, with cobbled alleys running picturesquely between old stone-roofed houses. A photogenic humpbacked bridge crosses to a wooded island mid-river, and from there to the west bank, where rises the campanile of **San Nicolao**, one of the most atmospheric of Ticino's many Romanesque churches. Its external walls are decorated with Lombardic designs, while inside is a fresco-decorated choir above a beautiful triple-apsed half-sunken crypt. After exploring the village, visit the *Osteria Giornico* on the main street (☎091 864 22 15; closed Wed) to pick up the keys for **La Congiunta**. This is an art gallery – though you'd never know from the outside: it looks like a concrete bunker, stuck in the fields 300m north of Giornico's little train station. The oddly tranquil interior holds three rooms of lumpy metal reliefs and bronze sculptures (dated 1950–91) by Zürich artist Hans Josephsohn. The deserted, deconstructed building, designed by architect Peter Märkli, perfectly suits the art.

Giornico has a couple of terrific *grotti*, both of them serving up deliciously simple, home-cooked food. The *Grotto dei Due Ponti* (ⓦ www.grotto2ponti.ch; closed Tues), on the mid-river island, is the one everyone goes to, its shaded terrace overlooking the rushing water. *Grotto Pergola* (ⓦ www.grottopergola .ch; closed Tues), tucked away on the west bank of the river and south of San Nicolao, though with a less alluring garden, serves even better food.

Airolo

Some 28km north of Giornico is **AIROLO**, first town in the Ticino for the millions who pour out of the Gottardo train and road tunnels each year heading south. Thankfully bypassed by the main routes, it's a quiet town with a handful of hotels serving as staging post for summer journeys up to the **Gotthard Pass** (see p.348), or into the **Val Bedretto** and up to the **Novena** (Nufenen Pass; see p.307). The town is also the trailhead for plenty of high-altitude walks, especially into the stunning **Val Piora**, outlined in the box on p.470. Winter sees Airolo transformed into a modest ski resort. The Leventina's **tourist office** is also here (℡091 869 15 33, ⓦwww.leventinaturismo.ch).

Locarno

Trains and often packed minor roads head west from Bellinzona for some 15km to **Lake Maggiore** and its principal Swiss resort, **LOCARNO**. This characterful old town enjoys a grand location, on the broad sweeping curve of a bay in the lake. The arcades and piazzas of the town centre are overlooked by subtropical gardens of palms, camellias, bougainvillea, cypress, oleanders and magnolias, which flourish on the lakeside promenades and cover the wooded slopes which crowd in above the town centre.

Locarno found its feet in the nineteenth century as the most elegant of Swiss resorts. In 1925 its backdrop of *belle-époque* hotels and piazza cafés served as the

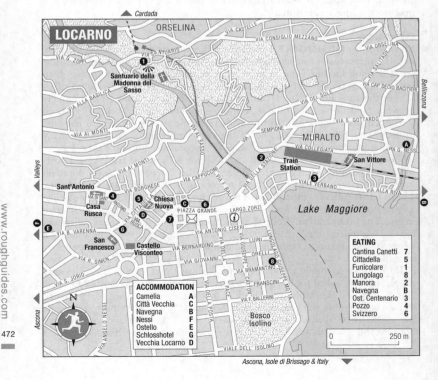

setting for the **Treaty of Locarno**, signed by the European powers in a failed effort to secure peace following World War I. These days, Locarno focuses its considerable resources on tourism, and draws in two very different sets of customers: one, from the German-speaking north, arrives to test out their hiking boots, while the other, from fog- and smog-bound Milan, comes to test out their sunglasses. The cobbled alleys of Locarno's Old Town, lined with Renaissance facades, can get overrun with the rich and wannabe-famous on summer weekends, yet still – in the midst of the hubbub – the place manages to retain its poise.

Turn to p.480 for an account of Locarno's neighbour, **Ascona**.

Arrival, information and accommodation

Locarno's **train station** is 100m north of the lakeshore landing stage and 150m northeast of Piazza Grande; mainline FFS trains depart from ground level, while the local transport company Ferrovie Autolinee Regionali Ticinesi – unfortunately abbreviated to **FART** – operates trains on the Centovalli line (see p.479) from a separate station below ground.

The **tourist office** is in the Casino complex on Via Largo Zorzi, 100m southwest of the station (Mon–Fri 9am–6pm, Sat 10am–6pm, Sun 10am–1.30pm & 2.30–5pm; ⊤091 791 00 91, ⓦwww.maggiore.ch); staff can make hotel bookings. Locarno's **accommodation** is strongest in the mid-range bracket: if you're after a spot of luxury, head over to Ascona (p.480) or Lugano (p.483), or head out towards Bellinzona for the wonderful *Fattoria l'Amorosa* agriturismo, described on p.466.

Campsite

Delta ⊤091 751 60 81, ⓦwww.campingdelta .com. Quality site, a 15min walk south along the lakeshore. March–Oct.

Hostels

Città Vecchia (see "Hotels" below). Good Old Town hotel with dorms. ❶
Ostello/Jugendherberge Palagiovani (HI hostel) Via Varenna 18 ⊤091 756 15 00, ⓦwww.youthhostel.ch. Modern hostel with dorms and bike rental, but it's in an awkward western location – take bus #31 or #36 to Cinque Vie. March–Nov. ❷

Hotels

Camelia Via Nessi 9, Muralto ⊤091 743 00 21, ⓦwww.camelia.ch. Elegant, eager-to-please family hotel set in fragrant floral gardens and offering spacious rooms, some with balconies and lake views. March–Oct. ❹
Città Vecchia Via Torretta 13 ⊤091 751 45 54, ⓦwww.cittavecchia.ch. Centrally placed B&B

hotel, with dorms and simple shared-bath rooms. March–Oct. ❶–❷
Navegna Via alla Riva 2, Minusio ⊤091 743 22 22, ⓦwww.navegna.ch. About 1.5km east of the centre, directly on the waterfront, with modern, stylishly renovated rooms, private parking and an excellent restaurant. March–Nov. ❺
Nessi Via Varenna 79 ⊤091 751 77 41, ⓦwww .garninessi.ch. Welcoming little family-run place a short way west of the centre, with pool and underground parking. Rooms are fresh and decent, with better, bigger ones on higher floors. Closed Jan. ❹
Schlosshotel Via San Francesco 7a ⊤091 751 23 61, ⓦwww.schlosshotellocarno.ch. Large, old-fashioned rooms in a well-kept Old Town pile. March–Nov. ❹
Vecchia Locarno Via Motta 10 ⊤091 751 65 02, ⓦwww.hotel-vecchia-locarno.ch. Scruffily characterful Old Town gem, with both shared-bath and en-suite rooms above a courtyard restaurant and wine-bar. March–Dec. ❷–❸

A **Swiss Pass** (see p.35) is valid for free bus and train transport in and around Locarno and Ascona (Lake Maggiore boats are excluded), and free admission to almost all museums reviewed in this book.

Boats run by NLM (April–Oct only; ⓦ www.navigazionelaghi.it) crisscross the Swiss shores of the exceptionally beautiful **Lake Maggiore**, as well as continuing down the lake into Italy. Note that Maggiore is the only major lake in Switzerland to be **excluded** from the Swiss Pass.

For all but the shortest hops, a **one-day pass** is the most economical choice: unlimited journeys within Zone A (Locarno to Ascona) or Zone B (Ascona to Brissago) costs Fr.15.80, or across Zones A and B Fr.25.50. For reference, a **point-to-point** ticket from Locarno to Ascona is Fr.8.40, Locarno to Isole di Brissago Fr.14.10. Examples of **international** journeys into Italy (and back) include Locarno to Stresa or the splendid island gardens of Isola Bella Fr.37, or Ascona to Cannóbio Fr.22.50. Using the hydrofoil – for which you must **reserve in advance** – adds Fr.3. Various **day-trip excursion** tickets into Italy are available, which include boat transport and admission fees for major attractions. Don't forget your **passport**.

Passes

A **Locarno Regional Pass** gives free transport in the Swiss waters of Lake Maggiore for one day, as well as other perks, including free use of buses, trains and cable cars around Locarno and Ascona and discounts on travel around Lake Lugano, for Fr.108 (7 days) or Fr.92 (any 3 days within a week). The combination ticket **Il Lago e la Montagna** (Fr.58; valid 10 days) includes a day pass for boats on the Swiss sector, admission to the Isole di Brissago, the funicular to Madonna del Sasso and the cable car to Cardada and Cimetta. A **Holiday Card** gives unlimited journeys on the whole lake, including Italy, for Fr.62 (3 days) or Fr.91 (7 days).

Lago Maggiore Express

For its simplicity, diversity and superb scenery, the **Lago Maggiore Express** ticket (ⓦ www.lagomaggioreexpress.com) is worth investigating. It comprises three sectors, all of them great journeys in their own right: a long **boat trip** on Maggiore, the stunning **Centovalli railway** between Locarno and Domodossola (see p.479), and a **fast train** on the historic Simplon line between Domodossola and Stresa.

The schedules are flexible: you can start and end wherever you like, making your own choice of connections, and you can also do the trip in either direction. The whole thing could take as little as six hours – or you could dawdle over it for a couple of days. It can be done in spring (mid-March to May Thurs–Sun), summer (June to mid-Sept daily) or autumn (mid-Sept to mid-Oct Sat & Sun). However, different timetables operate on **Wednesdays** to take account of the popular weekly market in the Italian lakeside town of Luino; check details carefully.

Note that this is not a tour: you are on your own, using **public transport**. You should carry your **passport** (the route crosses into Italy) and also check the time-tables carefully for the validity of each part of the trip. You must reserve ahead for any **hydrofoil** journeys (and pay a small supplement). On certain boats – marked on the timetables – **lunch** is available.

Fares are great value. The complete round-trip in **one day**, in either direction and from any starting point, costs Fr.48. The **two-day** pass, which allows you to break your journey overnight anywhere on the route and also includes free boat travel on the whole of Lake Maggiore, is Fr.58. Brochures and the website have full timetable listings.

The Town

The focus of town is **Piazza Grande**, an attractive arcaded square just off the lakefront that is lined with pavement cafés and serves as the town's meeting point, social club and public catwalk. Warm summer nights serve up some great people-watching, as exquisitely groomed locals parade to and fro, all the cafés abuzz and fragrant breezes bringing in the scent of flowers from the lakeside gardens.

From the west end of Piazza Grande, lanes run up to Via Cittadella in the **Old Town** and the Baroque **Chiesa Nuova**, adorned with a huge statue of St Christopher outside. The quiet arcaded courtyard, reached through a side door, is a charming spot to draw breath away from the bustle. Following the atmospheric Via di Sant'Antonio brings you to the rather sombre church of **Sant'Antonio**, dating from the seventeenth century but rebuilt following a fatal roof collapse in 1863. Beside the church, the eighteenth-century **Casa Rusca** (Tues–Sun 10am–noon & 2–5pm; Fr.7) houses a worthwhile art museum focusing on the twentieth-century Swiss artist Jean Arp.

Alleys lead south to the tall **San Francesco**, consecrated as part of a monastery in the fourteenth century. Sixteenth-century renovation added frescoes, most of which are now fading badly. Further down sits the stout thirteenth-century **Castello Visconteo**, now home to the **Museo Archeo-logico** (April–Oct Tues–Sun 10am–noon & 2–5pm; Fr.7), worth visiting if only for its collection of beautiful Roman glassware and ceramics.

On the other side of town in Muralto, 100m east of the station, is the austere twelfth-century Romanesque basilica of **San Vittore**, built over a church first mentioned in the tenth century and now surrounded by housing developments. Medieval fresco-fragments inside and the Renaissance relief of St Victor on the bell-tower are a diverting contrast to the views over the train station. From here, a pleasant walk along the *lungolago* (lakefront promenade) leads back into town and on south for 1km or so, past beautiful gardens, to the fragrant **Parco delle Camelie**, planted with 900 varieties of camellia.

Madonna del Sasso

Most striking of all Locarno's sights is the **Santuario della Madonna del Sasso** church (daily 6.30am–7pm), an impressive ochre vision floating above the town on a wooded crag – *sasso* means rock – and consecrated in 1487 on the spot where, seven years earlier, the Virgin had appeared to a Franciscan brother. The twenty-minute walk up through the wooded ravine of the

▲ View over Lake Maggiore from Locarno

Torrente Ramogno and past a handful of decaying shrines is atmospheric enough in itself; or you could take the **funicular** (every 15min) from just west of the train station. The low, Baroque interior of the church features a number of paintings, two of which stand out: Bramantino's emotionally charged *Fuga in Egitto* (Flight to Egypt, 1522) and local artist Antonio Ciseri's *Trasporto di Cristo al Sepolcro* (1870).

Cardada and Cimetta

When sweltering Locarno (210m) gets too much, it's easy to escape into the cool, wooded hills above. By the top station of the Madonna del Sasso funicular in Orselina (395m) is the base station – designed by architect Mario Botta – of a futuristic cable car that rises on an ear-popplingly steep course to the plateau of **Cardada** (1350m; ⓦwww.cardada.ch). A short stroll left from the top station, set amidst fragrant pine woods and fresh breezes, is the "Observation Platform", a gracefully designed catwalk suspended off a huge A-frame; an eagle-eye view takes in Ascona, the lake and the mountains. There's a couple of simple restaurants up here and some easy strolls in the pine forest – many of them wheelchair accessible.

Turn right from the top station, and it's ten minutes or so through the woods to a spectacular chairlift that whisks you even higher, right through the trees up to the flower-strewn meadows of **Cimetta** (1672m), where there's a restaurant/guesthouse with a terrace view that you won't forget in a hurry.

A return **ticket** from Orselina to Cardada is Fr.27, to Cimetta Fr.33. If you're coming up from Locarno, ask at the base station of the Madonna del Sasso funicular for a ticket to the top: this discounts the fare and includes half-price car parking in Locarno as well.

Eating and drinking

Piazza Grande is full of cafés and pizzerias buzzing from morning until after midnight, but **eating and drinking** is more atmospheric in the Old Town alleys. Fresh fish plucked from the lake is Locarno's speciality – look out for trout (*trota*), perch (*persico*), pike (*luccio*) and whitefish (*coregone*). See p.468 for details of the fine restaurant at the *Fattoria l'Amorosa* agriturismo near Gudo, roughly fifteen minutes' drive northeast of Locarno.

Cantina Canetti Off Piazza Grande. Plain local cooking (Fr.17) in a noisy diner, with the added bonus of live accordion on Friday and Saturday nights. Closed Thurs eve.

Cittadella Via Cittadella 18 ☏091 751 58 85. The popular trattoria section at ground level is excellent, serving pizzas, pasta and simple fish dishes for Fr.25 or less, while upstairs the formal

---

Festivals in Locarno and Ascona

Events and festivities run all summer long (see ⓦwww.ticino.ch). The season kicks off in May with Ascona's **Street Artists Festival**, followed in late June by the popular Ascona **New Orleans Jazz Festival**. In July, nearby Magadino holds an **International Organ Festival**, while Locarno hosts **Moon and Stars**, a run of open-air rock and pop gigs by major stars.

The top-class **Locarno International Film Festival** (ⓦwww.pardo.ch), in early August, is rated among the top five film festivals in the world. Catch major offerings on the huge open-air screen in Piazza Grande, playing to 7500 people nightly (Fr.22), or at one of the twelve daily screenings in the city's cinemas (Fr.15).

Over late August and September, Ascona presents its **Settimane Musicali** ("Music Weeks"), a series of prestigious classical concerts staged around the region.

restaurant concentrates on fish alone – and does it well (4-course *menu* Fr.75). Closed Mon.
Funicolare Beside funicular top station in Orselina. Quiet, simple place that benefits from a spectacular secluded terrace garden, overlooking Madonna del Sasso, in which to savour their inexpensive fish specialities. Closed Thurs in winter & Nov–Jan.
Lungolago Via Bramantino 1. Classy pizzeria, *paninoteca* and pub where locals go to flee the invasion of white-knee'd northerners.
Manora Via della Stazione. Good self-service salads and plain cooking in this busy spot across from the train station, open late and Sundays.
Navegna (see "Hotels"). A little way east in Minusio, but right on the lakefront and highly

acclaimed for its delicately prepared and presented Ticinese cuisine (*menus* Fr.50). Closed Nov–March.
Osteria del Centenario Lungolago 13, Muralto ☏ 091 743 82 22. One of Locarno's best, serving internationally acclaimed *nouvelle cuisine* in an appealing blend of French and Italian styles. A lakeside terrace and three-figure bills come as standard. Closed Sun.
Pozzo Piazza Sant'Antonio. Friendly local café-bar on a quiet Old Town square.
Svizzero Piazza Grande. Best of the many pizzerias and diners on the square, with affordable freshly made pasta, wood-fired pizza and plenty of Italian staples. Bustling from breakfast till the small hours.

Locarno's valleys

The valleys around Locarno are packed with hiking possibilities, and offer some of the most beautiful scenery in the whole canton. **Val Verzasca** and **Valle Maggia** both lead north from Locarno, while the gorgeous **Centovalli** runs west on one of Switzerland's most scenic and dramatic train rides. Locarno's neighbour **Ascona** is covered on p.480.

Adventure sports and activities

There are some excellent opportunities for **adventure sports** around Ticino, all of which need to be booked in advance. **Trekking Team** (ⓦwww.trekking.ch) is a top local operator that runs what is perhaps the star attraction: the highest bungee-jump in the world, off the 220m-high Verzasca Dam (see p.479), as performed by James Bond in the opening scene of *GoldenEye*. It takes some nerve just to venture out onto the dam to watch, let alone do the leap yourself. Your first jump costs Fr.255, including training and free drinks; a second on the same day is a cut-price Fr.125, and in high summer, you can jump by moonlight. They also do bungee-jumps off the seventy-metre Intragna railway bridge (see p.479; one Fr.125, two Fr.195), as well as canyoning in the Centovalli, Val Onsernone, Val Verzasca, Valle Maggia and elsewhere. **Swiss Challenge** (ⓦwww .swisschallenge.ch), based at Roveredo near Bellinzona, organizes canoeing around Cresciano and on Lake Maggiore, and canyoning in Val Malvaglia or around Cugnasco. **Swissraft** (ⓦwww.swissraft.ch) has an office near Bellinzona, organizing river rafting from Cama through Roveredo, canyoning, mountain biking and more. Locarno's **Wake Inn** (ⓦwww.watersports.ch) runs wakeboarding and waterskiing. **Adventure's Best** (ⓦwww.asbest.ch) is Lugano's biggest operator, with a full range of adventure sports including canyoning, rap jumps, freeclimbing, paragliding, mountain biking and more.

Walks around Locarno
The tourist office brochure *Sentieri della Collina* pinpoints the route of two pleasant walking paths on the hillside just above the town. The **Sentiera Collina Bassa** is 5.4km long, and takes you from the Madonna del Sasso funicular east through Orselina and onto the Via Panoramica through the suburb of **Brione** above Minusio, before gently coming down to the lakeshore in **Tenero** (1hr 40min), from where buses and trains return you to Locarno. The **Sentiera Collina Alta** runs for 6.3km from **Monte Brè**, the next hill west of Orselina (bus #32), on a scenic, winding path through the foothills to **Contra**, and down to Tenero (2hr).

Valle Maggia

The **VALLE MAGGIA** comprises a complex valley system stretching north of Locarno into the high Alps. About 30km into the main valley, roads split to follow three separate upper valleys, the Val Rovana, Val Bavona and Val Lavizzara, which are cut off from each other and which all eventually come to a stop against impassable rock. It is superb territory for **walking**: the long-distance route outlined in the box on p.470 passes through, and there are some fine short walks in remote corners.

North from Pontebrolla, a village above Locarno at the junction of the Centovalli, the valley is deep, rugged and very narrow. It opens out further along around Gordevio and the village of **MAGGIA**, home of the local tourist office (T091 753 18 85, W www.vallemaggia.ch) and fine local restaurant *Locanda Poncini* (W www.locandaponcini.ch). Across the river from Maggia at **Aurigeno** is the SB hostel *Baracca* (T079 207 15 54, W www.baracca-backpacker.ch; April–Oct; ❶), while the neighbouring hamlet of **Lodano** holds *Ca' Serafina* (T091 756 50 60, W www.caserafina.com; ❸), a beautiful guesthouse with five spacious, en-suite rooms and the warmest of welcomes from English-speaking owner, Alexa Thio.

At Cevio (416m), a road branches west into the **Val Rovana**, climbing to the village of **BOSCO/GURIN** (1503m). This is the highest settlement in Ticino, and also its only German-speaking community, founded in the Middle Ages by ex-mercenaries from the upper Valais; the locals still speak an odd combination of Oberwalliser and Locarnese dialects. With lift access up to 2400m, the remote village has become a centre for winter sports, and there are some good walks in summer in and around Grossalp (W www.capannagrossalp.ch).

Just 2km north of Cevio (30km north of Locarno) is **BIGNASCO** village (438m), where the valley divides. Of a handful of lovely restaurants here, the *Turisti* has excellent food and a shaded terrace, as well as some rooms (T091 754 11 65; ❶). Northwest from Bignasco, a road climbs into the wild **Val Bavona**, a strip of valley floor 10km long, hemmed in by sheer scarps on both sides. There are twelve rustic hamlets in the valley, including **Foroglio**, with a restaurant huddled next to a splendid waterfall. A short climb above **San Carlo** (960m), the final hamlet, characterized by tall, narrow sixteenth-century stone houses, is a cable car up to the eyrie of **ROBIEI** (1905m), overlooked by the Basodino glacier. The top station has a terrace restaurant with rooms and dorms (T091 756 50 20, W www.robiei.ch; ❶); one of the most scenic walks heads west into the Val Fiorina (45min).

From Bignasco, another road climbs northeast into the **Val Lavizzara**. After Peccia (849m) – renowned for its marble quarries and sculpture school – the switchbacks get tighter up to the hamlet of **MOGNO** (1180m), where, across the way on your right, you'll spot the tilted circular roof of the church of **San Giovanni Battista** through the trees. The church, reached by a short path climbing from a parking area, was designed by Mario Botta after an avalanche destroyed a pre-existing chapel on the same spot in 1986: Botta has said that the locals came to him saying they didn't want to give the future generation a place poorer than the one they knew. He responded by offering to build a church that would last a thousand years. His achievement, in this remotest of places, is dazzling. It is a small building, set on a marble plaza. The interior is supremely elegant, bare and silent, encircled in striped marble, the transparent roof bathing the altar in sunlight. Lingering here is mesmeric; walking back out into the pine forest, amidst chirping birds and log cabins, is a revelation.

Val Verzasca

About 1.5km east of Locarno on Lake Maggiore, **Tenero** stands at the head of the **VAL VERZASCA**, the shortest of the major valleys around Locarno. The southern end of the valley, high above Tenero, is blocked by the gigantic **Verzasca Dam**, scene of the world's highest bungee-jump (see box, p.477). Even if you're not jumping, it's worth stopping here to wander out into the middle of the dam; on one side is a dizzying 220-metre drop down to bare rock, on the other a tranquil blue lake is framed by classic Alpine scenery.

The road continues beyond the dam, passing below **Corippo** (530m) at the end of the lake, a beautiful cluster of old stone cottages crowned by a tall campanile; 3km north is **Lavertezzo**, site of perhaps the most photographed bridge in Switzerland, a graceful seventeenth-century double arch. Many quieter trails head off into side valleys from Lavertezzo, while the valley cuts deeper for another 14km up to **Sonogno** (909m), passing on the way through **Brione**, located on a plateau at a junction of valleys; the views are pretty and the church boasts fourteenth-century Giotto-style frescoes.

The Centovalli

Locarno is the eastern terminus of the scenic **Centovalli** railway (ⓦwww.centovalli.ch) running to the Italian town of Domodossola, known in its Italian section as the **Ferrovia Vigezzina** (ⓦwww.vigezzina.com). Little trains run by the FART company depart from beneath Locarno station into the spectacular valley – so named for its "hundred" side valleys – most of the time winding slowly on precarious bridges and viaducts above ravine-like depths. Sit on the left for the best views. The area is renowned for its natural beauty, and with a walking map from Locarno tourist office (also available at ⓦwww.procentovalli.ch) you could get out at any of the villages en route, pick up a trail and head off into the hills. There's no lack of *grotti*, cafés and simple accommodation. One neat way to see the route is with the **Lago Maggiore Express** pass (see p.474).

Past Pontebrolla, tiny **Verscio**, 4km northwest of Locarno, is a lovely stone-built village which houses the **Teatro Dimitri** (ⓦwww.teatrodimitri.ch), an international mime school founded by the Ascona-born clown Dimitri, a protégé of Marcel Marceau. The small theatre, in a cobbled lane off the village square, stages performances almost nightly (March–Nov). Also on site is the small **Museo Comico** (open on performance days 5pm–midnight; Fr.5, free with theatre ticket), with costumes and memorabilia.

Some 3km down the line, the train clanks over a graceful iron viaduct spanning the 75-metre gorge of the Isorno torrent. This was the scene of Switzerland's first-ever bungee-jump, in 1993, and remains a choice spot for leaping (see box, p.477), on the outskirts of **INTRAGNA**, its church marked by the highest steeple in Ticino (65m), built in 1775. A great walk starts from Intragna station, crossing a medieval bridge and joining a mule-track which climbs gently across the meadows to **Rasa**, an isolated stone-built hamlet with no road access, from where a tiny cable car swoops back over the valley down to **VERDASIO** station. From Verdasio, another cable car scales the opposite, northern valley wall to **Monte Comino**, 600m above (ⓦwww.comino.ch); from here, you could follow a two-hour circuit of the summit, or a more taxing six-kilometre path back to Intragna.

After Verdasio, the train rolls on through dense chestnut forests to the quiet border village of **Cámedo** (passport needed) and on through the rustic villages of the Val Vigezzo for the climb to **Santa Maria Maggiore**, the highest point of the line (830m), before easing down into Domodossola, 20km on.

Into the Gambarogno

The 13km of shoreline opposite Locarno and Ascona is known as the **Gambarogno**, and comprises a line of quiet shoreside villages backed by rugged mountains. **VIRA** holds the local **tourist office** (July & Aug Mon–Fri 8am–6.30pm, Sat 9am–noon & 3–5pm, Sun 9am–noon; rest of year Mon–Fri 8am–noon & 2–6pm, plus Sat 9am–noon in June, Sept & Oct; ☏091 795 18 66, ⊕www.gambarognoturismo.ch). On the hillside above Vira is the splendid **Parco Botanico del Gambarogno** (⊕www.parcobotanico .ch), showcasing one of Europe's finest collections of magnolias and camellias. From Vira, a tightly coiled road leads for 17km over the bleak **Alpe di Neggia** pass (1395m) – with an inn boasting spectacular views – up to the isolated hamlet of **INDÉMINI** (930m), on the mountain border with Italy. This stone-built village clinging to the valley sides has recently attracted artists and sculptors; workshops are often open, and the simple *Ristorante Indeminese* (☏091 795 12 22) is a great lunch stop. The road continues for 18km through some spectacular mountain terrain, with sensational viewpoints high above the lake, down to the Italian town of **Maccagno**, 9km south of the lakeside border at Pino/Zenna. Buses also serve Indémini from the ferry stop at Magadino, beside Vira.

Domodossola

The busy Italian town of **DOMODOSSOLA** stands at the fulcrum of three train routes: Swiss main line trains run west to Brig (see p.296) and Bern; Italian ones speed south to Stresa and Milan; and it is also the terminus for little mountain trains on the Centovalli line from Locarno (see p.479).

Pick up a map at the **tourist office** (Mon–Fri 9am–noon & 2.30–6.30pm, Sat 9am–noon; ☏0324.248.265, ⊕www.prodomodossola.it), or just walk away from the station on Corso Ferraris and Corso Fratelli di Dio into the old part of town, 200m west, set around a series of attractively crumbling arcaded piazzas. **Piazza Mercato** is the finest – conveniently laid with café tables – and also stages a Saturday market. From here, pedestrianized Via Briona leads to Piazza Cavour, from where Via Marconi returns to the station.

Via Briona has pleasant cafés and **restaurants**. *La Meridiana*, Via Rosmini 11 (☏0324.240.858; closed Mon), offers moderately priced Spanish specialities, as well as fish and pasta dishes. In front of the station, cheery *Piazzetta*, Piazza Matteotti 5, has good-value pizza. Walk 250m north of Piazza Cavour on Via Binda, then turn right to find *Pasticceria Grandazzi*, Via Castellazzo 23 (⊕www.pasticceriagrandazzi.com; closed Sun pm & Mon), a superb, innovative **chocolatier**: munch on their chocolate paintbrushes or take away a chocolate toolbox, complete with cocoa-dusted "rusty" nails.

Ascona

On the south-facing side of the Maggia delta, 3km southwest of Locarno, **ASCONA** has been a magnet for idealistic, sun-starved northerners for more than a century. The place was nothing more than a fishing hamlet until the 1890s, but since then it has grown into a cultured, artistically inclined small town, an enticing blend of character, natural beauty and good shopping.

But the influx of German-speakers, as summer tourists and second-home-owners, has been so great in recent years that Ascona can feel like it has lost its way. Since most of the visitors have, at best, rudimentary Italian, staff in hotels and restaurants are now accustomed to speaking to guests in German first. Even the poshest menus are bilingual. Shops frequently advertise special offers in German before Italian, and some cultural activities – readings or gallery openings – take place in German. With general Ticinese disquiet at German-speaking dominance of Swiss affairs, Asconesi are becoming uneasy: voices are being raised for the cantonal government to step in and force Ascona's businesses to use Italian.

The Town

Ascona's *tour de force* is **Piazza Motta**, the cobbled lakefront promenade, south-facing and fully 500m long: the airy views down the lake, flanked by wooded peaks, to the Brissago islands are sensational. There are few better places to watch the day drift by: the morning mists on the water, the clarity of light at midday, the sunsets and peaceful twilight are simply mesmerizing.

Word of Ascona began to spread a century or more ago, when a slow but steady influx began of philosophers, theosophists and spiritualists, most of whom believed that a return to nature was the best remedy for the moral disintegration of Western society. At the turn of the century the artists Henri Oedenkoven and Ida Hofmann established an esoteric, vegetarian artists' colony on the hill of **Monte Verità** beside Ascona. An array of European fringe intellectuals followed, including practitioners of the new arts of psychology and psychoanalysis. In 1913, Rudolf von Laban set up his nudist School of Natural and Expressive Dance within the Monte Verità community, attracting Isadora Duncan among others, and during and after World War I artists and pacifists flocked to Ascona. The buildings atop the peaceful wooded hill are now used mostly for conferences, but a few have been preserved as a **museum** of the movement (Tues–Sun: July & Aug 3–7pm; April–June, Sept & Oct 2.30–6pm; Fr.6; ⒲www.monteverita.org). It's a short walk up the hill from the bus stop (bus #33) to the **Casa Anatta**, with two floors of the original wooden house given over to papers and photos commemorating the artists' exploits. A walk past the main Bauhaus conference centre and into the woods brings you to the tiny **Casa Selma**, used as the community's retreat, and on further to the **Elisarion**, housing a circular painting by Elisar von Kupffer depicting the spiritual liberations of communal life.

Central Ascona's attractive cobbled lanes leading back from the lakefront are full of artisans' galleries, jewellers and craft shops. The **Museo Comunale d'Arte Moderna**, in a sixteenth-century *palazzo* at Via Borgo 34 (March–Dec Tues–Sat 10am–noon & 3–6pm, Sun 4–6pm; Fr.7; ⒲www.museoascona.ch), has a high-quality collection focused on Marianne von Werefkin, one of the many artists attracted to Ascona in its heyday and joint founder of Munich's expressionist *Blaue Reiter* movement; look out for her terrifying, Munch-like *Il Cenciaiolo* (The Rag-Man, 1920).

The **Italian border** lies 8km south of Ascona. Keep going through the uninspiring Swiss border village of **Brissago** to reach the characterful and attractive old Italian town of **Cannóbio** 5km further – well worth a visit.

Practicalities

Ascona's **tourist office** is at the top of the old quarter, Viale Papio 5 (Mon–Fri 9am–6pm, Sat 10am–6pm, Sun 2.30–5pm, restricted hours in winter; ☎091 791 00 91, ⒲www.ascona.ch). There are literally dozens of **hotels**, with nine on the waterfront Piazza Motta alone: a good three-star here is the characterful, family-run ⚘ *Tamaro* (☎091 785 48 48, ⒲www.hotel-tamaro.ch; ⑤), or a few

metres away is the four-star *Castello Seeschloss* (℡091 791 01 61, Ⓦwww
.castello-seeschloss.ch; ⑥), with romantic, tastefully appointed classic interiors.
If money's no object, aim for the *Eden Roc*,Via Albarelle 16 (℡091 785 71 71,
Ⓦwww.edenroc.ch; ⑨), one of Switzerland's top luxury hotels, where a south-
facing room is a cool Fr.800-plus a night, or the sensuously opulent five-star
spa retreat *Albergo Giardino*,Via Segnale 10 (℡091 785 88 88, Ⓦwww.giardino
.ch; ⑨), set in lavish gardens.

Eating is a case of following your nose: every waterfront café lays tables
outside.The *Tamaro* offers dining in a pleasant internal atrium, while the *Elvezia*
is a good spot for inexpensive pizza and fish dishes; Fr.30 will cover a meal at
either. *Della Carrà* (℡091 791 44 52, Ⓦwww.ristorantedellacarra.ch; closed Sun
& Mon) has an atmospheric courtyard off the cobbled Via Carrà dei Nasi,
serving excellent fish and pasta, and vaulted *Antico Ristorante Borromeo*, Via
Collegio 16 (℡091 791 92 81; closed Mon), offers a small menu, a private
garden and excellent service.

Isole di Brissago

Twin islands 4km south of Ascona, the **ISOLE DI BRISSAGO** (April–Oct
daily 9am–6pm; Fr.8 in addition to boat ticket; Ⓦwww.isolebrissago.ch) are
accessible by hourly boats from Locarno and Ascona, and by more regular
shuttles from **Porto Ronco**, the nearest point on the mainland.These tiny dots
of green in the shimmering lake overflow with luxuriant subtropical flora
basking in the hot sun (this is also the lowest point in Switzerland, 193m above
sea level).The main island, St Pancras – about ten minutes' stroll end to end – is
given over to a fine botanical garden. Note that the signs identifying each plant
species are in Italian, French and German – but not English. At one end is an
attractive 1929 villa, now a conference centre and quality **restaurant** (℡091
791 43 62, Ⓦwww.isolebrissago.org), with adjacent, lower-priced **bistro**: a long
lunch here, followed by a siesta under the palms, makes for a most un-Swiss-like
afternoon. A free boat shuttles over from Ascona for diners on summer evenings
(June–Aug 6pm–midnight) after the scheduled ferry service ends. The small
island, St Apollinaris, has no public access.

Sottoceneri

The **SOTTOCENERI** region south of Bellinzona and Locarno is more
developed than the Sopraceneri, with neat, prosperous towns crammed in
between the narrowing international borders to east and west. The principal
draw is the stylish city of **Lugano**, sited on a bay of the glorious **Lake Lugano**,
which twists out into Italy on both sides. Jutting out into the lake just a stone's
throw from the city is the sun-drenched **Ceresio peninsula**, dotted with
idyllic Italianate country villages and crisscrossed by some of the loveliest easy
walks in the canton.

North of Lugano, alongside the autostrada and rail exit from the Monte Ceneri tunnel, gondolas rise from the town of **RIVERA** (469m) up to **Alpe Foppa** (1530m), located on a shoulder of **Monte Tamaro** (1961m; ⓦwww.montetamaro.ch). By the gondola top station, alongside a restaurant and information centre, is the church of **Santa Maria degli Angeli**, designed by Ticinese architect Mario Botta. It's an effortlessly graceful building, with symmetrical stairs, arches and a long walkway, everything in beautiful porphyry stone. From the belvedere, a crucifix faces out over an infinite view above the Ticino valley. The intimate interior of the cylindrical chapel, with black plastered walls, is filled with indirect light and culminates in an ethereal blue fresco by Enzo Cucchi of two cupped hands.

The church is worth the journey by itself, but you'll also find plenty of walks – not least from Alpe Foppa up to the Tamaro summit (1hr 40min) or down to Rivera (2hr 15min). The most spectacular heads on an isolated route (4hr 30min) along a ridge west to **Monte Lema** (1624m; ⓦwww.montelema.ch), from where a cable car runs down to Miglieglia, linked by bus to Lugano.

Lugano

With its compact cluster of Italianate piazzas and extensive tree-lined promenades, **LUGANO** is the most alluring of Ticino's lake resorts, much less touristy than Locarno but with, if anything, double the chic. It's an exciting, sassy place, full of energy and style – less famous than its Italian near-neighbour Como, but smaller, cleaner and sexier. While Como looks north, Lugano basks on a south-facing bay of the cerulean blue **Lake Lugano**, framed on all sides by wooded, sugarloaf hills rising sheer from the water (some maps refer to the lake by its Latin name, **Ceresio**). Both **Monte Brè** to the northeast and **San Salvatore** to the south are served by funiculars, and both give stunning views over to the snowcapped Alps. Even Milanese urban style-junkies, who give very little quarter to their own provincial towns, are prepared to bring friends over to Lugano for some shopping, a lakeside drink and a good meal.

Lugano stands alongside Zürich and Geneva as a Swiss banking centre, and the city centre reflects this. These old alleys and winding lanes are full of commerce, whether in the form of enticing delicatessens and boutiques or graceful, villa-style hotels and apartment buildings. Explore churches and art galleries, or indulge in the simpler pleasure of a stroll under the lakeside palms. The twilight views over the lake from the summit of Monte Brè, with a warm southerly breeze blowing and the toot and rumble of cars rising from a bed of twinkling lights, could melt the hardest of hearts.

Arrival and information

Lugano's **train station** overlooks the town from the west. From within the station, a funicular (Fr.1.10) takes two minutes to trundle down to pedestrianized **Piazza Cioccaro** in the centre; if you prefer to walk, follow steps from the station down to Via Cattedrale, which connects to Piazza Cioccaro. Narrow lanes link this with the main **Piazza della Riforma**, one block back from the waterfront. The train station is also the arrival point for Palm Express **postbuses** from St Moritz; all other postbuses depart from Piazza Rezzonico, adjacent to Riforma in the centre. **Parking** is in short supply – make sure your hotel has spaces or resign yourself to shelling out Fr.25–30 per day at the long-term car parks flanking the train station.

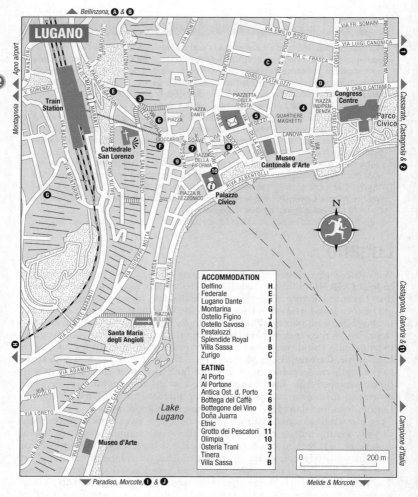

Bellinzona, **A** & **B**

LUGANO

Agno airport

Montagnola

Cassarate, Castagnola & **2**

Train Station

Cattedrale San Lorenzo

Congress Centre

Parco Civico

Museo Cantonale d'Arte

Palazzo Civico

Santa Maria degli Angioli

Castagnola, Gandria & **11**

PIAZZA B. LUINI

Lake Lugano

Campione d'Italia

Museo d'Arte

ACCOMMODATION

Delfino	H
Federale	E
Lugano Dante	F
Montarina	G
Ostello Figino	J
Ostello Savosa	A
Pestalozzi	D
Splendide Royal	I
Villa Sassa	B
Zurigo	C

EATING

Al Porto	9
Al Portone	1
Antica Ost. d. Porto	2
Bottega del Caffè	6
Bottegone del Vino	8
Doña Juarra	5
Etnic	4
Grotto dei Pescatori	11
Olimpia	10
Osteria Trani	3
Tinera	7
Villa Sassa	B

N

0   200 m

Paradiso, Morcote, **1** & **J**

Melide & Morcote

Lugano's little **airport** is 4km west of the city in Agno. Shuttle buses wait for flight arrivals; the driver will drop you at your hotel or any point in the centre (Fr.10 one-way including luggage). On departure, you must book a pick-up at least one hour in advance (☎079 221 42 43, ⓦwww.shuttle-bus.com). A taxi is around Fr.35. **Milan Malpensa** airport, 40km southwest of Lugano in Italy, is served by shuttles operated by Star Bus (☎091 994 88 78, ⓦwww.starstation .ch; daily hourly; Fr.60 return).

The **tourist office** is opposite the main landing stage, in the Palazzo Civico on Riva Albertolli (May–Sept Mon–Fri 9am–7pm, Sat 9am–6pm, Sun 10am–6pm, April & Oct Sat & Sun closes 5pm, Nov–March Mon–Fri 9am–noon &

A **Swiss Pass** (see p.35) is valid for free transport in and around Lugano, including boats on Lake Lugano, and free admission to almost all museums reviewed in this book.

Boats on Lake Lugano

Idyllic **Lake Lugano** merits taking to the water simply for the pleasure of it. SNL (℡091 971 52 23, ⓦwww.lakelugano.ch) names their main landing stage, opposite the tourist office, **Lugano-Centrale**; some services depart from **Lugano-Giardino** 100m to the east. Within the city, boats also call in at Cassarate and Castagnola further east, and Paradiso to the south.

Between April and October boats run roughly hourly to **Gandria**, while others depart less frequently south to **Campione d'Italia**, **Morcote**, **Porto Ceresio** and on around the peninsula to **Ponte Tresa**, stopping at most places on the way. One boat a day heads east to **Porlezza**, while one morning boat connects at **Capolago** for the rack-railway up to Monte Generoso. **Cruises** operate around various bays – or the whole lake – throughout the day, some with commentary in English, others offering on-board meals, drinks and/or music. In **winter**, a skeleton service operates to Morcote, with a few boats each week to Campione and Gandria.

Passes

Swiss Pass holders travel free. Otherwise, fares start from Fr.20–25, or a **lake pass** for unlimited journeys in one/three/seven days cost Fr.38/58/68. A **Lugano Regional Pass** gives free travel on Lugano's boats, buses, trains and cable cars, as well as half-price travel on buses in the Swiss part of Lake Maggiore and buses, trains and cable cars around Locarno and Ascona, for Fr.108 (7 days) or Fr.92 (any 3 days within a week).

The pass **Como e Lugano: Due Laghi per Sognare** ("Two lakes to dream about"; April–Oct only; Fr.46) outlines a circular trip around Lake Lugano and neighbouring Lake Como in Italy, using boats, buses and trains. It's a great-value way to get a flavour of the landscapes – and the ticket is valid for two days, meaning you can break the journey where you like. Check brochures for up-to-date timings before you set out – and don't forget your passport.

2–5.30pm, Sat 10am–12.30pm & 1.30–5pm; ℡091 913 32 32, ⓦwww.luganotourism.ch), with a branch inside the station (Mon–Sat 2–7pm). They run **free guided walks** in English (mid-March to mid-Oct only) around the city (Mon & Thurs 9.30am) and through parks and gardens (Sun 10am), each starting from the tourist office and lasting two and a half hours. Other trips include a full-day tour of vineyards and wine cellars (March–Dec Sat 10am–6pm; Fr.15; book 24hr ahead on ℡091 641 30 50).

If you don't already have a Swiss Pass, which grants free travel on boats and city buses, explore the terms of the good-value **Lugano Regional Pass**, outlined on p.461. Otherwise, a short bus ride costs Fr.1.60, a day pass Fr.5.

Accommodation

Lugano has a wide choice of accommodation: business-oriented hotels in the centre, holiday hotels on the lakeshore (including in the Paradiso district) and some luxurious hideaway options in the hills.

Campsite

La Piodella Muzzano ℡091 994 77 88. Lakeshore site 3km west of town near Agno airport – best of five that are in close proximity. Closed Nov.

Hostels

Montarina (see "Hotels", p.486). Good low-budget central hotel that also has dorms.

Ostello/Jugendherberge Figino (HI hostel) Via Casoro 2, Figino ℡091 995 11 51, ⓦwww.youthhostel.ch. A good alternative to the suburban Savosa hostel, located in a former fishing village on the Ceresio peninsula, offering dorms and rooms. Hourly postbuses from outside the Lugano tourist office go to Casoro, a stop beside the hostel (20min). Mid-March to mid-Oct. ❶

Ostello/Jugendherberge Savosa (HI hostel) Via Cantonale 13, Savosa ☎091 966 27 28, ⓦwww .youthhostel.ch. One of Switzerland's best hostels (complete with swimming pool), with dorms and rooms. Bus #5 to Crocifisso from the stop 200m left out of the train station. March–Nov. ❶

Hotels

Delfino Via Casserinetta 6 ☎091 985 99 99, ⓦwww.delfinolugano.ch. Pleasant, small family-run hotel, with secure private parking and a pool. Something of an institution, and with a good reputation to uphold; rooms are functional rather than characterful, and the food is of a high standard. Private parking. ❺

Federale Via Regazzoni 8 ☎091 910 08 08, ⓦwww.hotel-federale.ch. Classic old town house hotel set in a quiet leafy district immediately below the station, well away from traffic and with lake views from upper floors; rooms are characterful and good value. Private parking. ❺

Lugano Dante Piazza Cioccaro 5 ☎091 910 57 00, ⓦwww.hotel-luganodante.com. Quality option bang in the heart of the pedestrianized city centre (right by the funicular base station), with good service, comfortable rooms and no trouble from street noise. Private parking. ❻

Montarina Via Montarina 1 ☎091 966 72 72, ⓦwww.montarina.ch. Efficient little place in a nice garden just behind the station, with clean, all-new rooms and helpful management. Closed Jan. ❸

Pestalozzi Piazza Indipendenza 9 ☎091 921 46 46, ⓦwww.pestalozzi-lugano.ch. Very nice, renovated two-star in the centre, 150m from the lakeshore. Some rooms have balconies and lake views. ❸–❹

Splendide Royal Riva Caccia 7 ☎091 985 77 11, ⓦwww.splendide.ch. Lugano's premier city-centre five-star hotel, with traditionally styled public spaces and guest rooms that live up to the hotel's name. Accept nothing less than one of the vast rooms on the top floor, offering the best views in the city. Private parking. ❾

Villa Sassa Via Tesserete 10 ☎091 911 41 11, ⓦwww.villasassa.ch. An excellent modern four-star hotel in the hills just north of the city centre. Rooms – which are large, airy, quiet and with contemporary styling – look out onto the pool area, with a superb view over the city and lake. Service is cheerily efficient. Private parking. ❽

Zurigo Corso Pestalozzi 13 ☎091 923 43 43, ⓦwww.hotelzurigo.ch. Central, very clean and well-kept three-star, with renovated rooms, private parking and a trace of style. ❹

The Town

The centre of Lugano is the broad **Piazza della Riforma**, a huge café-lined square perfect for eyeballing passers-by over a coffee. The lake is a few metres

▲ View of Lugano from the water

Lugano's festivals

April's two-month **Lugano Festival** (ⓦ www.luganofestival.ch) features classical soloists and orchestras. In early July are the star-studded free concerts of **Estival Jazz** (ⓦ www.estivaljazz.ch), which in the 1950s and 1960s hosted luminaries such as Dexter Gordon and Ornette Coleman. The **Ceresio Estate** classical music season runs throughout July and August, flanking two big **fireworks** displays over the lake: the Italian enclave of Campione throws down the gauntlet in late July and Lugano responds on August 1 (Swiss National Day). The **Blues to Bop Festival** in late August (ⓦ www.bluestobop.ch) showcases international blues, jazz, rock and gospel artists.

away behind the Neoclassical **Palazzo Civico**, as are the characterful steep lanes of the Old Town on the opposite side of the square. Wandering through the dense maze of shopping alleys northwest of Riforma, you're bound to stumble on the photogenic Gabbani delicatessen, whose fame spreads far beyond Lugano – the interior is an Aladdin's Cave of fine *salsicce* made especially for the shop, cabinets full of Alpine cheeses from the farmers of Alto Ticino, pastries and foodie delights galore. From bustling Piazza Cioccaro just past the deli, the atmospheric stepped Via Cattedrale doglegs steeply up to **Cattedrale San Lorenzo**, characterized by an impressive Renaissance portal, fragments of fourteenth- to sixteenth-century interior frescoes, and spectacular views from its terrace.

The narrow **Via Nassa** – one of Switzerland's top addresses for chic, designer-label fashions – heads southwest from Riforma through a string of picturesque little squares to the medieval church of **Santa Maria degli Angioli** on Piazza Luini. This plain little building was founded in 1490 as part of a Franciscan monastery (suppressed in 1848 during Switzerland's civil war). Inside, the wall separating the nave from the chancel is entirely covered with a monumental Leonardo-esque fresco of the Passion and Crucifixion painted in 1529 by **Bernadino Luini**, as well as St Sebastian, graphically pierced by arrows. On the left-hand wall is another fresco by Luini, this time of the Last Supper.

In the lakefront park opposite is a bust of one "**Giorgio" Washington**, placed here by a nineteenth-century Swiss entrepreneur who'd made his fortune in the United States. Some 100m south on the lakefront is the **Museo d'Arte**, Riva Caccia 5 (Tues–Sun 10am–6pm; Fr.12; ⓦ www.mda.lugano.ch), which stages several major exhibitions a year, while five minutes' walk east from Piazza Riforma brings you to the **Museo Cantonale d'Arte**, Via Canova 10 (Tues 2–5pm, Wed–Sun 10am–5pm; Fr.7–12; ⓦ www.museo-cantonale-arte.ch), a fine old villa housing paintings by Klee and Renoir amongst work by Swiss and Italian artists.

Monte Brè

From Cassarate, ten minutes' walk east of the centre, a funicular rises to **Monte Brè** (ⓦ www.montebre.ch), a sheer 660m directly above the city (also accessible by car), offering spectacular views from the summit café over the lake, the curve of Lugano's bay overlooked by San Salvatore, and the snowy Monte Rosa

For details of the scenic journey to the top of **San Salvatore**, the sugarloaf mountain rising above Lugano's bay, turn to p.491.

massif. Bracing hikes lead off all over the mountain, while a short walk from the summit is Brè village, dotted with outdoor art installations (W www.montebre .com): the tourist office runs a **free guided walk** in English through the village (June–Sept Fri 2.30pm; 4hr; meet at funicular base station).

Eating and drinking

Lugano is blessed with plenty of pleasant, atmospheric places to **eat**. The many cafés and restaurants around Piazza Riforma all offer good, inexpensive food at lunch and dinner; for more characterful locations, head deeper into the city.

Cafés and snacks

Al Porto Via Pessina 3 W www.grand-cafe-lugano .ch. Venerable grand café in the lanes behind Piazza Riforma, built on the site of a medieval convent and boasting Florentine-style frescoes in the old refectory (now used for private parties). The patio, under its cupola, is the perfect place for genteel morning coffee or afternoon tea. Closed eves & Sun.

Bottega del Caffè Via Cattedrale 6. Modest café-bar dispensing espresso as it should be. Closed Sun.

Bottegone del Vino Via Magatti 1. Popular old-style wine-bar beside the post office, with waiters in proper aprons and a huge range of wines on offer by the glass or bottle. Closed Sun.

Olimpia Piazza della Riforma. A Lugano landmark, occupying one wing of the Palazzo Civico, and best of the many cafés around the main square for its good, inexpensive food. Meals of Italian staples, steaks or a few more interesting dishes rarely go for more than Fr.30.

Restaurants

Al Portone Viale Cassarate 3 T 091 923 55 11. Gourmet restaurant that manages to keep a pleas-antly relaxed ambience alongside its inventive new Italian cuisine. This kind of quality commands top prices. Closed Sun & Mon.

Antica Osteria del Porto Via Foce 9 T 091 971 42 00, W www.osteriadelporto.ch. Busy, amiable little riverside terrace restaurant by the marina, serving Ticino-inspired cuisine to a relaxed array of Luganesi families. *Menus* around Fr.45. Closed Tues.

Doña Juarra Via Vegezzi 4 T 091 922 03 65. Popular, well-respected evening and late-night bar-restaurant serving good-value, quality Mexican food (*menus* Fr.30 or so). Closed Mon.

Etnic Quartiere Maghetti, east of the post office. A great, inexpensive bamboo-and-candlelight café/bar/restaurant, tucked away in an unlikely looking mini shopping centre a few streets back from the lake. The menu is broadly Mediterranean, with Greek and Lebanese light

bites alongside tapas and pasta dishes. Eat for around Fr.20, or just plump for a beer or a cocktail from the bar instead. Either way, the atmosphere is cool, friendly and relaxed. Closed Sat lunch & Sun.

Grotto dei Pescatori Caprino T 091 923 98 67. Alluring little *grotto* (rustic tavern), located near the hamlet of Caprino, across the lake from Lugano – and inaccessible by road. The only way to get here is by boat: a handful head over from Lugano, and smaller craft shuttle across from Gandria. The means of arrival and the isolation are the main attractions, but the atmosphere of the place – and the food – match up: tables are laid out under the shade of the trees, directly on the waterfront. Plump for the succulent perch in butter and sage, or a heartier dish such as beef with polenta. Prices are moderate – around Fr.30. Closed Oct–April.

Osteria Trani Via Cattedrale 12 T 091 922 05 05. Friendly little local eatery, tucked away in a quiet corner off the cathedral lane, with a pleasant, skylit interior and tables laid out on the steps. Stop in for excellent pasta – including an innovative dish mixing gnocchi, ravioli and lasagne – as well as good perch, bass and vegetarian options. *Menus* around Fr.50. Closed Sun lunch.

Tinera Via dei Gorini 2. Popular rustic *grotto*-style restaurant, specializing in Ticinese and Lombard dishes such as *pollo alla cacciatora* (spicy chicken stew) and home-made pasta, along with an array of excellent local Merlots. Set *menus* around Fr.22. Closed Sun & Aug.

Villa Sassa (see "Hotels"). Outstanding *haute-cuisine* restaurant attached to this luxury hotel in the hills just north of the city centre. The restaurant terrace offers a spectacular view over the city and the lake. The romance is kept up by the service – white-tuxedoed waiters gliding by – and the food, formal European/inter-national cuisine with a North Italian twist: superb lake fish, delicately flavoured filled pastas and the like. Prices are high – rarely less than Fr.50 per head.

Around Lake Lugano

The possibilities for getting out into the countryside around Lugano are plentiful: the tourist office has sheets detailing fifty-odd cycling routes and walking trails out of the city, for all abilities. The best area to head for is the hilly countryside of the **Ceresio peninsula**, extending southwards behind the San Salvatore mountain opposite Lugano, and well served by boats and buses.

East of Lugano across the Italian border is a cluster of attractive villages on the way to **Porlezza** and then Menaggio on Lake Como. West of Lugano in the **Malcantone** district, before the border at Ponte Tresa, there's the memorable attraction of a Swiss chocolate factory at little **Caslano**.

Gandria and east to Lake Como

From Castagnola, just east of Lugano city centre, a pleasant stroll heads east around the base of Monte Brè, joining the Sentiero di Gandria footpath through the **Parco degli Olivi**, a Mediterranean-style lakefront park shaded by olive trees, cypress, laurels and oleander.

After less than an hour's walk from Lugano (or five minutes in the car), you come to picturesque **GANDRIA**, rising straight from the water 5km east of the city. There is no road access to the village – the slopes are far too steep. Parking areas are signed off the main road. Wandering down through the narrow alleys, past palm trees growing out of the rocky walls, you come to the landing stage (served by regular boats from Lugano), around which is crowded a handful of charming terrace **restaurants**: there are few quieter, more alluring corners at which to hole up. Views down this little-explored eastern arm of Lake Lugano frame the pinnacle of Monte dei Pizzoni – and, beside it, Monte Bronzone – sweeping down into the water, with precipitous wooded slopes opposite that are almost completely devoid of habitation. The silence is wonderful. Should you decide to **stay**, *Hotel Moosmann* can oblige with a lake-view room (☎091 971 72 61, ⓦ www.hotel-moosmann-gandria.ch; April–Oct; ❺).

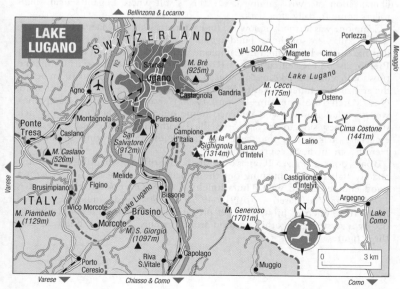

Opposite Gandria, with its own landing stage served by boats from Gandria as well as Lugano (there are no roads here), is the **Museo delle Dogane Svizzere** (Customs Museum; April–Oct daily 1.30–5.30pm; free), with an interesting collection of smuggler-related bits and bobs.

East into Italy: Porlezza

From Gandria, the main road heads east for 1.3km to the international border; after 500m of no-man's-land, you emerge into the **VALSOLDA**, a stretch of Italian lakeside villages headed by **Oria** and **Albogasio**, both of them cheerful little places – thoroughly Italian, and quite unlike Gandria just the other side of the frontier. **San Mamete** is especially picturesque, with its twelfth-century belltower.

A quarter-hour east of Gandria, and 8km from the border, is **PORLEZZA**, the main town on this Italian branch of Lake Lugano – a fairly uninspiring place, with sensational views west over the water but not much else to offer. Take a five-minute stroll through the old quarter, and a three-minute stroll along the lakefront, then settle down with an ice cream. **Menaggio**, on the shores of Lake Como, lies just 11km east.

Campione d'Italia

Visible across the lake from Lugano is the enclave of **CAMPIONE D'ITALIA**, which opted out of Ticino's independence campaign in 1798 and so remained Italian when all around it became Swiss. The village – for that's all it is, even though it's very swish – is part of the Provincia di Como; it has Italian police driving around in Swiss-registered cars and uses Swiss francs rather than euros. There is no passport control.

By road, you enter at a modern **arch**: there is a strict one-way system, so you must go right round the town centre before turning back along the lakeshore. Campione's landmark building is its giant **casino** (daily 3.30pm–3.30am or later; Ⓦ www.casinocampione.it). Unlimited stakes apply here, and – despite liberalization of Swiss gaming law – this is still where Lugano's many high rollers come to dally after dark.

Campione was formerly renowned for its stonemasons, the Maestri Campionesi, whose skills were sought for buildings all over northern Italy; the only example that has survived unscathed in Campione is the little glassed-in church of **San Pietro**, just off the central **Piazza Roma**. From here, Via Marco da Campione runs south along the lake, back to the arch. About 700m along, and 100m before the arch, is the church of **Santa Maria dei Ghirli** (April–Oct daily 9am–6pm; Nov–March Sat & Sun 9am–4.30pm). *Ghirli* ("swallows") refers to Campione's well-travelled masons, who returned home only rarely. The church – which shows its best side to the lake – is filled with thirteenth-century **frescoes**; especially striking are the scenes on the south wall, showing Salome and Herodias in medieval courtly dress.

Boats dock at Piazza Roma, opposite a row of busy, cheerful and unmistakably Italian cafés churning out the coffees and full meals: *La Taverna* is a good choice (closed Wed, Thurs lunch). Campione's poshest **restaurant** is *Da Candida*, Via Marco 4 (Ⓣ 091 649 75 41, Ⓦ www.dacandida.net; closed Mon, Tues lunch & July); the chef prepares his own foie gras, and imports his own oysters and other seafood from Brittany. Expect a bill well into three figures.

Monte Generoso

From alongside **Capolago** train station (274m) at the southern end of the lake (also accessible by boat from Lugano), a rack-railway climbs on a slow, scenic route up to **MONTE GENEROSO** (1704m; Ⓦ www.montegeneroso.ch). For the views alone, this trip is worth taking: from the summit – a short walk above the Vetta (top) station – you can see out across a sizeable part of northern Italy, in an amazing panorama. Milan and Turin are both visible; Bellagio on Lake Como is in plain sight, as is Arona on Lake Maggiore and the distinctive pyramidal Matterhorn; and you can even see as far as the mountain pass in the Apennines above Genoa. The restaurant by the top station is the starting point for an array of **walks**, including down to Mendrisio one way (2hr 40min) or Muggio another (2hr 15min); pick up maps and information at the ticket office in Capolago.

San Salvatore and around

From the district of Paradiso, ten minutes' walk south of central Lugano, a funicular rises to **SAN SALVATORE** (Ⓦ www.montesansalvatore.ch), a rugged rock pinnacle offering especially good 360-degree panoramas from the roof of the little church on the summit, a short climb from the funicular station. A terrace café by the top station attends to refreshment needs. This is also the starting point for walks south into the **Ceresio peninsula**: it's about an hour and twenty minutes through Carona village to Morcote (see below) on the tip of the peninsula.

On the top of the Collina d'Oro behind San Salvatore – named "Hill of Gold" for its sun-drenched tranquillity – sits **MONTAGNOLA** village. The writer Hermann Hesse lived in Montagnola from 1919 until his death in 1962, and wrote most of his classic works here, including *Steppenwolf* and *The Glass Bead Game*. His villa Casa Camuzzi now houses the **Museo Hermann Hesse** (March–Oct daily 10am–6.30pm; Nov–Feb Sat & Sun 10am–5.30pm; Fr.7.50; Ⓦ www.hessemontagnola.ch), an interesting little spot, though the displays – Hesse's umbrella, Hesse's table – are modest. What makes a visit worthwhile is an excellent 45-minute video in English on the writer's life in Montagnola that the staff can set up for you.

Melide: Swissminiatur

On the eastern side of the peninsula, at the point where the train tracks, main road and autostrada all cross the lake on a low bridge, sits the village of **MELIDE**, home to the kitschy **Swissminiatur** (mid-March to mid-Nov daily 9am–6pm; Fr.15; Ⓦ www.swissminiatur.ch). This small park features 1:25 scale models of just about every attraction in Switzerland, from Geneva's cathedral to Alpine peaks, with moving model boats, trains and cable cars livening up the static displays. A wander past all 113 exhibits could fill a slow hour or two.

Morcote and Vico Morcote

At the peninsula's southern tip, 4km south of Melide, lies the captivating village of **MORCOTE**, once a fishing community and now eking out a living as a lakeside attraction. Its photogenic arcaded houses – and slightly tacky antiques shops – are strung along the shoreline road, where you'll also find the small **Museo del Manifesto Ticinese** (March–Oct Tues–Sat 2–6pm; free), displaying vintage posters, and, nearby, the hillside **Parco Scherrer** (April–Oct daily 10am–5pm; July & Aug until 6pm; Fr.7), a romantic garden of lush flora and exotic follies. A web of stepped lanes leads up the hill behind to **Santa Maria del Sasso** (April–Oct Mon–Fri 8am–6pm, Sat & Sun 9am–6pm; Nov–March Mon–Fri 1.30–6pm, Sat & Sun 9am–6pm), an atmospheric church with sixteenth-century frescoes and great views.

Morcote's waterfront is shoulder-to-shoulder cafés – pleasant enough, but fairly generic (and often crowded). Aim instead for the tinier village of **VICO MORCOTE**, on the hillside above and 1km north: unlike in Morcote, here you can stand alone in the cobbled street to absorb the atmosphere. Two restaurants make the trip worthwhile. The rustic, family-run *Osteria Al Böcc* (☎091 980 26 27; closed Tues & Wed) specializes in polenta served seven different ways – expect a bill around Fr.25 – or wander over to the sleek *Ristorante La Sorgente* (☎091 996 23 01; closed Sun eve & Mon), with stone tables set out on a lovely little terrace and a cool, white-walled interior: lunch on salad and prosciutto (around Fr.25) or sample their handmade pasta alongside dishes such as grilled octopus (*menus* Fr.50 or more).

Porto Ceresio and around

From Capolago, a minor road cuts west through the medieval village of **RIVA SAN VITALE** and around the perimeter of **Monte San Giorgio**, a wooded mountain that is a UNESCO World Natural Heritage Site for its unspoilt environment and its fossils. From **BRUSINO ARSIZIO**, an attractive village 5km from Riva, with a handful of lazy terrace cafés that soak up the afternoon sun, a **cable car** rises to Serpiano on a shoulder of the mountain for lonesome forest rambling. Before you reach Brusino, the road rounds the headland of **Pojana**, occupied by the shady terrace of a simple café-restaurant, offering stunning views north past Lugano to the high Alps.

The Italian border lies 2km beyond Brusino; 1500m further brings you to the genial lakefront town of **PORTO CERESIO**, gazing back at Morcote. In a moment of inspiration, the town built itself a boardwalk on stilts over the water to facilitate the lovely late-afternoon *passeggiata*, which extends either side of the main lakefront **Piazza Bossi**, and takes in several enticing little pockets of west-facing sandy beach. There's not much else to do; boats stop in here two or three times a day from Lugano, but the town is more oriented towards its Italian neighbours – Varese lies just 10km south. The train station is opposite the landing stage, 300m around the lakeshore from Piazza Bossi.

The Malcantone

Little red trains start from open platforms opposite Lugano's main rail station on a scenic route west through the **Malcantone** district, bound for Ponte Tresa. After circling the pint-sized airport at **AGNO** – above which stands Monte Lema, end point of a long, beautiful hiking trail from Monte Tamaro (see p.483) – trains head on to the undistinguished town of **CASLANO**, unlikely home of the **Alprose chocolate factory** (Mon–Fri 9am–5.30pm, Sat & Sun 9am–4.30pm; Fr.3; ⓦwww.alprose.ch) on an industrial estate at Via Rompada 36; from Caslano station, follow the tracks in the direction of Ponte Tresa for about 200m and cut left. As you enter you're greeted, Willy Wonka–style, by a fountain bubbling with fragrant molten chocolate. The museum comprises some old coin-op machines and knick-knacks, plus the chance to watch the mixing machines and production line conveyor belts in action (Mon–Fri only). The full Alprose range is discounted in the onsite shop.

Caslano is loomed over by the bulbous **Monte Caslano**, which almost chokes this corner of the lake: there is just a narrow, reedy strait between the mountain and the opposite, Italian, shore allowing boats to access **PONTE TRESA**, the rail terminus 3km south of Caslano. This is a schizophrenic little place, divided by the **international border**. The Swiss half of town is placid and neat, but crossing the bridge over the River Tresa for which the town was named throws you into its Italian twin – a mini-maelstrom of cars negotiating a complex one-way system around busy shops.

From Ponte Tresa minor roads run parallel on both the Swiss and Italian river-banks for 10km west to Lake Maggiore. South around the lakeshore lies **Porto Ceresio** (see opposite).

The Mendrisiotto

South of Lake Lugano, main roads and trains shoot through the hot, dry region known as the **Mendrisiotto**, after **MENDRISIO**, largest town in the area and a major wine-growing centre. There's not a great deal to stop for in the town, although its centre is picturesque; the main draw is the giant **Foxtown outlet mall** (ⓦwww.foxtown.ch), prominently signposted alongside the autostrada, where you can pick up designer-label fashions – Prada, Gucci, Versace, Dolce & Gabbana, and more – at up to seventy percent off.

Near Mendrisio, the village of Morbio Inferiore marks a branch road that climbs into the last valley in Switzerland, the tranquil **Valle di Muggio** (ⓦwww.valledimuggio.ch). Thickly wooded, with seemingly inaccessible hamlets clinging to the steep side opposite the road, this is a lovely, rarely visited backwater; **MUGGIO** (666m), 7km in, has a few taverns where you can grab a bite, and a steep trail leading up to Monte Generoso. ⵏ *Osteria La Montanara* (ⓣ091 684 14 79; ❷) is a welcoming little family-run inn in **MONTE**, across the valley from Muggio. Rooms are simple and quiet – you feel hidden away out of sight here – and the food is hearty, home-cooked village fare.

Some 6km on, and 23km south of Lugano, the Italian frontier is marked by **CHIASSO**, an unprepossessing border town, with a large train station on the edge of a desultory town centre and swarms of motorized and foot traffic passing through during the morning and evening rush hours. Como's suburbs begin immediately on the other side.

Travel details

Full timetables for all trains, buses, trams, boats and cable cars in Switzerland – as well as international connections – are searchable at ⓦwww.rail.ch.

Trains

Bellinzona to: Airolo (hourly; 50min); Biasca (twice hourly; 15min); Locarno (3 hourly; 20min); Lugano (3 hourly; 25min); Zürich (twice hourly; 2hr 30min).
Locarno to: Bellinzona (3 hourly; 20min); Domodossola, Italy (approx. hourly; 1hr 45min); Zürich (approx. hourly; 3hr).

Lugano to: Bellinzona (3 hourly; 25min); Caslano (every 20min; 25min); Como, Italy (twice hourly; 45min); Lucerne (hourly; 2hr 40min); Zürich (hourly; 2hr 55min).

Buses

Ascona to: Brissago (every 30min; 10min); Locarno (every 15min; 15min).
Bellinzona to: Biasca (hourly; 25min); Giornico (hourly; 40min).
Biasca to: Bellinzona (hourly; 25min); Giornico (hourly; 10min); Olivone (every 2hr; 40min).

Locarno to: Ascona (every 15min; 15min); Bellin-zona (hourly; 50min).

Lugano to: Melide (approx. hourly; 15min); Montagnola (hourly; 20min); Morcote (approx. hourly; 30min); St Moritz via Italy (Palm Express; 1–3 daily; 4hr).

Boats

Following is a summary of April–Oct services. See Ⓦ www.navigazionelaghi.it (Lake Maggiore) or Ⓦ www.lakelugano.ch (Lake Lugano).

Ascona to: Isole di Brissago (hourly; 15min); Locarno (approx twice hourly; 20–30min).

Locarno to: Ascona (approx twice hourly; 20–30min); Isole di Brissago (hourly; 45min–1hr).

Lugano to: Gandria (approx every 45min; 35min); Morcote (every 2hr; 1hr).

Contexts

Contexts

History

Switzerland is often dismissed as an irrelevance in the broader picture of European history. Because the country is peaceful today, the assumption is that it either wasn't subject to the same tide of events as elsewhere, or that it is just somehow inherently tranquil. Both ideas are false.

The Swiss difference came in solving the same problems that everyone else had in often unique ways: decentralization, consultation and cooperation have been key Swiss attributes since the start of the country's history in 1291. Until 150 years ago, Switzerland was the most unstable country in Europe. The Alpine calm of today came at the price of almost a millennium of war.

Early civilizations

Near Appenzell and Schaffhausen are scattered remains of **Paleolithic** civilizations. Around 10,000 years ago, at the end of the last major Ice Age, hunter-fisherfolk built villages on the lakeshores at Zürich, Neuchâtel, Geneva and elsewhere. During the **Bronze Age** and early **Iron Age** villagers began to make contact with neighbouring regions. In the first millennium BC, the **Celts** advanced into Switzerland from the west, bringing with them a new culture, as exemplified in the fortified Celtic township discovered at **La Tène**, near Neuchâtel.

The Romans: 58 BC–400 AD

In 58 BC a **Roman** army under Julius Caesar defeated the **Helvetii**, a group of Celtic tribes resident in the fertile area between the Alps and the Jura. After also conquering **Rhaetia** (modern Graubünden), the Romans built the first roads over the major Alpine passes – most significantly the **Grand-St-Bernard** – and founded provincial towns at Nyon, Augst and Avenches, the last of which became the region's capital. Peace and prosperity lasted until 260 AD, when the **Alemanii** – Celtic tribes from the area of modern Germany – broke through the Romans' northern border. Amidst increasing turmoil, Helvetia and Rhaetia were reduced to impoverished frontier regions.

The roots of freedom: 400–1516

Around 400, Rome withdrew from Switzerland, and Germanic tribes moved in to take control. In the western regions, the **Burgundians** settled and adopted both Christianity and the Latin language. On the south side of the mountains, and in the closed Alpine valleys of Rhaetia, Lombardic and **Romansh** peoples retained close cultural and linguistic links with their former Roman overlords. Elsewhere, **Aleman** tribes from the north settled central and northeastern Helvetia, halting their advances at points where the land was already populated by Latin-speaking Burgundians. In this way, a **border** of language and culture developed, marking the easternmost limit of Latinate Burgundian territory and the westernmost limit of Alemanic territory. This language border survives today as the line between French- and German-speaking Switzerland.

Around 600, the **Franks** absorbed the Alemans and Burgundians into their empire under first **Merovingian** and then **Carolingian** kings. The Frankish Empire expanded Latin Christianity with a network of **monasteries**, including those which still flourish at Romainmôtier, Einsiedeln, Engelberg and St Gallen. **Feudalism** spread, as warrior nobles controlled an agrarian society of lords, vassals and peasants. Conflict erupted after **Charlemagne**'s empire was split in 870, with peace returning only around 1050.

The birth of the Confederation

During the twelfth century, noble dynasties – among them **Habsburg**, **Zähringen** and **Savoy** – established towns such as Bern, Fribourg, Murten and Winterthur from which to assert control over the increasingly prosperous countryside.

Around 1220, a road was opened over the **Gotthard Pass** and those communities lying on the northern approaches to the pass – specifically Uri and Schwyz – suddenly took on massive importance to the imperial rulers. A resurgence in **trade** with the Mediterranean led to luxury goods crossing the Alps into northern Europe. Merchants, princes and the valley communes squabbled for control of the lucrative pass routes until the Holy Roman Emperor himself stepped in, granting to Uri in 1231 and to Schwyz in 1240 the privilege of freedom from feudal overlordship. The proud folk farming these remote valleys remained self-reliant.

The death in 1291 of the ruler **Rudolf of Habsburg** sparked popular revolts. Several Swiss communities forged new partnerships, or renewed old ones, to give themselves a degree of protection against an uncertain future. The legendary **founding of the Swiss Confederation** at Lake Lucerne's Rütli meadow on August 1, 1291, by representatives of Uri, Schwyz and their neighbours in Unterwalden, was just one of these alliances. The anti-Habsburg legend of **William Tell**, set around this time, arose as a way to embody the concept of Swiss liberty.

After 1291 the Swiss called themselves **Eidgenossen**, a term untranslatable in English which connotes comrades bound into a cooperative by oath. Switzerland still calls itself the *Eidgenossenschaft*, and modern lexicographers give *Eidgenosse* as a synonym for "Swiss".

Consolidation and growth

Revolts continued against symbols of Habsburg power. In 1315 at **Morgarten**, Swiss peasants defeated an army of Austrian knights. The Habsburgs then tried to force **Lucerne**, a burgeoning market town and transport hub for the Gotthard route, to take up arms against its neighbours. It chose instead to partner them, joining the Confederation in 1332. Unable to bring the Swiss to heel, Habsburg bailiffs withdrew altogether in about 1350.

The feudal system then began to collapse as the increasingly prosperous peasants formed democratic communes. This matched a rise in the power of urban workers: **Zürich**, where the guilds had already overthrown the city's ruling nobility, joined the Confederation in 1351. **Glarus** and **Zug** followed, and then **Bern**. Suddenly, in a little over sixty years, the insignificant Swiss – born out of a pact of farming folk – were able to call on an army of over 100,000, and had control of a large swathe of former Habsburg territory across the northern foothills of the Alps.

Similar leagues of alliance among ordinary farmers in impenetrable Rhaetia to the east also developed into organized opposition to Habsburg rule. While blue-blooded Habsburg armies swept victorious through the great cities of Swabia, in southern Germany, the very same armies experienced crushing defeats in Switzerland, most notably at **Sempach** in 1386 and **Näfels** in 1388. The eight Swiss cantons formed an independent state ruled – uniquely – by urban burghers and merchants and founded on principles of social cooperation, at a time when elsewhere across Europe royalty and nobles held unchallenged sway.

Military conquest
In the fifteenth century Swiss forces crossed the Gotthard to seize the **Valle Leventina**, crushing the armies of the dukes of Milan. After 1460, Swiss **mercenaries** became feared throughout Europe for their skill fighting Charles the Bold of **Burgundy**. However, victories over Burgundy at Grandson, Murten and Nancy in 1476–77 led to the first of many disputes within the Swiss Confederation over the balance of power between towns and countryside. Rural cantons were loath to see Bern – principal victor against Charles – become any more powerful. **Fribourg** and **Solothurn** were only accepted into the Confederation in 1481 on condition that they arbitrated to moderate urban expansion. Following Zürich's victory in the **Swabian War** of 1499 – which ensured complete freedom from the German Empire – both **Basel** and **Schaffhausen** joined the Confederation, followed by **Appenzell**. The first Swiss parliament, the **Diet**, met regularly in Baden, coming to decisions – even at this early date – by majority voting.

Reformation and religious conflict: 1516–1798

The **Reformation**, which began in Germany in the early sixteenth century, was sparked in Switzerland by **Huldrych Zwingli**, a lay priest in Zürich. City after city overthrew ecclesiastical overlords in favour of the new **Protestantism**. In each place, once Catholicism had been ejected, city authorities gained new power over the countryside. When Zwingli proposed reorganizing the Confederation under the **urban** leadership of Zürich and Bern, many **rural** Catholics resisted, feeling their faith and political interests to be under threat. Conflict broke out in 1531: Zwingli was killed and the Catholics won a right of veto in the Diet.

The Reformation continued to spread. In 1536, the French priest **Jean Calvin** settled in Geneva (newly independent from Savoy), establishing a Protestant theocracy that spread the city's reputation for tolerance and religious zeal Europe-wide. In the 1560s, with the Reformation coalescing around Calvinist doctrine, the **Counter–Reformation** launched a bid to reassert Catholic rights. With the support of Spain – a major world power – the Catholic cantons retained their religious identity (in 1597 Appenzell split into two half-cantons, one Protestant and one Catholic), but they increasingly nurtured an inferiority complex towards the Protestant cities, which held a grip on political authority. In addition, Switzerland's urban economy was boosted by the arrival of skilled Huguenot and Veltliner artisans – **Protestant refugees** from Catholic regimes in France and Italy.

The seventeenth century
Only shared economic interests kept the Swiss Confederation together. A lucrative system of **textile processing** developed, in which merchants in the cities (generally Protestant) supplied raw materials to peasants in the countryside (generally Catholic), who worked up finished products and returned them for trading on. Politics, however, remained in deadlock. Catholic mistrust of a perceived Protestant agenda for domination of the Confederation prevented reorganization of jointly administered subject territories.

The continuing traffic in mercenaries entangled the Confederation in a complex web of **armed neutrality**. All the cantons had pledged to supply

France with manpower; in addition, the Catholic ones had links with Spain and Savoy, the Protestant ones with Holland and various German principalities. (The Battle of Malplaquet in 1709 between France and Holland is the most famous example of Swiss mercenaries taking to the battlefield against each other.) The Confederation stayed out of the **Thirty Years' War** (1618–48) – the first significant test of its neutrality – but still imposed new defence taxes. A **Peasants' Revolt** resulted in 1653, crushed with violence by the urban patricians of Bern and Lucerne, who then tried to rewrite the Confederate charter in favour of themselves. The Catholic rural cantons blocked this, then went to war against their compatriots.

The build-up to revolution

Protestant victory at Villmergen in 1712 resulted in a **social and economic shift** in favour of the cities. Catholic regions remained free from Calvinist restrictions on personal conduct but were industrially backward; Protestant areas benefited from better education and economic vitality. French Huguenots, their name a corruption of *Eidgenosse*, drove urban growth in **watchmaking** in the northwest and **textiles** in the east. During the Swiss industrial revolution of the eighteenth century, **commercial farming** also began to take hold.

The **Enlightenment** saw thinkers such as Jean-Jacques Rousseau and Heinrich Pestalozzi feeding a new spirit of Helvetic nationalism which brought Catholics and Protestants together in patriotic endeavour. Politics, however, ossified. Fearful of more peasant rebellions, urban patricians concentrated power in their own hands. Yet popular opposition to entrenched systemic injustice, fuelled by increasing prosperity and the influence of liberal philosophies, showed a grassroots desire for change.

Revolution and civil war: 1798–1848

The impact in Switzerland of the **French Revolution** of 1789 was enormous. The Confederation itself remained neutral in the battles that followed, but popular demonstrations spurred a full-scale **French invasion** in 1798 under Napoleon. Revolution swept the country. In Ticino, Aargau and lower Valais the patrician establishment was overthrown; Basel, Zürich and Schaffhausen announced equality before the law; and Vaud declared itself independent. On March 5, French forces entered Bern, marking the fall of the *ancien régime* in Switzerland.

Within weeks, Napoleon promulgated a constitution intended to replace the archaic patchwork of communities that had prevailed since the Middle Ages. His **Helvetic Republic** abolished cantons, vesting power (in centralized French style) nominally in the people but actually in a five-man executive. The Swiss broke the habit of centuries by coming together – liberal and conservative, Catholic and Protestant alike – in unanimous rejection. A series of *coups d'état* prompted the hurried withdrawal of French troops in 1802. Civil war broke out, resolved by the Swiss-conceived **Mediation**, which restored autonomous cantons (conferring full cantonal status on St Gallen, Graubünden, Aargau, Thurgau, Ticino and Vaud) and named the country the **Swiss Confederation**, the title it bears today.

After Napoleon

After Napoleon's defeat at Waterloo, the democratic balance in Switzerland collapsed. The 1815 **Congress of Vienna** reasserted old patrician privileges throughout Europe: in Switzerland aristocratic families regained control over local and federal politics and Geneva, Neuchâtel and Valais entered the Confederation as new cantons. Street-fighting in Paris in 1830 sparked in Switzerland the **Regeneration**: bands of peasants, urban merchants and artisans seized power, assuring universal political rights under new cantonal constitutions and instituting democratic elections to the cantonal governments. In 1831, the patricians of **Basel** condoned a localized civil war, and the division of the canton into two antagonistic half-cantons, rather than surrender any of their powers to radical activists.

Switzerland was nonetheless enjoying an **economic** boom. Unlike in Britain – the only country more industrially advanced – there was no rush to the cities by impoverished workers. Swiss factories were in rural areas, and drew their labour from the local peasantry, who often came to work after tending to their herds. Cottage industries, where textiles were processed or watches assembled by individuals working in their own homes under contract from urban suppliers, remained a mainstay of Swiss economic development. This piecemeal, individual-driven textile industry staved off competition from Britain's "dark satanic mills" throughout the first half of the century. New fields of expertise in chemical production, chocolate-making and tourism boosted both image and national confidence.

The Sonderbund War

Conflict between **radical** liberals and **conservative**, generally Catholic, activists continued. After Aargau overturned religious equality in 1841 and ordered all religious buildings in the canton to be shut down, outraged Catholics in neighbouring Lucerne nullified their own canton's liberal constitution and – in a move intended to provoke – invited the **Jesuit** order to run the schools. This, in turn, outraged radical opinion, which viewed Jesuit control of education as nothing less than a retreat into superstition.

Violent scuffles erupted. The Catholic cantons – Lucerne, Zug, Schwyz, Uri, Obwalden, Nidwalden, Fribourg and Valais – formed an illegal resistance force, the **Sonderbund** (Separatist League). Radicals seized control of more and more cantons until by 1847, with a majority in the Diet, they demanded the expulsion of the Jesuits, dissolution of the Sonderbund and a new democratic constitution. **Civil war** was inevitable, and – if only to head off foreign intervention – the federal commander-in-chief General Henri Dufour launched a lightning strike, rapidly regaining control and crushing the Sonderbund with minimal casualties.

Reconciliation: 1848–1919

The postwar **Federal Constitution of 1848** – still in effect today – marked the birth of the modern Swiss state. It enshrined a host of liberal measures designed to limit patrician power and encourage economic growth. For the first time, Switzerland had a **central government**, with a directly elected bicameral parliament. As revolutions broke out all over Europe during 1848, the liberals – conscious of centuries of Swiss conflict – shrewdly devised a constitution that defused the age-old Catholic fears of Protestant domination. **Federalism** – the devolution of political power to self-governing regions – permitted strong Catholic institutions at the cantonal level and strong Protestant institutions at the national level: Protestants and Catholics were now able to debate in the knowledge that each needed the other to survive. And the formal adoption in 1874 of the **referendum** as the prime tool for consultation of the people – on matters of local, cantonal and national interest alike – ensured that politicians remained directly accountable.

Steady economic growth in railways, tourism, chemicals, engineering and heavy industry fostered **national reconciliation**. Increasing numbers of Alpine tourists, huge celebrations in 1891 of the 600th anniversary of the Confederation and the unveiling in 1895 of an idealistic William Tell monument in Altdorf all contributed to the rise of a specifically **Swiss national identity**.

Yet even while unity was bolstered, **nationalism** threatened – paradoxically – to split the country apart. Alluringly woolly ideas of race, social Darwinism and the mystical destiny shared by people who spoke one language held a romantic appeal. German-speaking Swiss looked towards the achievements of Germany, with its booming economy, military prowess and advanced social-welfare policies, and felt themselves to be part of it, distanced from their French-speaking compatriots. Similarly, French Swiss looked towards the cultural achievements of *fin-de-siècle* France, and saw their Swiss–German neighbours as foreign. Italian-speaking Swiss felt the border between them and the "rest" of Italy to be absurd. By the dawn of the twentieth century, the Swiss had stopped talking to each other.

World War I and after

Officially, Switzerland stayed out of **World War I**. In practice, military commanders were passing intelligence to Berlin. French Swiss were outraged by their army's pro-German bias. Tough economic conditions were compounded by the need to maintain a frontier force and support a growing number of refugees and asylum-seekers. Lenin, Trotsky and Zinoviev were all resident in Switzerland, and their influence, as well as subsequent news of the Russian Revolution, spurred Swiss workers on to a **General Strike** in November 1918. The Federal Council called in the army, but the strikers had made their point: soon after, **proportional representation** became law for national elections, alongside welfare expansion and a 48-hour working week.

Neutrality and World War II: 1919–1945

As elsewhere, the economic bubble of the 1920s burst in the early 1930s, with **depression** halving output, decimating incomes and causing huge unemployment. At the same time, cosy domestic coalitions were breaking down under the influence of proportional representation, which brought numerous economic and political interest groups into parliament. After **Hitler**'s rise to power in Germany in 1933, Swiss Nazis gathered support from conservatives and the hard-hit middle classes. But a devaluation of the franc in 1936 (which boosted Swiss industry in the run-up to war) and a new partnership of liberals and social democrats were able to sideline these authoritarian movements in favour of continued democratic debate. As war became inevitable, Switzerland bolstered its institutions, affirming **Romansh** as a national language, authorizing widespread official usage of **Swiss German** as a distancing measure from the High German of the Third Reich, and showcasing home-grown achievements at a National Exhibition in 1939. Banking reforms introduced anonymous **numbered bank accounts** to protect the Swiss-held savings of German Jews from seizure by the Nazis.

Switzerland and the Jews

As across Europe, **anti-Semitism** worked its way into official Swiss policy over decades. Freedom of residence and legal equality had been granted to Jews in

Switzerland only in 1866. After Russian pogroms in the 1880s led destitute Jews to head west across Europe in search of safety, Swiss worries about **Überfremdung** (foreign infiltration) resulted in discriminatory immigration policies that required assimilation before civic protection could be conferred. In virtually all cases, Jews who applied for refugee status were deemed to be alien to Swiss society and thus unassimilable.

As the European situation worsened during the 1930s, Switzerland searched for a way to **keep the Jews out** – as did many European governments – without being seen to compromise their reputation for neutrality and tradition of providing asylum. In 1938, in response to a request made by Switzerland's police chief to the Gestapo, the passports of all "non-Aryan" Germans (that is, Jews) were stamped with a "J". German border guards were then instructed to refuse passage out of Germany for anyone holding a "J" stamp.

In August 1942, racial persecution was deemed to be insufficient grounds for emergency admission to Switzerland, and the borders were effectively closed. Only twelve Jews in each year of the war were granted Swiss naturalization papers, and of some 300,000 refugees who were accepted into Switzerland, just ten percent were Jewish. Surviving records testify to 25,000 Jews being turned back at the borders, but the real figure must have been vastly higher.

By autumn 1942, the Red Cross in Geneva knew of the systematic murder of Jews in Nazi death camps. Under pressure from the Swiss government, it did and said nothing. A few individuals within Switzerland were working against the policies of the government, but the official line was that – in the notorious words of Federal Councillor Eduard von Steiger – "the lifeboat is full".

World War II

In the summer of 1939, Switzerland mobilized between ten and twenty percent of its population in preparation for **war**. Germany had invaded Austria in 1938 under the pretext of "union" (*Anschluss*), and by June 1940, Denmark, Norway, Holland, Belgium, Luxembourg and France had all succumbed. Mussolini's Fascist Italy lay to the south. Switzerland was surrounded. An invasion by the Axis powers seemed imminent. On July 25 the Swiss commander-in-chief **General Guisan** assembled the entire officer corps at the Rütli meadow, venue of the 1291 foundation of the Confederation, and reaffirmed Switzerland's commitment to resistance and neutrality. All officers did the same.

And yet it is now clear that collaboration with Berlin continued apace, concealed beneath a glow of national pride and unity. The role of Switzerland in World War II is still controversial, but historians now accept that the country **escaped Nazi invasion** not simply through the dogged bravery of its soldiers (as Swiss history books long maintained). Both the Allies and the Axis powers were very well served by having an ostensibly neutral, stable Switzerland at the heart of war-torn Europe. Had Hitler invaded, traffic across the Alpine passes that linked Germany and Italy would have been threatened, and Germany was anyhow benefiting from Swiss industry, which continued to supply the Third Reich with arms.

But Switzerland was safe above all because of its pivotal role as a **banking and financial centre**: both sides needed resources, and during the war the only currency accepted for payment worldwide was the Swiss franc. The Bank of International Settlements – an organization of national banks, headquartered in Basel, with board members from the US, Britain, France, Germany and elsewhere – kept the wheels of international capitalism turning, and was the only place where **high-level meetings** continued (in extreme secrecy) between Allied and Axis officials. By the standards of both, such meetings were treasonous.

Right up until the fall of Berlin in 1945, the Swiss National Bank **bought gold** from Germany, knowing that the cash it paid to Berlin would be used to prolong the war, and that the ingots it was buying were of illegal origin – looted from the reserves of occupied countries and/or melted down from the possessions (and even the teeth) of dead Jews.

After the Rütli gathering, General Guisan ordered Swiss frontier defence positions to withdraw from the national borders in order to fortify positions within the high Alpine chain. The *réduit national* ("**Fortress Switzerland**") took shape: at almost any point after 1940, Hitler could have crossed the frontier and taken the entire populated lowlands – Basel, Zürich, Bern, Geneva and the countryside – without a fight. Independent Switzerland would have been reduced to a few snowbound bunkers. But such an invasion would have impoverished the Reich by opening Switzerland to Allied bombing. So Berlin instead ensured that Switzerland remained open for business, despite the war raging all around. The moral consequences of compliance with this for the purportedly neutral Swiss are only now becoming clear.

Sonderfall Schweiz: 1945–2001

Swiss historian Patrick Kury wrote: "After World War II, the lack of experience of war made Swiss people believe that they were a kind of chosen people living outside history. This strange belief goes together with the misconception that between 1933 and 1945 Switzerland had followed a humanitarian tradition, and had never practised an anti-Jewish [policy]. In the postwar period, neutrality – the number one state maxim – also helped to neutralize analysis and discussion."

National pride in having reached war's end unscathed – despite the fact that neither Allied nor Axis powers had had the slightest intention of invading, and that the Swiss themselves had done no fighting – left the country aglow. Switzerland felt itself to be special: the term **Sonderfall Schweiz**, or "Switzerland as a Special Case", is often used to describe the period.

While the postwar mood expressed itself in the establishment of the **United Nations** in 1945, Switzerland stuck tight to its neutrality and stayed out. With its intact industry, low taxes and sociopolitical stability, Switzerland was in a perfect position to cash in on European reconstruction, not least because it could draw on large capital reserves (thanks in large part, it is now clear, to the wartime policy of buying looted gold from Berlin).

With the **Cold War**, Swiss political parties that were already rooted in concordance moved together into a rock-solid national consensus. Dubbed after 1959 the "**magic formula**", this ensured two seats on the Federal Council went to the moderate-left Liberals, two to the moderate-right Christian Democrats, two to the left-wing Social Democrats and one to the right-wing People's Party. Four were reserved for German-speakers and three for French- and Italian-speakers, reflecting the language division in the country.

Along with most of the rest of Western Europe, Switzerland experienced a cycle of economic fortunes: consolidation in the 1950s, boom in the 1960s, recession in the 1970s, entrenchment and readjustment in the 1980s, streamlined growth in the 1990s. However, despite massive advances in personal and national wealth, and success in adapting traditional industries to the new era – exemplified by the launch of **Swatch**, a slick, new company that dragged the Swiss watch industry out of its fustiness – it took until the 1990s for

Switzerland to bring itself fully into line with European conceptions of social modernity. **Women** got the vote in national elections only in 1971, decades behind most other European countries; as late as 1991, one canton (Appenzell Inner-Rhodes) had to be forced to adopt universal suffrage by the Federal Supreme Court.

As the Western European powers drew together in a **common market**, the insular Swiss looked on, the national mood still one of "Fortress Switzerland". In 1986, a proposal for **United Nations** membership received a resounding "no" from 76 percent of Swiss voters. A vote in 1992 on joining the **European Union** was rejected narrowly, but analysis of the figures showed that 70 percent had voted yes in French-speaking areas, as against 44 percent voting yes in German-speaking areas. Further breakdowns showed that urban voters across the country were pro-EU, while rural voters were anti-EU. The figures reignited national soul-searching over the age-old social and linguistic divide, exploited by a new bloc of strident, right-wing opinion shaped by the notorious politician **Christoph Blocher**, who campaigned throughout the 1990s on a platform of anti-Europe, anti-immigration rhetoric, wrapped up in a cloak of pro-Swiss, pro-neutrality platitudes.

Amidst a floundering economy – Switzerland had the weakest growth rate in Western Europe in the period 1992–2001 – parliamentary time was taken up with endless amendments to bring Swiss law into line with EU law: regardless of the 1992 vote, Switzerland simply couldn't afford to ignore the direction its neighbours were heading in and, rather than joining the EU, instead drew up a series of bilateral accords with it.

Meanwhile, the cosy "magic formula" began to crumble in the face of a series of major **scandals**. Out of the blue, the squeaky-clean image that postwar generations had of themselves and their country was shown to have been an illusion. In 1989 **Elizabeth Kopp**, the first woman to serve as a Federal Councillor – and an icon of the new Switzerland – had to resign amid allegations of corruption. The same year it emerged that the Swiss **secret police** had been keeping files on 200,000 individuals, under the guise of monitoring anti-patriotic activity. An accountant under investigation in a multimillion-franc **fraud** case – the largest in Swiss history – turned out to be an intelligence agent, and claimed he had been acting under orders to fund the secret training of shadowy armed militias.

But the story that hit the international headlines, and brought Switzerland into the uncomfortable glare of global attention, concerned its **wartime** record.

Wartime reappraisal

With the end of the Cold War in 1989, former Communist countries in Eastern Europe opened their borders and their state archives. **Jews** who had survived the Holocaust began petitioning the governments in Warsaw, Budapest, Prague and elsewhere – often with the help of international Jewish organizations such as the New York-based **World Jewish Congress** (WJC) – for return of property that had been seized by the Nazis. In 1995, the fiftieth anniversary of the end of World War II prompted apologies from many Western governments for their activities during wartime. Swiss president Kaspar Villiger **apologized** for the introduction of the "J" stamp in the passports of German Jews and for Switzerland's closing its borders to Jewish refugees. Meanwhile, WJC researchers had been recording case after case of Holocaust survivors being refused access to their dead relatives' accounts in Swiss banks, often on spurious grounds such as not providing a death certificate. They uncovered records at the US National Archives showing that the Swiss banks were not just hoarding the assets of dead Jews, but that they had also accepted vast quantities of obviously looted **gold** amidst hitherto only guessed-at collusion with the Third Reich.

The story made global headlines and pressure grew for an official inquiry. In 1996 the **Swiss Bankers' Association** announced it had uncovered Fr.39 million in heirless accounts – a tiny sum. Activists continued to demand access to banks' archives. In 1997 a security guard working at UBS, **Christoph Meili**, made public the fact that the bank was secretly shredding large quantities of prewar documents. Meili was fired and prosecuted, but it was becoming clear to the Swiss establishment that the game was up: the president, Arnold Koller, tried to draw a line by proposing a Fr.7 billion fund, funded from Swiss gold reserves, to support victims of oppression and natural disaster – the so-called **Swiss Solidarity Foundation**. Then a newspaper revealed that Credit Suisse had opened an account for the Nazi SS during the war and that the Bank for International Settlements in Basel had acted as conduit for much of the Reich's looted gold. Documents were found in the US National Archive stating that **Japan**, wartime ally of the Nazis, had also used Swiss banks. The banks themselves continued scrabbling to prove their good faith: Fr.17 million that had lain in dormant accounts since the war was returned to the descendants of account holders.

The affair was souring international relations. Switzerland complained to the BBC over a documentary entitled "**Nazi Gold**". Canada admitted that it had laundered at least six tons of Nazi gold via Switzerland. The US granted the bank security guard Christoph Meili asylum; UBS dropped the case against him and apologized. The **Red Cross** admitted a "moral failure" in having remained silent during the war about the genocide of the Jews and later acknowledged regret over the fact that, in 1949, it had issued **Josef Mengele**, the infamous doctor at the Auschwitz death camp, with a permit to travel through Switzerland.

In 1997 a committee of historians chaired by **Jean-François Bergier** reported that, in addition to the $389 million of gold purchased from Nazi Germany by the Swiss National Bank (approximately $4 billion in modern terms), a further $61 million had been bought by the Swiss commercial banks (among which were UBS and Credit Suisse), three times more than previously thought. Under intense worldwide pressure to admit culpability, and desperate to see an end to the story, the three largest Swiss banks, Credit Suisse, UBS and SBC, offered $1.25 billion, the so-called **global settlement sum**, to settle all claims connected with Holocaust-era assets.

Switzerland's **Volcker Commission** unearthed almost 54,000 accounts that had been opened at Swiss banks between 1933 and 1945, and, in addition to the thousands of names already declared, advised the banks to publish a further 25,000 names of account holders suspected to have been victims of the Nazis. It estimated that, at current prices, these accounts might total as much as $440 million. Meanwhile the **Bergier Commission** confirmed that Switzerland had deliberately blocked the entry of refugees, condemning Jews and others to certain death. It identified a strain of "cultural, social and political" anti-Semitism in wartime Switzerland and stated explicitly that the country's refugee policy had "contributed to… the Holocaust."

The end of "Sonderfall Schweiz"

The whole sorry saga of the 1990s struck deep at the heart of Swiss self-confidence. The Bergier Commission's statement that "Switzerland declined to help people in mortal danger" contradicted all the notions of ethical behaviour that postwar Swiss generations learned from their parents, from each other and from their history books. The anger and disorientation felt, in particular, in the proudly nationalistic inner cantons has coincided with the rise of the right-wing demagogue Christoph Blocher, who has channelled it into an extremist political strategy directed against foreigners of all kinds, embodied by the EU and the many asylum seekers and guest workers resident in Switzerland.

Swiss self-confidence was further undermined in 2001, when the national airline **Swissair** – having squandered millions buying up failing European carriers – went bust. The failure of a core institution, and the sight of Swiss travellers marooned at foreign airports with the flag humiliated in public, felt to many Swiss like a national disaster.

In five short years, a devastating combination of scandal and national humiliation effectively punctured the self-assurance – and, some said, smugness – that had shaped Swiss national consciousness over the previous five decades. Commenting on the country's wartime role, the Geneva newspaper *Le Temps* finally spoke a painful truth: "The Swiss were no better or worse than anyone else." *Sonderfall Schweiz* was dead.

Switzerland today

Contemporary Switzerland has gained a new, rejuvenating humility, most tangibly expressed in the 2002 vote to end its isolation and join the **United Nations**. The same year, the Swiss government enacted seven **bilateral accords** between Switzerland and the EU, bringing liberalization on such matters as trade and free movement by 2014, whether the Swiss people ever vote for EU membership or not.

Asylum and immigration remains a hot topic, tied up with an inexorable rise in the use of **English** in education, business and popular culture. Much to the chagrin of those trying to build cultural bridges between the four language communities, English is increasingly seen as Switzerland's *lingua franca*.

Yet Switzerland continues to search for a contemporary identity. On the one hand, Swiss **architecture** and design lead the world, and a focus on environmental protection has channelled substantial public investment in **high–speed rail** to help shift pan-European freight off the roads. On the other hand, Switzerland remains a conservative, traditionalist and – perhaps most surprisingly – deeply militaristic society: it is now the only European country with **universal male conscription**. Switzerland has gained new self-knowledge and abandoned the old consensus politics, but it has also lurched to the right. The old guard are digging in.

Alpine flora and fauna

Switzerland hosts a wide range of wildlife and botanical habitats. Thanks to the huge difference in altitude, climate and vegetation zones, there's nearly always something of interest to see, whether you're a dedicated naturalist or just a visitor interested in the Alpine environment.

Fauna

In the distant past the Swiss Alps were inhabited by such creatures as the cave bear, cave lion and panther. Not more than a few hundred years ago the most prolific animals found in the Alpine valleys included the lynx and wildcat, and the wolf. The **Parc Naziunal Svizzer** (Swiss National Park) is a haven for numerous resident and migratory animals, and is perhaps the country's most rewarding location for the casual wildlife observer, since something like half of the seventy species of mammals found in Switzerland can be seen there. The following survey, by no means comprehensive, picks out the highlights.

Mammals

The **red deer** (*Cervus elaphus*) had disappeared from much of the country before the National Park was established in 1914, but natural migration from neighbouring regions of Austria saw a steady repopulation in the forested valleys of Graubünden. Fawns are born in May or June and are suckled for three or four months, remaining near forest shelter. In summer the adult coat is reddish brown, turning grey-brown in winter. The much smaller **roe deer** (*Capreolus capreolus*) has similar colouring and can be seen roaming around the upper timber line in the early morning or towards dusk, when they stray from tree cover.

The **red squirrel** (*Sciurus vulgaris*) favours a woodland habitat and is fairly common. The **European lynx** (*Lynx lynx*) was reintroduced into the Swiss Alpine forests in 1970, though casual sightings are extremely rare. The **wildcat** (*Felis silvestris*) is another elusive forest predator. The **Alpine hare** (*Lepus timidus*) has a wide distribution in northern Europe and is found in open country both below and above the tree line, to about 3000m. In winter its coat is white; in summer, brown with white patches. Thanks to the production of two, and sometimes three, litters a year, the hare manages to maintain its numbers.

Throughout the Alps the shrill, high-pitched alarm whistle of the **marmot** (*Marmota marmota* – or *Murmeltier* in German) will be heard from late spring until early autumn. One of the most widespread of all Alpine rodents, it remains wary: it is the chief food source of foxes and eagles. Living in burrows, mostly above the tree line, the marmot hibernates in a "nest" of dried grasses for as many as seven months a year in the upper regions around 3000m, or five to six months at lower altitudes. The young do not emerge much before the end of July, by which time they've grown fur and developed razor-sharp teeth to crop the coarse meadow grasses.

The **chamois** (*Rupicapra rupicapra* – or *Gemse* in German) can be seen, either singly or in herds, throughout the Swiss Alps as well as the lower Jura. Although sought by hunters in the autumn, in some areas it has enjoyed protected status since the sixteenth century. The Engadine is thought to have one of Europe's largest populations of this handsome antelope-like ruminant, noted for its agility, with short hooked horns and a russet coat sometimes lightening to fawn-grey in summer.

The stocky male **ibex** (*Capra ibex* – or *Steinbock* in German) has large, knobbly, scimitar-shaped horns which are used as weapons during the autumn rut. Although the chamois ranges high in the mountains, the ibex zone is even higher: some have been sighted at over 4000m. For the greater part of the year it lives above the tree line, often roaming to the high snows in summer, but occasionally descending to the forests in winter. Weighing up to 100kg, it negotiates narrow rock ledges with confidence. A sizeable herd roams above Pontresina in Graubünden; another can be seen above Val de Bagnes in Valais, often grazing close to the Sentier de Chamois hiking trail.

Birds

In woodlands of the Alpine foothills, and in the Jura, the bizarre call of the rare **capercaillie** (*Tetrao urogallus*) rattles in the early hours of a spring dawn. Its dark shape has easy camouflage in a beech, larch or pine wood where it can feed on berries, buds and needles, but where it can also fall prey to such predators as the fox and marten.

Game birds of the forest regions are notoriously difficult to observe except when accidentally flushed out of cover. The hazel hen (*Tetrastes bonasia*), black grouse (*Lyrurus tetrix*), ptarmigan (*Lagopus mutus*) and rock partridge (*Alectoris graeca*) are all found in the National Park, as is the long-billed woodcock (*Scolopax rusticola*), in marshy ground near the tree line. Other woodland birds found in Switzerland include the eagle **owl**, tawny, long-eared, pygmy, and small, golden-eyed Tengmalm's owl (*Aegolius funereus*), which takes over the abandoned nests of woodpeckers. The National Park hosts several species of **woodpecker**, notably the green, great-spotted, black and rare three-toed (*Picoides tridactylus*).

There's no shortage of songbirds, including mountain specialists such as the **alpine accentor** (*Prunella collaris*), whose nest has been discovered above 3000m and whose song resembles that of the lark. Another is the brightly coloured **rock thrush** (*Monticola saxitilis*) which returns to the Alps in mid-May after wintering in tropical Africa. Then there's the gregarious **alpine chough** (*Pyrrhocorax graculus*), whose aerial acrobatics, yellow beak and strident call are familiar to all who visit the hikers' huts in the high mountains.

The **golden eagle** (*Aquila chrysaetus*) builds its eyrie on inaccessible rock ledges; you have a fair chance of spotting one sailing over the high pastures. Although its summer diet consists chiefly of marmot, it will also strike grouse and mountain hare, and may even try to take the young of chamois and red deer.

Flora

Switzerland's range of **plants** is enormous: soil, habitat, climate and altitude vary from region to region and, in some cases, from one valley to the next. Igneous rocks may dominate in one district, with more plant-friendly limestone in another. Habitats vary from damp grassland to semi-arctic rockface, from desert-like scree to shady woodland, from glacial moraine to the marshy fringe of a mountain lake, from a sunny cliff or stretch of limestone pavement to an acid valley bog. Each has its own specific flora. Mountains create their own microclimate: one side may be damp, the other protected in a rain shadow. A south-facing hillside will be different from the opposite, north-facing slope, and on a mountainside the seasons change, not by the calendar, but by altitude. All these have an effect on the plant life, as do grazing and cultivation of the soil.

In the lower valleys **soldanellas**, **primulas**, **crocus**, **anemones** and others come into flower early in the year as the snow melts. Having bloomed, they wither and all but disappear. But as the season advances and the snow recedes, so the same flowers appear higher up the hillside. By mid-June or July, alongside many other plants, they colour the "alps" – the upper pastures – before cattle are brought up for summer grazing. Before the end of July most of the pasture flowers will have gone, but it is then that the screes, moraine walls and rockfaces display their own special Alpine flora.

The **pasque flower** comes in several forms. *Pulsatilla vernalis*, or the spring pasque flower, has its white petals often flushed a pale violet on the outside, while the alpine pasque flower (*Pulsatilla alpina*) is protected from the cold by a coating of tiny hairs. The tiny **alpine snowbell** (*Soldanella alpina*) has no apparent protection, even though it often pushes its way through the melting snowfields. Its tassled petals vary from violet to pink-blue depending on habitat: it may be found on sites as diverse as shallow pockets of limestone or damp pastures up to 3000m. The **lily** family is another pasture and meadowland favourite that comes in many forms, including asphodel, crocus, fritillary and scilla. The claret-headed martagon lily (*Lilium martagon*) appears in shady woodland glades of the Jura, while the showy orange lily (*Lilium bulbiferum*) adorns grassy terraces above Urnerboden.

The **gentian** is even more numerous, represented by such extremes as the great yellow gentian (*Gentiana lutea*), whose starry flowers burst from an upright stem, to the tiny, delicate blue favourite, the spring gentian (*Gentiana verna*), and deep royal blue trumpet gentian (*Gentiana kochiana*) that sometimes appears to have practically no stem at all, producing flowers almost as it emerges from the turf.

The low-growing, evergreen **alpenrose** shrub (*Rhododendron ferrugineum*) has a remarkably wide range, flowering pink to deep red on hillsides up to 3200m between June and August. The **creeping azalea** (*Loiseleuria procumbens*) is a member of the same family and has similar colouring, but prefers exposed peaty sites, often found on acid soils at altitudes of 1500–3000m. Forming cushions over rocks and screes, the eye-catching **moss campion** (*Silene acaulis*) is a mass of pink in a bed of deep green, while the rosettes of the **common houseleek** (*Sempervivum tectorum*) can decorate otherwise drab moraines when they produce their stalk of bright pink flower heads in summer.

Then, of course, there's the **edelweiss** (*Leontopodium alpinum*), whose woolly grey flowers have become famous. Found usually, but not exclusively, on limestone, it may be seen clustered in short grass overlooking a glacier, or thrusting from a cliff face, anywhere from the Engadine to the Bernese and Pennine Alps, flourishing as high as 3400m.

by Kev Reynolds

Books

I t can be surprisingly hard to find books about Switzerland. What follows is a personal selection of a few favourites; those with the 🏃 symbol are particularly recommended. Other good sources include **Bergli Books** (ⓦwww.bergli.ch), an English-language publisher based in Basel. **Pro Helvetia** (ⓦwww.prohelvetia.ch), Switzerland's publicly funded Arts Council, produces a range of English paperbacks giving erudite background on subjects including Swiss music, theatre, literature, film, media, architecture, politics, society, multilingualism and more. Order online or through any Swiss embassy.

Travel

Early travellers

Peter Arengo-Jones *Queen Victoria in Switzerland*. Absorbing transcript of Victoria's diaries from her incognito 1868 stay in Lucerne.

Trevor Braham *When the Alps Cast Their Spell*. Award-winning account of the early days of Alpine conquest, with detailed chapters on each of the major players – Stephen, Whymper, Mummery and the rest. Fascinating and comprehensive.

Mavis Coulson *Southwards to Geneva*. Well-researched survey of two centuries of English travellers' musings on Geneva, including excerpts from Boswell, Maria Edgeworth, Byron, Shelley and more.

Elma Dangerfield *Byron & the Romantics in Switzerland 1816*. Slim account of the travels, passions and writings of Byron, Shelley et al on their famous visit to Lake Geneva.

Alexandre Dumas *Travels in Switzerland*. Entertaining tales of Dumas's journeyings around Switzerland in 1832, at the age of 25.

🏃 **Heinrich Harrer** *The White Spider*. Classic mountaineer's tale of the first ascent of the North Face of the Eiger in 1938 by a four-man team from Germany. Full of thrills, spills and vivid writing.

Jim Ring *How the English Made the Alps*. Comprehensive account of

English involvement in Alpine travel and exploration, from the eighteenth century to the growth of winter sports in the mid-twentieth. The evocation of Victorian imperial ambition, set against the conquest of Alpine peaks and the rise in tourism, is outstanding.

Mark Twain *A Tramp Abroad* and *Climbing the Rigi*. Wry, witty tales of mountain climbing and exploration in the Alps when such a thing was the height of fashion.

Edward Whymper *Scrambles Amongst the Alps*. Modern reprint of the Victorian mountaineer's original account of the conquest of the Matterhorn.

Modern travellers and expat life

Paul N. Bilton *The Perpetual Tourist: In Search of a Swiss Role*. The diary of an Englishman in Switzerland attempting to bridge the cultural divide. As the blurb says: "The British look for humour in everything; the Swiss are brought up not to expect it." Also try *Laughing Along With the Swiss*, in similar vein.

🏃 **Dianne Dicks** (ed) *Ticking Along With the Swiss*, *Ticking Along Too*, *Ticking Along Free* et al. Entertaining collections of personal stories from travellers and expats, offering a sidelong glance at the people and the culture.

Eugene V. Epstein *Once Upon an Alp*. Wry vignettes of life in Switzerland through American/Swiss eyes, out of print since the 1960s and now republished.

🏃 **Margaret Oertig-Davidson** *Beyond Chocolate: Understanding Swiss Culture*. Outstanding dissection of the country and its mentality – one of the most insightful books on Switzerland available in English, and invaluable for digging beneath the stereotypes and the touristic images.

Susan Tuttle *Inside Outlandish*. Brief little book that playfully tries to bridge the expat gap, explaining the Swiss to outsiders and outsiders to the Swiss.

Guidebooks

🏃 **Peter Habicht** *Lifting the Mask*. Unassuming little volume that dissects the Basel *Fasnacht* (carnival) in minute detail. Written by a local historian and Fasnachtler, it gives unprecedented insight into this odd event.

Marcia & Philip Lieberman *Switzerland's Mountain Inns*. Lovingly folksy walking tour of many isolated *Berghäuser* tucked away in the remote Alps. Their *Walking Switzerland – the Swiss Way* has good trail information.

🏃 **Kev Reynolds** *Walking in the Alps*, *The Valais*, *The Bernese Alps*, *Central Switzerland*, *The Jura* (with R. Brian Evans), *The Engadine*, *Walking in Ticino*, *The Alpine Pass Route* and *Chamonix to Zermatt: The Walker's Haute Route*. The classic Swiss walking guides, vividly and knowledgeably written, containing detailed route descriptions and sketch-maps. *Walking in the Alps* is the largest, an amalgam of several long-distance routes; the others are neat little volumes concentrating on particular areas or hikes.

Alexander Schwab *Lake Thun*. Coffee-table tome (in English), evoking this most beautiful of Swiss lakes.

Peter Studer, et al *Berne: A Portrait of Switzerland's Federal Capital, of its people, culture and spirit*. Another interesting, photo-laden coffee-table book, written by Bernese insiders.

Elisabeth Upton-Eichenberger *Vaud* and *Zermatt*. Self-published guides, full of historical odds and ends and other delightfully long-winded material that gets edited out of most guidebooks.

History and society

Joy Charnley & Malcolm Pender (eds) *Images of Switzerland: Challenges from the Margins*. Slender collection of essays published by the Centre for Swiss Cultural Studies at Glasgow University, including a review of historical attitudes towards the Jews before World War II, and assessments of themes of marginalization in recent Swiss literature.

Clive H. Church *The Politics and Government of Switzerland*. Targeted at students of comparative European politics but fascinating for providing a digestible one-stop take on the make-up of the Swiss body politic.

Walter Dettwiler *William Tell: Portrait of a Legend*. Fascinating little study of the web of tales surrounding the Swiss national hero, and the many different ways the story has been told to suit the concerns of each particular age.

🏃 **Joëlle Kuntz** *Switzerland: How an Alpine pass became a country*. Chirpy little paperback dubbed "A historical primer for English-speaking visitors" that whisks through the major themes of Swiss history, very well illustrated with lots of colour. A good read and a fine souvenir. Published by the author (ISBN 9782881826139); only available in Switzerland.

Mitya New *Switzerland Unwrapped*. Fascinating delve into some skeleton-rich cupboards, including accounts of Swiss treatment of Jews and gypsies, attempts to solve Zürich's drug problems, and more, well written by a Reuters journalist.

Joachim Remak *A Very Civil War*. Illustrated chronicle of the Sonderbund war of 1847, drawing many parallels with the events of the American civil war that followed.

🏃 **Jonathan Steinberg** *Why Switzerland?* Outstanding overview of Swiss society, history and culture, learned yet anecdotal, rich with detail but strong on the wider picture, and packed with insight into why Switzerland is the way it is. Perfect train-journey reading.

Jean Ziegler *The Swiss, The Gold and the Dead*. Hard-hitting account of the Nazi gold scandal by an academic at the University of Geneva and former parliamentarian – hounded and now politically ostracized for remaining uncowed by the storm of protest his revelations unleashed. His calm condemnation of the Swiss establishment for their role in funding the Nazis, prolonging the war and refusing to help the Jews is devastating.

Literature

Switzerland in foreign fiction

Anita Brookner *Hotel du Lac*. A romantic novelist runs away from her impending marriage to a genteel lakeside resort (Vevey in all but name), and there finds what seems to be the start of a new life of freedom. Winner of the 1984 Booker Prize.

🏃 **Patricia Highsmith** *Small g: a Summer Idyll*. Highsmith – who spent her last years in Ticino – is best known for *Strangers on a Train* (made into a film by Alfred Hitchcock in 1951) and her Ripley series of crime fiction. *Small g* is focused on the characters who frequent a Zürich bar during one summer, with a story of love, sexuality and generosity expertly plotted around them. Highsmith died a month before its publication in 1995.

Henry James *Daisy Miller*. The novella that made James's name, a witty portrait of a young American visiting Lake Geneva who flirts and teases, and then travels to the Château de Chillon unchaperoned and so gets her comeuppance.

Thomas Mann *The Magic Mountain*. Seminal World War I novel of ideas that employs patients in a Davos sanatorium to discuss ideas of love, war and death, their tuberculosis symbolizing the sickness of European society as a whole. This and Mann's other books were later burned by the Nazis in his native Germany.

Mary Shelley *Frankenstein*. The famous tale of an idealistic doctor's dabblings with the elemental forces of life, written near Geneva in 1816 as Mary Shelley's offering in a ghost-story-writing competition dreamt up by Lord Byron.

Swiss authors

Max Frisch *Man in the Holocene*. The most striking of the six novels by Frisch, who was born in Zürich in 1911 and is acclaimed as one of the century's greatest writers. This is a haunting meditation on mortality, illuminating the slow decay of an old man's thought processes as he approaches death. Frisch's other novels are *Bluebeard*, *Gantenbein*, *Homo Faber*, his masterpiece *I'm Not Stiller*, and *Montauk*.

Hermann Hesse *Steppenwolf*. Hesse's best-known work, social deconstruction wrapped up as fantasy, which weaves strands of Eastern religion and mysticism into the compelling tale of a middle-aged misanthrope's progress towards social and spiritual maturity. Of his dozens of other works, *Siddhartha* is a graceful retelling of the legend of the Buddha; *Narziss and Goldmund* is a picaresque portrait of two monks, one a scholar, the other a bohemian; and *The Glass Bead Game* is a monumental utopian novel, set in a future where an elite group develops a game that resolves the world's conflicts.

Zoë Jenny *The Pollen Room*. An understated, mesmeric debut novel by this Basel author (born 1974), poetically chronicling a marriage break-up through the eyes of a child.

Liselotte Marshall *Tongue-Tied*. Tender novel of reconciliation, set in Péniel, a fictional Swiss Alpine resort, and centred on Rachel, an interpreter, who is forced to confront her painful wartime past.

Johanna Spyri *Heidi*. Perhaps the most famous book ever written about Switzerland, but a hopelessly moralistic, cloying tale for all that. Spyri expertly evokes the folksiness and stolid culture of the Swiss Alpine farmers and effortlessly pulls heart-strings for her cheese-munching, milk-quaffing heroine.

Beat Sterchi *The Cow*. Translated epic first novel set in a dairy farm and an abattoir, focusing on the experiences of a Spanish guest worker in Switzerland – Heaney-esque in its evocation of rural life. Praised by the *Guardian* for its "uncompromising magnificence as a work of art".

Robert Walser *Masquerade and other stories*. Improvised prose poems and poetic short stories from Walser's life in four cities (Zürich, Berlin, Biel and Bern) over the period 1899–1933, tracing influences on Kafka and other avant-garde modernists. *The Walk* is the best collection of his short fiction, or try the novel *Jakob von Gunten* (aka *Institute Benjamenta*), the dreamlike tale of a young man at a school for butlers. After 1933, Walser spent his last 22 years in an asylum near Appenzell. "I wrote nothing more," he said. "What for? My world had been obliterated by the Nazis." It later transpired that he wrote a great deal, but in a tiny, almost indecipherable script: his strange, shifting novel *The Robber* was published only recently, since it took decades for anyone to realize that the few pages of microscopic scribble comprised a complete novel. Hermann Hesse said of Walser: "If he had 100,000 readers, the world would be a better place."

Food and drink

Marianne Kaltenbach *Cooking in Switzerland*. Friendly trot through some traditional Swiss recipes, heavy on the meat and cream.

John C. Sloan *The Surprising Wines of Switzerland*. Best work in English on the variety of Swiss wines and

viticulture, exploring each area – and virtually each vineyard – with enthusiasm and expertise.

Sue Style *A Taste of Switzerland*. Splendid cookbook, with informed cultural background dotted in amongst the recipes.

Language

Language

Languages

Language is a thorny, often complicated topic in Switzerland. That said, it plays beneath the surface – invisibly to most visitors. Almost everyone you'll come across will speak at least a bit of English, and some Swiss are disconcertingly multilingual: fluency in four or five languages isn't rare.

Switzerland has four national languages. Broadly, **German** is spoken in the centre and the east; **French** in the west; **Italian** in the south; and **Romansh** in a few small areas of the southeast. The dividing lines between them (see map below) mostly stem from the movements of tribal peoples in medieval times, and generally have nothing to do with the cantonal boundaries, which were drawn up much later. Cantons Bern, Fribourg and Valais are all bilingual German/French, while Graubünden is trilingual German/Italian/Romansh. According to census figures, roughly 64 percent of the Swiss population consider German their main language, 20 percent French, 6 percent Italian and 0.5 percent Romansh (the rest are "others", principally English-speaking expats). However, more than one in ten of the Swiss population use English regularly every day alongside their own mother tongue.

All the spoken languages of Switzerland have differences from the orthodox standard versions used elsewhere. The German spoken in Switzerland, for instance, is completely different from that spoken in Germany or Austria, and has its own unique vocabulary, grammar and syntax. Its umbrella title "Swiss German" covers a multitude of regional **dialects** with marked differences both from each other and from standard German: the dialect of Basel is different from

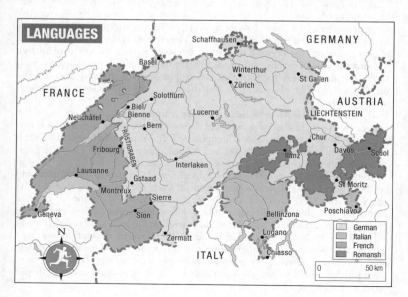

that of Zürich, which is different again from that spoken in the high valleys of Oberwallis. In addition, both the French and Italian of Switzerland have differences from the "pure" languages spoken over the borders. Romansh (see p.442) has detectably the same Latin roots as French and Italian, but is different from both of them.

Hoi: Your Swiss German Survival Guide, by Sergio J. Lievano and Nicole Egger, is published by Bergli Books (Ⓦwww.bergli.ch). Rough Guides produces handy *French*, *Italian* and *German* **phrasebooks**. Ⓦwww.mypledari.ch is an online Romansh translation tool.

German

Two forms of German are used in Switzerland. **High German** or *Hochdeutsch* (also known as *Schriftdeutsch*, "Written German") is the same language used throughout German-speaking Europe. **Swiss German**, or *Schwyzertütsch*, comprises dozens of regional dialects unique to Switzerland, and is unrecognizable to speakers of High German.

No one speaks High German in everyday situations in Switzerland: oral use of High German is restricted to school education, the mass media and public speaking. In all other situations, everyone naturally uses their own local dialect of Swiss German.

But Swiss German is hardly ever written. It's only relatively recently that a dictionary laying down agreed spellings has been compiled, and it's still open to some controversy: ask a Swiss person to write something in Swiss German and they'll probably struggle over the spelling. Everybody writes in High German (which is also the language of all signs and public notices) – but when reading out loud, they mentally transcribe the High German text into their own dialect of Swiss German as they're going along. People see the written word *Dienstag* (Tuesday), and say *tseeschtig*; or *Abend* (evening), and say *obik*. Many High German words simply aren't used: *guten Tag* (hello) is *grüezi* in Swiss German; *Straßenbahn* (tram) is *Tram*; *Fahrrad* (bicycle) is *Velo*; while regional differences mean that *Wiese* (meadow) is *Wise* in St Gallen but *Matte* in Bern. Add in a range of idiosyncratic regional **accents**; a tendency to stick the coy **diminutive** -*li* onto the end of nouns, and to use the throat-rasping **ch** (as in the Scottish *loch*) a lot; and a **stress pattern** that lays emphasis in unfamiliar places (usually on the first syllable of a word) – and the gulf from High German becomes unbridgeable.

To a speaker of *Hochdeutsch*, Swiss German sounds archaic and singsong – and this seems to delight the Swiss, who get their own back when they ask Germans to say the Swiss word for "kitchen cupboard". Transliterated as *chuchichäschtli*, it sounds, when spoken correctly, like a cat coughing up a hairball. Even the Swiss affectionately dub their own language *Mundart*, or "mouth skill".

Much has been written about the role of Swiss German as an emblem and symbol of Swissness, and how the accent of each region reflects that region's character: the taut, stretched vowels of *Baseldytsch*; the slow, loping tone of *Berntütsch*; the clipped efficiency of *Züridütsch*; and so on. No Swiss would dream of erasing these differences beneath a unified norm – and no such norm exists. We've picked a rough transliteration of **Bernese dialect** to use here, which will be universally understood, even if they do say things slightly differently elsewhere. Even if you stumble and splutter, the very fact that you're attempting to get your tongue around Swiss German pronunciation at all will prove a winner with the locals.

Swiss German pronunciation

Any attempt to lay down rules for Swiss German **pronunciation** is doomed to failure, since pronunciation (of vowels in particular) varies from district to district, and even from village to village. The following is only the loosest of guidelines.

In written German, note that all nouns begin with a capital letter, and that an umlaut (¨) over a vowel is sometimes replaced by an "e": Zürich can be written as Zuerich. In Switzerland, the German letter ß is always written out as "ss".

Vowels

Most of the time, pronounce all vowels: *grüezi* has a definite "eh" in the middle, and *Grossbrittanie* has two vowel sounds at the end. However, *eis* has only one vowel sound. In our transliteration, a double vowel, such as in *Määntig* or *Züschtig*, doubles the length of the sound.

a as in f**a**ther

ä is sometimes pronounced as in b**ea**r (eg Bärn) and sometimes as in p**ai**d (eg spät)

ai as in l**ie**

au as in h**ou**se

äu as in **oi**l

e as in d**a**y or w**e**t

ee roughly as in d**a**y

ei as in h**ei**ght or sometimes as in fr**ee**

eu approximates to an **ü** sound

i as in l**ee**k

ie as in fr**ee**

o as in b**o**ttom or r**o**se

ö is like the French eu, or the "urgh" in the middle of "colonel"

u as in b**oo**t

ü is like the French u, or a tight-lipped version of tr**u**e

y is a double-length **ee** – Schwyz is pronounced *shveets*

Consonants

There are no silent **consonants**. Differences from English include:

ch is a strong throaty rasp, as in the Scottish *loch*

gg is pronounced "ck": "Egg" is *eck*, and may even be written as Eck

j is like an English *y*: "Jura" is *yoora*

k has a throaty rasp attached to it: *danke* is transliterated as *dunkcha*

s is like a softened English *z*

sp at the start of a word is pronounced *shp*

st is always pronounced *sht*

w is like an English *v*

z is always pronounced *ts*

French

Swiss French dialect, though still used in the hinterlands of the Jura, has virtually died out. Differences do remain from standard French – principally in accent and inflection – but the Gallic aspirations of most locals mean that you can speak whatever French you know and be both understood and respected. You can even speak English with impunity. The surprising thing is that very few French Swiss speak or understand German. High German – dubbed *le bon allemand* – is taught in some schools beyond elementary level, but generally only as an optional subject. (On the other hand, most schools in German-speaking Switzerland teach French until leaving age.) French Swiss have virtually no opportunity to learn spoken Swiss German without going to live on the other side of the language border.

The most noticeable differences between Swiss–French and standard French are in just a handful of words: instead of *soixante-dix*, *quatre-vingts* and *quatre-vingt-dix*, "seventy", "eighty" and "ninety" are generally *septante*, *huitante* and *nonante* respectively. A PO box is a *boîte postale* in France but a *case postale*, or CP, in Switzerland. And in the Fribourg countryside, the *-ens* ending of place names such as Vuadens is pronounced in full (*voo-a-donce*) instead of the final *s* remaining silent.

French pronunciation

French **pronunciation** can be hard to master, not least because of the tight-lipped precision of many of the sounds compared with slack-jawed English, as well as the lack of any marked stress patterns: in French, equal stress is given to all syllables in a word.

Vowels

a as in h**a**t

au as in **o**ver

e as in g**e**t

é between g**e**t and g**a**te

è between g**e**t and g**u**t

eu as in h**u**rt

i as in mach**i**ne

o as in h**o**t

ô as in **o**ver

ou as in f**oo**d

u is a tight-lipped version of the English tr**ue**

The following are extra-tricky nasal sounds:

in/im like **an**xious

an/am and *en/em* like D**on**caster said through your nose

on/om like D**on**caster said with a heavy cold

un/um like **u**nderstand

Consonants

Consonants at the ends of words are usually silent: *pas plus tard* ("not later") is thus pronounced *pa-ploo-tarr*. However, when the following word begins with a vowel, you should run the consonant over: *pas après* ("not after") is *pazapray*. There are a few differences from English:

ch is an English *sh*

ç is an English *s*

j as in plea**s**ure: "Jura" is *zhoora*

h is silent

ll as in ba**y**onet: "billet" is *bee-yay*

r is growled rather than trilled

th is like an English *t* – "thé" is *tay*

Italian

In **Italian**-speaking Switzerland, written or High Italian is used less than the **Lombardic** dialect common to most of northern Italy. There are also several **Ticinese** dialects, different again from each other and from Lombardic. Almost all Ticinesi are effectively **quadrilingual**: to friends and family they speak the home dialect; on the street they chat in Lombardic; to strangers and in formal situations they speak High Italian; and most people are also proficient in German and/or Swiss German in order to communicate with the large numbers of tourists from the north. English, although spoken by some, remains well down the list.

The upshot of this is that, even if you happened to be fluent in Lombardic dialect, everyone you met in Ticino would anyway instinctively speak to you – a stranger and a foreigner – in standard Italian.

Italian pronunciation

Pronunciation is easy, since every word is spoken exactly as it is written and usually enunciated with exaggerated, open-mouthed clarity. The only slight difficulties come in the following **consonants**, which differ from English:

c before e or i is an English *ch*: "cioccolata" is *chokolata*

ch is an English *k*: "chiesa" is *kee-ay-za*

g before e or i is an English *j* – "Maggiore" is *madge-or-eh*, "giorno" is *jorno*

g before h as in **g**un

gli as in mi**lli**on: "figlia" is *feelya*

gn as in o**ni**on: "bagno" is *banyo*

h is silent

sci as in **shi**p

sce as in **she**d

z as in ba**ts**

Words and phrases

The basics

	Swiss German	French	Italian
good morning	guete Morge	bonjour	buongiorno
good evening	guete Obig	bonsoir	buona sera
hello/hi!	grüezi! (grüssech in Bern grüess Gott in the east)	salut!	salve!/ciao!
cheers! (toast)	proscht!	santé!	salute!
enjoy your meal	enguete	bon appétit	buon appetito
goodbye	of Widerluege	au revoir	arrivederci
bye!	tschüss!/ciao!	salut!	ciao!
yes	jo	oui	si
no	nei	non	no
OK	OK	ça marche	va bene
please	bitte	s'il vous plaît	per favore
thank you (very much)	merci/dunkcha (vielmol)	merci (beaucoup)	(molte) grazie
you're welcome	bitte	je vous en prie	prego
excuse me	entscholdigong	excusez-moi	mi scusi
I'm sorry	es tued mer leid	je suis désolé	mi dispiace
do you speak English?	reded Sii Änglisch?	parlez-vous anglais?	parla inglese?
I come from...	ich be vo...	je viens de...	vengo da...
Britain	Grossbritannie	Grande-Bretagne	Gran Bretagna
Ireland	Irland	Irlande	Irlanda
the US/Canada	d'Schtaate/Kanada	États-Unis/Canada	Stati Uniti/Canada
Australia	Auschtralie	Australie	Australia
New Zealand	Neuseeland	Nouvelle Zélande	Nuova Zelanda
I (don't) speak...	ich rede (ned)...	je (ne) parle (pas)...	io (non) parlo...
High German	Hochdütsch	allemand	tedesco
Swiss German	Schwyzertütsch	suisse allemand	svizzero-tedesco
French	Französisch	français	francese
Italian	Italiänisch	italienne	italiana
I (don't) understand	ich verschtoh (ned)	je (ne) comprends (pas)	(non) capisco

Directions and travel

	Swiss German	French	Italian
here/there	hier/dött	ici/là(-bas)	qui/li
left/right	links/rächts	gauche/droite	sinistra/destra
straight on	graduus	tout droit	sempre diritto
near/far	noch/wiit	près/loin	vicino/lontano
quick/slow	schnell/langsam	rapide/lent	rapido/lento
broad/narrow	breit/schmal	large/étroit	largo/stretto
train	Zug	train	treno
station	Bahnhof	gare	stazione
information	Auskunft	renseignements	informazioni
ticket office	Schalter	guichet	sportello
ticket	Billet	billet	biglietto
day card	Tageskarte	carte journalière	carta giornaliera
departure	Abfahrt	départ	partenza
arrival	Ankunft	arrivée	arrivo
which platform for the train to Zürich?	uf welem Gleis fahrt de Zog noch Züri?	sur quel quai part le train pour Zurich?	da quale binario parte il treno per Zurigo?
when does the train arrive in Geneva?	wenn chond de Zog z'Genf aa?	à quelle heure le train arrive-t-il à Genève?	quando arriva il treno a Ginevra?
change at Olten	umsteigen in Olten	changer à Olten	cambiare a Olten
lost-property office	Fundbüro	objets trouvés	oggetti smarriti
toilets	Toiletten/WC (spoken: vaytsay)	toilettes	gabinetti
women's toilet	Frauen/Damen	dames	signore
men's toilet	Männer/Herren	hommes	signori
postbus	Postauto	car postal	autopostale
bus stop	Haltestelle	arrêt	fermata
when does the bus to Chur leave?	wenn fahrt de Bus noch Chur?	à quelle heure part le bus pour Coire?	quando parte il auto-bus per Coira?
supplement	Zuschlag	supplément	sovratassa
tourist bus/coach	Car	autocar	pullman
(rental) car	(Miet)Auto	voiture (de location)	automobile (a noleggio)
parking area	Parkplatz	place de parc	parcheggio
covered car park	Parkhaus	parking	autosilo
available/full	frei/besetzt	libre/occupé	libero/occupato
(steam-)boat	(Dampf)Schiff	bateau (à vapeur)	battello (a vapore)
breakdown	Panne	panne	panna
boat travel	Schifffahrt	navigation	navigazione
(rental) bike	(Miet)Velo	vélo (de location)	bicicletta (a noleggio)
mountain bike	Mountainbike	vélo tout terrain (VTT)	rampichino
airport	Flughafen	aéroport	aeroporto
police	Polizei	police	polizia
fire service	Feuerwehr	pompiers	pompieri
ambulance	Ambulance	ambulance	ambulanza

Hotels and shops

	Swiss German	French	Italian
entrance/exit	Eingang/Ausgang	entrée/sortie	entrata/uscita
emergency exit	Notausgang	sortie de secours	uscita di sicurezza
push/pull	drücken/ziehen	poussez/tirez	spingere/tirare
reception	Empfang	réception	ricezione
do you have any rooms available?	händ Sii noh freii Zimmer?	avez-vous des chambres libres?	ha camere libere?
I reserved a room	ich ha es Zimmer reserviert	j'ai réservé une chambre	ho riservato una camera
have you got...?	händ Sii...?	avez-vous...?	avete...?
I'd like...	ich hätt gärn...	j'aimerais...	vorrei...
a single room	Einzelzimmer	chambre simple	camera singola
a double room	Doppelzimmer	chambre double	camera doppia
with a shower	mit Dusche	avec douche	con doccia
with a bath	mit Bad	avec bain	con bagno
with a balcony	mit Balkon	avec balcon	con balcone
with a mountain/ lake view	mit Blick uf d'Berge/ uf de See	avec vue sur les montagnes/sur le lac	con vista sulle montagne/sul lago
without	ohne/oni	sans	senza
how much is the room?	was choschtet s'Zimmer?	combien coûte la chambre?	quanto costa la camera?
with breakfast	mit Frühstück	avec petit-déjeuner	con prima colazione
with half board	mit Halbpension	en demi-pension	mezza pensione
dormitory	Massenlager	dortoir	dormitorio
campsite	Campingplatz	camping	campeggio
fully booked	voll/besetzt	complet	completo
big/small	gross/chli	grand/petit	grande/piccolo
new/old	neu/alt	nouveau/vieux	nuovo/vecchio
hot/cold	warm/chalt	chaud/froid	caldo/freddo
clean/dirty	suber/dräckig	propre/sale	pulito/sporco
quiet/noisy	ruhig/lärmig	silencieux/bruyant	silenzioso/rumoroso
open/closed	offen/geschlossen	ouvert/fermé	aperto/chiuso
opening hours	Öffnungszeiten	heures d'ouverture	orari d'apertura
day off	Ruhetag	jour de repos	giorno di riposo
VAT (sales tax)	MWST	TVA	IVA

Numbers

	Swiss German	French	Italian
0	null	zéro	zero
half	halb	demi	mezzo
1	eis	un	uno
2	zwöi	deux	due
3	drü	trois	tre

4	vier	quatre	quattro
5	füüf	cinq	cinque
6	sächs	six	sei
7	sibe	sept	sette
8	acht	huit	otto
9	nüün	neuf	nove
10	zää	dix	dieci
11	elf	onze	undici
12	zwölf	douze	dodici
13	drizää	treize	tredici
14	vierzää	quatorze	quattordici
15	föfzää	quinze	quindici
16	sächzää	seize	sedici
17	sibezää	dix-sept	diciasette
18	achzää	dix-huit	diciotto
19	nüünzää	dix-neuf	diciannove
20	zwänzg	vingt	venti
21	einezwänzg	vingt et un	ventuno
22	zwöiezwänzg	vingt-deux	ventidue
30	driisg	trente	trenta
40	vierzg	quarante	quaranta
50	föfzg	cinquante	cinquanta
60	sächzg	soixante	sessanta
70	sibezg	septante	settanta
80	achzg	huitante	ottanta
90	nüünzg	nonante	novanta
100	hondert	cent	cento
101	honderteis	cent un	centouno
200	zwöihondert	deux cents	duecento
1000	tuusig	mille	mille
2000	zwöituusig	deux mille	duemila
1st	erscht (1.)	premier (1er)	primo (1º)
2nd	zwöit (2.)	deuxième (2e)	secondo (2º)
3rd	dret (3.)	troisième (3e)	terzo (3º)
4th	viert (4.)	quatrième (4e)	quarto (4º)
5th	füüft (5.)	cinquième (5e)	quinto (5º)
once	einisch	une fois	una volta
twice	zwöimol	deux fois	due volte
three times	drümol	trois fois	tre volte

Telling the time

	Swiss German	French	Italian
what time is it?	was isch för Ziit?	quelle heure est-il?	che ora sono?
it's nine o'clock	es isch nüüni	il est neuf heures	sono le nove
1.05	füüf ab eis	une heure cinq	l'una e cinque

2.15	Viertel ab zwöi	deux heures et quart	le due e un quarto
5.45	Viertel vor sächsi	six heures moins quart	le sei meno un quarto
9.40	zwänzg vor zääni	dix heures moins vingt	le dieci meno venti
10.30	halbi elfi (ie half to 11)	dix heures et demie	le dieci e mezza
noon	Mettag	midi	mezzogiorno
midnight	Metternacht	minuit	mezzanotte
an hour	e Schtond	une heure	un'ora
half an hour	e Halbschtond	une demi-heure	mezz'ora

Days and months

Beware that abbreviations of the days (for opening hours posted outside museums or shops) can be confusing: "Di" in French-speaking areas means Sunday, but in German-speaking areas means Tuesday. "Do" is Thursday in German, but Sunday in Italian.

	Swiss German	French	Italian
Monday	Määntig (Mo)	lundi (lu)	lunedi (lu)
Tuesday	Ziischtig (Di)	mardi (ma)	martedi (ma)
Wednesday	Mettwoch (Mi)	mercredi (me)	mercoledi (me)
Thursday	Donnschtig (Do)	jeudi (je)	giovedi (gi)
Friday	Friitig (Fr)	vendredi (ve)	venerdi (ve)
Saturday	Samschtig (Sa)	samedi (sa)	sabato (sa)
Sunday	Sonntig (So)	dimanche (di)	domenica (do)
day	Tag	jour	giorno
in the morning	am Morge	le matin	la mattina
in the afternoon	am Nomitag	l'après-midi	di pomeriggio
in the evening	am Obig	le soir	di sera
at night	i de Nacht	la nuit	di notte
yesterday	geschter	hier	ieri
today	höt	aujourd'hui	oggi
tomorrow	morn	demain	domani
week	Woche	semaine	settimana
month	Monet	mois	mese
year	Johr	année	anno
spring	Früelig	printemps	primavera
summer	Sommer	été	estate
autumn	Herbscht	automne	autunno
winter	Wenter	hiver	inverno
January	Januar	janvier	gennaio
February	Februar	février	febbraio
March	März	mars	marzo
April	Aprel	avril	aprile
May	Mai	mai	maggio
June	Juni	juin	giugno
July	Juli	juillet	luglio
August	Auguscht	août	agosto

September	September	septembre	settembre
October	Oktober	octobre	ottobre
November	Novämber	novembre	novembre
December	Dezämber	décembre	dicembre

Swiss menu reader

Food and drink basics

	Swiss German	French	Italian
knife	Messer	couteau	coltello
fork	Gabel	fourchette	forchetta
spoon	Löffel	cuillère	cucchiaio
plate	Teller	assiette	piatto
napkin	Serviette	serviette	tovagliolo
bottle	Flasche	bouteille	bottiglia
glass	Glas	verre	bicchiere
cup	Tasse	tasse	tazza
menu	Speisekarte	carte	carta
bread	Brot	pain	pane
butter	Butter, Anke	beurre	burro
ham	Schinken	jambon	prosciutto
bacon	Speck	lardon	pancetta
cheese	Käse	fromage	formaggio
milk	Milch	lait	latte
whole milk	Vollmilch	lait entier	latte intero
skimmed milk	Magermilch	lait écrémé	latte scremato
buttermilk	Buttermilch	babeurre	latticello
yoghurt	Joghurt	yogourt	joghurt
cream	Rahm	crème	panna
egg	Ei	oeuf	uovo
jam	Konfitüre	confiture	marmellata
honey	Honig	miel	miele
tap water	Hahnenwasser	eau de robinet	acqua di rubinetto
mineral water	Mineralwasser	eau minérale	acqua minerale
juice	Saft	jus	succo
ice	Eis	glace	ghiaccio
a beer	e'Schtange	une pression	una birra
red wine	Rotwein	vin rouge	vino rosso
white wine	Weisswein	vin blanc	vino blanco
dry	trocken	sec	secco
sweet	süss	doux	dolce
sugar	Zucker	sucre	zucchero
salt	Salz	sel	sale

pepper	Pfeffer	poivre	pepe
oil	Öl	huile	olio
mustard	Senf	moutarde	senape
"waiter!"	"Bedienung!"	"Monsieur/Madame!"	"Cameriere/-a!"
"I'd like…"	"Ich nehme…"	"Je voudrais…"	"Vorrei…"
with	mit	avec	con
without	ohne	sans	senza
to eat	essen	manger	mangiare
to drink	trinken	boire	bere
non-smoking area	Nichtraucherzone	espace non-fumeurs	sezione non fumatori
breakfast	Frühstück, Zmorge	petit déjeuner	prima colazione
lunch	Mittagessen, Zmittag	déjeuner	pranzo
dinner/supper	Abendessen, Znacht	dîner	cena
the bill	die Rechnung	l'addition	il conto

Snacks and starters

	Swiss German	French	Italian
starters	Vorspeisen	hors d'oeuvres	antipasti
sandwich	Sandwich	sandwich	panino
chips (french fries)	Pommes frites	frites	patate fritte
crisps (potato chips)	Pommes Chips	pommes chips	patatine
omelette	Omelett	omelette	frittata
olives	Oliven	olives	olive
soup	Suppe	potage, consommé	zuppa, minestra
prawn cocktail	Krevetten Cocktail	cocktail des crevettes	cocktail di gamberi
green salad	Grüner Salat	salade verte	insalata verde
mixed salad	Gemischte Salat	salade mixte	insalata mista

Main courses

	Swiss German	French	Italian
main courses	Speisen	plats principaux	secondi piatti
meat	Fleisch	viande	carne
veal	Kalb	veau	vitello
beef	Rind	boeuf	manzo
pork	Schwein	porc	maiale
lamb	Lamm	agneau	agnello
chicken	Poulet	poulet	pollo

I am a vegetarian (m/f) Ich bin Vegetarier/-in Je suis végétarien/-ne Sono vegetariano/-a	Have you got any special dishes for vegetarians? Haben Sie spezielle Menus für Vegetarier? Avez-vous des menus spéciaux pour les végétariens? Avete menù speciali per vegetariani?

There's a survey of the various dialects of Romansh on p.442. Some similarities exist with Italian as regards pronunciation, but there are a few significant differences:

c before e or i is pronounced as in ba**ts**

ch before a or o is a palatal sneeze-like *tya* sound, almost an English *ch* but not quite; if there's a preceding *s*, Romansh separates the two with a hyphen – the Engadine town of Chamues-ch is pronounced something like *tyamwesh-tyuh*

ch before e or i is pronounced as in **c**at

g before e or i is pronounced as in **g**eranium

g before h is pronounced as in **g**arlic

gl before i and at the end of a word is like sta**lli**on

gn as in o**ni**on

h is silent

j is like an English y

qu before a, e or i as in **qu**ack

s before any consonant is like an English *sh*

tg is like an English *ch*: "notg" sounds like *notch*

The basics

hello	allegra	pardon!	perdunai!
good morning	bun di	excuse me	perstgisai
good afternoon or good evening	buna saira	I am	jau sun
		I'm from...	jau vegn...
goodbye	a revair	I'm sorry	i ma displascha
bye!	ciao!	I (don't) speak Romansh	jau (na) cur (betg) rumantsch
yes	gea		
no	na	I (don't) understand	jau (na) chapesch (betg)
OK	va bain		
please	anzi	Do you speak English?	Discurris Vus englais?
thank you (very much)	grazia (fitg)		

Travel, hotels and shops

train	tren	with a shower	cun duscha
station	staziun	with a bath	cun bogn
information	infurmaziuns	how much is the room?	quant custa la chombra?
ticket	bigliet		
Where can I get a postbus to Chur?	Nua partan ils autos postals per Cuira?	with breakfast	cun ensolver
		with half board	mesa pensiun
bus stop	fermada	dormitory	champ da massa
I'd like	jau avess gugent		
a single room	chombra singula	campsite	plazza de campar
a double room	chombra dubla		
with a basin	cun aua currenta	open/closed	avert/serrà
		day off	di da repaus

Eating and drinking

Could we have a table in a non-smoking section?	Pudessan nus ina maisa en ilsectur da nunfimaders?	game	selvaschina
		sausage	liongia
bread	paun	fish	pesch
butter	paintg	potato	tartuffel
cheese	chaschiel	vegetables	verdura
soup	schuppa	fruit	fritgs
beef	bov	water	aua
veal	vadè	white/red wine	vin alv/cotschen
pork	portg	a beer	ina biera
chicken	pulaster	cheers! (toast)	viva!

Numbers

0	nulla	11	indesch
1	in	12	dudesch
2	dus	13	tredesch
3	trais	14	quattordesch
4	quatter	15	quindesch
5	tschintg	16	sedesch
6	sis	17	deschset
7	set	18	deschdotg
8	otg	19	deschnov
9	nov	20	ventg
10	diesch		

Days and months

Monday	glindesdi	today	oz
Tuesday	mardi	tomorrow	damaun
Wednesday	mesemna	January	schaner
Thursday	gievgia	February	favrer
Friday	venderdi	March	mars
Saturday	sonda	April	avrigl
Sunday	dumengia	May	matg
day	di	June	zercladur
in the morning	la damaun	July	fanadur
at noon	a mezdi	August	avust
in the afternoon	il suentermezdi	September	settember
in the evening	la saira	October	october
at night	la notg	November	november
at midnight	a mesanotg	December	december
yesterday	ier		

horse	Pferde	cheval	cavallo
fillet	Filet	filet	filetto
a chop	Kotelett	côtelette	cotoletta
diced meat	Geschnetzelte	émincé	spezzatino
mincemeat	Hackfleisch	hachée	carne macinata
liver	Leber	foie	fegato
kidney	Niere	rognon	rognone
sausage	Wurst	saucisse	salsiccia
rice	Reis	riz	riso
boiled potatoes	Salzkartoffeln	pommes nature	patate bollite
pasta	Teigwaren	pâtes	pasta
noodles	Nudeln	nouilles	tagliatelle
mushrooms	Pilze	champignons	funghi
fish	Fisch	poisson	pesce
salmon	Lachs	saumon	salmone
trout	Forelle	truite	trota
tuna	Thunfisch	thon	tonno

Vegetables

	Swiss German	French	Italian
vegetables	Gemüse	légumes	verdure
tomato	Tomate	tomate	pomodoro
carrot	Rüebli	carotte	carota
cabbage	Chabis	chou	cavolo
cauliflower	Blumenkohl	choufleur	cavolfiore
corn	Mais	maïs	mais
cucumber	Gurke	concombre	cetriolo
asparagus	Spargel	asperge	asparagi
beans	Bohnen	haricots	fagioli
peas	Erbse	poix	piselli
sweet pepper	Peperoni	poivron	peperone
spinach	Spinat	épinards	spinaci
fennel	Fenchel	fenouil	finocchio
broccoli	Broccoli	brocoli	broccolo
onion	Zwiebel	oignon	cipolla
garlic	Knoblauch	ail	aglio

Cooking terms

	Swiss German	French	Italian
hot	heiss	chaud	caldo
cold	kalt	froid	freddo
smoked	geräuchert	fumé	affumicato
roast	gebraten	rôti	arrosto
rare	bluetig	saignant	al sangue

well done	gar	bien cuit	ben cotto
boiled	gekochte	bouilli	bollito
steamed	gedämpft	à la vapeur	al vapore
stuffed	gefüllt	farci	farcito
grilled	gegrillt	grillé	alla griglia
raw	roh	cru	crudo
baked	gebacken	au four	al forno
fried	gebraten, fritiert	frite	fritto
spices	Gewürze	épices	spezie
traditional cooking	gutbürgerliche Küche	cuisine bourgeoise	cucina casalinga
Swiss-German cooking	Schweizer Küche	cuisine suisse alémanique	cucina svizzero tedesca
Swiss-French cooking	Welsche Küche	cuisine romande	cucina romanda
Ticinese cooking	Tessiner Küche	cuisine tessinoise	cucina ticinese
Romansh cooking	Romanische Küche	cuisine romanche	cucina romancia
in the style of	art	à la	al/alla
home-made	Hausgemacht	fait à la maison	fatto in casa

Fruit and desserts

	Swiss German	French	Italian
fruit	Früchte	fruits	frutta
apple	Apfel	pomme	mela
pear	Birne	poire	pera
plum	Zwetschge	prune	prugna
peach	Pfirsich	pêche	pesca
cherry	Kirsche	cerise	ciliegia
grape	Trauben	raisin	uva
raspberry	Himbeere	framboise	lampone
strawberry	Erdbeere	fraise	fragola
apricot	Aprikose	abricot	albicocca
orange	Orange	orange	arancia
grapefruit	Grapefruit	pamplemousse	pompelmo
lemon	Zitrone	citron	limone
cake	Kuchen, Torte	gâteau, tarte	torta
chocolate	Schokolade	chocolat	cioccolata
ice cream	Glace	glace	gelato

Glossary

German

Abfahrt departure

Achtung! Beware!

Altstadt Old Town

Ankunft arrival

Auskunft information

Bach stream

Bahnhof station

Berg mountain

Bergführer mountain guide

Bergweg mountain path

Billets tickets

Blaue zone blue zone (city parking)

Brücke bridge

Deutschschweiz German-speaking Switzerland

Dorf village

Durchgang passageway

Fluss river

Fussgängerzone pedestrian zone

Gasse alley

Gefahr! Danger!

Gepäck baggage

Gipfel summit

Gletscher glacier

Gutbürgerliche traditional, solidly bourgeois

Hafen harbour

Hauptbahnhof main station

Hochsaison high season

Hof court or courtyard

Horn peak

Jass (*yass*) extremely complicated card game played in taverns by young and old using non-standard Swiss playing cards; suits are Rosen (roses), Schilden (shields), Eicheln (acorns) and Schellen (bells)

Jugendherberge youth hostel

Kantönligeist literally "little cantonal spirit": describes a stubborn Swiss parochialism, a blinkered pride in the attributes and culture of one's own town or canton above all others (with the same overtones as "Little Englander")

Kirche church

Kloster monastery or convent

Kulm summit

Kunst art

Kurverein tourist office

Massenlager dormitory

Matratzenlager dormitory

Mitenand friendly welcoming Swiss-German term for everyone in a group, with the same disarming overtones as "folks" in English: a hotel receptionist or maitre d' will greet a party with *grüezi mitenand* ("hello everyone"), a waiter will say *enguete mitenand* ("enjoy your meal, folks"), and so on

Münster minster or cathedral

Nachsaison post-season, low season

Nord north

Ober upper

Ost east

Platz town square

Rathaus town hall

Röstigraben informal name for the language border – a *Graben* is a military trench – between French-speaking Switzerland (where they don't eat the traditional potato dish *Rösti*) and German-speaking Switzerland (where they do)

Sammlung collection

SBB Swiss Federal Railways

Schloss castle or stately home

Schlucht gorge

Schweiz Switzerland

See lake

Strasse street

Stübe or Stübli A cosy, comfortable room with traditional decor, often in a restaurant or café

Sud south

Tal valley

Tessin Ticino

Tor gate

Tourismus tourist office

Touristenlager dormitory

Turm tower

Verboten! Prohibited!

Verkehrsverein tourist office

Vorsaison pre-season, low season

Wald forest

Wanderweg footpath

Welschland informal name for French-speaking Switzerland (the Swiss-German word Choderwelsch means "gobbledy-gook")

Westschweiz formal name for French-speaking Switzerland

Zeughaus arsenal

Zwischensaison between-season, low season

French

Auberge de jeunesse youth hostel

Basse-saison low season

Billettes tickets

Bois woods

CFF Swiss Federal Railways

Château castle or stately home

Chemin pédestre footpath

Col mountain pass

Église church

Est east

Forêt forest

Gare station

Haute-saison high season

Hôtel de ville town hall

Interdit! Prohibited!

Nord north

Office du tourisme tourist office

Ouest west

Pont bridge

Randonnée hike

Renseignements information

Romandie French-speaking Switzerland

Rue street

Ruelle alley

Sud south

Suisse Switzerland

Suisse alémanique German-speaking Switzerland

Suisse romande French-speaking Switzerland

Tessin Ticino

Tour tower

Vieille ville Old Town

Zone pour piétons pedestrian zone

Italian

Albergo hotel or inn

Alloggio accommodation

Alta stagione high season

Arrivo arrival

Bassa stagione low season

Biglietti tickets

Bosco forest or woodland

Capanna alpine hut

Castello castle

Centro storico Old Town

Chiesa church

Ente turistico tourist office

Est east

FFS Swiss Federal Railways

Fiume river

Ghiacciaio glacier

Grotto rustic country tavern

Lago lake

Nord north

Ostello per la gioventù youth hostel

Osteria rustic country tavern

Ovest west

Palazzo civico city hall

Partenza departure

Pericolo! Danger!

Piano floor or storey (in a building)

Piz peak

Ponte bridge

Rifugio alpine hut

Sentiero footpath

Sud south

Svizzera Switzerland

Svizzera romanda French-speaking Switzerland

Svizzera tedesca German-speaking Switzerland

Torre tower

Vetta summit

Via street

Vicolo alley

Vietato! Prohibited!

Zona pedonale pedestrian zone

Art and architecture

Apse semicircular termination at the east (altar) end of a church

Baroque exuberant architectural style of the seventeenth and early eighteenth centuries, characterized by ornate decoration, complex spatial arrangements and grand vistas. The term is also applied to the sumptuous style of painting of the same period

Biedermeier simple, bourgeois style of painting and decoration practised throughout the first half of the nineteenth century in German-speaking Europe

Capital the top of a column, usually ornate

Carolingian mid-eighth- to early tenth-century style of art and architecture named after Charlemagne

Chancel part of a church in which the altar is located

Choir part of a church where the service is sung, usually beside the altar

Fresco mural painting applied to wet plaster, so that the colours immediately soak in

Gothic architectural style of the thirteenth and fourteenth centuries, with an emphasis on verticality, characterized by pointed arches, ribbed vaulting and flying buttresses

Neoclassical late eighteenth- and early nineteenth-century style of art and architecture which returned to Classical

styles as a reaction against Baroque and Rococo excesses

Oriel projecting bay window

Renaissance fifteenth- and sixteenth-century Italian-originated movement in art and architecture, inspired by the rediscovery of Classical ideals

Rococo highly florid, light and graceful eighteenth-century style of architecture, painting and interior design, forming the last phase of Baroque

Romanesque solid architectural style of the late tenth to mid-thirteenth centuries, characterized by round-headed arches and a penchant for horizontality and geometrical precision

Rood screen screen in a Catholic church dividing the nave from the chancel (and thus separating worshippers from clergy)

Sgraffiti exterior house decoration of the Romansh-speaking Engadine Valley of Graubünden whereby designs or mottoes are etched into a white layer of plaster to reveal a darker-coloured layer beneath

Spandrel the underside of an arch

Stucco plaster used for decorative effects

Trompe l'oeil painting designed to fool the viewer into believing it is three-dimensional

Travel store

www.roughguides.com

nformation on over 25,000 destinations around the world

- **Read** Rough Guides' trusted travel info
- **Access** exclusive articles from Rough Guides authors
- **Update** yourself on new books, maps, CDs and other products
- **Enter** our competitions and win travel prizes
- **Share** ideas, journals, photos & travel advice with other users
- **Earn** points every time you contribute to the Rough Guide
  community and get rewards

Small print and

Index

A Rough Guide to Rough Guides

Published in 1982, the first Rough Guide – to Greece – was a student scheme that became a publishing phenomenon. Mark Ellingham, a recent graduate in English from Bristol University, had been travelling in Greece the previous summer and couldn't find the right guidebook. With a small group of friends he wrote his own guide, combining a highly contemporary, journalistic style with a thoroughly practical approach to travellers' needs.

The immediate success of the book spawned a series that rapidly covered dozens of destinations. And, in addition to impecunious backpackers, Rough Guides soon acquired a much broader and older readership that relished the guides' wit and inquisitiveness as much as their enthusiastic, critical approach and value-for-money ethos.

These days, Rough Guides include recommendations from shoestring to luxury and cover more than 200 destinations around the globe, including almost every country in the Americas and Europe, more than half of Africa and most of Asia and Australasia. Our ever-growing team of authors and photographers is spread all over the world, particularly in Europe, the US and Australia.

In the early 1990s, Rough Guides branched out of travel, with the publication of Rough Guides to World Music, Classical Music and the Internet. All three have become benchmark titles in their fields, spearheading the publication of a wide range of books under the Rough Guide name.

Including the travel series, Rough Guides now number more than 350 titles, covering: phrasebooks, waterproof maps, music guides from Opera to Heavy Metal, reference works as diverse as Conspiracy Theories and Shakespeare, and popular culture books from iPods to Poker. Rough Guides also produce a series of more than 120 World Music CDs in partnership with World Music Network.

Visit www.roughguides.com to see our latest publications.

Rough Guide travel images are available for commercial licensing at www.roughguidespictures.com

SMALL PRINT

Rough Guide credits

Text editor: Lara Kavanagh
Layout: Ajay Verma
Cartography: Alakananda Roy
Picture editor: Sarah Cummins
Production: Rebecca Short
Proofreader: Jan McCann
Cover design: Dan May and Chloë Roberts
Photographer: Chris Christoforou
Editorial: Ruth Blackmore, Andy Turner, Keith
Drew, Edward Aves, Alice Park, Lucy White,
Jo Kirby, James Smart, Natasha Foges, Róisín
Cameron, James Rice, Emma Traynor, Emma
Gibbs, Kathryn Lane, Monica Woods, Mani
Ramaswamy, Harry Wilson, Lucy Cowie, Alison
Roberts, Joe Staines, Peter Buckley, Matthew
Milton, Tracy Hopkins, Ruth Tidball; **Delhi**
Madhavi Singh, Karen D'Souza, Lubna Shaheen
Design & Pictures: **London** Scott Stickland,
Dan May, Diana Jarvis, Mark Thomas, Nicole
Newman, Emily Taylor; **Delhi** Umesh Aggarwal,
Jessica Subramanian, Ankur Guha, Pradeep
Thapliyal, Sachin Tanwar, Anita Singh, Nikhil
Agarwal, Sachin Gupta.

Production: Liz Cherry
Cartography: **London** Ed Wright, Katie Lloyd-
Jones; **Delhi** Rajesh Chhibber, Ashutosh Bharti,
Rajesh Mishra, Animesh Pathak, Jasbir Sandhu,
Karobi Gogoi, Swati Handoo, Deshpal Dabas
Online: **London** Faye Hellon, Jeanette Angell,
Fergus Day, Justine Bright, Clare Bryson, Aine
Fearon, Adrian Low, Ezgi Celebi; **Delhi** Amit
Verma, Rahul Kumar, Narender Kumar, Ravi
Yadav, Debojit Borah, Rakesh Kumar, Ganesh
Sharma, Shisir Basumatari
Marketing & Publicity: **London** Liz Statham,
Louise Maher, Jess Carter, Vanessa Godden,
Vivienne Watton, Anna Paynton, Rachel
Sprackett, Laura Vipond; **New York** Katy Ball,
Judi Powers; **Delhi** Ragini Govind
Reference Director: Andrew Lockett
Operations Assistant: Becky Doyle
Operations Manager: Helen Atkinson
Publishing Director (Travel): Clare Currie
Commercial Manager: Gino Magnotta
Managing Director: John Duhigg

Publishing information

This 4th edition published May 2010 by
Rough Guides Ltd,
80 Strand, London WC2R 0RL
14 Local Shopping Centre, Panchsheel Park,
New Delhi 110017, India
Distributed by the Penguin Group
Penguin Books Ltd,
80 Strand, London WC2R 0RL
Penguin Group (USA)
375 Hudson Street, NY 10014, USA
Penguin Group (Australia)
250 Camberwell Road, Camberwell,
Victoria 3124, Australia
Penguin Group (Canada)
195 Harry Walker Parkway N, Newmarket, ON,
L3Y 7B3 Canada
Penguin Group (NZ)
67 Apollo Drive, Mairangi Bay, Auckland 1310,
New Zealand
Cover concept by Peter Dyer.

Typeset in Bembo and Helvetica to an original
design by Henry Iles.
Printed in Singapore
© Matthew Teller 2010
Maps © Rough Guides

552pp includes index
A catalogue record for this book is available from
the British Library
ISBN: 978-1-84836-471-4

1 3 5 7 9 8 6 4 2

Help us update

We've gone to a lot of effort to ensure that the
fourth edition of **The Rough Guide to Switzerland**
is accurate and up-to-date. However, things
change – places get "discovered", opening hours
are notoriously fickle, restaurants and rooms raise
prices or lower standards. If you feel we've got it
wrong or left something out, we'd like to know,
and if you can remember the address, the price,
the hours, the phone number, so much the better.

Please send your comments with the subject
line "**Rough Guide Switzerland Update**"
to ⓔmail@roughguides.com. We'll credit all
contributions and send a copy of the next edition
(or any other Rough Guide if you prefer) for the
very best emails.
Have your questions answered and tell others
about your trip at ⓦwww.roughguides.com

SMALL PRINT

www.roughguides.com

541

Acknowledgements

The author would like to thank, in London, Evelyn Lafone, Roland Minder and colleagues at Switzerland Tourism for ever-present support, help and information; Greig Boyle and colleagues at Swiss International Air Lines for enthusiasm, flexibility and understanding; Andy Brabin and colleagues at Railbookers for vision and great ideas; Kev Reynolds for inspiration; Gavin Thomas for expert updating; and Lucy Ratcliffe for stepping in at a crucial moment. In Switzerland, many thanks to Hans Peter Kaiser and Joerg Leser in Zürich; Margrit Gontha in

Basel; Beat and Alex from citystroll.ch; Beatrice Candrian in Baden; and, of course, unfailingly helpful tourist office staff in locations all around Switzerland and Liechtenstein.

At Rough Guides, my editor, Lara Kavanagh, did a brilliant job – sharp, detailed and intelligent. She made the book better than I thought it could be. Thanks also to: Ajay Verma, Dan May, Chloë Roberts, Sarah Cummins, Alakananda Roy and Rebecca Short. And thank you to Han, for everything.

SMALL PRINT

Readers' letters

Thanks to all the readers who have taken the time to write in with comments and suggestions (and apologies if we've inadvertently omitted or misspelt anyone's name):

Thanks to: Valeria Akroyd, Laura Badertscher, Marianne & David Buehler, Steven Caldecourt, Eleanor Ciritci, Penny Collins, Daniel E. Coslett, Eddy le Couvreur, Susanne Daxelhoffer, Christine D'Incau, Aurélie Eichler, Anne-Laure Favre, Anthony Fitzsimmons, Neil Forsyth, Julia Geddes, Dave Gittins, Ian H. Gordon, Beat Graf and Alex Ulrich, Diane Gray, Markus Hauser, Audrey Hermanutz, Dr Martin Hussey, Natalie Jacobs, John and Rosemary Jamieson, Patrick Jansen, Bettina Jayawickrama, Michael Kaiser-Nyman, Brian Knox, Andrea Kuprecht, Mrs F. Landeryou,

Jane Lightfoot, Arthur Martensson, Don Maxwell, Paul McCarthy, John Medforth, Virginie Mottier, Georges Muller, Jürg Musfeld, David Nash, Tony Nichols and Yves Jatteau, Com O'Malley, Gé Ostendorf, Sue Poolman, Marilyn Roberts, Alison and Ivor Rowe, Annika Rullgard, Valerie Rulton, Dennis Schneider, Rebecca Scriven, Mr R. & Mrs B. Spencer, Venetia Stent, Joe Swan, Daniel Thomet, Roger Tonge, Erica and Emmanuel Trescher, Pierre Vanderhout, Guy Wachsman, Phill Wheaton, Carole Wood, Robert Wray.

Photographer, Chris Christoforou, would like to say a very big thank you to Severine Grossenbacher and all her colleagues at the Swiss tourist board in London and throughout Switzerland. Big thanks to Sarah Cummins and Nicole Newman for the opportunity. Thank you to the wonderful Therme Vals, who showed me such great hospitality, and to Terry and his lovely team at The Lazy Falken Backpackers in Interlaken. Finally, thanks to all the other wonderful people who helped make my time in Switzerland truly inspirational.

Photo credits

Selected images from our guidebooks are available for licensing from:

ROUGHGUIDESPICTURES.COM

Index

Map entries are in colour.

Map symbols

maps are listed in the full index using coloured text

-----	National boundary	⋔	Cliffs
—·—·—	Canton boundary	/'\	Hill shading
-----	Chapter boundary	🕈	Waterfall
▬▬	Motorway	⋇	Viewpoint
═══	Major road	Å	Campsite
───	Minor road	✈	Airport
------	Tunnel	◆	Point of interest
------	Footpath	⚜	Vineyard
⊪⊪⊪	Steps	⊞	Hospital
───	Wall	⊙	Statue
─■─	Railway	ⓘ	Tourist information
───	Metro line	✉	Post office
∷∷∷	Funicular railway	Ⓜ	Metro station
●----●	Cable car	🅿	Parking
─ ─	Ferry route	▬	Building
───	River	⬭	Stadium
⊃⊂	Bridge	─✝	Church/cathedral
⊐⊏	Viaduct	▦	Park
▲	Mountain peak	⊞	Cemetery
⊃⊂	Mountain pass	▨	Glacier

So now we've told you about the things not to miss, the best places to stay, the top restaurants, the liveliest bars and the most spectacular sights, it only seems fair to tell you about the best travel insurance around

WorldNomads.com
keep travelling safely

Recommended by Rough Guides